Czechoslov

D1138422

The principal sights:

Banská Bystrica (Neusohl) 372
Bratislava (Pressburg)...............334
Brno (Brünn) 296
České Budějovice (Budweis) ..161
Cheb (Eger) 216
Děčín (Tetschen).....................252
Františkovy Lázně
 (Franzensbad).....................220
Frýdlant (Friedland).................257
Hradec Králové (Königgrätz) 260
Jablonec nad Nisou (Gablonz) 258
Jihlava (Iglau)...........................313
Karlovy Vary (Karlsbad).........223
Karlštejn (Karlstein).................141
Kežmarok (Käsmark)...............399
Košice (Kaschau) 383
Krkonoše (Riesengebirge)
 (Giant Mountains)...............287
Kutná Hora (Kuttenberg).........152
Levoča (Leutschau) 394
Liberec (Reichenberg) 254
Litoměřice (Leitmeritz)............237
Mariánské Lázně (Marienbad) 230
Mělník (Melnik).......................148
Olomouc (Olmütz)..................322
Opava (Troppau) 329
Ostrava (Ostrau)......................321

Pardubice (Paradubitz).............263
Plzeň (Pilsen) 209
Praha (Prague) 36
 Charles Bridge.................... 56
 Charles Square 130
 Hradčany 83
 Josefov 62
 Loreto 119
 Malá Strana 72
 Nerudova............................. 76
 Old Town Hall.................... 45
 Powder Tower 42
 Týn 49
 St Vitus's Cathedral 87
 Vyšehrad..............................134
 Wenceslas Square 127
Prešov (Preschau).....................407
Spiš (Zips)................................389
Šumava (Böhmerwald) 196
Tábor (Tabor) 201
Teplice (Teplitz)......................246
Terezín (Theresienstadt)..........240
Trutnov (Trautenau) 285
Ústí nad Labem (Aussig).........235
Vysoké Tatry (High Tatras) ..402
Znojmo (Znaim) 306
Zvolen (Altsohl)......................375

< Lift flap for map

Zu drei böhmischen Bauer

U třech českých Sedlák

2

Erhard Gorys

Czechoslovakia

PALLAS GUIDES

Front cover: Houses in the market place, Telč (courtesy of Čedok)
Inside front cover: Telč (courtesy of Čedok)
Back cover: Beer sign on pub
Frontispiece: South Bohemian inn-sign, c.1850, "At the sign of the Three Bohemian Farmers"

ENGLISH VERSION PREPARED BY SEBASTIAN WORMELL

MANY THANKS TO PILSNER URQUELL (PLZEŇSKY PRAZDROJ), DISTRIBUTED IN THE UK BY SCOTTISH AND NEWCASTLE BREWERIES.

KIND SUPPORT FOR THIS BOOK HAS ALSO BEEN GIVEN BY:
ŽIVNOSTENSKÁ BANKA, LONDON
SAMACO LTD
TRAVELINES LTD AND ČEDOK, LONDON.

German edition first published by DuMont Buchverlag GmbH & Co, Cologne 1990.
English edition published by Pallas Athene, 59 Linden Gardens, London W2 4HJ.
© 1990, 1991 DuMont Buchverlag, Köln
Translation, adaptation and all additional material © Pallas Athene 1991

All rights reserved

ISBN 1 873439 03 7

All rights for all countries reserved by DuMont Buchverlag GmbH & Co., Limited partnership, Cologne, Germany. The title of the German original edition is: Tschechoslowakei, by Erhard Gorys.

Contents

Foreword... 9

History.. 11
Prehistory... 11
Celts and Germans.. 12
The Great Moravian Empire 14
The Přemyslids 16
Charles IV 18
The Hussite Wars (1419–1435)... 20
The Thirty Years' War (1618–1648)... 22
Eighteenth and Nineteenth Centuries.. 26
The Path to Nationhood 28
The Reich Protectorate of Bohemia and Moravia................................. 31
The Socialist Republic and its downfall 33

Prague (Praha).. 36
History of the city 36
Staré město (Old Town).. 40
   From the Municipal House to the Old Town Square 40   Old Town Square 44
   From the Old Town Square to the Charles Bridge 50   Josefov 62   Northern Old Town 66
   Southern Old Town 68
Malá strana (Lesser Town) 72
Castle Town (Hradčany).. 83
   Prague Castle 83   The Castle Town 115
Nové město (New Town) 124
Vyšehrad 134
Other districts 137

Central Bohemia (Střední Čechy)... 141
Karlštejn (Karlstein)... 141
Příbram, Svatá Hora 144
Křivoklát (Bürglitz) 146
Lidice 148
Mělník (Melnik).. 148
Kutná Hora (Kuttenberg) 152
Kolín (Kolin).. 156
Konopište (Konopischt).. 158

Southern Bohemia (Jižní Čechy) 161
České Budějovice (Budweis) 161
Hluboká nad Vltavou (Frauenberg) 164
Český Krumlov (Krumau) 166
Zlatá Koruna (Goldenkron) 193
Vyšší Brod (Hohenfurth) 193
Údolní nádrž Lipno (Lippener Stausee) 195
Prachatice (Prachatitz) 195
Šumava (Böhmerwald) 196
Volary (Wallern) 197
Stakonice (Strakonitz) 198
Písek (Pisek) 199
Zvíkov (Klingenberg) 200
Blatná (Platten) 201
Tábor (Tabor) 201
Jindřichův Hradec (Neuhaus) 204
Třeboň (Wittingau) 206

Western Bohemia (Západní Čechy) 209
Plzeň (Pilsen) 209
Klatovy (Klattau) 214
Domažlice (Taus) 215
Cheb (Eger) 216
Františkovy Lázně (Franzensbad) 220
Karlovy Vary (Karlsbad) 223
Loket (Elbogen) 228
Mariánské Lázně (Marienbad) 230
Jachýmov (St. Joachimsthal) 232

Northern Bohemia (Severní Čechy) 235
Ústí nad Labem (Aussig) 235
Litoměřice (Leitmeritz) 237
Terezín (Theresienstadt) 240
Lovosice (Lobositz) 242
Úštěk (Auscha) 243
Chomutov (Komotau) 243
Louny (Laun) 244
Žatec (Saaz) 245
Kadaň (Kaaden) 246
Most (Brüx) 246
Teplice (Teplitz) 246
Duchcov (Dux) 248
Osek (Osegg) 249

Chlumec (Kulm) 251
Děčín (Tetschen) 252
Česká Lípa (Böhmisch-Leipa) 253
Liberec (Reichenberg) 254
Frýdlant (Friedland) 257
Jablonec nad Nisou (Gablonz an der Neisse) 258

Eastern Bohemia (Východní Čechy) 260
Hradec Králové (Königgrätz) 260
Pardubice (Pardubitz) 263
Jičín (Jitschin) 282
Kuks (Kukus) 283
Český ráj (Bohemian Paradise) 284
Trutnov (Trautenau) 285
Teplice and Adršpach Rocks 286
Krkonoše (Riesengebirge, Giant Mountains) 287
   Vrchlabí (Hohenelbe) 288   Harrachov (Harrachsdorf) 290
   Špindlerův Mlýn (Spindlermühle) 290   Janské Lázně (Johannesbad) 290
   Sněžka (Schneekoppe) 290
Source of the Elbe 291
Náchod (Nachod) 291
Nové Město nad Metují (Neustadt an der Mettau) 292
Litomyšl (Leitomischl) 293

Southern Moravia (Jižní Morava) 296
Brno (Brünn) 296
Battlefield of Austerlitz 303
Mikulov (Nikolsburg) 304
Moravský Kras (Mährischer Karst) 304
Znojmo (Znaim) 306
Vranov nad Dyjí (Frain) 308
Jaroměřice nad Rokytnou (Jarmeritz) 310
Telč (Teltsch) 311
Jihlava (Iglau) 313
Staré Město at Uherské Hradiště (Ungarisch-Hradisch) 319
Zlín 320

Northern Moravia (Severní Morava) 321
Ostrava (Ostrau) 321
Hukvaldy (Hochwald) 322
Olomouc (Olmütz) 322
Bouzov (Busau) 328
Opava (Troppau) 329
Schönhengstgau 331
Kuhländchen 332
Hradec (Grätz) 333

Western Slovakia (Západní Slovensko) 334
Bratislava (Pressburg) 334
Devín (Theben) 358
Trnava (Tyrnau) 359
Piešt'any (Pistyan) 362
Trenčín (Trentschin) 364
Trenčianske Teplice (Trentschin-Teplitz) 366
Nitra (Neutra) 367

Central Slovakia (Střední Slovensko) 372
Banská Bystrica (Neusohl) 372
Zvolen (Altsohl) 375
Kremnica (Kremnitz) 376
Banská Štiavnica (Schemnitz) 378
Antol 380
Žilina (Sillein) 380
Orava (Arva) 381

Eastern Slovakia (Východní Slovensko) 383
Košice (Kaschau) 383
Herl'any (Herlein) 387
Jasov (Jossau) 387
Krásna Hôrka 388
Betliar 388
Domica jaskyňa (Domica caves) 389
Spiš (Zips) 389
  Spišsky hrad (Zipser Burg) 391   Spišska Kapitula (Zipser Kapitel) 391   Spišská Nová Ves
  (Neudorf) 393   Spišský Štvrtok (Donnersmarkt) 393   Poprad (Deutschendorf) 393
  Spišska Sobota 393   Gelnica (Göllnitz) 394   Slovenský raj (Slovak Paradise) 394
Levoča (Leutschau) 394
Kežmarok (Käsmark) 399
Vysoké Tatry (High Tatras) 402
  Tatranská Lomnica (Tatra-Lomnitz) 404   Starý Smokovec (Altschmecks) 404
  Štrbské pleso (Tschirmer See) 404   Ždiar 405   Spišská Magura (Zipser Magura) 405
Bardejov (Bartfeld) 406
Bardejovské Kúpele (Bad Bartfeld) 407
Prešov (Preschau, Eperjes) 407
Dukelský priesmyk (Dukla Pass) 409

Chronology 411
Czechoslovakia in brief 413
Glossary 415

Practical Information 417
Booklist 431
Index 435

Foreword

Czechoslovakia is the land of Smetana and Dvořák, of Kafka and Rilke; it is the heart of Europe, the heartland of the Holy Roman Empire, the cradle of the Reformation. Its capital, Prague, the Golden City, was the centre of European artistic and intellectual life for centuries. Italians, Flemings, many Germans and even some Englishmen flocked to the Czech and Slovak lands and created a culture of impressive richness. Perhaps in no other country has the splendour of wealthy towns, mighty castles and splendid châteaux survived better than in Czechoslovakia, almost untouched by the war and lovingly cared for ever since.

This Pallas guide is intended to be both a practical companion in Czechoslovakia, and a useful souvenir. It is as comprehensive as size permits, though inevitably inclusiveness has had to be balanced against detail. After all, there are some 300 castles and châteaux in Czechoslovakia, and some 30,000 other buildings of all styles that have undergone restoration and there are more than 70 historic town centres now designated as conservation areas.

The main section of the book, following the historical survey, begins with 'many-towered' Prague and continues with journeys through ten regions, each beginning with the regional capital. As well as information about art and architecture the reader will also learn about the romantic charm of Czechoslovakia's countryside, the teeming fishponds and lakes of southern Bohemia, the romantic wildness of the Bohemian Forest, the sophisticated spas of Karlsbad, Marienbad and Franzensbad, where kings and emperors met, the unusual volcanic peaks and rich vineyards on the Elbe and the Vltava, the Riesengebirge, home of the mountain spirit Krakonoš/Rübezahl, the bizarre landscape of the Moravian Karst with its many caves, the romantic Slovak Paradise with its waterfalls and ice-caves, the mighty peaks and secret 'sea eyes' of the High Tatras.

The official Czech or Slovak versions of place names and street names are used, to enable the traveller to refer to road maps and town plans. The old German names, (which in some cases are more familiar to English-speaking readers, particularly in the border regions, which until 1945 had an overwhelming German-speaking majority), or translations of the Czech names are usually given in brackets, and in Slovakia some of the old Hungarian names are also included in brackets. However, in view of recent political developments, it must be expected that many of these names will change. The names of some rivers and mountains are given in the form most familiar to English-speakers with the Czech or Slovak form in brackets if necessary, e.g. Danube (Dunaj), Elbe (Labe), Riesengebirge (Krkonoše), Bohemian Forest (Šumava) or High Tatras (Vysoké Tatry).

My thanks go to all who have given me advice and assistance: the ever-helpful Czechs and Slovaks, the friendly welcome at the national travel agency Čedok, the Prague press agency Orbis for their detailed information, and not least to my wife Christel, who has once again helped devise and evaluate the routes.

If this guide book contributes a little to making the wonderful charms of Czechoslovakia better known as one of Europe's most beautiful countries, then it will have fulfilled its purpose.

Erhard Gorys

History

Prehistory

The earliest human remains in the area that is now Czechoslovakia have been found at Gánovce in northern Slovakia. They include the impression of the skull of a pre-Neanderthal man, one of the hunter-gatherers who lived here about 120,000 years ago in the Eem temperate period, the period before the Würm cold period. (The original of this impression is preserved in the National Museum in Prague.) The Mousérian period, which extended into the Würm ice age, saw the emergence of Neanderthal man. Many remains of Neanderthal skeletons have been found in Moravia, e.g. in the Šipka cave near Štramberk and the Schwedenstuhl cave near Ochoz (c. 60,000 BC).

About 30,000 years ago, during an improvement in the climate within the Würm cold period known as the Aurignacian period, Cromagnon man appeared. He was probably the first human being to have a culture, live in village-like settlements and make fertility idols. In Dolní Věstonice (Unterwisternitz), in the Mikulov district in southern Moravia a mammoth-hunters' camp has been excavated which was inhabited for several generations. Between the bones of the killed mammoths archaeologists unearthed charming 'Venus statuettes' of ivory, and the famous 'Venus of Věstonice' made of fired clay 25,000 years ago, and hence the world's oldest piece of ceramic.

In Slovakia the earliest prehistoric work of art yet found is the extraordinarily naturalistic 'Venus of Moravany', carved from a mammoth tusk, 7.5 cm high and almost 23,000 years old. Not far away an early stone-age camp with huts, stone tools and bones of young mammoths, reindeer, cave-bears, Arctic foxes, lions and birds has been excavated.

The 'Neolithic revolution' – the transition from hunting and gathering to agriculture and domestication of animals – took place in the 6th millennium BC in central Europe. It resulted in settlements with durable dwellings and a division of labour. The *Danube Culture*, the first agricultural culture, developed in the 5th millennium BC with forest clearance by burning in the loess region, wooden long-houses and fired ceramics. Excavations near the village of Bylani near Kutná Hora revealed a settlement of Danube people covering 65,000 square metres and with several layers of occupation.

Around 3000 BC the potter's wheel reached the Balkans from the Near East, spreading to the region of present-day Slovakia and then to Moravia and Bohemia. Clay female figures representing a mother goddess who protected fertility were still made, but the Neolithic figurines were now strongly stylized, with tiny breasts and exaggerated hips and thighs, and the faces only summarily indicated. The Moravské muzeum in Brno contains more than a

The Venus of Věstonice (Aurignacian Period) and a footed clay bowl (c.700 BC)

hundred such statuettes from a 5000-year-old settlement near Střelice in the Znojmo district. Clay vessels in animal form, some of them with a funnel-shaped opening, were probably used in religious ceremonies. They have been found at Kroměříž and at Nrubčice, Prostějo district, (both in Moravia), and at Abraham in Slovakia.

A copper hoard found near Únětice (Aunjetitz) not far from Prague has given its name to the *Únětice Culture*, one of the most important groups of early bronze age cultures in central Europe. Clothes pins, neck rings and 'riveted daggers' were the favourite objects produced in this period which lasted from about 1900 to 1500 BC. In the late Únětice period active trading links via the 'amber route' developed with the Mycenaean world. Finally the Únětice Culture split into the Větěrov Culture of Moravia and the Mad' Arovče Culture of Slovakia.

Celts and Germans

The *Hallstatt Period* (c. 750–500 BC) can be divided geographically into a Celtic western part and a Thracian-Illyrian eastern part. The two cultures met in what is now Czechoslovakia: Celts settled Bohemia and Moravia, while Slovakia was under Illyrian influence. Among the most interesting objects from this period is a small bronze animal found on the sacrificial site in the Býčí-skála cave near Adamov in Moravia (c. 700 BC). Similar votive offerings, such as a small bronze horse from Obřany near Brno and a clay bowl with human feet from Lednice, Mikulov district, were also made c. 700 BC and are displayed in the Moravské muzeum, Brno.

The Hallstatt period was followed in the 5th century BC by the *Latène Period* (c. 500 BC to the birth of Christ), the greatest flourishing of Celtic culture which reworked Mediterranean influences and left its mark on non-Celtic neighbouring peoples. The Celts brought with them the potter's wheel, plough, sickle and scythe; they knew how to mine ore and make iron. From this warlike peasant people there emerged an aristocracy who lived in luxurious settlements protected by strong ramparts, and supervised trade with distant countries. Around 400 BC the Celtic *Boii* arrived from south-west Germany and for four centuries cultivated the regions between the rivers Ohře (Eger) and Tisza (Theiss) under the leadership of wise rulers. Some of them lived in *oppida*, fortified town-like settlements, and minted their own gold coins (known as 'rainbow bowls'). Archaeologists have found such *oppida* at Závist in west Prague (170 hectares), Stradonice in Beroun district (80 hectares), and Staré Hradisko near Prostějov. It was from the Boii that Bohemia took its name (from *Boiohaemum*, Boienheim, 'Boierland').

Striking examples of the art of the Boii include a very naturalistic sheep's head fibula from Panenský Týnec in Bohemia (c. 400 BC), the head of a man – probably a god or a priest – made of slate with a neck ring (c. 300 BC) from Mšecké Žehrovice near Slaný, a bronze belt plaque with a moulded mask head from Stupava in Slovakia (c. 300 BC) and a bronze statuette of a man from the *oppidum* at the earthworks which have been excavated at Stradonice near Beroun in Bohemia (c. 100 BC).

In 60 BC the Dacians under their king, Burebista, drove the Boii and Illyrii out of the region of present-day Slovakia. The Bohemian Boii defeated Caesar's Roman legions in 58 BC, and in 9 BC, after being defeated by the Romans, Marbod, duke of the *Marcomanni*, led his people from the Main to Bohemia. This was the beginning of the German settlement of the country: the *Quadi* settled in Moravia, the *Langobardi* occupied Slovakia. To counterbalance the power of Rome Marbod united the various tribes, who were linked by a common cult (Marcomanni, Quadi, Langobardi, Lugii, Hermunduri and Semnoni) to form the first empire of the Germans. In accordance with Celtic custom the German nobles made Marbod their king.

In the centuries that followed, the Marcomanni and Quadi repeatedly advanced into the Roman-occupied Danube provinces, finally forcing the Romans to give up the regions north of the Danube. However, the crushing of further advances of the Quadi in 375 and 395 led in the end to their fall. In 395 the Marcomanni, who had embraced Christianity under their princess, Fritigil, were settled by Stilicho, the Vandal regent of the West Roman Empire, in the region south of the Danube.

The Great Moravian Empire

The withdrawal of the Germans at the start of the 6th century marked the beginning of the occupation of the land by Slav tribes, which took place over several centuries. These tribes did not form a unified state, but a number of greater or lesser territorial communities. This period saw the development of the division of society into nobles, freemen and slaves, foreshadowing the feudal system. Under the protection of the nobles' castles, markets and settlements of merchants and craftsmen sprang up on the trading routes between the western kingdom of the Franks and the orient. In the second half of the 6th century the *Avars*, a fearsome Asiatic nomadic people, together with other ethnic groups (known as pseudo-Avars) attacked Europe and founded a state in the territory of present-day Hungary which exacted tribute from the surrounding Slav peoples.

Around 623-24 the Frankish merchant *Samo*, who despatched his trading caravans with a guard provided by his own formidable troops, united several Slav tribes, freed Bohemia and Moravia from Avar rule by stopping the payment of tribute, and founded the first Slav empire with territory extending as far as Thuringia and the upper Main. The Slavs made Samo their king. Meanwhile the Avars had concentrated on the capture of Constantinople which they besieged unsuccessfully in 626. The Franks, on the other hand, were worried by the presence of the new empire on their doorstep. A great battle took place in 631-32 near Wogastisburg, where Samo resided, in which Samo's Slav army defeated the expeditionary force of the Frankish king. The exact location of Wogastisburg has not yet been established, but it is believed to have been in northern Bohemia. After Samo's death in 658 the empire collapsed and the land once again came under the control of the Avars and later of the Franks under Charlemagne.

In 833 the Moravian prince Mojmir I united the principalities of Moravia and western Slovakia under his rule and refused to pay tribute to the Franks. When Mojmir sought to bring the Bohemian princes into his empire, fourteen of them went to Regensburg in 845 to pay homage to Louis the German, king of the East Franks, and ask for his help. Louis deposed Mojmir and enthroned Mojmir's nephew, Rastislav, from whom he expected greater loyalty. Rastislav, however, continued his uncle's policy of independence and exploited the conflicts within the East Frankish kingdom. His realm, which was centred on western Slovakia and eastern Moravia with Nitra as its capital, developed into the Great Moravian Empire, the leading power among the western Slavs. In 855 Rastislav repelled an attack from Louis the German who was attempting to correct his error of judgment in appointing him king, and in his pursuit of the Frankish troops Rastislav laid waste to large areas of the Ostmark (Austria).

In 861-62 Rastislav asked the Roman curia to separate the Great Moravian church from the East Frankish, but Rome refused. He then turned to the Byzantine Emperor Michael III, who despatched a mission under the leadership of Constantine the Philosopher (who later took the name of Cyril) and his brother, Methodios. These 'Apostles of the Slavs' brought a translation of the liturgical and pastoral texts to Moravia and created the Slavonic *Glagolitic* script. (This script, a sample of which can be seen on the 20 kčs bank note, should not be confused with the rather simpler Cyrillic alphabet derived from Greek uncials, which was also devised for transliterating Slavonic languages a little later – though not by Constantine/ Cyril.) In 867 the activities of Cyril and Methodios received the approval of Rome, and it was agreed that after a preliminary reading in Latin, preaching in the service could be conducted in the Slavonic tongue. More important, however, was that the Great Moravian church could now escape from Frankish influence. After the death of Cyril, Pope Hadrian II appointed Methodios archbishop of Moravia and Pannonia (the country around Vienna), which so enraged the Bavarian and East Frankish bishops that they threw him into prison, where he remained until freed by Pope John VIII in 873. The importance of the memory of Cyril and Methodius to the Slavs in general, and particularly to the Moravians and Slovaks, cannot be overemphasized. Their feast day is now a national holiday in Czechoslovakia.

In 870 Carloman, the eldest son of Louis the German, passed through the territory of the Moravian prince Svatopluk looting and burning. Svatopluk could think of no alternative but to go over to the Franks and deliver his uncle Rastislav to them, thus giving himself the opportunity of placing himself upon the throne of Great Moravia. But Carloman distrusted him and took him prisoner as well, provoking a bloody uprising of the Moravians and the expulsion of all Frankish clergy. Svatopluk was released, destroyed an East Frankish army of occupation, and attacked the Ostmark. Louis the German was forced to recognize a certain degree of autonomy for Great Moravia. The empire was extended by the addition of large parts of Silesia and Hungary as well as regions of Lusatia and the upper Vistula as far as Cracow (Kraków). Even the Bohemian princedoms had – more or less voluntarily – joined the empire. However, Svatopluk still had to pay homage to the East Frankish king and had certain tributary obligations. This meant of course that the influence the Frankish church grew once again. In 880 a Swabian, Wiching, was appointed bishop of Nitra, and when Methodios died in 885, Svatopluk banished all supporters of the Apostle of the Slavs from the country. In 894 King Svatopluk died, and within a few months later the Bohemian princes were paying homage at Regensburg to Arnulf of Carinthia (see p. 16), who in the meantime had become king of the East Franks. After the secession of Bohemia the Great Moravian Empire broke up.

At the beginning of the 10th century Bavarian and Bohemian armies attacked Moravia. Under the pressure of the Hungarian peril – the Magyars (nomads from the Urals) had settled in the central Danube basin in the late 9th century and from there threatened the neighbouring peoples – Moravia and Bavaria made peace. In 902 the Moravians had their last victory over the Magyars; five years later, on 4 July 907, the combined Bavarian and Moravian army suffered an annihilating defeat at the hands of the Magyars at the battle of Bratislava. Although around 949 the Byzantine Emperor Constantine VII Porphyrogenitus was still writing of 'Great Moravia', the empire had long since ceased to exist. Moravia became increasingly dependent on the Bohemian princes, and Hungary incorporated Slovakia which it retained – later as 'Upper Hungary' – until 1918.

The Přemyslids

In the 9th century, when the Slav tribes of Bohemia began to come together, three tribes vied for leadership: the Lučans on the middle Ohře (Eger), the Slavniks on the upper Elbe (Labe), and the Czechs in the Vltava region. Towards the end of the 9th century as the power of the Great Moravian Empire waned and the danger of an attack from the Hungarians grew ever greater, the Czech dynasty of the Přemyslids took control more or less by force. According to legend this dynasty was founded by Libuše (Libussa), who married Přemysl, the head of a neighbouring farming tribe. The earliest historical mention of the dynasty is when Duke Bořivoj, who had been baptized by Methodios, together with his wife, Ludmila of Pšov (who was later canonized), moved his residence from Levý Hradec to Prague. On Bořivoj's death in 895 his son Spitihněv (895–905) assumed the title of duke. He took Bohemia out of Great Moravia, which was in a state of collapse, and in the same year (895) travelled with his tribal princes to Regensburg to pay homage to Arnulf, king of the East Franks, and thus place himself under the protection of the Frankish kingdom. Spitihněv was followed by his brother Vratislav I (905–921) who fought off several Magyar attacks and consolidated the Bohemian state.

In 921 Vratislav's son Wenceslas I (Václav – the 'Good King Wenceslas' of the 19th-century English carol) ascended the throne of the Bohemian dukes. Wenceslas made the country Christian and strove for the ecclesiastical emancipation of Bohemia, but in 929 he was murdered on his way to Mass by his brother Boleslav – a senseless act, since Wenceslas was intending to ask his brother to take over the dukedom anyway, so that he himself could go to Rome to be consecrated and return as the first bishop of Bohemia. In the same century Wenceslas I was canonized, and he and his mother Ludmila were to become Bohemia's national saints.

The duchy of which Boleslav now took possession encompassed large parts of Silesia and stretched as far as Cracow. Otto the Great, the German king, used Boleslav's opposition to him as a pretext for leading an army to Bohemia in 950. Boleslav submitted and swore the oath of fealty which committed him to providing military support and attending court Diets ('Heerfahrt und Hoffahrt'). Bohemia thus became part of the Holy Roman Empire with the same status as the other duchies.

Boleslav II (972–999) fulfilled his uncle Wenceslas's wish to found a bishopric at Prague. The first bishop was a Saxon Benedictine, Thietmar, who was succeeded in 983 by the scion of a princely Slavnik family, Vojtěch (also known as Adalbert of Prague), who later went as a missionary to the Prussians and was martyred in 997 at the Frisches Haff on the Baltic. His death brought to an end the Slavnik dynasty, the last of the rivals to the Czech Přemyslids.

Around 990 Bolesław I Chrobry (the Bold), Duke of Poland, conquered the regions around Cracow and Lublin as well as the whole of Moravia, and between 1002 and 1004 he even occupied Bohemia. His intention was to create a great West Slav empire, but the German king, Henry II, the Saint, forced the Poles into subjection and restored the Přemyslids to their throne at Prague. The Poles, however, retained Silesia and Moravia until Duke Břetislav I (1034–1055) united Moravia with Bohemia for good in about 1029. When he sought to win back Silesia too and penetrated deep into Poland, King Henry III, the Black, forced him to submission. Břetislav was forced to go in penitential garments to Regensburg to receive his duchy as a fiefdom. It was not until the Treaty of Quedlinburg in 1154 that Silesia was ceded to Bohemia.

Břetislav's son Spytihněv II (1055–1061) was succeeded by his brother, Vratislav II (1061–1092), who became the first king of Bohemia, when the Emperor Henry IV, whom he had helped in the suppression of the Saxon revolt in 1075, crowned him as king in Mainz as a reward for his services. Vratislav's successors managed, in spite of the confusion of thrones and rapid change of rulers in the 12th century, to retain their royal crown, until finally in 1212 the Emperor Frederick II issued the 'Golden Bull of Bohemia' granting King Otakar II a number of privileges including the recognition of hereditary kingship for Bohemia.

By this time German settlers were playing an important role in the Czech lands. Vratislav II had already granted special rights to the German merchants in Prague, and a century later Duke Soběslav II (1173–1179), declared in the 'Sobislavum' of 1173: *Novesites, quod Theutonici liberi homines sunt* ('Know that the Germans are free men'). Otakar I Přemysl (1197–1230), the Bohemian 'founder of towns', summoned German miners, craftsmen and farmers to the country. The new communities formed at this time adopted German law, mostly following the codes of Nuremberg or Magdeburg. The silver produced in the predominantly German mining towns of Jihlava (Iglau) and Kutná Hora (Kuttenberg) did much to increase the power of the Bohemian rulers. The monasteries and the Czech nobility also brought Germans to the country, while in Slovakia during the 12th century and after the Mongol invasion of 1241 farmers, craftsmen and miners from Silesia, Saxony and Bavaria answered the call of the Hungarian kings and founded a flourishing community of towns in the Spiš (Zips) region with its own government and laws.

Bohemia achieved European significance in the reign of Otakar II Přemysl (1253–1278), who took possession of the Babenberg inheritance, annexed the Ostmark in 1251, Styria and parts of Slovakia in 1260, Egerland in 1266, and Krain and Carinthia in 1269. He supported the Teutonic Order against the Prussians, and in his honour the newly founded city on the Pregel was named Königsberg (now Kaliningrad). In 1273 he was beaten by Rudolph of Habsburg in his bid to become king of the Germans, and refused to do homage to the new king or to hand over the imperial fiefs, which he had occupied without authority. For this Otakar was outlawed and in 1278 was defeated at the Battle on the Marchfeld, where he was killed as he fled. His son Wenceslas II was still able to conquer a number of Polish regions and have himself crowned king of Poland at Gnesen (Polish: Gniezno), but the death of his grandson Wenceslas III (Václav; 1305–1306), murdered at the age of seventeen at Olomouc on the march to Poland, the Přemyslid dynasty died out in the male line. Albert I of Habsburg seized Bohemia as an Imperial fief and transferred it to his son Rudolph, who died only a few months later. For three years 1307–1310 Henry of Carinthia, the husband of Wenceslas II's eldest daughter, occupied the Bohemian throne until he was deposed by the decision of the princes of the Empire. Peter Aspelt, Archbishop of Mainz and Wenceslas II's chancellor, arranged the marriage between John of Luxemburg, the son of Henry VII, the German king and future emperor, and Elizabeth, Wenceslas II's younger daughter. John, a remarkable adventurer, German by birth and French by upbringing, became King of Bohemia (1311–1346), but his many other political interests caused him to neglect his new kingdom. In 1335 he refused the crown of Poland, but instead received the Duchy of Breslau (Wrocław), several Silesian princedoms and Masovia (the region around Warsaw) and acquired Egerland. His military career – a combination of the chivalrous and mercenary – took him all over Europe. In 1346 – by which time he was totally blind – he fought, together with his son Charles, in the army of French knights which faced the English at the Battle of Crécy, and was killed. His crest and motto are said to have been adopted by the Black Prince and so became the badge of the Prince of Wales:

'The Black Prince Edward at Cressy field ... tears
From the Bohemian crowne the plume he wears
Which after for his crest he did preserve
To his father's use, with this fit word, I SERVE.' (Ben Jonson)

Charles IV

Charles IV was born on 14 May 1316 in Prague, and his cosmopolitan upbringing imbued him with a strong sense of his Bohemian heritage, the sophisticated culture of the French court and the imperial tradition. He spent his early childhood at the Bohemian court with his parents John of Luxemburg and Elizabeth Přemysl. After his mother's death he went at the age of seven to live with his aunt Joanna, the wife of King Charles IV (the Fair) of France at Paris, where he gave up his baptismal name Wenceslas (Václav) and called himself Charles – in emulation of his hero, Charlemagne. In 1329 he married (the first of four wives) Blanche of Valois, the sister of the future King Philip VI of France. Two years later he accompanied his father on a campaign to Florence, but fell out with him after their return, and fled to Italy, where he served the Venetians as a *condottiere* (mercenary leader). After reconciliation with his father he was made governor of Bohemia and Moravia in 1333. This marked the beginning of the 'Golden Age' of these two countries. Before his death King John had already prepared for the election of his son as German King (and so successor to the emperor), and he was elected on 11 July 1346 at Rhens on the Rhine, the traditional meeting place for the German Electors. The following November, after his father's death, he was crowned at Bonn. In 1347 he also had himself crowned King of Bohemia, and in 1349 had himself crowned German King again in the hallowed setting of Aachen. In 1355 Charles IV travelled to Italy, where he received the iron crown of the Lombard kings at Milan, and the Imperial crown from Pope Innocent VI at Rome; his last coronation took place at Arles in 1365 when he received the crown of the Kingdom of Burgundy – the first Emperor to do so since Frederick Barbarossa nearly two hundred years earlier.

Charles IV entered his extensive dominions as an experienced ruler, with a wide education, self confident, magnanimous, yet thrifty. He spoke fluent Czech, German, Latin, French and Italian, and surrounded himself with the best men in the Empire. While England and France were being torn apart by the Hundred Years' War and Italy was fragmented and powerless, central

Charles IV, bust by Peter Parler in the triforium of St Vitus's Cathedral, Prague

Europe during Charles's reign experienced peace and relative prosperity, safeguarded by strong castles, fortified towns and a trained army. In his 'Golden Bull' of 1356 Charles laid down the basic law which was to remain the fundamental constitutional law of the Holy Roman Empire until 1806. It confirmed the right of the seven Electors to choose the German King, established the indivisibility of the electoral lands and male primogeniture, and granted the Electors unrestricted jurisdiction within their territories.

The economy and trade flourished. Charles expanded the network of great trading routes extending from Venice to Danzig, Riga and Novgorod, from Flanders to Kiev and Constantinople, and the waterways via the Vltava and Elbe to the North Sea. He strove for the close incorporation of Bohemia into the Empire, fostered close relations with Nuremberg, the south German metropolis, and with the Hanseatic league at Lübeck, encouraged the cultivation of unused land, as well as mining and manufacturing of all kinds. He orientated Imperial policy eastwards, whereas for centuries it had been mainly directed towards the south. Prague, his birthplace, he made the capital of the Holy Roman Empire, and the political, intellectual and economic centre of Europe. He adorned it with magnificent buildings and in his reign it became the third largest city in Europe after Rome and Constantinople. His architects were also active at Nuremberg, Aachen, Breslau, Brandenburg and countless other places. Charles was admired by Cola di Rienzo and Petrarch, who praised the emperor's 'angelic mind', and his court was a centre of early humanism. It was at Prague that in 1348 he founded the first university in central Europe.

He was also the greatest collector of art since antiquity. Like many of his contemporaries he had a passion for relics, believing in the supernatural powers of the material remains of the earthly life and passion of Christ and His saints. In 1355 he acquired in Italy the remains of St Vitus, to whom the cathedral at Prague was dedicated. The Byzantine Emperor John V Palaeologus sent him supposed bones of the Patriarchs Abraham, Isaac and Jacob. From the Hungarian King Louis the Great he received the table cloth used at the Last Supper, from the French Dauphin (the future King Charles V) two thorns from the Crown of Christ, and from Pope Urban VI a piece of Christ's loincloth. These precious relics were suitably housed in the gold-encrusted settings he created for them at Karlštejn and in St Vitus's Cathedral.

To gain the support of the Catholic Church for his ambitious plans, he increased its power and wealth. However, this extension of ecclesiastical power was eventually to lead to the crisis in society which brought about the Hussite Wars.

Charles was also able to safeguard and extend his territories: in 1335 he acquired the rest of Silesia, in 1368 Lower Lusatia, and in 1374 Brandenburg. In 1362 he married (as his fourth wife) Elizabeth of Pomerania. He came to an agreement over inheritance with the Habsburgs in 1364, and married his son Sigismund to the daughter of King Louis I of Hungary and Poland. He also made early arrangements for his succession, having his eldest son, Wenceslas IV, crowned King of Bohemia in 1363 at the age of two, and German King in 1376. Charles IV died on 29 November 1378 in his native city of Prague. He could be described as the last great ruler of medieval Europe and the first ruler of the modern age.

The Hussite Wars (1419-1435)

Wenceslas IV (Václav; 1378–1419), Charles IV's son, was too weak a personality to succeed in an age of religious and national upheavals. As his power declined so did the respect in which he was held, until in 1400 the four Rhenish Electors deposed him as King of the Romans, though he remained King of Bohemia. In 1382 Wenceslas had arranged the marriage of his sister Anne to King Richard II of England, a union which increased the contacts between Bohemian and English intellectuals. In the face of signs of moral decline among the clergy the theologian John Wycliffe in England was calling for radical reform. He argued that the Church should reject its property and its striving for secular power. The Czech Jan Hus (John Huss), Dean of the Philosophical Faculty at Prague University, took up Wycliffe's ideas, and combined his plans for church reform with Czech national aspirations. He created a Czech literary language, preached in Czech and struggled against the influence of the Germans.

In 1411 Hus was excommunicated and in 1414 appeared before the Council of Constance. King Sigismund, Wenceslas's successor on the Roman throne, had promised him safe-

IOHANNES
HEILIGE
HAT · MIT
SCHID · G
EIST · VN:
RE · VERSI
HEN · IM

HVSS · DER
MERTERER
SEINEM · AB ·
OTT · GEPR ·
SEINE · LEH ·
GELT · GSC ·
· 1 4 1 5 · IAR

· 1 5 6 5

B · I ·

3V · PRAG · PREDIGT · HVSS · IM · BEHMRLANT
WART · DARNACH · 3V · COSTENZ · VERBRA ·
VONS · TEVFLS · STATHALTER · DE · PAPI ·
BRACHT · IHN · IN · IREN · RAH · MIT · LISTN
WIR · DANCKN · VNSRM · HERRE · IESV · CRISI
SEIN · ASCH · GAR · WEIT · GSTOBEN · IST

Jan Hus as a holy martyr, from a book illustration, 1565

conduct, but the College of Cardinals disregarded this, claiming that Hus had obtained it only by obstinacy in his 'false doctrine'. They had him arrested and in 1415 burned at the stake as a heretic. The weak protest of King Sigismund was ignored. Hus was later to be regarded as the first great martyr of the Reformation.

On Wenceslas IV's death in 1419 King Sigismund succeeded him as King of Bohemia. He had himself crowned on the Hradčany, but the people of Prague kept the town gates shut. The Diet at Čáslav in central Bohemia declared Sigismund an enemy of the Bohemian nation because of his 'murder' of Hus, and in 1419 the First Defenestration of Prague at the town hall of the New Town in Prague (see p. 131) started an uprising against the Germans. They were forced to leave the country and their property was confiscated. The uprising was supported by the followers of Jan Hus (Hussites). They demanded poverty of the clergy, freedom in preaching, the distribution to the laity of both the bread and the wine in the Mass (the 'lay chalice'), and – perhaps most importantly – a national state for the Czechs. The Hussites set up their headquarters at the newly founded fortress town of Tábor in southern Bohemia. With chalice on their banners as a symbol of their cause, the Hussite armies , under their blind leader Jan Žižka, passed through Bohemia and Moravia, and through Austria, Hungary, Bavaria, Saxony, Silesia and Brandenburg, burning and killing as they went. They succeeded in inflicting several heavy defeats on the Imperial armies, notably at the Battle of Vitkov near Prague in 1420.

While the Council of Basle (1431–1439) was dealing with the Hussite leaders, the Czechs split into two camps: the more moderate *Utraquists* (from *sub utraque specie* 'under both forms', i.e. bread and wine), supported by the nobility, and the radical peasant *Taborites*. In 1433 in the 'Compactata of Prague' the Church conceded the lay chalice to the Utraquists, thus eliminating the idea that their demands conflicted with Catholicism. The Taborites, however, fought on under their commanders Procopius the Great (or Bald) and Procopius the Less, until they were defeated in 1434 at Lipany by a united army of Catholics and Utraquists. The full recognition of the Utraquists in the 'Compactata of Basle' of 1455 brought the Hussite Wars to an end.

The Hussite Wars had broken the power of the Catholic Church in Bohemia, the Germans were driven to the border regions of the country, the peasants remained poor and in bondage; only the nobility and the burghers had profited, increasing their property and power enormously. The nation state remained unrealized, but national consciousness had been strengthened. A pattern of Czech history had been laid, in which religious, ethnic and national aspirations were intertwined.

In 1437 Albert II of Habsburg, Sigismund's stepson, became King of Bohemia and Hungary, but he died two years later leaving a son, Ladislas Postumus, who was still a minor. The leader of the Utraquists, George of Poděbrady and Kunštát (Jiří Poděbradský; 1458–1471) governed as regent, before being elected King in 1458 after Ladislas's death. Before his coronation, however, the Estates demanded that he adopt the Catholic faith, and this he is alleged to have done secretly. After his death in 1471 the Bohemian Estates elected Władysław Jagiełło (Vladislav II, 1471–1516), a son of King Casimir (Kazimierz) IV of Poland, as King of Bohemia. At the Peace of Olomouc in 1479 he ceded the territories of Moravia, Silesia and Lusatia to King Matthias I Corvinus of Hungary. On Matthias's death in 1490 he inherited the Hungarian crown and the centre of government moved to Buda, but at the Peace of Pressburg (Bratislava) in 1491 he had to promise the Bohemian and Hungarian succession to the Habsburgs. So when Vladislav's son Louis died childless – he was drowned in the Danube after the defeat by the Turks at Mohács in southern Hungary – Bohemia and Hungary passed to the Habsburgs. The territories were to remain united with Austria until 1918.

The Thirty Years' War (1618–1648)

The first Bohemian King of the Habsburg dynasty was Ferdinand I (1526–1564). A younger brother of the Emperor Charles V, this talented statesman was elected as Roman king in 1531, and in 1556, following Charles V's abdication, was crowned Emperor of the Holy Roman Empire. He sought a lasting compromise between Protestants and Catholics, and summoned the Jesuits to Prague, where their Collegium Clementinum soon surpassed in importance the old university (Collegium Carolinum), which was also Catholic.

His son Maximilian II (1562–1576), Roman and Bohemian King from 1562 and Emperor from 1564, was unable to reconcile the increasingly bitter religious and political differences in Germany. By now almost 70 per cent of the population was Lutheran. The Emperor sympathized with the Protestants and would have liked to become a convert, had not the Catholic Church threatened him with disinheritance. In Bohemia at the end of the 16th century there are supposed to have been about 200 Catholic, 200 Utraquist and 1200 Protestant parishes. The Lutheran and Utraquist nobility sent their sons to the University of Wittenberg, while the Catholic nobility had theirs educated at the Jesuit college in Prague.

Rudolph II, contemporary engraving

The second emperor to choose Prague as the centre of the Holy Roman Empire was Rudolph II (1576–1612), the son of Maximilian II, born in Vienna in 1552. In 1572 he became King of Hungary, in 1575 King of Bohemia, and in 1576 Emperor of the Holy Roman Empire. Rudolph enjoyed life in Prague and transferred his residence from Vienna to the Vltava. Like Charles IV, Rudolph was a great collector. His agents throughout Europe sought to acquire the finest works of art for his collection, while the artists at his court in Prague created a distinctive 'Rudolphine Mannerism'. The scholars attracted to Prague by his patronage included not only Tycho Brahe and Kepler, but also the alchemists Dee and Kelley. But Rudolph did not evade his duty to preserve Christendom from the ever-present Turkish threat. Until 1593 he maintained an armistice with the Turks, but then they renewed their attacks, and for 13 years war raged with neither side gaining a decisive advantage. In 1605 Rudolph took over military command from his brother Matthias and in the following year made peace.

By 1608 Rudolph, always inclined to melancholy, was physically and mentally ill, and Matthias took over the rulership of Hungary, Moravia and Austria. In 1609 the Bohemian Estates compelled Rudolph II to issue a Letter of Majesty guaranteeing their full religious freedom and their inalienable privileges. In 1611 Matthias also became King of Bohemia, but Rudolph died in 1612, just before the Electors decided to revoke his title as Emperor. He was the last reigning Emperor to reside in Prague and to regard Bohemia as the heart of Europe.

He was not an outstanding ruler – his lack of interest in political matters and his increasing mental and physical frailty had caused his family to persuade him to renounce his title as king – but he had for a time made Prague a treasure house of art and a great intellectual centre of Europe.

Matthias (1611–1619), who succeeded his brother as Emperor, was also unable to defuse the growing tensions between the Catholics and the Protestants and Utraquists. The two sides formed alliances: the Protestant princes came together in the *Union*, the Catholics in the *League*. The Second Defenestration of Prague (see pp. 94f.) triggered the Bohemian War, which escalated into thirty years of European conflict.

Matthias was succeeded by Ferdinand II (1619–1637), a grandson of Ferdinand I. In 1618 he became King of Bohemia, in 1618 of Hungary and in 1619 received the Imperial crown. In the same year the Protestant Bohemian Estates proclaimed that they had the right to elect the ruler of Bohemia. Ferdinand was deposed, and in August 1619 the estates chose as King the Elector Palatine Frederick, the leader of the Protestant Union and husband of Elizabeth, the daughter of King James I of England. The League responded by forming an army under the command of Count Tilly, which in 1620 inflicted a crushing defeat on the troops of the Union at the White Mountain (Bílá Hora) near Prague. Frederick, called the 'Winter King' because he reigned for just a year, fled to the Low Countries and lost everything, including his title as Elector, which passed to Maximilian I of Bavaria, the leader of the League. Twenty seven Protestant leaders were executed in front of the town hall of the Old Town in Prague. The Protestant nobility of Bohemia were expropriated and forced into exile, and the leaders of Protestant sects, including the 'Bohemian Brethren' (later known as the Moravians), also had to leave the country.

Perhaps the most remarkable personality thrown up by the war was Albrecht von Waldstein, better known as Wallenstein (1583–1634). Born into a Protestant family of the Bohemian nobility, Wallenstein had become a Catholic in 1606 and, as an officer in Imperial service, had been granted a title and extensive estates, fought under Tilly in the victories at Wimpfen (1622), Höchst (1622) and Stadtlohn (1623). In 1625 he was made Duke of Friedland and in the same year raised an army of his own which defeated the Union several times and greatly increased the power of the Emperor. In 1630, under pressure from the envious Estates of the Empire, Ferdinand II dismissed him, but had to call on him again in the following year when Gustavus II Adolphus of Sweden entered the war and defeated Tilly at Breitenfeld. In 1632 the 'Friedländer', as he was known, was given supreme command *in absolutissima forma* (with the most extensive powers) over the Imperial armies. In the same year he fought the Swedes at the Battle of Lützen in which Gustavus Adolphus was killed. When Waldstein began to pursue his own foreign policy the Emperor dismissed him again, charged him with high treason and had him murdered in Eger (Cheb), before he could go over to the Swedish army. Whether Waldstein wished to bring about peace or was aiming to seize the Bohemian crown for himself remains unresolved, but his extraordinary energy and the grandeur of his ambition are evident in the massive palace he built in Prague and in the

Baroque Architecture in Bohemia

Baroque came to Bohemia with North Italian architects in the 17th century. Wallenstein's vast palace in Prague, begun in 1621, was designed by **Andrea Spezza**, and in the middle of the century **Francesco Caratti** (d. 1679) built the Černín Palace (1669–1689) on the Hradčany for Count Jan Czernín who had studied architecture at Rome, and introduced a new grandeur to the Bohemian capital with its giant attached columns and diamond rustication and the sheer length of the façade.

Italians, most notably **Carlo Lurago** (1618–1684) who built the Clementinum for the Jesuits, dominated the architectural scene, but the arrival of **Jean-Baptiste Mathey** (1630–1695) in Prague in 1675 brought a new French classicism, with his elegant Troja Palace and St Francis's church (Kreuzherrnkirche), both begun in 1679. 1679 also saw the arrival in Prague of the Theatine priest and architect Guarino Guarini to produce a design (unexecuted) for the church of St Maria of Altötting (Panny Marie ustavičné pomoci u kajetanů, in Malá Strana). Guarinesque spatial interpenetration was taken up and developed in the following century, particularly by **Christoph** and **Kilian Ignaz Dientzenhofer** (see p. 75).

Viennese court architects were active in the Czech lands: **Johann Bernhard Fischer von Erlach** with the mighty Hall of Ancestors at Vranov (1688) and the Clam-Gallas Palace (1715) in Prague, and **Johann Lukas von Hildebrandt** at Jaroměřice in Moravia. The influence of their work can be seen in buildings by local architects such as **Giovanni Battista Alliprandi** (1665–1720), the designer of the Lobkowicz Palace in Prague, who worked at Kuks for the remarkable patron Count F.A. Sporck (who also employed **Matthias Bernhard Braun** (1684–1738), Bohemia's greatest Baroque sculptor); **Ottavio Broggio** (1668–1742) whose activity was restricted to the environs of his native town of Litomerice (Leitmeritz); **Paul Ignaz Bayer** (1650–1733) and **František Maximilian Kaňka** (1674–1766).

Apart from the Dientzenhofers the greatest of the Bohemian architects in the early 18th century was Giovanni Battista Santini, whose family had been in Bohemia for three generations and who Germanized his name to **Johann Blasius Santini-Aichel** (1667–1723). The remarkable Gothic-Baroque he created for his monastic patrons at Sedlec, Kladruby and Žd'ár nad Sázavou seems to look forward to Art Nouveau. After his training in Italy Santini had visited England, and may have seen early Gothic revivalism there, but the character of his own work is quite unique and had no successors.

The great age of Bohemian Baroque architecture came to an end with the death of Kilian Ignaz Dientzenhofer. The remodelling of Prague Castle by the Viennese architect **Nikolaus Pacassi** (1716–1790) has a sterile and montonous classicism.

buildings he erected at Jičín (Jitschin) in eastern Bohemia, which he made the capital of his domains.

A heavy defeat of the Swedes at Nördlingen led to the 'Peace of Prague' concluded on 30 May 1635 between the Emperor and most of the Protestant Estates, which marked the beginning of the process of re-Catholicization in Bohemia and Moravia. But the war was still far from over: France became involved in the conflict in order to counter the superior power of the Habsburgs in Europe. The fortunes of war swung between the Imperial forces and the combined French and Swedish armies, until negotiations which had been underway since 1644 finally brought an end to the fighting with the 'Peace of Westphalia' in 1648.

Re-Catholicization and Baroque had been progressing hand in hand in Bohemia since the victories of the Imperial armies. The country lost its independence and Czech national consciousness was suppressed. The power of the Catholic clergy grew, together with the influence of the Germans who controlled the economy and supported the administration. From 1763 most lectures at Prague University were in German (previously the language used had been Latin), and from 1773 German was also established as the language of instruction in grammar schools.

18th and 19th Centuries

The Habsburg Emperors of the Holy Roman Empire of the German Nation continued to be also Kings of Bohemia: Ferdinand III (1637–1657), Leopold I (1658–1705), Joseph I (1705–1711), Charles VI (1711–1740). In the 'Pragmatic Sanction' of 1713 Charles VI declared that the Habsburg lands were indivisible and that succession could also pass through the female line. Nevertheless his daughter Maria Theresa (1740–1780) had a difficult task defending her inheritance in the War of the Austrian Succession (1740–1748) and the Silesian Wars (1740–1742, 1744-45). She was nevertheless able to repudiate Bavaria's claims to Bohemia. On 12 May 1743 she had herself crowned Queen of Bohemia in Prague, and although she resided mainly at Vienna, she had the castles at Prague and Bratislava (then still the capital of Hungary) remodelled as suitable royal residences.

The Emperor Joseph II (1765–1790), Maria Theresa's eldest son, ruled together with his mother until her death in 1780. The reforms which he introduced over the following years reflected his enlightened views. In 1781 he abolished serfdom, in 1782 he published the 'Edict of Toleration' which guaranteed freedom of belief (whereupon 80,000 people registered as Protestants in Bohemia). The Jews were allowed to leave the ghettos. In the course of a ruthless process of secularization Joseph dissolved more than 700 religious houses, and, in a move that was intended as a rationalization but was perceived by most of his non-German-speaking subjects as an affront, he made German the official language throughout the Habsburg lands. Joseph was, of course, also King of Bohemia, but unlike his mother he refused a coronation in St Vitus's Cathedral on the grounds that it was unnecessary. Leopold II (1790–1792) likewise did without a coronation at Prague. The infuriated Bohemian nobles are said to have spoken only Czech as a protest against the language policy of the Habsburgs, and in 1791 a chair in the Czech language was founded at Prague University.

Leopold's son Francis (1792–1835) was an Emperor twice over: in 1804 he founded the Austrian Empire as Francis I, and in 1806 as Francis II he renounced the title of Roman-German Emperor and declared the Holy Roman Empire abolished. Bohemia and Moravia remained almost undisturbed by the Napoleonic Wars. The only battle fought there was Austerlitz (Slavkov u Brna) in southern Moravia in 1805, in which Napoleon Bonaparte defeated the armies of the Alexander I of Russia and the Emperor Francis I. For the most part

Maria Theresa, by Martin von Meytens

Bohemia and Moravia were used as places of refuge and as a base for resistance against Napoleon.

Since Bohemia with Moravia had been part of the Habsburg Empire, its history now broadly follows that of Austria. Its flourishing economy made Bohemia a 'jewel in the Habsburg crown'. By the end of the 18th century – and especially in the 19th century – industrial businesses, both large and small, developed in the towns and in the countryside. The glass industry achieved European importance. In 1792 the first Bohemian porcelain factory was established at Karlovy Vary (Karlsbad). In 1796 the first English spinning machine was installed in northern Bohemia and in 1804 the first steam engine began working at Liberec (Reichenberg). In 1806 a Polytechnic was founded at Prague. The development of industry led to the growth of a Czech urban proletariat, which contributed to the re-awakening of the Czech national consciousness in the 19th century.

The Path to Nationhood

The revolutionary movement of 1848-49 spread from France to Germany and Austria did little to alleviate social and national tensions within the empire. Nevertheless, an imperial letter, signed by Emperor Ferdinand I and dated 8 April 1848 had declared: 'Bohemian Nationality must be considered a fundamental principle with complete equality of the Czech language with the German in all branches of State administration and public instruction.' And the constitution for all Austrian provinces of 26 April 1848 declared that 'the inviolability of nationality and language is guaranteed for all ethnic groups'. When the German National Assembly met on 18 May 1848 in the Paulskirche in Frankfurt-am-Main, the only Czech representatives present were from Moravia. Those from the Bohemian constituencies did not go; the historian František Palacký turned down the invitation to participate on the grounds that he was not a German. Afterwards the Moravian Diet, composed of 123 German and 124 Czech representatives, proclaimed the secession of Moravia from Bohemia.

At the 'Slav Congress' in Prague in June 1848 Palacký demanded the transformation of the Austrian Empire into a 'federation of peoples with equal rights'. The Czech uprising which then flared up in Prague was put down by troops of the General Commander in Bohemia, Prince Windischgrätz. Fighting at the barricades in Vienna (October 1848) caused the Emperor Ferdinand to flee to Olomouc (Olmütz) in northern Moravia (where on 2 December he was forced to abdicate), while the Austrian Reichstag, in which Palacký was the leader of the Slav party, moved to Kroměříž (Kremsier) in Moravia.

In 1866 the conflict between Prussia and Austria over the Schleswig-Holstein question escalated into a war into which all the other German states were drawn. The decisive battle took place at Königgrätz (Hradec Králové) in eastern Bohemia where the Prussians under Helmuth von Moltke were victorious. In Nikolsburg (Mikulov) in southern Moravia the two sides made a preliminary peace, which admitted none of the territorial claims of Austria and the adjacent south German states. The Peace of Prague ended the German War of 1866 conclusively.

In 1867 Austria conceded the nationalist claims of the Magyars and the Dual Monarchy of Austria-Hungary was formed, in which only foreign policy and war were to be conducted from Vienna. But the government in Vienna rejected similar demands from the Czechs. Emperor Franz Joseph I, the successor to Ferdinand I, who had abdicated in 1848, was crowned in Budapest as King of Hungary, but refused absolutely a coronation as King of Bohemia, although Prague Castle was redecorated in readiness for the event.

The national awakening saw a revival of Czech literature and music. The ardent nationalism was particularly evident in the operatic and symphonic works of Smetana. The Slovaks too were awakening. The Slovak romantic poet Jan Kollár (1793–1852) was the real founder of Pan-Slavism, a movement that was based on a sense of the brotherhood of all Slavs

Tomáš Garrigue Masaryk

and often looked to Russia as the only Slavic nation that was not under foreign rule. Ľudovít Štúr, a former Protestant pastor who took up the nationalist cause, created a Slovak literary language. An oppressive policy of Magyarization, by which the Hungarian authorities attempted to force all the inhabitants of Hungarian lands to speak Magyar and so become Hungarian, led to growing resentment in areas where the Slovaks were the majority.

Meanwhile in Bohemia Czech influence was growing. In the 1880's the Germans were replaced by the Czechs as the majority n the Bohemian Diet, and conflict between German and Czech representatives intensified in the Reichsrag and in the Diet. In 1882 Prague University was split into two universities, one German and one Czech, and in 1890 the Emperor founded the Czech Academy of Sciences and Arts at Prague. Around the turn of the century groups of ethnic Germans were beginning to argue for the incorporation of the German-speaking districts into the Reich, while the Czechs – especially the 'Young Czechs' under their leader Karel Kramář – demanded a Czech state within an Austro-Hungarian federation and union with a Slovakia liberated from Hungary.

After the outbreak of the First World War Tomáš Garrigue Masaryk (1850–1937), a professor at the Charles University in Prague and member of the Austrian Reichsrat, went abroad in order to lead the struggle of his land for independence. Masaryk was born in southern Moravia and had attended the German School at Brno (Brünn), studied philology and philosophy at Vienna and Leipzig, where he had met Charlotte Garrigue, an American student, who later became his wife. (After her death in 1923 he assumed her maiden name as a second forename.) In 1882 he was given a lectureship at the new Czech University in Prague.

In December 1914 he went to Rome, then to London, and finally to Paris, where with Edvard Beneš he founded a Czechoslovak National Council. 1917 saw the establishment of the 'Czech Legion', which fought with the allies against Germany and Austria-Hungary. On 30 May 1918 in the USA he concluded the 'Pittsburgh Agreement' with Slovak organizations, which envisaged the union of Czechs and Slovaks in a single state.

Since it was now becoming clear that Czechoslovakia would break away from the Dual Monarchy, Charles I, Emperor of Austria, declared on 16 October 1918 that he intended to transform the Monarchy into a federation of free nations. But it was already too late. In mid-October the Czechoslovak National Council in Paris had formed a provisional government, and on 28 October in Prague the *Czechoslovak Republic (ČSR)* was proclaimed. On 14 November the National Assembly in Prague elected Masaryk as the first President of the Republic, and Beneš was made Foreign Minister. The Slovaks and the Carpathian Ukrainians had joined the republic in return for the promise of an autonomous government in their regions.

After the departure of the Emperor on 11 November 1918 to exile in Switzerland, the Austrian National Assembly passed a resolution that the German-speaking regions of the former Habsburg Monarchy become part of the German Empire under the name of 'German Austria' ('Deutsch-Österreich'). The German-settled areas of Bohemia, Moravia and Austrian Silesia then declared themselves provinces of German Austria. But the Prague government insisted that the historic borders of the Czech lands be retained (not least because much of the country's industry was concentrated in the predominantly German-speaking border regions), and responded to this attempt to join the German Empire by sending in Czech troops and dissolving the German district and provincial governments. On 16 November 1918 the Hungarian People's Republic was proclaimed and Czech troops occupied Upper Hungary (i.e. Slovakia). The Treaty of Trianon (4 June 1920) confirmed the transfer of the 17 Upper Hungarian komitats to the Czechoslovak Republic, and the Treaty of Saint-Germain-en-Laye (10 September 1919) recognized the Czechoslovak Republic. At the same time the victorious powers forbade the use of the name 'German Austria' and the incorporation of the German-speaking areas into the German Reich.

According to the 1921 census the inhabitants of the multi-ethnic new republic consisted of 8.76 million Czechs and Slovaks, 3.12 million Germans, 750,000 Hungarians, 460,000 Ukrainians (Ruthenians), 180,000 Jews, 70,000 Poles, and 20,000 members of other ethnic groups: a total population of 13.36 million. The centralizing constitution (1920) and the long period in office of President Masaryk (1918–1936), the dominant personality of the republic although he stood aloof from party politics, ensured a peaceful and continual development. Although the minorities were involved in the work of government, the Slovaks and Carpathian Ukrainians were denied their promised autonomy. When the Slovak leader Vojtěch Tuka reminded the government of their promise in no uncertain terms, and threatened unilateral independence of his country, he was sentenced in 1929 to 15 years imprisonment for 'conspiring against the Republic'.

In 1933 Konrad Henlein, a bank official, founded the 'Sudetendeutsche Heimatfront' (Sudeten German Home Front) by uniting various German associations. Student unrest broke out in 1934, when the German University in Prague was forced to hand over its insignia to the Czech University – and was thus in effect abolished. Before the parliamentary elections in May 1935 the Sudetendeutsche Heimatfront had to change its name; it was known thereafter as the 'Sudetendeutsche Partei' (Sudeten German Party) and received 68 per cent of German votes, making it the strongest single party in Czechoslovakia. Masaryk retired at the age of 85 and was succeeded as President by Edvard Beneš. The Slovak Milan Hodža, a committed supporter of Czecho-Slovak cooperation, became head of government.

The Reich Protectorate of Bohemia and Moravia

In the autumn of 1937 Konrad Henlein demanded autonomy for the German-speaking areas of Bohemia and Moravia in the name of the Sudeten German Party. On 24 April 1938 he presented the 'Karlsbad Programme' in which, on Hitler's instructions, he deliberately asked for more than the Czechs were prepared to grant: autonomy, reparations, freedom to follow German traditions and equal rights. In the local elections in May the Sudeten German Party received 92 per cent of German votes. Henlein responded to the concessions of the Hodža government with a demand for incorporation into the Reich. In the late summer Lord Runciman conducted mediation discussions in Prague on behalf of the British government and in his final report recommended the transfer of the Sudeten German areas to the German Reich. After negotiations with Chamberlain Hitler set 1 October as the deadline for the handing over of the Sudeten German regions. Chamberlain and the French Prime Minister, Edouard Daladier pressed the Czechoslovak government to give way so that peace in Europe could be preserved, but Prague refused. Chamberlain asked Benito Mussolini to mediate. On 29 September Hitler, Chamberlain, Daladier and Mussolini met at Munich and decided that Czechoslovakia must cede the German-settled border areas to the German Reich (the Munich Agreement). The Soviet Union disapproved of this, but was not prepared to risk starting a war. Prague had no choice but to comply.

On 1 October 1938 German troops marched into the Sudeten German regions. These territories now formed the 'Reichsgau Sudetenland' (22,603 sq km, population: 2,943,187) with its capital Reichenberg (Liberec) and comprised three administrative districts, Eger (Cheb), Aussig (Ústí nad Labem) and Troppau (Opava). Konrad Henlein became Gauleiter and Reichsstatthalter (Reich-Governor). This signalled the break-up of the country. On 2 October 1938 Polish troops occupied the Olsa district, part of the old duchy of Teschen (Těšín; Polish: Cieszyn) which was in north Moravia but was inhabited mainly by Poles, and on 4 November Hungary annexed the border regions of Slovakia. On 5 October President Beneš resigned and left the country.

Meanwhile, under the leadership of Jozef Tiso, a Catholic priest, the Slovaks pressed for their country's independence. On 6 October 1938 (formally on 19 November) Slovakia was declared an autonomous state within 'Czecho-Slovakia' with Tiso as its prime minister. Thus the political settlement in the Czechoslovak region largely corresponded to the wishes of the various national groups, peace seemed to have been preserved, and Europe breathed again. But Hitler (in a secret military order of 21 October 1938) demanded more: the 'settling of the rest of Czechoslovakia'. In the early spring of 1939 Tiso demanded full sovereignty for Slovakia. On 13 March in Berlin he received the consent of Hitler who was supporting not only Slovak attempts at secession but also further territorial claims by Poland and Hungary. On 14 March Slovakia proclaimed its full autonomy; Jozef Tiso became its president, and Hungarian troops occupied Carpathian Ukraine.

Under the pressure of German military superiority, Emil Hácha, Beneš's successor as president, signed an agreement in Berlin creating the *Reichsprotektorat Böhmen und Mähren* (Reich Protectorate of Bohemia and Moravia) on 15 March. This 'Protectorate of the German Reich' covered an area of 49,000 sq km and had a population of 7.3 million. It had an autonomous government, legal system and culture, but had no control over foreign policy or defence.

On 23 March Slovakia placed itself under the protection of the German Reich, which formally guaranteed its political independence, but demanded close collaboration in foreign, defence and economic policy within a framework of 'protective friendship'. The 150,000 or so German citizens of Slovakia were given full cultural autonomy and were represented in the parliament and by their own secretary of state, while the more than 110,000 Slovakian Jews became the victims of increasing persecution and were eventually deported to extermination camps.

During the Second World War the Protectorate was developed as an industrial region of the Reich out of range of allied bombers, and it was here that many of the armaments, textiles, food, chemicals, vehicles, tyres, leather goods and optical instruments were produced. The workforce had full employment, good wages and relatively high food allocations, and consequently were not inclined to offer resistance. The leadership of the Protectorate used suppression mainly against the intelligentsia; after a student uprising the Czech universities were closed in the autumn of 1939, and professors and journalists were deported from 1941 onwards.

In 1941 Reinhard Heydrich, Chief of the head office of Reich security, took over the post of deputy Reich Protector. On 26 May 1942 Czech agents sent by the government in exile carried out an assassination attempt on Heydrich and he died as a result on 4 June. In retribution and as a deterrent the SS destroyed the village of Lidice and liquidated most of its population (see p. 148). If the intention of the Heydrich assassination had been to increase anti-Nazi feeling in the Czech population, it was successful.

Edvard Beneš had formed a 'Czechoslovak National Committee' in London in the autumn of 1939, which was recognized by the Allies as the provisional government. In 1943 this government concluded a pact of friendship and aid with the Soviet Union. It demanded the annulment of the Munich Agreement and the expulsion of the Sudeten Germans. On 18 August 1944 Soviet troops crossed the Slovak border. At the same time a revolt against the Tiso government broke out in the industrial region of Banská Bystrica. At Tiso's request German troops entered Slovakia and until the end of October brutally put down the uprising; the Soviet army did not intervene. On 4 April 1945 the Red Army entered

Bratislava. On 5 April 1945, after the withdrawal of the Wehrmacht, the Czechoslovak National Council proclaimed the unity of the Czech and Slovak peoples and the nationalizing of the basic industries, banks and insurance ('Košice Programme').

On 5 May 1945, three days before the end of the war, a general uprising broke out in Prague against the Germans. 2.9 million Sudeten Germans were expelled from the country. Of these 1.9 million found a new home in the Federal Republic of Germany, 800,000 in the GDR, and 140,000 in Austria. About 200,000 Germans were allowed to stay in Czechoslovakia. On 29 June the USSR took over Carpathian Ukraine as part of the Ukrainian SSR. Henlein committed suicide in Allied custody, Reichsprotektor Frick was condemned to death by the international Military Tribunal at Nuremberg, and Tiso, the former president of Slovakia, was executed on 18 April 1947.

The Socialist Republic and its downfall

In May 1945 the government of the Czechoslovak Republic (ČSR) under the Prime Minister Zdeněk Fierlinger began work in Prague. Beneš returned from exile in London and was once again President. At the election in 1946 the 'Communist Party of Czechoslovakia' (KPČ)

Wenceslas Square, Prague

won 37.9 per cent of the votes, more than any other party, a proportion similar to the post-war Communist vote in France. The communist leader Klement Gottwald took over from Fierlinger as Prime Minister.

After the 'Victorious February' coup of 1948 the KPČ seized political superiority, and the non-communist ministers resigned. A few days later the only non-communist left in the government, Tomáš Masaryk's son, Jan, was mysteriously found dead beneath a window in the Foreign Ministry. The new constitution of 9 May 1948 made the ČSR a centralized, people's democratic republic. At the rigged elections held on 30 May 89.3 per cent of the votes went to the KPČ-directed National Front. Beneš realized that the rôle of Czechoslovakia as a bridge between east and west was disappearing and resigned in June. Klement Gottwald became President, with Antonín Zápotocký as Prime Minister. In 1949 the ČSR joined the Council for Mutual Economic Aid (COMECON). In 1952 the purges of party members culminated in the notorious Slánský show-trials, which were reminiscent of Stalin's in the 1930's and were openly anti-semitic. Any idealism which communism had once attracted had by now evaporated. After Gottwald's death on 14 March 1953, a few days after that of his mentor, Stalin, Zápotocký succeeded as President, while Antonín Nóvotný took over leadership of the Party and Villem Široky, a Slovak, became Prime Minister. On Zápotocký's death in 1957 Nóvotný became President.

The new constitution of 11 July 1960 changed the People's Republic into a Socialist Republic – the ČSR became the ČSSR. The Slovaks were still denied self-government. A one-sided development of heavy industry led to economic difficulties, which resulted in internal conflicts between the 'orthodox' and the 'reformers' within the party. In January 1968 the reformers asserted themselves: Nóvotný was forced to resign; Alexander Dubček became Party leader, while the war hero Ludvík Svoboda became President, and the economic specialist Oldřich Černik took over as head of government. By implementing extensive economic reforms, guaranteeing civil rights, federalizing the Republic and acknowledging the rights of minorities the Party sought to win back the trust of the people. The new programme of the KPČ promised 'socialism with a human face'. The people looked forward to a 'Prague Spring', but the Soviet Union feared that Czechoslovakia would break away from the socialist block, while communist state and party leaderships in Berlin and Warsaw felt threatened by the changes in the ČSSR and demanded Soviet intervention. Leonid Brezhnev, General Secretary of the Communist Party of the Soviet Union, drew up the thesis of limited sovereignty of the states in the Soviet block (the 'Brezhnev Doctrine') and on the night of 20–21 August 1968 Warsaw Pact troops (USSR, GDR, Poland, Bulgaria and Hungary) moved into Czechoslovakia. The Soviet leadership brought President Svoboda, General Secretary Dubček, government leader Černik and Foreign Minister Smrkovský to Moscow to cancel all the reforms.

The 'Prague Spring' had by no means been a rejection of socialism, but the only one of its reforms which was retained was the federalization of the state: the changes to the Constitution of 1 January 1969 made the Czech and the Slovak Socialist Republics constituent parts of the *Federal State ČSSR* with a single head of state and federal parliament. In April 1969 Gustav Husák, a Slovak, removed Dubček from the leadership of the Party; fourteen months later Dubček was expelled from the Party. In January 1970 Černik was forced to resign as head of government in favour of Lubomir Štrougal. The treaty with the Soviet Union of 6 May 1970 ensured a return to the Soviet course. Increasing economic difficulties led to discontent among the population, and an attempt was made to overcome the difficulties by modernizing industry.

In 1977 Czechoslovak civil rights campaigners such as the former foreign minister Jiří Hájek, the dramatist Václav Havel and the philosopher Jan Patočka published 'Charter 77', a programme for the democratization of Czechoslovakia, which, despite all the attempts of the state at repression, was followed by about fifty other documents.

In 1988 Ladislav Adamec became head of government on the resignation of Štrougal. From then on the timid economic reforms of the ČSSR followed the aims of the Soviet leader Mikhail Gorbachev. At the same time the opposition to the government came into the open. In August 1988, on the twentieth anniversary of the entry of the Warsaw Pact troops into Prague, 10,000 students demonstrated in Wenceslas Square. It was also predominantly students who took part on 17 November 1989 in an authorized procession commemorating the events of November 1939 (when nine students were shot by the fascists, 1200 were taken to Sachsenhausen concentration camp and all Czech universities were closed). The Prague police broke up the demonstration with extreme violence. Two days later, on 19 November, members of the civil rights movement 'Charter 77', headed by Václav Havel, joined with other dissident groups to form *Civic Forum* as a voice for the Czechoslovak democracy movement. It was through the daily mass rallies held in Prague, Bratislava and other cities that the political changes in Czechoslovakia took place: the 'Velvet Revolution' – a peaceful, people's revolution. On 24 November the Communist Party General Secretary Miloš Jakeš resigned, and a few days later Prime Minister Adamec also stepped down. The Vice-Premier, Marián Čalfa formed a new government, in which the Communist Party no longer had a majority. On 9 December President Husák resigned, and on 29 December the National Assembly elected Václav Havel as the new head of state. On 29 March 1990 the Parliament decided that the country should now be known as the *Czech and Slovak Federative Republic* (ČSFR).

In the first elections for the Federative Assembly and National Council, held on 8 and 9 June 1990, the Czech *Civic Forum* and the Slovak *Public Against Violence* were confirmed as the strongest parties. President Havel entrusted Marián Čalfa, a Slovak, with forming a government. Alexander Dubček, the most famous of the 1968 reformers, became the Speaker of the Parliament. On 5 July the Federative Assembly voted to continue Václav Havel's presidency.

Prague (Praha)

Prague – the 'City of a Hundred Spires', the 'Golden City', 'Bohemian Rome', the ancient 'Mother in Israel' to the Jews, 'little mother' to all Czechs – has always been the main attraction for visitors to Bohemia. No other city in Europe has such a wealth of unspoiled architecture from so many periods, of which the marvellous works of the Late Gothic and Baroque are the most remarkable, though the Art Nouveau and Modernism are scarcely less important. It is undoubtedly one of the most beautiful cities in the world, its magnificent buildings covering the hilly landscape either side of the river. The friendly atmosphere of its pubs and wine bars, restaurants and cafés is appealing – all the more so since the Revolution of 1989 has lifted the oppressive pall of forty years of Communist rule.

Prague is the capital of Czechoslovakia, the capital of Bohemia, the administrative centre of the region of Central Bohemia, and a self-governing city with a population of 1,186,000. It now covers an area of 185 square kilometres in the river basin at the confluence of the Berounka (Beraun) and Vltava (Moldau) rivers. It is the most important crossroads and the biggest industrial and financial centre in Czechoslovakia.

The nucleus of the city is the *Old Town* (Staré město). The other old districts – *Malá strana* (Lesser Town; German: Kleinseite), the Castle Town or *Hradčany* (German: Hradschin), and the *New Town* (Nové město) – were all independent towns until their amalgamation in 1784. In 1786 the population of Prague was 73,000; in 1890 183,000; and in 1930 (after the incorporation of many suburbs) 849,000.

History

The hills around Prague were inhabited in neolithic times (6th millennium BC). From the 3rd millennium onward a trading station was established at the ford across the Vltava at the intersection of the amber and salt trade routes.

Around the year 700 the legendary Slav princess and prophetess Libuše (Libussa), who was living a few miles downstream, prophesied that a great city would arise at the ford: 'I see a city whose glory shall reach to the stars...' The city was called *Praha* because a 'sill' (*prah*) in the river bed was used as the ford. Libuše wedded the ploughman Přemysl (the story is told in Smetana's opera *Libuše*) and founded the Přemyslid dynasty, which ruled Bohemia for the next six hundred years. Her earliest recorded descendant, Prince Bořivoj (850–895), and his wife Ludmila, who had been baptized in Moravia by Methodios, the Apostle of the Slavs,

View of Prague in 1493, from Schedel's World Chronicle

founded a castle, the Hradčany, on the hill west of the ford, and later transferred their residence there. Within the precincts of the castle they erected a church in honour of the Virgin Mary on a pagan site of sacrifice and cremation called Žiži. Christianity had not, however, completely triumphed. After the death of her husband Ludmila was murdered by order of her pagan daughter-in-law, Drahomíra of Stodor, thus becoming Bohemia's first martyr. Her son, Vratislav I, built the Basilica of St George around 920, and in 925 his son, Duke Wenceslas (Václav), founded the Rotunda of St Vitus. Wenceslas – the 'Good King Wenceslas' of the 19th-century English carol, who was genuinely good, though never a king – was planning to renounce his dukedom in favour of his brother Boleslav I ('the Cruel') in order to become the first bishop of Prague, but in 929 his plan was preempted by the pagan Boleslav, who had him murdered on the way to mass. It was not until 973 that Mlada, the sister of Boleslav II ('the Pious') received the foundation charter for the bishopric of Prague from Pope John XIII in Rome. She later founded the first monastery in Bohemia next to St George's Basilica on the Hradčany. By the beginning of the 13th century there were more than fifty churches in Prague.

In the 10th century more and more Jewish and German merchants settled in the city, attracted after 1178 by legal and fiscal privileges. These were increased by King Otakar II Přemysl, who in 1267 laid out the *Lesser Town* for the German settlers. Around 1300 the royal mint started producing the Prague groschen, which was legal tender throughout the Holy Roman Empire.

Prague's golden age started with the return of Charles IV to his mother's native city. It was not promising: '... we had no place to stay, save in a house like any other burgher. The castle of Prague had been so devastated, dilapidated and destroyed since the time of Otakar that it had been wholly levelled to the ground. There we ordered the building, at heavy cost, of the spacious and stately palace.' Part of this rebuilding was St Vitus's Cathedral, begun in 1353, in keeping with the city's new status as an archbishopric which Charles had energetically negotiated. Five years earlier, Charles had founded the first university in Central Europe, named the Carolinum after him. Charles also planned the New Town and gave the crossing of the Vltava worthy expression with the massive stone bridge now called the Charles Bridge. Prague was now the third largest city in Europe after Rome and Constantinople, with a population of 40,000. From 1355 it was the capital of the Holy Roman Empire.

Charles's son Wenceslas IV (Václav) moved his residence from Hradčany to the Old Town. Theological and social tensions grew as Jan Hus and his supporters attacked both the clergy's pursuit of power and property, and the privileges and preferential treatment given to the Germans. Under pressure from Hus Wenceslas IV was forced to change the voting rights in Prague University in favour of the Czechs by the Decree of Kutná Hora (Kuttenberg), which was followed by the departure of the German students and professors. On 30 July 1419 the First Defenestration of Prague, when Catholic town councillors were thrown out of the window of the town hall of the New Town by an enraged mob led by the Hussite preacher Jan Želivský (p. 131), started the Hussite Wars, which caused severe damage and put a stop to all building work until the final victory of the moderate Hussites (Utraquists) at Lipany near Prague in 1434. George of Poděbrady re-established peace and order, and building activity was able to start again in Prague. His successor, the Polish Vladislav II Jagiello (1471–1516) gave the Castle its crowning glory with the great Vladislav Hall.

In 1556 Ferdinand I summoned the Jesuits to Prague and strengthened the position of the Catholic Church. His successor, Rudolph II (1576–1612), once more made Prague the splendid capital of the Holy Roman Empire, summoning artists and scholars from many lands to work at his court. On 23 May 1618 the Second Defenestration of Prague, when Protestant nobles threw two Imperial councillors and their secretary out of one of the

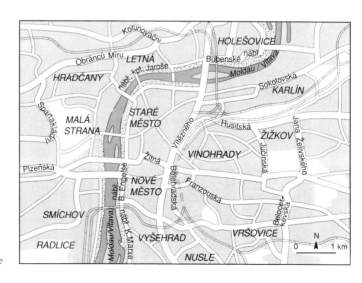

Central Prague

windows of the castle into the moat, started the Bohemian War which led to the Thirty Years' War. In the 'Battle of the White Mountain' near Prague (8 November 1620) the Imperial forces defeated the army of the Estates. The Protestant leaders were executed in the Old Town Square on 21 June 1621.

The Thirty Years' War left its mark on Prague. The property of the Protestant nobility was confiscated and a new Catholic aristocracy quickly moved in, accompanied by many who had made their fortune in the wars. Vast new palaces and religious houses were imposed on Prague, starting with the unprecedented proportions of the Waldstein Palace in the Malá Strana, built by Albrecht von Wallenstein, the imperial generalissimo. The devastation of Bohemia and Moravia was reflected in the fortunes of the capital; the population declined and the city was briefly occupied by Swedish troops – when the students of Prague put up a brave resistance. Yet Catholicism had triumphed, and with it the Baroque style which was to give Prague so many glorious buildings.

During the War of the Austrian Succession (1740–1748) and the Seven Years' War (1756–1763) Prague was the scene of heavy fighting on several occasions. In 1741 the Saxons, Bavarians and French besieged the capital for almost two months before taking it by storm in the night of 26 November. The capture was followed by looting. On 6 May 1757 Frederick the Great defeated the Austrians in the 'Battle of Prague' and once again besieged the city until the defeat at Kolín forced him to retreat.

Under Maria Theresa many churches, palaces and houses were given a classical appearance, and Prague Castle was renovated and extended. In 1784 Joseph II united the four independent towns of Prague to form a single city. The abolition of serfdom encouraged many Czechs to come to seek their fortune in Prague. Factories and tenements developed, and, as the Czech proportion of the population increased, so Czech national consciousness grew. In the 18th and 19th centuries several important Czech institutions were established: the Learned Society (1771), the Gallery of Patriotic Art-Lovers (1796), the Academy of Arts (1816), the National Museum (1818), the first Czech public library (1835). Yet even in 1857 half the population of the city was German. In 1861 the Germans lost their majority in the City Parliament for the first time, and in 1882 the Charles University was split to form two universities, one German and one Czech. Bohemia's rôle as the industrial heartland of the Austro-Hungarian Empire was shown in the great Industrial Exhibition held in Prague in 1891, of which several structures still remain on the Petřin. Prague was expanding energetically, and beautifying herself. The most striking example is the razing of the ghetto on the grounds of public sanitation, and its replacement by tall blocks in the latest Art Nouveau taste.

After the collapse of the Habsburg Empire at the end of the First World War the Czechoslovak Republic was proclaimed in Prague on 28 October 1918 by Tomáš Masaryk. This brief flowering of independence and prosperity was expressed in some remarkable modernist architecture, both public and domestic; but just under 21 years later, on 15 March 1939, units of the Wehrmacht occupied Prague and it became for six years the capital of the

'Protectorate of Bohemia and Moravia'. Of the 40,000 Jews in Prague, 36,000 went to the gas chambers of Auschwitz. On 9 May 1945 the Soviet Army marched into Prague.

The city has naturally been the focus of post-war Czechoslovak history. Here, in the Old Town Square, Gottwald staged the rallies that preceded the Communist coup of 1948; here the economic difficulties of the 1960's led to the Prague Spring of 1968, so quickly crushed by the tanks of the Warsaw Pact. Here, finally, the brutality of the dying regime and the courage of the masses in the Velvet Revolution of 1989 brought about the collapse of Communism, and created a new democracy.

Throughout all these events, the city of Prague has been more than just a setting; and the constant presence of the city in the political life of Czechoslovakia, from the grandiose town-planning of Charles IV's empire, and the Baroque glorification of the Catholic Church triumphant, to the resurgent Czech ambitions of the National Theatre dominating the Vltava, and of the soaring Cathedral completed in the heart of the bland, oppressive Habsburg castle, culminates perhaps in the revolutionary slogan *Havel na Hrad* – Havel to the Castle – which has made the absurdist playwright the successor to the Přemyslids and Luxemburgs, Habsburgs and Masaryks, in the great building that looms over the city.

Staré město (Old Town)

In the 10th century a group of settlements of merchants and craftsmen between the Vltava bend to the north and the ford to the west united to form a single settlement, the Old Town. In 973 the Jewish merchant Ibrahim ibn Jakub came to Prague from Arabic Spain and praised it as the greatest market in the Slavic lands: 'In the city of Prague saddles, bridles and shields are made ... cloths woven as thin as nets ... are used as money by them (the inhabitants of Prague) and they possess chests full of them. The most precious things can be bought for these cloths: wheat, slaves, horses, gold and silver ...'

The settlement was still under the immediate control of the lord of the castle, and the market people were under the jurisdiction of the duke's court. In the 12th century traffic increased considerably, churches were built and St Mary of Týn became the main marketplace church. In the 13th century more and more German merchants acquired sites in the marketplace. The danger of attack by the Turcomans made it necessary to fortify the small settlement, which gradually assumed the functions of a town. In 1338 King John granted the Old Town the right to regulate its own affairs.

From the Municipal House to the Old Town Square

The **Municipal House** (Obecní dům) has a much longer history than the appearance of the building might suggest. It stands on the site of the Royal Court, the residence of the rulers of Bohemia for much of the 15th century. King Wenceslas IV acquired a number of houses by

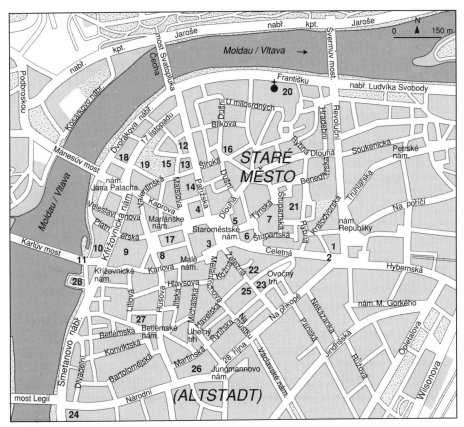

Old Town (Staré město)
1 Obecní dům   2 Powder Tower   3 Old Town Hall   4 St Nicholas   5 Kinsky Palace   6 Týn
Church   7 Ungelt   8 Clam-Gallas Palace   9 Clementinum   10 St. Francis (Church of the Knights of
the Cross)   11 Old Town Bridge Tower   12 Old-New Synagogue   13 Jewish Town Hall and High
Synagogue   14 Maisel Synagogue   15 Klausen Synagogue and Jewish Cemetry   16 Spanish Syn-
agogue   17 New Town Hall   18 House of Artists   19 Museum of Applied Arts   20 Convent of St.
Agnes   21 St. James   22 Carolinum   23 Tyl Theatre   24 National Theatre   25 St. Gall   26 St.
Martin in the Wall   27 Bethlehem Chapel   28 Smetana Museum

the walls of the Old Town and built a palace to which he moved from Prague Castle in 1383.
The most important occupant of the Royal Court was probably George of Poděbrady, the
Hussite king. Vladislav Jagiello had the ruined Hradčany rebuilt and since it was more secure
he returned to it in 1484. In 1631 Archbishop Ernst Harrach founded an archiepiscopal
seminary in the Royal Court, and after 1777 the area was used as barracks and later as a cadet
school.

In 1902–1903 the site was cleared and in 1906–1912 the leading architects and artists of Czechoslovakia created the Municipal (or Representative) House, a magnificent example of the Czech Secession style intended to express the aspirations of the emergent Czech nation. The building was designed by Osvald Polívka and Antonín Balšánek. The mosaic above the main entrance representing a *Homage to Prague* was made after a design by Karel Špillar. The groups of statues representing the *Humiliation and Resurrection of the Nation* are by Ladislav Šaloun. Karel Novák created the decoration on the façade, including figures on the balcony holding up the delightful polyhedral lamps. The central thrust of the building is similar to many Prague Baroque buildings, and like them the Obecní dům juggles with classical elements. But its essential modernity is unmistakeable in the decorative use of electric lights.

All the original charm and details of the interiors have been preserved. There is an attractive café, a restaurant, a wine bar, a tavern and six halls. The central *Smetana Hall* is used for concerts, balls and the annual opening of the 'Prague Spring' music festival. The *Primator's (Mayor's) Hall* is decorated with allegorical paintings by Alfons Maria Mucha, the master of Art Nouveau. The Czechoslovak Republic was founded in the Primator's Hall in October 1918, and it was also here that the Communist Party and Civic Forum negotiated the end of socialism in Czechoslovakia. Landscapes and national motifs and allegories appear in the other rooms, the *Sladovský*, *Rieger* and *Grégr* Halls.

The magnificent towered gateway next to the Obecní dům is the **Powder Tower** (Prašná brána) commissioned by Vladislav II Jagiello around 1475, and intended as a counterpart to the Old Town Bridge Tower (see p. 55). The old 13th-century gate was demolished and the 'New Tower' (Nová věž) was built by Matouš Rejsek. When Vladislav moved his residence back to the Hradčany in 1484 building work ceased and the gate was given a temporary roof. Like many buildings in Prague it was used at the end of the 17th century to store gunpowder. In 1757 the building was severely damaged during the Prussian siege and gradually fell into ruin. From 1875 to 1886 the restorer Josef Mocker combined a restoration of the Powder Tower with the sensitive completion of its upper parts, adding a gallery, hipped roof and architectural decoration in Late-Gothic-Jagiellon style. The statues on the two principal façades were added at this time: Otakar II (left) and Charles IV (right) on the west side; George of Poděbrady (left) and Vladislav II Jagiello (right) on the east.

The Powder Tower and Old Town Square are linked by **Celetná ulice**, one of the oldest streets in Prague, which follows the course of the ancient trade route to the east. Its name comes from the bakers who baked their *calty* ('Zelten': small flat cakes) here. Originally Celetná was a street of small merchants and craftsmen, but from the 15th century, when the Bohemian Kings were residing at the Royal Court (now the Obecní Dům), town councillors and royal officials began to build here, and later the nobility added their great town houses.

The first major building is the **Pachta Palace** (No. 31/585), on the right. The original palace was a small one, built in 1689 by Count Seeberg on the site of four medieval houses destroyed in a fire that swept through the district. It was altered by Kilian Ignaz Dientzenhofer for Baron Joseph Langer between 1737 and 1740, and it is probably to Dientzenhofer that the central thrust of the building and its handsome portal are due. Stucco busts of Maria Theresa and her husband, the Emperor Francis I, can be seen in the medallions above the first-floor windows. In 1801 the palace was bought by the Pachtas of Rajov; how they managed to afford such a very big house may be related to the fact that their immediate forebear, František Josef Pachta, was Master of the Mint. It was he who commissioned the handsome projecting building diagonally opposite. This new **Mint** (Mincovna; No. 36/587) was built in 1755 by Johann Josef Wirch, and its function is illustrated by the silver-miners who support the balcony. The first skirmishes of 1848 took place here, with the forces of repression under General Windischgrätz, who retreated to the Lesser Town after his wife was killed in the drawing room by a stray bullet. Later the Mint was used as a law court , and its labyrinth of corridors is the prototype for angst in *The Trial*. A few yards farther, on the same side, and mangled only by a brutal ground floor façade, No. 30 is one of Prague's more enchanting 19th-century follies; Italico-gothico-mooresque in style, it sports little dragon gutters. The large building opposite at No. 17/595 is the **Menhart Palace**, built by F.M. Kaňka. The doorway is inscribed 1700, and leads to a courtyard with two ugly Baroque statues and a wine bar.

The foundation walls of the house at the sign of the **Golden Vulture** (U zlatého supa; No. 22/563) date from the 14th century, when a brewery occupied the spacious ground floor – where today there is a comfortable ale house. In the 18th century the house was acquired by the University, and in 1804 it received its Neo-Classical appearance; only the main entrance remained Baroque. In the cellar of the **Caretto-Millesimo Palace** (No. 13/597) restoration has revealed 12th-century Romanesque masonry. The wings flanking the courtyard and the two brick gables are Gothic but since 1755 the overall appearance of the building has been Baroque. Count Johann Caretto de Millesimo bequeathed the house to a foundation for impoverished nobles. The **Hrzán Palace** (No. 12/558) was designed by G.B. Alliprandi in 1702, using the oversized keystones which also appear in the work of Santini-Aichel. The Baroque faces are unusually cross. Beyond the corner of Štupartská ul. are two fine old houses: the **Týn Presbytery** (Týnská fara; No. 5/601) and the house of the **Three Kings** (U tří králů; No. 3/602). In the 12th century the Týn Presbytery was a hostel for foreign merchants, and from 1365 it belonged to the Týn Church. In 1424–1471 Jan Rokycana, the religious leader of the Hussites lived here, and in the 16th century the Týn Presbytery was the seat of the highest administrative authority of the Hussite church. The house of the Three Kings is still Gothic from foundations to roof; the two gables and the roof timbers of spruce date from the 14th century. On the other side No. 8 is one of Prague's most splendid doorways, with a great staring sun. The last house before the Old Town Square is the **Sixt House** (No. 2/553), a Romanesque building of c. 1200 with Early Gothic additions, remodelled in Late Gothic style in 1523. Charles IV's Florentine apothecary Angelus lived

The Old Town Square

here, where he welcomed Petrarch and the real Doctor Faustus. In 1567 Sixt von Ottersdorf, a leading Utraquist politician and chronicler, acquired the house for his library and collection of paintings; later it belonged to the Catholic defenestratee Philip Fabricius. The sculptures of emperors on the attic storey are from the workshop of Bernhard Braun.

Old Town Square (Staroměstské náměstí)

All the trade routes that crossed the Vltava at Prague met in the Old Town Square, the heart of Prague (colour plate 6). Here merchants from near and far displayed their wares and it was around the marketplace that the first settlers made their homes in the 10th century. Soon the square was also being used as a place of assembly and law courts and for executions. It was the scene, too, of tournaments and coronation processions. Demonstrations here in 1918 and 1948 heralded political upheavals. Most of the buildings around this enormous square (9000 sq metres) are still Gothic despite their spirited Baroque façades.

In 1338 the 'old town of Prague' was granted autonomy in municipal affairs by King John of Luxemburg. For this a Town Hall was needed, but there was no money available for a new building. So the community bought the Early Gothic house of Wölflin vom Steine (Kámen) and added another storey to it. When Charles IV made Prague capital of the Holy Roman

Empire, the **Town Hall of the Old Town** (Staroměstská radnice) soon became too small. Adjacent plots occupied by clothmakers' shops were bought to make room for a two-storey extension. In 1364 the massive corner tower and the eastern extension were completed (colour plate 1). Around the turn of the 15th century the architect Matouš Rejsek gave the town hall complex a unified Late Gothic appearance. In 1835 the House at the sign of the Cock (which is in fact Romanesque) became part of the town hall, and in 1896 the House of the Minute (Dům U minuty; plate 13) which projects far in front of the façade. Impressive sgraffito decoration with classical and biblical motifs covers the white walls between the windows. The sgraffiti date from the first half of the 17th century, the house itself from the 14th century. From the end of the 18th century the stone lion at the corner of the house was the sign of the apothecary at the White Lion (U bílého lva). A loggia links the forecourt of the town hall with the Malé náměstí (Little Square) (see p. 50).

The tower of the town hall, 59.5 metres high, houses the *astronomical clock* (Orloj; colour plate 3). A clock was first installed in 1410 by Mikuláš of Kadaň, and rebuilt in 1490 by Master Hanuš of the Charles University. Guides still tell the dubious story of how Master Hanuš was blinded by order of the town council, so that he could not repeat his feat elsewhere, and how he then climbed up and stopped his clock's mechanism, which consequently could not be repaired for many years. The upper face, called the 'sphere', shows the time in 24 arabic numerals (counting from sunset to sunset: old Bohemian time) and in two sets of twelve roman numerals. As well as this the month is shown by the signs of the zodiac, and the phase of the moon, even the position of the planets can be read from the curved lines. Four small figures stand on either side of the sphere: Vanity with a mirror, Avarice with a money bag, Death with an hour-glass and funeral bell and a Turk with his turban. The lower face is a 'Calendarium' with the arms of the Old Town in its centre surrounded by the signs of the zodiac and scenes showing the labours of the months. The great Czech painter Josef Mánes painted these scenes in oils on copper in 1865 (the ones on the clock are now a copy; the originals are kept in the Museum of the City of Prague). Every hour just before the hour the automata come rather slowly to life: Death raises his hour-glass, the symbol of transcience, and rings the funeral bell. Then the twelve Apostles pass by the narrow windows, pausing for a moment to look thoughtfully down at the crowd. The cock crows, the Turk shakes his head threateningly (it was a long time before the Ottoman danger was past), the Miser gloats over his gold, the vain man gazes at his mirror, and finally the bell strikes the hour. The figures were destroyed in 1945 and were replaced a few years later with new carvings by the Czech sculptor Vojtěch Sucharda.

On the east side of the tower is a *chapel* built in 1381 and dedicated to the Virgin Mary, a jewel of Prague Gothic, possibly designed by Peter Parler. Its apse forms a decorative five-sided oriel window on the façade. The windows have fine tracery and an ornamental gable. After the First World War it was turned into a memorial to the war dead. The white crosses set in the paving stones in front of the town hall mark the site of the scaffold where 27 Protestant leaders, 17 Czechs and 10 Germans were executed as 'rebels' against the Catholic

Habsburgs on 21 June 1621, after being broken on the wheel. A bronze plate below the oriel commemorates the bloody court in Prague which condemned them, while an earlier execution, the beheading of the Hussite preacher Jan Želivský in 1422 (see p. 131), is commemorated by a bust.

A large part of the town hall was destroyed by the Germans on 8 May 1945 during the Prague Uprising. The south wing was soon rebuilt but the site of the east wing has been left as an open space awaiting a suitable modern replacement.

The *main portal* of the town hall, left of the astronomical clock, dates from the second half of the 15th century, when the clarity of Gothic lines was beginning to disintegrate. Next to the portal the double window of the entrance hall is in the same style. The splendid Renaissance window in the central part of the façade bears the arms of the Old Town with the proud inscription carved in 1520: *Praga caput regni* ('Prague, capital of the kingdom').

The *entrance hall* is decorated with wall mosaics (1934–1939) after designs by the Czech painter Mikoláš Aleš (1852–1913): *The Slav Peoples Paying Homage to Prague*, *Libuše Prophesying the Rise of Prague*, *St Wenceslas*. The hall leads to the Late Gothic *Council Chamber* with its magnificent wooden ceiling, rich wooden doors and the emblems of the 42 guilds of Prague on the panelled walls. Also shown is the 17th-century *Gemeindestube* and the *Assembly Hall* of 1879 with works by the history painter Václav Brožik: *Hus before the Council of Constance*, *George of Poděbrady Elected King of Bohemia*. The Old Town Hall is used today for city events and is a registry office, museum and art gallery with temporary exhibitions.

The massive **Jan Hus Memorial** in the north-east corner of the Old Town Square was unveiled on 6 July 1915, the five hundredth anniversary of the death of the reformer and national hero. The sculptor Ladislav Šaloun used his personal mixture of Impressionism and Art Nouveau to depict a people passing from defeat to rebellion in the face of oppression. Between the groups stands the tall figure of Jan Hus; on the plinth are inscribed his famous words *Pravda vitězí* ('truth prevails'). The monument has become a symbol of the Czech nation; the triumphant Nazis draped it with swastikas in 1939, and it was draped in black when the Warsaw Pact tanks rolled into Prague in 1968. British academics sent by the Jan Hus Foundation to conduct a sort of flying university in the later years of communist rule were met clandestinely by their hosts at the statue.

The houses surrounding the Old Town Square date back to the Romanesque or Early Gothic. In the course of their history they have undergone several renovations and alterations and now almost all of them have early Baroque (17th century) façades. A few examples from this recently restored ring of houses may be briefly mentioned. Near the entrance to Celetná is **Štorch House** (No. 16/552), originally a Gothic house of c. 1400, renovated in 1897 in Neo-Renaissance style. The picture on the façade showing St Wenceslas on horseback is after a design by Mikoláš Aleš. Kafka learnt about relativity in this house, at a private lecture given by Einstein. The patrician house at the sign of the **Golden Unicorn** (U zlatého jednorožce; No. 20/548) on the corner of Železna ul. was built in the 12th century. In the 14th century it was remodelled in the Gothic style and in the 15th century in the Late Gothic style, and in the 18th century the house received its present High Baroque appearance. Bedřich Smetana opened his first music school in this building in 1848. The famous wine tavern U Bindrů in the house of the **Blue Star** (U modré hvězdy; No. 25/479) was already in existence in the 16th century. The vestibule shows evidence of its Romanesque origins, the loggia contains Gothic features, and the 17th-century façade is Early Baroque.

In the north-west corner of the square is the **Church of St Nicholas** (Kostel sv. Mikuláš). The first church dedicated to St Nicholas was founded on this site by German merchants at the beginning of the 13th century. In the 14th century it was enlarged and given a tower; at this time it was the parish church of the Old Town, the Týn having not yet been completed. Here the reformer Jan Milič of Kroměříž preached in Latin for gentlefolk, and the church was a centre of Hussitism from 1414 until the Battle of the White Mountain; it is used today by the modern Protestant Czechoslovak Church, which claims its descent from Hussitism. The present church was built for the Benedictines by K.I. Dientzenhofer in 1732–1735 and has been called his most intensely expressive building. It was finished immediately before the other St Nicholas (built by Dientzenhofer and his father) in the Malá Strana (see p. 74). The main front facing Old Town Square consists of a very high portal and two towers; everything seems to pull out and up. The beguiling statues on the Old Town Square façade are by Anton Braun. Inside, the extreme complexity of concave and convex lines can be appreciated by looking up at the pediments from directly below; the whole effect is to show the pressures of the building's mass, and the energy of its conception, buckling and stretching out the walls and pillars. The impression of height is enhanced by the cunning use of artificially small statues in the topmost storey. The plasterwork, by B. Spinetti, is particularly delicate, with sugar-sweet angels flanking the (restored) evangelists in the corners, and the capitals decorated with St Nicholas's three barrels. The dome, chancel, and side chapels were painted by the Bavarian Peter Asam the elder; the chandelier was given by the Russian Orthodox community, who used the church between 1870 and 1914, and was made in Harrachov in eastern Bohemia. A little votive chapel next to the entrance is filled with glass-fronted safeboxes.

Prague, St. Nicholas in the Old Town, plan

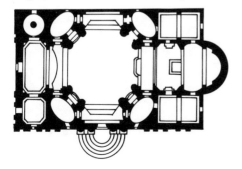

Outside the church, and marked by a large bust on the corner of the building, is the birthplace of Franz Kafka. The area beyond is the old ghetto, or Josefov. In fact the Kafkas tended to turn their backs on the ghetto: the father and son crossed the square daily, the former to work in his haberdashery shop on the ground floor of the great

Kinský Palace on the other side of the Hus monument, and the latter to study at the Altstädter Deutsches Gymnasium (Old Town German Grammar School) in the same building, where many of Prague's German-speaking writers were educated. (Kafka's connections here are even more elaborate. His grandparents also lived in the Kinský Palace; he himself lived for a while at No. 20, the Golden Unicorn, was a member of a Zionist salon at No. 18, and spent his last, tragic year at No. 5 opposite.) The Kinský Palace was also designed by Kilian Ignaz Dientzenhofer and was executed after his death by his son-in-law Anselmo Lurago for Count Johann Ernst Goltz between 1755 and 1761. Beneath it are the cellars of two houses, one Romanesque and the other Early Gothic. In 1786 the palace passed to Prince Rudolf Kinský, who remodelled the interiors in the Neo-Classical style and added a second courtyard at the back. It remained in the possession of the Kinský family (the family also of the actors Klaus and Natassia Kinsky) until 1945. The author Bertha von Suttner, née Kinský (1843–1914), the founder of the Austrian pacifist movement who encouraged Alfred Nobel to found his Peace Prize and herself won it in 1905, spent her childhood here. It was from the balcony of the Kinský Palace that the Communist leader Klement Gottwald addressed jubilant crowds on 21 February 1948 as a prelude to his coup. Today the building houses the National Gallery's *Prints and Drawings Collection* with a permanent exhibition from its large collection.

Adjoining it on the right and set back is the house of the **Stone Bell** (U kamenného zvonu; No. 13/605) which was converted in the 14th century into a town palace for King John of Luxemburg. The statues which covered its façade sadly vanished during the Baroque remodelling in the 17th century. On the corner of the building the house sign, a stone bell, can be seen. Between 1973 and 1987 the house underwent a controversial de-baroquization which restored its Gothic appearance.

There are two buildings in front of the Týn Church: the **Týn School** (Týnska škola) and the house of the **White Unicorn** (U bílého jednorožce). Romanesque vaults in the cellar show the great antiquity of these two houses. From the size of the arcades, the fenestration and the shape of the gables it seems that they were originally four houses. The Gothic loggia was added in the 14th century. In the 16th century there was a remodelling in the style of the Venetian Renaissance. The house of the White Unicorn was given Late Baroque additions in the 18th century, and in the 19th century the building of another storey resulted in the disappearance of its two gables. From the 14th until the mid– 19th century the northern building was

Prague, Týn Church, plan

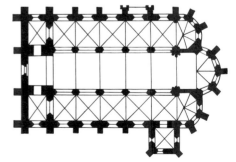

occupied by the Týn School, a parish school which achieved a high reputation in the 15th century.

Rising behind these buildings are the medieval spires of the **Týn Church** (Týnský chrám; German: Teynkirche; plate 2), among Prague's best known landmarks; at night they look like a candle-covered Christmas tree. The 'Church of Our Lady Before the Týn' (Kostel Panny Marie před Týnem), to give its full name, is reached by a small passageway under the arcades. The first church on this site was the *ecclesiae S. Mariae de hospitale* mentioned in 1135, a church attached to a hostel for foreign merchants who stayed in the neighbouring Ungelt. In the 13th century the Romanesque church was replaced by an aisled Early Gothic building. In 1339 the architects Peter Schmelzer and Otto Scheuffler began work on the present Gothic church. From 1390 they presumably had assistance from the workshop of Peter Parler to which the grand *doorway* on the north side of the church is attributed (between 1400 and 1410). It is richly furnished with plinths and canopies; the tympanum has scenes from the Passion of Christ: Flagellation, Crowning with Thorns, and Crucifixion (now replaced by copies). The spires had not yet been built when the Hussite Wars broke out, and it was not until the reign of George of Poděbrady (1458–1471) that work was resumed on the two towers. These are typical of Prague High Gothic with their staggered projecting turrets which give the church a fortified appearance. The towers were completed under Vladislav II (1471–1516). George of Poděbrady had decorated the façade with a statue of himself with a gold chalice, the symbol of the Utraquist cause. In 1626, after the triumph of Catholicism, the chalice was melted down to make the gold crown, sceptre and halo of the Virgin now in the gable.

Altogether the church is a good place to sense the various currents of Bohemian religious history. Famous reformers preached here in the 14th century, including Waldhauser and Milič of Kroměříž. The tall, slightly gaunt interior was given a Baroque vault after a fire of 1679. The half columns are topped by excellent Baroque saints, and the vault itself is decorated with colourful ecclesiastical coats of arms. At the end of the nave, the high altar was constructed in 1642–49 (though the St Michael at the very top was not added until 1679). The painting is by Karel Škréta. The altar replaced a medieval rood screen, whose figures are now kept at the end of the north aisle, the Christ being from the first quarter of the 15th century, the Virgin and St John from the second. Also here, in the sedilia, are two little busts of King Wenceslas IV and his wife, Joanna of Bavaria. The elaborate 17th century memorial tablet commemorates Shimon Abrams Abelles, a Jewish boy who was reputedly killed by his father for converting to Catholicism. All round the church there are superb grave stones, but the most famous is undoubtedly that of Tycho Brahe (1546–1601), which is on the last pillar of the nave to the south, facing the high altar. Brahe was the first man to understand the necessity of continuous detailed observation of the heavens to any successful scientific astronomy. His obsessive and expensive work was carried out in his native Denmark until even the Danes tired of his imperious character; so he moved to the intellectual and mystical court at Prague under Rudolph II. Here he met Johann Kepler, who was able to transform

Brahe's tables of observations into the universe we know today. Shortly after their first meeting, Brahe's pride forbade him from leaving the heavy-drinking table of Peter Vok Rožmberk, a magnate almost as learned and rich as the emperor, and he died within a week of a burst bladder. The tomb shows him as a member of the noble military caste, though his hand rests not only on the usual helmet, but on a model of the heavens. The line on the bridge of his nose is not a fault in the stone: it represents the nose of silver and gold which he wore after losing his first nose in a duel. His last words, to Kepler, were: 'Let me not seem to have lived in vain'; and his epitaph is full of superlatives, mostly referring to himself, but some to the heavens he explored.

Turning to face the west end, the visitor's eye will be caught by the majestic early Baroque organ; some of its tracery is charmingly gothic, and the two suns spin when it is played. Gluck was organist here in the 1730's. On the north side of the nave is a large baldaquin (1493) by Matouš Rejsek (who taught architecture at the Týn School outside); this originally covered the tomb of the Utraquist bishop Augustin Lucian, but now houses a rather insipid 19th-century altarpiece. Opposite, the Gothic pulpit stands next to one of the finest carved limewood altarpieces in Bohemia, signed only with the monogram IP (c. 1600). In this south aisle, the pewter font at the end was made in 1414 and is the oldest in Prague; it is contemporary with the wooden Madonna nearby, whose colours were unfortunately removed by 19th-century restoration. Before leaving the church, the visitor should not miss the presence of two outsiders; the town executioner, who as an unclean person could only observe the services from the balcony with a grille high up on the north-west corner; and Franz Kafka, whose window, second along the south wall, allowed him to watch the alien worship from rooms he occupied while writing *The Trial*.

East of the Týn Church is the extensive complex of the **Ungelt (Týn)** bounded by Týnská, Štupartská and Malá Štupartská ul. In the 11th century, and perhaps earlier, the Týn ('enclosed area') was fitted out as a hostel and warehouse for foreign merchants. Shortly afterwards workshops, a hospice and a church were added. In the 14th century the Týn Court developed into a profitable customs house, from which the name *Ungelt* (meaning something like 'duty-free' in German) is derived. After the abolition of duty the court passed into the hands of the former tax collector Jakob Granovský of Granov. Around 1460 he transformed the buildings into a Renaissance palace with an arcaded courtyard showing Tuscan influence. The fragmentary frescoes above the arcades are of biblical motifs. The Ungelt is at present being converted into a luxury hotel.

From the Old Town Square to the Charles Bridge

The Royal Way continues across **Malé náměstí** (Little Square) to Karlova. In the centre of the intimate little triangular square is a well with a Renaissance wrought iron grille made in 1560, though the lion was added a hundred years later. The houses around the square, which since the 14th century had been a fruit market, are all built on Romanesque foundations, and some of the 12th-century cellar vaults have survived. In the loggia on the east side were the shops of the 'Kränzler' who sold women's head-dresses. **Pezold House** (No. 10/4), remodelled c. 1600 in the style of the Late Renaissance, preserves remains of a Romanesque portal and staircase, and is decorated with Renaissance sgraffiti. **Richter House** (No. 11/459) diagonally opposite was created c. 1760 out of two Gothic houses. In 1353, during Charles IV's reign, a Florentine pharmacist opened the first pharmacy in Prague here. Next door at the **Golden Lily** (U zlaté lilie; No. 13/458) is the oldest shop front in Prague (14th century), and the lily, already recorded in 1405, suggests that it was originally the seat of the French community. The most striking house in Malé náměstí is the **Rott House** (No. 3/142) built in 1897 for the Rott firm of ironmongers. Its Bohemian Neo-Renaissance façade was profusely decorated with wall paintings to designs by Mikoláš Aleš in the 1890's. The house sign of Three White Roses (U tří bílých růží) can be seen high on the gable. Here in 1488 Jan Pytlích published the first Czech translation of the Bible. The Rott House preserves unusually rich Romanesque cellars.

Turning into Jilská ul. which connects Malé náměstí with Karlova ul., one should first enter Husova ul. (Hus Street) a few metres to the right. Here the most striking features are the Hercules atlantes flanking the two doorways of the **Clam-Gallas Palace.** In 1713 Count Johann Wenzel (Jan Václav) Gallas, field marshal, Imperial ambassador in London and Rome, and later Viceroy of Naples, commissioned the Viennese Baroque architect Johann Bernhard Fischer von Erlach to build the palace. The architect incorporated into his extensive building parts of the Gothic palace in which Margrave John Henry (Jan Jindřich) had lived in the 14th century. The magnificent atlantes and the statues of gods on the attic storey were made by Matthias Bernard Braun (the originals – 17 in number – are now in the National Gallery). The impressive staircase, one of the airiest spaces in Prague, was also created by Fischer von Erlach, its sculptural decoration is by M.B. Braun, and the ceiling fresco showing *Apollo in the Chariot of the Sun* is by Carlo Carlone, who was also responsible for the ceiling paintings in the two rooms on the second floor: *Olympus, The Coronation of Art and Learning* and in the Library, *Luna, Helios and the stars.* Today the building houses the Archive of the City of Prague.

Retracing our steps to Karlova we continue to the next corner dominated by the house at the sign of the **Golden Well** (U zlaté studně; No. 3/175) which projects ebulliently across the entrance to Seminářská ul. As a thanks offering for surviving the plague its owner commissioned Johann Ulrich Mayer in 1701 to make stucco reliefs of the patron saints of Bohemia and of the plague saints for the narrow façade. The lower double window is flanked by St Sebastian and St Roch. Above them is the miraculous image of Our Lady of Stará Boleslav (Altbunzlau). Next to the double window on the middle storey are St Wenceslas and St John Nepomuk, the national patron saints, and the upper window has the Jesuit saints Ignatius of Loyola and Francis Xavier, with St Rosalia, the Palermitan plague saint, reclining on a bed of skulls above them.

The massive complex of buildings opposite on the north side of Karlova is the **Clementinum.** The Jesuit college was once the spiritual power-house of the Counter-

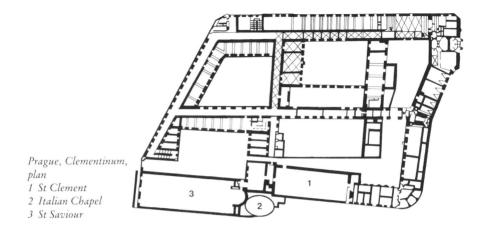

Prague, Clementinum, plan
1 St Clement
2 Italian Chapel
3 St Saviour

Reformation in Bohemia. From 1232 the Dominicans had a small friary next to the Romanesque parish church of St Clement. Its almost complete destruction in the Hussite Wars was followed by a makeshift rebuilding, and in 1556 the site was given to the Jesuits, who had been summoned to Bohemia by Ferdinand I. The college they founded, with Papal permission, was at first modest, but after the Battle of the White Mountain (1620), the Jesuits placed themselves at the head of the Counter-Reformation in Bohemia and their first act was an unparalleled expansion of their headquarters in Prague. This was to be a centre of scholarship and orthodoxy which would extirpate Protestant heresy from the land. Between 1653 and 1660 Carlo Lurago built the first range in Křižovnická ul. after designs by Francesco Caratti, and from 1660 to 1664 Domenico Orsi erected the north range of the college on Platnéřská. Building work continued into the 18th century. In 1721–1727 František Maximilian Kaňka built the east range which includes the schools, the Astronomical Tower and the famous Library with its barley-sugar columns and illusionistic allegorical ceiling frescoes by Johann Hiebl (1727). The Jesuits were fearless readers. Amongst all the white vellum bindings is one case of books bound in black: books on the Index which only the fathers were permitted to read. They brought together the most complete collection in the world of Wycliffiana, including the only known writing in his own hand. In the Malá Strana Gradual, a book of Catholic instruction made in 1572, the progress of reform is shown as a strip cartoon, Wycliffe rubbing two stones together to make the spark, Hus lighting his candle with it, and Luther brandishing a torch. The Society of Jesus also had a reputation for destroying knowledge, but the stories that one father alone in the 17th century was responsible for burning 80,000 books are probably untrue. The worldliness of the Jesuits is also demonstrated by the two magnificent globes they commissioned, now part of a collection assembled in the library.

After the suppression of the Jesuit Order in 1773 various institutions occupied the Clementinum. Today it houses the Czech State Library, including the University Library, the Library of the Technical University and the Slavonic Library.

The Romanesque church of **St Clement** (Kostel sv. Kliment) was replaced by Kilian Ignaz Dientzenhofer's Baroque building (1711–1715). The interior is one of the clearest and lightest of the great Baroque spaces. The visitor will probably first notice the striking ceiling fresco (Johann Hiebl) in which St Clement is thrown from an ample boat into the Black Sea. The Bohemians, always short of a sea-coast, tended to enjoy marine paintings. Though St Clement was not saved by God from drowning, the angels loved him and built his tomb underwater; and they reappear in great cascades over all the side altars. The painting above the *St Linhard Altar* is by Peter Johann Brandl. Like the Church Fathers in the first bay, and the Evangelists in the second, the sculptures of these side altars are by Matthias Bernhard Braun, and they make up the finest sculptural ensemble in Prague. As if to point up this virtuosity, the high altar is a trompe-l'oeil. The west end is taken up by an organ, with gold-wreathed putti and urns. Underneath it, a winsome angel blows the Last Trump. The carved confessionals below the gallery have a lightheartedness reminiscent of Boucher. The church was restored a few years ago and is now used by the Greek-Catholic community. Attached to St Clement's is the **Italian Chapel** (Vlašské kaple; Ger. Welsche Kapelle) built in 1590–1600 for the Italian colony and dedicated to the Assumption. With its oval ground plan it was the first Baroque centrally planned building in Prague. The portico and superb ironwork in front of the chapel doorway were designed by František Maximilian Kaňka.

Opposite the chapel is the **House of the French Crown** (Dům U francouzske koruny; No. 4/188), the setting for one of the great encounters in the history of science. Wackher von Wackenfels, so excited that he had to lean out of the coach window, arrived shouting the news that Galileo of Padua had looked through a Dutch spy-glass and discovered four new planets. Kepler wrote that 'I experienced a wonderful emotion while I listened to this curious tale. I felt moved in my deepest being ... Wackher was full of joy and feverish excitement; at one moment we both laughed at our confusion, the next he continued his narrative and I listened intently – there was no end to it.' Kepler had just finished his *Astronomia Nova*, where he elaborated his first two planetary laws describing the elliptical shape and variable speed of planetary orbits, in this house. Ten months after Wackher came with his news (which would lead to the Third Law, describing the orbits in relation to the sun: a visionary contribution to human thought which was published in the fateful week of the Defenestration in 1618) John Donne wrote:

'Man has weaved out a net, and this net throwne
Upon the Heavens, and now they are his owne.'

The Church of **St Saviour** at the end of Karlova dates from before the expansion of the college. It is the oldest Jesuit church in Prague and the largest and most important example of Renaissance church architecture in Bohemia. With the building of St Saviour between 1578 and 1602 on the site of the Gothic church of St Bartholomew the Jesuits marked the arrival of the Counter-Reformation in Bohemia. The church's plan was based on that of the Gesù in Rome. In 1602 work began on the Baroque interior. In 1638 Carlo Lurago added the galleries, in 1653 Francesco Caratti built the imposing portico on the façade – a triumphal arch symbolizing the victory of the Catholic Church and in particular of the Jesuits. The stone sculptures were designed by Johann Georg Bendl: on the gable is Christ the Saviour over the IHS between the four Evangelists, on either side of the gable are the Jesuit saints Ignatius of Loyola and Francis Xavier. In the central niche stands the Immaculate Virgin. On the balustrade of the portico are the four Fathers of the Church, Augustine, Gregory the Great, Ambrose in billowing robes and Jerome naked and with his lion, flanked by St Clement and St Adalbert (Vojtěch) of Prague; below these are charming putti sitting down. The towers were added by František Maximilián Kaňka in 1714. Inside, the ceiling above the high altar shows the four quarters of the world. There is some very fine ironwork.

St Saviour's Church faces one of the prettiest squares in Prague, Křižovnické nám., which offers a superb view of the Charles Bridge, the Lesser Town and Hradčany.

In 1252 St Agnes of Bohemia, a sister of King Wenceslas I, founded the hospitaller order of the 'Knights of the Cross with the Red Star' and built them a hospice with a church at the bridge gate on what was then the Judith Bridge. At the same time the King entrusted the Knights of the Cross with the protection and upkeep of the bridge as well as the collection of duty and tolls. The order's greatest period was the 16th and 17th centuries when for almost 150 years (1561–1694) its Grand Masters were also Archbishops of Prague.

In 1679–1789 on the foundations of the Knights' Early Gothic church Giovanni Domenico Canevale built the Church of **St Francis** (Kostel sv. Františka) to designs by Jean Baptiste Mathey. This was the first of Prague's many domes. This muscular Baroque, however, with firm rustication between giant pilasters, gained no following in Prague. Parts of the medieval structure form a grotto-like crypt beneath the Baroque church. The high attic storey is surmounted by five angels holding the instruments of the Passion by Matthäus Wenzel Jäckel (now copies). The vehement statues of Sts Agnes, Vitus, Francis, Wenceslas and Ludmila in the niches on the façade are attributed to Andreas Philipp Quittainer, while the portal statues of the Immaculate Virgin (1756) and John of Nepomuk (1758) are by Richard Georg Prachner. On the right-hand corner of Křižovnická ul. is the *Wine-growers' Column*, originally part of the Wine-Growers' guild building in the square, with a statue of St Wenceslas by Johann Georg Bendl (1676). The rough paving around the column is almost all that survives of the first bridge here, the 12th-century Judith Bridge. Inside the church, the *high altar*, an elaborate Descent of the Holy Spirit, by Jäckel and Dobner, together with the painting of *St Francis Receiving the Stigmata* (1700-01) by Johann Christoph Lischka make up one of the great works of High Baroque in Prague. The other statues, by C.M. and J. Süssner and by Jäckel again, are ten years earlier but almost as fine. The cupola fresco of the *Last Judgment* is by Wenzel Lorenz Reiner. The pulpit is by Quittainer, and Mozart played the organ here.

The Old Town Bridge Tower

The Neo-Gothic *Monument to Charles IV* in front of the church was designed by the sculptor Ernst Julius Hähnel (1811–1891) of Dresden and erected in 1848 on the 500th anniversary of the foundation of the Charles University by the Emperor. On the pedestal are allegorical figures representing the first four faculties.

The magnificent **Old Town Bridge Tower** (Staroměstská mostecká věž) was built at the end of the 14th century (c. 1370–1380) to the designs of Peter Parler and his cathedral workshop. The tower-gateway was intended as an ornament to the new bridge over the Vltava, while at the same time forming part of the city defences. Massive, yet appearing almost weightless, the elegant tower stands on one of the bridge's piers. The present earth embankment dates from the 19th century. The high broad passageway gives the building a fragile appearance, but it managed to withstand a two-week bombardment by the Swedes in 1648. (Some of the stones used in this bombardment, and in the courageous defence mounted by the students, can be seen in the first courtyard of the Clementinum, with a statue of the hero of the hour, J. Plachý.)

The Swedes did, however, succeed in destroying the sculpture on the west face of the tower so that Parler's elegant decoration survives only on the east side. High up in a tracery gallery are the two national patron saints Adalbert (Vojtěch) and Sigismund. Below them are the enthroned portraits of Charles IV (on the left, with sword) and his son and successor Wenceslas IV (on the right, with sceptre), the king who had John of Nepomuk thrown from his father's bridge, a few hundred yards further on. The structure between them on which St Vitus stands is a stylized representation of Charles Bridge. Flanking the saint are the arms of the Holy Roman Empire (the Eagle) and the ancestral lands of the Luxemburgs (the Bohemian Lion). The little emblem that recurs all over the tower is a kingfisher enclosed by a veil tied in a bow – the badge of Wenceslas IV. The boss in the net vault above the passage is in the form of the Bohemian Royal Crown. For ten years after the Battle of the White Mountain the heads of twelve of the anti-Habsburg rebels were displayed in iron baskets on this tower. On the river side is a long inscription praising Ferdinand III's Golden Peace at the end of the Thirty Years' War. 'Old Prague', it says, was saved from the Goths and the Vandals by this Gothic tower. Josef Mocker (the Czech Viollet-le-Duc) sensitively restored the Old Town Bridge Tower in 1874–1878. The present roof is entirely his work.

The passage through the tower leads onto the **Charles Bridge** (Karlův most), Prague's most famous monument. Its lower half is an unequalled feat of Gothic engineering, its upper an ecstatic procession of gesticulating saints. It reminded Rodin of a centaur. In the early period of the city's history the merchants travelling to or through Prague had to cross the Vltava at a ford thought to have been located just downstream, where the Mánes Bridge stands today. In the 11th century the great increase in traffic made the construction of a bridge necessary. This first wooden bridge, already mentioned by 1118, spanned the river about 200 metres north of Charles Bridge. After a flood swept it away in 1157, Vladislav II Přemysl built a stone bridge, which he named after his wife, Judith of Thuringia, but in 1342 it too was destroyed by a flood. In 1357 the Emperor Charles IV, inspired perhaps by the Pont Neuf in Paris, commissioned Peter Parler to build a new stone bridge. Until 1836 it was the only crossing over the Vltava and was originally called simply the Stone Bridge or Prague Bridge – it was not officially named the Charles Bridge until 1870 (colour plate 7). The bridge is 520 metres long and has 16 arches; the slight S-curve is the result of re-using parts of the Judith Bridge. It is also broad enough to take four carriages abreast. Legend has it that Charles was anxious to make his bridge as strong as possible by mixing the mortar with eggs. Eggs poured in from all over the kingdom – one village even sent theirs hard-boiled to stop them going bad.

For three hundred years the simple form of the bridge was enough – the only sculptural decoration was a *Crucifix* (the present one by Wolf Ernst dates from 1629 – the flanking figures are 19th-century additions). Then in 1683 the citizens of Prague set the first statue on the central pier on the north side: *St John of Nepomuk*. St John of Nepomuk (c. 1350–1393) was the vicar general of John of Jenzenstein, Archbishop of Prague. In the course of a conflict between the Archbishop and King Wenceslas IV concerning the election of the Abbot of Kladruby he was tortured by order of the King before being drowned in the Vltava. Another version of events – assiduously cultivated by the Jesuits – played down the political conflict of church and state. It claimed that John in fact suffered martyrdom because he refused to reveal to the king what the queen had said in the confessional. In 1961 the Roman Catholic Church formally admitted that this version was untrue. These scenes from John's martyrdom are shown in the reliefs, where the saint's head is bright with repeated touching for good luck. The actual spot where he was thrown in is marked a little further along by a small starry cross let into the parapet. John is said to have floated in the water for some time while five stars played around his head, and miracles took place. Ironically, perhaps, he is now the tutelary saint of bridges, and his statue is to be found on them all over Central Europe. The creator of the one on the Charles Bridge – probably the most beautiful and best known of the statues there – was Matthias Rauchmüller (1645–1689). His terracotta model (now in the National Gallery, Prague) was used by Johann Brokoff as the basis for a wooden model (now in the church of St John of Nepomuk on the Rock, Vyšehrad), which was used by the master founder Wolff Hieronymus Heroldt for casting the statue in bronze at Nuremberg. This statue was a great success, and in the fifteen years between 1698 and 1713 another 21 were installed by the leading Prague masters, Matthias Bernhard Braun, F.M. Brokoff and others. This statuary followed the principle of unrelenting Catholicization. No true believer could cross the bridge without crossing him or herself at every statue; and no one of Hussite sympathies could escape the repetitive triumph of the Church victorious. Werfel called it a monstrous clockwork. (It is perhaps fair to point out that the regularity is the result of the 19th-century impulse to complete a job and tidy up; all the gaps left in the original campaign of 1707–1720 were filled by the Max brothers and others with statues of unusual insipidity and earnestness.)

The programme of the sculpture is not a unified, logical whole, but it does follow a fairly clear line. All the major religious orders are represented (many paid for by their Prague houses): the Jesuits, Dominicans, Theatines, Servites, Cistercians, Premonstratensians, Augustinians, Franciscans, Trinitarians. There is also a strong emphasis on preaching, conversion, and ecstatic love of Christ. Woven in are strands of Bohemian nationalism, and a certain concern for the poor.

Some of the more interesting details are pointed out below, starting from the Old Town.

First pier:
St Ivo on the left was a Norman lawyer of such honesty that the common people, whom he protected, would cry out as he passed: 'A miracle! A miracle! a lawyer who's no thief!' He is the patron saint of judges and is shown dressed as one, with a blindfolded executioner as an extreme representation of Justice. The *Virgin* on the right is shown with *St Bernard* accompanied by a complete set of instruments of the passion, including the dice, the cock and the centurion's gauntlet. This is the Cistercian contribution.

Second pier:
Here the *Virgin* on the right is accompanied by Dominicans: *St Dominic* himself, with his dog (the Dominicans were, in the medieval pun, Domini canes – the dogs of God) and *St Thomas Aquinas* with a beehive, perhaps as Doctor Mellifluus, the honeyed teacher,

Statues on the Charles Bridge

Lesser Town

St Wenceslas J.K. Böhm, 1858	The Saviour, Sts Cosmas and Damian J. Mayer, 1709
St John of Matha, St Felix of Valois and the Blessed Ivan and a figure of a Turkish guard F.M. Brokoff, 1714	St Vitus F.M. Brokoff, 1714
St Adalbert F.M. Brokoff (?), 1709 (copy 1973)	St Philip Benitius M.B. Mandl, 1714
St Luitgard M.B. Braun, 1710	St Cajetan F.M. Brokoff, 1709
St Nicholas of Tolentino J.F. Kohl, 1708	St Augustine J.F. Kohl, 1708

Roland Column

St Vincent Ferrer and St Procopius F.M. Brokoff, 1712	St Jude Thaddaeus J. Mayer, 1708
St Francis of Assisi in ecstasy E. Max, 1855	St Anthony of Padua J. Mayer, 1707
St Ludmilla and St Wenceslas B. Braun (workshop), c. 1720	St John Nepomuk M. Rauchmüller, J.M. Brokoff, 1683
St Francis Borgia F.M. Brokoff, 1710	St Wenceslas, St Norbert, St Sigismund J. Max, 1853
St Christopher E. Max, 1857	St John the Baptist J. Max, 1857
St Francis Xavier F.M. Brokoff, 1711 (copy 1913)	SS Cyril and Methodius with allegorical figures of Moravia, Slovakia and Bohemia K. Dvořák, 1938
St Joseph J. Max, 1854	St Ann with the Infant Jesus M.W. Jäckel, 1707
Pietà E. Max, 1859	Crucifix, 1629 figures: E. Max, 1861
St Barbara, St Margaret and St Elizabeth F.M. Brokoff, 1707	The Virgin with St Dominic and St Thomas Aquinus M.W. Jäckel, 1708 (copy 1961)
St Ivo M.B. Braun, 1711 (copy 1908)	The Virgin with St Bernard M.W. Jäckel, 1709

Old Town

(though the epithet is more properly St Bernard's) or perhaps as a symbol of his industry. Opposite, princesses who overcame all opposition to affirm their Christian faith; St Barbara with her chalice, a favourite in Bohemia as the patron saint of miners, St Margaret with a tiny-winged, copper-tongued dragon, St Elizabeth of Hungary (who was born at Bratislava) giving succour.

Third pier:

Inscriptions in German, Czech and Latin record that this *Crucifix* (1629) was decorated with gold lettering in 1696 at the expense of a Jew caught blaspheming against the Holy Cross. The figures are by Emanuel Max, who also made the complementary *Pietà* opposite.

Fourth pier:

The Holy Family: a dreary 19th-century *St Joseph* on the left, and a lively *St Anne, the Virgin and the Infant Jesus* on the right.

Fifth pier:

This was the Jesuit pier. On the left *St Francis Xavier*, the 'Apostle of the Indies and of Japan' is shown bringing the faith to the Indians. The sculptor seems to have got his Indians confused: their king, kneeling before St Francis's cross, is dressed in what appears to be Central American Indian costume, and is in any case a Moor. Two more 'Indians' support the group, accompanied by two suspiciously Chinese-looking Japanese, complete with queues and whiskers. Opposite stood the statue of the other great luminary of the Jesuits, their founder St Ignatius. This, however, collapsed into the river during the floods of 1890, and is now in the National Museum. It was replaced by K. Dvořák's statue of the Apostles to the Slavs, as a suitable counterpart to St Francis Xavier. *Sts Cyril and Methodios* are seen bringing the Gospel to allegorical figures of Moravia, Slovakia and Bohemia.

Sixth pier:

St Christopher (left) and *St John the Baptist* (right), both uncontroversial 19th century additions.

Seventh pier:

The aristocratic *St Francis Borgia* on the left (the heap of skulls refers to the recommended Jesuit Spiritual Exercise of contemplating death), and, on the right, another three aristocratic saints: *Wenceslas, Norbert* and *Sigismund*, all related to the Premonstratensians.

Eighth pier:

Bohemia's national, Catholic consciousness: on the right, *St John of Nepomuk* described above; on the left *St Ludmila* and *St Wenceslas*. St Ludmila was the first Christian martyr of Bohemia; she is shown trampling a pagan altar. She teaches her grandson how to read in the Book, a metaphor of his induction into Christianity. An angel shows an image of the Virgin and Child in case the comparison has been missed. What the new religion has in store for the little boy is shown in the martyrdom relief below, where the angel comes to bestow the palm and crown to the murdered prince.

Ninth pier:

The Franciscan pier: *St Francis* himself is shown in ecstasy. This was commissioned as a mark of gratitude for the Emperor Franz Joseph's safe escape from an attempted assassination. *St Antony of Padua* is the Franciscan patron saint of lost objects and travellers. He was such a great preacher that at his exhumation his tongue was found to be perfectly preserved, though the rest of his body had been entirely consumed.

Tenth pier:

St Jude Thaddaeus on the right, patron saint of desperate emergencies and of friendship; *St Vincent Ferrer* and *St Procopius* on the left. St Vincent was celebrated for his conversions, some of which are listed here, and for inspiring flagellants, one of whom is shown. The numbers are impressive: the base mentions 8000 Saracens next to the figure of a disgruntled Turk, 25,000 Jews, next to a Jew in a ruff and hat, and an uncounted number of demons to the right. St Procopius, abbot of Prague and buried in St Vitus's Cathedral, overcame the devil, and made him plough rock, as shown on the relief.

Below this group is the figure of *Roland* (called Bruncvík in Czech) with the arms of the Old Town symbolizing the fact that the rights of the town extended as far as the Kampa. The Old Town followed the laws of Nuremberg, while Malá Strana had the laws of Magdeburg. The original Roland column dating from the 16th century was replaced by a copy in 1884.

Eleventh pier:

The Augustinian pier. *St Augustine of Hippo*, the Church Father, is shown on the right holding a flaming heart, symbol of religious fervour. The Augustinian *St Nicholas of Tolentino*, patron saint of teachers and invoked against the plague, represents the capacity for living up to the teaching represented by Augustine.

Twelfth pier:

A pier of ecstatic love. On the right, *St Cajetanus* with the Sacred Heart, a devotion that was gathering momentum; this fairly recent saint (1691) was the founder of the Theatine order, noted for poverty, humility and charity to the sick. Opposite him is *St Luitgard*, a blind Cistercian nun to whom Christ miraculously shows His wounded Heart.

Thirteenth pier:

St Adalbert (known to Czechs as Vojtěch), Apostle of Bohemia and Bishop of Prague, on the left, and *St Philip Benitius* on the right, greatest general of the Servite order, and another recent saint (1671).

Fourteenth pier:

St John of Matha, St Felix of Valois, the Blessed Ivan with a Turkish guard and prisoners.

St John founded the Trinitarian order, for the redemption of prisoners, to whom he is seen bringing succour, with St Felix of Valois, who is accompanied by his stag. The Blessed Ivan was a locally revered hermit. The Turkish guard is morose rather than fierce, despite the cat o' nine tails behind his back. Under communism, flowers were often left in the prisoners' little cage as a gesture of solidarity with the prisoners of the regime. Opposite is *St Vitus* on a hillock with lions emerging from their dens. Although after his martyrdom St Vitus's body was protected by a wolf or lion until it could receive Christian burial, the real reason for this pride seems to have been that the sculpture was given by a man named Löwenmacht ('lion strength'). St Vitus is the patron saint of those who have trouble getting up early in the morning.

Fifteenth pier:

The Saviour with *Sts Cosmas and Damian*: the two saints were doctors and wear medical costume; they were known for the generosity to the poor, from whom they demanded no fee for their services. The *St Wenceslas* opposite is dreary, but the spot is good for observing the little lewd face above the shop on the left of the bridge.

The Charles Bridge and the towers of the Old Town

Charles Bridge ends at the two **Lesser Town Bridge Towers**. The lower south tower guarded the wooden bridge and then the stone Judith Bridge; in 1591 it was rebuilt in the Renaissance style. The taller north tower was built by King George of Poděbrady in 1464, in place of a ruinous Romanesque tower, as an architectural counterpart to the Old Town Bridge Tower.

People who go over dark bridges
past the saints -
with faint little lights -
Clouds that travel over the grey sky,
past the churches -
with darkening spires -
One who leans over the parapet
- and looks into the evening water,
his hand on old stones.

FRANZ KAFKA, 1903

Josefov

There have been Jews living in Prague for more than a thousand years – it has even been said that there were Jews here before the Czechs arrived. They witnessed the awakening of the city and fostered its economic and cultural development. In 965 the Jewish merchant Ibrahim ibn Jakub from Arab Seville visited the Jewish settlements at the foot of the Hradčany and Vyšehrad: by 1091 Jewish traders were living near what was to become the Old-New Synagogue. When Pope Urban II rallied Christians to the crusade in 1095 the crusader armies passed through Prague and forced the Jews there to be baptized. Duke Břetislav II (1092–1100) allowed the Jewish quarters to be looted and surrounded the 'Jewish Town' (later called the 'ghetto') north of the Old Town Square with a wall (1098). On 18 April 1389 the biggest pogrom of medieval Prague left more than 4000 dead, many of them in the Old-New Synagogue, where they had crowded for safety. In the reign of Rudolph II (1575–1612) Mordechai Maisel, the wealthy mayor of the Jewish Town and confidant of Rudolph II, paid for the paving of the streets in the Jewish Town out of his own money. Known as 'Philanthrop', he founded a hospital with a public bath, a talmudic university, and built the Jewish Town Hall.

In the 17th and 18th centuries Imperial edicts had led to harassment and humiliations, but Maria Theresa eventually abolished the requirement that the Jews should live in the ghetto and Joseph II's Patent of Tolerance of 1781 improved their legal status. Yet it was not until 1849 that Franz Joseph I repealed the 'numerus clausus' which determined how many Jewish families were allowed to live in a particular region (8600 in Bohemia, 5400 Moravia); Jews were at last allowed to marry and have children freely. The ghetto was abolished, and the

'Jewish Town' was henceforth known as 'Joseph Town' (Josephstadt, Josefov) after Joseph II. In the next ten years the Jewish proportion of the population of Prague increased from 7.2 to 11 per cent.

Around the turn of the century the former ghetto was 'sanitized', i.e. demolished for hygienic reasons and rebuilt. Only the Jewish Town Hall, six synagogues and part of the old cemetery were preserved. The dense network of little streets was replaced by palatial blocks of flats in the attractive historicizing styles of the period. The finest of these line the broad avenue, the Pařížská třída (Paris Street), which runs through the neighbourhood from the Old Town Square to the Vltava.

After the Protectorate of Bohemia and Moravia was proclaimed in 1939 life for the Jews of Prague continued unchanged until 1941 when the National Socialists created the ghetto at Theresienstadt (Terezín). In 1942, after the Wannsee Conference in Berlin had decided on the 'final solution of the Jewish question', all the synagogues within the protectorate were abolished. The Jewish self-governing body brought all synagogal objects to Prague to protect them from vandalism. The Nazis then decided to found a Jewish Museum in Prague which was intended 'not to impress with sensational curiosities, but by means of a complete and balanced collection of material to give a picture of the social, economic and cultural development of Jewry.' It was supposed to be a 'museum of an extinct ethnic group'. Thus

In the Jewish Cemetery

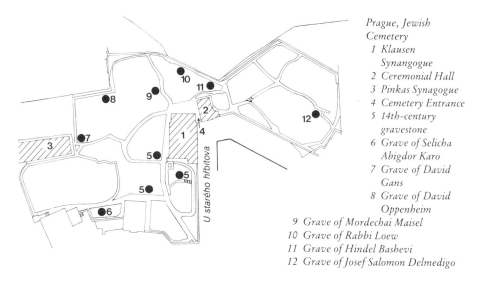

Prague, Jewish
Cemetery
1 Klausen
   Synangogue
2 Ceremonial Hall
3 Pinkas Synagogue
4 Cemetery Entrance
5 14th-century
   gravestone
6 Grave of Selicha
   Abigdor Karo
7 Grave of David
   Gans
8 Grave of David
   Oppenheim
9 Grave of Mordechai Maisel
10 Grave of Rabbi Loew
11 Grave of Hindel Bashevi
12 Grave of Josef Salomon Delmedigo

the 'Jüdisches Zentralmuseum' was formed with more than 100,000 exhibits (Torah scrolls, Torah mantels, candlesticks, temple curtains, archives), the largest and most complete Jewish Museum in the world. Prague Jews set up the museum, and the Josefov synagogues were carefully restored for it. Since 1945 it has been run by the Czechoslovak state as the 'State Jewish Museum'. Ninety per cent of Prague Jews died in Nazi concentration camps. Today there are fewer than 2000 Jews living in Prague.

The **Old-New Synagogue** (Staronová synagoga; plate 15) – the strange name may indicate that the synagogue was built on the remains of an earlier one – on Pařížská třída (entrance in Červená ul.) is the oldest surviving synagogue in Europe (since the destruction of the Worms synagogue in 1935), as well as being one of the first Early Gothic buildings in Prague. 'Many of the tenderest legends', in the words of one Jewish writer, 'are connected with this synagogue.' Most of these attempt to exaggerate its great age, so that it is said to be part of the Temple of Solomon, brought to Prague by angels, or, slightly less fancifully, by the Jews fleeing from Palestine. It was probably built in the reign of Otakar II Přemysl (1230–1278) who granted the Jews considerable privileges. The architects, however, were not Jews but Cistercians. The longitudinal vestibule with its pointed barrel vault dates from the time the synagogue was built (mid–13th century), and the double-aisled prayer room was added at the end of the 13th century. The master of the Cistercian workshop had to add a fifth rib to the cross-rib vault in order to avoid making the shape of the Christian cross, but the number twelve recurs throughout, symbolizing the twelve tribes of Israel. The capitals and springers are crisply carved with plant motifs. Narrow windows which splay outwards let in only a little light since 'the light should flow out of the synagogue into the world'. In the middle of the room, surrounded by a wrought iron railing, is the 'almenor', a sort of pulpit from which the Torah (the five Books of Moses) are read. The Torah shrine on the east wall in which the Torah scroll is kept has a pediment with Early Gothic carving. The red flag with the yellow star of David was granted to the Jews in Prague by the Emperor Charles IV, though whether anything of the original banner survives the repairs made over the centuries (and commemorated in an inscription) must be uncertain.The so-called 'Swedish Helmet' shown in the middle of the star represents the hat that the Jews had to wear at that time. This flag was carried in all ceremonial processions around the town by thirteen men at the head of the Jewish guilds. In coronation processions a young man would sit on the flag pole and lead the cheering of the new ruler. One of Prague's worst pogroms took place here in 1389, commemorated in a great poem by Abigdor Karo. Rabbi Löw is only one of the famous preachers who have spoken here.

Opposite the Old New Synagogue is the **Jewish Town Hall** which Mordechai Maisel had built at the end of the 16th century by the Italian architect Panacius Rodero (Pankraz Roders). It is the only Jewish town hall outside Israel. In 1763 the Town Hall was baroquized by Josef Schlesinger and given a tower with a clock and a bell. (Another clock has Hebrew numerals and hands that go anti-clockwise, since Hebrew is read from right to left.) The Town Hall has assembly rooms and administrative offices and is still used by the Jewish community in Prague; it also has a simple and attractive restaurant. Adjoining the Town Hall is the **High Synagogue** (Town Hall Synagogue; entrance in Červená ul.) also designed by Panacius Rodero at the end of the 16th century. It now contains an exhibition of synagogal textiles. The **Maisel Synagogue** on Maislova ul. was founded by Mordechai Maisel. It was rebuilt after a fire in 1689 and was given its present Neo-Gothic appearance by Alfred Grotte in 1892–1905. In the synagogue are displays of Jewish religious objects: candlesticks, plaques, bowls, cups – including some superb examples of silverwork from Bohemia and Moravia.

The continuation of Červená ul. beyond Maislova is called U starého hřbitova (At the Old Cemetery) and ends at the **Klaus Synagogue** which was built in 1694 on the site of three small buildings (prayer house, school and hospital). In 1884 the Baroque building was remodelled. It now houses a collection of old Hebrew manuscripts and printed books. The small castle-like building nearby is the **Ceremonial Hall** (Červená No. 3/243) built here in 1906 in a Romantic Romanesque style on the site of a previous building. It contains a display of harrowing drawings done by children in the concentration camp at Theresienstadt (Terezín).

Between the Klaus Synagogue and the Ceremonial Hall is the entrance to the **Old Jewish Cemetery** (plates 17 and 18), known in Hebrew as Beth Chaim, 'House of Life', one of Prague's most remarkable sights. From the 15th century until 1787 all Prague Jews were buried here. The earliest of the c. 11,000 gravestones bears the name of the great poet of Jewish suffering in the pogroms, Selicha Abigdor Karo, and the date of his death, 23 April 1439. The best-known grave, however, is that of Jehuda ben Bezalel, the Chief Rabbi Löw, who died in 1609 (plate 16), who is connected with the legend of the Golem. He was supposed to have made a figure out of clay into which he breathed life by whispering the names of the Lord. The Golem worked as his servant, uncovering Christian plots against the Jews – and in particular protecting them against the slanderous accusation of the ritual murder of Christian children. The Golem was also accident-prone and many legends have grown up around him, which eventually inspired an early film and Gustav Meyrink's eerie novel *Der Golem* (1915). Also worth visiting are the graves of the fabulously wealthy leader of the Jewish Town, Mordechai Maisel (d. 1601), who financed Rudolph II's court; the historian David Gans (d. 1613); the physician, astronomer and philosopher Josef Salomon Delmedigo (d. 1655), and the collector David Oppenheim (d. 1736), chief rabbi of Bohemia, whose collection of Jewish prints and documents is now in the Bodleian Library in Oxford. Since the cemetery could not be extended, and exhumation was unthinkable for religious reasons, the graves rose upwards as earth and sand were piled on. Up to twelve layers of graves have been counted. However, the most valuable gravestones always managed to rise to the top. It is estimated that the total number of those buried here is more than 100,000. In 1903 the Jewish community had to relinquish 1900 square metres of the cemetery as part of the rebuilding campaign. The bones were reburied forming a small hill (*Nefele*), and the gravestones were moved to the remaining part. It was while wandering in this 'mortal wilderness' (W. White) that Einstein first came to reflect on the meaning and importance of his Jewishness.

The **Pinkas Synagogue** between the cemetery and Široká ul. has foundations dating back to the 11th century, when a *mikve* (ritual bath) stood on the site. It is named after Pinkas, a 'court Jew', the financier of King Otakar II Přemysl (1252–1278). The Late Gothic vault dates from the enlarging of the synagogue in 1535; the south extension and women's gallery are 17th century. Between 1950 and 1958 the synagogue was converted into a memorial for the Jewish victims of Nazi rule in Bohemia and Moravia. Inside, the walls are covered with 77,297 names of the dead and missing. The memorial has, however, been closed to the public for over twenty years. The **Spanish Synagogue** (Spanělská synagóga) was built between 1822 and 1893 in the pseudo-moorish style popular for synagogues in this period. It is built on the foundations of an early 12th-century synagogue. Jews who had fled the Christian Reconquista in Spain in the 15th century gave the synagogue its name. F.J. Škroup, the composer of the Czechoslovak national anthem, was choir-master here.

Northern Old Town

On perambulations through the Old Town the visitor will cross Mariánské nám (Marienplatz) with the **New Town Hall** (Nová radnice) designed in 1908–1911 by Osvald Polívka, the creator of the Obecní dům, in the late Art Nouveau style. Stanislav Sucharda and Josef Mařatka were responsible for the sculptural decoration, while Ladislav Šaloun made the sculptures of the 'Iron Knights' and 'Rabbi Löw' at the corners. The north side of the square is dominated by the **Municipal People's Library** (Městská lidová knihovna) built in 1930 in an imposing functionalist style, while the east side is occupied by the Clementinum (see p. 52). On the wall of the Clam-Gallas Palace on the south side of the square is the **Vltava Fountain** with a delightful allegory of the river made by Václav Prachner in 1812. The original figure of 'Terezka' (little Teresa) – as the girl is popularly known – is in the National Gallery.

Mánes Bridge (Mánesov most) is built approximately on the site of the ford through which the merchants' carts rolled across the river in Prague's earliest times. The bridge, built 1911–1914, is named after Josef Mánes, one of the greatest Czech painters, who was born and died in Prague (1820–1871). Mánes, a pupil of the painter Peter Cornelius of Düsseldorf, incorporated influences from German Romanticism and Belgian history painting into his work. He chose themes from Bohemian history and folklore, as well as painting landscapes and portraits. A large proportion of his work is displayed in the Convent of St Agnes (see below). At the Old Town end of Mánes Bridge is nám. Jana Palacha. This was formerly Smetana Square and until recently Red Army Square, with red flowers planted as a star-shaped bed in the middle. The renaming after the student martyr of 1969, Jan Palach, who was a student at the philosophy faculty here, was the first such change of name after the 1989 revolution. The square is dominated by the **House of Artists** (Dům umělců; often known as the Rudolfinum). Apart from the National Theatre (see p. 124) this is the most important example of Neo-Renaissance architecture in Prague and was designed between 1876 and 1884 by Josef Zítek and Josef Schulz as an arts centre for the Czech-speaking community. Between 1918 and 1938 (and in 1945-46) the Czechoslovak National Assembly met here. The large concert hall (Dvořák Hall) is the focus of the annual 'Prague Spring' music festival.

Opposite the House of Artists, on the other side of the wide ul. 17. listopadu (Street of 17 November) stands the **Museum of Applied Arts** (Uměleckoprůmyslové muzeum – UPM), built in 1897–1901 by Josef Schulz. Among its many varied exhibits its famous collection of glass, the largest in the world, makes it particularly worth a visit.

A walk through the picturesque winding streets of the Old Town takes us to the **Convent of St Agnes** (Anežský klášter) in the north of the Old Town on the bank of the Vltava. This was the earliest group of Gothic buildings in Bohemia. The Přemyslid Princess Agnes (Anežka; 1211–1282), the sister of King Wenceslas I, had rejected the hand in marriage of the Emperor Frederick II and of the English King Henry III in order to emulate her cousin St Elizabeth of Hungary (d. 1231). She admired Francis of Assisi, corresponded with his disciple Clare, and in 1233 induced the king to found a convent in Prague for the female Franciscan Order, the Poor Clares. A few years later the Minorites (Franciscans of the First Order) were established very close by. On 12 November 1989, after many years of Beatitude, the Blessed Agnes was eventually canonized by the present pope.

The nucleus of the convent is the double-naved church of *St Francis*. Around 1280 the church of *the Saviour* was added to the east end of the north nave. St Saviour is the most important surviving example of early Bohemian Gothic. The choir was completed in 1350, the square cloister in 1360. The capitals of the portal linking the Church of the Saviour with the chapter house have five heads of Bohemian queens. It is presumed that from the time of Wenceslas I the convent was the burial place of the Přemyslids. Besides the king's grave, the tomb slabs of Guta II, the daughter of Wenceslas II, and of Kunhuta (Cunegunda), Otakar II's wife, have come to light. The grave of St Agnes is still being sought; according to an ancient prophecy, when her body is found Bohemia will experience a golden age.

In 1782 Joseph II closed down the Convent of St Agnes together with over 700 other 'useless' religious houses as part of his programme of rationalization. It was used as a reformatory, warehouse, and finally – when it was half-ruinous – a hide-out for the homeless. In 1892 restoration work started, and it has continued with interruptions until the present day. Since 1980 the *National Gallery* has shown its impressive collection of 19th-century Czech Painting in the beautiful rooms of the reconstructed part of the convent, with works by Josef Navrátil (1798–1865), Josef Mánes (1820–1871), Mikoláš Aleš (1852–1913), Antonín Slavíček (1870–1910) and many others, reflecting the artistic revival which accompanied the awakening of Czech national consciousness in the 19th century. Chamber music recitals are held in the Mánes Hall.

East of the Ungelt of Týn, in Jakubská ul. stands the **Church of St James** (Kostel sv. Jakuba), the longest church in Prague, after St Vitus. The monastery of St James was founded for the Minorites (Friars Minor or Franciscans) by Wenceslas I (1230–1253) with a small Romanesque church. In 1318 they began building a larger, Gothic church, which was consecrated in 1374. It was burned out in the great fire of 1689 and was immediately restored and baroquized by Jan Šimon Pánek (Panetius) in 1690–1702. The building was given a new barrel vault, about 5 metres lower than the original, and galleries in the two aisles. The surviving Gothic façade was decorated by the Italian sculptor Ottavio Mosto with reliefs showing St James flanked by St Francis and St Anthony of Padua. The most impressive feature of the interior is the Baroque splendour of the nave, the huge pilasters by Christian Schatzmann, the plasterwork of Abondio Bolla, the ceiling paintings by Franz Guido Voget, and the massive high altar by Matthias Schönherr with the Life of the Virgin. Wenzel Lorenz Reiner painted the monumental altarpiece *The Martyrdom of St James*. In the north aisle is one of the finest Baroque tombs in Bohemia: that of Count Jan Václav Vratislav of Mitrovic, Supreme Chancellor of the Kingdom of Bohemia, designed by Johann Bernhard Fischer von Erlach. Because of its remarkable acoustic, St James's Church is also used for concerts and organ recitals.

Southern Old Town

From the town hall of the Old Town (see pp. 45ff.) Melantrichova ul. leads southwards to the Gall district (Havelské Město). The printer and publisher Jiří Melantrich of Aventino (1511–1580), whose shop was an important centre of Czech humanism, gave the street its name. Two strainer arches mark the entrance to this shortest route between the Old Town Square and Wenceslas Square. Just at the beginning of the street is the house of the **Golden Jug** (U

The Seal of the Charles University

zlaté konvice; No. 20/477) which contains a typical old Prague wine tavern in a Gothic cellar. Around the corner of Kožná ul. (Leather Street) is the house of the **Two Golden Bears** (U dvou zlatých medvědů; No. 1/475; plate 8) the birthplace of the journalist and writer Egon Erwin Kisch (1885–1948). The house was originally Gothic but was remodelled in the late 16th century in Renaissance style and was given an Empire façade around 1800. The two bears are part of the elaborate carving of the Renaissance portal (c. 1590).

A peculiarity of Prague is the network of passages which run through houses connecting streets and forming a sort of secret street-plan. In the neighbourhood of Melantrichova, and near the Ungelt, there are many such passages, which are not noticed by the visitor hurrying past. They provide a route through from Kožná to Melantrichova and on to Michalská and Jilská, and from Malé náměsti to Hlavsova.

On 7 April 1348 Charles IV founded the **Carolinum** (or *Collegium Carolinum*), named after him, the first university in central Europe. At the outset no special building for teaching was provided, masters and students meeting in monasteries and private houses. It was not until 1383 that Wenceslas IV acquired the palace of the Master of the Mint, Johlin Rotlöw (Jan Rotlev), in Železná ul. (Iron Street) which had been built in about 1370. When František Maximilián Kaňka baroquized the Carolinum for the Jesuits in 1718, he left only the old oriel window of the Rotlev house in its High Gothic purity. In the course of extensive restoration work Josef Mocker re-gothicized the building in 1881–82, and between 1946–1950 Jaroslav Fragner returned the whole complex of buildings, including the interiors, to their original form.

The *Aula* (Great Hall) which was extended by Fragner is worth a visit for a large tapestry made in 1947 by Vladimir Sychra depicting *Charles VI presenting the University to St Wenceslas*. The larger than life-size bronze statue of the emperor is by Karel Pokorný. In the courtyard of the Carolinum the statue of Jan Hus, who was rector here until 1412, is by Karel Lidický (1959).

Železná, one of the oldest streets in Prague, also passes the **Tyl Theatre** (Tylovo divadlo), a Neo-Classical building erected in 1781–1783 to designs by Anton Haffenecker. The inauguration took place on 21 April 1783 with a performance of Lessing's *Emilia Galotti*. In 1786 Mozart received enthusiastic applause from Prague audiences for his new opera buffa

The Marriage of Figaro, which had had a cool reception from the Viennese public. 'My Praguers understand me,' wrote Mozart rapturously, and his next opera, *Don Giovanni*, was given its première here, on 29 October 1787, to the same enthusiasm. Carl Maria von Weber was opera director here between 1813 and 1816. In 1834 *Fidlovačka* (Spring Festival), a comedy by Josef Kajetán Tyl (1808–1856), was first performed in the theatre; the song 'Kde domov můj?' ('Where is my home?') from this play became the Czech national anthem. The theatre was named after Tyl in 1945.

The magnificent building at Rytířská 29 became the Klement Gottwald Museum after the president's death in 1953 and illustrated the development of the workers' movement in Czechoslovakia. It has now closed. The massive Neo-Renaissance-style building was built in 1892–1894 for the Prague Savings Bank by the architects Antonín Wiehl and Osvald Polívka, and was decorated by leading Czech artists. On this site once stood the earliest theatre in Prague, where German comedies and Italian operas were performed from 1738 until the opening of the Tyl Theatre.

The great pogrom against the Jews in 1098 left a gap in the commercial life of the city that was to be filled by the German business community, which henceforth grew in strength. In 1173 Duke Soběslav II granted it great privileges and gave them the area south of the Old Town Square. At the centre of the German quarter was the Romanesque church of **St Gall** (Kostel sv. Havel). When the head of St Gall came to Prague from the Swiss monastery of Sankt Gallen in mid–14th century the Church of St Gall was remodelled in the High Gothic style. The greatest reforming preachers of their age were active in St Gall's: Konrad Waldhauser (1358–1369), Jan Milič of Kroměříž (Kremsier; 1369–1373) and lastly Jan Hus. In 1627 the Calced Carmelites moved into the church, and in the late 17th century they had it remodelled in the Baroque style by Giovanni Domenico Orsi. The façade was altered by Johann Blasius Santini-Aichel in 1723–1738. Inside, the pietà is probably by Ferdinand Maximilian Brokoff. Karel Škréta, whose paintings are found in many Prague churches, is buried here.

In Charles IV's time St Gall's Church already dominated the long St Gall Market (German: Gallimarkt), which at that time extended from Ovocný trh (Fruit Market) to Uhelný trh (Coal Market). In 1372 to the west of the church a market hall 200 metres long was built, called *Kotce* with shops on either side of a broad central passage. In 1795 the hall was demolished and burghers' houses built on the site of the shops so that now the St Gall Market consisted of three streets: Havelská ul., V kotcích and Rytířská ul. In Havelská there is still a vegetable and flower market, and textiles are sold in V kotcich, but the egg market in Rytířská disappeared at the end of the 19th century. The beautiful arcades in Havelská in front of what are originally Gothic houses (Nos. 3/511, 5/510, 7/509 and 9/508) take the visitor back to the end of the 14th century. At the Platyz in the Coal Market (Uhelný trh 11) the drunken Liszt had to be helped to his rooms by Berlioz, and dissuaded from fighting duels with fellow topers who claimed to have drunk more. Leaving Uhelny trh by Martinská the visitor should pause to notice the two houses either side of the street: Da Ponte stayed on the top floor of one to write the libretto of *Don Giovanni*, which he then passed through the window to Mozart, who was writing the music on the top floor of the other. A little further down is the church of **St Martin in the Wall** (Kostel sv. Martina ve zdi) which is among the earliest Romanesque buildings in Prague. It was probably founded by Adelaide (Adelheid), the wife of Prince Soběslav I in about 1130. The unaisled church divided the Czech parish of St Martin (Ujezd sv. Martina) from the German Gall district. When the Old Town wall was built in the mid–13th century the church was built into the ramparts. In the 14th century it was remodelled and extended in Gothic style, and in 1488 the two aisles were added. The tower took on its present appearance after the fire of 1678. In 1784 the church was converted into a warehouse with dwellings and shops. It was here in 1414 that for the first time Holy Communion was distributed to the laity in both kinds, i.e. the Host *and* the Wine. Today St Martin's belongs to the Evangelical Brethren.

Nearby is perhaps the greatest centre of the Czech Reformation: the **Bethlehem Chapel** (Betlémská kaple) in Betlémské nám., a tall, two-gabled building founded in 1391 by Johann (Hanuš) of Mühlheim, a favourite of Wenceslas IV, so that sermons could be preached there in the Czech language. In 1402–1413 Jan Hus made the chapel the centre of the Reformation movement. In 1521, four years before his execution, the Protestant theologian and later leader of the Peasants' Revolt in Germany, Thomas Müntzer, preached in the Bethlehem Chapel and there wrote the 'Prague Manifesto', the first testimony of his radical social doctrines. In the 17th and 18th centuries the chapel was given to the Jesuits. After the suppression of the order in 1773 it was closed down and demolished 13 years later. In the 19th century a dwelling house was built on its foundations, but in 1948–1954 the Bethlehem Chapel was reconstructed from old plans and prints, the Communist authorities favouring the project because of the connection with the revolutionary Müntzer. Restoration work was also done on the preacher's house next door where Hus lived and worked. It is now a museum with documents relating to the great reformer and his work, and also preserves remains of a settlement here in the 11th century.

From the Smetanova nábřeží (Smetana Embankment) there is the finest view of Malá strana (Lesser Town), Hradčany, Charles Bridge and the former **Old Town Mills**. This delightful group of buildings projects far into the Vltava from Novotného lávka (Novotný Footbridge). The mills were built in the 14th century, the Late Gothic water tower (colour plate 5) c. 1489, and the building at the end of the footbridge was built in Neo-Renaissance style by Antonin Wiehl in 1885 as the headquarters of the Prague Waterworks. Since 1936 it has housed the *Bedřich Smetana Museum*. Bedřich Smetana (1824–1884), the composer of the opera *The Bartered Bride* and the symphonic poem *Má vlast* (My Country), was the director of a music school in Prague in 1848–1856, and in 1866 was made conductor at the Czech National Theatre. Despite being a German-speaker who never fully mastered Czech, Smetana was an ardent Czech nationalist, and his was a great part in the national awakening. On the façade are sgraffiti by František Ženíšek and Mikóláš Aleš showing the battle of the people of Prague against the Swedes on the Charles Bridge in 1648. In front of the building facing the Vltava, which flows through so much of his music, stands a memorial to the composer by the sculptor Josef Malejovský, erected in 1984.

Malá strana (Lesser Town)

The Charles Bridge links the Old Town with Malá Strana, perhaps the most attractive district of Prague. The area on the west bank of the Vltava was already settled by the 9th century, but it was not until 1257 that King Otakar II Přemysl made it the second town of Prague (after the Old Town). The town was first called *Nova civitas sub castro Pragensi* (New Town below Prague Castle), but from the 14th century it was known as *Minor civitas Pragensis* (Lesser Town of Prague), from which the name Malá strana and its German form 'Kleinseite' are derived. The Lesser Town was surrounded by a wall and mainly inhabited by German merchants and craftsmen brought to the country by Pitrolf, the royal *lokator* (the royal official charged with founding new settlements). In 1360–1362 Charles IV enlarged the town by building new walls. A disastrous fire swept through the district in 1541 destroying many buildings and clearing the way for a profusion of princely palaces. After the Thirty Years' War and the expropriation of the Protestant nobles' estates, Catholic nobility from all over the Empire settled in Malá Strana, which now took on its Baroque appearance with the building of splendid churches and residences. In 1784 it lost its independence and was joined with the Old Town, the New Town and Hradčany to form a single municipality. Since 1918 official bodies and foreign embassies have occupied the palaces of Malá Strana and thus preserved the aristocratic grandeur of the district between the Vltava and the Castle.

Mostecká ul. follows the route of the old Royal Way between the Charles Bridge and the Lesser Town Square (Malostranské náměstí). Attached to the smaller bridge tower at the end of the bridge is the former Customs House (No. 1/56), a Renaissance building of 1591. At first floor level a Late Romanesque relief (1254) shows the reconciliation of Wenceslas I with his son Otakar II Přemysl following the latter's unsuccessful coup d'état in 1249.

The **Lesser Town Square (Malostranské náměstí)** was the political and business centre of Malá Strana from the foundation of the town in 1257. In the square stood the Romanesque Wenceslas Rotunda, part of the strong outer fortifications of Hradčany. In 1283 the Gothic church of St Nicholas was built and, together with several houses, it divided the large square in two, a lower square and an upper square. This division remained when the Jesuits later enlarged and rebuilt the church in the Baroque style.

The old houses, originally Gothic but now almost all with Neo-Classical façades, survive only on the south side of the square, on the left as the visitor comes from the Charles Bridge. In their vaulted cellars wine taverns and pubs were established, e.g. *U Glaubiců* ('at the Glaubices' – Glaubic was a mayor of Malá Strana) at No. 5/266 and *U mecenáše* ('Maecenas') at No. 9/262. (The lovely Neo-Classical-Baroque house at No. 6/265 belonged to the architect Palliardi.) The sites on the other sides of the square were bought by the nobility who

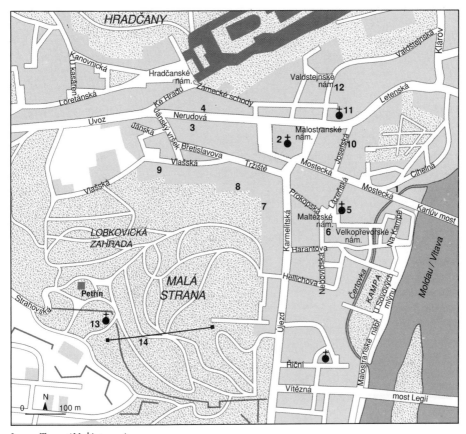

Lesser Town (Malá strana)
1 Customs House and Old Town Bridge Tower   2 St Nicholas   3 Morzin Palace   4 Thun-Hohenstein
Palace   5 St Mary   6 Nostitz Palace   7 St Mary of Victory   8 Vrtba gardens   9 Lobkowicz
Palace   10 St Joseph   11 St Thomas   12 Waldstein Palace   13 St Lawrence   14 Cable Railway

built a number of grand palaces. The **Liechtenstein Palace** (No. 13/258), which takes up the upper (west) side of the square, beyond the church, was built by the brutal Habsburg governor, Karl von Liechtenstein, who had the Protestant leaders executed in 1621. Its later history was no less repressive, as the headquarters of the Swedes for their assaults in 1648, and of Windischgrätz for his repression of the 1848 revolts, and it was here too that the intelligence officer Colonel Alfred Redl had his headquarters when his treachery was discovered in 1913. In the **Smiřický Palace** (No. 18/6), on the north side with two little turrets, the Bohemian Estates resolved on 22 May 1618 to rise against the Habsburgs; and the **Sternberg Palace** (No. 19/7), next door, supported by heavy buttresses and identified by a large star, was where the Czech Society of Sciences was founded by Goethe's great friend, the naturalist Count Kaspar Sternberg; Goethe promised on many occasions to visit him, but in the event never came to Prague. The last building on this side sports a little Renaissance oriel.

Then, on the opposite corner, past the spire of St Thomas, is the **Town Hall of the Lesser Town** (Malostranská beseda; No. 21/35), the centre of the political, economic and cultural life of Malá Strana from 1478 until 1784. It became famous in 1575 when the representatives of the religious groups drew up the 'Bohemian Confession' there (commemorative plaque on the façade).

In the middle of the lower square stands the **Grömling Palace**, two houses built in the 16th century from a group of butchers' market stalls. It was here that in 1874 the 'Radetzky-Café' was opened, named after the Austrian field marshal (of Czech extraction), whose monument stood in front of the café until 1918, when it was removed as a symbol of Habsburg rule. In the 1920's the café was known as the 'Malostranská kavárna' ('Kleinseitner Kaffeehaus') and it was there that the circle of German Jewish literati met: Franz Kafka, Max Brod, Franz Werfel, Willy Haas and others. The plain mass behind is the former **Jesuit College**, a house for novices, was built for the order in 1674–1691 by the architect Giovanni Domenico Orsi on the site of twenty houses; the Jesuits replaced the Romanesque Wenceslas rotunda at the north-west corner of the college with their new church of St Wenceslas.

But unmistakably the centrepiece of the Lesser Town Square is **St Nicholas in the Lesser Town** (Kostel sv. Mikuláše; German: St. Niklas auf der Kleinseite; ills. 19, 20). This is arguably the most beautiful religious building in Prague, next to St Vitus's Cathedral. The first church dedicated to St Nicholas was built in 1283 as the parish church of Malá Strana. It became particularly associated with Hussitism and rebellion, and when the Protestant leaders were taken to execution in 1621, it was the preacher of St Nicholas who accompanied them. His book, *Koruna neuvadlá*, 'The Crown has not Faded' became a rallying point for the cause. Unsurprisingly, therefore, his church was placed in the safest Catholic hands: the Society of Jesus. The Jesuits moved into the Gothic building in 1625, and built their college next door to it. In 1703–1711 Christoph Dientzenhofer built a new nave with the west front,

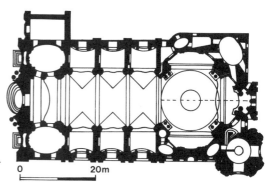

Prague, St Nicholas in the Lesser Town, plan

0   20m

The Dientzenhofer family of architects

The Dientzenhofers, who came originally from near Aibling in Upper Bavaria, were the greatest masters of the German Late Baroque. Five sons of Georg Dientzenhofer, a mountain farmer, moved to Prague to learn the art of architecture there in the workshops of Abraham Leutner and Carlo Lurago. Four of them then returned to southern Germany, where they built a number of well-known abbeys and churches: *Georg* (1643–1689) built the magnificent Trinity Church at Kappel, the Cistercian abbey church at Waldsassen and St Martin at Bamberg; *Wolfgang* (1648–1706) worked at Amberg and built the abbeys of Speinshart and Michelfeld; *Leonhard* (1660–1707) was responsible for the Neue Residenz at Bamberg and Ebrach Abbey; while *Johann* (1663–1726) built Fulda Cathedral and Schloss, Pommersfelden Abbey and the famous abbey church of Banz.

Christoph Dientzenhofer (1655–1727), the only brother to remain in Prague, perfected Guarini's ingenious concept of interpenetrating vaults. Together with his son Kilian Ignaz he left his mark on townscape of Prague, as well as building some architectural gems in southern and western Bohemia. Between 1689 and 1751 father and son built more than 120 works, mostly churches and abbeys, but also including châteaux, palaces, fortifications, gates, dwellings and farms. Among Christoph's major works are the abbey church of St Clare in Cheb (Eger) (see p. 219), the pilgrimage church of Chlumec (Maria Kulm) near Cheb, the monastery of Teplá (Tepl) near Mariánské Lázne (Marienbad), the nave and façade of St Nicholas in Malá strana, Prague, and the abbey churches at Obořiště and Břevnov, Prague (see p. 138).

Kilian Ignaz Dientzenhofer (1689–1751), born and died in Prague, became even more famous than his father and was one of the greatest masters of the Late Baroque. Among his works are St John Nepomuk on the Rock in Prague (see p. 132), the church of St Mary Magdalene, Karlovy Vary (Karlsbad; see p. 227), St Francis Xavier at Oparany, and lastly the completion of St Nicholas in Malá strana, Prague, one of the world's most beautiful Baroque churches, a symphony of sweeping spaces.

and the choir and dome were built in 1737–1752 by his son, Kilian Ignaz Dientzenhofer, one of the greatest of all Baroque architects. Father and son created a masterpiece: a dizzying play of curves and interpenetrating ovals, with an extraordinary undulating vault rising above a complicated ground plan. Painting, architecture, sculpture are all confused into a single ecstatic experience. Anselmo Lurago, Kilian Ignaz's son-in-law, added the bell-tower in 1755, and in 1760–61 Johann Lucas Kracker of Vienna painted the impressive ceiling fresco in the nave, the *Glorification of St Nicholas*, covering 1500 square metres and one of the largest paintings in Europe. St Nicholas of Myra – Santa Claus – is seen in the centre, blessing the congregation. Elsewhere an acolyte distributes miraculous oils, the saint gives money to a poor man who would otherwise have to sell his daughter, and he saves three Romans from execution. The rocky coast refers to the saint's protection of seafarers. Another miracle, the bringing to life of three murdered boys in a brine barrel, is suggested by the stucco image of three little barrels within a gold scroll at the base of the drum of the dome. The dome itself is painted with a *Celebration of the Holy Trinity* by Karl Palko, 1752–53. The sculptural decoration, such as the statue of St Nicholas above the high altar, is almost entirely by Ignaz Platzer, who also made the gigantic Church Fathers on the piers, and the rather smaller virtues above them. The pulpit (Richard and Peter Prachner, 1765) is especially spectacular, with a liquid execution of St John the Baptist, and two angels pulling back gold curtains. Standing by it, the visitor will have a good view of the hordes of angels flying round the organ. The Gothic image of the Virgin above the side altar on the left was brought to Prague by the Jesuits in 1629 from the Belgian Marian shrine of Foyen, and the painting in the second chapel on the left is by the Neapolitan master, Francesco Solimena.

The Plague Column in the upper square was designed in 1715 by the architect Giovanni Battista Alliprandi as a token of gratitude for the end of an epidemic. The sculpture representing the Trinity was made by Johann Ulrich Mayer and Ferdinand Geiger.

From the upper part of the Lesser Town Square **Nerudová ulice** leads fairly steeply up to Hradčany. The street is named after the Czech writer Jan Neruda (1834–1891) who lived here and immortalized the Malá Strana in his work. Its attractive burghers' houses make Nerudová one of the most beautiful streets in Prague. Because the houses had no numbers, only names, they needed clearly visible signs to identify them. Almost every house in Nerudová has one of these 'name badges': the Red Eagle (U červeného orla; No. 5/207), the Three Little Fiddles (U tří housliček; No. 12/210; plate 7) – these are real fiddles, put up by a family of violin-makers; the Golden Cup (U zlaté číše; No. 16/212), St John Nepomuk (U sv. Jana Nepomuckého; No. 18/213), the Golden Key (U zlatého klíče; No. 27/243); the Golden Lion (U zlatého lva; No. 32/219) where there is a fine Empire pharmacy, now a museum; the Golden Horseshoe (U zlaté podkovy; No. 34/220) – the horse is oddly twisted to show the (real) horseshoe in the lucky position, though it has since disappeared; the Red Lion (U červeného lva; No. 41/236), the Green Lobster (U zeleného raka; No. 43/235); the Two Suns (U dvou slunců; No. 47/233) – Neruda's house – and the White Swan (U bílé labutě; No. 49/239). On the corner of Janský vršek the Baroque house with the grey Rococo façade is the **Bretfeld Palace** (No. 33/240), or 'Summer and Spring House'. Famous balls were held here in the 18th century; at one of them, Mozart, on his first night in Prague, in 1787, came face to face with his fame. He was too tired, he wrote, to dance, and too bashful to flirt, but 'I looked on with the greatest pleasure while all those people flew about in sheer delight to the music of my "Figaro" arranged for quadrilles and waltzes. For here they talk about nothing but Figaro. Nothing is played, sung or whistled but Figaro. Nothing, nothing but Figaro. Certainly a great honour for me!' Such was his popularity that he returned ten months later for the première of Don Giovanni at the Estates Theatre (now the Tyl), and stayed this time at the Bretfeld palace, in the company of Casanova.

Nerudová is also, in a sense, Santini-Aichel's street: the great master of the Baroque and of the Baroque-Gothic, born in Prague as the crippled son of a stone mason, lived at No. 14/211, to which he gave its present façade. He also built the two palaces that interrupt the burghers's houses on either side of Nerudová, and the church a little further up the street. The **Morzin Palace** on the left (No. 5/256) is now the Rumanian Embassy, and the **Thun-Hohenstein Palace** (No. 20/214; c. 1720) opposite, the Italian Embassy. The portal of the Morzin Palace is held up by two moors, a pun on the owner's name; the central keystone is carved as their quiver. The sculptor was Ferdinand Maximilian Brokoff, who also made Day and Night further up, shown as a beaming Apollo with the sun on his breast, facing Night as the weary moon; the attic has figures of the Continents, Europe serious and wise with an owl, Africa astride a crocodile, Asia wearing a pagoda in her hair. On the other side the two mighty eagles of the Thun-Hohenstein Palace are by Matthias Bernhard Braun. Something of Santini's waywardness can be seen in the little peaked pediments over the first-floor windows; these can be compared with the crushing keystones over the windows of the **Theatine Church**. (The Theatines originally engaged Guarini to design this church, which is dedicated to Our Lady of Perpetual Succour, and it is conceivable that Santini was able to examine his plans.)

Nerudová ends at the ramp to the Castle (Ke Hradu), which rises steeply up to Hradčany. The continuation of Nerudová becomes the Uvoz (the Cutting). Parallel to Nerudová is **Zámecké schody** (New Castle Steps) which date from the 16th century. There was a steep path here in the 13th century; the steps were added in the 15th century. In the 16th and 17th centuries craftsmen and artists had their shops on either side. The steps are very quiet now, but they end with a flourish at Jože Plečnik's grand balustrade, marking the entrance to the Castle Gardens.

Immediately in front of the larger of the towers at Malá Strana end of the Charles Bridge is the famous House of the **Three Ostriches** (U tří pštrosů; No. 1/76). In 1606 the owner, Jan Fux, extended the Renaissance building (erected in 1585), and had the ostrich motifs painted on the façade because he was a dealer in ostrich feathers, which had come into fashion at that time. In 1657 the house was baroquized. Deodat Damajan, an Armenian, founded the first coffee-house in Prague here in 1714.

Čertovka (Devil's Stream), a branch of the Vltava, separates the island of **Kampa** from Malá Strana. The island used to be subject to frequent flooding and it was not until the 15th

View of Prague

century that it was built on and then only at the end near Charles Bridge. The southern part remained a garden and is nowadays a popular park. Since the 13th century the Čertovka powered several mills of which the mill-wheels of the Grand Priory Mill and the Mlýn Hut' (Works Mill) south of the Charles Bridge are preserved to some extent. North of the bridge are houses rising straight from the water; the area has been known since the 16th century as 'Prague Venice'. Crossing back into the Malá Strana over a little bridge, the visitor will find himself surrounded by palaces in **Velkopřevorské náměstí** (Grand Priory Square). *Hrzán Palace* (No. 1/490) in which Josef Bohuslav Foerster (1859–1951), the Czech composer of the operas *Deborah* and the *Bagpiper of Strakonice*, was born; *Buquoy Palace* (No. 2/486), home of the French mercenary who created the victory at the White Mountain and now the French Embassy (Paul Claudel worked here during the First World War), and the **Grand Prior's Palace** (No. 4/485), built by the Grand Prior Johann von Rosenberg (Jan of Rožmberk)

in 1516–1532. Its Baroque façade by Bartholomäus Scotti dates from 1725–1727 and was built for one of the energetically Catholic Dietrichsteins. There is a delightful staircase carved by M.B. Braun, leading up to a museum of old musical instruments and the music archive of the National Museum. The **Grand Priory Mill** (No. 7/489), whose workings could be seen from the bridge, was in operation from the 13th century until 1936. The calm of this little square is a strange setting for the rainbow shrine of John Lennon, on the Grand Priory wall, which became a focus for the frustration of the young under communism.

Lázeňská leads from Velkopřevorské nám. past the church of **St Mary below the Chain** (Kostel Panny Maria pod řetězem) at the corner of Lázeňská in Maltézské nám. (Maltese Square), a reminder of the Hospitallers of St John (who later became the Knights of Malta), for whom King Vladislav I founded a house in 1160. The community owned all the land around under its own jurisdiction. The three-aisled church originally built in 1169–1182 was considerably larger than the present building. It was gothicized in the 13th and 14th centuries and was given its Baroque appearance by Carlo Lurago in the mid–17th century. Karel Škréta painted the high altarpiece c. 1660 representing the victory of the Maltese Knights against the Turks at Lepanto (1571) aided by the Mother of God and John the Baptist. The church was restored in 1965–1985.

In the north-west corner of the little square outside the church there is a pretty wrought-iron balcony, and a memorial plaque to Beethoven. The building was an inn, clearly in particular favour with Beethoven's patron, Prince Lichnowsky, since he had also brought Mozart to stay here. Burney, investigating the musical scene in Bohemia a few years earlier, on the recommendation of J.C. Bach, was serenaded here at dinner by the street musicians. (Further down Lázeňská, towards the Charles Bridge, the visitor may notice a memorial to Chateaubriand, who stayed at Lázeňská 6/283, then the Im Bad hotel, which also welcomed Peter the Great, the exiled Charles X of France, and Bismarck; later as a lecture hall it was often used by Masaryk). **Maltézské náměstí**, one of the friendly little squares so typical of Prague and particularly of Malá Strana, was a particular favourite of Rilke's, and appears in much of his work. The statue of John the Baptist in the centre, which originally formed part of a fountain, was made by Ferdinand Maximilian Brokoff in 1715. The house at the sign of the **Painters** (U malířů; No. 11/291), built in 1531 on the remains of Malá Strana town walls, now contains a pleasant wine tavern. The **Stará pošta** (Old Post Office; No. 8/481) is a Baroque building in which the first post office in Prague was housed in the 15th century. **Nostitz Palace** on the south side of Maltese Square was built in 1658–1660, probably to a design by Francesco Caratti, with statues by Brokoff (now copies). In 1765 Anton Haffenecker gave the building its Rococo portal. The palace is now divided between the Dutch Embassy and the Dobrovský Library. The linguistic and literary writings of Josef Dobrovský (1753–1829), the founder of Slav philology, contributed to the rise of Czech national consciousness. The Nostitz Library is famous for its collection of Copernicus manuscripts. Down the street to the left, Nosticova, No. 465 was the house Christoph Dientzenhofer built for himself in 1702; it was later lived in by the architect Anton Affenecker whose major work was the Nostitz Riding School opposite.

Prokopská and Harantova both lead to the main street of Malá Strana, **Karmelitská ulice**, which has been lined with palaces since the 17th century. From the beginning of the 14th century a convent of Magdalenes, of the 'Order of St Mary Magdalene of Penitence', stood there, and in 1604 the Dominicans arrived. The **Rohan Palace** (No. 8/386) presents an Empire appearance; the **Sporck Palace** (No. 14/382) has Baroque garb, while Baroque and Neo-Classicism are combined in the **Muscon Palace** (No. 16/380), which began life as a Renaissance building at the beginning of the 17th century.

Rising above Karmelitská is the church of **Our Lady of Victory** (Kostel P. Marie Vítězné), the earliest Baroque building in Prague. Originally dedicated to the Holy Trinity, it was built in 1611–1613 for German Lutherans by Giovanni Maria Filippi, an architect from Trentino in northern Italy. During the Counter-Reformation the church passed to the Catholic Order of Discalced Carmelites in 1624 and received its new dedication to the 'Virgin of Victory' in remembrance of the victory of the White Mountain. Extensive remodelling from 1636 to 1644 gave the church a new orientation.

Noteworthy is the tall façade with figure of the victorious Mother of God, in a round-arched niche above the portal, as the Queen of Heaven with crown, sceptre and glory – the prototype for innumerable statues of the Virgin throughout Bohemia and Moravia. The interior of the aisle-less, barrel-vaulted church is plain and enlivened only by the elaborately furnished side niches. The high altar in the form of a Roman triumphal arch is the work of Johann Ferdinand Schor (1723), the altar paintings (*St Joseph*, *St Joachim and St Anne* and *St Simon Stock* are by Peter Johann Brandl. The modern Madonna is by the painter and writer Josef Čapek (1887–1945) who died in Belsen.

The particular curiosity in the church, and the reason why it is the goal of countless pilgrims from all over the world, is the miraculous *Holy Infant of Prague*, 'Bambino di Praga' or 'pražské Jesulátko', a two foot tall wax figurine, richly clothed and in a silver shrine. When Maria Manriques de Lara married a Bohemian nobleman, Vratislav of Pernstein, in the second half of the 16th century she brought the doll with her to Prague. She gave the family heirloom to her daughter Polyxena on the latter's marriage to the Chancellor Zdeněk Popel of Lobkowicz. When Polyxena of Lobkowicz was widowed in 1628, she presented the statuette to the Carmelites for their Church of Our Lady of Victory. In 1784 Joseph II closed down the Carmelite friary, and the church now comes under the direct control of the Archbishopric of Prague.

The **Vrtba Palace** (Karmelitská No. 25/373) was formed from two Renaissance houses joined together by Count Vrtba in 1631. The remarkable feature of the palace is its garden (Vrtbovská zahrada), one of the most beautiful gardens in central Europe, which rises in terraces on the slope above. It was built for the burgrave Jan Josef of Vrtba to the designs of František Maximilián Kaňka, the sculptures were made in the workshop of Matthias Bernhard Braun, and the wall paintings by Wenzel Lorenz Reiner. Work on the garden lasted from 1715 to 1720. On the lowest of the four terraces a *giardinetto* with little fountains links the *sala terrena* with the palace. Two portals lead up to the next terrace from which a double flight of steps rises to the third terrace with statues of the Olympian gods. The upper terrace has a wonderful view of Prague Castle across the roofs of Malá Strana.

In Vlašská ul. (Welsche Gasse; No. 19/347) stands the handsome **Schonborn Palace** with its amusing windows, perhaps by Santini-Aichel. (It was while living in a flat here that Kafka first became aware of his fatal tuberculosis; as the American Embassy the house is now the home of Shirley Temple.) A little further up is the **Lobkowicz Palace**, now the German Embassy. It was built in 1702–1705 by Giovanni Battista Alliprandi and its most impressive feature is the magnificent garden front. In 1753 the Lobkowicz family acquired the site with its enormous garden stretching up as far as Petřín hill. It was down this hill in 1989 that the East German refugees crept towards sanctuary in the gardens of the Lobkowicz Palace; all other approaches were guarded by Czech police. The ensuing crisis precipitated the collapse of communism in Eastern Europe. The two gate piers at the entance to the garden are surmounted by groups of statuary representing *Hades abducting Persephone* and *Boreas, the north wind, abducting Oreithyia*. Also noteworthy is the splendid entrance with the ceiling roundel of *Chronos hovering*.

Turning east from the Lesser Town Square into Letenská ul., the visitor comes almost immediately to the church of **St Thomas** (Kostel sv. Tomáse), its façade all the more dramatic for its cramped position. It was founded together with a monastery of Augustinian hermits by King Wenceslas II in 1285. Within 90 years a Gothic basilica had been built in two building campaigns. Around 1600 this was renovated in the Renaissance style, and then in 1727–1731 given a Baroque remodelling by Kilian Ignaz Dientzenhofer. Rubens's altar paintings of *St Augustine* and *The Martyrdom of St Thomas* (1639) are now in the National Gallery. Next door to the church in Letenská is the **St Thomas Brewery** founded in 1358 with a pleasant cellar and garden tavern, famous for its dark beer.

Opposite the south doorway of St Thomas is Josefská ul., which has a particularly interesting example of Prague Baroque: the church of **St Joseph** (Kostel sv. Josefa), built for the Discalced Carmelites by Jean-Baptiste Mathey and Abraham Paris in 1687–1692 as an Early Baroque church on a centralized elliptical plan. The narrow façade with vigorous horizontal bands was designed by Johann Raas of the Tyrol (Father Ignatius à Jesu).

Backtracking slightly, the visitor will find other famous taverns in Tomášská ul., such as U Schnellů (No. 2/27) and the Three Storks (U tří čápů). The visitor should certainly take a look at the house of the **Golden Stag** (U zlatého jelena; No. 4/26). Its magnificent Baroque façade was designed by Kilian Ignaz Dientzenhofer in 1725–26, and the house sign, made by the sculptor Ferdinand Maximilian Brokoff, showing *St Hubert with the stag* is perhaps the most elaborate in the whole of Prague. The composer Václav Tomášek (1774–1850) lived at Tomáškův palác (Tomášská 15/15); known as the pope of Prague because of his influence on the musical life of the city, he must have been one of the few people to have known both Mozart and Wagner.

Valdštejnské nám. (Waldsteinplatz) is dominated by **Waldstein Palace** (Valdštejnsky Palác) the first Baroque building built in Prague. In 1621 Albrecht Wenzel Eusebius von Waldstein (better known as Wallenstein), the commander of the Imperial Catholic army, then still a mere count but immensely wealthy after the purchase of property confiscated from the Protestant nobility (see pp. 257f), acquired a Renaissance mansion together with 23 surrounding houses at the foot of Prague Castle. In 1623 a group of Italian architects under the direction of Andrea Spezza began work on the palace which was intended to be bigger and more splendid than the Royal Palace on Hradčany. The monumental building with its five courtyards and vast garden was completed in 1630 – by which time the Emperor Ferdinand III had created Wallenstein Duke of Friedland (Frýdlant), Prince of Sagan and Duke of Mecklenburg.

The grand engaged gates may have been directly inspired by the Matthias Gate at the Castle, and may indeed in turn have inspired Pacassi's later incorporation of the Matthias gate into his first range. The carving on the Waldstein gates is of very high quality. Although the exterior of the palace is surprisingly modest, the large windows hint at the unusual magnificence of the interior, particularly the two-storey *Hall of the Knights* in the centre of building, with its plasterwork ceiling with a fresco by Baccio Bianco (1630) depicting Wallenstein in the guise of a triumphant figure of Mars, the god of war. A chapel in the north wing of the castle occupies the whole height of the building and contains frescoes of scenes from the life of St Wenceslas, also by Baccio Bianco.

Unlike the palace, which now houses the Ministry of Culture and the Comenius Museum, the adjacent *Waldstein Garden* is regularly open to the public (entrance in Letenská ul.). The high point of the garden is the monumental *sala terrena* with its three tall arcades, designed by Giovanni Pierroni in the Ligurian style. The ceiling paintings by Baccio Bianco depict scenes from the Trojan War. The delicate fountain in front of the *sala* is surmounted by a copy of the Venus cast in 1599 by Benedikt Wurzelbauer of Nuremberg for the garden of Lobkowicz Palace. The original was brought to the Waldstein Garden in 1630, carried off to Sweden in 1648, and brought back in 1889, since when it has been kept in the Castle Gallery. The path through the garden from the *sala* is lined with copies of works by the Dutchman, Adriaen de Vries, who had been court sculptor under Rudolph II. The originals were taken in 1648 to Sweden where they still remain at Drottningholm, the Swedish Kings' summer palace. They are: *Wrestlers, Venus and Adonis, Laocoon, Neptune, Bacchus* and *Apollo*; the sculptures in the basin, *Hercules and Naiads* and an allegorical group which cannot be precisely identified, are also by de Vries.

Hradčany (Castle District)

Prague Castle (Pražský Hrad)

In the course of its thousand year history Prague Castle (colour plate 2) has been the seat of princes, dukes, kings, bishops and archbishops and the centre of the Holy Roman Empire. Today it remains the political and symbolic centre of the Czechoslovak state.

Around the year 890 the Přemyslid prince, Bořivoj, moved the seat of his princedom from Levý Hradec to Prague which was beginning to develop as a lively trading centre. On the hill above the Vltava he built his palace with a wooden church dedicated to the Virgin, the second Christian sanctuary to be built in Bohemia (the first, a church dedicated to St Clement, had been built by Bořivoj at his previous residence). His sons, Spitihněv and Vratislav I, encircled the vast area of the castle with strong ramparts built of tree trunks and stones, and replaced the wooden church with a stone structure. In about 915 Vratislav I founded a second church to St George, and some ten years later Prince Wenceslas (later canonized) began work on the massive Rotunda of St Vitus.

973, when Prague was raised to a bishopric, also saw the foundation, next to St George's Basilica, of the first monastery in Bohemia. A massive wall of ashlar masonry was built round

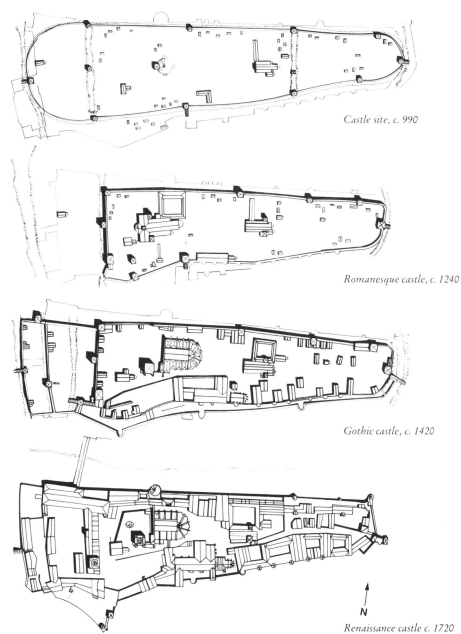

Castle site, c. 990

Romanesque castle, c. 1240

Gothic castle, c. 1420

N

Renaissance castle c. 1720

Development of Prague Castle

the castle after 1041 with towers to protect the gates and corners. In 1096 the new Basilica of St Vitus on the site of the old Rotunda, was consecrated by the Bishop of Prague. Soběslav I renovated the whole system of defences, which was to last for almost 500 years.

Hradčany reached the apogee of its splendour under Emperor Charles IV, who enlarged the castle after a disastrous fire in 1303. It now became the centre of the Holy Roman Empire, and, with Charles's patronage, the Parlers made St Vitus's Cathedral one of Europe's greatest Gothic buildings. From 1382 onwards, however, the Castle was deserted. On the occasions when he was in Prague Wenceslas IV preferred to reside in the Old Town, and the Hussites drove out the clergy and ravaged the churches and monasteries. It was not until 1484 that King Vladislav II Jagiello moved back into the Castle, and he started a tradition of grandiose works that continued under the Habsburg Emperor Ferdinand I and his son, Archduke Ferdinand of the Tyrol, Governor of Bohemia; the Castle slowly became a residence worthy of a Renaissance prince. The work was continued by Emperor Rudolph II, who made Prague a great centre of the arts and sciences.

After the victory of the Imperial forces in the Battle of the White Mountain (1620) the Habsburgs made only occasional visits to Prague. Maria Theresa, who was crowned in great pomp with the Bohemian Crown in 1748, ordered an extensive remodelling of the Castle in 1753. Later, however, the buildings became increasingly deserted, and it was all too appropriate that it should have been the last home for the simple-minded Emperor Ferdinand I from his abdication in 1848 until his death in 1875. After the foundation of the Czechoslovak Republic in 1918 Prague Castle became the seat of the head of a democratic state and this ideological sea change was marked by Jože Plečnik's quirky additions, created in collaboration with President Masaryk himself.

There are three official entrances to Prague Castle: from the north across the Powder Bridge, from the east via the Old Castle Steps and from Hradčany Square through the main entrance into the First Courtyard. The **First Castle Courtyard** was built in 1763–1771 as part of the extension and rebuilding programme under Maria Theresa. Her initials can be seen over the central gateway. The designs were prepared in Vienna by the Court Architect Nikolaus Pacassi, and construction was under the direction of Anselmo Lurago, Anton Kurz and Anton Haffenecker. This team was responsible for the appearance of the whole castle as it is seen from the rest of Prague. Before this huge campaign the Hradschin had been a motley assembly of buildings of all periods, serving all purposes, and not many of them royal. Some of the tensions beneath the Pacassi straitjacket can be sensed by looking at the uneven lines of the roofs as they smooth over different buildings. Few writers have had much good to say about the homogenization; most of them echo Walter White's remark in 1857 that the Hradschin is 'an imposing mass of building in the factory style of architecture'. Yet from a distance it does create a rhetorical statement from the bulk of the castle rock, and works as a powerful frame to the cathedral; closer to, it sets off features such as the Matthias Gate with considerable dignity.

The first courtyard is separated from Hradčany Square by high railings with gate piers

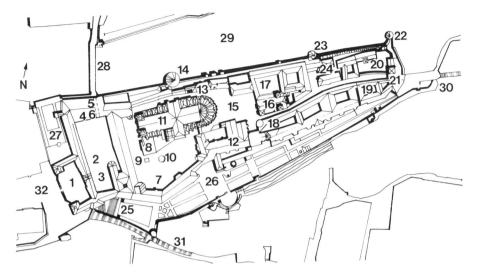

Prague Castle
1 First Castle Courtyard   2 Second Castle Courtyard   3 Chapel of the Holy Cross   4 Spanish Hall
5 Rudolph Gallery   6 Art Gallery   7 Third Castle Courtyard   8 Old Provost's Lodge   9 Obelisk   10 St
George and the Dragon   11 St Vitus's Cathedral   12 Royal Palace   13 Old Deanery   14 Mihulka
Tower   15 St George's Square   16 Basilica of St George   17 Convent of St George   18 Rožmberk
Palace   19 Lobkowicz Palace   20 Burgrave's House   21 Black Tower   22 Daliborka Tower   23 New
White Tower   24 Golden Alley   25 Paradise Garden   26 Rampart Garden   27 Bastion Garden
28 Powder Bridge   29 Deer Moat   30 Old Castle Steps   31 New Castle Steps   32 Hradčany Square

surmounted by sculptures of *Fighting Giants* by Ignaz Platzer (1768; now replaced by copies), who also made the trophies. On the flanking piers, putti ride the Bohemian Lion and shelter under the Imperial eagle. The building surrounding the courtyard contains the state rooms of the President. This Neo-Classical construction incorporates Prague's earliest secular Baroque building, the Matthias Gateway (1614, by G.M. Philippi). This was originally free-standing, a gateway on one of the earthworks which defended the exposed western end of the castle. Between the triglyphs in the entablature above the gateway are the arms of the lands of Empire in the time of Emperor Matthias; the panel below the pediment contains the Imperial arms with an inscription recording the Emperor's titles. The two tall tapering flagpoles are by Plečnik and echo the mannerist obelisks of the Matthias Gateway. Inside this first range, a staircase by Pacassi on the right leads to the President's apartments, and one on the left by Rothmayer (1948) to Plečnik's Hall of Columns which rises through the entire height of the building, the topmost capitals squeezing out under the weight of the roof.

The Matthias Gate leads to the **Second Castle Courtyard** created in the late 16th century outside the Romanesque west wall and dominated by the Chapel of the Holy Cross, also by

Anselmo Lurago to a design by Pacassi (1756–1763). Again Platzer is responsible for the altar statues. The Neo-Baroque interior is a remodelling carried out in the 1850's. Since 1961 the chapel has housed the *Treasury of St Vitus*, a collection of liturgical objects, reliquaries and vestments dating from the 8th to the 19th century.

Past the Baroque well-house, the north side of the Second Courtyard contains the Spanish Hall and the former Rudolph Gallery. The **Spanish Hall** measuring 48 metres long, 24 metres wide and 12 metres high, was built in 1601–1606 and remodelled in 1748–1750 by Kilian Ignaz Dientzenhofer. It was modernized in 1865–1868 for the planned coronation of Emperor Franz Joseph I as King of Bohemia, which was eventually called off. The **Rudolph Gallery** was built in 1586–1598. Both rooms are now used for state functions.

In the north gateway is the entrance to the **Art Gallery** of Prague Castle which since 1965 has used part of the west range and the ground floor of the north range for displaying its collection. As it is today it represents only a fragment of Rudolph's extraordinary collection, world famous at the time, though accessible to only a handful of people. Most of the works were sold to Dresden, moved to Vienna or auctioned in Joseph II's notorious sale of 1782. A surprising number of paintings have nevertheless survived, often to be rediscovered under layers of overpainting, and the collection still includes works by the great Venetians, and by Rudolph's favourites, Giuseppe Arcimboldo, Adriaen de Vries and Bartholomäus Spranger.

A passage (through the earliest fortifications, some of which can be seen) links the Second Courtyard with the **Third Castle Courtyard**, the nucleus of the castle, entirely dominated today by St Vitus's Cathedral. Here was the beginning of the main street of the Slav settlement. In front of the south-west corner of the cathedral is the 11th-century Bishop's Palace, now known as the **Old Provost's Lodge,** which was given a Baroque exterior in the 17th century, though the original windows can be seen at the back. The doorway and statue of St Wenceslas are by Johann Georg Bendl. The obelisk, 18 metres tall, was set up by Plečnik in 1928 on the tenth anniversary of the foundation of the Czechoslovak Republic. At the other end of the courtyard is his canopied stairway down to the Rampart Gardens. The delicate bronze **equestrian statue of St George** was made by the brothers George and Martin of Klausenburg (Kolozsvár, now Cluj, in Transylvania) in 1373 (the original is in the nearby monastery of St George beyond the cathedral).

The **Cathedral of St Vitus** (Katedrála sv. Vita; plate 1). Duke Wenceslas I ('Good King Wenceslas' and also a saint) founded the pre-Romanesque Rotunda of St Vitus around 925 as the court church of the Přemyslids. From 835 the main centre of the cult of St Vitus (who suffered martyrdom in Sicily around 313) was the Frankish Benedictine abbey of Corvey on the Weser, and from there it spread to Prague. Charles IV acquired the bones of St Vitus at Pavia in 1355 and made Prague the focus of the saint's cult. After the foundation of the bishopric in 973 the court church became the principal church of the bishops of Prague. In 1060–1096 the Frankish rotunda was replaced by a three-aisled Romanesque basilica, whose foundations can be seen, behind Plečnik's bars, between the Provost's Lodge and the Golden Gate. Prague was raised to an archbishopric by Pope Clement VI in 1344 at the

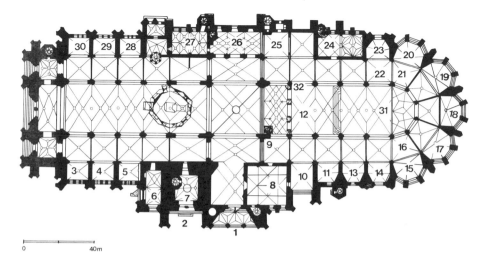

Prague, St Vitus's Cathedral, plan
1 Golden Gate   2 Tower   3 Chaper of St Ludmila   4 Chapel of the Holy Sepulchre   5 Thun Chapel   6 Chapter Library   7 Hasenburg Chapel   8 Chapel of St Wencelas   9 Schlick Tomb 10 Chapel of St Andrew (Martinic Chapel)   11 Chapel of the Holy Cross, and entrance to Royal Vault 12 Royal Mausoleum   13 Royal Oratory   14 Waldstein Chapel   15 Chapel of St John of Nepomuk 16 Tomb of St John of Nepomuk   17 Reliquary Chapel   18 Lady Chapel   19 Chapel of St John the Baptist   20 Archiepiscopal Chapel   21 Schwarzenberg Tomb   22 Wooden Relief of the Flight of the Winter King   23 Chapel of St Anne   24 Old Sacristy (St. Michael's Chapel)   25 Chapel of St Sigismund   26 Choir Chapel   27 New Sacristy   28 New Archiepiscopal Chapel   29 Schwarzenberg Chapel   30 Bartoňs of Dobenin Chapel   31 Choir and High Altar   32 Pulpit

insistence of Charles IV (then merely Margrave of Moravia), and Charles with his father, John the Blind of Luxemburg, laid the foundation stone of a massive Gothic cathedral on 21 November 1344. The design of the building was entrusted to Matthias of Arras, a Frenchman who had been headhunted from the Papal court at Avignon, and it followed the pattern of the southern French cathedrals. He built the apse with its ambulatory and the eastern part of the choir, and after his death in 1352 the work was continued by Peter Parler (c. 1330–1399), who completed the choir and built, to his own design, the south transept with its porch, the lower storey of the main tower and parts of the nave. These are some of the high points of Gothic. Parler's sons, Johann, Wenzel and Paul, continued work on the tower, but during the Hussite Wars, work could go no further than the completed east end which was closed off with a temporary wall. In about 1500 Vladislav II Jagiello built himself an Oratory in the Cathedral, which he connected to his bedroom in the castle by the little bridge just beyond the Golden Gate. The tower was completed sixty years later by Bonifaz Wohlmut with exterior galleries and an onion dome, which was altered again, by Pacassi, in 1770, making the construction we see today. Work on the main structure of the cathedral was not resumed until 1873, and continued until 1929 – Josef Kranner, Josef Mocker and Kamil Hilbert bringing almost 600 years of work to a close.

Exterior: The 19th-century statues on the west front (saints, Charles IV and other significant figures; by Stanislav Sucharda), the bronze reliefs on the west doors with scenes from the lives of St Adalbert (Vojtěch) (left) and St Wenceslas (right) and from the building of the cathedral (centre) are by Otakar Španiel after designs by the painter Vratislav Hugo Brunner. On the south side is the famous *Golden Gate*, the ceremonial entrance (plates 3, 4) by Peter Parler himself (1367) with lacy staircages and eddying poly-foil decoration. The much restored but still pretty dim mosaic (1370–71, by Italian craftsmen) shows the Last Judgement with the patron saints of Bohemia, and Charles IV with his fourth wife, Elizabeth of Pomerania (Eliška Pomořancká).

Left of the Golden Gate is the *Tower*, almost 100 metres high. The sudden switch from Gothic to Renaissance and Baroque is clearly visible in its upper parts. On the first floor hangs the Sigismund (Zikmund) Bell (18 tonnes), made in 1549, the largest bell in Bohemia. The glorious ironwork on the first floor was installed by Rudolph II, whose monogram can be seen above.

Tour of the Cathedral (anti-clockwise starting from the West door; see colour plate 4): *Chapel of St Ludmila* (3) with a Baroque font (17th century), on the Neo-Gothic altar is a statue of St Ludmila (Emanuel Max, 1845), stained-glass window of the *Descent of the Holy Spirit* (Max Švabinský); *Chapel of the Holy Sepulchre* (4) with stained-glass window showing the *Works of Mercy* (Karel Svolinský, 1932); *Thun Chapel* (5) with a stained-glass window illustrating the text *Who sows in tears will reap with joy* (František Kysela, 1928/29); the *Hasenburg Chapel* (7; usually closed) contains the entrance to the tower with the bells, clock and exterior gallery. There are some fine tombs on the walls here, with muscular figures. The window by Cyril Bouda depicts the *Laying of the Foundation Stone of the Nave* (1934).

The jewel of the cathedral is the *Chapel of St Wenceslas* (8) built by Peter Parler between 1362 and 1367. It is the fullest expression of Charles IV's piety, taste and political aspirations, as he sought to associate the Luxemburg dynasty with the prestige and holiness of the previous dynasty, the Přemyslids, his mother's family. (There is a parallel with the beautification which Henry III of England lavished on Edward the Confessor's shrine at Westminster a century earlier.) The chapel's political significance was still potent when Ferdinand was elected King of Bohemia here, fatefully inaugurating the 350 years of Habsburg rule. In a sense the chapel is still the centre of Bohemian sovereignty, since it guards the talismanic Crown Jewels – something Heydrich understood very well, when he demanded that the keys be handed ceremonially to him as Deputy Reichsprotektor. The chapel is built directly above Wenceslas's original shrine in the southern apse of the Rotunda of St Vitus. Here Boleslav had buried the brother he had murdered on his way to mass; the 14th century ironwork of the chapel door incorporates the ring to which the saint had clung in his agony. Wenceslas's otherworldly meekness shines from the limestone statue by Heinrich Parler (1373). He is shown flanked by the angels who appeared either side of him at the Imperial Diet of the Saxon King Henry. The upper register of paintings (1509) by the Master of the Litoměřice Altarpiece shows the king's good deeds – demolishing gallows and prisons – and his untimely end. The lower register has Charles IV's decoration: paintings of the Passion (1372) by Master Oswald of Prague surrounded by semi-precious stones – crosses of amethyst, chalcedony, jasper, chrysoprase and agate, 1372 of them altogether – in imitation of the Heavenly Jerusalem of the Apocalypse. Oswald's paintings are very fine; there is a charming Ascension on the south wall, and on the east wall Charles himself is seen kneeling to the left of the Calvary, opposite his last wife. (The other great builder, Vladislav Jagiello, is shown above, very much larger, with his only wife, Anne of Foix.) The Wenceslas candelabrum in the corner was made by the bronze founder Hans Vischer of Nuremberg in 1534 for the Prague maltsters' guild. The panel painting on the pier near the entrance by an unknown painter (initials 'I.W.') shows the murder of St Wenceslas at Stará Boleslav. Above the Chapel of St Wenceslas, behind seven locks, is the *Crown Chamber* with coronation regalia of the Bohemian kings: the Crown of St Wenceslas (14th century), which Charles IV had reworked from the old crown of the Přemyslids, the Coronation Sword (14th century), the sceptre and orb (16th century), Coronation Mantle and Stole (18th century). The regalia are displayed only on special occasions.

On the south-east crossing pier opposite the Wenceslas Chapel is the Baroque memorial to Count Leopold Schlick (1723; 9), based on a design by Joseph Emmanuel Fischer von Erlach with architectural details by František Maximilián Kaňka and sculpture from the workshop of Matthias Bernhard Braun. The Chapel of St Wenceslas adjoins the *Chapel of St Andrew* (Martinic Chapel, 10) with a beautiful grille (1748) and the tomb on the south wall of Jaroslav Martinic, Governor of Bohemia, who was thrown out of the window of his office on 23 May 1618 but survived almost unscathed (see p.94). Beyond it is the *Chapel of the Holy Cross* (11) with a spectacular silver antependium (1729) on the altar, and the entrance to the Royal Vault (sarcophagi of Charles IV; his son, Wenceslas IV; his four wives in a single sarcophagus; Ladislav the Posthumous and George of Poděbrady; the Empire-style sarcophagus of Maria Amalie, daughter of Empress Maria Theresa, the pewter coffin of Rudolph II, and others). Just next to the Royal Vault the foundations of the rotunda and of the basilica have been uncovered. Projecting into the choir directly above the Royal Vault is the marble *Royal Mausoleum* (12). Ferdinand I is seen flanked by his wife Anna Jagiello and his son Maximilian II; on the side of the tomb medallions show the kings and queens of Bohemia buried below; Charles IV is solemn with his four wimpled wives. The mausoleum, started in Innsbruck in 1564 by the Netherlandish sculptor Alexander Colin, was not finished here until 1589; the lovely grille had been made some thirty years before by a blacksmith from the Lesser Town. The *Royal Oratory* (13) was designed by Benedikt Rieth for King Vladislav II Jagiello, to connect with the king's new bedchamber in the castle. The king's monogram W can be seen on the boss. The bewildering branchwork decoration was created in 1493 by Hans Spiess of Frankfurt. Stylistically it has parallels with the Powder Tower in the Old Town (see p. 42)

The Parlers and the 'Schöner Stil'

In 1353 **Peter Parler** (1330–1399), was called to Prague at the age of twenty-three to take charge of the construction of St Vitus's Cathedral. He is the most prominent member of a famous family of German masons, who revolutionized architecture and sculpture in central Europe in the 14th and early 15th centuries.

The Parler family tree is difficult to unravel, especially since the family name was simply the German word for 'foreman', but we know from an inscription in St Vitus's that Peter's father was **Heinrich** of Cologne, the architect of the Heiligkreuzkirche at Schwäbisch Gmünd in Swabia, which marked the beginning of the Late Gothic style, 'Sondergotik' ('Unusual Gothic') in Germany. It was in Prague, at the Parler workshop under Charles IV's patronage, that this style took root.

Under Parler's direction St Vitus's became a centre of architectural experimentation. The triforium, for instance, is glazed, making the interior unusually bright, and above all there are the extraordinary vaults. The choir vault is not divided into cross-rib bays, but unifies the space with its net-like web, while the south porch and the western chapels have complex rib patterns, flying ribs and pendant bosses. The only precedents for such vaulting are in England a few decades earlier.

The Charles Bridge demonstrates Peter's skill as an engineer, while the fine sculpture produced by his workshop can be seen on the Old Town Bridge Tower and in St Vitus's. The Parlers helped create the courtly style known as the International Style (because it was fashionable all over Europe) or the *Schöner Stil* ('Beautiful Style'). Peter's greatest achievement in sculpture is the superb series of busts in the cathedral triforium. These are idealized images, but they are still strikingly convincing as individual portraits. The finest of all, the bust of Peter Parler himself, may be the first real self-portrait of an artist in western art. In contrast, the statue of St Wenceslas (1373) in the Wenceslas Chapel, the work of another **Heinrich** (probably Peter's nephew, architect to the Margrave of Moravia), has an exquisite gracefulness.

Johann of Gmünd, probably Peter's brother, worked on the minsters at Freiburg and Basle, while another brother, **Michael** is mentioned as a stone mason at Zlatá Koruna and Prague. Peter's sons **Wenzel**, **Paul** and **Johann** succeeded him as cathedral architects. Another **Heinrich** of Gmünd, a member of the Ulm branch of the family, acted as consultant to the builders of Milan Cathedral in 1391.

which was built at the same time. The Oratory is a good place to get to know the local heraldry. From left to right the shields represent: Dalmatia, Upper Lusatia, Bosnia, Poland, Hungary, Bohemia, Moravia, Luxemburg, Silesia and Lower Lusatia.

The most extraordinary feature of the Oratory, and a wonderful example of the Bohemian felicity in combining the Late Gothic and the Baroque is M.B. Braun's statue of a miner (one of two) who bursts from the pier to offer the light of his lamp to the *Tomb of St John of Nepomuk* (16) in the aisle. It was in fact a tax on the (Hussitish) silver-miners of Kutná Hora that raised the money for this magnificent confection, emblematic too of the richness of Bohemia's natural resources. The main purpose of the shrine was to celebrate John of Nepomuk's recent (1729) canonization and thus, like the Wenceslas Chapel earlier, to bolster the political dispensation by a display of religious and artistic extravagance. Designed by Johann Bernhard Fischer von Erlach c. 1736, the tomb chest was cast by Antonio Corradini and J.J. Würth, and shows the Saint hearing the Queen's confession, the secrecy of which he preserved even unto martyrdom – according to the version of his story which the Jesuits promoted. He is guarded by Justice, Strength, Wisdom and Reticence, who are probably by I.F. Platzer. The massive structure seems to be borne weightlessly by angels towards heaven; other slightly later angels hold up the drapes of a baldacchino (given by Maria Theresa).

Returning to the chapels, the *Waldstein Chapel* (14) contains the tombs of the builders of the cathedral, Matthias of Arras (d. 1352) and Peter Parler (d. 1399). In the choir is the first of a pair of wooden reliefs by Kasper Bechteller (1631); this one shows the *Looting of the cathedral and of the shrine of St John of Nepomuk by the Calvinists* in 1619. Next is the *Chapel of St John of Nepomuk* with the reliquary of St Adalbert. The *Reliquary Chapel* (17) containing the Gothic tombs of the two Přemyslid kings Otakar I and Otakar II from the Parler workshop; the *Lady Chapel* (18) at the east end contains two further tombs from the workshop, those of the princes Břetislav I and Spitihněv II; the *Chapel of St John the Baptist* (19) with the tombs of the Bohemian princes Břetislav II and Bořivoj II (the bronze 'Jerusalem Candelabrum', a masterpiece of Romanesque metalwork, is supposed to have been looted by Bohemian troops from Milan in 1158); the *Archiepiscopal Chapel* (20), where the archbishops of Prague are buried (plate 5) is noteworthy for the Renaissance tomb of the High Chancellor Vratislav of Pernštejn (Vredeman de Vries; 1582); in front of the chapel is the sculpture of the Cardinal Archbishop Friedrich (Bedřich) Josef Schwarzenberg (Josef Václav Myslbek; 1895). Next is the second of Kasper Bechteller's reliefs showing the *Flight of the Winter King after the Battle of the White Mountain* (22), the well-deserved recompense for the iconoclasm depicted opposite. We see Prague one chill morning in 1618: the river flows choppily under the bridge, the bells are ringing as the line of waggons and horsemen rush through the town; there are deer still in the Deer Moat, and peasants sit and talk unconcernedly in the hills. In the *Chapel of St Anne* (23) is an Early Gothic reliquary panel from the church of St Martin at Trier (1266) set in the Neo-Gothic altar; the *Old Sacristy* (St Michael's Chapel; 24) with a particularly fine star vault, the *Chapel of St Sigismund* (25) with relics of the saint which Charles IV brought to Prague in 1365. This is also known as the Černín Chapel; it contains the tomb of Jan Humprecht Czernín, who originally commissioned the huge palace further up in the Hradčany, and the dramatic altar is by F.M. Kaňka (sculpture by F.I. Weiss) c. 1735, who was also modifying the palace. The grille, contemporary with the altar, has the Czernín monogram. Next, the *Choir Chapel* (26) has the organ above it in Bonifaz Wohlmut's gallery (1557–1561) which originally stood at the west end of the cathedral until the building of the nave in the 19th century, the *New Sacristy* (27), and finally the *New Archiepiscopal Chapel* (28) in which the archbishops of the present century have been laid to rest amongst the Utraquist tombstones. The strikingly beautiful window with scenes from the lives and works of the national saints was designed by Alfons Mucha (1931). The central section shows Cyril and Methodios baptizing Slavs, and, below,

Ludmila inspiring her grandson Wenceslas to saintly deeds. The altarpiece triptych of the *Adoration of the Three Kings* in the Schwarzenberg Chapel was made around 1500. Finally, the *Barton Chapel*, like St Ludmila's opposite, has a fine grille made in 1938.

Below the clearstorey of the choir a *triforium* runs round the cathedral. Here Peter Parler placed portrait busts of members of the royal family and others who had made a contribution to the building of the cathedral, including the emperor, his wives, archbishops of Prague, and the architects, Parler himself and Matthias of Arras – whose presence, apparently on an equal footing with their imperial and episcopal patrons, is remarkable evidence of the high status of these masters. The 21 busts, the work of the Parler workshop (1374–1385) show a striking realism not found elsewhere in 14th century sculpture; although the triforium is inaccessible, casts of the busts can be seen in the Royal Palace and at Karlštejn. The series was continued with busts in the Neo-Gothic part of the triforium showing the people involved in the completion of the cathedral in the 19th and 20th centuries by Ladislav Kofránek, Bohumil Kafka and other Czech sculptors.

Leaving the Third Courtyard under the bridge that connects the palace with the cathedral, and past the statue of St John of Nepomuk (I. Platzer) on the ouside of his chapel, the visitor will see the great windows of the Vladislav hall on the other side of the sunken courtyard – windows that have been called (with some justice) 'the first apostles of the Renaissance in Central Europe'. Their date can just be made out over the one on the far left. The Gothic buttresses are part of an earlier hall, built by Charles IV. The **Old Royal Palace** (Královsky palác) was the residence of the kings of Bohemia from the 11th to the 16th centuries. From the 16th to the 18th century it was the seat of the central government offices of Bohemia. Since then the buildings have been used only for special occasions (e.g. sessions of the Diet). The reconstruction of the Royal Palace was begun in 1924.

Peter Parler, Self-Portrait, in the triforium of St Vitus's Cathedral

In front of the entrance to the Royal Palace stands the *Eagle Fountain* (1) designed in 1664 by Francesco Caratti. To the left of the *vestibule* (2) is the *Green Chamber* (3) where lawcourts were held in Charles IV's time and where the Kammergericht and Hofgericht met from 1512. Its function is reflected in the Baroque fresco of the Judgment of Solomon (transferred here in 1960). Beyond this is the *Bedchamber of Vladislav* (4), a Late Gothic room with a magnificent multi-coloured vault.

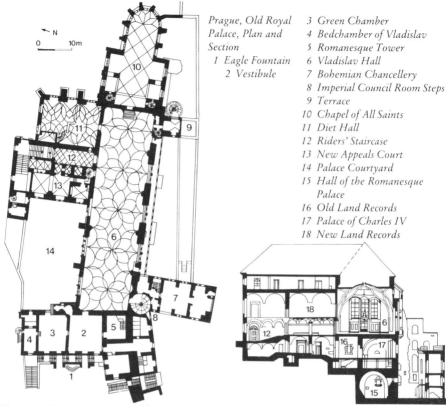

Prague, Old Royal
Palace, Plan and
Section
  1 Eagle Fountain
  2 Vestibule
  3 Green Chamber
  4 Bedchamber of Vladislav
  5 Romanesque Tower
  6 Vladislav Hall
  7 Bohemian Chancellery
  8 Imperial Council Room Steps
  9 Terrace
 10 Chapel of All Saints
 11 Diet Hall
 12 Riders' Staircase
 13 New Appeals Court
 14 Palace Courtyard
 15 Hall of the Romanesque
     Palace
 16 Old Land Records
 17 Palace of Charles IV
 18 New Land Records

The 'W' above the windows is the initial of Vladislav Jagiello (old spelling: 'Wladislaw'), who also gave his name to the splendid *Vladislav Hall* (6). Originally built in the reign of Charles IV, the Hall was remodelled by Benedikt Rieth (1493–1502), an architect of almost Baroque sensibility, who plays here with the vocabulary of Late Gothic to create vaulting of wilful lightness and almost sensuous plasticity. The hall is 62 metres long, 16 metres wide and 13 metres high. Coronation ceremonies and important assemblies, knightly tournaments and balls were held in it; it was used as a luxury market in the 16th century; the Kings of Bohemia were elected here, as is the President of the Republic (since 1934). Changes to the constitution are enacted in the hall, including the promulgation of the 1948 Constitution, and the 1970 pact of Friendship, Cooperation and Mutual Assistance with the Soviet Union.

To the south of the Vladislav Hall is the *Ludvík Wing* containing the rooms of the *Bohemian Chancellery* (Benedikt Rieth, 1502–1509) (7). It was from the east window of the furthermost room that the supporters of the Estates threw the imperial governors, Jaroslav Martinic and Wilhelm Slavata of Chlum, with their secretary, Philipp Fabricius, on 23 May 1618, triggering off the Thirty Years' War. A dung-heap fortuitously broke their fall and all three survived. A spiral staircase (8) leads up to the *Imperial Court Council Room* where the 27 ringleaders were sentenced to death, a sentence which was carried out in the Old Town Square on 21 June 1621. An excellent view of the Ludvík Wing is to be had from the terrace (9) at the end of the Vladislav Hall.

The steps at the end of the Vladislav Hall lead up to the *Chapel of All Saints* (10) built by Peter Parler after 1370 and rebuilt in 1579–80 after the fire of 1541. The painting of All Saints on the Baroque high altar is by Wenzel Lorenz Reiner (1732). The altar on the north side of the chapel contains the relics of St Procopius (c. 1004–1053), who founded a monastery in the Sázava valley not far from Prague, and is the subject of the cycle of twelve paintings by K. Dittmann. The altar on the south side has an unusually anatomical All-Seeing Eye.

In the north-east corner of the Vladislav Hall a doorway leads to the *Diet Hall* (11), a part

Vladislav Hall, c. 1607

of Charles IV's palace. The original room was also built by Rieth, at the same time as the Vladislav Hall, but did not survive the great fire of 1541, which destroyed so much of Hradčany and the Lesser Town. Bonifaz Wohlmut's replacement (1559–1563) was conceived in direct emulation of Rieth's Vladislav Hall, though it is busier, and the Gothic ribs spring rather oddly from classical pilasters. Wohlmut's true sympathies come out in the structure in the left corner, a rostrum for the use of the Chief Clerk of the Land Records, which were an essential part of the business of the Supreme Provincial Court sitting here. The furniture is arranged as it might have been for sessions of the Diet after the War of the Estates in the early 17th century: the king on the throne, the Church on his right, headed by the Archbishop, the judiciary on his left, the nobility in front of him. The little gallery by the window is standing room for the representatives of the royal towns, an essential part of the King's independent power but allowed only a single, collective vote in the Diet. Next to the Diet Hall is the Riders' Staircase (12) with Late Gothic vaulting by Benedikt Rieth (c. 1500) up which knights could ride their horses from St George's Square to tournaments in the Vladislav Hall.

The lower storeys contain rooms of the medieval palace. A stairway leads from the palace courtyard (14) down to the *Hall of the Romanesque Palace* (15) of the Princes Soběslav I and Vladislav I (first half of the 12th century). In the vestibule are remains of what is thought to be the first Slav castle on the site. Above the Romanesque palace are the rooms of the Gothic palace: first, the *Old Land Records* (16), a large room dating from the time of Otakar II, with an Early Gothic vault springing from two thick-set cylindrical pillars. It was used for storing the 'land records', books in which were recorded important decisions of the Diet and changes in the ownership of property of the nobility, clergy and towns. Two halls of the *Palace of Charles IV* (17) dating from the first half of the 14th century lie directly below the Vladislav Hall. Beyond them are the *Old Registry* and the *Wenceslas IV's Hall of Columns* with an asymetric vault springing from two slender cylindrical piers (15th century).

Vikářská ul. to the north of the cathedral links the Third Castle Courtyard with St George's Square (Jiřské nám.). In Vikářská stands the High Baroque building of the **Old Deanery** (No. 2/37), the residence of the deans of St Vitus's Cathedral since 1483. The round **Mihulka Tower** (or Prašna věž) projects far over the Deer Moat; it was built as an artillery position by King Vladislav Jagiello towards the end of the 15th century Here Rudolph's alchemists were set to work finding the philosopher's stone. The Old and New Vicarages (Nos. 1, 4/38, 39) were joined together in 1969 and opened as the 'Vikářská' restaurant and wine bar. The 19th-century houses where Vikářská runs into St George's Square are by Josef Mocker.

The main building in the square is the **Basilica of St George** (Bazilika sv. Jiří), founded by Prince Vladislav I around 915. When a monastery was established next to it the basilica was extended to form a three-aisled building. The two towers were added after the fire of 1142, and in 1657–1680 the church was given its Early Baroque exterior. St George is seen high up in the pediment, and the two leading pilasters are crowned with statues of Vratislav II and

PRAGUE St Vitus's Cathedral

2   PRAGUE View of the Old Town with the Týn Church and the Castle. ▷

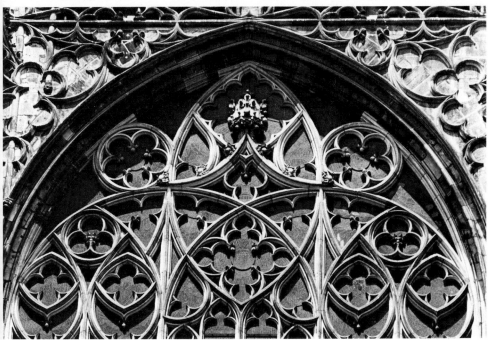

4 PRAGUE St Vitus's Cathedral, Tracery on the Golden Gate
3 PRAGUE St Vitus's Cathedral, Golden Gate
5 PRAGUE St Vitus's Cathedral, Archiepiscopal Chapel

6 PRAGUE House 'At the Leaping House'

7 PRAGUE House 'At the Three Little Fiddles'

8　Prague Doorway of the House 'At the Two Golden Bears'

9   PRAGUE St Nicholas in the Old Town

10   PRAGUE National Theatre

11   PRAGUE Loreto

12   PRAGUE Kinský Palace

13 PRAGUE House of the Minute

14 PRAGUE Powder Tower

15   PRAGUE Old-New Synagogue and Jewish Town Hall

16 PRAGUE Grave of Rabbi Löw in the Old Jewish
Cemetery

17,18   Graves in the Old Jewish Cemetery

20   PRAGUE St Nicholas from the gardens of the Vrtba Palace

Princess Mlada, the convent's founder, and first superior. Next to the basilica is the little chapel of St John of Nepomuk (1717–1722) with a statue of the saint by F.M. Brokoff and interior decorations by W.L. Reiner. Like St Vitus's Cathedral, St George's Basilica has a magnificent south portal built in the early 16th century by the workshop of Benedikt Rieth. The tympanum has a lively sculpture of the saint slaying the dragon under the anxious gaze of the king and queen (the original is now in St George's Convent). The interior of the church, which is used for concerts, has preserved its austere Romanesque beauty. The arcades date from the 10th and 11th centuries, the gallery windows from the 12th. The choir vault is painted with a Romanesque Heavenly Jerusalem. Archaeological excavations between 1958 and 1962 revealed the tombs of early Přemyslid princes and patrons: Vratislav I (d. 921) in a splendid 15th-century wooden tomb chest and Boleslav II (d. 999) with a tomb dating from around 1730. The frescoed *Chapel of St Ludmila*, the first female martyr of Bohemia and 'Mother of the Bohemian people', dates from the early 13th century. It contains the grave and relics of the saint; the impressive tomb was made by the Parler workshop c. 1380.

The **Convent of St George** (Klášter sv. Jiří) founded by Mlada, the sister of Prince Boleslav II the Pious, in 973, was the first monastic house in Bohemia. Mlada persuaded Pope John XIII in Rome that Bohemia needed its own bishop to promote and safeguard the Christian faith. Prague got its bishop and Mlada became the first abbess of the convent of Benedictine nuns at St George's. Over the centuries the convent was altered and extended several times, with the basilica. In 1782 it was closed by Joseph II and turned into barracks. Since 1976 it has been part of the National Gallery; this is the place to discover the splendours of Bohemian Art from Gothic to Baroque, including many of the panel paintings painted by Master Theodoric between 1357 and 1367 for the Holy Cross Chapel in Karlštejn Castle (see pp. 143f.) and examples of Rudolphine Mannerism. The *Chapel of St Anne*, part of the convent, was built over the grave of the Blessed Mlada (d. 994).

Since the Castle was the heart of Bohemia, it is not surprising that the great nobles should set up court there like the King, whose near-equal they often were. In the 16th century the Rožmberks (Rosenbergs) acquired the site on the corner opposite St George's, pulled down several houses and built the magnificent **Rožmberk Palace**. This became a centre of political and social life in Prague, but the gradual impoverishment of the Rožmberks as they slipped towards extinction in the person of the melancholy and erudite Peter Vok, gave the Emperor Rudolph II a chance to swap this palace for the Schwarzenberg Palace in the square opposite the Castle. This was one of the first of the Emperor's depredations, foreshadowing the wholesale takeover of the Rožmberk inheritance after Peter Vok's death. The palace was not given its present form, including the entrance, until the mid–18th century, when Maria Theresa had it converted to an Institute for Impoverished Gentlewomen. The conversion was carried out in 1754-55 by Anselmo Lurago to the plans of Pacassi, as a prelude to their larger work of homogenizing the Castle itself. In the process, the Chapel of All Saints at the end of the Vladislav Hall was incorporated into the institute.

The **Lobkowicz (Lobkowitz) Palace** (19) at the south-east corner of the castle was built by the High Chancellor Vratislav of Pernštejn around 1570. In 1602 the property was acquired by Zdeněk Popel of Lobkowicz as a dowry. Wenzel Eusebius of Lobkowicz, minister under Emperor Leopold I, commissioned Carlo Lurago to remodel the palace in the Early Baroque style in 1651. Its outer appearance, however, dates from 1791. Today the palace, with its fine Great Hall, is a branch of the National Museum and displays 'memorable events from the national past'.

In the 12th century the **Black Tower** was the eastern gate to the Castle. Wenceslas I had the gate walled up and a new one built to the south of it. In front is a terrace made from a 16th-century artillery position, which consequently has an excellent view. The 'Old Castle Steps' (Staré zámecké schody) link the Castle with the Lesser Town. The wall to the north-east is strengthened by two strong artillery towers: the Daliborka and the New White Tower. The **Daliborka Tower** was built by Benedikt Rieth in 1496 together with the new fortifications. Its name recalls Dalibor, a knight, who was the first prisoner to languish in the windowless dungeon of the tower, for having granted protection to rebellious peasants at his castle at Litoměřice. The plaintive notes of his violin charmed the people of Prague until his execution; the story was retold in Smetana's opera *Dalibor*. The **New White Tower**, also built for artillery in 1584, was mainly used as a state prison. The charlatan alchemist Edward Kelley was kept here after failing to make gold for Rudolph II, while the treasurer, Caspar Rutský, who had been stealing the emperor's genuine gold, hanged himself here with his chain of office. It was here that the 27 leaders of the Revolt of the Estates awaited their execution. Along the wall between the two towers is the **Golden Alley** (Zlatá ulička). The castle marksmen lived in the small brightly-coloured houses in the 16th century, and the street owes its name to the goldsmiths who replaced them in the 17th century, not to the dubious transmuters of gold patronized by Rudolph II. In the 18th and 19th centuries the Golden Alley was a poor area, favoured by artists and poets. Franz Kafka lived in No. 22 during 1917, and in the 1920's the Czech poet Jaroslav Seifert, winner of the 1984 Nobel Prize for Literature, also lived in the alley (in a house that has since been demolished).

In 1562 Archduke Ferdinand of the Tyrol, Governor of Bohemia, had the moats and earthworks in front of the south walls of the Castle levelled and turned into gardens. These were remodelled between 1920 and 1930 by Jože Plečnik and, when restoration is complete, these may be the best place in Prague to get to know his interesting work. Plečnik was a Slovene, and a pupil of Otto Wagner; he had a robust sense of space that he constantly undercut with a strange assortment of freak ornaments.

Outside the north gate, where there is another Early Baroque gate submerged in the Pacassi homogenization, the **Powder Bridge** (Prašný most) crosses the deep **Deer Moat** (Jelení příkop), which was a deer park from the 16th to the 18th century. In 1769 the wooden bridge was replaced by an embankment. The view back to the castle and the cathedral is one of the best. Beyond the moat on the left is the **Riding School** (Jízdárna) of Emperor Leopold I (Jean-Baptiste Mathey, c. 1694), an exhibition space for modern art since 1949.

The eastern side of the path called U Prašného mostu (To the Powder Bridge) is occupied by the **Ferdinand Stables** dating from 1534. Here also is the **Lion Court** (Lví dvůr) designed by the architect Udalrico Aostali in 1581–1583 for Rudolph II. In the courtyard the emperor kept lions, tigers, bears, wolves and other exotic beasts, in heated cages; it is now a restaurant. The **Royal Garden** (Královská zahrada) extends along Deer Moat from the Lion Court to the Belvedere and contains the Great Tennis Court (1567–1569) designed by Bonifaz Wohlmut and now used for state functions.

To the east the Royal Garden ends at the **Belvedere** (Belvedér, Kralovský Letohrádec). This Summer Palace was commissioned by Ferdinand I for his wife Anne (he can be seen in one of the reliefs in the colonnade giving her a flower). Built in 1535–1564 to designs by the Genoese architect Paolo della Stella and completed by Bonifaz Wohlmut, it is perhaps the most authentic work of Italian Renaissance architecture north of the Alps with its arcade and graceful curving roof. In the centre of the charming Renaissance *giardinetto* stands the *Singing Fountain* by Francesco Terzio, cast in bronze in 1564 by Tomáš Jaroš. The jets of water falling into the two basins create a resonant vibration which gives the fountain its name.

Hradčany (Castle Town)

A settlement soon developed in the area west of the castle, mainly inhabited by those employed there. Around 1320 the burgrave Hynek Berka granted this settlement, which extended as far as the present U kasáren street, the status of a town under the burgrave's protection, and a few decades later, from 1360 to 1362, Charles IV surrounded a vast area including the Petřín Hill and the Strahov Monastery with the 'Hunger Wall' (see p. 123). The Hussite Wars around 1420 and the great fire of 1541 destroyed the Gothic Hradčany, but it rose from the ashes with neat burghers' houses and Renaissance palaces. From 1598 to 1784 Hradčany was a royal town and thereafter a part of the city of Prague.

From 1541 **Hradčanské náměstí** (Hradčany Square), the centre of the Castle Town, was surrounded by the palaces of the nobility and clergy. The garden in the middle of the square contains a plague column with a statue of the Virgin surrounded by the eight national patron saints, by Ferdinand Maximilian Brokoff (1726). Starting at the south corner, the Empire style palace (No. 1/186) was built between 1800 and 1810 by the Archbishop of Prague Wilhelm Florentin von Salm, whose initials can be seen over the doorway. It was acquired in 1813 by Prince Philipp Schwarzenberg, who connected it with his own family palace next door. The **Schwarzenberg Palace** (No. 2/185) itself (now a military museum) was built by Augustin Vlach from 1545 to 1563 for Jan of Lobkowicz, on the site of a number of burghers' houses destroyed in the 1541 fire. The façades of the impressive Renaissance building are decorated with ornamental sgraffiti reminiscent of Italian palace architecture, and the interiors have magnificent mythological paintings. This palace was the last Prague home of the Rožmberks; it was here at a banquet given in October of 1601 by Peter Vok Rožmberk, the last of his line, that the great astronomer Tycho Brahe fatally overestimated his capacity for drink, and staggered up the hill to his deathbed, in a house just beyond the Loreto.

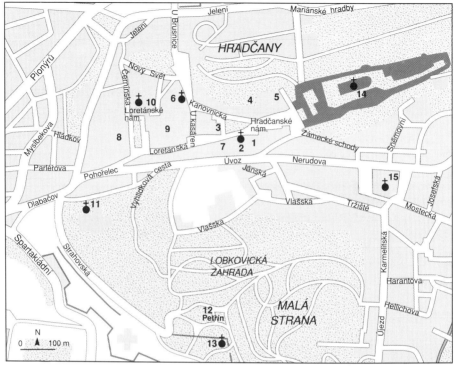

Hradčany
1 Schwarzenberg Palace   2 St Benedict   3 Tuscan Palace   4 Sternberg Place (National Gallery)
5 Archbishop's Palace   6 Church of St John of Nepomuk   7 Town Hall   8 Černin Palace   9 Loreto
10 Capuchin Monastery   11 Strahov Monastery   12 Petřin Tower   13 St Lawrence   14 St Vitus's
Cathedral   15 St Nicholas in the Lesser Town

As early as 1353 the church of **St Benedict** (Kostel sv. Benedikta) was the parish church of Hradčany. It was altered several times, the last being c. 1720. In 1626 the church and adjoining small convent (No. 3/184) came into the possession of the Discalced Carmelite nuns. Since 1960 the monastic buildings have been used to accommodate state guests.

On the opposite corner is the palace built for Michael Oswald Count Thun-Hohenstein by Jean-Baptiste Mathey in 1689–1691. It was acquired by Grand Duchess Maria Anna of Tuscany in 1718 and has been known ever since as the **Tuscan Palace** (No. 5/182). The pleasing symmetry of the façade with its two striking doorways is further emphasized by the roof pavilions. The allegorical statues on the attic represent the liberal arts, and like the two massive coats of arms of Tuscany above the portals and the statue of Neptune in the courtyard, are by Johann Brokoff (1689–1691), while the figure of St Michael at the corner of the building is the work of the Italian sculptor Ottavio Mosto and dates from around 1694.

Walking clockwise round the square we come next to the **Canons' Houses** (No. 6/65 and No. 7/68), which have ground plans that go back to their medieval predecessors, and at the corner of Kanovnická ul. the **Martinic Palace** has delightful sgraffiti from the late 16th and early 17th centuries, showing the story of Joseph and Potiphar's wife and other scenes, as well as casually executed decorative panels. The decoration is continued in the courtyard with scenes of Samson and Hercules, and one of Prague's more attractive modern fountains. The palace is now the office of the Prague city architect. The next buildings, with their charming façades, all belonged at various times to the archdiocese; some of them are still marked with its coat of arms, a plain red band on a black background. A lane between these houses and the Archbishop's Palace leads to the **Sternberg Palace** (No. 15/57) built by Giovanni Battista Alliprandi, using designs by the Viennese architect Domenico Martinelli, for Count Wenzel Adalbert von Sternberg (1698–1707). Since 1950 this has been the home of the National Gallery's fine collection of non-Bohemian European art. Among the works exhibited are Italian paintings of the 14th to 18th century, German paintings, 17th-century Dutch paintings, and a particularly good collection of French paintings from Romanticism to Cubism. But the most famous painting here is Dürer's *Festival of the Rose Garlands* (1506) painted in Venice and intended to rival the works of the Venetian masters; its poor condition may be due to its journey in 1606 from Venice to Prague, when Rudolph, who had acquired the painting out of obsessive admiration for Dürer's work and veneration of his ancestor Maximilian I, insisted that it be carried by hand across the Alps wrapped in carpets, rather than go by cart, which he considered unsafe.

The nucleus of the **Archbishop's Palace** can be traced back to the house built before 1538 for Florian Griesbach, Secretary of the Bohemian Chancellery. From 1562 to 1564 the architect Udalrico Aostali de Sala extended it for Archbishop Antonin Brus, the first Catholic archbishop after the Hussite Wars, to form a Renaissance palace which had to be further extended in 1599. After 1675 alterations in the Baroque style were made to the palace by Francesco Lurago after designs by Jean-Baptiste Mathey. The present Rococo façade was added in 1764-65 by Johann Joseph Wirch and since 1989 has been restored to its original splendour. Much of the interior decoration of the palace (which is only open to the public once a year, on Maundy Thursday) is also Wirch's work; among the sumptuous furnishings is a set of French tapestries (1753-1756) showing flora and fauna of the East and West Indies.

Continuing along Kanovnická ul. we come to the church of **St John of Nepomuk** (Kostel sv. Jana Nepomuckého; 1720-1729), the first of Kilian Ignaz Dientzenhofer's churches. In 1737 he added a convent (No. 5/72) for the Ursuline order. In 1784 the convent was turned into barracks and the church became a storehouse; the top of the steeple had to be altered in 1815. In 1861 it was made a Protestant garrison church, becoming a Catholic church again in 1902. Inside, the ceilings are painted with the life and miracles of John of Nepomuk by Wenzel Lorenz Reiner (1728), and the altarpieces are by J.C. Lischka.

Immediately behind the church begins **Nový Svět**, the 'New World', a picturesque, but poverty-stricken district that first grew up in the 16th century. Today its colourful little houses are popular with artists and writers. The Golden Pear (U zlaté hrušky; No. 3/77) is now a popular wine tavern, the Blue Bunch of Grapes (U modrého hroznu; No. 5/78) has a fine baroque façade, and Brahe is associated with the house at the Golden Griffin (U zlatého noha; No. 5/78).

Loretánská ul., which links Hradčany Square with Loreto Square (both of which, incidently, have superb green-painted cast-iron street chandeliers), contains the former **Town Hall** of Hradčany (No. 1/173). In the 15th century the presbytery of St Benedict's church had been adequate for council meetings, but when Hradčany was made a royal town in 1598 it needed its own town hall. This was built by Kaspar von Oemlichen of Saxony (1601–1604). Three smaller palaces stand in Loretánská: the **Martinic Palace** (No. 4/181), built in 1700–1705 for Count Jiří Adam Martinic, the Imperial ambassador at Rome; the **Trauttmansdorff Palace** (No. 6/180) dating from the 16th century and remodelled in Neo-Classical style in the late 18th century; and the **Hrzán Palace** (No. 9/177), which dates from the Gothic period, belonged to Peter Parler, and has been modified in practically every architectural style over the centuries.

Loretánské nám. (Loreto Square) is one of Prague's most unusual squares, flanked as it is by the gigantic bulk of Černín Palace, the low Loreto sanctuary and the inconspicuous Capuchin monastery. **Černín Palace** (1669–1692) was built for Jan Humprecht Czernín von Chudenitz, the Imperial ambassador at Venice. The great architect and sculptor of Baroque Rome, Gian Lorenzo Bernini, is supposed to have made a preliminary design, but the detailed planning was the responsibility of Francesco Caratti. The Emperor Leopold I was aghast at the scale of the building, despite Czernín's insistence, when the emperor visited the uncompleted palace, that it was 'just a barn' – a barn for which two whole streets were demolished. Nugent, writing in 1749, was suitably impressed: 'that which exceeds all other palaces as to its magnificence is the palace of the prince *Tschernin*; the stair-case, and a suite of rooms in it are very grand; one bed-chamber is entirely hung and furnished with cloth of gold, adorned with silk *Indian* work.' Of the wall paintings and ceiling paintings by the Bohemian artist Wenzel Lorenz Reiner (1689–1743) only the *Fall of the Giants* (1718) on the staircase has survived. All the other frescoes and the sculptures by Matthias Bernhard Braun were destroyed by French troops in 1742. František Maximilián Kaňka, who modified the palace in the 1720's, also added an orangery, itself modified by Anselmo Lurago, who restored the palace after French damage and completed it with a balcony extending across the central bays of the façade above the three doorways. Above the high basement storey with its diamond rustication – Czernín was obviously determined to outdo the sgraffito diamond rustication of the other grand palaces on the Hradčany – the façade is a staggering 150 metres long, articulated by 30 half columns and 29 window bays with triangular and segmental pediments. The only touch of mannerist levity are the unusually grotesque masks concealed in the Corinthian capitals. In the 1851 the palace was turned into barracks, and in 1929–1934 Pavel Janák extended the building by adding a new wing. During the Second World War it was the headquarters of the Reichsprotektor; since 1945 it has once again been the foreign ministry. It was from an upstairs window of this building that the foreign minister Jan Masaryk, the son of the founder of the republic and the only non-communist left in the government after the February coup, fell mysteriously to his death on 10 March 1948.

By complete contrast, the building opposite the vast mass of the Czernín Palace is an exercise in overpowering charm: the **Loreto** (Loreta). Following the Battle of the White Mountain (1620) and the onset of the Counter-Reformation, the Roman Church sought every means to bring the predominantly Protestant population back to the old faith and sponsored a revival of the Marian cult of Loreto. According to the legend angels were supposed to have carried the house of the Holy Family from Nazareth to the central Italian province of Ancona in 1295 and placed it in a laurel grove. This *Casa Santa* in the laurel grove (Latin: *lauretum*, hence Loreto) became one of the most famous pilgrimage shrines in Christendom. In the 17th century around fifty Loreto shrines were founded all over Bohemia, of which the one in Prague (plate 11) was by far the most important. Princess Benigna Kateřina Lobkowicz, inspired by the work at Mikulov of the zealous Catholicizer, Cardinal Dietrichstein, founded this Loreto in 1626 on land bought cheap from fleeing Protestants. The Loreto soon generated a whole complex of buildings, of which the façade and the towers are some of the latest, being erected in 1721–25 by Christoph Dientzenhofer, and after his death in 1722, by his son Kilian Ignaz. The sculptural decoration is by Jan Kohl, including the delightful symbols of the Evangelists either side of the chapel gables. The putti on the staircase are by A.P. Quittainer (some modern copies). The tower contains an

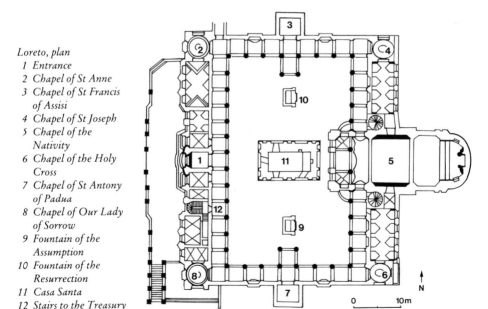

Loreto, plan
1 Entrance
2 Chapel of St Anne
3 Chapel of St Francis
  of Assisi
4 Chapel of St Joseph
5 Chapel of the
  Nativity
6 Chapel of the Holy
  Cross
7 Chapel of St Antony
  of Padua
8 Chapel of Our Lady
  of Sorrow
9 Fountain of the
  Assumption
10 Fountain of the
  Resurrection
11 Casa Santa
12 Stairs to the Treasury

Amsterdam carillon of 1694, which is now made to play only 'A Thousand Times we Greet Thee' every hour on the hour.

The inner courtyard is taken up with the *Casa Santa* itself, flanked by two fountains, showing the Resurrection and the Ascension (J.M. Brüderle, 1740). All round runs a covered passageway, built in 1634–1640 to protect the pilgrims from inclement weather. The most popular is *Our Lady of Sorrows* in the south-west corner, which houses an early 15th-century Pietà, as well as the arresting image of St Wilgefortis, a fictitious Portuguese princess who, having taken a vow of virginity, prayed that she might be spared from the marriage her father had arranged for her with the King of Sicily. God answered by making her grow a beard overnight; her enraged father was sufficiently impressed to have her crucified. Two disembodied arms – her own – reach up to the statue from the altar. The Casa Santa itself, in the centre of the complex, was built by Giovanni Battista Orsi of Como, consecrated in 1631, and slightly later had its exterior walls decorated by Italian craftsmen with plaster reliefs, somewhat inferior versions of Sansovino's originals in Italy. The scenes from the life of the Virgin on the interior walls were painted by František Kunz in 1695; the figure of the Virgin in a niche was made by the Prague goldsmith Markus Hrbek in 1671, and the altar is of silver.

The magnificent *Church of the Nativity* on the east side of the cloister was created from 1717 by Christoph Dientzenhofer out of the existing chapel of St Anne. It was extended westward in 1722 by his son Kilian Ignaz, and eastward by his stepbrother Johann Georg Aichbauer twelve years later, but it retains a satisfying unity nevertheless. The ceiling paintings are by Wenzel Lorenz Reiner (*The Presentation*, 1735) and Johann Anton Schöpf (*Adoration of the Shepherds* and *Adoration of the Kings*, 1742); the plasterwork is by T. Soldati; the sculpture is by Matthias Schönherr and Richard Georg Prachner (the side altars). The pulpit is a choppy sea of cherubs, rivalled only by the glorious organ. The pièce de résistance, however, may well be the pair of shrines either side of the main altar, which contain, dressed up and carefully posed, the complete skeletons of St Felicissimus and St Marcia. Next to them are exceptional paintings by the Venetian trained Antonín Kern of *St Agatha* (right) and *St Apolena* (left), shown in exactly the same poses as the skeleton saints. The visitor may well feel that here, at least, art is more attractive than reality. In 1746-47 Kilian Ignaz Dientzenhofer added an upper storey to the arcaded ambulatory of the church and renovated the façade.

Stairs lead from the ambulatory to the *Treasury* on the first floor, outside which is a portrait of the withered foundress, Benigna Kateřina Lobkowicz. The Treasury has some very fine pieces, but its glory is the famous 'Diamond Monstrance' (also known as the 'Prague Sun') a receptacle for the consecrated host measuring 90 cm high and weighing 12 kg, of silver gilt set with 6222 diamonds from the wedding dress of the donor, which carried 6500 diamonds (the difference being the craftsman's fee). Far too heavy though it may have been to use, this object is the most graceful monument of the Baroque to be seen in Prague. It was designed by J.B. Fischer von Erlach and made by the Viennese court jewellers Matthias Stegner and Johann Känischbauer in 1699. The star simply floats above the Virgin; hidden in its pulsating rays is a tiny enamelled Dove. Though the monstrance has always been here, its failure to inspire similar airy flights of fancy is evident from its magnificent, but pedestrian companions in the Treasury.

Joined to the Loreto by a first floor corridor is the **Capuchin Monastery**, with its typically inconspicuous little church. This was the first Capuchin monastery in Bohemia, founded in 1602 by St Lawrence of Brindisi, the general of the order. Anyone visiting Prague during the Christmas season should go to see the impressive Baroque crib from Naples that is installed here. The visitor should return to the main road by climbing up the Loreto staircase, to enjoy the angels and the view of a particularly fine Rococo doorway.

The road from Hradčany to the Strahov Monastery passes through **Pohořelec** (Fire Square), a long square with fine old houses. In 1375 deputy burgrave Aleš of Malkovitz (Malkovice) laid out this district within the town wall ('Hunger Wall'), which had been completed in 1362. It was only later that the square received its present name after the houses had several times gone up in flames: first in 1420 during the fighting between the Hussites and the forces loyal to the Emperor, and then in the great fire of 1541 which destroyed almost the whole of the Lesser Town and all of Hradčany. It went up again during the French assaults in 1741. Most of the present houses were built in the 16th or early 17th centuries, like the **Kučera Palace** (No. 22/114), which was later refaced in the purest Rococo style.

On the corner of Parléřova and Keplerova not far from the tram stop is the stolid **Brahe and Kepler Monument** made by the sculptor Josef Vajce in 1984. This was the site of the small Renaissance palace of Jakob Kurz von Senftenau, where the Danish astronomer lived until his death in 1601.

From Dlabačov ul., which joins Pohořelec, a Baroque gateway leads into the **Strahov Monastery** (Strahovský klášter; colour plate 8). The statue of St Norbert surmounting the gate is by Johann Anton Quittainer (1755). Norbert (c. 1082–1134), a canon of Xanten, Archbishop of Magdeburg, and Chancellor of the Holy Roman Empire, founded the order of Premonstratensian canons in 1120 at Prémontré near Laon. Around 1140, canons from the house at Steinfeld in the Eifel came to Prague and on 'Mount Zion' built a three-aisled Romanesque church dedicated to the Assumption together with monastic buildings. In 1258 the whole precinct was destroyed by fire but was rebuilt within a few years. Abbot Kaspar Questenberg restored the monastery in the Renaissance style (1614–1629), and Jean-Baptiste Mathey completely remodelled the abbey in the Baroque style (1682–1698). The monastery suffered severe damage during the siege of Prague by the French in 1741. In the last quarter of the 18th century the Strahov Monastery acquired its famous library. Since its restoration (1950–1953) the former abbey has housed the 'Museum of Czech Literature'. In 1990 Premonstratensians returned to the monastery.

In the forecourt beyond the gateway stands the small *Church of St Roch* (Kostel sv. Rocha), built by Abbot Jan Lohelius (1603–1612). The centrally planned Gothic building with Renaissance elements was founded by Rudolph II and dedicated to St Roch, the plague saint, as a thanks offering for being spared in the terrible epidemic of 1599. Until 1784 St Roch

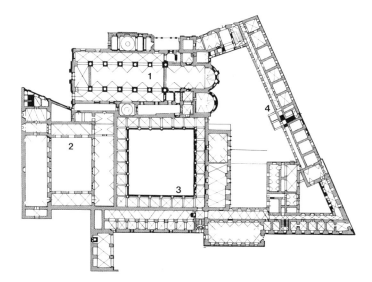

Prague, Strahov
Monastery, plan
1 Abbey Church
2 Library
3 Convent
4 Prelature

was the parish church of the Strahov quarter, after which it fell into decay; it was not restored until the 1970's. Since then it has been used as an exhibition hall.

The church of the *Assumption of the Virgin* (Kostel Nanebevzeti Panny Marie; 1148), despite all the alterations it has undergone, is still essentially the Romanesque basilica of 1148. In 1258–1268 the three-aisled church was given Early Gothic vaulting, a transept and two side-chapels. Around 1601–1606 the church was remodelled in the Renaissance style and at the end of the 17th century received Baroque alterations by Jean-Baptiste Mathey. The church was given its façade and towers, and the interior its present appearance after the artillery bombardment of 1742. The interior frescoes are by Georg Wilhelm Neunherz (1743/44). Johann Anton Quittainer made the sculptural decoration of the side altars (1750–1764), and the high altar was created by Josef Lauermann and Ignaz Franz Platzer (1763). Mozart played the organ here.

The *Strahov Library*, now part of the Museum of Czech Literature, owes its present form to the expansionist plans of Abbot Václav Mayer – a freemason in such tune with the times that he even included a portrait of the enlightened Emperor Joseph II, the great destroyer of the monasteries, on the façade of his monastic library. Perhaps this was also due to the fact that the opportunity for expansion was given by the secularization of the Premonstratensian monastery at Louka (Klosterbruck) near Znojmo and the transfer of its library to Strahov. Entering through this façade (by Ignaz Michael Platzer, son of Ignaz Franz Platzer), the visitor climbs stairs to the anteroom of the *Philosophical Hall*, a two-storey room built by Ignaz Johann Palliardi between 1783 and 1790, and a magnificent example of the transition from the Baroque to Neo-classicism. Its dimensions were determined by the booty from Louka, since the books came with their sumptuous shelving (by Johann Lachofer) and even the library's floor. The subject of the ceiling fresco (an allegory of the search for perfection in philosophy and science from the earliest days and their shared discovery of eternal wisdom in Christianity) reflects the enlightened religion of abbot and emperor. The fresco was painted in six months by the great Viennese Baroque painter, Franz Anton Maulpertsch, then in his seventies. The Hall contains a revolving desk, a large cabinet given by Marie Louise, wife of Napoleon, in 1812, while the innocuous Baroque table near the door converts into steps, or a chair and desk. The corridor (extended by a trompe l'oeil mural) leads to the *Theological Hall*, built by the Italian architect Giovanni Domenico Orsi between 1671 and 1679, just before J.B. Mathey remodelled the entire abbey. The room was originally shorter, but was increased by two bays in 1721, and then given its decoration of stucco and paintings by Siard Nosecký, illustrating the search for True Wisdom. This hall was sufficient to contain the monastery's entire collection until the acquisition of the Louka library, when it was reserved for theology.

Enlightenment monks were not satisfied with books alone. The corridor and anteroom show their many other interests: charming Rococo cases filled with Roman lamps, pots, mammoth tusks, a dried-out hammerhead shark. The visitor should not miss the collection of bark and lichen, nor the Crucifixion in a bottle.

After the Second World War nearly all the monastic libraries in Czechoslovakia were closed and their contents brought together at Strahov. Officially the library now contains over 500,000 volumes, but in fact only 130,000 are kept at Strahov, including many unique copies, incunabula and manuscripts. Among the library's greatest treasures are the 9th-century Strahov Gospels. Further exhibition rooms of the museum are in the cloister and the adjacent rooms of the former monastery. Exhibits cover the whole of Czech history and include charters of the Přemyslids, facsimiles of the 'Vyšehrad Gospels' and the 'Cosmas Chronicle' and texts from the Hussite period.

From the Strahov Monastery there is a pleasant walk along the **Hunger Wall** across Petřín Hill. Charles IV is said to have had this Gothic town wall built in order to bridge a period of hardship by giving the poor of Prague an opportunity to earn their living; it was financed by expropriations from the Jews. The battlemented wall still stands to its full height in many places. **Petřín**, a foothill of the White Mountain (Bílá Hora), is now a vast public orchard. Its main landmark, an iron viewing tower (Rozhleda), a six-sided version of the Eiffel Tower 60 metres tall, was built in 1891 for the Prague Industrial Exhibition. From its gallery (384 metres above sea-level) there is an incomparable view of Prague and its immediate surroundings. Also built at this time was the **Mirror Maze** (Bludiště) situated next to a panorama showing the students of Prague resisting the Swedes in 1648, painted by Karl and Adolf Liebscher and Vojtěch Bratoněk in 1898.

Near the viewing tower stands the church of **St Lawrence** (Kostel sv. Vavřince) which gave the Petřín hill its old German name, Laurenziberg. The small aisle-less church, mentioned as early as 1135, was incorporated as the choir of a new Baroque church by Ignaz Johann Palliardi (1735–70). Just beside it is the *Calvary Chapel* with sgraffito decoration on its façade showing the Resurrection of Christ, after a design by Mikoláš Aleš. The chapel contains a Baroque Crucifixion group. The *Holy Sepulchre Chapel* of 1732 follows the pattern of the Holy Sepulchre in Jerusalem and forms the final station in a Way of the Cross leading up from the Lesser Town to the Petřín. A funicular railway links the Újezd with the summit of Petřín. The views here at night are magnificent.

Nové město (New Town)

In 1348–1350 Charles IV enclosed an area covering two sq km south of the Old Town and extending as far as Vyšehrad with a long wall. The town he built within it is a magnificent example of medieval urban planning. All the streets, market places, churches and monasteries, as well as the private lots and even the height of the houses were precisely laid down. Most of the settlers in this 'New Town' were craftsmen who poured in from all parts of Bohemia to enjoy the advantages of living in the imperial capital. Until 1784, when it was amalgamated with the three other towns of Prague, *Nové město* was an independent town with its own council.

When the New Town was laid out the southern part of the Old Town wall was no longer important and so was demolished. The moat was replaced by broad streets, the present-day business thoroughfares Na příkopě (At the Moat), 28. října (28 October) and Národní třída (National Street). The buildings – banks, insurance companies, department stores – which now stand in these streets mainly date from the end of the Habsburg period. They include the National Bank, Na příkopě, No. 14/854; Dům elegance, Prague's oldest department store, Na příkopě, No. 4/847 (1871); Rapid offices, 28. října, No. 13/377 (1902) and the Máj department store, Národní, No. 26/63 (1975). Two art nouveau offices in Národní, Nos. 7/1011 and 9/1010 deserve a close look: they were both built in 1907-08 by Osvald Polívka, one for the former insurance company Praha with façade reliefs by Ladislav Šaloun, and its neighbour for the publishers Topič. The house at the sign of the **Black Rose** (U černé růže; No. 12/853) has an arcade designed by Oldřich Tyl (1929) which contained the entrance to the public typing room, where people had to type when the communist government kept a strict control on the ownership of typewriters. In the arcade at Kaňka's House (No. 16/118) is a bronze memorial to events of 17 November 1989, when student demonstrators were beaten up here by the police.

At the end of Národní, on the banks of the Vltava stands the **National Theatre** (Národní divadlo; plate 10), the pre-eminent symbol of 19th-century Czech national resurgence. Built by Josef Zítek from 1868 to 1881 and paid for entirely by contributions from the Czech people, it opened on 15 July 1881 with a performance of Smetana's opera *Libuše*, but less than a month later it was gutted by fire. The city and even the Emperor donated considerable sums for its restoration, and the theatre was ready to reopen as early as 1883. The statues of *Apollo* and the nine *Muses* on the attic storey are by the sculptor Bohuslav Schnirch, as are the two

Smetana, Dvořák, Janáček

Music had a central place in the great Czech cultural renaissance in the 19th century. The Czech musical world earlier this century was split over the respective merits of the two leaders of this musical revival, Smetana and Dvořák. Was Smetana's music too personal and poetic? Was Dvořák's too formalistic and conservative? Traces of this schism remain today.

Although his first language was German, **Bedřich Smetana** (1824–1884) was above all a Czech nationalist and sought in his opera *Libuše* (1869–1872) and sequence of symphonic poems *Má Vlast* (My Fatherland; 1874–1879) to portray Czech history and landscape with new grandeur (Performances of *Má Vlast* in the years of Habsburg, Nazi or Soviet domination were always an expression of Czech nationhood.) He regarded his immensely popular folk opera *The Bartered Bride* (Prodaná nevěstá; 1866) as secondary to his great nationalist works. His two autobiographical string quartets, written after deafness had marked the onset of his long final illness, are the precursors of Janáček's intimate late quartets.

Antonín Dvořák (1841–1904) was less overtly nationalistic, though he played the viola in the orchestra under Smetana's baton, and his *Slavonic Rhapsodies* (1878) captured the spirit of the country's folk music (though, like Smetana, he made little use of actual folk tunes). Dvořák was more outward-looking than Smetana and more open to influences from beyond Bohemia, particularly from Brahms, who greatly admired him. He enjoyed great success in England, especially with his choral works (he was made a Cambridge D.Mus. in 1891), and his homesickness during his time in America in the 1890's gave rise in his Symphony No. 9 (*From the New World*; Z noveho světa) to some of his most Czech music – though he was also influenced by the music of the American blacks, with whom he sympathized as an oppressed people. Through his son-in-law, the composer **Josef Suk** (1874–1935), Dvořák started a musical dynasty which continues today with his great-grandson, the violinist Josef Suk.

The music of Dvořák's friend, **Leoš Janáček** (1854–1928), a fervent nationalist, was deeply rooted in his close study of the folk music and of the rhythms of the language of his native Moravia – and thus closer to a truly national music than either Smetana or Dvořák. As director of the Organ School he was an important musical figure at Brno, but it was not until the success of his opera *Jenůfa* at Prague in 1916, and the championing of his work by Max Brod (Kafka's friend), that he became known to the wider world. The last decade of his life saw a great burst of creative activity with the operas *Kat'á Kabanova*, *The Cunning Little Vixen*, *The Macropoulos Case* (based on a story by K. Čapek) and *From the House of the Dead* (based on Dostoevsky), the *Glagolitic Mass* and his finest chamber music.

bronze chariots. On the side entrance facing the Vltava the two statues representing *Opera* and *Theatre* were designed by Josef Václav Myslbek. The interior of the theatre has recently undergone drastic restoration. In 1977–1983 the architect K. Prager extended the theatre complex by building the **New Stage**, a group of three interconnecting steel-framed buildings comprising a theatre, an administrative and office building and a restaurant. Opposite the National Theatre is the Lažanský Palace. Here Smetana wrote *Dalibor* and *The Bartered Bride*, and in the Café Slavia on the ground floor, Jaroslav Seifert and other avant-garde poets between the wars dreamt that the Vltava was another Seine (helped perhaps by the view of the pint-sized Eiffel Tower on the Petřin opposite).

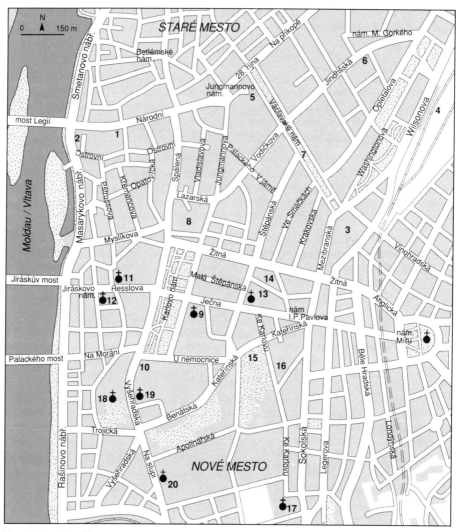

Nové město (New Town)
1 Church and Convent of St Ursula   2 National Theatre   3 National Museum   4 Main Station   5 Our Lady of the Snows   6 St Henry   7 Wenceslas Square   8 Town Hall of the New Town   9 St Ignatius   10 Faust House   11 Sts Cyril and Methodius   12 St Wenceslas   13 St Stephen   14 Rotunda of St Longinus   15 St Catherine   16 Villa Amerika (Dvořak Museum)   17 Karlov   18 Emmaus Monastery   19 St John of Nepomuk on the Rock   20 St Mary na slupi

Národní třída ends at **Most Legii** (Legion Bridge) which has spanned the Vltava since 1901, cutting across the end of **Střelecký ostrov** (Marksmen's Island). This island was already being used by the citizens of the Old Town for shooting practice in 1472. In 1890 the workers of Prague held the first May Day celebrations in Bohemia there. Another bridge links Masarykovo nábřežní (Masaryk Embankment, as it has recently been renamed) with **Slovanský ostrov** (Slav Island – named after the Slav Congress held here in 1848). On this island in the 19th century stood the 'Sophiensaal', a hall in which Hector Berlioz, Franz Liszt, Richard Wagner and Jan Kubelík all gave concerts. The **Šitkovský Water Tower** of 1495 is a reminder of the watermills that stood next to Slav Island: it was given its Baroque onion dome at the end of the 18th century. On the site of the mills the **Mánes Building** was built in 1930 by Otakar Novotný as the headquarters of the Union of Artists. It has a restaurant with a fine view. Masarykovo nábřeží continues, with magnificent Art Nouveau architecture, becoming Rašínovo nábřeží after the Jiráskův Bridge. Two blocks down is the little square around the stupendous memorial to the Czech historian and naturalist František Palacký (1789–1876) made by S. Sucharda and A. Dryák (1905–1907).

Outside the Old Town walls Charles IV laid out a 'Horse Market' (Koňský trh) in 1348, which was to become the centre of the inner city of Prague. Since 1848 it has been called **Wenceslas Square** (Václavské nám.). Measuring 750 metres long and 60 metres wide, it is one of the largest and most attractive town squares in the world – though it is in fact more of a boulevard than a square. There are more hotels, restaurants, cafés, cinemas and shops here than anywhere else in the city, and nowhere are there such crowds of people. They come here to stroll, argue and sometimes to demonstrate. Huge crowds occupied the square in the Velvet Revolution of 1989, addressed by Václav Havel from the balcony opposite the Mir building.

There was a stone statue of St Wenceslas in the Horse Market as early as 1680, but it was removed to Vyšehrad in 1878. The present **Wenceslas Memorial**, a large equestrian statue, was made by Josef Václav Myslbek in 1888 and set up at the upper end of the square in 1912. Just below the Wenceslas Memorial is the spot where the Republic was proclaimed in 1919, and where fifty years later, in protest at the lack of resistance in Czechoslovakia to the Soviet Tanks, the student Jan Palach burned himself to death in January 1969. (His gesture may have been inspired by the Buddhist protests against the Vietnam War, and it was followed by other self-immolations in Czechoslovakia.) A small shrine has been set up here, with pictures of Palach, his emulators, and the Masaryks; this was the rallying point of the Velvet Revolution. The oldest building in Wenceslas Square is the Hotel Adria (No. 26/784), a Baroque building (c. 1789), but nearly all the many large shops and office buildings, hotels and houses were built within the last hundred years. Besides the Art Nouveau splendour of the Hotel Evropa (No. 25,27/825,826), built from 1903 to 1905, there are also several important examples of Czech modernism, including the Tatran Hotel (No. 22/782; formerly the Juliš Hotel) built from 1925 to 1926 by Pavel Janák; Dům obuv (No. 6/774; House of Shoes, formerly the offices of Baťa) by Ludvík Kysela (1928–1929); Peterka House (No. 12/777) by Jan Kotěra

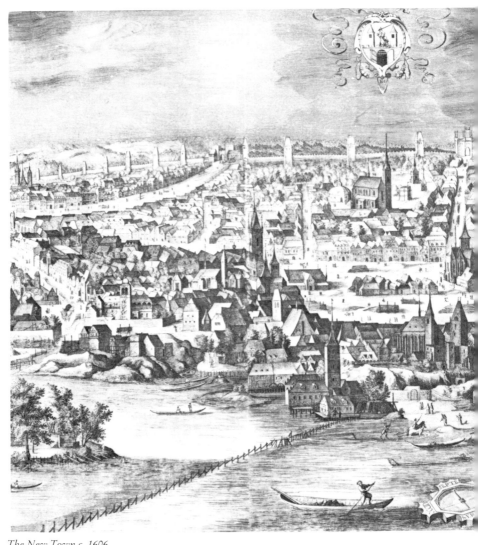

The New Town c. 1606

and V. Thierhier; and at the bottom of the square, the Palác Koruna (No. 1/846) by Antonín Pfeiffer (1912–1914). Kafka worked at No. 19/832, the Assicurazione Generali, as did Joseph K. in *The Trial*.

The grand but rather dull building closing the view at the top end of Wenceslas Square is the **National Museum** (Národní muzeum), which mostly contains historical and scientific

collections. The department of history and archaeology has a large collection of coins and medals, and displays illustrating the history of the Czech theatre and puppet theatre. It was built by Josef Schulz (1885–1890), and like the National Theatre was intended as an expression of the Czech national revival. Anton Wagner designed the allegorical figures on the ramp and the reliefs (*The Foundation of the Zbraslav Monastery*, *The Foundation of Charles University* and *Rudolph II Receiving Scholars and Artists*) on this enormous façade and, in collaboration with other artists, the allegories of the sciences on the side towers. The entrance hall and staircase are decorated with bronze statues by Ludwig Schwanthaler of Munich dating from the 1840's; Libuše, Přemysl, Otakar II, Wenceslas II, George of Poděbrady, Archbishop Ernest of Pardubice. The *Pantheon* or ceremonial hall of the museum has mural paintings by František Ženíšek and Václav Brožík; it houses statues and busts of Czech heroes.

The road in front of the museum is Wilsonova (named after President Woodrow Wilson, whose vision of a post-war Europe in 1918 included autonomous development for the peoples of Austria-Hungary, and so helped bring about the creation of Czechoslovakia), the main traffic artery through the Prague inner city. It passes the monumental **Federal Assembly Building** (No. 6/52) built in 1973 above the old Prague stock exchange (J. Rössler 1936–1938), hence its extraordinary bridging shape; it is the seat of the highest legislative body, comprising a Chamber of the People and a Chamber of the Nations. A little further on is the **Smetana Theatre** (Smetanovo divadlo), formerly the Neues Deutsches Theater, built to replace a wooden theatre in 1886/87. Then the road passes the **Main Railway Station** (Hlavní nádraží), an Art Nouveau gem built by J. Fanta (1901–1909) which has been lovingly preserved through the recent extension and modernization (1980). Somewhat further is Šverma Park (Švermovy sady) with the **Museum of the City of Prague** (Muzeum hlavního města Prahy), which includes a wooden model of Prague in the 1830's, useful for a view of buildings hidden behind high walls.

In 1347 Charles IV founded the church of **Our Lady of the Snows** (Kostel Panny Marie Sněžné), with its friary of Discalced Carmelites, as the main landmark of the New Town, but work did not begin on building the church until 1349, after the death of his first wife, Blanche of Valois. (The church's strange dedication of the church goes back to the old Marian legend of the miraculous fall of snow showing where Santa Maria Maggiore was to be built in Rome.) In the 19th century the enormous building (the chancel is 35 metres high) still dominated Wenceslas Square. It was originally intended as a vast coronation church, larger than St Vitus's at more than 100 metres in length, but after the completion of the chancel the Hussite Wars brought building work to a standstill. Jan Želivský, a former Premonstratensian who became one of the most radical advocates of Hussite teachings, preached in Our Lady of the Snows. It was from this church that he led the mass demonstration which gave rise to the First Defenestration of Prague in 1419 (see p. 131). After his execution on 9 March 1422 he was buried in his church, which itself was badly damaged in the ensuing Hussite disturbances. From the 15th century the building fell into decay. It was not restored until the Franciscans took it over at the beginning of the 17th century.

The best view of the tall church of Our Lady of the Snows surmounted by its tiny tower is from the Franciscan garden which adjoins it to the south and which still contains a few of the old convent buildings, but the entrance to the church is from Jungmannova nám. Josef Jungmann (1773–1847) whose memorial has stood here since 1878, was the author of a dictionary and a history of Czech which laid the foundations of the new Czech literary language; he also translated *Paradise Lost* into Czech.

Just past the Cubist lamp (Vladislav Hofmann, 1913), the north portal leading to the churchyard is surmounted by a badly damaged 14th-century Gothic tympanum with the Coronation of the Virgin surmounted by the Trinity and flanked by Charles IV and his wife, Blanche of Valois (or possibly his father, John of Luxemburg). The height of the interior is impressive, but it was even taller before the original vaulting collapsed in 1611 and had to be replaced by the present vault. The pewter font dates from 1459. The 16th-century high altarpiece, the tallest in Prague, has a painting of the *Annunciation* by Wenzel Lorenz Reiner (1724).

Jungmannova has a collection of impressive modernist buildings, starting with the **Adria Palace** (P. Janák and J. Zasche) for the Riunione Adriatica di Sicurta. The basement is the home of the world-famous Laterna Magica, which combines theatre, dance and cinema; during the frenetic weeks of the revolution in 1989 this was the headquarters of Civic Forum. Jungmannova leads to **Charles Square** (Karlovo nám.) developed from the second biggest marketplace of the New Town, the Cattle Market (Dobytčí trh). Charles IV decided on its location and extent, and set up a wooden tower in the middle of the square from which to display the coronation regalia to the people on certain feastdays. The square's present name dates from 1848; it was laid out as a slightly shapeless public garden between 1843 and 1863.

The north side of the square is occupied by the **Town Hall of the New Town** (Novoměstská radnice). It is first mentioned in 1377, but must have been built shortly after 1348. Originally there were two wings: the one facing Charles Square contained the state rooms and council chambers, while the one facing Vodičkova had offices and the prison. In 1411–1418 the town hall was enlarged by Martin Friček and given an arcaded courtyard; the massive corner tower was added in 1452–1456. In 1559 the building was remodelled in the Renaissance style after a fire. After the amalgamation of the four towns of Prague in 1784 it was used as a criminal court and prison. Today it houses departments of the city administration including the registry.

The town hall was the site of the First Defenestration of Prague. The procession of armed Hussites led by Jan Želivský arrived outside the building on 30 July 1419 brandishing a monstrance and demanding the release of their imprisoned co-religionists. The sight of the host provoked the newly appointed German-speaking, Catholic councillors; a stone was flung from the town hall. At this the building was stormed and the councillors hurled out of the windows to be lynched by the mob below. Two weeks later King Wenceslas IV, after a last attempt to find a compromise between the religious parties, died of a heart attack, and for the next fifteen years the country was torn apart by the Hussite Wars.

The **Jan Želivský Monument** in front of the town hall, made by J. Lukešová in 1960, commemorates the Defenestration. Other statues of famous Czech scientists, writers and scholars stand in the square.

Half way down on the left stands the church of **St Ignatius** (Kostel sv. Ignáce) built as the headquarters of the Jesuits in the New Town in 1665–1687 by Carlo Lurago to designs by Giovanni Domenico Orsi; this meant that the order now had establishments in each of the towns of Prague. The tower was erected at the end of the 17th century by Paul Ignaz Bayer who also added the splendid portico to the west front with its statue of *St Ignatius in glory*. In the relatively severe interior, rich architectural plasterwork (by T. Soldati) forms the main decoration, and frescoes have a very limited place. The visitor should not miss the death's-head chapel on the right, not the chapel on the left, where one of the few remaining red stars in Prague points the way to a Marian grotto. The soot-shrouded painting on the high altar also depicts *St Ignatius in Glory* and is by Johann Georg Heintsch (1688), a pupil of Škréta. A few years before work began on building the church 23 houses were demolished to make way for the Jesuit College, which after the suppression of the order in 1773 became a hospital. Today the huge building is used by the medical faculty of Charles University.

The **Faust House** (Faustův dům) on the south side of the square (No. 40/502) has its origins in a 14th-century Gothic palace. The house was altered on several occasions, the last being in the 18th century in the Late Baroque style. The inhabitants of the New Town soon associated the house with the Faust legend, because in the years when it was occupied it was also used as a laboratory. It is reputed to have been the workshop of Edward Kelley, the English alchemist, whose charlatanism eventually became apparent even to Rudolph II. Today the building is still a chemist's, but is now attached to a hospital. The road on the right of the Faust house, Vyšehradská (the old road from Vyšehrad castle to Hradčany) leads down the hill, leaving the garden of **St John of Nepomuk on the Rock** (Kostel sv. Jana na Skalce; 1730–1739), one of most delightful of Kilian Ignaz Dientzenhofer's churches and perhaps the most perfect example of the plastic dynamism of his architecure. A double flight of steps leads up to the church from the street. The portal, flanked by two towers set at an angle and with tall caps, opens into an octagonal room with gently concave walls. Inside, the indifferent fresco of the *Ascension of St John of Nepomuk* by Karel Kovař (1798) is interesting for the picture of the artist at his easel, talking to patrons. On the high altar is the wooden model made by Johann Brokoff for the bronze statue of St John of Nepomuk on Charles Bridge (see p. 56f). There is a charming and unexpectedly powerful organ.

Opposite St John is the **Emmaus Monastery** (Klášter na Slovanech), founded by Charles IV in 1347, next to the old church of Sts Cosmas and Damian (the parish church of the village of Podskalí); it was charged with fostering Slavic culture within the Empire. Croatian Benedictines were brought to preserve the Slavonic liturgy and the Glagolitic script that had been created by Cyril and Methodios five hundred years earlier. The new abbey church was consecrated to the Virgin and the patron saints of the Slavs on Easter Monday 1372, when the theme of the consecration service was the meeting of the resurrected Christ with the apostles on the road to Emmaus. Consequently the monastery gained its other name, 'Emmaus'. This was preferred by the German community, while the Czechs call it 'na Slovanech' ('at the Slavs'). It became a centre of Hussitism. After 1636 Benedictines from the Spanish abbey of Our Lady of Montserrat moved in and remodelled the building in the Baroque style. In 1880 Benedictines from Beuron Abbey regothicized it all in the 'Beuron School' style. In February 1945 the monastery was destroyed during the bombing of Prague by the US Air Force, the only major architectural casualty of the war in Prague.

In 1950 a number of research institutes of the Czechoslovak Academy of Sciences were established in the monastic precinct. When the church was rebuilt a deliberate decision was made not to build copies of the two towers, but to make the west front an expressive combination of Gothic and Modern architecture. The result is two intersecting wings of concrete pointing heavenwards (architect: František M. Černý). The Gothic wall paintings (1360–1370) in the monastery cloister are some of the most important in all Bohemia. Nikolaus Wurmser, the Master of the Emmaus Cycle, and Master Oswald worked in the style of a *Biblia pauperum* (Bible of the poor): the lower registers show scenes from the Old Testament that foreshadow the events from the New Testament shown in the topmost register. This 'typological' system was used at a very early date in Bohemia in the Vyšehrad Gospels (10th century). The frescoes are in very poor condition, but there are passages of great beauty.

Vyšehradská třída continues beyond the church as Na slupi. According to legend in heathen times a column (*sloup*) bearing the god Svatovit stood there. The Christians replaced the heathen god with the Virgin Mary. When the Servites built their monastery here in 1330–1365 they made the Svatovit or Virgin column the central support of their Gothic church of **St Mary 'Na slupi'** ('at the column'; also called Kostel Panny Marie Na trávníčku, St Mary on the Lawn). It is, however, doubtful whether the present pillar which stands in the centre of the building supporting the vault is in fact the same heathen column. The Servite monastery, which has undergone many alterations, now houses a research institute of the Charles University.

The church of **Sts Cyril and Methodios** (Kostel sv. Cyrila a Metoděje), in Resslova ul. which runs from Charles Square to Jiráskovo nám. on the Vltava embankment. It was built to designs by Kilian Ignaz Dientzenhofer from 1730 to 1736 and originally dedicated to St Charles Borromeo, but was given to the Orthodox church in the 1930's. It achieved unhappy notoriety in the Second World War. In 1942 the assassins of Heydrich hid in the crypt of the church, but their hiding place was betrayed. All attempts to storm the building failed, and the Nazis tried to flood the crypt. The men fought on to their last bullet, and then committed suicide. There is a monument on Resslova. The small church opposite was the Romanesque parish church of a village standing here before the New Town was created; remains of this first structure can just be made out, even though the church has since been gothicized, baroquized and re-gothicized.

Štěpánská ul. runs south from Wenceslas Square, crosses the broad Žitná thoroughfare and reaches the church of **St Stephen** (Kostel sv. Štěpána), a Gothic basilica built by Charles IV in 1351–1394 as the parish church of the upper New Town. Despite many alterations it has preserved its Gothic character both within and without. Noteworthy are the pewter font (1462) and several paintings by the Baroque master Karel Škréta (*Baptism of Christ*, *St Wenceslas*, *St Rosalia*, all mid–17th century). The great Baroque sculptor Matthias Bernhard Braun lies buried here. In the garden behind the church is the **St Longinus Rotunda** (Rotunda sv. Longina), a small round parish church built in the 12th century for the hamlet of Rybníček ('Fishponds'). Before the neighbouring church was built, the rotunda was dedicated to St Stephen; afterwards the dedication was changed to St Longinus, who is unusually prominent in the altarpiece *Crucifixion*.

The nearby convent of Augustinian nuns with the church of **St Catherine** (Kostel sv. Kateříny) was founded by Charles IV in 1354 in thanks for his first victory in 1332 at San Felice in Italy when he was but sixteen. The Hussites destroyed the convent and church, but both were rebuilt in 1518–1522. In 1737–1742 Kilian Ignaz Dientzenhofer and František Maximilián Kaňka replaced the Gothic church with a Baroque one, but the octagonal tower goes back to the Gothic period; it is known as the 'Prague minaret'. Almost all the wall paintings in St Katherine's are by the Baroque painter Wenzel Lorenz Reiner; the stucco is the work of B. Spinetti. The convent is now a psychiatric hospital, while the church houses the municipal *Lapidarium* or sculpture museum.

The charming summer villa in Ke Karlovu street is an early work of Kilian Ignaz Dientzenhofer, built for Count Jan Václav Michna of Vacinov between 1717 and 1720. It originally stood amidst gardens and parks but is now surrounded by hospitals. The elegance of the central pavilion shows evidence of Dientzenhofer's recent training in Vienna under the Court Architect Johann Lukas Hildebrandt. The great hall on the first floor has a frescoed ceiling showing *Apollo, Pegasus and the Arts* by the Innsbruck painter, Johann Ferdinand Schor. The sculptures in the garden are from the workshop of Anton Braun, nephew of Matthias, and represent the *Four Seasons* (1734). In the 19th century the villa was a restaurant called the *Villa Amerika*, and has kept this name ever since. Today it houses the **Antonín Dvořák Museum**.

Nearby in Na Bojišti street stands **U kalicha**, the Chalice tavern, made famous by Jaroslav Hašek as the local of the Good Soldier Švejk, and now something of a tourist trap with interiors heavily decorated with Švejk imagery.

To the south Ke Karlovu ends at **Karlov**, with its church of the Assumption and St Charles (Kostel Nanebevzeti Panny Marie a Karla Velikého), another of Charles IV's foundations for his New Town. He founded this monastery for Augustinian canons in 1350, the year after his coronation at Aachen as King of the Romans, and it was consecrated in 1377. The church is partly dedicated to Charles's predecessor and namesake, Charlemagne (canonized in 1165), and takes its octagonal plan from Charlemagne's palatine chapel at Aachen. The stellar vault, spanning 22.75 metres with no central support, was completed by Bonifaz Wohlmut in 1575. In 1708 a *scala santa* was built on the north side of the church to the designs of Johann Santini Aichel. Between 1733 and 1738 the interior underwent a Baroque transformation at the hands of František Maximilián Kaňka with life-size tableaux of the *Visitation* and of *Pilate and Christ before the People*, by J.J. Schlansovský; some at least of the remarkable colour scheme also dates from this period. (It is some of the very last such decoration to survive in Prague, similar painting in the Vladislav Hall and elsewhere having been cleaned up in this century.) In the crypt is a 'Bethlehem' or Holy Grotto, a triumph of Baroque fantasy. Until the 1989 Revolution the conventual buildings housed the unique Museum of the Interior Ministry with its collection of exhibits showing the patriotic work of the police and border patrols under the Communist regime.

Vyšehrad

According to legend the prophetess Libuše and the first Přemyslid rulers were supposed to have lived on Vyšehrad ('High Castle'), a massive outcrop by the Vltava. Historians and archaeologists have discovered, however, that Vyšehrad had no fortifications until the first half of the 10th century, and consequently Prague Castle must be older and must have been the home of the first Přemyslids before they crossed the river to Vyšehrad. Nevertheless, Vyšehrad has a central place in Czech national consciousness and romanticism, perhaps best summed up by Smetana's symphonic poem, which opens his patriotic sequence, 'Ma Vlast'.

Vyšehrad, c. 1606

In the 11th century Vratislav II, with the support of Pope Gregory VII, founded a church dedicated to St Peter and St Paul on the cliff, and soon after this a royal palace was built. The collegiate chapter was an important centre of culture. Only the round church of St Martin survives from this period.

From Vladislav II Přemysl (1140–1172) the Bohemian rulers again governed from Hradčany, and the 'High Castle' fell into decay. However, Charles IV's order of coronation stipulated that the coronation ceremonies had to begin on Vyšehrad, which meant that all buildings there including the fortification had to be restored. From here the coronation procession followed the old route through Charles Square to the Old Town Square, across the Charles Bridge and up to the cathedral in Hradčany. In 1420 the Hussites took Vyšehrad Castle and destroyed it. In the following decades many burghers' houses were built on the cliff, and by 1467 there is mention of a 'town of Vyšehrad hill'. Around the middle of the 17th century the strategically important town castle was transformed into a strong Baroque fortification with tall brick fieldworks and massive corner bastions. The fortress was dismantled in 1866, and completely razed in 1911. Since then archaeologists have been at work on the steep rocky hill, which has now become a park.

The **Tábor Gate** in the south-east was built in the Early Baroque style around 1655. Just 100 metres behind it are masonry remains of the **Špička Gate** (1348–1350), part of Charles IV's restorations. A portion of Gothic castle wall about 140 metres long is also preserved. The **Leopold Gate**, built by Carlo Lurago around 1678, forms the inner entrance to the castle. The original drawbridge was replaced by an embankment in 1842.

The **Rotunda of St Martin** (Rotunda sv. Martina), the earliest surviving building on Vyšehrad, and one of the earliest Christian buildings in Bohemia, was built in the reign of Vratislav II in the last third of the 11th century. Later, when the fortress in Vyšehrad was in use, the church was used as a powder magazine. In 1876–1880 the entrance on the west side was walled up and a Neo-Gothic portal was created on the south side. The door and interior walls were decorated with motifs taken from the Vyšehrad Codex. In the mid-18th century the neighbouring chapel of **Our Lady in the Fortifications** (Kaple P.Marie v hradbách) was built. Passing the **New Deanery** (1877–1879), which contains an exhibition of the history of Vyšehrad, the road leads to the **Basilica of St Lawrence**, beneath which archaeologists have discovered a pre-Romanesque church from the late 10th century. In the 15th century the basilica became a canons' house and parts of its masonry were later incorporated into the chapter deanery.

The huge but rather dull towers of the church of **St Peter and St Paul** (Kostel sv. Petra a Pavla) date from 1902. The church was built by Vratislav II between 1070 and 1080 as a three-aisled basilica. The collegiate church has been restored several times, the last occasion being in 1885–1903 by Josef Mocker and František Mikš. The decoration of the façade and the interior furnishings date almost entirely from the turn of the century. The Romanesque stone sarcophagus, which probably contained the remains of one of the Přemyslids, is c. 1100. According to tradition Vratislav II (d. 1092), Konrad I Otto (d. 1092) and Sobeslav I (d. 1140) were buried here. Charles IV donated a panel painting of the Virgin Mary, the celebrated 'Vyšehrad Madonna' (in the third chapel of the south aisle), often called 'Our Lady of Rain' because the Bohemian peasants prayed to her in times of drought.

The **National Cemetery** next to the church contains the 'Slavín' (or Pantheon). In the 1870's the parish graveyard of the Vyšehrad collegiate church was turned into a national burial place. Henceforth all persons of distinction were to be buried there with gravestones carved by the leading Czech sculptors. The writers Karel Čapek and Jan Neruda, the painter Mikoláš Aleš, the sculptors Václav Levý and Otakar Španiel, the composers Antonín Dvořák, Bedřich Smetana and Zdeněk Fibich are all buried here. In 1889–93 the *Slavín* itself was built to house the remains of the very greatest Czechs: the painter Alfons Mucha, the sculptors Josef Václav Myslbek, Bohumil Kafka and Ladislav Šaloun, the violinist Jan Kubelík, and about 50 other national worthies – but no soldiers or politicians.

The site on which the royal palace stood, south of the cemetery, has been since 1927 a well-tended park. In it stand the monumental sculptures by Josef Václav Myslbek, which until 1948 formed the decoration of Palacký Bridge (Palackého most). Their themes are taken from Czech legends: *Lumír and the song, Ctirad and Šarka, Záboj and Slavoj, Libuše and Přemysl*. A walk along the former gun emplacements on the edge of the cliff is recommended for its fine view. Since the age of Romanticism a gothic ruin on the cliff side has been identified as 'Libuše's Bath'.

Beside Vyšehrad metro station, which has a spectacular view over the city, the visitor will find two characteristic examples of modern Czech architecture: the **Palace of Culture** (1981) intended for Party Congresses, but also Prague's biggest cultural venue, and the **Hotel Forum**.

Other districts

A magnificent view of the Old Town, Hradčany and the bridges over the Vltava can be obtained from the **Letná Plateau**. It was here in 1955 that the government erected a giant statue of Stalin – the largest in the world – only to blow it up in 1962. The dictator was shown leading the people, thus earning the monument its nickname of 'the bread queue'. To the north-east of Letná is the vast **Stromovaka** park and the **Exhibition Ground** (Vystaviště) laid out for the 1891 exhibition. The iron **Congress Palace** by Bedřich Münzberger dates from 1891, as does the **Prague Pavilion**, which now contains the National Museum's *Lapidarium*, a collection of pieces of sculpture and architecture dating from the 11th to the 19th centuries. The circular **Panorama Pavilion** (1908) has a representation of the Battle of Lipany fought between the Hussites and the imperial forces on 30 May 1434. The **Exhibition Pavilion** designed by F. Cubr, J. Hrubý and Z. Pokorný won the gold medal at the 1958 World Exhibition at Brussels. The park also has a planetarium, a sports hall, a swimming pool (1976), several open-air theatres and a panoramic cinema.

On the other side of the Vltava, which makes a great loop before continuing its course westwards, is the Prague **Zoological Gardens** (Zoologická zahrada). Among its more remarkable inmates is a unique herd of Przewalski horses (Equus przewalskii), a primitive type of horse, standing only 135 cm high. East of the zoo stands **Schloss Troja** (Trojský zámek) a Baroque building in the style of a Roman villa built in 1679–1685 at the foot of the Vltava heights opposite Prague Castle by Jean-Baptiste Mathey for Count Wenzel Adalbert von Šternberk, the imperial Chamberlain and the head of one of the leading Bohemian aristocratic families. The nucleus of the long red and white building is a two-storey banqueting hall with a ceiling fresco representing the *Victory of Emperor Leopold I over the*

Prague, Hževda, or Star Palace, plan

Turks by Francesco Marchetti and the brothers Abraham and Isaak Godyn. This central section is flanked by lower wings each with a staircase tower. Curving up from the French garden to the banqueting hall is a double flight of steps decorated with sculptures representing a *Battle of Giants* by the Dresden court sculptor Johann Georg Heermann and his nephew, Paul (1685–1703). The château has recently undergone extensive restoration.

National Road No. 7 to Karlovy Vary (Karlsbad) passes round Hradčany and by **Břevnov Monastery** (Klášter sv. Markéty) in the suburb of Břevnov. Adalbert (Vojtěch), the second bishop of Prague, and Prince Boleslav II founded this Benedictine abbey in 993, the first monastery in Bohemia. Around 1040 the abbey church was dedicated to St Margaret (sv. Markéta); the 11th-century crypt survives. In 1708 work to give the church its present Baroque appearance was started by Paul Ignaz Bayer and completed seven years later by Christoph Dientzenhofer, whose son Kilian Ignaz was responsible for the interior decoration. Dientzenhofer's design has been praised as one of the most organic creations of the entire Baroque for the energy of the space created by the interpenetrating ovals that look, from the outside, like a balloon tied in by the single giant order of pilasters. The interior vaults were painted by Johann Jakob Steinfels, and the altar paintings by Peter Johann Brandl. The conventual buildings have recently been returned to the Benedictines after being used for state archives. The most remarkable feature is the ceiling fresco in the Prelates' Hall by Cosmas Damian Asam (1727) depicting *St Günther and the miracle of the peacock*.

West of the monastery is the **White Mountain** (Bílá Hora) – at 381 metres it is really not much more than a hill. It is dominated by the **Hvězda (Star) Summer Palace** (Letohrádek Hvězda) set within a large walled game park (*obora*), which was transformed into an English park in 1787. The English traveller Fynes Moryson came to this place in 1592, 'called Stella, because the trees are planted in the figure of starres, and a little faire house therein is likewise built, with six corners in forme of a starre. And in this place the Emperor kept twelve Cammels, an Indian Oxe, yellow, all over rugged, and hairy upon the throat, like a Lyon' as well as two leopards, that would join the chase, sitting just behind the huntsman on his horse. Archduke Ferdinand of the Tyrol, son of Emperor Ferdinand I and Governor of Bohemia, built this star-shaped Renaissance hunting lodge in 1555-56. The archduke himself provided the sketch plan and the building work was directed by Juan Maria del Pambio and Giovanni Lucchese. Despite its completely bare exterior the carefully restored palace is worth visiting not only on account of its extraordinary ground plan, but also for the unique plasterwork on the ceilings of the ground floor, showing scenes from classical history and mythology, by the Italian stuccatori, Giovanni Campion and Andrea Avostolis del Pambio (1556–1563). Like so many buildings in Prague the Star Palace spent the 18th century as a powder magazine. It is now an uninspiring museum of the lives and work of the writer Alois Jirásek (1851–1930) and the painter Mikoláš Aleš (1852–1913) who did much to strengthen the national consciousness of the Czech people.

South-west of the enclosure is the site of the *Battle of the White Mountain* which took place on 8 November 1620; the artillery took their sights from the star. The clash between the Catholic-Imperial army of Maximilian of Bavaria under his commander Count Tilly (and with the young Descartes as a very junior officer), and the Protestant army of the Bohemian Estates lasted only an hour, before the Estates forces took to flight. The next morning Frederick and his English wife, Elizabeth, the Winter King and Queen, fled from Prague. The defeat ended the 'Bohemian War', the opening round of the Thirty Years' War: the Protestant cause was lost in Bohemia and with it the opportunity of creating a Czech nation state in the 17th century. It was followed by the arrival of the Counter-Reformation which led to a partial re-Catholicizing of the country, as well as a strengthening of Habsburg power as the Protestant nobility had their property confiscated by the emperor.

Immediately after the Battle of the White Mountain the Imperial side erected a votive *chapel* on the battle field dedicated to the Virgin Mary. In 1704–1730 the chapel was enlarged to a church and given a cloister; it then became a centre of Marian pilgrimage. The ceiling frescoes are by Cosmas Damian Asam, Wenzel Lorenz Reiner and Johann Anton Schöpf.

In the Smíchov district the visitor will find the **Villa Bertramka**, a farmhouse dating from the second half of the 17th century in which Mozart stayed with his friends the Dušeks and completed *Don Giovanni* in 1787. Today the house contains the **Mozart Museum** and concerts are held in the garden in the summer.

The way to the **National Memorial on Mount Žižkov** (Národní památník na vrchu Žižkově) leads from the Main Station across Husitská and U památníku (approx. 2 km). On 14 July 1420 the Hussite commander Jan Žižka of Trocnov (Tratzenau) defeated the massively superior forces of King Sigismund. The Hussites advanced singing their great chorale 'Ye who are God's Warriors'; the Catholic nerve failed completely, and Sigismund's forces were routed. At that time the mountain – or rather hill – was called Vítkov (Vítus Hill). The memorial was built in 1929–1932 and has since been enlarged several times. In 1955 it received the grave of the Unknown Soldier and became the mausoleum for Klement Gottwald and other Communist leaders; their remains were removed in 1990. In 1950 an equestrian statue of Jan Žižka, 9 metres high, by Bohumil Kafka was erected here. There is a magnificent view over Prague from the terrace.

Central Bohemia (Střední Čechy)

Karlštejn (Karlstein)

Only 25 km from Prague, hidden between five hills, stands **Karlštejn**, one of the most perfect castles in Europe (plate 23). Charles IV, when he was King of the Holy Roman Empire, commissioned the French architect Matthias of Arras to build a fortress here in the midst of impenetrable forests, as a place of relaxation and inner reflection, and as a treasury for the Imperial jewels and relics. The forbidding exterior gives little indication of the splendour within, where seven churches and chapels emphasized the religious power of the king and emperor.

The foundation stone was laid by Ernest of Pardubice, archbishop of Prague and the king's closest friend, on 10 June 1348, just four years before work began on the building of St Vitus's Cathedral. By November 1355 the residential quarters were completed and Charles IV was able to move in. On 27 March 1357 the Holy Cross Chapel, the heart of the castle, was consecrated in his presence. It was then that the emperor gave the castle its name: Karlstein. Work on the decoration continued until 1367. In 1587–1596 Udalrico Aostali remodelled the castle in the Renaissance style, but in 1887–1899 Josef Mocker and Friedrich Schmidt returned it to its original Gothic appearance and completed the towers.

The road rises steeply from the village of Budňany (now a part of Karlštejn village) to the first gateway on the north side of the castle. Nowadays the castle is entered through the *Ursula (Voršila) Tower*, a fortified corner tower of the lower outer bailey; the original gateway lay to the east. About 100 metres further on the path passes through the second gateway into the Burgrave's Court (Pukrabský dvůr), the upper bailey containing the long Late Gothic *Burgrave's House*. From here a path leads to the *Well Tower* at the furthermost western corner of the precinct. The inmates of the castle used a large wooden treadwheel to draw the water from a depth of 79 metres. Guided tours begin in the Burgrave's Court, and it is also used for theatrical performances on summer evenings.

A large gateway leads to the castle courtyard containing the *Imperial Palace* (Císařský palác), a three-storey building 46 metres long by 12.5 metres wide. Above the stables on the ground floor is the *Vassals' Hall*, a banqueting hall reached up a flight of steps. The Chapel of St Nicholas is a semi-circular extension of the hall eastwards; it has a late 14th century figure of the saint. The emperor's state and residential rooms are on the second floor: his study and bedroom with its small oratory, the private chapel in which the emperor said his morning and evening prayers. On the same floor there was also a hall 'where the emperor's lineage was painted'. An anonymous 'Master of the Family Tree' created this gallery of ancestors of

Charles IV in the 14th century. The third floor was the empress's; her bedroom contains a portable diptych by Tommaso da Modena (c.1370) and a Gothic statue of the Virgin (c.1350).

The residential building is linked by a wooden bridge to *St Mary's Tower* (Mariánská věž). Right at the bottom is a dungeon, above which is the little *Church of St Mary*. Here the wooden ceiling and the walls are decorated with paintings probably by Charles IV's court painter, Nikolaus Wurmser of Strasbourg. The south wall has scenes of Charles receiving relics, while the east wall is painted with an Apocalypse Cycle. On the Neo-Gothic altar is a wooden Gothic statue of St Catherine (after 1400). A pointed arch in the south-west corner of the church leads to a narrow passage called the 'Sepulchre of Christ', which opens through another portal into the tiny *Chapel of St Catherine*, set into the thickness of the south wall of the tower. The chapel is connected with the church by two little openings in the wall; the

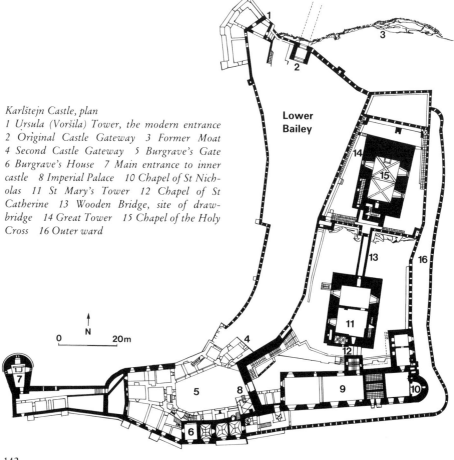

Karlštejn Castle, plan
1 Ursula (Voršila) Tower, the modern entrance
2 Original Castle Gateway   3 Former Moat
4 Second Castle Gateway   5 Burgrave's Gate
6 Burgrave's House   7 Main entrance to inner castle   8 Imperial Palace   10 Chapel of St Nich-olas   11 St Mary's Tower   12 Chapel of St Catherine   13 Wooden Bridge, site of draw-bridge   14 Great Tower   15 Chapel of the Holy Cross   16 Outer ward

Lower Bailey

N
0   20m

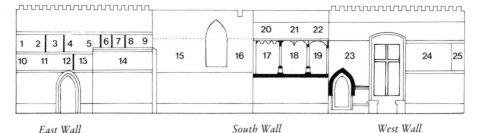

East Wall   South Wall   West Wall

Karlštejn Castle (Karlstein) Church of St Mary
East Wall 1 The Four Angels on the bank of the Euphrates 2 The Horsemen 3 The Mighty Angel gives John the Book to eat 4 John measures the Temple with the Rod 5 The Prophets Enoch and Elijah preach to the people 6 & 7 The Beasts strangle Enoch and Elijah, who lie unburied in the street of the city 8 Enoch and Elijah are taken up into Heaven 9 The City destroyed by an earthquake 10 The Seventh Trump 11 God's temple in Heaven is opened 12 Earthquake 13 The dragon threatens the Woman who is about to give birth 14 The battle between the angels and the devils
South Wall 15 The Four Horsemen of the Apocalypse 16 Souls of the Martyrs below the altar 17 Charles IV with the Dauphin 18 Charles IV with the King of Jerusalem 19 Charles IV with reliquary cross 20–22 Charles IV and Blanche of Valois pray to the Trinity
West Wall 23 The seven choirs of angels 24 The dragon pursues the Women who flies into the wilderness 25 The Woman clothed with the sun

upper one was probably used to pass the oil lamp through and the lower one for exchanging news and orders, since Emperor Charles IV used to spend whole nights in the chapel meditating and pondering political decisions. Around 1365 he had wall paintings in the chapel covered up with semi-precious stones. Above the entrance are portraits of the emperor and his third wife, Anne of Schweidnitz, shown with the relic of the true cross. The stone at the centre of the boss in the vaulted ceiling is a Late Roman head of Medusa dating from the first half of the 4th century.

Leaving the Tower of St Mary through the sacristy vestibule, we then cross a wooden bridge to the massive keep of the castle, the *Great Tower* (Velka věž), 37 metres high, on the uppermost terrace of the castle. With walls up to 6 metres thick, and a drawbridge instead of the present fixed bridge, this tower was once a fortress in its own right – a castle within the castle. A spiral staircase with mural paintings of the legends of St Wenceslas and St Ludmila (c.1360, but altered by 19th-century restorers) leads up to the *Chapel of the Holy Cross* (Kaple sv. Kříže; also called the Chapel of Christ's Passion), the secular and spiritual centre of the castle, the 'Tresor' in which the Imperial crown jewels and relics were kept behind four doors with 19 locks. The treasure – the best guarded in the world – included the golden crown of Emperor Otto the Great, the golden Imperial orb, the silver Imperial sceptre, rings, spurs, a censer and ceremonial robes. The Chapel of the Holy Cross also contained some extremely precious relics, among them a golden ceremonial sceptre set with precious stones and containing a nail and a splinter from the True Cross as well as the point of the lance that pierced His side.

A gilded grille divides the oblong chapel into two halves. The sanctuary with the altar could be entered only by the emperor and the priests. The cross vault of the chapel is covered with gilded discs of Venetian glass in the form of sun, moon and stars. The lower part of the walls is clad with a wide strip encrusted with semi-precious stones – mainly jasper, chalcedony, amethyst, onyx, carneol and agate – set in gilded plaster. Above this are three rows of panel paintings, 128 in all, by Master Theodoric of Prague (Magister Theodoricus), the founder of the Bohemian School of painting and the first Master of the Guild of St Luke at Prague. The patriarchs, prophets, apostles, martyrs, knights, kings and dukes, virgins and widows, together with the suffering Saviour, represent the Company of Heaven. (At present the panels are in the National Gallery in the Convent of St George in Prague Castle.)

The altarpiece triptych of the *Madonna with St Wenceslas and St Palmatius* was painted by Tommaso da Modena in the third quarter of the 14th century. (These are the patron saints of Charles's coronations: St Wenceslas, his Přemyslid predecessor in Bohemia, and St Palmatius, with whose iron crown Charles was made King of Lombardy at Milan in 1355.) The light of 1333 candles reflected from the precious stones and glass discs would have created an effect of unimaginable luminosity, a picture of the Heavenly Jerusalem.

Even after the present restoration is completed the Chapel of the Holy Cross will not be open to visitors, since its condition is simply too delicate. Instead all the details of the chapel will be shown to visitors on video screens with multi-lingual commentary.

Karlštejn Castle was impregnable to the techniques of medieval warfare: in 1422 the Hussites were forced to withdraw after a fruitless siege. They had nevertheless shaken the Bohemian rulers' trust in the fortress's invincibility and five years later, when the Hussite Wars were still raging, the Imperial regalia were removed to Hungary. They never returned to Karlštejn and are now kept in the Treasury of the Hofburg in Vienna; the Bohemian crown jewels are in St Vitus's Cathedral in Prague.

Příbram, 23 km south-west of Prague, was already an important mining town in the 14th century. The silver mined here earned it the protection of the archbishops of Prague from 1348 until the Hussite Wars. To protect the silver ore that had been extracted Ernest of Pardubice, the first archbishop, built a castle, the nucleus of which still survives (ul. Na přikopech). The deanery church of St James the Great dates from the 13th century; major alterations were completed in 1795 and 1869. In 1579 Příbram was granted the status of a Royal mining town. A mining academy was founded here in 1849 which survived for almost a century. Its work is now continued by the College of Mining at the Moravian town of Ostrava (Ostrau). In 1875 the Adalbert Shaft (Votěšská šachta) was the first mining shaft in the world to reach a depth of 1000 metres. Nowadays lead, zinc and uranium ores are extracted and processed at Příbram.

On the south-eastern edge of Příbram rises **Svatá Hora** ('Holy Mountain'), the oldest and most famous Marian shrine in Bohemia. The shrine (colour plate 11) on the hill (586 metres high) developed from a small 14th-century Gothic church. This was taken over around the middle of the 17th century by the Jesuits, who had it altered in 1661–1687 to designs by the

Karlštejn circa 1840

Italian architect Carlo Lurago. The enlarged buildings stood on a high terrace built of ashlar blocks and were enclosed by a fortress-like arcaded ambulatory for the parties of pilgrims. Since 1658 a covered 'Scala Santa' (Holy Stairway), altered in 1727-28 by Kilian Ignaz Dientzenhofer, has led up from Příbram to the shrine.

The *arcaded ambulatory* with rich sculptural decoration contains four octagonal chapels, eight niche-shaped chapels and a bell-tower. There are two gateways leading to the shrine: the *Prague Portal* to the east was created in 1702–1705 by Johann Brokoff, while the *Březnic Portal* to the south was built by Andreas Philipp Quittainer in 1707. The (newly restored) ceiling paintings showing scenes from the life of the Virgin and the history of the Holy Mountain are by Josef Mathauser (1880–1890). On the north side of the ambulatory is the residence of the Jesuits, who still run the pilgrimage shrine.

The *Church of Our Lady* is notable for the three arcade chapels on its east side (the corresponding chapels on the west side were walled up around the middle of the 18th century). The chapel on the left is dedicated to St Anne, that on the right to St Joseph and middle one to the Visitation. On the terrace balustrade are a large number of statues of angels and saints. The church itself consists of a rectangular sanctuary with a sacristy (chapel of St Francis Xavier) to the north and the chapel of St Ignatius to the south. An interesting Late Gothic statue of St Anne (after 1500) can be seen in the porch.

Křivoklát (Bürglitz)

About 50 km west of Prague, on the left bank of the Berounka river in the middle of thickly wooded hills stands the magnificent castle of **Křivoklát** (plate 24), formerly called **Bürglitz** (or Pürglitz). One of the oldest and most interesting fortresses in Bohemia, it has been painstakingly restored and lovingly furnished.

The vast forests in the region of Rakovník were a favourite hunting ground of the Přemyslid princes in the 9th and 10th centuries. One of their hunting lodges was Křivoklát, which was still a fortified homestead in the 11th century, but was converted by Vladislav I at the beginning of the 12th century into a defensible castle where the prince incarcerated his recalcitrant cousin and rival for the dukedom of Bohemia, Otto II of Moravia, for three years. King Otakar I Přemysl (1197–1230) liked to stay at Křivoklát. In the mid-13th century his son, Wenceslas I, replaced the wooden buildings with a stone castle, which from 1241 bore the German name *Burglin*, or later *Burgleis*. The royal hunting castle became the setting for lavish festivities and the elaborate performances of the minnesingers. The remarkable castle chapel in the south range was founded by Otakar II Přemysl.

Between 1316 and 1323 the future Emperor Charles IV spent his childhood in the castle, where he was literally and metaphorically kept in the dark by his father, John of Luxemburg. After his wife's death, however, John sent the seven-year-old Charles to France. He did not return to Burglin until 1334, when as Governor of Bohemia and Moravia he was accompanied by his young wife, Blanche of Valois, who wrote: 'It came to pass in the year of Our Lord 1334 in the middle of spring that my lord and husband brought me to Beheim (Bohemia). The land was indeed charming, and the people everywhere were of cheerful and honest mind. They must indeed have loved us and I sought to repay them with kindness. In March of the following year I was delivered of my daughter Margaret. My husband had nightingales trapped throughout the land and placed in the woods at the foot of the castle so that I might take pleasure in their song. They too obeyed his will, and nested there forthwith and their notes filled the air and people's hearts.'

The German king, Sigismund, took advantage of the Hussite Wars to plunder the richly appointed castles of Bohemia, especial Křivoklát. At the end of the 15th century and beginning of the 16th century the Jagiellon kings, Vladislav II and Louis (Ludvík) II remodelled the castle in the Late Gothic style. From 1548 to 1564 Jan Augusta, the bishop of the Bohemian Brethren, and his companion Jakub Bílek languished in the castle dungeons. At the same time (1559–1564) Archduke Ferdinand of the Tyrol and Philippine Welser, the beautiful daughter of an Augsburg merchant, hid in the castle until the Habsburg Emperor Ferdinand I agreed to recognize their secret, morganatic marriage. Philippine bore her husband three children there. Rudolph II also liked to spend time at Bürglitz.

In 1597 and again in 1643 Křivoklát went up in flames and seems to have fallen into ruin, since the Habsburgs now resided only at Vienna. In 1685 the Imperial court sold the castle to Count Waldstein, and it finally passed by marriage to the princely family of Fürstenberg, who repaired it in 1826, and between 1882 and 1923 had it reconstructed and restored in the

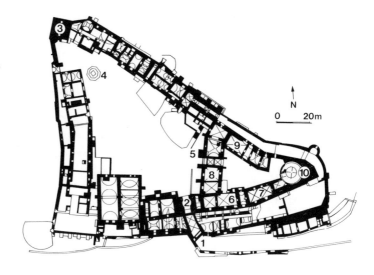

Křivoklát (Bürglitz), plan
1 Gatehouse
2 Entrance Tower
3 Huderka Tower
4 Well
5 Sentry loggia
6 King's
    apartments
7 Chapel
8 Royal Hall
    (Knights' Hall)
9 Queen's
    apartments
10 Round Tower

style of the Jagiellon period by Josef Mocker, Humbert Walcher von Moltheim and Kamil Hilbert. In 1929 Křivoklát was acquired by the Czechoslovak state.

The visitor enters the castle through a porch with the arms of the family of Vladislav II displayed above the portal leading to the *Passage Tower*, an imposing square gate tower. Its counterpart is the *Huderka Tower* at the north-west corner of the outer bailey. The buildings in the south, west and north ranges of the outer bailey (kitchen, soldiers' lodgings, burgrave's office, captain's house and brewery) were almost all built in the time of the Jagiellons. The east range of the enclosed court is occupied by the *Main Castle*. The Early Gothic entrance to the inner bailey is flanked by a sentry post (loggia), on the upper corner of which are two shields, held up by angels and bearing the letter 'W', the cypher of King Vladislav II Jagiello (which the visitor may have seen in Prague on the King's Oratory in St Vitus's). Projecting from the façade above the gateway is the delightful oriel window of the Royal Hall on the first floor; below the oriel are reliefs with the busts of Vladislav II and his son Louis II. The Royal Hall is linked to the Passage Tower by a magnificent balcony. On its inner side the west range of the Main Castle is surmounted by a wooden gallery on tall arches. The south range consists of the king's residence and the *Castle Chapel* built by Master Hans Spiess in 1499–1516. The net vault is supported on stone corbels decorated with curiously carved and colourfully painted heads. The magnificent winged altarpiece in the sanctuary is a fine example of Late-Gothic woodcarving (c. 1490) depicting the Coronation of the Virgin and scenes from the life of the Virgin. Also noteworthy are the stained-glass windows (c. 1500) of St George and St Wenceslas. Below the chapel is the gloomy *Augusta Prison* where Bishop Jan Augusta was held for sixteen years, and which today houses a collection of beautifully designed instruments of torture and execution.

The three-aisled *Royal Hall* (also called the Great Hall or Knights' Hall) with its high star vaults and delightful figured corbels, each of them different, was part of the Přemyslid palace and is now used for an exhibition of Gothic painting and sculpture.

A balcony with filigree-like vaulting connects the Knights' Hall with the queen's residence in the north range of the castle, which was repaired in 1516–1522 following a fire. The present building was recreated by Kamil Hilbert in 1921 in the Late Gothic style, and some of the rooms still have their original early 20th-century furnishings from the time when the Fürstenbergs lived there. The tallest building in the castle precinct is a massive four-storey *Round Tower* guarding the eastern side of the castle. Parts of its masonry date back to 13th century, and the early days of the castle as a Přemyslid hunting lodge.

10 km north-west of Křivoklát is the château of *Lany*, the summer residence of the Presidents of Czechoslovakia and the burial place of the first President, Tomáš Garrigue Masaryk, and his son Jan. Even when the Masaryks were removed from history by the Communists, their graves rarely lacked a flower or two; and now the pilgrimage is a popular outing.

On 10 June 1942 all 184 male inhabitants of the mining village of **Lidice** (about 20 km north west of Prague) were shot by SS units, the 198 women were transported to the concentration camp at Ravensbrück, and the 98 children taken to be 'Germanized' in SS families or sent to extermination camps. The SS burned the village and razed it to the ground. Only 143 women and 16 children returned after the war.

The massacre was carried out in revenge for the assassination of Reinhard Heydrich, the Deputy Reichsprotektor of Bohemia and Moravia, who died of wounds on 4 June. Seven members of the Free Czechoslovak Army with orders from the government in exile had parachuted in near Prague; and two of them had thrown a bomb into Heydrich's convertible. All seven committed suicide after being holed up in the church of Sts Cyril and Methodius in Prague; the baffled Germans seized flimsy evidence to justify wiping Lidice off the map. In this they did not succeed, since countless villages and mining communities over the world joined the campaign vowing that 'Lidice shall not die'.

A large, plain cross with a barbed wire wreath now marks the centre of the former village, and masonry foundations mark the sites of some houses. Young people of many countries planted 3000 rose bushes on the plot next to the little museum, and a new village was built a little further north. Lidice is now a national memorial, a place of international understanding and a warning to all peoples to resist every sort of repression.

Mělník

To the north of Prague, at the point where the Vltava joins the Elbe (Labe) stands the beautiful old castle of **Mělník** set on a high hill planted with vineyards, and with it a town with a population of approx. 22,000. As early as the 9th century a residence of the Pšovan princes stood on this strategically important height on the north bank of the Elbe, the settlement connected with the castle was called *Pšov*. Towards the end of the 9th century the Pšovan prince Slavibor gave his daughter Ludmila (later canonized) in marriage to the Přemyslid prince, Bořivoj. After Slavibor's death the lands of the Pšovans passed to the Přemyslids, an early step towards the unification of Bohemia. Ludmila liked to stay at the Pšovan castle and brought up her grandson Václav (later St Wenceslas) there. In the 10th century Pšov developed into a sort of dower house for widowed Bohemian princesses. The settlement became a town and was given the name *Mělník*. Around the year 1000 Princess Hemma, the widow of Boleslav II, even had a mint producing silver coinage at her residence at Mělník. The wooden fortress gave way to a Romanesque stone castle, and at this time a small castle church dedicated to St Peter was built. This was enlarged c. 1126 to a three-aisled collegiate church dedicated to the apostles Peter and Paul.

At the beginning of the 13th century high walls were built around the town, and the castle was remodelled in Early Gothic style (west range). In 1274 King Otakar II Přemysl raised Mělník to the status of a royal town, giving it the laws of Magdeburg. The castle remained a widows' residence, and after Otakar's death his wife Kunhuta lived in the castle. Charles IV declared Mělník a royal 'dower town', which was inalienable and in times of emergency could not be sold, but only mortgaged.

When Charles was crowned King of Burgundy at Arles in 1365 he brought vine-growers from there to the Elbe to plant vineyards on the warm southern slopes that were sheltered from the wind. The red burgundy of Mělník is still prized, even outside Czechoslovakia. During the Hussite Wars (1419–1435) Mělník, which by now had a predominantly Czech population, stood resolutely on the side of the Reformers. In 1438, 1439 and 1442 congresses of the Utraquist party were held in the castle. Under George of Poděbrady and the Jagiellons the town experienced an economic boom and the wine-growers made good profits. In 1475 Johanka of Rožmitál, George of Poděbrady's widow, died at Mělník castle, bringing to an end its almost 600 year old tradition as a royal dower house. Thereafter the castle changed owners, the town freed itself from castle rule and by the end of the 15th century tensions between town and castle had reached such a pitch that fortifications were built between the two. In 1542 Zdislav Berka of Dubá built the north wing, turning the Late Gothic castle into a Renaissance schloss. In 1646 the by then dilapidated building was acquired by Heřman Czernín of Chudenice who restored it. The Baroque south wing was added in the 1690s. In 1753 the schloss with its estates passed by marriage to the Lobkowicz princes. Since they resided in Prague, the stylistic development of the schloss was frozen. Henceforth it was used for wine-growing and in 1895 even the hill on which the schloss stands was made into a terraced vineyard.

The *schloss* is approached through the inconspicuous main gate (Hlavní brán) at the southeast corner of the complex, which from the outside looks like a large block of flats. The gateway was given its present appearance in the 1690's, when the wooden superstructure above the Late Gothic ground floor was removed and the masonry wall continued up to the height of the neighbouring south wing.

In the courtyard the visitor is aware of three architectural styles: the long *west range* is basically Gothic with Baroque alterations of the late 17th century; the *north range* preserves the purity of its Renaissance features (loggias with arcades on both floors and delicate sgraffito decoration across the whole façade); while the *south range* is Baroque, even though the massive arcades at ground floor and first floor level have certain parallels with the north range. The east side is closed by a wall with a defensive passage running along it. Inside the schloss is a museum with interesting exhibits connected with wine growing and folklore, and a gallery with Baroque Czech painting, as well as a terrace restaurant with a spectacular view over the Elbe, the Vltava and the surrounding vineyards, and a wine bar.

The provostal church of **Sts Peter and Paul** (Kostel sv. Petra a Pavla) developed from the 11th-century castle chapel; the rectangular tower on the south-west side of the present church is still pure Romanesque. Construction of the church began in the first half of the 14th century, around 1380 a Gothic presbyterium was built, and after 1480 the three-aisled hall-nave. Between 1485 and 1488 Hans Spiess of Frankfurt on Main erected the great façade tower, though the present turrets and onion domes date from 1681. The most precious treasure in the church is a Late Gothic silver-gilt monstrance, made in Prague at the end of the 15th century, with statuettes of the Madonna, St Catherine and St Dorothy, St Wenceslas and St Vitus.

The spacious market place (colour plate 18) is worth a visit, with its smart arcaded houses

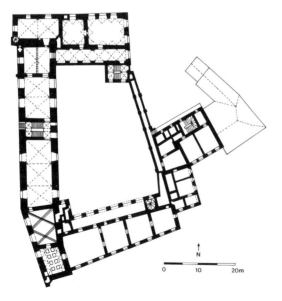

Mělník Castle, plan
first floor

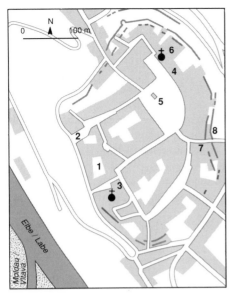

Mělník
1 Castle   2 Charles IV Monument   3 Provostal Church   4 Town Hall   5 Wine Harvest Column   6 Capuchin Monastery with Church of the Fourteen Auxiliary Saints   7 Prague Gate   8 Town walls

and its town hall, which is distinguished from its neighbours by its clock tower and two curved gables. Other points of interest are the *Prague Gate* (Pražská brána) on the eastern side of the old town, and the remains of the town fortifications dating from the 13th century.

7 km north-west of Mělník, also on the right bank of the Elbe and surrounded by vineyards, is the town of **Liběchov** (Liboch) with its carefully restored 16th-century château of the same name. At the beginning of the 18th century the Renaissance building was extended with a new Baroque wing facing the park (probably by František Maximilián Kaňka). In the first half of the 19th century Baron Veith gathered around him at Liběchov a circle of patriotic scholars and artists influenced by the teachings of the priest and founder of Slavonic philology, Josef Dobrovský (1753–1829). The philosopher Bernhard Bolzano (1781–1848) belonged to this group as did the painter Josef Navrátil (1798–1865), who decorated the château in 1838–1843 with scenes from the Czech national epic *Vlasta* (Fatherland) by Karl Egon Ebert. Temporary art exhibitions are held at the château.

17 km north-east of Mělník is the rocky **Kokořín Valley** (Kokořínský důl) formed by the river Pškova, now a nature reserve and favourite place for excursions. It is dominated by the formidable yet picturesque Kokořín (Kokorschin), a Gothic fortress dating from the first half of the 14th century. The castle was damaged in the Hussite Wars and fell into ruin. In 1911–1918 it was restored by the architect Eduard Sochor for the industrialist Špaček von Starburg, and another restoration was carried out in 1975–1977. In the castle is a display of memorabilia of the Czech Romantic poet Karl Hynek Mácha (1810–1836).

15 km west of Mělník, rising from fertile farmland, is a 459 metre high basalt mountain: the **Říp** (Georgsberg). According to a legend Čech, the ancestor of all the Czechs, took possession of Bohemia from here and gave the land his name. Since 1126 the Romanesque *Rotunda of St George* has stood on the mountain, a reminder of the victory of Duke Soběslav I of Bohemia over the army of Emperor Lothar at Chlumec (Kulm) in 1126.

14 km south-west of Mělník stands the Renaissance château of **Nelahozeves** (Mühlhausen) on the Vltava, begun in 1553 for Florian Griesbach, Secretary to the Chancellor of Bohemia. Its exterior has splendid sgraffito decoration, while the fine interiors now house the Central Bohemian Gallery, with European paintings from Bohemian collections. The village below the château contains the birthplace of the composer Antonín Dvořák (1841–1904), whose father was a butcher here; it is now a museum.

20 km south-east of Mělník, overlooking the River Jizera (whose frequent floodings give this area the nickname of the Bohemian Venice) is the castle of **Benátky**, which Rudolph II gave to the Danish astronomer Tycho Brahe. Here on 4 February 1600 Johann Kepler and Brahe finally met: co-founders, in Koestler's words, of a new universe.

Kutná Hora (Kuttenberg)

With the exception of Prague, **Kutná Hora**, because of its attractive situation in the deep valley of the river Vrchlice and its fine old buildings, is perhaps the most interesting town for

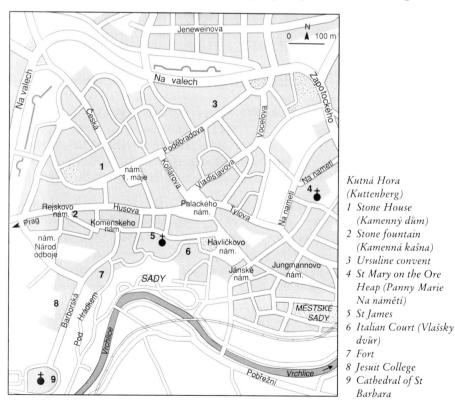

Kutná Hora (Kuttenberg)
1 *Stone House (Kamenný dům)*
2 *Stone fountain (Kamenná kašna)*
3 *Ursuline convent*
4 *St Mary on the Ore Heap (Panny Marie Na náměti)*
5 *St James*
6 *Italian Court (Vlašsky dvůr)*
7 *Fort*
8 *Jesuit College*
9 *Cathedral of St Barbara*

visitors to Bohemia. The rich silver deposits soon led to the expansion of the settlement to become the second largest town in Bohemia after Prague, even though its revenues were siphoned off by Charles IV to make Prague a metropolis worthy of the Empire. The first mention of Kuttenberg is in 1276 when exploitation of the silver mines was increasing. Silver ore had, however, been dug here earlier: there is evidence that at the end of the 10th century coins were being minted on the Vrchlice river for the princely dynasty of Slavnik. Around 1300, eleven years after Kutná Hora had been raised to the status of a town, work began on the construction of the Vlašský dvůr (Italian Court) as the royal mint. Here coiners from Florence struck the 'Prague groschen', a silver piece that became recognized and highly prized throughout Europe for its high silver content.

The Bohemian kings often resided at Kutná Hora. On 18 January 1409 the 'Kuttenberg Decree' was signed here by Wenceslas IV at the instigation of Jan Hus, changing the statutes of Charles University in Prague in favour of the Czechs and causing an exodus of the German professors and students, who then founded a new university at Leipzig. In 1471 the Bohemian Estates, meeting in the Italian Court, elected Vladislav Jagiello, the son of the Polish king, as king of Bohemia. The 16th century saw a decline in silver mining at Kutná Hora, and while the mint continued to function until 1726, the status of the town diminished.

The centre of Kutná Hora is the main square, Palackého nám., surrounded by fine Renaissance buildings including the Old Town Hall. In Šultyskovo nám. the large *Plague Column*, dedicated to the Virgin, was made by F. Baugut (1713–1715) to commemorate the plague of 1713. Jan Šultys, after whom the square is named, was mayor of Kutná Hora and one of the 27 Protestant ringleaders executed on 21 July 1621 in front of the Town Hall in the Old Town Square in Prague (see p. 45). In nám. 1. máje stands the Late Gothic *Stone House* (Kamenný dům), built in 1485–1495 by an unknown architect with a loggia, oriel and tall gable. The sculptures are attributed to Brixi, a stonemason from Breslau (Wrocław): the patron saints of Bohemia decorate the oriel, a statue of the Virgin is on the gable; Adam and Eve were added by the restorers, Jan Kastner and František Hnátek in 1900–1902. The Stone House is now the Town Museum (Městské muzeum).

In Husova třída František Maximilián Kaňka built the beautiful church of *St John of Nepomuk* (Kostel sv. Jan Nepomuckého) between 1734 and 1754. The twelve-sided Late Gothic *Stone Fountain* (Kamenná kašna) (1493–1495), in Rejskovo nám., with its rich blind arcading, is probably a work of the great architect and sculptor Matouš Rejsek, who gave his name to the square. The *Marble House* (U Marmorů) in the south-west corner of the square has a fine Renaissance portal.

The former *Ursuline Convent* (Klášter uršulinek) in Poděbradova was built by Kilian Ignaz Dientzenhofer in 1733–1743 for Countess Eleonora Trauttmansdorff. The Baroque building is decorated with statues of saints by Jan Brázda, and the oval staircase in the corner between the two wings of the complex is surmounted by a dome. The Neo-Baroque convent

Inn-sign in Kutná Hora

church was built by the Viennese architect Friedrich Ohmann in 1898–1901. In Na náměti street on the east side of the old town the Gothic church of *Our Lady on the Ore Heap* (Panny Marie Na náměti) contains the grave of the Peter Johann Brandl (1668–1735), one of the greatest and most dynamic of Bohemian Baroque painters.

Above the river Vrchlice in a square called U Vlašského dvora (At the Italian Court) stands the Gothic church of *St James* (Chram sv. Jakuba; 1330–1420). The window tracery suggests that the Parler workshop was involved in its construction. In 1567 Master Augustin built the north tower which has five storeys and is 83 metres high; it was not until 1737 that it was given its Baroque onion dome roof; the south tower remained unfinished. The interior of the church is impressive for its rich furnishings. The magnificent high altar is the work of Georg Riedl; the paintings of St James (1752) and the Holy Trinity (1734) are by Franz Xaver Balko and Peter Brandl. The copy of Annibale Carracci's Pietà is by Karel Škréta (1673). The *Last Supper* (1515) is the work of Hans Efeldar, and the Early Baroque group of *Christ and the Sons of Zebedee* was carved by Kaspar Eigler in 1678.

At the end of the 13th century Wenceslas II summoned coiners from Florence to Kutná Hora. In the *Vlašský dvůr* (Italian Court) they struck the famous Prague groschen. Some remains of the early mint can still be seen in the masonry of the north and west wings of the building. The Italian Court was constantly changing its appearance; the final remodelling took place in 1898. The most interesting parts of the complex, which was later also used as a royal residence, were built in the reign of Wenceslas IV. Between 1390 and 1400 he erected the east wing with residential quarters, the tower at the front, and the chapel. The *Chapel of St Wenceslas* is reached up an exterior spiral staircase. The four vaulting bays of the square room spring from a central pier, and there is a polygonal chancel. The walls are decorated with representations of the 'Wenceslas Legend' by the Art Nouveau painter František Urban (1900). The three Gothic winged altarpieces were made around 1500 and depict the Death of the Virgin. The *Council Chamber* in the residential quarters contains a Late Gothic 'Ecce Homo' (Christ with the Crown of Thorns) and an elaborately carved bench (both early 16th century), while in the *Cellars* are representations and tools connected with minting in the middle ages.

The *Fort* (Hrádek) on Barborská ul. goes back to a 14th-century wooden fortress. It was replaced in the 15th century by a stone building which was intended as a royal castle but was in fact used as a second mint, since the kings preferred to reside at the Italian Court. In the same street is the former *Jesuit College* (Jezuitska kolej), a monumental building by Domenico Orsi (1626–1667), which was used as a barracks from the late 18th until the early

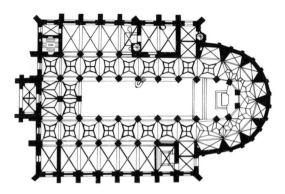

Kutná Hora (Kuttenberg)
Cathedral of St Barbara, plan

19th centuries. The thirteen Baroque statues on the balustrade, extending as far as St Barbara's, were made by F. Baugut.

The five-aisled *Cathedral of St Barbara* (Chrám sv. Barbory; plate 25) dedicated to the patron saint of miners, was commissioned by the mine-owners of Kutná Hora. The plans were made by Peter Parler, who began work on the building in 1388. After interruption because of the Hussite Wars, construction was continued from 1481 to 1489 by Master Hanuš; from 1489 to 1506 Matouš Rejsek was working on the cathedral, and from 1512 to 1547 Benedikt Rieth. The work was completed in 1558. The building was last altered in 1884–1893 by Josef Mocker and Ludvík Lábler.

The glorious, tent-like roof was built over the hall-nave and choir by Master Vaněk in 1532. The interior of the cathedral has an impressive 'loop-star' vault over the aisled hall by Benedikt Rieth, while the net vaults in the choir were designed by Matouš Rejsek, who filled the interstices between some of the ribs with the arms of the lands belonging to the Bohemian kingdom of the Jagiellons and to the guilds of craftsmen in Kutná Hora.

The high altarpiece with St Barbara on its left wing is a replica of the original Baroque altarpiece. The Smíšek Chapel contains some valuable wall paintings: the *Cumaean Sibyl*, the *Arrival of the Queen of Sheba* and the *Crucifixion* (before 1490). A triptych shows the Virgin surrounded by saints. Kutná Hora's economy is represented by a wall statue of a miner in the costume of the period around 1700, with his miner's lamp, tools and bag. Other working men, this time striking coins in the mint (third quarter 15th century) can be seen above the Passion scenes in the south aisle. The Gothic statue of the enthroned Virgin and Child in the northern part of the choir ambulatory was made around 1380 and given Baroque decorations (sceptre, orb and polychromy) in the 18th century.

The former Cistercian monastery of *Sedlec* (Sedletz) on the north-eastern edge of the town dates from 1142. It was closed down in the Josephine reforms in 1784, eventually being converted into a tobacco factory in 1812. Its buildings include the Gothic church of *St Mary* (Chrám Panny Marie), the remarkable first work of Johann Santini-Aichel. The original church (c. 1300) had been destroyed in the Hussite Wars, and it was precisely to emphasize the return to the pure Catholic faith that the Cistercians chose to revive the Gothic style (just as the Jesuits chose to revive the cult of St John of Nepomuk). The result, built between 1699 and 1707, is breathtaking, and almost surrealistic, as Santini-Aichel exploits a new material – stucco – to draw architectonically impossible or useless lines over his vaults. Rieth's vault at nearby Kutná Hora was clearly an inspiration. In the monastery cemetery (about 400 metres north of the church) is a 12th-century Gothic chapel, which was used as an ossuary after the great plague of 1318. In the lower part of the two-storey chapel all the furnishings (altar, candelabrum, coats of arms etc.) are made of human bones.

Kolín, a small town on the Elbe, is famous for a battle during the Seven Years' War in which the Austrians defeated the Prussians on 18 June 1757. The town was founded in the early 13th century, on the site of a fortified Slav settlement, by German colonists summoned to Bohemia by King Otakar I Přemysl. By 1261 work had begun on the three-aisled church of St Bartholomew, which was dramatically extended in the 14th century by Peter Parler with a High Gothic choir, one of the most beautiful works of ecclesiastical architecture in Bohemia. In 1421 the town came under Hussite rule and the Germans lost their majority in the town council.

The old town has the grid street-plan typical of the German colonial towns. Its large market place is lined with Baroque burghers' houses, mostly designed by the local architect Josef Jedlička after a great fire in 1734. A particularly fine example is No. 46. The Neo-Renaissance town hall was built in 1887.

View of Kolín from Merian's Topography

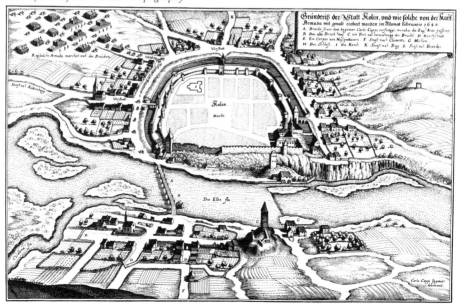

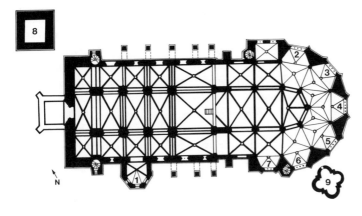

Kolín, Cathedral of St
Bartholomew, plan
1 Kokov Chapel
2 Bakers' Chapel
3 Brewers' Chapel
4 Butchers' Chapel
5 Sperlinkov Chapel
6 Chapel of St John
7 Chapel of St
    Wenceslas
8 Belltower
9 Ossuary

The church of *St Bartholomew* (Chrám sv. Bartoloměje), the most important building in Kolín, stands at the highest point in the old town. The three-aisled hall-church with its two octagonal towers (70 metres high) was built in 1261–1300 on the site of the Slavic fortifications. Romanesque remnants, such as a crypt, indicate that there was a church here even before the Early Gothic building. In 1349 a fire swept through the town damaging the cathedral. Ten years later Emperor Charles IV entrusted his court architect Peter Parler, who had been working since 1352 on St Vitus's Cathedral and since 1357 on Charles Bridge, with the restoration of the church at Kolín. Parler demolished the old chancel and built a new choir with seven chapels and richly traceried windows. In 1378 St Bartholomew's was consecrated. The massive, free-standing belltower was built in 1504, and the Baroque ossuary in front of the south-east side of the church in 1733. In 1796 the Gothic high altar, together with a number of side altars, the organ and many paintings and sculptures, was destroyed by fire, and in 1797 the cathedral had to be given a temporary roof. It was not until 1904–1910 that this was replaced by a permanent structure in keeping with the style of the building. The Neo-Gothic high altar also dates from 1910. The painting of the *Martyrdom of St Bartholomew* in the Šperlinkov Chapel is by Peter Brandl (1734).

Brandl is commemorated in the name of the street next to the cathedral. At Brandlova ul. 35 is the town *Museum*, which includes one of the most important collections of prehistoric objects in Bohemia. The collection was founded by Dr František Dvořák (1896–1943), a doctor from Kolín, who was executed at Dresden because of his involvement in a resistance group. There are excavated objects dating from the palaeolithic to the medieval period: palaeolithic stone tools, neolithic funnel beaker ceramics, bronze weapons of the Bylan Culture, Celtic coins, Marcoman jewellery, and grave goods of the early Slavic period. A special section of the museum commemorates Jean Gaspard Debureau (1796–1846), the 'King of Pierrots', the most famous mime of the 19th century. His father, Philippe Germain Debureau, was a Frenchman who came to Kolín as a soldier in the Austrian army and married there. After the birth of Jean Gaspard he worked at first as a barber before travelling the world as an acrobat. In 1813 the whole family appeared at the Théâtre des Funambules in Paris as a troupe of tight-rope artists. Jean Gaspard mimed the part of Bajazzo and many other characters, but was most famous as Pierrot. His work developed mime, bringing it recognition as a branch of ballet and thus preparing the way for his great French successors Jean-Louis Barrault and Marcel Marceau.

Not far beyond the town the National road No. 12/E15 to Prague crosses the *Battlefield of Kolín*. In May 1757 Frederick the Great of Prussia began the siege and bombardment of Prague. In an attempt to force the king to raise the siege the Austrian Field-Marshal Leopold Josef von Daun took his army past Prague on the eastern side so that he could attack Frederick from the rear. Early on the morning of 18 June the two armies clashed west of Kolín. Frederick lost the battle, and was forced to give up the siege of Prague and leave Bohemian territory. In thanks for the victory the Austrian empress instituted the Order of Maria Theresa. There are monuments commemorating the battle near the villages of Krečhoř and Vítězov and on Vysoká hill.

5 km west of Plaňany a road branches southwards to the little town of **Kouřim** 6 km away. Although it shows little evidence of its long history, Kouřim was founded in 1260 as a royal town. Dating from this period are the remains of the town walls, the archidiaconal church of St Stephen, and Prague Gate. Near the town archaeologists have uncovered an old Slavic defensive earthwork enclosing an area of 40 hectares. The town *Museum* in the large market place is worth a visit, as is the open-air *Museum of Village Life* with examples of rural architecture from the 17th and 18th centuries, which opened in 1972.

Konopiště (Konopischt)

One of the most beautiful castles in Bohemia, **Konopiště** (colour plate 17) was the summer residence of Archduke Franz Ferdinand, the heir to the Austrian throne, who was assassinated with his wife Sophie by a Serbian nationalist at Sarajevo on 28 June 1914.

Despite the castle's many changes of owners – Sternbergs, Hodějovskýs, Vrtbas, Lobkoviczes processing through, as the various religious and political conflicts kept Bohemia alight – since it was built in the 1280's by the Benešov family, it is the Archduke's personality alone that dominates. Here he was able to indulge a fine talent for landscape gardening, a delicate taste in statuary, and an insatiable bloodthirstiness as a shot. Here too Franz Ferdinand enjoyed domestic happiness with his adored morganatic wife, the Czech Countess Sophie Chotek, away from the disapproval of his family and the scorn of the Viennese aristocracy.

Konopiště's present appearance is due to the ubiquitous Josef Mocker; its interiors were designed by Franz Schmoranz. The rich collections, based on Franz Ferdinand's Italian

Konopiště, engraving by V.A. Berger, 1802–1804

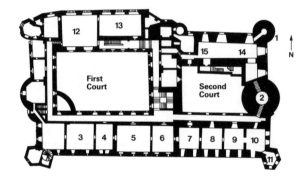

Konopiště Castle, plan
First Floor
1 Václavka   2 East Tower   3 Columned Saloon   4 Reception Room   5 Great Dining Hall (Lobkowicz Hall)   6 Pantry   7 Tirpitz Saloon   8 Bedroom of Grand Admiral Tirpitz   9 Bedroom of Kaiser Wilhelm II   10 Vrtba Sallon   11 Tower Chamber
Second Floor
12 Smoking Room   13 Library   14 Chapel
Third Floor
15 Armoury (above chapel)

inheritance from the d'Estes has, however, been creamed off in favour of the National Gallery and the Museum of Military History in Prague.

From the car park beside a large modern restaurant the walk up the drive to the château takes about 10 minutes. A magnificent *Baroque gateway* designed by František Maximilián Kaňka in 1725 stands alone in front of the bridge across the moat. The actual gateway to the château is flanked by statues of *Bellona* and *Mars* by Matthias Braun. The bronze statue of a man with dogs was made around 1900.

The seven round towers of the French Gothic castle, all of equal height and projecting at various distances from the wall, have only partly preserved their original form; they were integrated into the castle complex, the upper parts were altered with angular additions or greatly increased in height (East Tower). The only round corner tower is the *Václavka*, named after King Wenceslas (Václav) IV, who was held captive by the Czech nobility in the tower towards the end of the 14th century. Above the west portal are the coats of arms of Přech Hodějovský (a golden carp on a blue ground) and his wife Dorota of Harrachov (Dorothea von Harrachsdorf). The date 1605 above the portals and window mouldings refers to the year when the building work undertaken by the Hodějovskýs was completed.

The interior of the château contains lavishly furnished rooms reflecting the luxurious lifestyle of the archduke: the columned Saloon, the *Great Dining Room* (Lobkowicz Room) with two tapestries made at the royal Gobelin factory in Paris (1774) depicting scenes from Cervantes's *Don Quixote*; the Tirpitz Saloon; Kaiser Wilhelm II's Bedroom; the Vrtba Saloon; and the Smoking Room. The original dedication of the *Castle Chapel* of Konopište to St Giles was changed in the Baroque period to St Hubert, the patron saint of huntsmen. The walls of the staircase and corridors are covered with thousands of hunting trophies and natural history engravings with German inscriptions. The *Armoury* displays historic arms and armour from the 15th to the 19th centuries.

At the end of the 19th century famous garden architects such as Mössmer from Vienna, Marchant from England, and Rozínek from Prague created a wonderful *Park*, which now covers an area of more than 225 hectares with pools, lakes and game reserves. The terraced garden on the south side of the château, however, is 18th century and is on the site of the filled-in moat. Immediately in front of the Baroque gateway are gleaming white statues of gods which stand out against the green of the gardens. The highlight of the park is the *Rose Garden*, created in 1906–1913 with more than 200 varieties of roses to delight the visitor; scattered amongst them is more attractive garden sculpture: statues from Modena, the Venetian vases, the busts of fauns, obelisks, and in the middle a classical column with a statue òf Cleopatra. The statue of Poseidon in the eastern part of the park was formerly part of the decoration of the gardens of Catajo near Padua. The Way of the Cross here was laid out by Countess O'Kelly (née Vrtbová) in memory of seven of her serfs fatally wounded in an uprising in 1775.

Southern Bohemia (Jižní Čechy)

České Budějovice (Budweis)

České Budějovice with a population of almost 100,000 is the regional capital of South Bohemia. Its chief attraction is its large quadrangular market place – one of the finest squares in Europe – surrounded by old arcaded houses including the magnificent town hall. Its many interesting buildings and the medieval fortifications, as well as the former butchers' stalls in which the visitor can sample the town's famous Budvar beer, better known as Budweiser, make České Budějovice worth an extended visit.

It was in 1265 that King Otakar II Přemysl, in his quest to build up a power base independent of the great feudal lords, granted a town charter to the German colonial settlement of Budweis at the confluence of the Malše with the Vltava. It was on one of the major salt routes, and salt remained one of the most important elements in Budějovice's economy. At the same time Otakar also founded a Dominican friary here. In the 14th century the town developed into the main trading centre for southern Bohemia and in 1358 Emperor Charles IV granted it *Stapelrecht* among other privileges, which meant that all merchants passing by had to put their goods on sale at Budweis for a specified time before they could continue their journey. Perhaps such marks of royal favour ensured Budweis's staunch Catholicism during the Hussite troubles. In the 16th century the discovery of substantial deposits of silver led to the establishment of a royal mint and a mining office. At that time Budweis was the third largest town in Bohemia, after Prague and Plzeň, and the largest market for grain and wood in the south of the country. In 1631, during the Thirty Years' War, Budějovice was still unshakeably Catholic, a fact recognized by the Imperial side who brought the Royal crown and the land records (see p. 96) to safety within its walls. Since 1785 Budějovice has been the seat of a bishop, whose diocese covers the whole of southern Bohemia. In 1827 the first horse-drawn railway in Europe was opened, between Budweis and Linz. Industrialization in the 19th century brought increasing numbers of Czechs to the town with the result that the population's German majority dwindled until Germans were outnumbered at the turn of the century. Today České Budějovice (or 'Czech Budweis', so called to distinguish it from the small town of Moravské Budějovice, or 'Moravian Budweis' or 'Budwitz') is a lively industrial town with the Tesla electrical works and a metal foundry belonging to the Škoda works.

The old town, a historic conservation area, is laid out – like all the German colonial towns – on a chequerboard plan. The ramparts to the north and east are now parks and a remnant of the moat forms the Mlýnská stoka (Mill Canal). The main square of old Budweis, **nám.**

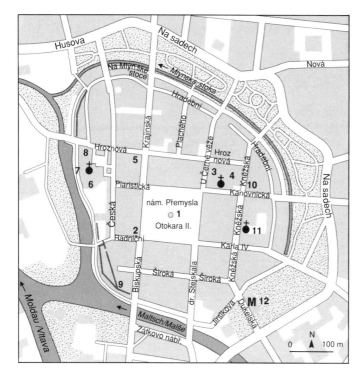

České Budějovice
(Budweis)
1 Samson Fountain
2 Town Hall
3 Black Tower
4 Cathedral of St
  Nicholas
5 Butchers' Stalls
6 Dominican Friary
7 St Mary
8 Salt House
9 Town Walls
10 Kneisl House
11 St Anne
12 South Bohemian
   Museum

Přemysla Otakara II, has uninterrupted sides of 133 metres, longer than any other blocks of houses in the town. At its centre is the great **Samson Fountain** (Samsonova kašna) designed in 1727 by Josef Dietrich (diameter 17 metres), with very fine mask spouts. This was originally the town's only water supply.

The whole square is bordered with arcaded houses which have been lovingly restored. Some date from the 13th century, though their façades have been altered over the centuries in a succession of styles (Renaissance, Empire, Neo-Classical). The Baroque **Town Hall**, with its three towers, in the south-west corner of the square was built in 1727–1731 by the Viennese court architect, Anton Erhard Martinelli, to replace a Renaissance building. The **Bishop's Palace** (Biskupská rezidence), also built in the 18th century dominates the neighbouring Biskupská ul.

Rising behind the houses at the north-east corner of the market place is the **Black Tower** (Černá věž), the free-standing clock tower of the cathedral. This Renaissance tower (1550–1577) is 72 metres high and 360 steps lead up to the gallery under its slightly squat onion dome, which gives a magnificent view over the town and surrounding area – on clear days as far as the Alps. The Baroque **Cathedral of St Nicholas** (Katedrála sv. Mikuláše; 1649) replaced the Gothic town church which dated from the period after King Otakar's charter.

Of the original building only a part of the choir survives. Behind the cathedral is the **Chapel of Christ's Agony** (Kaple Smrtelných úzkosti Páně).

The 16th-century **Butchers' Stalls** (Masné krámy) in Krajinská (Province street) at the corner of Hroznova ul. now contain the cosy and popular 'Masné krámy' restaurant.

On the backwater of the Vltava (slepé rameno Vltavy) to the west of the the old town stands the former **Dominican Friary** (Dominikánský klášter) founded by Otakar II Přemysl in 1265. The present building was erected by the Parler workshop between 1340 and 1370. Although the monastery is now used as a teaching institute, it is still possible to visit its beautiful Gothic cloister with cross-rib vaulting springing from mask-shaped corbels and polygonal piers. In the courtyard stands a polygonal well-house. Along the north range of the cloister is the Gothic church of St Mary (Kostel Obětování Panny Marie). The choir was built at the end of the 13th century, and the three-aisled hall-nave was completed in the late 14th century.

Near St Mary's church stands the **Salt House** (Solnice) dating from 1531, occasionally also used as the town's arsenal (Zbrojnice). It is an imposing building that reflects the importance of salt to Budějovice. The steps of its gable are mock battlements; three very curious stone faces stare out of the wall.

In the south-west of the old town, on the bank of the Malše, are the remains of the medieval

The town square of České Budějovice in the second half of the 17th century

Town Fortifications: the swallow-tail bastion (Otakarova bašta) with the Iron Maiden tower (Železná panna). At the north-west corner, on the Mill Canal, the sturdy Rabenstein Tower (Rabenštejnská věž) still stands, which also dates from the second half of the 14th century.

It is worth taking a stroll through the town's picturesque alleyways; everywhere there are fine old houses, such as the sgraffito-decorated **Kneisl House** (Kneislův dům; 16th century) in Kanovnická ul. next to the cathedral. In Kněžská ul. the newly restored former church of **St Anne** which was first built during the Bohemian War (1615–1621) on the site of the Capuchin monastery, is now a teacher training college. In Dukelská in the south-eastern part of the ramparts is the **South Bohemian Museum** (Jihočeské muzeum) with displays illustrating the natural history, history and present-day life of Southern Bohemia.

Hluboká nad Vltavou (Frauenberg)

8 km north of České Budějovice, on a rock 83 metres above the Vltava, stands **Hluboká** (colour plate 12), the most visited castle in Czechoslovakia.

Around the mid–13th century King Wenceslas I built a royal fortress on this easily defended site, which after the death of Otakar II Přemysl in 1278 was acquired by Otakar's arch-enemy Záviš of Falkenstein. Záviš married the king's widow, Kunhuta (Kunigunde), becoming the most powerful man in Bohemia, and attempted to oust Wenceslas II. In 1290 the king was able to regain power and had Záviš executed at the foot of *Fronburg* (Vroburc, or 'Lord's Castle', as Hluboká was then called; the Czech name was not used until after 1918).

From 1450 owners of the castle changed in quick succession until the castle passed to Wilhelm of Pernstein. Wilhelm devoted himself intensively to forestry and also created many fishponds which are still a feature of the landscape around Hluboká. The complications of Bohemian history ensured a rapid turnover of owners until in 1661 Johann Adolph von Schwarzenberg, who was made a Reichsfürst (prince of the Empire) in 1670, acquired 'Frowenburg' (the name is derived from 'Fronburg'). The Schwarzenbergs stayed here until 1945, providing diplomats, ministers and soldiers to the Habsburgs and beyond: Václav Havel's chancellor is the present Prince Schwarzenberg. Frauenberg was the main seat of the Schwarzenbergs, and centre of their great estates; with the advent of communism it 'passed into state ownership'.

The castle was comprehensively baroquized in 1728 by Paul Ignaz Bayer, who restored the chapel and created the two-storey ballroom, which Georg Werle decorated with paintings. It was even more comprehensively gothicized in the middle of the 19th century for Eleonore Schwarzenberg. From 1839 to 1871 the architects, Franz Beer and Ferdinand Damian Deworetzky, completely reshaped Frauenberg giving it the something of the appearance of the restored Windsor Castle – English Picturesque Gothic transferred to Bohemia.

The interiors of Hluboka magnificently evoke the spirit of the Victorian age: the mechanical excess, the inflated cosiness and cluttered grandeur are repeated through all the 41

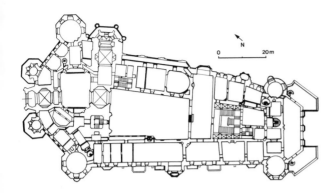

*Hluboká (Frauenberg)
Castle, plan*

rooms (out of a total of 140) shown to the visitor. Many of the fittings are very fine: the Renaissance ceiling in the great dining hall, for instance (from Český Krumlov, another Schwarzenberg possession); the superb Brussels tapestries after Jordaens cartoons, and the Baroque bookshelves from Schloss Schwarzenberg at Scheinfeld, Franconia. The handsome panelling of the ogival Hamilton room supports hunting pictures by second-generation Scottish emigré Johann Georg de Hamilton. In the plethora of works of art two early paintings stand out: an *Adoration of the Christ Child* by the Master of the Třeboň (Wittingau) Altarpiece (c. 1380) and a *Madonna with St Bartholomew and St Margaret* (South Bohemian school, c.1400).

Many visitors will also be interested in the castle's early central heating system, which has been in operation since 1855 without needing any major repairs. It is fuelled by wood and the temperatures of the rooms are regulated by small brass doors. Running water and bathrooms were installed as early as 1735.

The remodelling of the castle included the construction of an elaborate iron and glass *Winter Garden*, which links the castle with the Neo-Gothic Riding Hall and Stables. These were converted in 1955 to house the *Aleš South Bohemian Art Gallery* named after the Czech painter, Mikoláš Aleš (1852–1913), which contains paintings and sculpture by South Bohemian artists from the middle ages to the present day – the largest art collection in Bohemia after the National Gallery in Prague.

The castle grounds were transformed by the Schwarzenbergs into an English *Park* with many fishponds, wooded hills and pheasantries, exotic trees and shrubs, centuries-old oaks and bronze statues.

2 km south-west of Hluboká, Paul Ignaz Bayer, the Schwarzenbergs' architect, built the Baroque **Ohrada Hunting Lodge** (Zwinger) between 1703 and 1713, in the middle of a game park on the south shore of the Munický rybník pond. It now houses a museum of hunting, fishing and forestry, plenty of tables and chairs made of antlers, and a superb rug made out of over fifty wolves.

30 km west of České Budějovice (past the very fine and unspoiled village of Holašovice) is **Kratochvíle (Kurzweil)**, a pleasure castle built for the last but one of the Rožmberks, Vilém, in 1583–1588. Little can have changed in the next hundred years, before it was painted by Heinrich von Verle, and nothing has changed since. The sgraffitoed exterior, the naive expression of the stucco reliefs (mainly classical scenes, interspersed with the occasional medieval Rožmberk in apotheosis) by Antonio Melana (1588) and the lovely paintings by Georg Widmann make a perfect Renaissance ensemble, now used as a museum of Czech animated film.

Český Krumlov (Krumau)

The remarkable setting of the medieval town of **Český Krumlov**, on either side of a narrow loop in the Vltava, squeezed in on the edge of Blanský les (Plansk Forest), inspired some of Egon Schiele's finest paintings. To the left of the narrow river on a rocky height is the second largest castle in Bohemia (after Prague Castle) and to the right the town has spread out in almost all directions. Český Krumlov was the main residence of three noble families in succession, the Rožmberks (1302–1611), the Eggenbergs (1622–1717) and the Schwarzenbergs (1717–1945) who each made it the centre of an economic empire.

'In his later years he had yet one great joy, when his son Witiko began to build a castle on the rock at the Krumme Au, which now belonged to Witiko's family.' So ends *Witiko*, the historical novel by Adalbert Stifter (1805–1868) set in 12th-century Bohemia, and so begins the history of the castle and town of Český Krumlov. Around 1240 the noble house of the Witigons (Vítek) founded the castle above the loop in the Vltava, or 'curved meadow' ('krumme Au' – hence the name Krumau). The first documentary mention of the castle is in 1253. German colonists from Bavaria and Austria settled at the foot of the castle and opposite in the area protected by the bend in the river. By 1274 the settlement had become a town. In 1302 Henry of Rožmberk, a member of what was then the most powerful noble family in Bohemia, took over the castle and town. In 1497 the Rožmberks set up a stonemasons' lodge and began digging for silver in the surrounding hills of the Bohemian Forest; success was such that in 1526 the Jagiellon King Louis II granted the town a coat of arms and a seal, and gave the Rožmberks the right to establish their own mint at Krumau. The Rožmberks remodelled the castle as a splendid Renaissance residence. When the silver mines were exhausted towards the end of the 16th century the dynasty found itself in financial straits, and in 1600 Peter Vok of Rožmberk was forced to sell the lordship of Krumau to the Emperor Rudolph II, and to move to Třeboň with twenty-three chests full of books.

In 1622 the Emperor Ferdinand II gave Krumau, together with the estates belonging to it, to Ulrich, Baron Eggenberg in gratitude for services rendered during the Thirty Years' War. When the last Prince Eggenberg died in 1717, his widow Maria Ernestine, Princess Schwarzenberg, inherited the property. From then on the Schwarzenberg family ruled at Krumau, until in 1947 ownership of the castle was transferred to the town and it has since served as a museum and state archive.

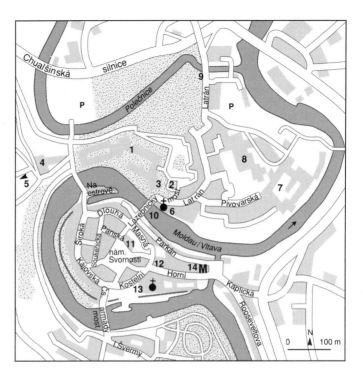

Český Krumlov
(Krumau)
 1 *Castle*
 2 *Latran Gate*
 3 *Castle Tower*
 4 *Castle Theatre*
 5 *Castle Park*
 6 *St Justus*
 7 *Brewery*
 8 *Minorite and*
   Poor Clares
   Convents
 9 *Budějovice*
   Gate
10 *Vltava Gate*
11 *Town Hall*
12 *Chaplaincy*
13 *St Vitus*
14 *Museum*

High above the Vltava the *Castle* with its massive tower dominates the town. The extensive complex of buildings, consisting of the outer bailey, the lower castle and the upper castle, dates back to the 13th and 14th centuries but were altered in the 16th century by Vilém of Rožmberk. The *Latrán Gate* forms the entrance to the castle. Bears play in the deep moat in front the gate. The *Burgrave's Office*, a two-winged Renaissance building dating from 1578 has impressive chiaroscuro painting on its façades. The *Mint* was designed by Anton Erhard Martinelli in the first half of the 18th century. The centre of the courtyard is occupied by a three-storey Renaissance building, the *Little Castle* (Hrádek); it is the successor to the living quarters of the original castle, and was later used as a residential and administrative range. The massive round *Castle Tower* dates from the middle of the 13th century and was given its Renaissance cap and arcaded gallery in 1588–1590. This gallery offers a spectacular view over the town and the delightful foothills of the Bohemian Forest.

A late 16th-century bridge links the Lower Castle with the *Upper Castle* which consists of a long building with two courtyards. The building dates from the 14th century and was altered in the 16th century by Antonio Eritzer and Baldassare Maggi da Arogno. The wall paintings in the back court depict the planets, the virtues and Ovid's *Metamorphoses* (1588). The Upper Castle was the splendid residence of the lords of the castle. Their lavishly furnished domestic and state rooms, offices and chapels can still be seen today. In the *Masquerade Hall* an 18th-century fancy dress ball surrounds the spectators with trompe l'oeil pierrots, Turks, Chinamen, tricornes, dominoes and assignations (Joseph Lederer, 1748). The room inspired Rainer Maria Rilke for a scene in his novella, *Die Geschwister*. Next comes the *Chinese Cabinet* with fine porcelain of the K'ang-hsi period (c. 1700), then galleries of paintings and works of art. The Eggenberg Coach (Eggenbersky kočar) makes a surprising appearance here; it was used by an Eggenberg acting as an imperial envoy to the Vatican. The 28 tapestries hung in the finest rooms in the Upper Castle are mostly Brussels work of the 16th–18th centuries; particularly notable is the cycle of scenes from Virgil's *Aeneid*. The *Great Castle Chapel* (Chapel of St George) dating from the Gothic period was baroquized by Matthias André between 1750 and 1755, while the *Little Castle Chapel* has retained its Gothic appearance, with net-vault and a winged altarpiece.

Statues of St John of Nepomuk, St Wenceslas and St Anthony by Johann Anton Zinner stand on the bridge, built in 1764 to connect the Upper Castle with a miraculous survival, the Baroque *Castle Theatre*. The first theatre was built in 1675-1682 by the Salzburg theatre architect, Johann M. Schaumberger. In 1766-67 the Viennese architect, Laurenz Makh built a new wooden building for Joseph Adam Prince Schwarzenberg, which still contains the scenery by the Viennese stage designers, Johann Wetschel and Leo Merkel; their ceiling painting shows *Zeus crowning the Muses presented to him by Apollo* (1766).

The upper passage of the castle bridge leads to the very large *Park* in which stands the *Bellaria* summer house, built in 1706–1708, but later given a Rococo appearance. Andrea Altomonte and Johann Anton Zinner created the splendid Neptune Fountain between 1745 and 1765. Mention should also be made of the open-air theatre (1958) with a rotating auditorium for an audience of 500, and another typical *fishpond* on the south-western end of the castle garden.

Spreading out at the foot of the castle is the old quarter of *Latrán*. The monks in the 14th century are supposed to have regarded the walled settlement as a *Castellum Boni Latronis* (Fort of the Good Robber), remembering the repentant robber who died next to Jesus on the cross. Places of interest in this part of the town include the former church of St Justus (Kostel sv. Jost) dating from the 14th century and restored in the 16th century, the Brewery (Pivovar) in a 16th-century arsenal, the sgraffito-decorated former Latrán Town Hall, the Minorite friary, the neighbouring convent of Poor Clares, the church of Corpus Christi (used by both communities) which was built in the 14th century but given a Baroque remodelling in the 17th century, and lastly the České Budějovice Gate, the only entrance for vehicles to the guarded car park (parkoviště).

The Vltava bridge links Latrán to the *Old Town*. Passing along Radniční ul. the visitor

1   PRAGUE, Old Town Hall ▷

2   PRAGUE, View of Hradčany ▷▷

3   PRAGUE, Astronomical Clock at the Old Town Hall   4   PRAGUE, St Vitus's Cathedral

5   PRAGUE, Old Town Mills and Water Tower

6   PRAGUE, Old Town Square

7 PRAGUE, Charles Bridge and Lesser Town Bridge Tower

8 PRAGUE, Gate to Strahov Monastery

9 Castle at LOKET (Elbogen) ▷

10 MARIÁNSKÉ LÁZNĚ (Marienbad) Main Colonnade

11 PŘÍBRAM Holy Stairway (Svatá Hora)

12 HLUBOKÁ (Frauenberg) Schloss

13   Pardubice (Pardubitz) Pernstein Square

14   Telč (Teltsch) Market Square

15   Litoměřice (Leitmeritz) Chalice House

17   The Castle at KONOPIŠTĚ (Konopischt)
16   Rock formation ADRŠPACH (Adersbach)

18   MĚLNÍK Main square with Town Hall ▷

20 Moated Castle, BLATNÁ
19 BRATISLAVA (Pressburg) Michalská brána

22 LEVOČA (Leutschau, Löcse) Thurzo House
21 LEVOČA (Leutschau) Town Hall   23 HIGH TATRAS, Popradské pleso (Poppersee) ▷

reaches the *Town Square* (nám. Svornosti, Square of Unity) with its Marian *Plague Column*. The *Town Hall* on the north side of the square has a Gothic loggia, and the façade is decorated with a Renaissance frieze and large coats of arms of Bohemia, Český Krumlov, and the Eggenberg and Schwarzenberg families.

Horní ul., which runs eastwards from the square, passes the Chaplaincy (Kaplanka) with its fine oriel window (1514–1520), the Prelature with Rococo stairs in the courtyard, the former Jesuit College, built in 1586–1588 (now a hotel), the Theatre (originally the Jesuit Theatre) built in 1613, and then the Town Museum with an interesting collection of Gothic art, a 17th-century shop and and memorabilia of the writer and painter Adalbert Stifter. A reminder that the German population was once the majority here are the gravestones with German inscriptions outside the museum, which was built in 1650–1662 as a Jesuit Seminary.

South of the Chaplaincy stands the church of *St Vitus*, the archidiaconal church of Český Krumlov, built in 1407–1439 to replace an earlier Gothic church founded by Peter of Rožmberk in 1309. The architect of the present three-aisled hall-church, with its tall slender west tower, was Master Linhart of Aldeberg. The net-vault of the nave rests on arcades of four piers, and the Late Gothic gallery is supported on four arches with star-rib vaults. The wall paintings include Gothic works: *The Crucifixion*, *St Veronica*, *St Elizabeth*, *St Mary Magdalene with Donor* and *St Bartholomew* (c. 1430) in the north aisle. The early Baroque high altar was made by Johann Worath between 1673 and 1683.

The České Budějovice road passes the Cistercian monastery of **Zlatá Koruna** (Goldenkron), founded by King Otakar II Přemysl in 1263 to celebrate his victory over the Hungarians. The original wooden buildings were replaced by a handsome stone building at the end of the 13th century in the reign of Wenceslas II. In 1420 the abbey was burned down by the Hussites and remained a ruin for more than 200 years, before being restored and baroquized in 1663 as a symbol of Catholic loyalty. The monastery was closed in 1785 by the Emperor Joseph II , and its buildings were later used as a factory and for residential purposes. Various restorations have taken place this century.

The centre of the monastery is the 14th-century St Mary's Church, its four aisles now reduced to three. The Parler lodge was responsible for some of its construction. The three-bay choir was baroquized in the 17th century and renovated in the 18th century. On what is now a Neo-Classical high altar are statues of Cistercian saints by Jakob Eberle and a painting of the *Assumption of the Virgin* by Karl Philippot. A cenotaph in the choir commemorates the founder, Otakar II Přemysl.

The fortified Cistercian monastery of **Vyšší Brod** (Hohenfurth) goes back to its foundation in 1259 by Peter Vok of Rožmberk who intended to have his family tombs here. (It was also

Český Krumlov, engraving by K. Postl from a drawing by L. Janscha

the Rožmberk response to Otakar II's moves to establish a power base at Budějovice and even Zlatá Koruna, which the king hoped to link up with newly inherited lands in Austria. The centre of Rožmberk domains was the castle at **Rožmberk nad Vltavou**, 8 km north east, built on a bend of the river like Český Krumlov, and with some important Renaissance frescoes.) The last of the line, another Peter Vok, was buried at Vyšší Brod in 1611; the symbol of the rose was broken over his coffin as it was lowered into the ground.

All the monastic buildings are squeezed into the narrow space within the walls: the gate tower, the abbey church dedicated to the Virgin, the cloister, two conventual buildings, the prelature, the novitiate and the infirmary. The church was built between 1360 and 1380. The five-bay cross-rib vault in the nave and aisles springs from polygonal piers. The high altar is Early Baroque, in the two side chapels of St Roch and St Barbara stand some Late Gothic winged altarpieces (1524-25). Two memorials commemorate Peter Vok of Rožmberk (1539-1611) and Jan Zrinský, the first abbot of Vyšší Brod. Adjoining the south aisle is the Gothic cloister on the east side of which is the Early Gothic *chapter house*, a square room with a central clustered pier with a carved base supporting the four cross-rib vaults; the windows have Late Gothic tracery.

The dazzling library contains numerous manuscripts and incunables. There is an art gallery with works by Dutch masters of the 17th–18th centuries and a postal museum. But the most valuable treasures of the monastery, the famous *Vyšší Brod Madonna* (c. 1420), the nine panels by the Master of the Vyšší Brod Altarpiece (c. 1350) and the Záviš cross, goldsmith's work of the first half of the 13th century, have been kept in the National Gallery or St Vitus's Cathedral in Prague since 1945, after spending the war in a Nazi salt mine.

The Vltava rises on the eastern slope of the Černá hora (Schwarzberg) (1314 metres), and is harnessed for hydro-electric power at the foot of the Bohemian Forest (Šumava) by a dam forming the **Údolní nádrž Lipno** (Lipensská přehradní nádrž; Lipno Reservoir). The waters, imprisoned in a 25-mile-long reservoir, no longer roar as they do in Smetana's 'Ma Vlast', but the northern shore of this lake is now a popular resort with camping sites, bathing facilities and marinas.

At the upper end of the Lipno Reservoir is **Horní Plana** (Oberplan), an ancient little town which was granted the right to a market in 1349. The church of St Mary Magdalene dates from the 13th century. This little village full of sunseekers was the birthplace of the German-speaking writer and painter Adalbert Stifter (there is a gallery of his paintings in Vienna). The house where he was born is now a memorial, and there is a bronze monument to him in the town park.

The picturesque little town of **Prachatice** (Prachatitz) lies in a valley basin surrounded by forests, at the foot of Libín mountain (1091 metres). It was the centre of the salt trade that flourished in Bohemia in the middle ages. Already in 1010 Frankish sources mention the 'Golden Way', the old trading route linking Bavaria and Bohemia, which passed through the Bohemian Forest. This *via aurea* or *via bohemica* started at Passau and ended at Prachatice. Fine textiles, spices, wines and arms came to Bohemia in return for grain, butter, honey, wax and skins to the west. The main commodity traded was salt, of which Bohemia has no natural supply, and Prachatice developed into the salt store for the whole country. The salt office survives in the main square. The town received its charter in 1323 and soon afterwards came under the control of the powerful Rožmberk family, which proved very advantageous for the development of the community. In 1608 the burghers gained the title of a free royal town, but because Prachatice had supported the Bohemian Estates at the outbreak of the

Adalbert Stifter

Šumava (Böhmerwald; the Bohemian Forest)

The Bohemian Forest is different from the wild harshness of the Krkonoše (Riesengebirge; Giant Mountains) or the gentle landscape of the Krušné hory (Erzgebirge; Ore Mountains). It has an austere beauty, endlessly wide and unspoiled, covered with dense forests and moorland; the mountains are suitable for walking in all seasons, but particularly in late summer and autumn, when the sun shines more constantly and the air is crystal clear. Acid rain is, however, an increasingly serious problem here as elsewhere in Czechoslovakia.

The name Bohemian Forest (Böhmerwald) occurs as 'Behaime Walt' as early as the beginning of the 12th century. Since the 16th century the Czechs have called it *Šumava* (from *šumet* to murmur), because the wanderer on the broad highlands hears only the rustling of the wind in the tops of the trees. Strictly speaking Šumava refers only to the larger, wilder south-eastern part of the Bohemian Forest, the homeland of the writer Adalbert Stifter. The north-western part is called *Český les* (Czech Forest).

Since 1963 Šumava, with an area of 1630 sq km, has formed the largest conservation area in Czechoslovakia. About a quarter of this area consists of plateaux 1000–1100 metres above sea-level. Above these forested *pláně* with their bogs, peat and moors, rise unspectacular summits such as Plechý (Böhmischer Plöckenstein; 1378 m). There are six specially protected nature reserves: Lipka; Jezerní slat' (from *slatina*, moor); Buková slat'; Boubínský prales (*prales*, primeval forest); Mrtvý luh ('dead meadow'), a low moor at the confluence of the Teplá Vltava and the Studená Vltava (the Warm Vlatva and the Cold Vltava); and Trojmezná hora (*hora* means 'mountain').

Thirty Years' War, it suffered reprisals at the hands of General Buquoy, to whom many of the Rožmberk lands were eventually given. However, salt was still needed and the town continued to flourish until 1692, when Leopold I introduced an imperial monopoly. Henceforth salt for Bohemia was to travel from Gmunden in Upper Austria to České Budějovice, and Prachatice declined into insignificance. The 'Säumerglocke' ('pack-horse driver's bell'), which used to direct merchants to the town who had lost their way, still rings at 10 o'clock every evening.

It is obvious even to today's visitor that Prachatice was once a rich town. Nowhere else are there more lavish façades to the burghers' houses, decorated with sgraffiti and frescoes, around the market square and in the surrounding streets. Above the cornices of the houses rise imposing attics, and Venetian arch motifs or volute shapes ornament the façades. This Renaissance Prachatice arose after the destruction of the Gothic town centre by fire in 1507.

Standing close together around the slightly sloping market square are: the Latin school attended by Jan Hus and possibly the Taborite leader Žižka (the house where Hus was born on 6 July 1369 in the small neighbouring town of Husinec is now a memorial); the Salt Office, later called the Rumpál House; the brew house; Zd'árský House, now a folk museum; and the old Town Hall dating from 1571. Until the Rožmberk family died out at the beginning of the 17th century this was their town palace. The façade is covered with sgraffito scenes with inscriptions: just below the roof are the eight virtues, and below them classical and biblical scenes, some of them taken from Holbein. The German motto has a sarcastic ring:

Das Recht, es gleicht dem Netz der Spinnen,
der Käfer sprengt's, die Fliegen hängen drinnen.
(The law is like the spider's net:
The beetle bursts it, but flies get caught.)

The Gothic diaconal church of *St James* with its immensely steep roofs, is a three-aisled hall-church built between 1410 and 1513 (with interruptions). Squeezed in between the two towers – the north tower remains unfinished – is the porch with a fine star and net vault (late 15th century). An elaborately carved Late Gothic oak door opens onto the nave. The sanctuary dates from the previous church, an early 14th-century basilica. The furnishings of the church are basically Baroque, although parts of the high altar, such as the carvings of the life of the Virgin by the Master of the Zvíkov (Klingenberg) Lamentation (c. 1520), date from the Late Gothic period.

The extensive remains of the Gothic *Town Fortifications* of the 14th and 16th centuries are still impressive. On the Písek Gate, a double gate on the north side of the town, is a fresco showing Wilhelm von Rosenberg (Vilém of Rožmberk) on horseback, below the red rose that was the family's emblem.

The best known health resort in the southern Bohemian Forest is **Volary** (Wallern) 750 metres above sea-level. Colonists from the Tyrol founded it as a resting place on the 'Golden Way' and left their mark on the place with their wooden Alpine houses with low roofs weighted with stones, and their picturesque galleries. A few of these houses still survive today. Using their royal privilege the Wallinger forced the merchants passing through to spend the night in their community. They had to provide lodging, stabling and food. Any commercial traveller caught attempting to sneak past the town without sampling its hospitality had to pay a hefty fine, half of which went to the town and half to the local lord.

At the junction of three countries, Germany, Austria and Czechoslovakia, the Plechý (Böhmischer Plöckenstein) rises to a height of 1378 metres. To the south-east of it glitters Plešné jezero (Plöckensteinsee), the lake made famous by Adalbert Stifter's stories. On a rock overlooking the lake stands a memorial to the writer.

One of the many castles guarding the 'Golden Way' and its subsidiary roads is **Vimperk** (Winterberg), built in 1264 by Otakar II Přemysl in the romantic valley of the Volyňka (Wolinka). The king granted it as a fiefdom to a trusty comrade-in-arms, Purkart of Janovic (Burkhart of Janowitz). The settlement attached to the castle developed into a small town where the first printing press in Bohemia was established in 1484 – only a few decades after Gutenberg's invention. Here Johannes Alagrav printed calendars and Christian texts. The tradition was later continued by the Steinbrenner press, and today prayer books for almost all religions are still sent from Vimperk all over the world. In 1554 the Rožmberk family assumed the lordship of Winterberg and transformed the Gothic castle into a Renaissance schloss. Later it passed to the Schwarzenbergs, who gave the property a Baroque renovation between 1728 and 1734. Though burned down in 1857 the schloss was quickly rebuilt to the old plans. It was expropriated by the state in 1947.

The little town of Vimperk is the main town of Šumava (the southern part of the Bohemian Forest), and is now a popular resort in both summer and winter.

Strakonice (Strakonitz)

Strakonice, famous for its fezzes, started off, like so many Bohemian towns, as a castle and a religious foundation. In the first quarter of the 13th century Bavor I founded a castle on a spur of land at the confluence of the Volyňka (Wolinka) and the Otava (Wottava). Soon afterwards, in 1243, he made it over to the order of Knights Hospitaller of St John, who established a priory there and made the castle the headquarters of the order in Bohemia, which it remained until 1694. The town developed at the same time as the castle.

The *Castle* occupies a spacious triangular site, with at its centre the Romanesque hall-range (palas), which later became the 'commandery', or headquarters, of the Hospitallers. The single-storey building contains the chapter house; the wall paintings here date from the first half of the 14th century. Next to it is the simple church of St Procopius, a Romanesque building which was renovated in the Gothic style c. 1300. The sacristy rises into a residential tower in the castle walls. The altarpiece of St Anne in the church was carved c. 1520 by the Master of the Zvíkov (Klingenberg) Lamentation. Between the church and the hall-range a cloister was built c.1280, the walls of which were painted at the beginning of the 14th century. A Romanesque columned portal leads from the cloister to the chapter house in the hall-range.

Písek, lithograph by Č. V. Gottman after a drawing by J. Rattay, c. 1820

In the south-west corner of the castle site stands the two-storey New Palas, built around 1260–1280 and exceptionally well preserved. Since 1930 it has been used as a museum of archaeology and art, with other sections dealing with the history of the motorcycle and the manufacture of the fez, Strakonice's principal exports. The Old Palas and New Palas have been linked since 1421 by the commandery (administrative offices) of the Hospitallers. Also in the south-western part of the castle is the massive round main tower dating from the period around 1300; its name, *Rumpál* indicates that in the past it contained a winch for raising loads. The burgrave's office with a Late Gothic gable was built on Romanesque foundations in 1500. Above the castle moat rises the *Jelenka* ('stinkhorn'), a rectangular tower with oriel windows. Strakonice was restored in 1936 as a typical example of a medieval castle complex.

At the royal town of **Písek** the oldest stone bridge in Bohemia crosses the Otava on the old trading route from Passau to Prague. The gold-bearing sand which the Otava brings down from the Bohemian Forest was already being washed by the Celts to obtain the precious metal. At some time the gold-washers' settlement was given the Latin name *Arena* meaning 'sand'. Later, in the 8th century the Slavs too called the place 'sand' or *Písek*; and when the German colonists arrived here in the 13th century they also could think of no other name but Sand. However, it was not the gold dust, which by the 13th century was being extracted in very small quantities (though still enough to justify building a gold ore mill here, recently discovered), that moved Otakar II Přemysl to grant the settlement the status of a royal town in 1254, but its important position on the road between the Prachatice, the centre of the salt trade, and Prague. He spanned the dangerous ford with a stone bridge, at the same time building a defensive castle to protect the bridge and its traffic.

The main square is surrounded by several fine old burghers' houses. These have Renaissance, Baroque or Empire gables but the core of the buildings is Gothic. The Baroque *Town Hall* with its two towers was built in 1737–1766. Hidden in its courtyard is the Gothic hall (*palas*), the last remnant of the 13th-century royal castle, the rest of which was destroyed by fire in 1532. The hall range now houses the town museum.

Among the most interesting buildings in Písek is the parish church of *St Mary*. The building work was under the direction of the royal masons' lodge of Zvíkov, which was also building the castle and the stone bridge. In 1489 Master Mikuláš built the tower (74 metres high), which was altered after the fire of 1555. In 1741–1746 the Baroque chapel of St John of Nepomuk was added to the south transept. The church's treasures include the *Madonna of Písek*, a Gothic panel painting from the end of the 14th century, and a pewter font dated 1587. On the middle piers the great restorer, Josef Mocker, uncovered an Early Gothic picture cycle dating from the end of the 13th century.

But the most attractive feature of Písek is certainly its provincial version of the Charles Bridge in Prague. In fact the *stone bridge* is older than Charles's – it dates back to the mid–13th century – and it has only a few Baroque saints on the piers. Until the floods of 1768, it also had a little bridge tower, now replaced by a seventh arch.

High on a rock between the Otava and the Vltava, 24 km north of Písek, stands **Zvíkov** (Klingenberg) castle, called the 'Queen of Bohemian castles' because of its majestic situation, though nowadays the Orlík dam (Orlická přehradni nádrž) has filled the deep valleys and deprived the castle of much of its romantic charm.

Prehistoric man built earthworks on the site of the present building from which to control the traffic of goods on the two rivers. In 1234 King Wenceslas I built an Early Gothic castle, which was extended by the masons' lodge of Otakar II Přemysl in 1255–1270. Around the middle of the 16th century the Renaissance architect Hans Vlach remodelled the castle in the style of the period, but in 1759 it was so badly damaged by fire that it remained uninhabited for more than a century and fell into ruin. In 1880 Marchetti began an uncharacteristically low-key restoration for the Schwarzenbergs, and the result has a genuinely medieval austerity and calm far removed from their energetic Neo-Gothicisms elsewhere. In 1947 Zvíkov was nationalized and is now a protected monument.

The deep moat is spanned by a bridge leading to the Písek Gate with a round, late 13th-century, watchtower above it, which was given its present roof in 1554. The nucleus of the castle is the mid–13th-century residential quarters (*palas*), a beautiful arcaded courtyard. The lower arcade is open while the upper one is filled with tracery. The *Wedding Hall* on the upper floor of the west range is decorated with contemporary scenes of dancing and elaborate greenery (c. 1500). The very good Late Gothic relief of the *Lamentation of Christ* which forms the altarpiece in the *Chapel of St Wenceslas* has given its name to its anonymous creator: the Master of the Zvíkov (Klingenberg) Lamentation. Adjoining the south range of the palace is the tall castle keep (Hlizová věž, 'Boil Tower'), also dating from the 13th century.

On a little island in the river Lomnice in the middle of an overgrown park stands the medieval castle of **Blatná** (Platten; colour plate 20). In the 13th century a fortified manor house belonging to the lords Bavor of Strakonice stood on the site of the present castle. The foundations of its Romanesque chapel were excavated in 1926. By the time the property passed to the Rožmitál family in 1391, the house had already become a castle. The new masters built the long Gothic living quarters (*palas*) and the massive gate tower. All the buildings were remodelled and decorated with wall paintings in the course of the following centuries. In the first half of the 16th century the celebrated architect Benedikt Rieth strengthened the fortifications and built a new Renaissance *palas*. A third *palas* was commissioned by the Rozdražov family who owned Blatná from 1579.

At present the castle is closed for restoration, but when this is completed the visitor will be able to visit the upper part of the gate tower and see the earliest Bohemian depiction of a town (1480). In the *Old Palas* are Late Gothic frescoes with a variety of subject matter: figures from classical antiquity as well as from the Old and New Testaments, a knightly tournament, the Garden of Love, Samson and Delilah, a depiction of the castle and others.

The little town of Blatná is surrounded by fishponds and is famous for its fragrant roses which are exported all over the world. In the market place stands the Gothic church of St Mary, built by Bavor of Strakonice between 1290 and 1300 on the site of an earlier Romanesque church. The present Late Gothic parish church was built in 1414–1444. Its long choir has a rib vault in the Parler style and a polygonal east end. Dating from the period around 1500 are a Crucifix with a Madonna at the foot of the cross, and a statue of the Virgin.

Tábor (Tabor)

About 90 km south of Prague on a hill between Jordán and Lužnice stands the old Hussite town of **Tábor**. Everything in the town is a reminder of the radical reformers of the 15th century, Master Jan Hus and the military commander Jan Žižka. In 1420, five years after the execution of Jan Hus and a few months after the Defenestration in the New Town of Prague (see p. 131), several thousand men with their families gathered at Kotnov castle under the banner of the chalice to move against Emperor and Church. The tent encampment developed into a fortress, and the fortress became a town, which the supporters of Hus named Tábor after the mountain of the Transfiguration of Christ in the New Testament. From Tábor the blind Jan Žižka of Trocnov led the Hussite army back and forth across Bohemia, defeating the imperial forces at Vítkov near Prague in 1420 and at Havlíčkův Brod (Deutsch-Brod) in 1422. After the great Žižka was killed in 1424 his place was taken by other leaders who continued the fight against Catholicism and the Germans, and ultimately even against their more moderate fellow reformers, the Utraquists, until defeat at Lipany (1434) marked the end of the uprising.

After the Hussite Wars avid building activity started at Tábor. Most of its population remained 'Bohemian Brethren' or moderate Utraquists and outside the Catholic Church. Others too – 'Nicolaitans', 'Arians', 'Manichaeans', 'Nestorians', 'Waldensians', 'Poor Men of Lyons' – sought truth in their own faiths here. Bar Catholicism all religions were tolerated, up to a point: Žižka, did, however, personally supervise the burning of sectarians such as the Adamites who practised nudity and worse. If in the 16th and 17th centuries serfs rose against their masters in Bohemia there were always citizens of Tábor present waving their black banners with the emblem of the red chalice.

Not surprisingly the town joined the uprising against the Habsburgs after the Second Defenestration of Prague in 1618, and following the Battle of the White Mountain it was the last town to fall to the victors (1621). The Catholic clergy did everything they could to bring the inhabitants back to the true faith, but their efforts were in vain. Even today Tábor has the lowest percentage of Catholics in the country.

The centre of the town is Žižkovo nám. with a monumental bronze statue of the Hussite leader by the sculptor J. Strachovský (1877). Also in the square are two stone

The Hussite commander, Jan Žižka

tables, one in front of the town hall and the other in front of Ctibor House (No. 6), at which the Hussite Holy Communion is thought to have been distributed. There is also a Roland fountain. Old, well-restored burghers' houses line the quadrangular square. Running beneath the square and the whole of the old town is a labyrinth of underground passageways used by the Hussites as magazines and arsenals and for refuge. Some of these passages can be visited.

On the west side of the square stands the former *Town Hall* built in 1440–1521 but later altered several times and remodelled in Neo-Gothic style in 1878. The building now contains a museum of the Hussite movement. The splendid municipal coat of arms is framed by statuettes of the Hussite heroes:

View of Tábor from Merian's Topography

Jan Hus, Jan Žižka, Procopius the Great (or Bald) and Jerome of Prague, as well as a group of Adamites. (This sect, according to a mythology that Speed repeated in 1631, practised 'promiscuous whoredom and incest at their Divine Service. When the priest pronounceth the word of *Genesis* (as his custome is), *Crescite, et multiplicamini et replete terram*, the lights are suddainely popt out, and without any respect had, to alliance and kindred, or reverence to their exercise, they mingle like Beasts, and when they have acted their wickedness, and are returned to their seates, the Candles are againe lighted, and they fall to their pretended prayers, as if there had been no harm done.') Inside the town hall, the two-storey council chamber is particularly striking, with a net vault on octagonal piers, and bosses carved as human and animal figures.

The north-west corner of the square is dominated by the *Church of the Transfiguration of Christ* (Chrám Proměněni Krista Pána) with its tower 77 metres high. The church was begun in 1440 and consecrated in 1516. Behind the town hall is the Augustinian church of 1662 with its monastery.

On Prážská ul., which begins in the south-eastern corner of the square are several fine *Renaissance houses*, such as No. 220 with its tall gable and overhanging upper storey corbels, and its neighbour No. 221 with an arched gable. For reasons of defence all the streets in the old town have a curve in them before they reach the town walls, which are still well preserved on the northern side. From the south-western corner of Žižkovo nám. Klokotská ul.

('Nightingale Street') leads to *Kotnov Castle*, of which all that is left is a massive round tower next to the Bechyně Gate.

The *Jordán Pond* to the north-east was created in 1492 to provide a water supply for the town – the oldest dam in Bohemia. In this pond – the 'Jordan' – the Taborites used to baptize their children.

Jindřichův Hradec (Neuhaus)

Not far from the Austrian border, on the little Nežárka river and lake Vajgar stands the beautiful old town of **Jindřichův Hradec** with its strong castle and neat burghers' houses. This was a family castle, never sold or mortgaged, changing hands only through inheritance or marriage, and it has a family ghost, the famous 'Woman in White'.

Around 1220 Henry, the son of Vítek (Witigo) of Prčice, built a castle which he named *Nova domus* ('New House' or Neuhaus) but which his Czech subjects gave the name *Jindřichův Hradec* ('Henry's Castle'). It was a Romanesque stone building with wooden superstructures, surrounded by the water of the Vajgar (Weiher) lake. Between 1260 and 1270 the Romanesque fortress was replaced by a Gothic building. Over the following centuries the lords of Jindřichův Hradec were continually making additions to the building, adding more storeys and modernizing it. In the second half of the 16th century Italian architects transformed the castle into a magnificent Renaissance schloss.

The castle had been followed by a settlement, the schloss by a town. In 1710 a certain Count Rechtskron came to Jindřichův Hradec with French workmen and founded a mirror factory which gained a worldwide reputation. The town became an important and popular post station between Vienna and Prague, and was patronized by the aristocracy.

The centre of the town, which slopes gently up from the lake, is the triangular market place with Baroque and Neo-Classical burghers' houses. In the centre of the square is the *Trinity Column* made by M. Strahovsky in 1764. The Gothic Town Hall on the north side of the square was renovated in 1801-1807, after the fire which swept through the town.

North of the market place is a Minorite (Franciscan) friary dating from the 13th century and now used as a hospital. The Franciscan *Church of St John the Baptist* (Kostel sv. Jana Křtitele) was built as a two-aisled basilica in the third quarter of the 13th century. It has been altered several times and restored after fires, most recently in 1891-1895. The choir has some Gothic paintings of the second half of the 14th century: scenes from the life of Christ and a *Misericordia* (Christ as the Man of Sorrows) with the donors on the north wall and images of saints on the south wall. *St Francis receiving the stigmata* and the *Preaching of St Capistranus* on the north side of the nave date from the period around 1480. The church's interior has a Baroque appearance, although there is a Gothic chapel next to the choir. On the north side of the church is the cloister with Late Gothic frescoes and two chapels: the Cloth-makers's Chapel (before 1375) and St Mary's Chapel (1761-1778). The hospital is a Renaissance building of 1560-61.

The aisle-less *Church of St Mary Magdalene* was founded by the Teutonic Knights in the 13th century. In the 14th century it was altered by the order, which in 1594 handed it over to the Jesuits, who erected a large college with four ranges designed by Antonio and Domenico Battista Cometa (1595–1605). By 1635 they had added a seminary. In 1615 after a fire the church was rebuilt in Late Renaissance style, and was given Baroque decorations by Francesco Caratti. In 1788 the church and religious house were dissolved in the Josephine reforms, and the conventual buildings were converted into barracks. Today the seminary and church house the Jindřichův Hradec *town museum*. The *Nežárka Gate* next to the museum is part of the town's former fortifications.

Rising on the western edge of the old town is the mighty *Castle*; its various parts built between the 13th and 18th centuries illustrate architectural development from Early Gothic to Baroque. The three castle courtyards are of interest, particularly the inner court with its Renaissance arcades by the Italian architect Antonio Cometa (1586–1592). Below these 'Great Arcades' is a wrought-iron gate leading to the castle garden. On the south side of the garden is one of the greatest achievements of the Renaissance in Central Europe, the castle Rotunda (Giovanni Maria Faconi and Antonio Cometa 1591–1593). A solid but energetic building on the outside, its slightly ponderous Italianism is relieved by very Central European gables. Inside the white and gold stucco (Pietro Martriola, 1594–1596) was the latest in Mannerist sophistication, full of perspective tricks but never losing its poise. The castle itself has some fine ceilings, and collections that include paintings by the great Baroque artists, Karel Škréta (1610–1674) and Peter Brandl (c. 1630–1680), as well as the Gothic *Madonna of Hradec*, and furniture and faience of various periods. In the chapel of the old residential quarters (*palas*) the walls are decorated with an Early Gothic cycle of scenes from the legend of St George (1338).

People in Jindřichův Hradec still have tales to tell about the 'Woman in White', Berta (Perchta) of Rosenberg (Rožmberk), who was born in 1430 and grew up to be one of the most beautiful and richest maidens in the land. (Her portrait hangs in the gallery of the castle.) Her father married her to Count Liechtenstein from Styria, but Berta was in love with the young Bohemian Count Sternberg. During the wedding festivities at Jindřichův Hradec she called Sternberg to her room and bade him a tearful farewell. Her husband surprised the couple and from then on treated his wife worse than a maidservant. Not until many years later did she return to Jindřichův Hradec as a widow, beautifying the castle and every year on Maundy Thursday distributing a concoction of oatmeal, warm beer and honey to the poor of the town. People only ever saw her in her white widow's weeds and called her the 'Woman in White'. On her death the whole town went into mourning, but because her husband had never pardoned her she was compelled to continue roaming the castle as a ghost. She is supposed to have foretold good and bad events, births and deaths, riches and poverty to her descendants and the later owners of the castle by appearing wearing either white or black gloves.

About 12 km north of Jindřichův Hradec in the middle of a lake surrounded by forest, stands **Červená Lhota** (Rothlhota), one of the prettiest moated country houses in Europe. In the 16th century the original Gothic castle was rebuilt as a small Renaissance schloss which has since been restored several times. Karl Ditters von Dittersdorf, the highly successful composer of numerous *singspiele*, operas, oratorios, concerti and chamber works during a lifetime as kapellmeister at various princely courts, died at Červená Lhota on 24 October 1799. His grave in the cemetery of the neighbouring village of Deštna (Deschtna) is marked by an obelisk and a cast-iron cross. In the schloss is a valuable collection of furniture, tapestries, paintings, porcelain and pewter.

Třeboň (Wittingau)

The medieval town of **Třeboň** is delightfully situated between undulating hills, deep valleys and a large number of ponds. Since 1975 the historic town centre has been a conservation area, and in 1979 the unique surrounding countryside with some 270 fishponds was made a nature reserve under UNESCO protection.

The German name of the town recalls the fact that around the middle of the 13th century the castle and town were founded by the noble family of Witigo (Vítek). The Rožmberks (Rosenberg), descendants of the Witigons, were the lords of Wittingau from 1366 to 1611 and shaped the town, castle and landscape. Peter Vok, the last of the Rožmberks, died at Wittingau castle surrounded by his famous library and a selection of alchemists, astrologers and poets. His court had been second only to Rudolph II's in grandeur and intellectual lustre. The English magus John Dee stayed here for several years (as did Edward Kelley), transmuting base metals into gold as a symbol of his conversations with the archangel Uriel, and of the transcendent harmony of the universe – the goal also of his contemporary and fellow researcher Kepler. Dee's son Arthur, however, remembered playing at quoits as a child with the pieces of gold obtained through projection, as it was called, while Kelley bamboozled the magus into experimenting with universal harmony in the form of wife-swapping. This was a mistake; Mrs Dee objected, and the angels expressed their disapproval by never speaking to Dee again. During the Thirty Years' War Swedish landsknechts carried the library off to Stockholm, and it was later donated to the Vatican by Queen Christine after her conversion to Catholicism in 1655.

The lordship of Třeboň passed by an inheritance settlement in 1611 to the Protestant Schwanbergs, but in 1623 it was confiscated by the Emperor Ferdinand II and given to his brother, Archduke Leopold William of Austria. The archduke in turn transferred it in 1658 to another new owner, the Bavarian Count Johann Adolf zu Schwarzenberg, in order to wipe out a large debt. Their acquisition of Třeboň marked the first entry of the Schwarzenbergs into Bohemia.

The *Main Square* of Třeboň (nám. Julia Fučika) is framed by fine Renaissance and Baroque houses. On the north side is the Renaissance house Bílý koníček (the White Horse) built in

The Fishponds

In the 12th and 13th centuries the first colonists settled in the then marshy region of southern Bohemia and built canals and fishponds so that they could enjoy fish in this land-locked country. This work reached its climax in the 15th and 16th centuries when the pond-builder Josef Štěpanek Netolicky and his successor Jakob Křcín of Jelcany, with the financial support of the Rožmberks, developed a fish-farming system of such perfection that it has needed practically no modification to the present day. From 1571 they created the **Rybník Svět** (World Pond) with an area of 208 hectares. The builders of the pond nicknamed it 'Ingratitude' because it was always attempting to break its banks. In 1581 Rybník Svět was fished out for the first time. Now a popular health resort has developed on its shore; peat rich in sulphur and iron is used to treat rheumatism, arthritis and nervous disorders, and there are facilities for swimming and rowing.

The **Rožmberk Pond** (Rožmberkský rybník) in the north of the town covers 721 hectares and is the largest fishpond in Czechoslovakia. Its walls are 2430 metres long, 80 metres wide at its foot and up to 12 metres high. Every two or three years the pond is drained in autumn and the fish are taken. This event attracts many thousands of visitors, who come to watch 'St Peter's harvest' seething in the last remnant of water; from the Rozmberk Pond alone the fishermen can expect to catch the 100 tonnes of carp which are exported all over the world before New Year's Eve (or 'Silvester', which, like Christmas Eve, is a traditional day for carp-eating in much of central Europe). The 16th-century **Golden Canal** (Zlatá stoka) runs south of Třeboň from the Luznice river, linking many of the fishponds before rejoining the river 45 km further downstream.

There are some 6000 fishponds near Třeboň, in all an area of 41,000 hectares being farmed. The average annual production is 15,500 tonnes. Tench, pike, zander, trout, catfish and whitefish are farmed, but carp make up the largest part of the harvest. Fifteen per cent of the fish caught are exported to Germany, Austria, France, Italy and Belgium.

1544 with a loggia and a stepped gable with tiny turrets. The building is now a hotel. Also worth mentioning is the house of Štěpanek Netolický, who developed fish farming under the Rožmberks (commemorative plaque). The Town Hall on the south side of the square was built in 1566 and renovated between 1802 and 1820; its tower dates from 1638. The square contains a fountain (1569) and a Marian column (1780).

In the south-west corner of the square the visitor will find the entrance to the *Castle* with its fine Renaissance staircase and elegant courtyards. The castle is now used as a hospital and only the Heraldic Hall of the Rožmberks, the Hall of the Courtiers and the well-maintained park are open to the public.

The church of *St Giles* (Chrám sv. Jiljí) in Husova třída is the main church of Třeboň. It belonged to the third house of Augustinian canons founded in Bohemia, after Prague and Roudnice nad Labem (Raudnitz). The first church was built, together with its monastic buildings, in the third quarter of the 13th century. After 1367 it was replaced by a two-aisled hall-church, which in 1781 underwent Baroque alterations in the course of which the church lost the famous *Altarpiece of the Master of Třeboň (Wittingau)* (c. 1380-90). The panels of the altarpiece were distributed among surrounding churches. Three of them, the *Agony in the Garden*, the *Entombment* and the *Resurrection* survive and are now in the National Gallery in Prague. The works of the Třeboň Master are impressive for their novel effects of light and shade, the elongated proportions of the figures and the gentle fall of the draperies; they mark a preliminary stage in the development of the the 'Schöner Stil' (International Style). This style influenced art throughout Europe around 1400; another celebrated example is the *Madonna of Třeboň*, a Gothic limestone sculpture of the period c. 1390. There are also some impressive 15th-century wall paintings: the *Foundation of the Monastery*, *Apostles*, *St Christopher* and the *Last Judgement*.

The *Town Walls* have survived almost in their entirety and still have the three town gates: the Hradécká brána (Hradec gate) to the east, the Svinenská brána (Sviny gate) and the Novohradská brána (Novo Hrady gate) to the south.

Western Bohemia (Západní Čechy)

Plzeň (Pilsen)

Plzeňský Prazdroj, Pilsner Urquell, 'Pilsen's Original Source': the original fount of all lagers, and never equalled. Few towns are as completely identified with their product as **Plzeň** (Pilsen). Yet it was not the breweries but the Škoda armaments factory that once gave Plzeň, the sixth biggest town in Czechoslovakia (population 180,000), its industrial muscle and the nickname of the 'Bohemian Krupps'. The coal and iron ore mined here in large quantities led to the development of the powerful steel industry, while the presence of very pure kaolin encouraged a high-quality ceramics industry. Nevertheless there is much in the historic town centre to attract the foreign visitor; in particular the impressive Gothic Church of St Bartholomew, the decorated Renaissance town hall and the magnificent medieval burghers' houses.

In the 10th century the ducal castle of *Plzenec* (Pilsenetz) stood in the valley of the Úslava on a rocky spur called Hůrka. The adjacent town was already a place of some importance, boasting three churches and five chapels, the remains of which date back to the origin of the settlement (c. 1266). But when in the 13th century the trade routes linking Regensburg and Nuremberg with Prague and Saxony increased in importance, it was not Plzenec that profited, but a settlement that had developed about 10 km north-west of the old castle, at the crossroads of the trade routes on the confluence of the Mže and Radbuza rivers. In 1295 Wenceslas II made this the royal town of *Nova Plzna*. His lokator Heinrich (Jindřich) settled Bavarian craftsmen and merchants there, who laid out their new town on a strict chequerboard pattern: a network of streets and alleys forming 22 rectangular blocks. Soon all of these blocks were filled with 300 half-timbered and stone houses, most of them one storey high. The Franciscans and Dominicans each built a friary with a church. Two blocks in the middle of town were kept empty as a market and assembly place, and it was here that the big parish church was built. Earthworks and a wall with towers and the two little rivers enclosed the town, which covered approximately 22 hectares. Nova Plzna became Plzeň (pronounced 'Pilsen'), while the town next to the castle on the Úslava was given the name *Starý Plzenec* (Altpilsenetz, 'Old Pilsenetz'). The name Plzeň is derived from the boggy ground (*plzký*, slippery) in the region of the four rivers, the Radbuza (Radbusa), the Mže (Mies), the Úhlava (Angel) and the Úslava, which join at Plzeň to form the Berounka (Beraun) which itself flows into the Vltava.

During the Hussite Wars Plzeň backed the Hussites. In 1419 Jan Žižka built the town into a fortress and destroyed all its monasteries. In the spring of 1420 the Imperial army laid siege

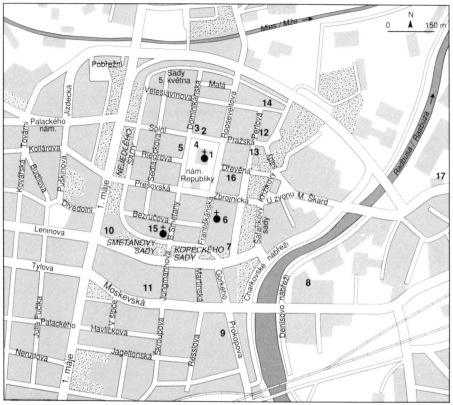

Plzeň (Pilsen)
1 St Bartholomew   2 Town Hall   3 Emperor's House   4 Plague Column   5 Archdeaconry   6 Church
of the Assumption   7 West Bohemian Museum   8 House of Culture   9 Chamber Theatre   10 Tyl
Theatre   11 Children's Theatre   12 Watertower   13 Butchers' Hall   14 Museum of Brewing   15 St
Anne   16 Gerlach House   17 Plzeň Brewery

to it. When Žižka realized that he could not hold the town, he surrendered it on condition
that the defenders were given free passage. Henceforth Plzeň was a bulwark of Catholicism
which the Hussites were unable to recapture despite several sieges. Because of its loyalty the
Emperor Sigismund freed the town from any taxes, and this resulted in a remarkable
economic boom. In the wars of succession in the late 1440's Plzeň opposed the Utraquist
George of Poděbrady and as a consequence Pope Paul II granted to this 'most faithful
Catholic town' the right to add two keys and a knight with half an eagle to the its coat of arms.

From 1496 to 1561 Plzeň was ruled by the Sternberg family, and thereafter came directly
under the king. The prosperity and importance of the town grew with a flourishing trade in
cloth and lifestock. Merchants, craftsmen and artists from the German-speaking countries

settled here, and architects from northern Italy arrived bringing with them the new ideas of the Renaissance. In 1599 the Emperor Rudolph II fled from the plague in Prague with his court and foreign ambassadors, and for nine months Plzeň was the rather overstretched centre of the Holy Roman Empire.

During the Revolt of the Estates Plzeň was fiercely fought over, while maintaining its Catholic and pro-Habsburg stance. In 1618 after a siege lasting several months it was captured by an army of the Estates, but on 26 March 1621 the Imperial general Tilly retook the town. Shortly before his murder at Cheb (Eger), some 80 km northwest, Wallenstein had established his winter quarters at Plzeň (1633-34), and it was here that hubris overtook him and, in an act that amounted to treason against the emperor, he compelled his officers to swear personal loyalty to him (the 'Pilsner Schüsse').

In the 17th and 18th centuries Plzeň was a peaceful country town. The Czech proportion of its population increased constantly and by 1800 it reached almost 80 per cent. At the beginning of the 18th century the first small factories were established and in the 19th century industry developed. In 1842 the brewers of Plzeň joined together to create the Prazdroj (Urquell) beer, and by the 1860's Plzeň was connected by railway with Bavaria and central Bohemia.

In spring 1945 General Patton halted the Allied army's advance at Plzeň, since by an agreement made the previous year Czechoslovakia was to be occupied by the Red Army.

The nucleus of the old town is nám. Republiky, formerly the 'Ring', measuring 139 metres by 193 metres, the largest town square in Bohemia. In it stands the massive Gothic **Church of St Bartholomew** (Chrám sv. Bartoloměje), the main parish church of Plzeň. Construction of this hall-church began shortly after the founding of the town in 1297 but was not completed until around 1476. In 1310 King Henry of Carinthia placed the church under the patronage of the Teutonic Order of Knights, whose shields carved in stone still decorate the exterior of the choir. The main portal at the west end is flanked by two towers. The slender green spire of the north steeple reaches a height of 103 metres, the tallest in Czechoslovakia. In 1663 the main

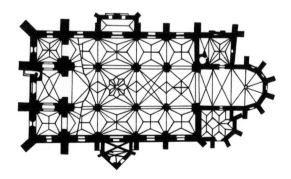

Plzeň (Pilsen), St. Bartholomew's Church, plan

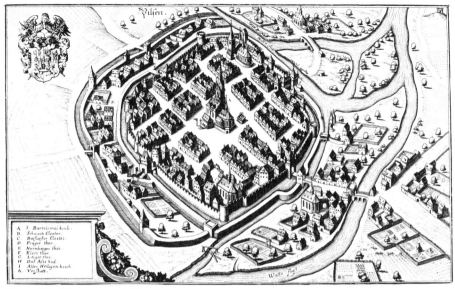

View of Plzeň from Merian's Topography

portal was given a crucifixion group and the façade a statue of St Bartholomew. The star vault of the nave and aisles rests on plain, unadorned piers. The high altar dates from 1883 but is decorated with the 'Plzeň Madonna' a Gothic statue made c. 1390 in the 'Schöner Stil' (International Style). In the early 16th century the Sternbergs, recently enriched by George of Poděbrady, founded the chapel that bears their name, which was built by an anonymous master on the south side of the choir. Its remarkable vault with a pendant boss make it one of the most exciting works of the Late Gothic, while its wall paintings are Renaissance (c. 1600). A wrought-iron grille on the exterior of the choir protects the magnificent carving of the *Agony in the Garden* (16th century).

On the north side of the square, with its ranks of little gold pennants and exuberant sgraffito decoration stands the *Town Hall* (plates 22, 28) built between 1554 and 1559 by an Italian from Lugano, Giovanni de Statio. It is one of the most splendid Renaissance buildings north of the Alps, although in fact most of the present sgraffiti were made between 1908 and 1912. Plzeň is full of sgraffito art, many of the houses having been decorated by the great painter Mikoláš Aleš. Adjoining the town hall is the *Emperor's House* (No. 290) where Rudolph II resided during his stay at Plzeň (the date 1565 is above the door). On its façade is a statue of the knight Žumbera, a kind of Roland figure, which used to surmount a fountain. Some identify him as John of Luxembourg. The neighbouring *corner house* (No. 289), built after the great town fire of 1507 on the site of two residential houses, has a Neo-Classical exterior. Both houses are now joined to the Town Hall, the official seat of the mayor. Town council meetings and weddings are held in the building, and the great ceremonial hall is used for degree ceremonies, chamber concerts and other events.

The *Plague Column* (Mariánsky morový sloup) between St Bartholomew's Church and the Town Hall was made by Christian Widemann in 1681. On the north, east and south sides of the square are more Gothic houses remodelled in the Renaissance and Baroque periods. Opposite the west portal of the church the *Archdeaconry* (Arciděkanství; No. 234) is perhaps the finest Baroque building in Plzeň. It was acquired in 1344 by the Teutonic Order for the town's priest, and rebuilt in the Baroque style by Jakob Auguston in 1710.

In Františkánská ul. which runs south from the south-east corner of the square is the *Church of the Assumption* (Kostel Nanebevzetí Panny Marie) of the former Franciscan friary. The Gothic building suffered considerable damage during the Hussite troubles and the Thirty Years' War and was eventually restored in the Baroque style. On the east range of the beautiful cloister is the delightful chapel of St Barbara with frescoes painted c. 1460 depicting scenes from the life of the saint.

The *West Bohemian Museum* (Západočeské muzeum) in Kopeckého sady (Kopecký Park) contains works of art from the 14th century to the present day, as well as collections of porcelain, ceramics, glass, clocks, furniture and arms. South of the park in Prokopova ul. stands the *Chamber Theatre* (Komorní divadlo), formerly the 'Deutsches Theater'. To the west Kopecký Park continues as Smetana Park (Smetanovy sady) which in turn becomes Nejedlý Park (Nejedlého sady) at the beautiful *Tyl Theatre* (Divadlo J.K. Tyla), in front of which stands a monument to the dramatist Josef Kajétan Tyl (1808–1856) who died in Plzeň; Tyl's real fame is for writing the song that would become the Czech national anthem, 'Kde domov můj?' – 'Where is my home?'. The *Children's Theatre* (Divadlo dětí) at Moskevská 17 is in the tradition of the great puppeteer Josef Skupa (1892–1957) who created his famous puppets 'Spejbl' and 'Hurvínek' at Plzeň. His pupil, the book illustrator and film director Jiří Trnka (1912–1969), gave Czech puppet film its worldwide reputation.

In Pražská ul. which runs eastwards from the north-east corner of the square are several Renaissance houses with Gothic origins. The old *Water Tower* (Stará vodárenská věž; early 16th century) at the east end of the street was intended to strengthen the town walls near the Prague Gate. The Gothic *Butchers' Stalls* (Masné krámy) opposite the tower are now used by the West Bohemian Museum for temporary exhibitions and as a concert hall. Veleslavínova ul. contains a Late Gothic malt house which is now the *Museum of Brewing* (Pivorarské muzeum) with interesting exhibits from the history of the Plzeň brewing industry. The ethnographical department of the West Bohemian Museum is housed in the *Gerlachovský dům* in Dřevěná ul., whose façade, stretching over two burghers' houses, is a pot-pourri of Gothic, Renaissance and Baroque elements. In ul. B. Smetany stands the Baroque *Church of St Anne* built in the 18th century by Jakob Auguston.

East of the old town the road to Prague – beyond the Radbuza it is called U Prazdroje – leads to the *Západočeské pivovary* (West Bohemian Brewery) founded in 1842 as a 'civic brewery' by the combined brewers of Plzeň; it is the oldest, biggest and most famous Plzeň brewery. In the large beer tavern beside its grand entrance gates – erected in 1892 for the firm's 50th anniversary and shown on every label – the visitor can sample the 'Prazdroj' (Urquell) beer. The inimitable flavour and bouquet of this celebrated beverage is said to be due to the excellent quality of the Plzeň water, the home-dried malt, the particularly aromatic Žatec (Saaz) hops and above all to the microclimate created in the cellars, which have more than 9 km of passages, where the beer is matured. At present the brewery produces more than 25.5 million hectolitres –560 million Imperial gallons– of *Plzěnský Prazdroj* a year, with an original gravity of 12%.

The *Škoda Works* to the north of the town employ 35,000 people. The small metalwork factory developed in the 19th century into one of the biggest steel works in the world. Today nuclear reactors, turbo aggregates, rolling mills, metallurgical plant, electric motors, electric locomotives and automatically controlled production centres are made here and exported to about 70 countries in the world. Volkswagen have recently bought a large stake.

At **Starý Plzenec** about 10 km south of Plzeň are some remains of the Přemyslid castle on the Hůrka: the Romanesque rotunda of St Peter dating from the 10th century (remodelled in the 16th century) and foundations of the castle which is first mentioned in 976. A nature trail links the most interesting features of this historic site.

Near Plzeň are two major works by Johann Santini-Aichel: the Cistercian abbey of **Plasy** (Plass), 20 km to the north, offers a rare opportunity to see his painting, which decorates buildings by his mentor, the French architect J.-B. Mathey; and at **Kladruby** (Kladrau), 23 km west, the flower of his career. Like Sedlec (see p. 155) this Benedictine abbey had been razed by the Hussites and again in the Thirty Years' War; Santini-Aichel began work on its restoration in 1712. The abbot was determined to create a 'hitherto unheard-of Gothic manner', a symbol of the return to the true faith. On the outside crocketed pinnacles, lancet and trefoil windows fulfil his vision, and inside the ribs draw crosses, stars and flowers across the vaults with high-pitched virtuosity like a jazz fugue. The climax of the church is the high altar, where swooning Baroque saints and angels perch on a flight of buttresses. The winged ox's head and other symbols of the Evangelists should be noted.

Klatovy (Klattau)

The fragrance of carnations is the characteristic feature of **Klatovy** (population 23,000), the district capital and northern 'gateway to the Bohemian Forest'. It was founded as a royal town by that intensive improver, King Otakar II Přemysl, in 1260. The citizens of Klatovy were later active particants in the Hussite troubles and destroyed their Dominican friary. Their refusal in 1547 to give any military support to Emperor Ferdinand I resulted in the loss of their privileges for some time. Today the inhabitants of Klatovy work mainly in the textile, machine, leather and timber industries, as well as in carnation cultivation.

On the large market place stands the Renaissance *Town Hall* completed in 1559 and incorporating the dour *Black Tower* built between 1547 and 1557 by Master Anton of

Klatovy and contains a starvation dungeon and a torture chamber; the clock dates from 1759, and the roof from 1872. The tower is 75 metres high and has a panoramic view over the town and the nearby Bohemian Forest from the lookout's gallery. Its blackness was the result of repeated burnings.

Next to the Town Hall are the altogether more charming towers of the Early Baroque church of *St Ignatius* built for the Jesuits by Carlo Lurago and Domenico Orsi between 1654 and 1679, and completed by Karl Ignaz Dientzenhofer in 1717. The splendid doorway dates from 1720. In the crypt are the mummified bodies of Jesuits who were laid to rest here until 1674. The Gothic collegiate church of *St Mary* was built after 1260 and altered many times in the following centuries. It has a freestanding belltower called the *White Tower*. In the market square the visitor should take a look in the former *Pharmacy* (Lékárna) dating from the first half of the 18th century: its rich Baroque furnishings, made by the cabinet and woodcarver Josef Gschwendt, and its equipment are intact. Parts of the 14th–15th century *town fortifications* are in a good state of preservation.

The medieval town of **Domažlice** (Taus), encircled by hills, 57 km from Plzeň and 14 km from the German border, is the main town of Chodsko (Chodenland). This has been for centuries the homeland of the Chods, an unusual Slav ethnic group with their own dialect and customs. On the first weekend after 10 August, St Laurence's Day, Chods from all the surrounding country gather on Svatý Vavřineček (582 metres high) on the western edge of Domažlice to celebrate their colourful church festival with bagpipe music, dancing and song.

Domažlice was founded around 1260 by Otakar II Přemysl as a customs post on the road from Regensburg to Prague. It was settled by Chods and soon afterwards made a royal town. Almost all the important buildings of the town date from the third quarter of the 13th century, including the fortifications with their gates, and the castle. The centre of the picturesque old town of Domažlice is its long market place which divides the town into two parts, north and south. Arcaded houses of the Renaissance, Baroque and Empire styles line the square. On its north side stands the decanal church of the *Nativity of the Virgin* (Kostel Narození Panny Marie). The 13th-century building was renovated in 1747 by Kilian Ignaz Dientzenhofer after a town fire. The uncompromising clock tower, which was also built in the 13th century, was formerly used as a watch tower, and its gallery still gives a good view over the surrounding country. Every evening a trumpeter plays an old Chod melody.

Opposite the church stands the *Town Hall* which was restored in the Neo-Renaissance style. The north-west corner of the main square is occupied by the former Augustinian monastery with its Gothic-Baroque church. To the east the square extends as far as the solid *Lower Gate* (Dolní brána) which was built c. 1270 as part of the town fortifications. Near the Augustinian monastery the 13th-century *Chodský hrad* (Chod castle) with its massive tower is a reminder of the great times of the free Chods. The Chod burgrave resided in the castle, as well as the Royal Chod judges and scribes. Every four weeks the Chod court would meet in the castle and the hereditary judges from all the surrounding Chod villages came to attend it.

In the castle the banners of the Chods, their seals and the charters guaranteeing their privileges were kept. The building, which underwent a Renaissance remodelling, now houses a *Museum* with extensive historical and ethnographic collections. An extensive collection of Chod folk art is also to be found at the Jindřich Jindřich Museum, named after the composer and collector.

The Chods

Nobody knows exactly who the Chods are and where they come from. They are Slavs – this much is undisputed – and indeed the westernmost Slavic groups; they were so warlike and reliable that Duke Bretislav I, who in 1040 had had some difficulty in repulsing an army of the German king (and future emperor) Henry III which penetrated the northern part of the Bohemian Forest, settled them as sentries on the Bohemian-Bavarian border. At that time they were given the name 'Chods' from the Czech word *chodit* meaning to walk about or patrol. It was the Chods who guarded the border region, safeguarded the important road over the Schafberg Pass to Regensburg and escorted merchants' caravans. Their weapon was the *cakan*, the Slavic fighting axe. In return for their difficult and responsible task they enjoyed special privileges. They were freemen for life and subject to no lord but the king of Bohemia; no nobleman could acquire property in Chodsko; and the Chods had no forced labour to perform for feudal lords. They were allowed freely to use the forests they tended, for hunting and cutting wood. Because of the dog's head which adorned their banner as an emblem of loyalty and watchfulness, the Chods were also called – more in respect than mockery – the 'Dog's Heads'. The first mention of them as free farmers of the king was in 1325 by John of Luxembourg. Just how feared the Chods were was demonstrated in 1431 when these 'Bohemian border guards' under the Hussite leader Prokop the Great attacked the imperial army in front of Domazlice. Scarcely had the Chods started singing the Hussite war song 'Those who are God's warriors' ('Kroz jsů Boži bojovnici') than the imperial army, which outnumbered them ten to one, fled in panic back to Bavaria, together with the papal legates.

In 1618 the Chods sided with the Estates and so after the Battle of the White Mountain they lost all their privileges. Their free land came under the control of Wilhelm Lamminger von Albenreuth, called Lomikar, who exacted the hardest forced labour from the Chods. In the end the Chods under their leader Jan Sladký Kozina rebelled, but Lomikar with the assistance of imperial troops suppressed the uprising bloodily and in 1695 Kozina was condemned to death. Beneath the gallows in Plzeň market place he prophesied the death of his adversary 'after a year and a day'. The following year on the anniversary of Kozina's execution, as Lomikar was holding a glittering banquet at his castle of Trhanov and scornfully recalling the prophecy, he suddenly collapsed from a stroke. The Czech writer Alois Jirásek (1851–1930) described the bitter struggle of the Chods to regain their royal privileges in his historical novel *Psohlavci* ('The Dogs Heads').

Cheb (Eger)

The district town of **Cheb** (population 32,000) situated not far from the German border on the banks of the river Ohře (Eger) is impressive for its medieval town centre and the remains of its imperial palace. It was at Cheb that Wallenstein, the great commander in the Thirty Years' War, was murdered in 1634, and the great Baroque architect, Balthasar Neumann, was born in 1687.

Traces of Únětice Culture indicate that there was an early settlement on the site (1800–1600 BC) and, on a rock high above the ford, a Slavic castle was built in the 10th century on the foundations of Celtic and Germanic defences. In the 11th century German merchants settled near the castle and founded the village of *Egire*, which in 1149 obtained the right to hold markets. In the same year at Eger the young Swabian duke Frederick married Adela (Adelheid) the daughter of the lord of the castle. In 1167 the castle passed into the possession of the same duke who in the meantime had become the Emperor Frederick I, nicknamed Rotbart or Barbarossa. He extended the castle on a grand scale and held court Diets there. It was one of the series of palaces he established throughout his empire as a means of imposing effective administration over his domains. Eger received its charter as an imperial market town in 1179 and this new status resulted in a great increase of population, while outside the south gate a large Jewish settlement developed. The town was also of importance to Frederick's successors. His son, Henry VI, regularly spent Christmas here, and Henry's son, Emperor Frederick II, summoned court Diets at Eger on five occasions. On 12 July 1213 in the 'Golden Bull of Eger' he was forced to guarantee the status of the Papal States and give up any influence in the election of bishops and other rights in the Church in return for Papal help in his struggle for the German crown.

Several times Eger was occupied by the Kings of Bohemia, but it was not until 1322 that the Imperial city together with the surrounding region of Egerland fell to the Bohemian crown. The German King Louis IV had mortgaged Eger to John of Luxemburg for 20,000 silver marks 'while guaranteeing the full independence from the kingdom of Bohemia'. And indeed the town did preserve a certain amount of independence until the Thirty Years' War, but thereafter Eger was administratively part of Bohemia, then of Austria-Hungary, and since 1918 of Czechoslovakia. Since 1945 the town has officially been called by its Czech name Cheb (bend in the river), which first appears in the sources in the 14th century and was used after 1920 as a second official name for the town besides Eger.

Historic **Egerland** bordered by the Ore Mountains and the Kaiserwald, Böhmerwald and Fichtelgebirge, extended from Kadaň (Kaaden) and Žatec (Saaz) in the north as far as Horšovský Týn (Bischofteinitz) in the south. Until 1945 its predominantly German-speaking population preserved ancient traditions with splendid regional costumes, distinctive half-timbered houses and a peculiar dialect. Eger was also a centre for German resistance to Czech nationalism, and its population welcomed incorporation into the Third Reich. The majority was, in consequence, forced to leave in 1945, and the town has never recovered.

The centre of Cheb is the former market place, now called *nám. krále Jiřího z Poděbrad* (King George of Poděbrady Square) with its fine old houses. The former *Town Hall* on the east side was built by Giovanni Battista Alliprandi in the Baroque style between 1722 and 1728. In the

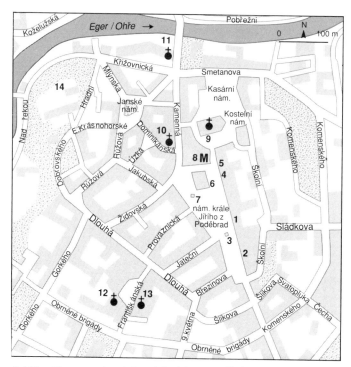

Cheb (Eger)
1 Town Hall
2 Schiller House
3 Roland Fountain
4 Schirnding House
5 Gabler House
6 Špaliček
7 Hercules Fountain
8 Municipal House (Municipal Museum)
9 St Nicholas
10 Dominican Church (St Wenceslas)
11 St Bartholomew
12 Church of the Assumption
13 St Clare
14 Imperial Palace

Schiller House to the right of the Town Hall the poet stayed in 1791, having come here to write his *Wallenstein* trilogy. The *Schirnding House* in the north-east corner of the square stands out because of its tall gable. Goethe lodged in 1821 at the neighbouring *Gabler House* on the left, a Late Gothic burgher's house baroquized in 1783.

The square is adorned with two fountains, the *Roland Fountain* ('Röhrkastenwastl'; 16th century) in front of the Town Hall, and the *Hercules Fountain* ('Wilder-Mann-Brunnen') in front of the *Špaliček* (Stöckl; plate 27), a group of originally eleven houses dating from the 13th century which were at that time inhabited by Jewish merchants. The houses developed from market stalls which were first built of wood and later half-timbered and could have storeys added as need arose ('aufgestöckelt' – hence the German name). Hidden behind the Špaliček is the former *Municipal House* built at the beginning of the 17th century by Mayor Pachelbel. It was in this house that Albrecht von Wallenstein was murdered on 25 February 1634. An imperial decree issued by Ferdinand II three days earlier had declared the generalissimo a traitor and commanded that he be captured dead or alive. Wallenstein's end was planned by colonels Butler (an Irishman) and Lesley (a Scot) and the commandant of Eger, John Gordon (also of Scottish descent). The generalissimo had risen from his sickbed when the assassins entered his room, and was struck down at the window by the English cavalry captain, Walter Devereux, who was richly rewarded. The Municipal House is now the Town Museum which has a varied and extensive collection. Its most precious,exhibit is the 'Eger Antependium', a large altar frontal (218 by 90 cm) with beaded embroidery on silk, made c. 1300 by the Poor Clares of Cheb for the castle chapel.

The archidiaconal church of *St Nicholas* (Kostel sv. Mikuláš; plate 26) is a medley of styles. Remains of the original Romanesque structure (1230–1270) can be seen in the west portal and the lower part of the eastern towers. The Early Gothic choir was built towards the end of the 13th century; the church was given a Late Gothic remodelling in the third quarter of the 15th century, and Baroque alterations in the 18th century, the latter carried out by Balthasar Neumann.

In the 13th century a number of religious orders settled at Cheb: the Teutonic Order of Knights moved in next to St Nicholas, the Dominicans at St Wenceslas (Kostel sv. Václava; now Early Baroque: 1674–1689), the Knights of the Cross with the Red Star at St Bartholomew's (completed in 1414 and now a gallery of Cheb Gothic art), the Minorites (Franciscans) at the Church of the Assumption (Kostel Nanebevzetí Panny Marie; completed in 1285), and the Poor Clares at *St Clare's* (Kostel sv. Klara). The present church

Murder of Wallenstein

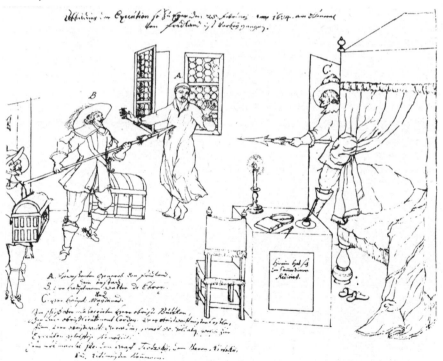

of St Clare was built between 1708 and 1711 to designs by Christoph Dientzenhofer. In this plain and monumental church it is possible to see how the real character of Baroque is not decoration but the strength and fluency of the use of space: here two ovals juxtaposed and energized. It is used for concerts and exhibitions.

On a rock overlooking the river Ohře are the ruins of Frederick Barbarossa's *Imperial Palace* (Kaiserpfalz). At the beginning of the 12th century a Romanesque castle had been built on the site of a Slavic fortress and it was expanded between 1167 and 1175 by the emperor. The nucleus of Barbarossa's palace is the massive hall range (*palas*) with its banqueting hall, 24.5 metres long, 12.8 metres wide and 6 metres high, of which the north wall and part of the east wall with Romanesque round-arched windows are still extant. Two rooms adjoined the hall and beyond them was the kitchen. Below the hall were storage rooms, servants' rooms and a prison. Between 1475 and 1490 the range was given an upper storey with half-timbering. Thereafter the west wall adjoined the house of the commandant of the castle and it was there, a few hours before Wallenstein's murder, that his four closest confidants, Field-Marshal Freiherr von Ilow, Count Trčka, Baron Kinský and Captain Neumann were stabbed to death. The *castle keep* was built between 1180 and 1190 of basalt blocks and hence is called the 'Black Tower'. Its walls are 3.16 metres thick and enclose a rectangle measuring 9.2 by 8.9 metres rising to a height of 18.5 metres. In the 15th century a brickwork addition raised the height to 21 metres. The heavy casemates beside the tower date from the Thirty Years' War.

Still standing complete and carefully restored is the Romanesque *Palace Chapel* (1179–1188). It is a two-storey chapel, as was usual in all imperial palaces (e.g. at Nuremberg Castle), and appears plain and block-like from the outside. The heavy, dark lower storey with cross vaults on massive piers with block capitals, was intended for the servants; the ornamented upper storey is a bright contrast, the cross-rib vaults here resting on four slender polygonal pillars with richly carved capitals. This was reserved for the emperor, his family and his entourage. The two storeys are linked by a wide octagonal opening . A wooden bridge connects the chapel with the residential quarters.

5 km north of Cheb is **Františkovy Lázně** (Franzensbad) with a population of 5000, the smallest of the three famous Bohemian spas and the one which has best kept its Victorian charm. 24 mineral springs (10.1–12.5°C) and radioactive mud have made it a world famous health resort for cardiac, rheumatic and gynaecological ailments. Goethe, for one, called it Paradise on earth.

In the 16th century 'Egerer Säuerling' was already widely known – even Paracelsus tested the water – and the 18th century saw the beginning of the export of mineral water, which is still of importance. In the later 18th century the town physician of Eger (Cheb), Dr Bernhard Vinzenz Adler (1753–1810) promoted the development of the small community into a spa (1793), and in 1807 the town was named 'Kaiser Franzens Bad', or 'Franzensbad' for short, after the Austrian Emperor Francis I. In 1848 the town achieved independent status and in

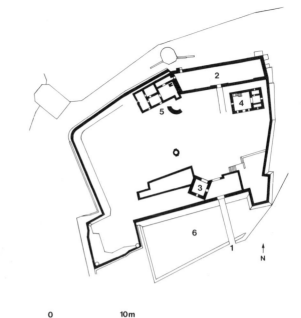

Cheb (Eger) Imperial Palace, plan
1 Entrance
2 Hall Range (palas)
3 Black Tower
4 Castle Chapel
5 House of Castle Commandant
6 Castle Graveyard

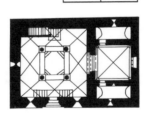

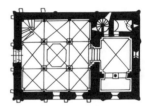

a Double Chapel, section   b Lower Chapel, plan   c Upper Chapel, plan

1865 was even granted a charter, but until 1914 the springs and spa facilities belonged to the town of Eger.

The centre of Františkovy Lázně is the park-like nám. Miru ('Peace Square', formerly Kurplatz with the Colonnade (1912–1914), the Gas-Bath (dry carbon dioxide), the Assembly House (Společenský dům; 1876/77) and the Francis Spring Pavilion (Františkův pramen) dating from 1832. A sculpture shows Eros with a fish, the symbol of fertility. Women who touch the boy-god are supposed soon to become pregnant.

West of the Kurhaus stands *Bath-House I* (Lázně I) built in 1827 which adjoins Dvořákovy sady (Dvořák Park, formerly Kaffeegarten) with the large round wooden pavilion of the *Louise Spring* (Luisin pramen) and the *Cold Spring* (Studený pramen). Also in

221

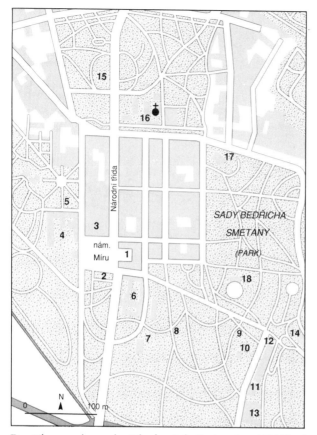

*Františkovy Lázné
(Franzensbad)*
1 *Colonnade*
2 *Francis Spring*
3 *Kurhaus*
4 *Bath I*
5 *Louise Spring and Cold
  Spring*
6 *Bath II*
7 *Hall of Glauber Salts
  Springs III and IV*
8 *New Spring*
9 *Adler Spring*
10 *Adler Memorial*
11 *Meadow Spring*
12 *Salt Spring*
13 *Bath III*
14 *Bath IV*
15 *Music Pavilion*
16 *Catholic Church*
17 *Theatre*
18 *Hotel Imperial*

Dvořákovy sady are the *Glauber Salts Springs I and II* (Glauberův pramen I a II) and the *Sun Spring* (Sluneční pramen). Glauber salts, a sodium sulphate also known as *Mirabilit* (from Latin *mirabilis*, wonderful), are named after the pharmacist Johann Rudolph Glauber (1604–1670); they are a proven laxative.

Next to the Francis Spring stands Bath-House II (Lázně II) behind which nestles the *Hall of Glauber Salts Springs III and IV* (Dvorana Glauberových pramenů III a IV; plate 32) in a park where the visitor will also find the *New Spring* and the *Adler Spring*, named after the founder of the spa. Not far from the spring is a memorial to the doctor. The Colonnade of Czech-Soviet Friendship (kolonáda Československo-sovětského přátelsví) contains the *Meadow Spring* (Luční pramen) and, shrouded in unpleasant odours, the *Salt Spring* (Solný pramen), which are flanked by *Bath-House III* (Lázně III) to the south and *Bath-House IV* to the north.

From the main square the broad Národní třída (formerly Goethestrasse), lined mainly with grand houses from the turn of the century, runs through the centre of the regularly planned town centre. The house of the *Three Lilies* (U tří lilií; No, 10) dates from 1794 and is one of the first boarding houses to be built in Franzensbad. Beethoven stayed nearby, and there is a memorial of his visit in 1812. The northern end of Národní třída reaches the Kurpark itself, with a particularly beautiful music pavilion built of finely joined woodwork.

Adjacent to the town centre to the east is Sady Bedřicha Smetany (Bedřich Smetana Park) with the Goethe Fountain, the cubist Town Theatre (1906) and Municipal Museum. The imposing Hotel Imperial is still one of the leading hotels of the town.

Karlovy Vary (Karlsbad)

' "It's a Matlocky sort of a place," cried a young lady as I passed an elegant party, who were sauntering about the pleasant grounds behind the *Theresienbrunn*, "it's a Matlocky sort of a place!" and a merry laugh followed the iteration of her ingenious adjective.' Walter White, *A Summer's Holiday*, 1857.

Karlovy Vary or **Karlsbad** is the best known of the spas in the West Bohemian triangle above the confluence of the river Teplá (Tepl) with the Ohře (Eger). The hot springs were used in the middle ages, but it was from the 18th century onwards that Karlsbad achieved world fame when emperors, kings and tsars, Russian grand dukes, politicians and statesmen, Turkish princes, Indian maharajas and international financiers met here.

The history of the spa began with Charles IV who gave the place his name. A legend describes how the emperor discovered the steaming springs one day when his hounds were hunting a fine stag. The stag attempted to escape by leaping with a mighty jump from a high rock and the hounds sprang after it but began to howl horribly when they landed in the hot spring water. There is more solid historical evidence that the emperor's personal physician, Baier, tested the water, found it curative and recommended the foundation of a bath at the springs. In 1349 the settlement was given the name 'Karlsbad' (the Czech name means 'Charles's Boilings'). As early as 1370 Charles IV granted his 'beloved Karlsbaders' a town charter with the laws of the nearby town of Elbogen (Loket), and he came frequently to the Teplá to bathe in the 'miraculous waters'.

In the 15th century prominent visitors began to frequent the spa, including the margraves of Kulmbach and Bayreuth, and in the 16th century the princes of Brandenburg and Saxony, Archduke Ferdinand of the Tyrol, the Dukes of Pomerania and Mecklenburg, as well as sundry Italian and Polish counts, all spent time at Karlsbad. At the beginning of the 16th century the physician Dr Wenzel Payer introduced the drinking of the waters as a cure; before then they had only been used for bathing.

A terrible flood in 1582 marked the beginning of a century of hardship for the town: in 1604 almost all its 162 houses were destroyed in a fire; in 1627 Emperor Ferdinand II confiscated the property of the Protestant town. It was only after the citizens had reverted to the Catholic faith that the emperor confirmed its old privileges. In 1632 the Polish and Croatian troops plundered the town, and in 1640 and 1646 the Swedes wreaked havoc in the Teplá valley.

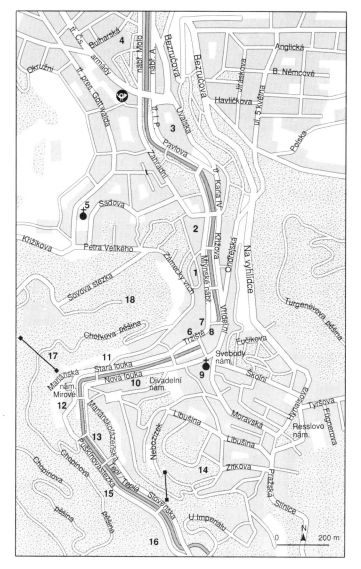

Karlovy Vary
(Karlsbad)
 1 Mill Spring
   Colonnade
   (Kolonáda
   Mlýnská)
 2 Bath III
 3 Thermal
   Sanatorium
 4 Bath V
 5 Russian Church
 6 Market Colonnade
   (Tržní kolonáda)
 7 Castle Tower
 8 Sprudel (Vřídlo)
 9 St Mary
   Magdalene
10 Municipal Theatre
11 Stará Louka
12 Hotel Pupp
13 Bath I
14 Sanatorium
   Imperial
15 Puškinova stezka
16 Art Gallery
17 Funicular Railway
   to Friendship
   Heights
18 Hirschensprung
   (Jelení skok)

Towards the end of the 17th century the spa achieved world fame: in 1682 Elector Johann Georg III of Saxony came here, and he was followed by Augustus the Strong of Saxony and Poland, Frederick III of Brandenburg and Duke Ernst August of Hanover. In 1707 Emperor Joseph I made Karlsbad a royal free town. In 1711 and 1712 'the great Tsar Peter' met

Wilhelm von Leibniz here to 'make learning, arts and sciences flourish in the Russian Empire'. Bach came here twice (in 1718 and 1720) in the suite of the Duke of Anhalt-Cöthen. By the 1730's Karlsbad was on the itinerary of both the Imperial court and ordinary tourists. Nugent's *Traveller's Guide or Grand Tour* specifies that 'the course of drinking the waters, bathing and sweating, is very severe and disagreeable'. Consequently much effort was expended on the entertainment, with lavish balls, concerts and torch processions. Goethe, who visited Karlsbad thirteen times between 1785 and 1823, knew of 'no more pleasant or more comfortable stay'. He wrote to Wilhelm von Humboldt in 1812: 'Weimar, Karlsbad and Rome are the only places where I would like to live.'

Absolutism took a turn for the worse here too, when in 1819 the Austrian Chancellor Metternich invited the representatives of the 'trustworthy' states to Karlsbad and with them issued the 'Karlsbad Decrees'. The assassination at Mannheim on 23 March 1819 of the dramatist Kotzebue by a theology student served as a pretext for the wholesale repression of pan-Germanist and liberal agitation, which within the century would destroy the old Europe so deftly reassembled at the Congress of Vienna in 1815. The agitation was focussed on the universities and these were henceforth to be subject to strict supervision. Revolutionary teachers were dismissed, the student Burschenschaft (the pan-German student fraternity) prohibited, and censorship intensified.

In the 19th and early 20th centuries anyone who was anyone made their way to Karlsbad: King Gustav IV of Sweden, Archbishop Count Genga (later Pope Leo XII); Prince Blücher arrived in 1816 in Napoleon's carriage which he had captured at Waterloo; Beethoven, Liszt, Weber, Robert Schumann and Frédéric Chopin. There seemed to be no better place for political meetings than Karlsbad: in 1863 King Wilhelm I of Prussia arrived incognito as Count Zollern, bringing with him his minister Otto von Bismarck. In 1864 the two met Emperor Franz Joseph I of Austria. Between 1874 and 1876 Karl Marx wrote part of *Das Kapital* at Karlsbad. The battlelines of the First World War were laid here with a succession of meetings: between Clemenceau and Edward VII to establish the Entente Cordiale, and, in May 1914, between the German and Austrian chiefs-of-staff, Helmut von Moltke and Conrad von Hötzendorf, to coordinate their armies.

The centre of the spa is the *kolonáda Mlýnská* (Mühlbrunnkolonnade; Mill Spring Colonnade, 1871–1881; plate 31), sometimes called Zítek Colonnade after its architect, Josef Zítek (who also built the National Theatre in Prague), and sometimes the Czechoslovak-Soviet Friendship Colonnade. The end pavilions are surmounted by twelve allegorical statues by Otto Mentzel , representing the months. The building replaces a Baroque bath-house of 1792 and a Neo-Classical colonnade of 1811. No less than four of the most important thermal springs (42–62°C) are here: the Rusalka Spring (Rusalčin pramen), the Prince Wenceslas Spring (Knížete Václava pramen), the Libuše Spring (Libušin pramen) and the Mill Spring (Mlýnský pramen) itself. If the taste of the waters does not seem to have improved since Nugent's time, it can be banished by munching the local sweet wafers (oplatký, Karlsbader

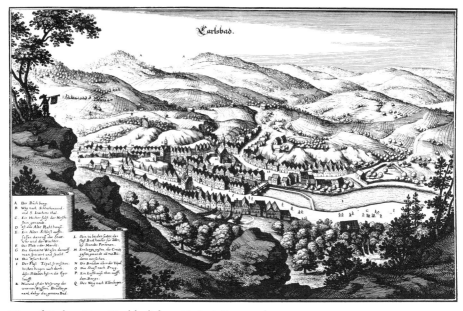

View of Karlovy Vary (Karlsbad) from Merian's Topography

Oblaten) baked here since the 19th century, or by sipping what is known as the thirteenth spring: Becherovka. This remarkable digestive tonic, made from 19 varieties of herbs, was created in 1805 by a pharmacist named Joseph Becher in collaboration with Dr Frobzig, personal physician to the Reichsgraf von und zu Plettenberg-Mietingen.

North of the Mill Spring Colonnade rises the Neo-Gothic *Bath III* (Lázně III), built between 1864 and 1867 as a Kurhaus. Then comes the *Park Spring* (Sadový pramen) next to the slender cast-iron Art Nouveau colonnade of 1880 (a survival from a larger complex) and *Dvořák Park* (Dvořákory sady) with a sculpture of the Czech composer.

The cultural and bathing centre of modern Karlsbad is the impressive *Thermal Sanatorium* built between 1966 and 1977 on the right bank of the Teplá. Further north, opposite the main post office, in the small Smetana Park (Smetanovy sady) is *Bath V* (Lázně V), formerly the Elizabeth Bath, a massive building in a Empire Revival style completed in 1906, the largest balneo-therapeutic establishment in Czechoslovakia.

Above the Mill Spring Colonnade is the Park Spring (Sadový pramen). Not far from it Sadova třída (Park Street), lined by tall trees and magnificent villas, rises steeply to the neo-Byzantine *Russian Church* (1893–1898).

South of the Mill Spring Colonnade *Mlýnské nábřeží* leads to *Tržiště* (the Market Square) with the wooden Market Colonnade (Tržní kolonáda) of 1878, which contains two further thermal springs: the *Emperor Charles IV Spring* (Pramen Karla IV) and the *Market Spring*

(Tržní pramen). The Baroque *Trinity Column* was made by the sculptor Oswald Wenda of Luditz (Žlutice) in 1716. In an artificial grotto above the market square is the *Lower Schloss Spring* (Zámecký pramen dolní); a circular building dating from 1913 protects the *Upper Schloss Spring* (Zámecký pramen horní). The tall *Castle Tower* (Zámecká věž) is part of the town castle built by Emperor Charles IV in 1358.

The spacious modern Vřídelní kolonáda (Sprudel Colonnade) leads to the *Sprudel* (Vřídlo), the oldest and hottest of the Karlsbad springs. The water, 73°C, shoots up to a height of up to 12 metres in powerful thrusts: 2030 litres a minute, about 3 million litres a day with over 19,000 kg of minerals (6.46 grams a litre). Since these minerals soon solidify and block the outlet of the spring the Sprudel has always been seeking new openings over the centuries. It has been tamed by means of subterranean structures, overflow towers, and annual re-boring of the passages. Nowadays Sprudel water is mostly processed to produce 'Karlsbad Salts' which have a worldwide reputation as a laxative. Among the popular souvenirs of Karlsbad are flowers and fashion jewellery petrified in Sprudel water, or mosaics of Sprudel stones.

It is surprising in this town so redolent of the Belle Epoque to find Kilian Ignaz Dientzenhofer's masterpiece, *St Mary Magdalene* (Kostel sv. Maří Magdaleny) in nám. Svobody, built between 1732 and 1736 for the Order of the Knights Hospitaller to replace the town's parish church of 1485. Closely related to his Prague church of St John on the Rock (see p. 132), the Karlsbad church nevertheless expresses a longitudinal thrust more clearly: the oval nave is the essential unit of articulation, both inside and out. Its structure, together with that of the sanctuary, another oval set at right angles to the nave, is backlit by the subsidiary chapels. The towers of the façade were rebuilt in 1861. The high altar, shaped like a portal, is decorated with works by the west Bohemian sculptor Jakob Eberle: statues of *St Jerome, St Augustine, Sts Peter and St Paul*, the *Assumption of the Virgin* and the *Trinity with an Angel* (1759). The painting of *St Mary Magdalene* is by Johann Hermann of Vienna (1847). Bernard Hoffmann made the pulpit (1751).

The *Municipal Theatre* (Divadlo Vítězslava Nezvala) in Divadelní nám. (Theatre Square) was built in 1886. Karlsbad had its own theatre by 1717, and the first references to

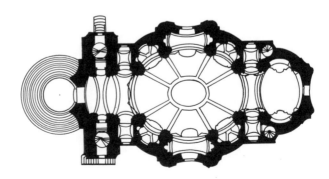

Karlovy Vary (Karlsbad)
St Mary Magdalene, plan

performances here go back even earlier, to 1602. The present theatre is named after an important Czech dramatist and lyric poet, Vítěslav Nezval (1900–1958).

The street leading along the Teplá from the market place is now once again called *Stará louka* (Alte Wiese; Old Meadow), after being named for several decades after the Heroes of the Dukla Pass (see p. 409). This famous and popular promenade, which was once lined with branches of all the leading European shops, opens into Mírové nám. (formerly Goetheplatz), where the greatest of all spa hotels, *Grand Hotel Pupp* (until recently renamed 'Hotel Moskva') still stands. Around the middle of the 18th century the great places of entertainment in old Karlsbad were grouped at this southern end of the spa: the Saxon Hall (Sächsischer Saal) (1701), the Becher'sches Lusthaus (1726) and the Böhmisches Saal (1728). In 1760 the confectioner Johann Georg Pupp came to Karlsbad, found a job at the Mitterbacher Konditorei, married the boss's daughter and in 1775 acquired the Böhmischer Saal which developed in the course of a century into the world-famous Pupp Hotel. The present building dates from 1872. Diagonally opposite it the Viennese architects, F. Fellner and H. Helmer, took a break from constructing theatres to build the grandiose *Bath I* (Lázně I), formerly called the 'Kaiserbad', between 1893 and 1895 in the style of the French Renaissance. Within it the 'Fürstenbad' (Prince's Bath) and the 'Zandersaal' are worth seeing. From Divadelní nám. and from Slovenská třída funicular railways (Lanovka) go up to the enormous *Sanatorium Imperial* (1910–1912) with 320 rooms. This was a meeting place for international finance, while the aristocracy preferred the Pupp.

Puškinova stezka (Pushkin Way; formerly Goetheweg) leads southwards past the numerous memorial plaques and monuments, including a bust of Goethe by Adolf Donndorf (1883) and a monument to Schiller (1905), to the *Art Gallery* (Galerie umění) with exhibitions of modern Czech artists.

Behind the Hotel Pupp a cable railway (signposted 'Lanovka') leads to Výšina Přátelství (Friendship Heights) with a viewing tower and restaurant, 174 metres above the town. From the stop quiet woodland paths lead to the *Petrova Výšina* (Peter Heights) over which Peter the Great is supposed to have ridden bareback. From here there is a spectacular view over the spa district of Karlovy Vary. To the east the walker will find *Jelení skok* (Hirschensprung; Deer's Leap), a steeply projecting cliff with a bronze chamois buck (Kamzík) on top. Another footpath runs across Gogolova pěšina (Gogol Way) to Three Crosses Mount (U Tři Křížů; 551 metres) and up to the *Goethovo Rozhledna* (Goethewarte; Goethe viewing point; 636 metres) with an observation tower. A more curious monument is the Findlater Temple, like the Anglican Church (1877) a forlorn reminder of times when Bohemia was more to the English than Neville Chamberlain's 'far-away country of which we know little'.

11 km south-west of Karlovy Vary on the other side of Road 6/E48 the Ohře makes a narrow loop, somewhat like an elbow, around a high granite rock with the charming little town of **Loket** (Elbogen – both names mean elbow), which rises in terraces at the foot of a splendid castle. Goethe called Elbogen 'a work of art in landscape'. On his journeys to Karlsbad and

Karlovy Vary (Karlsbad)

Marienbad he always stopped several days in the little town with its picturesque market place, coming here for the last time in 1823 to celebrate his 74th birthday with his last love, Ulrike von Levetzow (see p. 230). She was only 21.

The castle (colour plate 9) was built by Otakar I Přemysl at the end of the 12th century to protect the western border of Bohemia. In 1227 Elbogen was already mentioned as a *civitas* (town). Around 1237 Wenceslas I enlarged the fortress to receive the German king, Conrad IV, and c. 1240 he made the settlement around the castle a royal town. In 1376 Emperor Charles IV held court at Elbogen. After the Thirty Years' War the castle fell into decay and from 1822 it was used as a state prison.

The narrow market square is crowded with medieval houses behind Gothic, Renaissance and Baroque façades. A memorial plaque in the inn *U bílého koně* (Zum weissen Ross; the White Horse) in the market square commemorates Goethe's visits to Elbogen (there is also a monument to him outside the town walls, made by Willy Russ in 1932). The Late Gothic church of *St Wenceslas* (13th century) was remodelled in the 18th century. The *Town Hall* is the work of Abraham Leuthner (1682–1686), and the Trinity Column, 15 metres high, is by Oswald Wenda. The *Margrave's House* of the castle now contains a museum with collections of glass, porcelain and pewter; a meteorite weighing 108 kg allegedly found in the castle well is known as the 'petrified burgrave'.

Mariánské Lázně (Marienbad)

No less well known than Karlsbad in the 19th and early 20th centuries was **Marienbad** (colour plate 10), the most recent of the three great West Bohemian spas. The 43 cold mineral springs (9–12°C) of various mineral compositions, and the mud rich in iron sulphate are used as cures for ailments of the stomach and intestines, gall bladder, kidneys and bladder, skin, respiratory tract and nerves. Marienbad's altitude (623 metres above sea level) and its extensive network of well-kept footpaths are added attractions when balneological therapy palls. In the late 19th century Marienbad was the most progressive of the spas. Work here inspired the development of balneology as a valid field for academic research, a status which was confirmed by the Charles University in Prague when it founded the first chair in this subject. It was at Marienbad that mudbaths, which are now used everywhere, were prescribed for the first time.

In 1341 the Premonstratensian abbey of Teplá (Tepl), which means 'warm', founded the village of *Auschowitz* near the springs. In 1710 Abbot Raimund II of Teplá arranged for the cleaning of the springs, to which the ill and infirm were flocking in ever increasing numbers, and built a pilgrims' hostel there. The abbey sold the healing waters in barrels to Vienna and other large towns. In order to reduce the transport costs the monastery's pharmacist, Damian Schulz, started evaporating the water to produce 'Tepl Salts' and erected a cross next to the 'Salty Spring', which thereafter was known as 'Cross Spring'. In 1791 the monastery physician, Dr Josef Nehr, built the first bath house, a crudely built wooden structure with four bathing rooms. He later came to be regarded as the founder of the spa. Fourteen years later another, larger bath house was built to satisfy the growing demand.

Near another spring grateful visitors to the spa hung an image of the Virgin on a tree, which gave the spring the name 'Marienquelle' (St Mary's Spring). Because of this, Abbot Chrysostomus Pfrogner of Teplá named the rapidly developing spa town 'Marienbad'. In 1812 it became a self-governing community, and in 1818, at the request of Abbot Karl Reitenberger, it was granted the status of a 'spa town of the Austrian Monarchy'. Reitenberger used all his efforts to promote the young spa, until in 1827 he was voted out of office for his extravagance in 'throwing the abbey's money into the marsh'.

Goethe, intrepid spa-seeker that he was, first came to Marienbad briefly in 1820, when the spa had only been officially established for two years. In August of the following year he returned and met the nineteen-year-old Baroness Ulrike von Levetzow. The two were together almost every day, and again in the following summer of 1822. By August 1823 Goethe's fatherly affection for Ulrike turned into a passionate love, and he asked for her hand in marriage, but her mother refused. His *Marienbad Elegy* is a touching expression of his renunciation. Goethe never returned to Marienbad, nor to Karlsbad or the other Bohemian spas, and only letters and small gifts were exchanged by the lovers. Ulrike never married. 'It was a good time,' she declared in her old age, 'that we spent with the kind old man. I can assure you that Goethe never kissed me, except in parting.' Still more restrained was the

*Mariánské Lázně
(Marienbad)*

1 New Bath (Nové
   Lázně)
2 Casino
3 Ambrose Spring
4 Central Bath
5 Mud Bath
6 St Mary's Spring
7 Rudolph and
   Ferdinand Springs
8 Main Colonnade
9 Cross Spring
   (Křížový)
10 Church of the
   Assumption
11 Goethe House
12 Hotel Weimar
13 Lutheran Church
14 Municipal Theatre
15 Forest Spring
   (Lesní pramen)
16 Town Hall
17 English Church
18 Russian Church

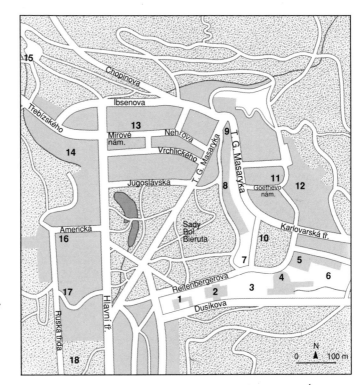

courtship of Kafka and Felice Bauer, a few months of happiness stolen in Marienbad from tuberculosis and the war.

Marienbad soon achieved a worldwide reputation. Magnificent hotels replaced the modest boarding houses, luxury shops were established around the spa gardens and in the colonnades. The future Napoleon III came in 1823, Carl Maria von Weber in 1824, and in 1833 Louis Spohr wrote his waltz *Erinnerung an Marienbad*. Chopin, Wagner, Bruckner and Spontini were all on the 19th-century guest list. Before the First World War Clemenceau and Iswolsky, the foreign ministers of France and Russia came over from Karlsbad several times to confer with Edward VII and his ministers. Indeed Marienbad was a favourite resort of King Edward in his later years; he travelled incognito as Duke of Lancaster and he used his visits for some informal diplomacy. The communists removed his monument in 1948, and the church where he worshipped, though still standing, is sadly dilapidated.

Hlavní třída (Main Street) runs for half a mile through Marienbad to the beautiful spa *park* (Sady Boleslava Bieruta). On the southern edge of the park Reitenbergerova passes the imposing *Nové lázně* (New Bath) and the *Casino*, the former Kurhaus. Both buildings were built around the turn of the century in a Neo-Renaissance style; the New Bath was completed in 1896, the Casino in 1901. East of the Casino is the *Ambrose Spring* (Ambrožův pramen) the water of which contains iron. To be precise there are three springs, of which it is jokingly said the first is for single, the second for married and the third for divorced visitors. Further east are the three-storey Ústředni lázně (Central Bath), the mud bath, and between them the *Marienquelle*, which spouts water containing carbon dioxide and because of its hydrogen sulphide content was known in Goethe's time as the 'Stinkquelle'.

In a recently restored colonnade to the north of the Ambrose Spring is the *Rudolf Spring* (Rudolfův pramen) with a muddy, diuretic water, and the *Ferdinand Spring* (Ferdinandův pramen) with water containing Glauber salts, a remedy for consumption. From here the park rises to the Main Colonnade of the Cross Spring Rotunda (Kreuzbrunn-Rotunda). Once called the 'New Colonnade', this magnificent cast-iron construction, measuring 120 metres long by 12 metres wide, was built between 1884 and 1889 by the Viennese architects, Miksch and Niedzielski. The many thousands of iron braces were cast at the Blansko ironworks near Brno (Brünn). In front of the colonnade stands a bronze statue of Abbot Karl Reitenberger of Teplá (1879), and the 'Singing Fountain' (1988) which has a computer to control the changing actions of the water. By contrast the Rotunda with the *Cross Spring* (Křízovy pramen; 1818) was here in Goethe's time. The water of this, the most important spring in Marienbad, helps cure constipation.

Behind the Catholic church of the Assumption (1844–1848) the garden-like Goethovo nám. (Goethe Square) slopes up to a row of old villas and hotels. The centre of this row is the *Goethe House* (Dům Goethe), formerly the Golden Grapes (U zlatého hroznu). The Neo-Classical building now houses the town museum of Mariánské Lázně. It was built in 1818 and five years later Goethe stayed there. In the garden in front of the house where his statue once stood (until it was removed in 1945 by the retreating Germans) there is now a memorial plaque with an inscription in several languages, though not in German, a reminder of the difficulties of the Czechoslovak-German relationship.

To the north Hlavní třída ends at Mirové nám. (Peace Square, formerly Franz-Joseph-Platz) which contains some large hotels and a fountain (1913). From the town theatre, which until 1990 bore the name of the Russian dramatist Nikolai Gogol, Třebízského ul. leads to the *Forest Spring* (Lesní pramen), the alkaline water of which is taken to alleviate asthma.

At the foot of the Krušné hory (Erzgebirge, Ore Mountains), in a romantic valley below one of its highest peaks, Klínovec (Keilberg) lies the straggling resort of **Jáchymov** (St. Joachimsthal) the first radium spa in the world.

In the 14th century *Konradsgrün*, a farm with a hammer-mill, stood in the valley. The discovery of huge deposits of silver led in 1516 to the founding of a settlement named after St Joachim, which three years later Louis of Bavaria made into a royal mining town, granting the Barons Schlick the right to mint silver gulden there. These 'Joachimsthaler gulden' were valued throughout the Holy Roman Empire and it was from them that a later unit of

The Joachimsthaler (16th century)

currency, the 'Taler', took its name – eventually becoming the dollar. By 1540 St. Joachimsthal grew to become the second largest town in Bohemia with a population of 18,000. Approximately 8000 'Knappen' (miners) and 800 'Steiger' (overmen) were then working in the silver mines. After the Thirty Years' War the deposits were exhausted and St. Joachimsthal reverted to insignificance.

A by-product of silver mining was black pitchblende, a mineral used in the 19th century for the production of dyes for porcelain and glass. Marie Curie-Sklodowska, the Polish physicist working in France, discovered that pitchblende was three to five times more radioactive than pure uranium, whose radioactivity had only just been discovered by Antoine Becquerel in the flurry of activity that followed Röntgen's first observation of X-rays. The Austrian government presented Marie Curie with a ton of residues from the State Manufactury at Joachimsthal, and by a laborious (and though she did not know it, very dangerous) process of fractionation, Marie Curie and her husband Pierre isolated the radioactive element polonium in 1898, and, two years later, radium. Becquerel and the Curies won the Nobel Prize for Physics in 1906 (and Marie Curie won the Nobel Prize for Chemistry in 1911 for her researches into radioactivity). The discovery of radioactivity marked the beginning of a new period of prosperity for St Joachimsthal, for scientists soon discovered that the radioactive mine water had curative qualities. At the beginning of the present century the Joachimsthal master baker Kuhn built the first primitive bath house, and in 1906 St Joachimsthal was officially recognized as a spa.

After the Second World War uranium mining took priority. But the deposits of ore were soon exhausted, and the isolated little town in the middle of forests was able to resume its activity as a spa. Today Jáchymov's business is booming, despite the unsavoury history of its uranium mines, used as forced labour camps in the 1950's.

The historic town centre with its long town square and ancient houses with their fine portals is in the northern part of Jáchymov. The *Town Hall* with its octagonal tower and two stepped gables dates from the 16th century. In the same century (1526) the town *Church of St Joachim* was built; it was restored in 1876. In the old mint behind the town hall the Joachimsthaler were struck; today it houses an interesting museum of mining and minting.

The spa gardens are situated in the southern part of the town, beyond the road that runs through the town. The warm (26–34°C) radioactive (10.5 kBq/l) spouts up from 550 metre deep tunnels at a rate of 400 litres a minute. It is piped to the baths where it is used particularly for ailments of the motor system and the peripheral nervous system. The main building of the early period is the elegant *Radium Palace Sanatorium* (now often called the Madame Curie-

Sklodowska Sanatorium), built between 1910 and 1912 in the Sezession style with a concert hall, several restaurants, a bar and wine cellar. In the park below the Radium Palace is a monument to Marie Curie. The modern counterpart to the Radium Palace is the *Academician Běhounek Sanatorium*, built in 1975 and named after a pupil of Marie Curie. Other spa facilities are under construction.

Northern Bohemia (Severní Čechy)

Ústí nad Labem (Aussig)

Ústí nad Labem (Aussig on the Elbe), population 94,000, is the regional capital of North Bohemia. Its situation at the mouth of the river Bílina (Biela) gave the town its Czech name *Ústí* (mouth). Chemical industry, machine building, glass and porcelain production, textile and clothing industry, and above all its status as the second largest port on the Elbe after Hamburg helped the town become the economic centre of the north-west of the country.

Ústí is first mentioned in 993 as a customs station on the Elbe and on the old trade route between Prague and Meissen. In the second half of the 13th century German colonists migrated here, and in 1260 King Otakar II Přemysl granted the rising settlement its town charter. In spring 1426 the Hussites besieged Aussig, which was defended by Saxon troops. To relieve the town a 20,000 strong 'Crusader army' advanced. A large part of the 24,000 Hussite 'warriors of God' under Procopius the Great (also known as the Bald) formed a massive defensive circle of waggons west of Aussig. On 15 July battle was joined. The Catholic cavaliers broke through the first line of waggons and already sensed victory when 'the heretics [i.e. the Hussites] shot with their guns, of which they had great numbers, and they had long hooks with which they pulled the nobles and their pious men from the horses and killed them.' So wrote the Thuringian Johann Rothe in 1733. The Hussites moved to the counter-attack and the Catholics turned to flight. 'And as they thus retreated the heretics pursued them and killed many of the Christians. And many suffocated, for the weather was very hot and there was much dust ... And of those who escaped each returned to his own land with sorrow. And there was much grief in the land of Meissen, Thuringia and in Hesse ...' The Battle of Aussig is said to have left 10,000 dead; a Catholic nursery rhyme runs: *Prokop der Kahle frisst dich zum Mahle!* ('Bald Prokop's hungry chops Seek a sinner for his dinner!')

On the night of the battle the Hussites occupied Aussig: 'In the year 1426 this town was besieged by Praguers and Taborites and stormed on 6 June, so the Germans wished to relieve it; a bloody battle began on 15 June very early on a holy Sunday and continued until nightfall, when in the end the German army was beaten in flight. And still in the same night this town of Aussig was taken by the Bohemians, all were murdered, the child in the cradle was not spared, and the town was at last burned to the ground' (Merian, 1650). Not until years had passed after its destruction by the Hussites was Aussig rebuilt. Its recovery was difficult and it was only in the 16th century that it returned to economic prosperity. In 1547 it was given a seat in the Bohemian Diet. Like the rest of northern Bohemia the Aussigers converted to Lutheranism, but were re-Catholicized after the Battle of the White Mountain (1620). In

1848 Aussig played a central part in the Bohemian Pan-Germanism; the town's importance was underlined by an economic boom in the late 19th century.

On the north side of the *main square* of Ústí nad Labem, nám. Míru (Peace Square), stands the Town Hall. The plague column dedicated to St Anthony of Padua on the east side of the square was erected in 1708. The archidiaconal church of the *Assumption* (Kostel Nanebevzetí Panny Marie) dates from the 14th century. In 1426 it was destroyed by the Hussites, then rebuilt and received Late Gothic alterations in the late 15th and 16th centuries. Of interest are the 15th-century winged altarpiece and the pulpit of 1574. The church of *St Adalbert* (Kostel sv. Vojtěcha) of the Dominican friary to the east of the archidiaconal church, also dates from the 14th century. Around 1731 it was rebuilt in the Baroque style by the architect Ottavio Broggio of Litoměřice (Leitmeritz). The beautiful *Municipal Theatre* in the Sezession style was built in 1910. One of the old Elbe boats which so contributed to Aussig's prosperity has now become a café (*Kavárna Karla*) near the Nikos Bělojannis Bridge.

An 85 metre high cliff of phonolite (volcanic rock) 2 km upstream from Ústí, is the

The Crossing at Schreckenstein, oil on canvas, by Ludwig Richter, 1837

picturesque setting of **Střekov Castle** (Burg Schreckenstein) built in 1319 by King John of Luxemburg to keep the insubordinate nobles in northern Bohemia in check. The German name 'Schreckenstein' is derived not from the German *schrecken*, meaning 'horror' (despite all the fighting that has taken place here), but from the Old High German *screckan*, meaning 'cracked' – indeed the rock on which the castle stands is split in two. Towards the Elbe the rock falls away almost vertically, a feature that has given rise to many legends. The castle passed from owner to owner, from family to family, until finally in 1563 Emperor Maximilian II gave it to Wenzel von Lobkowicz, who restored the building in the Renaissance style. In the 18th century the Lobkowicz family left Schreckenstein, but the castle remained their property until 1945.

Not surprisingly the castle cast a powerful spell on the German Romantics, most powerfully on Richard Wagner: 'I obtained a tiny room in which a bed of straw was made up for me to sleep on at night. Daily ascent of the Wostrai, the highest peak in the area, revivified me in such a way that, on one moonlit night, I clambered around the ruins of the Schreckenstein castle wrapped only in a sheet, thereby hoping to provide myself with the ghost that was otherwise lacking, and delighting myself with the thought that some nearby wanderer might see me and be terrified.' Wagner was thus sufficiently inspired to start work on *Tannhäuser*.

The castle keep, 17 metres high, has been restored, as have the residential quarters (*palas*) in the upper bailey, the remains of the heated chamber and a linking range, the chapel, part of the castle walls with two watch towers, as well as the Knights's Hall and the kitchen (now a restaurant) in the lower part of the castle.

Litoměřice (Leitmeritz)

The town of **Litoměřice** lies, surrounded by vineyards and hop fields, on the north bank of the Elbe opposite the mouth of the Ohře (Eger). Its population of about 20,000 is mainly employed in the food industry. Litoměřice has the only Catholic seminary in Bohemia and Moravia. Among its most famous sons are the Slav philologist, Josef Jungmann (1773–1847), and the Expressionist artist, Alfred Kubin (1877–1959).

Sickles, daggers and other bronze objects found here indicate that the cathedral hill was already inhabited in Celtic times; its obvious strategic and economic value has always been control of the Elbe crossing already heavily used by merchants' caravans. The Celtic Boii were followed by the Marcomanni, who in their turn were followed by the Slavs. The Slavic Ludomeric tribe – whose name Litoměřice preserves – in the 9th century refortified the earthworks on the hill as a castle for the district. Settlements developed both inside and outside the fortifications. Around the middle of the 11th century the Přemyslid duke Spitihněv II founded the collegiate chapter of St Stephen which in 1057 replaced the heathen tribal shrine with a church. From 1118 onwards German craftsmen and merchants migrated to the settlement in increasing numbers, and its economic strength is proved by the

Litoměřice (Leitmeritz Market Square with Town Hall, Churches and Chalice House)

establishment around 1200 of a mint. In 1227 the castle settlement was the second settlement in Bohemia (after Prague) to be granted a town charter, using the Magdeburg code. During the reign of Charles IV a new town wall was built (1377) which made allowances for Litoměřice's rapid expansion, but it was not until 1452 that the first bridge was built across the Elbe. Although the Minorites (Franciscans) and Dominicans exerted a strong influence in Litoměřice, the town was able by making clever deals with the Utraquists to come through the Hussite Wars relatively unscathed. However, the inhabitants were less fortunate in the Thirty Years' War: when the war ended only 68 of the town's 563 houses were left in a habitable state.

The centre of Litoměřice is the large *Market Square* (the town square or 'Ring') now called Mirové nám. It is one of the largest and most beautiful town squares in Bohemia. In the middle ages annual fairs were held here with merchants coming from Prague, Nuremberg and Saxony. The fruit and grain markets were the biggest in the country: barley and lentils were sent as far afield as Hamburg and Paris. The centre of the market place would be dominated by a *plague column* erected by the grateful citizens after the great epidemic of 1681, if it were not obscured by lime trees. Atop a tall corinthian column sits the Virgin enthroned, while at the foot the four 'plague saints', Bartholomew, Sebastian, Francis Xavier and Roch, stand guard.

The majestic arches of the *Town Hall* date from the original construction of the late 14th century. Between 1537 and 1539 the building was enlarged and remodelled by Master Paul and Carpenter George, who created the complex Renaissance banding of the gables. The figure of Roland on a buttress on the left-hand corner of the building dates back to these alterations. This Roland, a small, powerful man with a club in his hand and a money-bag on his shield, is the symbol of royal free towns and 'Stapelrecht'. The column is decorated with the arms of the town with the date 1539 and reliefs of the more important mayors ('primators'). At its foot is the iron 'Leitmeritz (Litoměřice) cubit' placed there as a standard measure for those attending the market. A stone column on the right-hand corner of the town hall with the heads of two men grimacing with pain is a reminder of the pillory which once stood there.

Inside, the town hall (now a town museum) has a fine staircase and magnificently panelled council hall (1542). It was in this hall that Ferdinand I, King of Bohemia and Hungary, and King of the Romans since 1531, called on the Bohemian Estates for help against the Protestant Elector Johann Friedrich of Saxony. Their limited agreement was the first of a series of failures of nerve which eventually led to the triumph of Habsburg-Catholic authority in Bohemia. The Saxons, abandoned by their natural allies in Bohemia, were defeated at Mühlberg and Ferdinand returned victoriously to Litoměřice. About a hundred years later the 'Peace of Leitmeritz', paving the way for the Peace of Westphalia which ended the Thirty Years' War, was signed in this council hall.

To the right of the town hall, and separated from it by Dlouhá ul., the decanal town church of *All Saints* has stood since 1235. In 1570 it was enlarged and between 1704 and 1731 given its present Baroque appearance by Ottavio Broggio. The church has an interesting three-part pyramidal roof over its long choir, which has a polygonal east end. The most precious of the internal furnishings is the panel painting of the *Agony in the Garden* by the Master of the Litoměřice (Leitmeritz) Altarpiece (c. 1500). Other paintings are by Jan Čech, the carvings were done by an anonymous Teplice (Teplitz) master around 1510. The massive *Town Tower* next to All Saints' Church is a remnant of the fortifications which date from the first half of the 13th century.

The finest *burghers' houses* are those that survive on the south side of the square, which escaped destruction in the fire of 1712: the corner house opposite All Saints', the *Golden Star* (No. 1/9), the *Golden Serpent* (No. 2/10) and the *Black Eagle* (Černý orel; No. 3/11), a Renaissance house with an attractive sgraffiti-decorated façade which until the mid–19th century was a pharmacy. The *Königsburg* inn (No. 4/12) became the property of the town as the community house in 1726; in 1822 the small town theatre was built in its courtyard. Nos. 5/13 and 6/14 were butchers' shops.

The symbol of the town is the *Mrászovský dům* (No. 7/15; colour plate 15) with its chalice-shaped roof. It was built between 1581 and 1584 by the Italian architect Ambrosio Balli for the Utraquist patrician, Mráz of Milešovka (Mras von Milleschau). The chalice-shaped tower on the roof, a masterpiece of architectural woodwork, is intended to recall the Holy Communion and the Utraquist demand for the cup to be given to the laity. Beneath the building is a large wine cellar which extends far under the town square. In 1655 the town took over the 'Chalice House' to use it for stores and salt.

Almost all the houses on the north side of the square were destroyed by the 1712 fire, and the present burghers' houses on this side are all 18th century, or later. Notable are Biener's house (No. 33/160) and its neighbour, the Golden Crown (No. 34/161). Both houses have been licenced to brew beer ever since they were built and together they form the Hotel *Zum Roten Krebs* (the Red Crayfish). Also of interest are the *Old Kamerale* (No. 23/150), the former finance office, the *Black Dog* (No. 27/154) and the *House of the Town Clerk Paul Stransky* (No. 31/158), who once said of his fellow citizens: 'He is a fortunate man who comes away from Saaz without being insulted, from Laun without being beaten up and from Leitmeritz without being drunk.'

The church of the *Annunciation*, south of All Saints', was built by the Jesuits between 1689 and 1701, with a splendid portal and a rich interior, dominated by the massive high altar. After the suppression of the Jesuit Order in 1773 the Leitmeritz brewers took over the church as a storehouse for forty years. Attached to the church is the former Jesuit college. The church of *St Ludmila* belongs to the Capuchin friary (1647–1649). Another church connected with a religious house is the Dominican church of *St James*, a Baroque building erected between 1730 and 1740 by Ottavio Broggio.

West of the town centre, in the oldest part of the town, on a low hill sloping down to the Elbe, stands the Baroque *Cathedral of St Stephen*, built between 1664 and 1681 by Bernardo Spineta and Giulio Broggio, father of Ottavio. Until the remodelling in the 17th century the cathedral furnishings included a winged altarpiece, sadly no longer complete, by an anonymous artist known as the 'Master of the Litoměřice Altarpiece'. It can now be seen in the Litoměřice art gallery. The most famous of its panels is the *Flagellation of Christ*. The rich interior decoration also includes a picture of *St Anthony* by Lucas Cranach and several paintings by Karel Škréta.

North-west of the cathedral Ottavio Broggio built the interesting little church of *St Wenceslas* (Kostel sv. Václava) between 1714 and 1716, a picturesque Baroque building with a long oval nave and a polygonal chancel. The dome rises on a high drum above the bulbous extension of the nave. The pediment of the portal is decorated with a statue of St Wenceslas by F. Dollinger.

Litoměřice is linked by a bridge across the Elbe with the Late Baroque fortress town of **Terezín** (Theresienstadt), which achieved unhappy fame in the Second World War when it was made the ghetto and transit camp for Czech Jews.

Because of the repeated attacks by the Prussians against Bohemia under the incurably aggressive Frederick II, the Austrian generals decided to build a fortress 3 km south of Litoměřice to block their advance. The Emperor Joseph II personally laid the foundation stone on 10 October 1780, after the population of two villages, Trabschitz and Deutsch-Kopist had been moved elsewhere. The emperor named the town 'Theresienstadt' after his mother, the Empress Maria Theresa.

The fortress was conceived by the architect Mezières, using the very latest developments in the science of fortifications, as an elongated octagon with eight bastions, each of which was

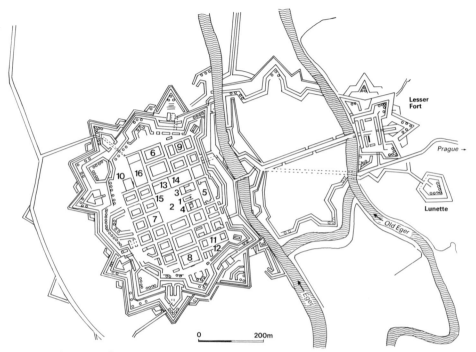

Terezín (Theresienstadt)
1 Garrison Church 2 Parade Ground 3 Fortress Commandant's House 4 Officer's Pavilion
5 Hospital 6 Arsenal (Artillery Barracks) 7 Engineers' Building 8 Catering Depot 9 Infantry
Barracks 10 Officers' Mess 11 Cavalry Barracks 12 Riding School, stables 13 Town Hall
14 School 15 Post Office 16 Colloredo Park

provided with a 'cavalier' (a higher defensive work). A broad glacis with four gates surrounded the main fortress, the nucleus of which was to form a town measuring 700 metres by 500 metres. The Neo-Classical blocks of houses are divided into 20 squares: barracks, arsenals, magazines, engineers' buildings, hospital, commandant's headquarters, dwellings for craftsmen and traders. The monumental Empire-style *garrison church of the Resurrection* was built between 1805 and 1810. The muster and parade ground in the centre of the town (now a well-kept park) measured 110 by 70 metres. The builders of the fortress created a branch of the Ohře (Eger) 4 km long and 50 metres wide to run in front of the main fortress. There were 13 km of underground tunnels linking the defences with each other and with the Little Fortress and with the 'lunettes' (fieldworks).

The town and fortress were completed in 1784. 15,000 people moved into the houses, and the garrison was made up of 16,000 men. Theresienstadt was the biggest and most modern fortress of the 18th century, but it was never to be put to the test, and in 1886, a century after its completion, it was closed. The Little Fortress continued to be used as a state prison of the

Austro-Hungarian Monarchy. It was there that the Serbian nationalist Gavrilo Princip was imprisoned in 1914 after his assassination of Archduke Franz Ferdinand. He died there in 1918, reportedly saying: 'If I had not done it, the Germans would have found another excuse'. In 1940 the Prague Gestapo made the Little Fortress into a police prison.

In 1941 the SS removed the population of Theresienstadt elsewhere and created a *Ghetto* for several thousand Jewish citizens of Bohemia and Moravia. To begin with the ghetto was largely self-governing with cultural facilities, schools, and activities of all kinds, including theatrical and opera performances. However, from 1944 onwards Theresienstadt merely served as a transit camp where the selection was made for transport to the extermination camps. By the end of the war about 33,000 people had died at Terezín and 87,000 taken to their deaths elsewhere. The former military casemates in the *Little Fortress* (Malá pevnost) had been filled by the Gestapo mostly with 'enemies of the state', most of whom were executed. In front of the gateway to this fortress, between the Ohře and the Old Ohře, is the vast graveyard of Jews and victims of the Nazis who died at Terezín.

A tour of the building, which is now a memorial (*Památník Terezín*), takes the visitor past the workroom, guardroom, the office of the prison commandant and the room for prisoners' clothes, into the first courtyard with 17 shared and 20 single cells. Above the courtyard gate the motto of the concentration camps still announces: 'Arbeit macht frei'. The nearest single cell has been turned into a memorial to Princip. The washroom, sickroom and mortuary come next. The visitor then goes through a subterranean passage – part of the old fortress – to the place of execution where, from the end of 1943, around 250 prisoners were shot or hanged. (In August 1945 the remains of 601 bodies were found in the nearby mass grave.) Condemned prisoners passed through the 'Gates of Death' to reach the place of execution.

The fourth courtyard at the eastern end of the Little Fortress was fitted with prison cells when the original cells could no longer contain the new intake of prisoners. The SS would cram up to 12 prisoners into single cells, while up to 600 prisoners would squeeze into the communal cells. In the middle of the Little Fortress were the barracks for the 150 guards. In the 18th-century 'Herrenhof' the commandant lived with a few guards and their families. The second courtyard contained the workshops and guards' canteen, and the third courtyard was used from 1942 onwards for holding woman prisoners. On 8 May 1945 the prisoners of Terezín were freed by Soviet tank detachments.

Only a few kilometres west of Terezín is the town of **Lovošice** (Lobosit), a centre for wine-production and fruit-growing but also for industry. Here, at the point where the Elbe takes a sharp turn northwards to enter the České středohoří (Central Bohemian Range), the Porta Bohemica, Frederick the Great of Prussia fought the first battle of the Seven Years' War on 1 October 1756. The town, which developed from a prehistoric fishing settlement, has a pleasant *market place* surrounded by burghers' houses in the Empire style and dominated by the Baroquized Gothic church of St Wenceslas. The Early Baroque *Castle* was rebuilt by the Schwarzenbergs on the site of an earlier building.

About 16 km north-east of Litoměřice in the midst of hop-fields and fruit gardens lies the town of **Úštěk**, known in the middle ages as Auscha. In the 11th century there is mention of a Slavic castle here called *Husz* or *Usch*. In the 13th century the settlement around it became a market town. At that time it belonged to the Counts Michelberg, but when in 1384 Úštěk received its town charter, it passed into the possession of the lords Berka of Dubá, who converted the castle into a Renaissance schloss. A great fire in 1765 left almost the whole of the town in ashes.

The *market place* (Marktanger) of Úštěk runs through the old town centre. Standing in the middle at its broadest point is the parish church of *St Peter and St Paul*. The present building was built by the Jesuits between 1765 and 1769, but retains the altarpiece painted for its predecessor by the Baroque painter Karel Škréta of Prague. The Town Hall set in a row of old houses was also rebuilt in 1773. Opposite it stands the inconspicuous castle, whose Renaissance residential wing was occupied by the Jesuits after the Thirty Years' War. A few decades later a brewery was established in the building. The finest burghers' houses, some of them with delightful Rococo plasterwork and deep loggias, are on the north side of the market place. From the old town fortifications there are remains of masonry and towers, including the *Picards' Tower*, named after the refugees from Picardy in northern France who, like many similar groups, came to Bohemia in the late 16th century to escape religious persecution. In the Bohemian suburb of the town (west of the Bohemian Gate) a few shaky wooden houses survive of a type whose Czech name *ptačí domky* – 'bird houses' – suggests how they cling precariously, like swallows' nests. They were mostly lived in by Jewish families.

Chomutov (Komotau)

At the foot of the Krušné hory (Erzgebirge; Ore Mountains), at the junction of several important roads is the industrial town of **Chomutov** (Komotau), the centre of which is still interesting. In 1252 the village of Komotau came into the possession of Teutonic Order, which developed it into their most important 'commandery' (headquarters) in Bohemia. Hordes of German colonists followed in the wake of the order, and the Czechs in the neighbouring villages coined the caustic saying: 'Everywhere people, but in Komotau Germans.' In 1335 Komotau received its charter. In 1421 the Hussites under their leader Jan Žižka drove out the Teutonic Knights and destroyed them together with the town; only a few inhabitants escaped the slaughter. Just under a hundred years later Komotau came into the possession of the Lobkowicz family, who introduced Jesuit teachers in order to bring the predominantly Protestant population back to the Catholic faith. The young Christoph Willibald Gluck, whose father was a forester on the Lobkowicz estate, attended the Jesuit grammar school between 1725 and 1730.

In the historic town centre of Chomutov is the *market place* with Late Gothic, Renaissance and Baroque arcaded houses, and, of course, a plague column. The arcade at No. 9 is a very

View of Chomutov (Komotau) from Merian's Topography

fine example of Late Gothic Czech vaulting. The 13th-century church of *St Catherine* was the first Early Gothic church to be built in Bohemia. Attached to the church was the Kommende of Teutonic Knights, on the foundations of which the Lobkowiczes built a Renaissance palace around 1520. After Komotau had become a royal town in 1607 the palace was used as the town hall (today it is the town museum). The church of the *Assumption* (Kostel Nanebevzetí Panny Marie), the Late Gothic parish church of Komotau was built by Josef Schremmel between 1516 and 1545. *St Ignatius* is by Carlo Lurago (1688).

At the beginning of the 13th century German cloth-makers founded a settlement on a terrace on the bank of the Ohře (Eger), which received its town charter in 1260 and was fortified. During the 15th-century wars of religion **Louny** (Laun), together with Žatec (Saaz) and Slaný (Schlan), took the side of the Hussites. After the town was destroyed in 1517 by a fire, reconstruction work was under the direction of the celebrated architect Benedikt Rieth, who was above all responsible for the design of the rebuilt church of *St Nicholas* (1520–1538). Rieth himself died here in 1534, before the work was finished. Only the Gothic belltower had survived almost unscathed and was integrated (at a slight angle) into Rieth's three-aisled hall-church. The castellated gallery of the tower gives a splendid view over the town. The south side of the church was given a portal in the style of the 'Romanesque Renaissance'. The tall building is surmounted by a triple pyramidal slate roof. The magnificent 'loop-star' vaults springing from three pairs of polygonal pillars, are a fine example of Rieth's liquid vaulting. The interior of the church has a Late Gothic stone pulpit (1540) and three gorgeously carved Baroque altarpieces (1701–1704).

Situated on a hill on the right bank of the Ohře (Eger) is the town of **Žatec** (Saaz), famous for its cucumbers and above all for its 'green gold', the bitter aromatic hops used to add flavour not only to Pilsner Urquell but also to many other beers of the world. One can still see the old hop-drying kilns, and in late summer a festival is still held at which the 'queen of the cucumbers' is chosen.

On the hill in the 10th century stood a Slavic castle of the Lučans, which by 1004 was already a princely seat of the Prague branch of the Přemyslids. Just a few decades later the Přemyslids built within the castle precincts a church dedicated to the Assumption. Below the castle – which is now the brewery – there developed a settlement which was occupied by German craftsmen and merchants in the reign of Otakar I Přemysl at the beginning of the 13th century. It grew rapidly, gaining the right to have a market in 1228, and being raised to the status of a town twenty years later, in 1248, and to that of a royal town in 1266. Moreover, by the 14th century, if not before, the farmers of Saaz were beginning to grow hops, which were soon in great demand outside Bohemia.

Between 1378 and 1411 Johann von Saaz (c. 1350–1414), also known as Johannes von Tepl, was town clerk and notary at Saaz, where in about 1401 he wrote the first literary work in the Modern High German language: *Der Ackermann aus Böhmen*. This prose disputation between the 'Ploughman' and Death, who has taken away his wife, sprang from personal experience: Johann's own young wife Margarete had just died in childbirth. Although God pronounces in favour of Death, the Ploughman's arguments in favour of this present life, citing classical sources and even Plato, show an emerging humanism influenced by the New Learning that had flourished at the court of Charles IV.

The 18th century saw the beginning of the town's most flourishing period as it concentrated on brewing and became the trading centre for northern and central Bohemian hops. Locally, hop shoots were even used as a salad, the favourite dish of Goethe when passing through Saaz which he called a 'truly beautiful town'. It was outside Saaz that a huge rally of Sudeten Germans acclaimed Konrad Henlein as their leader in 1933.

In the *market place* the principal building is, naturally, the Town Hall, built in 1559 and given its slightly squat Baroque onion-domed tower in 1770. Burghers' houses of various periods with fine gables, and some also with arcades, line the square, which also has a Trinity column surrounded by statues. The church of the *Assumption*, originally built in the 11th century, was converted into a three-aisled Gothic hall-church. The rectangular bell-tower was built on the south side in 1380. After 1738 the church was given a Baroque façade with two flanking towers and the Chapel of St John of Nepomuk was added. The tympanum of the west portal (early 13th century) is filled by a Romanesque scupture of St Peter. The altarpiece of the *Assumption* and the paintings on the side altars were painted by Anton Stevens in 1668. The altarpiece of the high altar was carved by Veit Styrl, the frescoes in the choir and gallery are by Leopold Reimboth. The *Marian Column* in front of the church was carved in sandstone by the Saaz sculptor Johann Karl Vetter in 1736.

The most beautiful *watch tower* of any Bohemian town is in the old town of **Kadaň** (Kaaden) on the middle Ohře. The 15th-century tower, with its solid base suddenly enlivened by battlements and with crockets on the spire, dominates the market place, which has fine medieval arcaded houses and a heavily populated plague column dating from the 18th century. The Gothic parish church was baroquized by Johann Christoph Kosch.

In front of the *Holy Gate* (Svatá brána), part of the old town fortifications, the Franciscans founded a friary around 1470 next to a 14th-century Gothic chapel. Between 1473 and 1480 they built the friary church of the *Fourteen Auxiliary Saints*, a Late Gothic three-aisled basilica which may have been designed by Johann Baptist Bauer of Eger (Cheb). The church contains the marble sarcophagus of Johann of Lobkowicz who died around 1517.

According to an old Bohemian-German saying *In Brüx ist nix, in Dux ist Jux, und in Komatau ist der Himmel blau* ('There's nowt in Brüx, there's fun in Dux, and in Komatau the sky is blue'). And indeed **Most** (population 65,000), as Brüx is now called, has almost nothing to offer the visitor beyond a modern shopping and residential district on the edge of the biggest open-cast brown coal mine in Europe. The old Brüx disappeared under the shovels of the giant excavators digging out the rich coal seam on which it stood. The new town of Most grew up alongside, as the most modern town in Czechoslovakia. Of the old town only a single building was saved from the pit: the parish church of the *Assumption*, a masterpiece of the Late Gothic and Early Renaissance. This massive structure was simply moved to the edge of the coal mine in 1975 – an extraordinary technical feat which was reported world-wide.

The church was designed at the beginning of the 16th century by Jakob Heilmann of Schweinfurt, the most famous of Benedikt Rieth's pupils; its original site was that of the earlier Gothic parish church, burnt down in 1515. Heilmann's plans were executed by the architect Jörg von Maulbronn between 1517 and 1548, and the glorious vault was built by Master Peter. The plain exterior and low-key window tracery of the church is a striking contrast with the richness of its interior. This consists of a large galleried hall divided into three by seven pairs of piers with delicately hollowed-out sides; they hold up one of the finest 'loop-star' vaults in Bohemia.

The church made its way to its new site in September-October 1975 at an average speed of 120 cm per hour. The massive piece of masonry 31 metres high, 30 metres wide and more than 60 metres long, held in a steel corset, was moved on 53 railway waggons along the 841-metre stretch. Stabilizing and restoration work lasted until autumn 1988. Since then the former parish church has housed an exhibition of north Bohemian art from the 14th to the 18th centuries.

Teplice (Teplitz)

Teplice, called Teplitz-Schönau until 1945 in the Biela (Bílina) valley at the foot of the Krušné hory (Ore Mountains) is the oldest spa in Bohemia and at the same time a busy, blighted, industrial town (textiles, machinery, glass, ceramic products) with a population of 58,000. Tsar Peter the Great, Goethe, Beethoven, Fichte, Kleist, Clemens Brentano, Schopenhauer, Richard Wagner, Paganini, Chopin, Liszt, Empress Marie Louise, the Duchess of Sagan: unbelievable as this may now seem, all of these took the cure at Teplitz or at its elegant suburb of Schönau (Šanov). The alkaline, saline, and partly radioactive springs bring relief to sufferers from gout, sciatica, rheumatism, paralysis and external injuries. After the great Lisbon earthquake of 1755 the hot springs dried up for a short time, and the mining disaster at Osek (Ossegg) in 1879 led to another short-term cessation.

According to legend a swineherd of the knight Kolostuj is supposed to have stirred up the healing springs in 762 and wallowed in them. There is more solid historical evidence that in 1156 Queen Judith, the Thuringian wife of Vladislav II Přemysl, founded a house of Benedictine nuns dedicated to St John the Baptist, a daughter house of St George's at Prague, *ad calidas aquas* ('at the warm waters'). At that time the Benedictine sisters were the only religious order who were expressly permitted to take baths. Next to the convent there soon sprang up a settlement named 'Teplitz' (from *teply*, warm), which from the 13th century onwards was under the rule of the Counts Kinský. In 1426 the Hussites reduced the convent to rubble. In the second half of the 16th century the Kinskýs built a palace on its ruins. Even at that time the great physician Paracelsus was recommending the waters of 'Döpplitz'. At the beginning of the 17th century a regular cure industry began. In 1607 the physician Caspar Schwenckfeldt gives a long list of spas for the 'gentle' and 'common' folk, most of them established by the Kinský family. In 1681 Teplitz drew up a 'cure list', the first such list of spa-visitors in Bohemia. The heyday of the spa began with the 19th century when grand Empire-style buildings were erected in the spa district. It was at Schloss Teplitz on 9 September 1813, immediately before the 'Battle of the Nations' at Leipzig, that Tsar Alexander I of Russia, Emperor Francis I of Austria and King Frederick William of Prussia concluded the 'Holy Alliance' against Napoleon.

The old *market place* in the centre of the town (plate 38) still has a few historic buildings, for example the town hall (1545), but most have been demolished and replaced. (The reshaping of the old town centre and its link to the spa gardens has not yet been completed.) The *schloss* in Zámecké nám. was built between 1585 and 1634 on the site of the old Benedictine nunnery. It was remodelled in Baroque style in 1751 and in the Empire style at the beginning of the 19th century. Adjoining the north side of the schloss is the church of the *Exaltation of the Cross*, a Renaissance building which underwent a Neo-Gothic remodelling in the late 19th century. Archaeologists have uncovered the convent's foundations nearby. The neighbouring schloss church is the decanal church of *St John the Baptist*, originally 12th century but renovated in the Baroque style between 1700 and 1703; its rich furnishings include paintings by Peter Johann Brandl and Wenzel Lorenz Reiner. The *Trinity Column* (Plague Column) was made in 1718-19 by the great Baroque sculptor Matthias Braun. *At the Old Post Office* (Zur alten Post) (Zámecké nám. No. 3/69) is the house where Tsar

Alexander I, the instigator of the Holy Alliance, stayed in 1813. Later Richard Wagner and Franz Liszt also lodged there.

South of the schloss is the English-style *Schloss Garden* (Zámecká zahrada) with old trees and large ponds. The schloss theatre was built for Count Franz Wenzel Clary-Aldringen in 1751 as a private theatre; its early programmes included plays by the young Goethe.

North of Zámecké nám. is the well-tended *Spa Park* (Lázeňsky park) with the Steel Bath, the Kurhaus, the Ore Mountains Theatre and the House of Culture. In the *Steel Bath* (Lázeňské ústavy Pravřídlo a Fučík) 25,000 hl a day of warm water (42.8°C) are pumped out of the 'Urquelle' (Pravřídlo) and piped to other bath centres such as the Stone Bath and the Snake Bath.

Lipova třída runs east to the Sady Československé armády (Park of the Czechoslovak Army), formerly Kaiserpark, which contains the *Stone Bath* (Kamenné lázně), the *Emperor Bath* (Cisařské lázně) and the *Snake Bath* (Hadí lázně). In 1839 the *New Bath* (Nové lázně) with its own spring was built. These baths are in the Šanov (Schönau) district of the town which was united with Teplice in 1894.

To the east of Teplice on Doubravská hora (Eichenwaldberg) are the ruins of *Doubravka Castle*, built between 1478 and 1486 and destroyed in 1644. In the 19th century the castle underwent a romantic restoration, and the keep was transformed into an observation tower.

Just 10 km from Teplice on the edge of the north Bohemian brown coal field stands the old town of Dux, now called **Duchcov**. This small industrial town of 10,000 inhabitants has a schloss memorable for having sheltered Casanova for the last thirteen years of his life. It was here that he wrote his famous memoirs.

The town was founded in about 1250 with the name *Hrabišín*. The schloss was built at the end of 16th century, and in the 18th century passed into the possession of the Counts Waldstein, a collateral branch of the famous Wallenstein's family. Jean-Battiste Mathey extended the original Renaissance building in 1707, and the magnificent French garden was created between 1716 and 1728.

In 1785 Giacomo Girolamo Casanova took up a post as librarian to Count Karl Josef Waldstein, who regarded the Italian adventurer as no more than a witty conversationalist for his guests. Casanova, the self-ennobled Chevalier de Seingalt, had become famous for his bold escape from the Piombi beneath the Doges' Palace in Venice in 1756. He was a doctor of law, a cardinal's secretary in Rome, an officer in Venice, a theatre violinist, a lottery ticket seller for the King of France, a secret agent, a lion of the salons, a confidence trickster and of course a ladies' man par excellence. There was hardly a person in politics or society with whom he was not closely acquainted and who did not value his extraordinary talents as a raconteur. In his *Memoirs* Casanova meticulously portrays social conditions in the decades before the French Revolution, liberally punctuated with erotic episodes, for 'the cultivation of sensual pleasure was the main occupation of my life; there has never been anything more important to me.' Casanova died on 4 June 1798 at Schloss Dux, and is commemorated by the contemporary statue in the schloss park. At the Chapel of St Barbara, in the old cemetery, a tombstone near what is presumed to be his grave bears the inscription: 'Jakob Casanova Venedig 1725 – Dux 1798.'

Between 1812 and 1818 the Waldstein family had the Baroque schloss remodelled in the Neo-Classical style. In accordance with the taste of the time the splendid Baroque gardens were turned into an English park with several ponds and an artificial hill. In 1956 the brown coal mining reached as far as Schloss Dux, swallowed up a large part of the park and several buildings including the Baroque hospital designed by Ottavio Broggio, the local architect from nearby Litoměřice. The area which the coal excavators have worked out has now been replanted and the former Baroque gardens recreated.

Schloss Duchcov now has a Neo-Classical façade. A wrought-iron fence with vases and sculptures from Braun's workshop (Hercules, Minerva and Mars) divides the outer courtyard from the cour d'honneur. The grandiose interior decoration of the schloss were made by the greatest Baroque masters in the land: Wenzel Lorenz Reiner, Matthias Bernhard Braun and Ferdinand Maximilian Brokoff. The schloss now contains a comprehensive collection of furniture from Romanticism to Cubism, together with paintings from the former Waldstein collection, including a portrait of the generalissimo Wallenstein himself by Anthony van Dyck. There is also some Casanova memorabilia.

In 1967-68 the *Schloss gardens*, called the 'Fürstengarten' (Princes' Garden) was reconstructed in its Baroque form with the aid of old plans and engravings, as a French garden of severely symmetrical composition with regular flowerbeds, green hedges, rose-covered supporting walls, basins and decorative fountains. A double flight of steps leads up to the schloss. In the niche stands Braun's sandstone sculpture of the *Rape of Beauty by Time* in the mythological form of the wind god Boreas abducting Oreithyia, the daughter of King Erechteus of Athens.

15 km from Teplice is the little town of **Osek** (Ossegg) with its Cistercian monastery founded shortly after 1200, the most important Baroque monastic complex in northern Bohemia. The Cistercians were established in the late 10th century as a reformed offshoot of the Benedictine order which had become rich and ostentatious. They sought a spiritual revival based on a return to poverty. By the first half of the 14th century 700 monasteries had been founded from the first house at Cîteaux in Burgundy. All these monasteries were rich, not because of endowments but from the intensive farming of the order's land. In 1196 Cistercians from the Bavarian abbey of Waldsassen moved first to Maštov (Maschau, in the Saaz basin) and shortly afterwards to Rýzmburk (Riesenburg) and in 1199 founded the monastery of Osek.

Between 1206 and 1266 the Cistercians built first a church, a three-aisled basilica in a Burgundian Gothic style. After the completion of the church the order then proceeded to replace the makeshift wooden conventual buildings with stone buildings. The south range with the chapter house (c. 1230) and part of the cloister were then built. In 1248 the army of

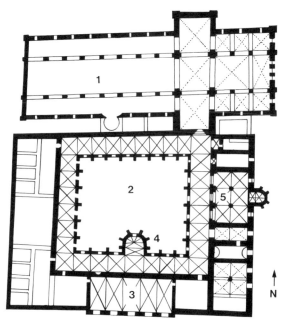

Osek (Osegg) Cistercian Abbey, plan
1 Abbey Church of the Assumption
2 Cloister
3 Refectory
4 Fountain Chapel
5 Chapter House

Otakar Přemysl, fighting in the attempt to topple his father, King Wenceslas I, caused serious damage to the monastery. In 1278 it was looted by the victorious allies of Rudolph of Habsburg after the Battle of the Marchfeld. When the monastic buildings were burned down in 1341, King John granted the Cistercians the right to collect royal taxes in Brüx and Leitmeritz for ten years. In the 15th and 16th centuries, however, the abbey's finances were depleted by looting, Hussite troubles and mortgages to such an extent that in 1580 Pope Gregory XIII dissolved the monastery which by now was totally mortgaged.

In 1642 Osek abbey was revived as part of the re-Catholicizing of Bohemia. Endowments, bequests, returns from monastic farms and a textile mill (the oldest in Bohemia), as well as taxes enabled the abbey to undertake extensive rebuilding and expansion between 1693 and 1732 and to have the church remodelled in the Baroque style by Ottavio Broggio. The two Silesian Wars (1740–1742 and 1744) and the Seven Years' War (1756–1763) left their marks on Osek (the damage was estimated at 200,000 gulden), but this was paid for by increased taxes from the faithful.

The abbey was not adversely affected by the Josephine reforms: on the contrary, like Strahov in Prague, it was chosen to receive libraries and collections of paintings from monasteries that had been dissolved. In 1950 it was taken over by the state and since then part of it has been used as a retirement home for nuns of various orders. At present the only parts open to the public are the former abbey church, which is used for organ recitals, the cloister, the chapter house and the abbey courtyard.

The *Abbey Church of the Assumption* as it appears today is Ottavio Broggio's most important work. The task of baroquizing the church and monastery was given to him in 1712 and concluded in 1718 (plate 41). The impressive three-storey west front with heavy volutes and a projecting porch is his work; the sculptures on the façade (saints of the Cistercian order, Evangelists and patron saints of Bohemia) are by Franz Anton Kuen, while the statue of St John the Baptist with Angels is by Edmund Johann Richter (1713).

Inside the church the form of the three-aisled Romanesque building is still apparent beneath its Baroque cladding: the barrel vault in the nave, the transepts, the articulation of the walls by pilasters. The plasterwork (cartouches, medallions) is by Giacomo Antonio Corbellini. The frescoes are mostly by Wenzel Lorenz Reiner; the *Descent of the Holy Spirit* and other frescoes in the nave are the work of Johann Jakob Steinfels. The principal picture on the altarpiece was painted by Michael Willmann (after 1702), the other paintings of the high altar were done by Johann Christoph Lischka (*Beheading of John the Baptist*). The altars of St Bernard were also decorated by Reiner.

Adjoining the church on its south side are the conventual buildings around a *cloister* (completed 1350) which has retained its Gothic appearance. Its south range contains the Refectory with Baroque plasterwork by Corbellini, opposite which is the Fountain Chapel (c. 1300) which projects into the cloister garth. A pointed arch with tracery leads from the east side of the cloister into the Early Gothic *Chapter House* (c. 1230), which also escaped baroquization. The six low-set cross-rib vaults are supported on two columns with battlemented and florid capitals. Cistercian austerity is expressed by the cut-off shafts on the walls, whose curves are echoed by the knotted stem of the lectern, with its relief carving of a lamb (c. 1230). The wall paintings by Johann Peter Molitor (1756) show legends of saints of the order. The polygonal sanctuary was built in to the east wall c. 1520.

2 km north of Osek stand the ruins of the 13th-century **Rýžmburk** (Riesenburg) castle, now called Hrad Osek. At the edge of the forest outside Osek is a monument commemorating 142 miners killed in an accident in the Nelson III shaft in 1934.

The old military and trade road, known in German as the 'Kulmer Weg' or 'Sorbensteig' ('Sorb path' – the Sorbs, or Wends, were a Slavic group who settled in Lusatia), runs between Bohemia and Saxony via **Chlumec** (Kulm) and the Tiské sedlo (Nollendorfer Pass). The broad undulating countryside around Chlumec was often the scene of military conflict, between the Bohemian Duke Soběslav I and the German King, Lothar of Saxony (1126), for instance, and at the Battle of Kulm (29 August 1813) the allied army of the Prussians, Austrians and Russians trapped the army of the French Marshal Dominique-René Vandamme, who was forced to surrender with 10,000 men. This weakening of the French army played a decisive part in its defeat six weeks later at the 'Battle of the Nations' at Leipzig, which opened the way to France. The Battle of Kulm is commemorated by several monuments.

Further on, in the direction of Děčín, are some massive fissured sandstone rocks which loom melodramatically over the village of Tisá (Tyssa). They are known as the **Tiské stěny** (Tyssaer Wände; 'Tisá Walls'). The groups called the 'Doctor' and the 'Mayor' are particularly impressive.

Děčín (Tetschen)

'At last we caught sight of the towers of Tetschen Castle, we came nearer and there it stood before us in all its splendour. On a tall rock it looms above the town, of which at first one is quite unaware. It was a delightful moment when our boat rounded a rocky corner and all its beauty now lay before us,' wrote the young German poet Theodor Körner (1791–1813) in his diary. Děčín (Tetschen) lies on the Elbe (Labe) at the point where it begins its course through the gorge that cuts through the Elbe sandstone mountains (Děčínské stěny) towards Saxony. The town's convenient situation on the river and railway facilitated the early development of various industries there.

In 1128 there is mention of a Přemyslid castle on the rock above the right bank of the Elbe. On the north side of this castle a settlement grew up, and under the rule of the Counts Wartenberg (1305–1511) it obtained a market and a town charter. The Wartenbergs were followed by the Salhausens and the Protestant Bünaus, who in 1620 were forced to flee the country because of their religion. The lordship of Tetschen was then purchased by the Counts Thun who came from the South Tyrol. On the opposite bank the village of Bodenbach (now Podmokly) developed in the 19th century into a rising industrial centre – after Aussig (Ústí) it was the second biggest trans-shipment centre for coal and industrial goods to Germany. The two towns were amagamated as 'Tetschen-Bodenbach' in 1943, and since 1945 have been known as Děčín.

Set on a sandstone cliff 50 metres above the Elbe stands the *Schloss* of the Counts Thun-Hohenstein. In the mid–17th century they remodelled the Renaissance building, which had developed from a 13th-century castle, and around 1790 Johann Wenzel Koch made alterations in a transitional style between Late Baroque and Neo-Classicism. Leading up to the schloss is a ramp carved out of the rock, called the 'Dlouhá jízda' ('long ride'). To the east extends the terraced *Rose Garden* (Růžova zahrada) with Baroque stairs. Count Maximilian Thun-Hohenstein enriched the garden in the last quarter of the 17th century by the addition of a *sala terrena* and a three-storey gloriette. The gloriette has a double flight of steps leading up to the landing and then continuing as a single flight up to a terrace with a pavilion which is open on all sides. Abraham Felix Kitzinger decorated the gloriette with allegorical figures of the seasons, goddesses and gladiators in 1683. The schloss itself is now a barracks, and therefore closed to the public, though the gardens are open.

Beside the ramp up to the castle stands the church of the *Holy Cross* (Kostel sv. Kříže), a Baroque building of 1687–1691 with wall paintings of 1792. The church of *St Wenceslas* (Kostel sv. Václava) was built between 1754 and 1778. To the south of it is the town square with an Art Nouveau fountain of 1906.

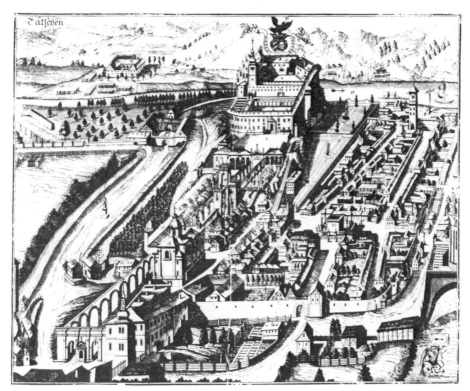

View of Děčín (Tetschen)

The centre of the industrial quarter of Bodenbach, now called **Podmolky** is Husovo nám., formerly the town square. The Late Baroque church of *St Wenceslas* in the Rozbělesy district was the Catholic parish church until 1934, when this function was taken over by the Neo-Romanesque church of St Francis Seraphim in the town square. The church of St John, renovated in the Neo-Gothic style, contains the family vault of the Thun-Hohensteins.

Near Kamenický Šenov on the way from Děčín to Nový Bor is the basalt rock formation of **Panská skála** (Herrnhausfelsen; plate 34) with basalt crystals 10 to 15 metres high set in rows like organ pipes, the Bohemian version of the Giant's Causeway in Ulster. It is now a protected natural site. **Nový Bor** (Haida) at the foot of a 961 metre tall phonolite cliff has been an important centre of the Bohemian glass industry since 1427.

Between the volcanic hills of the České středohoří (Central Bohemian Uplands) and the chalk sandstone hills of the Jizer (Iser) plateau is the district town of **Česká Lípa** (Böhmisch Leipa) on the river Ploučnice (Polzen), a busy industrial centre (textiles, machines, electrical goods, musical instruments) with a population of 16,000. The most interesting building in the

---

Děčínské steny (Elbe sandstone rocks)

To appreciate the magnificence of the Elbe sandstone rocks on the Czech side of the border the visitor should travel from Děčín on the right of the Elbe to Hřensko (Herrnkretschen) just before the German border and from there walk to **Dolní souteška** (Edmundsklamm) and **Divoká souteška** (Wilde Klamm) on the river Kamenice (Kamnitz), a tributary of the Elbe (excursion with boat trip 3–4 hours). The **Pravčická brána** (Prebischtor), the largest natural rock gateway in Europe, is particularly worth a visit: 20 metres above a chasm two pillars of rock are linked by a sandstone block 15 metres long and 3 metres thick, from which there is a breathtaking view.

---

town is the *Red House* (Červený dům), a small Renaissance palace built in 1583 and decorated with arcades and sgraffiti. It was used as a hunting lodge by the Berka of Dubá und Leipa family.

The church of *St Mary Magdalene*, the oldest church in the town was built after 1200 by Cistercians from Plasy (Plass) abbey, and was altered in the 16th, 17th and 18th centuries. The church of the *Holy Cross* dating from 1381 has also undergone many alterations, but it retains its Gothic portal. The church of *All Saints* is part of the Augustinian monastery founded by Albrecht von Wallenstein in 1627; its interior is decorated with paintings by Johann Georg Heintsch and others. The Baroque church of *St Mary* was built in 1714.

A few kilometres north of Česká Lípa in the midst of a delightful landscape with ponds, valleys with mountain streams and volcanic hills stands the ruined castle of **Sloup**, a rock massif 40 metres high, called 'Bürgstein' or 'Pirkenstein' in old sources. The castle was built in the 14th century by Vinzenz of Oybin, became the seat of a robber baron in the 15th century and was destroyed by an army levied from the federation of the six towns of Upper Lusatia. There are dungeons hewn deep into the rock and an armoury with columns carved in relief (probably the origin of the castle's Czech name: *sloup*, column).

Liberec (Reichenberg)

Liberec, the gateway to the Jizerské hory (Iser Mountains), is situated on the Lužická Nisa (Lausitzer Neisse) river. Since medieval times it has been the centre of the north Bohemian textile industry, and was known encouragingly as the 'Bohemian Manchester'. The annual Liberec fair (Liberecké výstavní trh, LVT for short) presents the textiles, home furnishings, glassware and jewellery produced in the area to an international market. Liberec now has a population of 105,000.

Founded somewhere around 1300 and mentioned for the first time in 1352, (as *Reychinberch*) the town, which belonged to the Redern (Raedern, Rödern) family, who imported Flemish linen weavers and their families. The Redern lords gave the weavers all the necessary freedoms and in the 14th century the settlement developed into a flourishing centre of textile production. The Flemings were joined by German weavers, knotters and dyers.

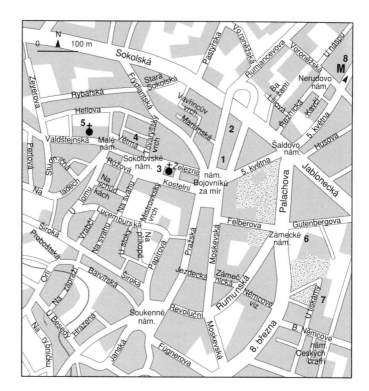

Liberec (Reichenberg)
1 Town Hall
2 Town Theatre
3 St Anthony Abbot
4 Wallenstein Houses
5 Church of the Holy
   Cross
6 Renaissance Schloss
7 Art Gallery
8 North Bohemian
   Museum

In 1577 Emperor Rudolph II raised Reichenberg to the status of a town, and by the end of the 16th century its cloth was being exported to Saxony, Bavaria and Austria. The town suffered during the Thirty Years' War at the hands of bands of plundering mercenaries, and the great plague of 1680 also contributed to its decline. It was not until the 18th century that the town recovered with the revival of the textile industry. And while the other European weaving centres collapsed in the 19th century under the competition of the new machinery, Reichenberg's textile king, Johann Liebig, expanded production, introduced the most modern machinery while ensuring that no weaving jobs were lost as a result, built housing estates for his employees and so increased the prosperity of the town and its citizens. True, he could not prevent the tensions that now developed because of the increasing social disparities among the town's population, tensions which made Reichenberg the cradle of both the German and the Czech workers' movement in Bohemia. It was also the centre of German nationalism, and the base of Henlein's Sudeten German Party.

The heart of the town centre of Liberec is the *nám. Bojovníků za mír* (Peace-fighters' Square; formerly Altstädter Platz). In its centre is the enormous *Town Hall* (plate 39) built between

1888 and 1893 by the Viennese architect Franz von Neumann in the Flemish Baroque style, consciously recalling the New Town Hall in Vienna. There is a fine view from its central tower (56 metres high). The fountain in front of the town hall was made in 1927 by the sculptor Franz Metzner. Behind the town hall is the *Town Theatre* (Divadlo F.X. Šaldy) built by the Viennese specialists in theatre-building, Ferdinand Fellner and Hermann Helmer, and now named after a Liberec playwright and writer, František Xafer Šalda (1867–1937). Almost all the houses in the old town centre were built in the late 19th and early 20th centuries, but here and there a fine burgher's house has survived from the 18th century. A particular house type, known as the 'Liberec (or Reichenberg) house' is characterized by pretty plaster decorations in the gables, in the form of flowers, garlands and fruit, as well as religious or mythological scenes. A good example of this type is No. 15 in the old town square, dating from 1795.

Kostelní ul. (Kirchgasse; Church Street) connects the old town square with Sokolovské nám. (formerly Neustädter Platz), in which stands the archidiaconal church of *St Anthony* (Arcidĕkanský chrám sv. Antonína), completed in 1579 and remodelled in Neo-Gothic style in 1879. Some of the surrounding houses have façades of the Empire period. Three narrow alleys run westwards to Malé nám. (Kleiner Platz; Little Square). The northernmost of these, Vĕtrná ul. (Windgasse) has some picturesque early 17th-century half-timbered houses known as the Valdštejnské domky (Wallenstein houses).

The church of the *Holy Cross* (Kostel sv. Kříže) on the north side of Valdštejnská ul., which runs into Malé nám., is a Baroque building dating from 1733–1756, designed by Johann Josef Kunz. Inside there are some fine paintings including one of *St Anne, the Virgin and the Christ Child* (c. 1520) possibly by Dürer. The *Plague Column* behind the church of the Holy Cross is by Matthias Braun (1719).

Between 1582 and 1615 on what is now Gutenbergova ul. the Counts Clam-Gallas built a Renaissance *schloss* with the beautiful chapel of the Saviour (1604–1606), whose furnishings are among the greatest of Liberec's treasures. The high altar, oratory, choir and coffered ceiling bear witness to the high standard of Reichenberg woodcarving. When the Clam-Gallas family remodelled the park in 1779, Emperor Joseph II personally ploughed a furrow as a symbol of the peasant origins of his dynasty. (Přemysl, the ancestor of the Bohemian kings, was ploughing when Libuše's emissaries appeared.)

The *Picture Gallery* (Oblastní galerie) at U tiskárny 1, containing works by Bohemian, French and German painters, was founded by the industrialist Johann Liebig. The *North Bohemian Museum* (Severočeské muzeum) founded in 1873 provides an excellent – and charming – overview of the culture and economy of northern Bohemia. There are special collections devoted to glass, porcelain, faience, textiles, furniture, artistic woodwork and metalwork, and 22 tapestries woven by Flemish artisans in medieval Reichenberg. The museum building was built in 1897-98. *5. kvĕtna* ends at the large *Park* (Lidové sady Petra Bezruče), named after the Czech poet Petr Bezruč (1867–1958), with a Park of Culture (Park kultury a oddechu), botanical and zoological gardens (Botanická zahrada, Zoologická zahrada) and an open-air theatre (Létní divadlo). The Botanical garden has an international reputation for its tropical flora and extensive collection of orchids. The zoo, although not founded till 1906, is the oldest in Bohemia.

South-west of Liberec **Ještěd** (Jeschken) hill rises steeply to a height of 1021 metres. Since 1973 the summit has been crowned by a space-age tower 92 metres high, for which the architect, Karel Hubáček, received the Auguste Perret Prize of the International Union of Architects. The futuristic building contains a restaurant, hotel and viewing terrace, from which one can see as far as the Sněžka in the Krkonoše Mountains and as far as Prague. From Horní Hanychov in Liberec it is possible to reach the summit by footpath, road or cable car (Visuta lanova dráha).

14 km north of Liberec in the foothills of the Jizer mountains **Frýdlant** rises majestically from a basalt outcrop. This castle was Albrecht von Wallenstein's powerbase. After the generalissimo was transformed into a doomed Romantic hero in Schiller's trilogy (1797–1799), the castle became a focus of the public imagination and was opened to visitors by its owners, the Counts Clam-Gallas, as early as 1801. It is thus Central Europe's first stately home museum.

The knight Ronovec, a forebear of the Berka of Dubá family, founded Friedland castle on a tall basalt rock above the river Smědá (Wittig). A powerful round tower formed its core. In 1278 the castle passed to the noble Biberstein family from Meissen. At the end of the 15th century the Bibersteins strengthened the castle defences with bastions and modernized the residential quarters of the castle in the Renaissance style. When the Friedland branch of the family died out around the middle of the 16th century the castle reverted to the Bohemian crown. In 1558 the Silesian Baron Friedrich von Redern bought the lordship of Friedland and his Italian architect Marco Spatio transformed the Gothic outer ward into a magnificent Renaissance schloss (the 'Lower Castle'), adding a chapel between 1598 and 1602 and reinforcing the castle entrance with strong outworks. The Baron's family was Lutheran and endeavoured to promote both Lutheranism in the Friedland region and the German element there. In 1619 Christoph von Redern, the lord of Friedland at that time, supported the uprising of the Bohemian Estates against the Habsburgs and the Catholic clergy. Following the defeat of the Estates' army at the Battle of the White Mountain he only escaped execution by fleeing abroad. Friedland and all the property attached to it was confiscated by the emperor.

In 1620 the successful commander of the Imperial forces, Albrecht von Wallenstein became the successor to the Rederns. Friedland was only a small part of the possessions he held throughout northern and eastern Bohemia, but since the generalissimo particularly enjoyed staying at the castle, the Emperor Ferdinand II made it an hereditary princedom in 1624 and a dukedom a year later. After Wallenstein's fall and murder in 1634 Friedland passed to the Imperial commander Matthias Gallas, who was, however, unable to enjoy his new possession for a time since Friedland remained in the battle zone and was continually being plundered alternately by French and Imperial troops.

Albrecht von Wallenstein

Frýdlant Castle is now in an excellent state of repair, since it was lived in until 1945 and parts of it have been a museum for almost 200 years. Restoration of the Renaissance façades covered with sgraffito decoration in the *Lower Castle* with its octagonal stair tower crowned by a Baroque cupola, was completed in 1960. The *Knights' Bridge* links the Lower with the *Upper Castle*, the original Gothic fortress with its massive round tower which was given two top-lit domed turrets in the Renaissance period.

The tour of the castle goes through richly decorated salons, the Hall of the Knights with its overpoweringly pompous fireplace, the court hall and the Heraldic Hall, which has a painted plaster ceiling decorated with the coats of arms of all the lords of the castle. The picture gallery is famous and contains works by important masters: the *Martyrdom of St Stephen* by Karel Škréta, the *Portrait of Count Franz Anton Sporck* (the builder of Kuks) by Peter Brandl, landscapes by Wenzel Lorenz Reiner, portraits of Wallenstein himself by Christian Maulpertsch, and of his successor Count Matthias Gallas by Franz Leux. Moreover the rooms of the castle also contain unusual collections of weapons, glass and ceramics, as well as furniture of many styles.

The castle was given its present fortification by the Swedish garrison in occupation between 1645 and 1647 during the closing stages of the Thirty Years' War. When they left, their commandant left the following inscription on the gateway of the barbican: *Pax bello potior, sequar trahentia fata! Benjamin Magnus Nortmann svaecus Capitaneus et p. trc. Friedland. Praefectus Anno 1647* (Peace is stronger than war, I shall follow the destiny that beckons me!)

The church of the *Holy Cross* contains a spectacular monument to the Redern family: Christopher on the right, with his father (an Imperial Marshal) and his mother, proud, sinuous bronze figures, moving through a frame of coloured marbles. Two Turkish prisoners cower below them; King David and Judas Maccabeus ride above. The whole monument (1605–1610; by the Dutchman C.G. Heinrick) breathes an almost decadent confidence, and thus a sense of doom.

The centre of the well-known Jablonec glass and jewellery industry is the town of **Jablonec nad Nisou** (Gablonz an der Neisse), a flourishing town with a population of 48,000. The first mention of the settlement of *Gablonz* occurs in 1356, but in the Hussite Wars of the 15th century it was razed to the ground. The site remained uninhabited until in the 16th century German glass-makers from the Erzgebirge came here and settled in the surrounding forests (considerable quantities of charcoal being required for the manufacture of glass). In the 18th century the Gablonzers began to make imitation precious stones and pearls out of glass. This marked the beginning of a rapid development. In 1808 Gablonz was granted the right to hold a market, and in 1866 it became a town.

In 1945 all the Germans, who comprised the overwhelming majority of the population, were forced to leave. At Kaufbeuren in Bavarian Swabia they founded a part of the town called Neugablonz (New Gablonz) and continued the manufacture of glass and jewellery in a modern plant there. At Jablonec nad Nisou too production started again in 1948. The traditional industries have been supplemented by machine building and the manufacture of trucks and plastics.

Jablonec's great prosperity before the war is reflected in its extraordinary mass of Secessionist and Constructivist buildings, all now in a sad state of decay. The imposing *Town Hall* (Nová radnice) in nám. Jana Švermy (formerly Unterer Platz) was built between 1929 and 1933 by the architect Karl Winter. The *Municipal Theatre* in Leninova is a late work (1906/07) by the Viennese theatre architects Fellner and Helmer. A visit to the *Museum of Glass and Jewellery* (Muzeum skla a bižutérie) in U muzea street is highly recommended. The museum shows the development of the production and working of glass from the earliest examples found in the Mediterranean up to the present, and there are displays of work by great Czech glass artists.

Between 1930 and 1932 in what is now nám. Rudé armády Joseph Zasche built the church of the *Sacred Heart* (Kostel Nejsv. srdce Páně), the parish church of Gablonz, an elegant brick building with Constructivist forms. The former parish church of *St Anne* (Kostel sv. Anny) in Dukelské nám. dates from the 16th century and underwent Baroque alterations between 1685 and 1687.

Eastern Bohemia (Východní Čechy)

Hradec Králové (Königgrätz)

At the confluence of the Orlice (Adler) and the Elbe lies **Hradec Králové** (Königgrätz), the administrative capital of East Bohemia. As an industrial centre and junction of communications it has increased considerably in importance in recent decades, but large parts of the old town centre are conservation areas and illustrate its urban development from the 14th to the 20th century. The town became famous for the Battle of Königgrätz (Sadova) which sealed the victory of the Prussians in the Austro-Prussian War of 1866 for dominance in Germany.

In the 10th century the headland between the two rivers was already surmounted by a Slavic earthwork, at the foot of which a settlement developed. Around 1225 this became one of the first Bohemian communities to receive a town charter. At the beginning of the 14th century Elizabeth (Ryksa Elżbieta) of Poland, the wife of Wenceslas II and then of Rudolph I made the town her dowager residence, and gave it the name *Gretz* (from *hrad*, castle) which later became Königgrätz (or Hradec Králové). In the 15th century the town, itself a centre of the Hussite movement, supported the Taborites, whose great commander, the blind Jan Žižka, died of the plague here in 1424 and was buried temporarily in the church of the Holy Ghost. 'The famous Captaine of the Bohemians' was already a mythical figure by 1592, when Fynes Moryson remarked that 'he did lead the Hussites valiantly, and being ready to die, wished them to make a Drumme of his skin, ominating that the sound thereof would bee so terrible to the enemies as they would run away.'

After 1620 the Jesuits re-Catholicized the townspeople, and forty years later Emperor Leopold raised Hradec Králové to an episcopal see. Between 1766 and 1789 Empress Maria Theresa surrounded the town with massive bastions and the suburbs were demolished for defensive reasons.

On 3 July 1866, just three weeks after the outbreak of the Austro-Prussian War (see p. 28), 221,000 Prussians with 702 guns under the command of the legendary Chief of the General Staff, Helmuth von Moltke, clashed with 206,000 Austrians and Saxons with 650 guns led by General Ludwig August von Benedek. Not only did the Prussians have superior numbers, they also had superior military technology – 'the terrible needle gun' – while the Austrians artillery still had the old front-loaders. Benedek therefore decided from the outset to fight a defensive battle and accordingly built his positions east of the Bistritza marsh. But the Prussians managed to break through the Austrian positions and put Benedek's troops to flight. The Battle of Königgrätz (also called the Battle of Sadova) was followed by a peace treaty (the 'Peace of Prague') which left the territories of the Danube Monarchy untouched

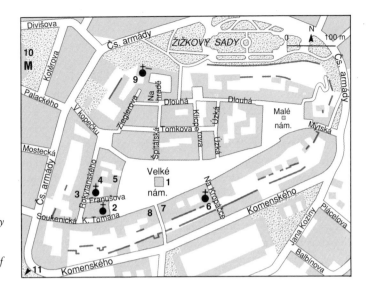

Hradec Králové
(Königgrätz)
1 *Plague Column*
2 *Cathedral of the*
   Holy Ghost
3 *White Tower*
4 *St Clement*
5 *Old Town Hall*
6 *Church of the*
   Assumption and
   Jesuit College
7 *Špulak House*
8 *Bishop's Palace*
9 *Episcopal Seminary*
   and Church of St
   John of Nepomuk
10 *Wooden Church of*
   St Michael

(though it lost Venice which was incorporated into the Kingdom of Italy), but allowed Prussia to annex Hanover, the Electorate of Hesse, Hesse-Nassau, Frankfurt and Schleswig-Holstein. In 1867 Prussia assumed the leadership of the newly founded North German League, and Austria definitively lost all influence in Germany. The Viennese poet Franz Grillparzer (1791–1872) reproached the victors: 'You believe you have given birth to an empire, but all you have done is destroy a people!'

In 1884 the history of the fortress of Königgrätz came to an end; the bastions and earthwork were demolished almost without trace, and from then on the town expanded on an unprecedented scale with some exemplary town planning by the architects V. Rejchl and O. Liška in 1909. Work continued on the new town after the foundation of the Czechoslovak Republic; it includes some fine examples of Czech Modernism by Jan Kotěra and Josef Gočar.

The core of the old town centre is the triangular *Žižkovo nám.* (Žižka Square; plate 29), formerly the market place, in which stands a Baroque *Plague Column* commemorating the epidemic of 1714. The column, 19 metres high and surmounted by a statue of the Virgin is surrounded by the plague saints and the patron saints of Bohemia. In the south-west corner of the market place is the tall brick Gothic *Cathedral of the Holy Ghost* (Katedrála sv. Ducha; ill. 42) founded by the Dowager Queen Elizabeth, the widow of Wenceslas II (Ryksa Elżbieta or, in Czech, Eliżka Rejčka) in 1307, and built between 1339 and 1360 as a twin-towered basilica. The church was remodelled and altered several times, made a cathedral, baroquized, re-gothicized in the 19th century and finally restored between 1934 and 1941.

The stained glass is after designs by Josef Scheiwl and the wall paintings in the choir date from the second half of the 19th century. The handsome pewter font, the oldest in Bohemia, was made in 1406. In 1494 the Master of the Hradec Králové (Königgrätz) Altarpiece made the Late Gothic triptych with scenes from the life of the Virgin. The painting of St Antony is by Peter Brandl (c. 1730). In the choir the Late Gothic tabernacle with its original iron grille is a work of Matouš Rejsek dating from 1497.

North of the cathedral, in ul. Rokytanského, rises the *White Tower* (Bílá věž), built as a belltower between 1574 and 1585. Tacked on to the tower is the little church of *St Clement* (Kostel sv. Klimenta), a Baroque building (1714–1717) but with Gothic origins. Also on the west side of Žižka square is the *Old Town Hall* (Bývalá radnice), a two-towered 16th-century Renaissance building. The Early Baroque church of the *Assumption* (Kostel Nanebevzetí Panny Marie) on the south side of the square was built for the Jesuits by Carlo Lurago. Its interior decoration includes several paintings by Peter Brandl. To the right of the church is the former *Jesuit College* (Jezuitská kolej; 1671–1710), built by Johann Santini-Aichel and Paul Ignaz Bayer. After the suppression of the order in 1773 the college was used as barracks. To the west of it, on the corner of the stepped street called *Bono Publiko*, stands the *Špulak House* (U Špuláků; No. 34), a Renaissance building which was given its present Baroque appearance around 1750.

The *Bishop's Residence* (Biskupská rezidence) on the other side of the steps dates from 1709–1716 and was renovated in the High Baroque style in 1777. The building now contains the regional art gallery with works by old masters, and a collection of antiquities. The streets behind the cathedral have some old Renaissance and Baroque canons' houses (ul. Karla Tomana Nos. 44–51). Špitálska ul. and Na hradé run from Žižka Square northwards to the former *Episcopal Seminary* and the church of *St John of Nepomuk* (Kostel sv. Jana Nepomuckého) behind it, both built in the first quarter of the 18th century and replacing the castle that once stood there. The eastern end of Žižkovo nám. opens into *Husovo nám.* (Hus Square) with a fountain of St John of Nepomuk (Kašna se sochou sv. Jana Nepomuckého; 1718) and fine burghers' houses, originally Gothic but remodelled during the Renaissance (Nos. 6 and 10–14).

On the bank of the Elbe in the old town centre stands the muscular Art Nouveau *East Bohemian Provincial Museum* (Krajské muzeum východních Čech) built between 1908 and 1912 by Jan Kotěra. The undressed and forbidding figures that flank the entrance are allegories of *History* and *Industry*, made in 1912 by Vojtěch Sucharda to suggest the themes of the museum's interesting displays.

Road 35 to Prague passes through the *Battlefield of Königgrätz (Sadova)*. About 10 km beyond Hradec Králové a turning leads to the village of **Chlum** (1 km), scene of bitter fighting and now the site of a museum, a viewing platform, with a prospect of the whole battlefield where the Austrian officer corps was mown down as they led bayonet charges against modern artillery, an ossuary and a little Prussian cemetery with tall trees in the middle of fields. This is one of the many graveyards strewn over the battlefield. In a single day the Austrians lost 24,000 men killed or wounded and 13,000 taken prisoner.

Pardubice (Pardubitz)

Pardubice in eastern Bohemia is renowned for its delicious gingerbread and good ice hockey; and also Semtex explosive, which is produced nearby at Semtin. Devotees of the turf may also be familiar with the annual Grand Pardubice Steeplechase, the hardest race of this kind run in continental Europe. The growing industrial town (radio and television sets, chemicals, food) with its fascinating old town centre – now a conservation area – is situated where the river Chrudimka flows into the Elbe. It has a population of 98,000.

In 1491 the Moravian lord, Vilém of Pernštejn acquired the town, which had been founded in 1340, and made the old castle into a smart Late Gothic residence. After a great fire in 1507 he rebuilt the town more splendidly than before – hence the old Bohemian saying: 'It shines like Pardubice.' In 1538 the town was destroyed by fire a second time and this time it was Vilém's son, Jan, who financed the rebuilding in the elegant style of the local Renaissance. In 1560 the Royal Chamber bought the town of Pardubice from the bankrupt Pernštejns and governed it for the next 300 years. The building of the railway in 1845 marked the beginning of the economic and urban expansion of the community.

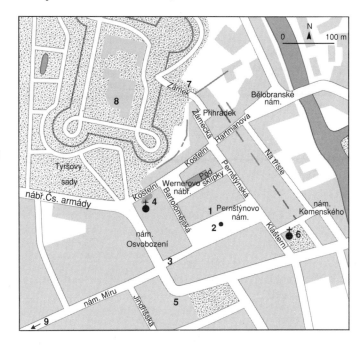

Pardubice (Pardubitz)
1 *Town Hall*
2 *Plague Column*
3 *The Green Gate*
  (Zelená brána)
4 *St Bartholomew*
5 *East Bohemian*
  Theatre
6 *Church of the*
  Annunciation
7 *Embankment path*
8 *Schloss*
9 *Church of St John*
  the Baptist

Since the Pernštejn family left their mark on the town to such an extent, it is not surprising that its main square bears their name: *Pernštejnské nám.* (colour plate 13). None of its neat burghers' houses is earlier than 1507, when this square was created in its present form. The relief decoration on several of the houses is justly famous (ill. 47). Since it was not until the second half of the 19th century that the town was able to free itself from rule by the Royal Chamber, it was very late in acquiring a *Town Hall* of its own (1893-94). This is a Neo-Renaissance building, on the façade of which are sgraffito decorations designed by the celebrated Mikoláš Aleš. In the centre of the square is a *Marian Column* dating from 1695 but given a Rococo restoration between 1773 and 1777 by Jakub Teplý.

On the gateway to Bartolomějská ul. a carved relief, which in fact belongs to the portal of the castle, shows the legendary origins of the Pernštejn family. The charcoal-burner Věnava, the ancestor of the dynasty, led an aurochs by the nose to Brno and there cut its head off with a single blow. The head of the aurochs with a tether through its nose is on the Pernštejn coat of arms. (Depictions of this legend are found also in other Bohemian towns, e.g. Litomyšl.)

The *Green Gate* (Zelená braná), an imposing gate tower erected between 1507 and 1534 and formerly called the Prague Gate (Pražská brána), links Pernštýnovo nám. with the long narrow nám. Ovobození (Liberation Square). At its northern end stands the town's parish church of *St Bartholomew* (Kostel sv. Bartoloměje). Originally a monastic church founded in 1295, it was destroyed in 1421, rebuilt in Late Gothic style between 1507 and 1514, and was given Renaissance alterations not long after in 1538. In the course of its restoration in 1912/13 a fine mosaic after a design by Mikoláš Aleš was added to the façade. The *East Bohemian Theatre* (Východočeské divadlo; plate 40) at the other end of the square was built by the Sezession architect Antonín Balšanek between 1906 and 1909. Its two façade mosaics by František Urban show the *Judgment of Libuše* and *Žižka before Prague*.

In Klášterní ul., which runs southwards from Pernštýnovo nám., stands the Gothic church of the *Annunciation* (Kostel Zvěstování Panny Marie), first mentioned in 1359, and renovated in 1507. Pernštýnská ul. continues northwards with two old burghers' houses (Nos. 11 and 12), which are basically Gothic in origin, becoming Zámecká ul. (Castle street) before opening through a gateway into a tiny square; the houses here occupy the site of the original outer bailey of the castle. A passage leads to an embankment, where the bridge once crossed the moat whose waters were designed to run mills as well as protect the Pernštejns – there is still a statue of the bridge saint, John of Nepomuk. The embankment ends in front of the portal of the Renaissance *Schloss* which replaced the original 13th-century Gothic castle in 1529. Quantities of reliefs decorate the castle, of various degrees of sophistication; the bridge sports wild men and cross-legged horses, as well as the Pernštejn aurochs' head. The relatively narrow castle courtyard is surrounded by two-storey arcades. (The schloss is at present undergoing restoration.) A path runs through the former moat past the remains of the town walls to the Tysršovy sady (Tyrš Garden) and the nám. Osvobozeni.

Třída míru (Peace street) is the main shopping street of Pardubice, linking the historic town centre with the modern part of the town. Branching off it is ul. bratranců Veverků

23 The Castle at KARLŠTEJN (Karlstein)

◁ 22 PLZEŇ (Pilsen) Town Hall

24 The Castle at KŘIVOKLÁT (Bürglitz)

25   KUTNÁ HORA (Kuttenberg) Cathedral of St Barbara

26   CHEB (Eger) St Nicholas

27 CHEB (Eger) Špalíček

28 PLZEŇ (Pilsen) Sgraffito decoration on the Town Hall

29 CHEB (Eger) Doorway of the Gabler House

POTENS VIRGO CARENS LABE, ÆDIS HVIVS CVRAM HABE

505

6
MĚSTO
507

507

Drobné
zboží
Cheb

30 KARLOVY VARY (Karlsbad) Taking the waters

31 KARLOVY VARY (Karlsbad) Mill Spring Colonnade

32 FRANTIŠKOVY LÁZNĚ (Franzensbad) Glauber Salts Spring

33 FRANTIŠKOVY LÁZNĚ (Franzensbad) Spa Buildings

34 Panska Skala (Herrrenhausfelsen) near DĚCÍN

35 In the Giant Mountains (KRKONOŠE, Riesengebirge)

36   Landscape near Spišský Hrad

38   Teplice (Teplitz) Castle Square ▷

37   The Giant Mountains near Peč

40 PARDUBICE (Pardubitz) East Bohemian Theatre
◁ 39 LIBEREC (Reichenberg) Town Hall
41 OSEK (Osegg) Abbey Church of the Assumption

43 Jičín (Jitschin) Town Square
◁ 42 HRADEC KRÁLOVÉ (Königgrätz) Cathedral of the Holy Ghost
44 CHEB (Eger) Market Place

45 The Elbe at Hřensko

46 In the Giant Mountains, near Hradec Králové

47 PARDUBICE (Pardubitz) House on Pernštejnske náměstí ▷

Pardubice (Pardubitz)
Carving over
Castle doorway

(street of the Veverka brothers) in which stands the Gothic church of *St John the Baptist* (Kostel sv. Jana Křtitele). Between 1563 and 1570 it was remodelled in the Renaissance style. Near St John's church stands a monument to the brothers Václav and František Veverka, who invented the mechanical plough in 1832.

National road 11 from Hradec Králové to Prague runs through the village of **Chlumec nad Cidlinou** (Chlumetz) with the Baroque schloss of *Karlova Koruna* (Karlskrone), one of the most beautiful country houses in Bohemia. Its name goes back to Charles VI who spent three

The Pardubice Steeplechase

Every October the Grand Pardubice Steeplechase (Velká Pardubická) draws the riding elite and race-goers to Pardubice – in 1990 it was run for the hundredth time. After the Grand National at Aintree in England it is the most famous, most difficult and most exciting steeplechase in the world. Steeplechases developed in England in the 19th century as horse races across country (they were so called because originally the aim of such a race was to reach a church steeple after crossing all the intervening obstacles) or round a course over artificial fences. From 1856 the Counts Kinský introduced such a race at Pardubice, and in 1875 a proper steeplechase was run for the first time on a specially terraced course here.

'The race is run over 4 miles of complex, unrailed country, including long stretches of plough, and there are 29 fences including open waters, banks, post and rails, and the notorious Taxis fence, which consists of a hedge 5 foot high and 6 foot wide flanking 16 foot of water. It is quite common for the whole field to be felled by this obstacle, and though the riders usually remount, there have been two occasions, 1909 and 1920, when the race has been declared void because no-one finished within the time limit.' (P. Smyly, *Encyclopaedia of Steeplechasing*, 1973.) The first running in 1874 was won by an English rider, Sayers, and in 1973 an English rider, Chris Collins, revived this tradition with a famous win.

days here in 1711 at the time of his coronation as King of Bohemia. In 1721 Ferdinand Count Kinský commissioned the architect Johann Santini-Aichel to create a suitably grand residence from an unimpressive medieval moated castle. Santini-Aichel turned to a project by Fischer von Erlach for a garden pavilion to create this light structure of three square wings leading off a central rotunda. Inside there are many valuable exhibits illustrating the development of Bohemian Baroque from its beginnings in the 17th century up to its high point in the first quarter of the 18th century, including works by the great Baroque masters, Karel Škréta, Peter Johann Brandl, Johann Kupetzky and Matthias Bernhard Braun.

Jičín (Jitschin)

The little town of **Jičín** on the Cidlina, a tributary of the Elbe, the birthplace of the German-speaking satirist and critic Karl Kraus, is the gateway to Český ráj (the 'Bohemian Paradise'). The first mention of Jičín is in 1293 as the property of Queen Jitka (Guta of Habsburg), the wife of Wenceslas II, so it is assumed that the town took its name from the queen. She mortgaged the town, however, and it later came into the possession of the lords of Wartenberg. In the Hussite Wars the town was unscathed because its inhabitants soon sided with the reformers, and in the 16th century under the Trčka of Lipa family the town experienced a boom.

Just how dramatic the history of the ruling Bohemian aristocratic families can be is demonstrated by the fate of the Smiřicky family, one of the wealthiest aristocratic dynasties in Bohemia at the turn of the 17th century. Zikmund of Smiřic, at that time the owner of Jičín, learned one day that his daughter, Eliška Kateřina, was having an affair with a blacksmith, so he shut her up in the dungeon of Kumburk Castle. Soon afterwards he died of grief. In 1611 and 1618 two of his sons died, leaders of the rebellion of the Bohemian Estates against the Habsburgs. His second daughter, Markéta Salomena, then ruled his vast estates as regent for his youngest son, Jindřich, who was still a minor. In 1619 Otto von Wartenberg attacked Kumburk, freed Eliška from the dungeon, and married her; at the same time he took over the possessions of the Smiřickýs. Markéta took the case to law and won. During the ensuing inventory of Jičín a powder store exploded, killing Eliška. Markéta, however, had little time to enjoy her victory. As a Protestant she was forced to leave the country in 1620 and thereafter lived in Hamburg. After Markéta's emigration Albrecht von Wallenstein took over the guardianship of her brother Jindřich. After the young Jindřich's sudden and unexplained death Wallenstein expropriated almost all the property of the Smiřický family.

Wallenstein made Jičín the capital of his duchy of Friedland (Frýdlant), and set about improvements with his usual energy. He bought a number of houses in the town square and demolished them to build a schloss. He founded a new church, a Jesuit college, a grammar school, built himself a pleasure house near Valdice (Walditz), established a mint at Jičín and even intended to found a bishopric and a university here. His murder in 1634 spelled the end of Jičín's heady part in history.

When the Napoleonic troops marched into Austria and Bohemia in 1806, the imperial treasure was secretly brought from Prague and Vienna to Jičín, where it was safely hidden in the churches of the town. In 1813 in the conference hall of the Wallenstein schloss Tsar Alexander I of Russia, the Emperor Francis I of Austria and King Frederick William III of Prussia signed the 'Holy Alliance' against Napoleon I. This last, successful attempt at cooperation marked the beginning of the end for Napoleon.

The south side of the broad and handsome town square (Valdštejnovo nám.; ill. 43) with its arcaded houses is dominated by the *Wallenstein Schloss* built between 1625 and 1633 in the Late Renaissance style. With its loggia and two corner oriels it fits in almost unnoticed between the neighbouring burghers' houses. The castle now contains a museum and a painting gallery. Also shown to visitors is the Conference Room where the three rulers met in 1813.

The towerless Early Baroque church of *St James the Great* (Kostel sv. Jakuba Většího) next to the schloss dates from 1627 and is one of the earliest centrally planned Baroque churches in Bohemia. The design is by G.B. Pierroni, the dome fresco and altar paintings are by Josef Kramolín. The *Valdice Gate* (Valdická brána) in the south-east corner of the square is all that survives of the imposing town fortifications (1568-1570). In 1768 the gate-tower was repaired and in 1840 it was given a gallery and a roof in the Neo-Gothic style. In 1939-40 it was carefully restored. The church of *St Ignatius* (Kostel sv. Ignáce) in the south-west corner of the square dated from the 14th century. The square contains a Baroque *Plague Column* (Mariánský sloup) of 1702, an *Amphitrite Fountain* (Kašna se sochou Amfitrité) made by the sculptor Jan Sucharda in 1835, and the *Coronation Fountain* (Korunovační kašna) in honour of Ferdinand V who passed through Jičín on his way to his coronation in 1836, the last coronation of a King of Bohemia. Since 1934 the fountain has been used as a meteorological station.

North-east of the old town centre an avenue of linden trees (Lipové stromořadí), all planted simultaneously by Wallenstein's superbly drilled soldiers, each issued with a shovel and a tree, leads to the pleasure lodge of *Libosad* situated about 2.5 km from the town. Its loggia is a magnificent example of Italian Mannerism (by Sebregondi, 1632). Near **Valdice** (Walditz) Wallenstein commissioned his architects, Spezza and Sebregondi, to build a Carthusian monastery (Kartouzy). Here his body rested between 1642 and 1785 when it was removed to its present resting place beside his first wife, Lucretia of Landek, in the chapel of St Anne in the castle church of Mnichovo Hradiště (Münchengrätz).

Kuks (Kukus)

Between Trutnov and Hradec Králové on both sides of the Elbe stretch the expressive Baroque remains of what was once the famous spa town of **Kuks**. In 1695, exploiting the vicinity of three mineral springs, Count František Anton Špork (Franz Anton von Sporck) began to create this extraordinary watering place. There was a schloss for himself and his

Český ráj (Bohemian Paradise)

North-west of Jičín begins the **Bohemian Paradise** (Český ráj), a nature conservation park covering 1300 sq km with bizarre rock formations, pine forests and many castles. The most delightful parts of the Paradise are the **Prachov Rocks** (Prachovské skaly) with a dense network of signposted footpaths. The ruins of **Trosky Castle** (Hrad Trosky) are also worth a visit. Here stand two tall sheer basalt crags called the *Panna* (Virgin; 57 metres) and *Baba* (Grandmother; 47 metres) towers. The castle dates from the 14th century, but it only received its present name, *Trosky* ('rubble') in modern times.

Kost Castle is one of the best preserved medieval castles in Bohemia. Built in the second half of the 14th century by the lords of Wartenberg, the Gothic parts of the castle include the large rectangular *Tower* at the south-west corner of the trapeze-shaped courtyard, the old residential range (*Old Palas*) on the south-west side and the *Chapel of St Anne* to the south-east. In the early 16th century the lords of Schellenberg added the Late Gothic *New Palas* (now the best preserved), and around the middle of the 16th century there followed a third residential range for the lords of Biberstein. The Early Baroque *sala terrena* near the main tower was built in 1629 in the time of Wallenstein. The Lobkowicz family added an outer bailey and a brewery. In 1635 the castle was burned down, in 1686 the *Old Palas* collapsed and was replaced by a granary. Since 1953 the castle has been restored in its original style, and now contains an interesting collection of Late Gothic art.

Further sights of interest in the Bohemian Paradise are the Baroque **Humprecht Hunting Lodge**, an odd circular construction now a literary museum, the ruins of **Valdštejn Castle**, the ancestral seat of the Waldstein (Wallenstein) family, the 'rock town' of **Hrubá Skála** with a castle of the same name, and the rock formation known as *Drábské světničky* ('lackeys' chamber').

distinguished guests, several bath houses and guest houses, a 'Comoedienhaus' or theatre, and other facilities of the amusement of spa guests, such as a 'pleasure house', a 'bird shooting stand' and a 'ring track'. The young Tyrolean sculptor, Matthias Bernhard Braun was commissioned to populate the terraces and gardens with allegories of the virtues and vices and other strange figures. Kuks spa quickly developed into a centre of social life in northern Bohemia, even rivalling celebrated Karlsbad. Festivals, hunts, concerts, theatrical performances followed each other in quick succession, the spring water fortifying the visitors.

After the death of the count in 1738 the crowds no longer came and the spa fell into decline. In 1740 a disastrous Elbe flood swept away some of the buildings. Today the park has regained its Baroque appearance, and a few bath houses have been restored, the oldest of them dating from 1699. Above the right bank of the Elbe rises the vigorous church of the *Holy Trinity* with the nearby *Hospital of the Brothers of Mercy*, built between 1707 and 1717 by Giovanni Battista Alliprandi. The large crypt serves as the family vault of the Counts Sporck. The former hospital on either side of the church contains a refectory and a pharmacy which remained in uninterrupted business from 1740 until 1946, as well as a museum with the original sculptures from the Braun workshop. On the terrace the visitor will find many more stone figures (good copies like all the sculptures in the open air). Braun's vices, to the right of the church, are particularly energetic.

Trosky Castle, engraving by K. Postl after a drawing by L. Janscha

To the west of Kuks in the middle of the forest near the village of *Stanovice* (Stangendorf) Braun and his workshop carved a number of biblical scenes in the living rock, including a Nativity, from which the place took its name **Betlém** (Bethlehem).

Trutnov (Trautenau)

The picturesque district town of **Trutnov**, the centre of flax spinning in Bohemia, is known as the 'pearl of the Krkonoše (Riesengebirge or Giant Mountains)' or sometimes as the 'gateway to Krakonoš's (or Rübezahl's) domain' (see below). It was founded by German settlers on the orders of Otakar II Přemysl as *Trautenau* on the Úpa (Aupa), a small tributary of the Elbe. From the 13th century it was the property for life of the dowager queens of Bohemia, who drew their income from it. Under John of Luxemburg (1310–1346) Trautenau received its charter and developed to become the most important town in the Krkonoše Mountains. During the Thirty Years' War (1618–1648) the Swedes sacked the town several times, and the inhabitants also inevitably suffered during the three Silesian Wars (1740-1742; 1744-45; 1756-1763) and in the War of the Bavarian Succession (1778-79). On 27 June 1866,

Teplice and Adršpach Rocks (Teplicko-adrspasské skaly)

From Trutnov a road follows the rails of a branch line in a north-westerly direction to **Adršpach** (Adersbach; 18 km) and Teplice nad Metuji (Wekelsdorf; 24 km). These two villages are famous for their extraordinary 'rock cities', the **Teplicko-adršpašské skaly**. Over millions of years the strangely shaped formations, 70 metres tall – rock towers, rock needles, rock bridges – have been created by geological pressure forcing up the massive sandstone plate which rests on the primary rocks, causing it to crack. Water and wind, frost and heat then moulded the projecting stone.

The Adršpach rocks were discovered in 1734, but it was not until 1824, following a big forest fire, that the Teplice rocks appeared. They almost immediately became important tourist attractions. Since 1933 both have been protected areas, mainly on account of their rare flora and fauna. There are signposted routes around the rocks which take 2 or 3 hours. The visitor who wants to make do with visiting just one of the 'rock cities' should choose the Adršpach rocks with their particularly bizarre shapes, the weirdly beautiful rock lake and the Krakonoš (Rübezahl) Waterfall.

The Rock City of Adršpach (Adršpachšské skály; colour plate 16) comprises about sixty listed rock formations, all of them given fanciful names such as the *Sugarloaf* (Homole cukru), *Krakonoš's Tooth* (Krakonošův zub), the *Lovers* (Milenci), the *Crocodile* (Krokodýl), the *Cossack* (Kozák), the *Mayor and Mayoress* (Starosta a Starosová), the *Svidnice Tower* (Svidnická vez) and *Krakonoš's Armchair* (Krakonošova lenoška). You can punt across the fairy-tale beauty of the Adršpach lake in which the rocky scenery is reflected. At the *Goethova deska* rock is a plaque commemorating Goethe's visit. In front of the waterfall (Vodopád) a little further on children shout three times 'Krakonoš! Krakonoš! Krakonoš!', and Krakonoš answers their call by swelling the meagre trickle of water to a thundering cascade. This is a tourist trick well over a century old: Krakonoš is in fact impersonated by an attendant operating the sluice gate at the outlet from the lake. A shout at Echo Point (Ozvěna) will return several times over.

six days before the Battle of Königgrätz (Sadova; see p. 260), the Austrians beat off a Prussian army division – their only victory in the Austro-Prussian War of 1866. On Gablenzberg stands a victory monument to Field Marshal Ludwig von Gablenz (1868).

A tour of Trutnov can be restricted to the pleasant town square surrounded with fine arcaded houses from the Renaissance and Late Baroque periods. In the square stands the *Trinity Column* 11 metres high (1704) and the *Krakonoš Fountain* dedicated to the mighty spirit of the Giant Mountains. *Krakonoš*, as he is known to the Czechs (the Germans call him Rübezahl), appears in legend for the first time around the middle of the 16th century on the Silesian side of the mountains. Friendly and humorous, he is said still to help the poor and oppressed, but whoever offends him is severely punished. Otherwise Krakonoš is always ready to play pranks, as he showed in the nearby Adršpašské skále (Adersbach Rocks; see above). The inhabitants of the Giant Mountains have many tales to tell about this bearded man, a collection of which was made in the 17th century by the Leipzig scholar, Johannes Praetorius in a book called *Daemonologia Rubinsalii Silesii*.

The Late Baroque church of the *Nativity of the Virgin* was built by Leopold Niederöcker between 1755 and 1782 in place of a 13th-century parish church. The *town hall* has a Neo-

Renaissance front and a pleasant wine tavern and restaurant in its cellars. The *museum* (Muzeum Podkrkonoší) with historical, art and ethnographical collections is an Empire-style building occupying the site of the former castle, the residence of the dowager queens.

Krkonoše (Riesengebirge; Giant Mountains)

Since 1963 approximately 385 sq km of the Bohemian Giant Mountains have been a national park. Together with the 55 sq km of park on the other side of the Polish border it forms the largest single conservation area in central Europe (plates 35, 37, 46). Flora, fauna and geology are protected, and any departure from the excellently signposted footpaths results in a fine. Nevertheless there is such pressure on the landscape that some of the most popular routes have to be closed for a whole year for nature to recover.

The Bohemian part of the Giant Mountains consists of two ranges: the main or border range and the Bohemian range. The main range begins in the west with Violík (Veilchenspitze, 1471 metres), continues with Vysoké Kolo (Hohe Rad; 1506 metres) and the Velký Šišák (Grossen Sturmhaube; 124 metres), then down to the Mužské a Divčí kameny (Mann- und Mädelstein; 1416 metres and 1414 metres) and the Špinlerovo sedlo (Spindlersattel; 1198 metres), rises to the Malý Šišák (Kleinen Sturmhaube; 1440 metres) and the Stříbrný hřbet (Lahnberg; 1490 metres), and reaches the highest point in the Giant Mountains, Sněžka (Schneekoppe; 1602 metres) before going down to the Pomezní Boudy (Grenzbauden; 1050 metres). The Bohemian range rises through the Plešivec (Plessberg; 1210 metres) and Lysá hora (Kahleberg; 1344 metres) to Kotel (Kesselkoppe; 1435 metres) and Zlaté návrší (Goldhöhe; 1333 metres), is interrupted beyond the Medvědín (Schüsselberg; 1235 metres) by the deep Elbe valley (Labský důl), and picks up beyond the valley with the Kozí hřbety (Ziegenrücken: 1389 metres) and then continues as part of the main range. The Bohemian range has some southern foothills: Přední Žalý (Heidelberg; 1019 metres) near Vrchlabí; Bönischberg, Jelení (Hirschberg; 1024 metres) near Černý Důl (Schwarzental) and Černá hora (Schwarzer Berg; 1299 metres) near Janské Lázně. Between the main range and the Bohemian range are the two most beautiful valleys in the Giant Mountains: the Labský důl (Elbgrund) with the waterfalls on the Elbe and the Pancava (Pantsche), and the Důl Bílého Labe (Weisswassergrund).

A distinctive feature of the Giant Mountains are the *Boudy* (Bauden). They are refreshment places where the walker can obtain drinks of all kinds, fortifying and tasty food, and usually also simple overnight accommodation (notification in advance is recommended). Many are picturesque and old, though there are also some very modern ones, and they have their origins in the shelters for livestock. Most have retained their simplicity, though some have grown into multistorey super-hotels, such as the new Labská bouda (Elbfallbaude). Starting points for walks are the little towns of Rokytnice nad Jizerou and Vrchlabí in the southern foothills of the Giant Mountains, as well as the mountain resorts of Harrachov, Špindlerův Mlýn, Pec pod Sněžkou and Janské Lázně.

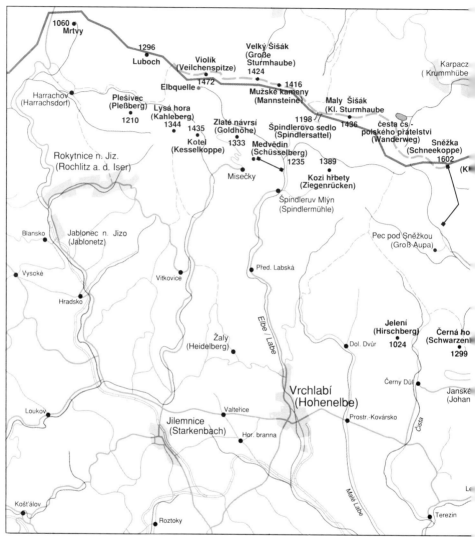

The Giant Mountains

Vrchlabí (Hohenelbe) was founded in the 13th century and given the status of a mining town in 1534. Mining was later supplemented by weaving and timber processing as meagre sources of income; and it was not until the emergence of tourism that the economic position of the inhabitants improved. Here in 1886 Guido Rotter founded the world's first youth hostel. Of

interest is the Renaissance *town hall*, built in 1581 and baroquized between 1732 and 1735. On the road to Špindlerův Mlýn there are still some old *timber-framed arcaded houses* of the 17th and 18th centuries. The *schloss* of the Counts Czernín-Morzin was built between 1546 and 1614. The architect, Christoph von Gendorf, a Royal Bohemian miners' leader, complied with the count's love of number symbolism: the four towers symbolize the four seasons; the twelve gates the twelve months; the 52 rooms the weeks and the (supposedly) 365 windows the days of the year. The schloss is now the seat of the administration of the Krkonoše National Park. In 1941 the *Augustinian Monastery* in Husova, founded in 1705, was used to house the historical and natural history collections of the Deutscher Riesengebirgsverein, which are still exhibited there in a modern display on the theme of 'Stone and Life' (Krkonošské muzeum).

Harrachov (Harrachsdorf) is situated in the middle of coniferous forests at the southwestern foot of the Krkonoše Mountains in the valley of the Mumlava (Mummel). The village was founded in the 17th century and in the 18th century was given the name of the ruling family, the Counts Harrach. In the neighbouring village of **Nový Svět** (formerly Neuwelt) the count built a glass factory in 1712, and its products were much sought after even beyond the borders of Austria-Hungary. It was in Neuwelt that the famous glass-cutter Dominik Biemann (1800–1857) began his career; later he went to Prague and finally to Franzensbad, where he cut glass portraits of Goethe, Beethoven and members of the Imperial house and the aristocracy. His works are to be seen in many museums in Europe. Today at the glass factory of Harrachov highly skilled craftsmen still cut crystal glass on the old cutting benches ; their work can be bought at the shop, and the work of their predecessors admired in the museum. Harrachov now welcomes international visitors as a winter sports centre with ski jumping, numerous ski lifts and ski slopes.

Špindlerův Mlýn (Spindlermühle), is a climatic health resort, 750–850 metres up, founded in the 17th century by Tyrolean foresters. The name of the town derives from the water mill of a man called Spindler. Until 1630 silver and copper were mined from the mountain. Today Špindlerův Mlýn is the centre of tourism in Krkonoše. **Janské Lázné** (Johannesbad), the 'Badgastein of the Giant Mountains', was founded in 1677 by Johann Adolf Prince Schwarzenberg in the valley of the Úpa (Aupa). There is a hot spring (29.6°C) and a number of ferrous springs which are used for the treatment of nervous disorders and muscular ailments, and a stay can be combined with walking and winter sports. Footpaths and a cable car go up to Černá hora (Schwarzenberg; 1299 metres). The 550 metre ascent can be made on foot by following the Lobkowicz path to the Zrcadlovky and from there to the summit with the Sokolská bouda and the Horský hotel. Thence it continues to the Černohorská rašelina, the highest area of moorland in the Krkonoše and a conservation area. A nature trail 4 km long runs through the reservation.

Sněžka (Schneekoppe), at 1602 metres the highest mountain in the Krkonoše, is best reached from Pec pod Sněžnou. There is a chair-lift next to the carpark in Obří důl (Giants Valley) above the village. At the summit, on the border between Poland and Czechoslovakia, stands the *Česká bouda* built in 1868. On the Polish side of the border a former *weather station* built of wood in 1900 sways in the wind. Also built of timber is the round *chapel of St Laurence* founded by the Silesian Count Schaffgotsch on the mountain. The site of the former Silesian Koppenbaude is now occupied by a modern *mountain hotel* with a built-in

Excursion to the source of the Elbe

If in a car, drive from the turn-off at Jilemnice (Starkenbach) northwards as far as Mísečky (Schlüsselbauden), leaving the car in the big car park at the end of the road and changing on to the bus to Vrbatova bouda. From here there is a signposted footpath to the Pancava Waterfall (Vodopád Pančavy), the highest waterfall in the Giant Mountains (130 metres), and on to the **Labská bouda** (Elbe bouda) on the steep slope of the **Elbe Meadow** (Labská louka), a high moor (1386 metres) with mountain pines. There is no spring as such – the waters that flow from the Elbe Meadow join to form a stream – but the **Elbe Spring** (Labská studanka or pramen Labe) symbolizes the source. A bronze plaque is dedicated to Jan Buchar, the greatest advocate of rambling in the Krkonoše Mountains. The two rows of coats of arms are those of all the towns which the Elbe passes through on its way to the North Sea. To the north-east of the Labská bouda the path leads to the 40 metre high **Elbe Waterfall** (Labský vodopád), from which the new river rushes through the 8 km of the **Elbe valley** (Labský dul), the romantic region of the 'Seven Valleys', where in 1762 the last bear in the Krkonoše was shot. At the level of the Myslivna restaurant the Elbe joins the White Elbe (Bílé Labe) and approaches Špindlerův Mlyn. The **Harrach Path** which accompanies it was created in 1879 by Count Harrach who made the Labský dul a nature reserve as early as 1904.

weather station. The view from Sněžka is famous: on a clear day it extends as far as the television tower at Liberec, to Zobten in Silesia, and even to the White Mountain near Prague.

Dominating the town of **Broumov** (Braunau), 30 km east of Trutnov near the Polish border is a great Benedictine monastery with an extraordinary courtyard by Kilian Ignaz Dientzenhofer (1726–1738). The pedimented centrepieces on all sides bulge forward with a dynamic plasticity that is Dientzenhofer's hallmark. There are churches by K.I.Dientzenhofer at Vernerovice and Hermankovice nearby.

North-east of Hradec Králové is the little industrial town of **Náchod (Nachod)**, whose church of St Lawrence has curious clapboard towers, dominated by the massive castle of the Piccolomini family. The Florentine Ottavio I Piccolomini-Pieri (1599–1656) entered Wallenstein's service as a bodyguard in 1627. In 1632 he was made an officer in Wallenstein's army, but betrayed Wallenstein's secret plans to Ferdinand II. The emperor entrusted him with the capture of the commander. In 1634 Wallenstein was killed at Cheb (Eger; see p. 218f). Ferdinand II appointed Ottavio Piccolomini Imperial field marshal and presented him with the lordship of Náchod.

The imposing castle, which grew from a border castle (c. 1250) of Count Hron of Náchod, was given a Renaissance remodelling between 1554 and 1614. At this time the *Smiřický Castle* was built in the south of the precincts. Of the Gothic construction only the massive round tower survives. Piccolomini had the castle renovated between 1650 and 1659 by Carlo Lurago who also added the *Piccolomini wing*. This contains a *chapel of St Mary* with

Dwarf in the Castle
entrance, Nové Město

magnificent Early Baroque plasterwork by Domenico Rossi and Andrea Cyrus. Between 1729 and 1731 Anton Brath added two office buildings to the north of the ensemble. The grand Piccolomini portal was designed by Severin Storař. The north side was terminated in the 17th century with a round bastion. The *Spanish Hall* created by Lurago in the Smiřický castle, was remodelled in the Rococo style around the middle of the 18th century. The slightly pedestrian *Apotheosis of Ottavio I Piccolomini* on the ceiling (by F. A. Scheffler) is made up for by the eager little angels in the lunettes and the brilliant plasterwork (by C.G. Bossi).

The castle contains some interesting furnishings including a series of Brussels tapestries after designs by Jacob Jordaens (first half of the 17th century). In 1792 Duke Peter of Kurland bought the castle and lordship of Náchod. Having lost his Baltic province in the Third Partition of Poland he settled in Bohemia as a wealthy and knowledgeable patron of art and added valuable paintings to the Piccolomini collection, which now includes a superb array of Flemish flower pictures.

At the north-western foot of the Orlické hory (Adlergebirge, Eagle Mountains) on a mountain spur round which flows the river Metuje (Mettau) stands the town of **Nové Město nad Metují** (Neustadt), which is worth a visit for the sake of its castle alone. Little is known about the origins of the town, though it was granted its town charter around 1501. After being destroyed by fire in 1526 it was rebuilt in the Renaissance style under the new rulership of the Counts Pernštejn. The medieval fortress was transformed by the Pernštejns into the grand castle that still dominates the town.

The *Market Square* is surrounded by houses with vigorous gabling and unusually majestic arcades, dating from the 16th century, including a splendid *town hall*. The parish church too dates from the early 16th century, its squat cupola less like an onion than a handbell. From the market place a bridge crosses the former castle moat to the Renaissance *castle* whose tall, round tower also has a low cupola; hence its name, the *Máselnice* (butter churn). Between 1655 and 1661 Carlo Lurago gave the castle its Baroque appearance. In the 19th century it was deserted and became dilapidated, until in 1908 the textile magnate Josef Bartoň bought it and commissioned the Slovak Dušan Jurkovič to restore it. This was done in an individualistic Art Nouveau, some of the interiors being completely remodelled. In 1910 Jurkovič linked the castle terraces to the gardens below the castle with a playful wooden bridge, before setting off on a wholesale recasting of the gardens and the park. Appropriate antiques were also bought, notably in 1932 the 24 dwarves along the terrace wall made by the workshop of Matthias Bernhard Braun after drawings by Jacques Callot. Braun's dwarves also stand on either side of the bridge in front of the moat.

The castle contains valuable collections, including Flemish masters, but above all Czech art of the 19th and 20th centuries, with paintings by Julius Mařák, Max Švabinský and Antonín Hudeček, sculptures by Josef Václav Myslbek, Jan Štursa and František Úprka, tapestries, ceramics and Cubist furniture.

Litomyšl (Leitomischl)

Like Nové Město **Litomyšl** is mainly worth visiting for its castle, within whose superb

Bedřich Smetana

Litomyšl (Leitomischl)
1 Smetana Memorial 2 Church of the Exaltation of the Cross 3 Church of the Invention of the Cross 4 Town Museum 5 Jirásek Memorial 6 Castle 7 Smetana Birthplace 8 Interhotel Dalibor

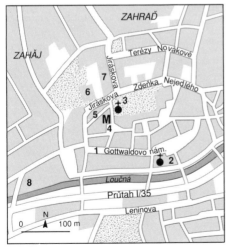

Renaissance walls is the Museum of Czech Music, since Litomyšl is the birthplace of the greatest Czech composer, Bedřich Smetana.

In the 10th century the Slavnik dynasty built a castle and church on what is now the castle hill. Before 1150 the Premonstratensians founded a monastery near the castle, and transformed it in the 14th century into a cathedral chapter. From 1344 until the Hussite Wars Litomyšl was the seat of a bishop. Its bishops settled the Hřebečsko (Schönhengstgau; see p. 331) with German farmers and craftsmen. In 1568 the Pernštejns converted the castle into a monumental Renaissance schloss.

The nucleus of Litomyšl is the long market place containing the Smetana monument. It is lined with particularly well-preserved

View of Litomyšl (Leitomischl)

Renaissance and Baroque houses with arcades and fine gables. The Knights' House, by the local stone mason Blažek is an extraordinary combination of rustic grandiose with almost Byzantine sophistication: griffins, lions, sea-monsters of all kinds, writhing corbels, knights, merchants and a pumpkin. The church of the *Exaltation of the Cross* dates from the third quarter of the 14th century and was renovated in the 17th century. The Baroque Piarist church of the *Invention of the Cross* was built by Giovanni Battista Alliprandi between 1714 and 1726. Adjoining the church is the 17th-century *Piarist College* which is now used for weddings and other ceremonies, and which contains the small but beautifully furnished town *Museum*, whose most precious exhibit is a Gradual (church song book) of 1563. The portal of the college dating from 1618 is worth the visitor's attention. It contains the coats of arms of the Trauttmansdorffs (blossom and star) and the Pernštejns (an aurochs's head with a tether through its nose).

The Renaissance *schloss* of Litomyšl, whose outer walls sport naive figural sgraffiti, was built for the Chancellor Vratislav Pernštejn by the brothers Giovanni Battista and Udalrico Aostali between 1568 and 1573. On the second floor of the south range, which includes the main gate, is a long open gallery, which forms part of the great arcaded courtyard. In the last decade of the 18th century a new owner, Count Georg Josef von Waldstein-Wartenberg had the interior remodelled in the Neo-Classical style. Only the chapel, the great dining hall and the 'Hall of Battles', which Count Trauttmansdorff had decorated with pictures of the battles of Prince Eugene of Savoy around 1730, remained as they were.

On the ground floor of the west range a new *theatre* was built in 1796–97, after two earlier theatres had been destroyed by fire within a short time. With the theatre of Český Krumlov (see p. 168) this is one of the oldest surviving playhouses in central Europe. It was decorated by Dominik Dvořák, who had also painted charming rural scenes in the new Neo-Classical interiors of the palace. The wings were designed by the most famous theatre painter in the

Habsburg Empire, Josef Platzer. Only the drawings survive of the scenery he designed for Vienna and Prague, but Litomyšl still has the originals of all the sets he designed for it, where, despite the heaviness of the forms, an incurable lightness of spirit seems to have survived. It was here that the young Smetana made his debut as a pianist.

Apart from the theatre the *Museum of Czech Music* in the state rooms of the castle should be visited. This is an annexe of the National Museum in Prague and shows the development of Czech music from the early middle ages to the present. There are taped musical examples from each period for the visitor to play.

Opposite the Castle stands the plain building of the schloss brewery, which was *Bedřich Smetana's birthplace*, with a small memorial. In this Renaissance building, which has undergone many modifications over the centuries, the composer was born on 2 March 1824, the son of the master brewer (see p. 125). The bust of the composer in the room of his birth is by Otakar Španiel (1924).

Music in Bohemia

Bohemia's reputation as a land of musicians was well established by the 18th century. Charles Burney was impressed by the high level of musical education: 'not only in every large town, but in all villages, where there is a reading and writing school, children of both sexes are taught music'. The musical training provided by the Jesuit colleges was good, and music was fostered by the church and by noblemen such as Count J.A. Questenberg at Jaroměřice nad Rokytnou, and Count F.A. Sporck, who put on Italian operas (some with Czech themes) at his theatres at Prague and Kuks, introduced the French horn to Bohemia, and published collections of religious folk songs. However, many fine instrumentalists went to work abroad: the violinist **Johann Stamitz** (1717–1757) moved to Mannheim, and **František Benda** (1709–1786) to Berlin. The prolific opera composer **Josef Mysliveček** (1737–1781) spent much of his career in Italy, and the pianist and composer **Jan Ladislav Dušek** (1760–1812) pursued a peripatetic career round Europe.

Prague cherishes its link with **Mozart**, who greatly enjoyed his stay there in 1787, when the city was Figaro-mad. His Symphony No. 38 ('the Prague') was first performed then, and *Don Giovanni*, specially written for Prague, had its première there in the same year. Mozart returned there in 1791, shortly before his death, to supervise his last opera, *La Clemenza di Tito*, hurriedly written (mostly on the coach journey to Prague) for the coronation of Leopold II as King of Bohemia.

A number of German-speaking composers had Bohemian or Moravian connections: **Christoph Willibald Gluck** (1714–1787), whose childhood was spent in northern Bohemia; **Karl Ditters von Dittersdorf** (1739–1799), who is buried near Jindřichův Hradec (Neuhaus); and **Gustav Mahler** (1860–1911), who spent his early years at Jihlava (Iglau), before going to study at Vienna in 1875.

Southern Moravia (Jižní Morava)

Brno (Brünn)

Brno (Brünn), the old capital of Moravia, is now the administrative capital of the South Moravian district. The third largest city in Czechoslovakia (population 395,000), it is situated at the foot of the Špilberk (Spielberg) and at the confluence of the Svratka (Schwarzawa) and Svitava (Zwittawa). It is one of the most important industrial centres in the country (textiles, machinery, electrical, chemical) and hosts the largest industrial fair in Czechoslovakia, but the old town centre, now surrounded by three broad ring-roads, still preserves many medieval buildings.

The history of Brno goes back, however, much further, to the Palaeolithic Brno man (Homo fossilis) 30,000 years ago. Brno man was part of Aurignacian culture. Around 400 BC Celts gave the settlement the name *Brynn*, which the Slavs (who followed the Quadii) turned into *Brno*. Around 800 they built a castle on Petrov (Petersberg), which is first mentioned as the seat of the Margraves of Moravia in 1091. In the 12th and 13th centuries large groups of Germans moved to the settlement, which they called *Brünn*. In 1243 King Wenceslas I raised it to the status of a town, and its privileges were confirmed and extended by Otakar II Přemysl and Wenceslas II.

In the 14th century the Margraves of Moravia built themselves a new residence on the Špilberk, and it was here that Charles IV resided during his formative years as the Margrave, before his coronation as king. During the Hussite Wars Brno remained true to the Emperor; it was besieged by the Taborites in 1428 and 1430 but was not captured. In 1642 Brno replaced Olomouc as capital of Moravia. After devastation by the Swedes (1645) and the Turks (1663) massive defences were built, and these proved effective enough to withstand the attack of Frederick the Great in 1742. On 2 December 1805 Napoleon lodged at Brno before the Battle of Austerlitz (see p. 303); but in 1809 he was able to have the citadel on the Špilberk dismantled. In 1860 the town walls too were demolished and their place taken by parks and boulevards. Only the Měnín Gate remained intact. In the late 18th and especially in the 19th centuries coal-mining and sheep farming turned Brno into such a great industrial town that it was known as the 'Moravian Manchester'. Brno gave the first two letters of its name to the Bren gun, which was originally made here, before production at Enfield.

The old town centre of Brno has several central squares of which Zelný trh (Krautmarkt; 'vegetable market'), also known as Horní trh (Oberring; upper square), at the foot of the castle is the largest and oldest and has the most character. In its centre is the foaming splendour of the *Parnassus Fountain* designed by Johann Bernhard Fischer von Erlach (1693–

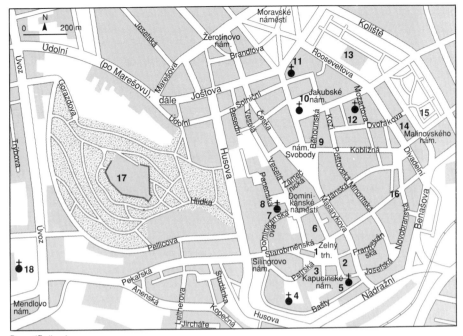

Brno (Brünn)
1 Parnassus Fountain   2 Reduta   3 Moravian Museum   4 Cathedral of St Peter   5 Church of the Invention of the Cross   6 Old Town Hall   7 Dominican Church of St Michael   8 New Town Hall   9 Folk Museum   10 St James   11 St Thomas   12 Jesuit Church of the Assumption   13 Janáček Theatre   14 Mahen Theatre   15 House of Artists   16 Měnín Gate   17 Špilberk   18 Augustinian Church of the Assumption

1695) with carvings by Adam Tobias Kracker and Bernhard Höger: allegories of the Four Seasons, Hercules fighting Cerberus, Amphitrite and various animals. The square, true to its name, still has fruit and vegetable stalls. The *Trinity Column* dates from 1729–1733. The *Redoute* (Reduta) in the south-east corner of the square is the oldest theatre in Brno, founded in 1670. Between 1918 and 1945 it was well known as the German-language theatre 'Kammerspiele am Krautmarkt'.

The south-west corner of Zelný trh is dominated by the *Moravian Museum* (Moravské muzeum), which was created as early as 1818, as the Franzensmuseum, from the Dietrichstein Palace (17th century) and the neighbouring old Bishop's Palace (15th-16th centuries). It was from this palace that Cardinal Prince Franz von Dietrichstein organized the re-Catholicizing of Moravia after the Battle of the White Mountain. The museum is famous for its archaeological and natural history collections, which include the stone-age 'Venus of Věstonice' (see p. 12) and the largest collection of cicadas in the world. The museum's gallery of paintings has works by Cranach, Rubens, Teniers, Maulpertsch, Hugo Lederer and modern Moravian painters, as well as an interesting picture cycle from the first half of the 15th century. The *Špaliček*, a group of tightly packed burghers' houses, reconstructed between 1969 and 1973, is a fine example of medieval building. It now contains a collection of modern sculpture.

Petrská ul. leads from the square up to Petrov Hill (Petersberg, also called Franzensberg), where the *Cathedral of St Peter* (Dóm na Petrově; also called Sts Peter and Paul) stands. It is built on the foundations of an old Slav castle and the Romanesque church (1131). The 15th-century High Gothic building was badly damaged by the Swedish bombardment, and was renovated in the Baroque style by the Bavarian architect Mauritz Grimm in the 1740's. At the beginning of the 20th century it was re-gothicized and two delicate towers were added. The exterior pulpit on the north side of the cathedral (the 'Capestrano pulpit') is a reminder of the great 15th-century Franciscan itinerant preacher, Johannes Capestrano.

The midday bell of Brno Cathedral rings at 11 instead of 12 o'clock, a tradition which goes back to the Swedish siege in 1645. After several weeks the Swedish commander decided to raise the siege if the town was not captured by noon the following day. The cathedral bellringers got to hear of this and so, when the Swedes seemed about to break through, they rang the midday bell an hour earlier than usual. The Swedes immediately ceased their attack and withdrew. In gratitude for this the midday bell has been rung at 11 ever since.

The *Mercury Fountain* in the cathedral courtyard was built by Brno merchants in 1693 for the lower market and placed in its present position in 1867.

The church of the *Invention of the Holy Cross* (Kostel Nalezení sv. Kříže) in Kapucinské nám. (formerly Kohlenmarkt, coal market), formed part of the former Capuchin friary and was built by the architect Otto Erna between 1648 and 1651. Its gabled façade is decorated with an image of the Empress Helena discovering the True Cross. The crypt of the church is enriched by some fifty well-preserved mummies of monks and benefactors; among them, in a glass coffin, is the colonel of the fearsome Pandurs, Baron Trenck (1711-1749).

Two streets lead northwards from the square: Mečová ul. and Radnická ul. Between them stands the *Old Town Hall* (Stará radnice) which was given its present appearance after the fire of 1311. From the 13th century almost without interruption until 1945, this was the seat of the town council of Brno. Its imposing tower dates from 1489 (there is a fine view from its gallery), and about 20 years later the magnificent Renaissance loggia in the town hall courtyard was built.

The elegant Late Gothic superstructure (plate 49) above the main doorway facing on to Radnická was created in 1511 by Master Anton Pilgram of Brno, the architect of St Stephen's in Vienna. It is a fragile piece of sandstone architecture with five sculptures (two armed figures, two burghers and, in the centre, an allegory of justice), each with its pinnacled canopy. The topmost pinnacle is bent and seems about to fall. Legend relates that this is because Master Pilgram used only part of his advance for materials and spent most of the money on wine – so it was not surprising that the pinnacles on his designs began to twist and turn. The stone masons who executed the work did not dare point out this peculiarity to the master, so the councillors were furious when they saw the completed portal and refused to pay the rest of the fee. Master Pilgram corrected the portal at his own expense, but the town council still refused to pay him. The artist flew into a rage and cursed the portal so that the middle pinnacle immediately twisted again. (The observant visitor will notice that two of the other pinnacles are also slightly bent.) Master Pilgram's curse is still supposed to strike anyone who dares to try to straighten the pinnacles.

In the passage to the town hall courtyard hangs the 'Brno Dragon' (Brněnský drak), also called the 'lindworm', a female alligator which is the subject of many legends. The dragon is supposed to have ravaged the country outside the walls of Brno, eating the peasants' livestock and the townspeople's children. Nobody was able to kill the creature, until at last a young journeyman mason had an idea. He filled a sack with unslaked lime, put it in the skin of a freshly killed goat and set it out as bait. The dragon ate the skin with the lime inside and, when it went to quench its raging thirst in the Svratka river, the water slaked the lime until the dragon burst. Guides still show visitors the scar on the alligator's belly.

A more accurate version of the dragon's history relates how Archduke Matthias was staying at Brno in 1608 to stir up the Moravian nobility against his brother, the Emperor Rudolph II. At the same time a Venetian showman was displaying a stuffed alligator which aroused the archduke's interest. The alligator was presented to him and he then gave it to the town as an expression of gratitude for its hospitality. The 'Brno Dragon' was then hung in the public passageway of the town hall where it has been now for nearly four hundred years. The visitor should also see the 'Brno cart wheel' (Brněnské kolo), made in 1636 and described in a contemporary source as 'four foot and ten inches high, which the master wheelwright Georg Birk for a wager of 12 reichsthaler not only made from freshly felled timber, starting at six o'clock in the morning, but also drove on the same day from Eisgrub (Lednice) to here (five miles)'.

Mečová leads to Dominikanské nám. (formerly also called Fischmarkt), with the *Dominican church of St Michael* (Dominikánský chrám sv. Michala), a two-towered Baroque building built after 1655 from a 13th-century Gothic church. The adjoining Dominican friary with 19th-century additions is now used as the *New Town Hall* (Nová radnice). In 1582 a Renaissance building for the Moravian administration was built above the cloister and was used for town councils and courts until 1784. In the 17th century the Sundial range was built, and between 1726 and 1733 Mauritz Grimm gave the town hall its present Baroque appearance and created the magnificent Estates Hall. In Dominikánská a medieval market hall has survived, the *Schmetterhaus*.

The counterpart to Zelný trh is the triangular *nám. Svobody*, formerly known as the Lower Market, or Great Square (Velký náměstí) or Viktoriaplatz, with its Early Baroque Marian Column (1680). The only survivor of the fine burghers' houses around this, the oldest square in the city, is the four-storey Renaissance house of the merchant Karl Schwarz (No. 17 in the south-west corner), built between 1589 and 1596. The doorway and the loggia in the

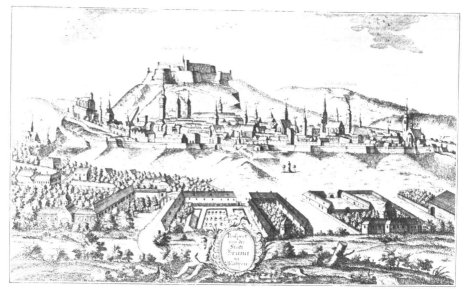

View of Brno (Brünn), engraving after F. B Werner

courtyard are particularly worth noticing. The house 'of the Four Caryatids' (Dům u čtyř mamlasů; No. 10) was built in 1901 by an industrialist.

In Minoritská is the Minorite friary with the Baroque church dedicated to the *Two Saints John* (1723–1733). The foundation for noble ladies and respectable burgher maidens in Kobližná was built in the 1670's. Today it contains the *Ethnographical Section* of the *Moravian Museum* (Národopisné muzeum) with applied arts, including wonderful Late Gothic vestments from Brno Cathedral dating from 1495.

To the north of nám. Svobody, třída 9. května (May 9th Street) passes the church of *St James* (Chrám sv. Jakuba), the parish church of the town with its slender tower 92 metres high. The Early Gothic church built at the command of Prince Vladislav in 1220 was destroyed in a fire in the 15th century, and the present Late Gothic aisled nave was built in the first half of the 16th century. Master Anton Pilgram worked on the building for a time (sacristy with oriel window). The tower was built around 1590 by the master carpenter Simon Tauch; in 1901 the wooden tower was replaced by an iron construction. The splendid net vault is supported by 18 slender compound piers. Except for the Late Gothic stone pulpit (1526) and the Early Baroque choir stalls (1707) the furnishings are all Neo-Gothic. There is a beautiful silver and black organ. Behind the high altar is the tomb of Raduit de Souches, the French soldier of fortune who galvanized Brno's defence against the Swedes. On the south wall of the tower is the 'rude little man' baring his backside towards the cathedral. Only recently a photographer has discovered that the man is in fact embracing a beautiful townswoman completely hidden from the pious churchgoers at street level.

Třída 9. května opens near the church of St Thomas (Kostel sv. Tomáše) into Moravské nám. The Augustinian church here was founded in 1350 by Margrave John, who entrusted the Parler workshop with its construction. Around 1737 Mauritz Grimm made Baroque alterations. The picture of St Thomas above the high altar was painted in 1764 by Franz Anton Maulpertsch. The conventual buildings attached to the church are now the seat of the district administration of South Moravia.

The *Jesuit church* dedicated to the Assumption (Kostel Nanebevzetí Panny Marie), was built between 1589 and 1602 to replace a 13th-century Gothic church. It was remodelled in 1734 by the Viennese architect J.G. Schauberger and is now one of the most beautiful Baroque churches in Brno.

In Rooseveltova třída stands the *Janáček Theatre* (Janáčkovo divadlo) for opera and ballet performances, opened in 1965. To the south is the *Mahen Theatre* (Mahenovo divadlo) in Malinovského nám., built in the second half of the 19th century by the Viennese theatre architects Ferdinand Fellner and Georg Helmer in a French Renaissance style. It was the first theatre in Europe with electric lighting. 100 metres to the east, in the gardens of the former ramparts, is the *House of Artists* (Dům umění) built in 1911 by Heinrich Ried.

Around 1270 King Otakar II Přemysl built a castle on the Špilberk (288 metres above sea-level) to the west of the city, which was strategically better sited than the old castle on Petrov. In 1640, during the Thirty Years' War, the Italian architects, Giovanni Pierroni and Andrea Erna converted the castle into a mighty citadel that withstood even the onslaught of the Swedes. Later in the notorious subterranean dungeons of the fortress many opponents of the Habsburgs languished, among them the Pandur colonel, Freiherr von der Trenck (1746–1749), and the Italian poet and leader of the 'Carbonari' secret society, Count Silvio Pellico (1822–1830). In 1783 the Emperor Joseph II had himself locked in the deepest and darkest dungeon, and said after emerging: 'I was the last person in these rooms. From now on no one shall ever again cross this threshold.' Nevertheless in 1820 the whole of the Špilberk citadel was turned into a prison for the enemies of the Austro-Hungarian Monarchy, where conditions were so appalling that Pellico's revelations closed it, apparently for good, in 1857. It turned out, however, to be suitable for the SS. Today the visitor can see the remains of the old fortifications which Napoleon razed in 1809, and visit the subterranean prisons, where thousands were tortured and executed in the last war.

At the south-western foot of the Špilberk stands the former *Augustinian monastery*, a foundation of Queen Elizabeth in 1323. It was in this monastery that Gregor Johann Mendel (1822–1884) carried out his famous experiments on peas, beans and bees, and from them deduced the laws of heredity, which were later called the 'Mendelian laws', when his achievement was posthumously recognized. There is a monument erected to the great cleric in 1910. Leoš Janáček received some of his early musical training as a chorister here in the 1860's. The abbey church of the Assumption, a three-aisled basilica, was founded in 1356 by the Margrave John Henry, a brother of Charles IV. It is a brick building, baroquized between 1661 and 1666 by Giovanni Pierroni, who preserved the old Gothic masonry in its original state except for the façade. In the niches of the façade he set statues of the patron saints of the order. The greatest treasure in the interior is a *pietà* (c. 1385) attributed to Heinrich Parler the younger, nephew to Master Peter.

The *abbey church of Maria Saal* in the district known as Staré Brno (Altbrünn; Old Brno). This convent of Cistercian nuns was founded in 1323 by Wenceslas II's widow, Elizabeth, who was buried there in 1335. The church – towerless, as the austere rules of the Cistercian order required – is the oldest brick building in Czechoslovakia. The greatly venerated panel painting on the Augsburg silver tabernacle is the 'Virgin of Brno' or 'Black Mother of God', a Byzantine work of the second half of the 13th century. The story that the icon dates from the 9th or 10th centuries, and that at the Sack of Milan it came into the hands of the Emperor Frederick Barbarossa who presented it to Vladislav II is without foundation. In fact it was acquired by the Emperor Charles IV who passed it on to his brother John Henry, who in turn donated it to the Augustinians at their monastery of St Thomas, who brought it with them when they migrated to Staré Brno in 1783.

The **Výstaviště** (Exhibition Ground) on the west side of the city was created in 1928 for a large exhibition devoted to Czechoslovak culture, in celebration of the tenth anniversary of the republic, which was to be a showpiece of modern architecture. The work of many of the leading Czechoslovak functionalist and constructivist architects of the time can still be seen here. Appropriately the site also contains the earlier **Schloss Bauer** (Zámeček), built in 1925 for a local sugar magnate by the pioneer modernist Adolf Loos (1870–1933), who was born in Brno.

A major work by a younger contemporary of Loos, the German Ludwig Mies van der Rohe, was commissioned by another wealthy Brno industrialist family, the Tugendhats. The elegant **Tugendhat House** at Černopolní 45, in a north-eastern suburb of Brno, with its unified living space, rich marble panelling and exquisite detailing, was built in 1930.

Two churches near Brno are among Johann Santini-Aichel's finest works, though neither of them is in his Baroque-Gothic style: 10 km north-east is the Premonstratensian pilgrimage church at **Křtiny** (Kiritein; 1713–1735), a centralized building on a Greek cross plan with an impressive galleried interior rising to a great frescoed dome; 10 km south is the collegiate church of **Rajhrad** (Raigern; 1722–1724), the architect's last work, built around a series of three domed elliptical spaces.

Pernštejn Castle (Pernstein)

25 km north-west of Brno stands the family castle of the lords of Pernštejn (originally Bärenstein), one of the largest castles in Moravia. First mentioned in 1285, it was extended and strengthened several times by the Pernštejns. The core of the complex is the heavy Romanesque round tower, called 'Barborka', to which other buildings were added over the centuries. In the first half of the 16th century Vílem of Pernštein converted the massive fortress into a grand family seat. The many oriel windows built then give the building a

picturesque appearance. Impressive diamond vaults are to be found in the entrance hall. Somewhat incongruously, there are also Rococo interiors, including a lemon-coloured bedroom with pastorals in the French taste. The castle chapel of the Conversion of St Paul was completed in 1570 and baroquized in the 17th century.

It was in 1866 in the Knights' Hall of the castle that Otto von Bismarck and the Prussian General Karl Friedrich von Steinmetz negotiated with the Austrians over the Peace of Nikolsburg. Between 1818 and 1948 Pernštejn Castle belonged to the Counts Mitrovský. It is now a protected monument.

Between Brno and Pernštejn is the small town of **Tišnov**, where the Early Gothic (1240) Cistercian abbey (Předkláštěří u Tíšnova) has a superb portal, reflecting its Latin name *Porta Coeli*: Christ in a mandorla with donors, the Apostles in rows on either side, and six elaborately carved arches.

21 km east of Brno lies the little town of **Slavkov u Brna** (Austerlitz) with the great Baroque schloss of the Counts Kaunitz. Austerlitz was the site on 2 December 1805 of the 'Battle of the Three Emperors' in which the French under Napoleon inflicted a heavy defeat on the allied armies of the Austrians under Francis II and the Russians under Alexander I. Alexander was easily hoodwinked by Napoleon into thinking that the French were falling back; and Francis had slept soundly while Napoleon was using the night to inspect the battlefield from Zmán Hill (small monument). The eager allies overstretched themselves and Napoleon was able to crash through their centre on Pracký Hill and attack from the rear: a classic manoeuvre carried out with an unprecedentedly large army. In memory of the 40,000 soldiers who fell in the battle a monument (1910-11)in the form of an old Slavic tomb was erected 9 km west of Slavkov on Mohyla míru, the hill where the fiercest fighting took place.

The château of **Bučovice**, 9 km east of Slavkov, is one of the high points of the Renaissance. An arcaded courtyard, of sparkling lightness, has spandrels and bases decorated with delicate reliefs (by Pietro Ferrabosco or Pietro Garbi; 1568). Everything is redolent of the pleasures of a summer pavilion, though the fountain in the middle suggests grosser joys: the twisting figure of Bacchus, staggering under the weight of a hairy wine-skin, while below him crouching mermen with wings slump under the weight of dog-faced shells open in lecherous grins. The enchantment of Bučovice comes with the *Hare Room* (Zaječí sál), where hares act out the courtly, martial life of the 16th-century aristocracy, and the *Emperor's Room* (Cisařský sál), where grotesques even more quicksilver than the hares are outshone by the stucco figures of Mars, Diana, Europa and the Emperor Charles V (in full jousting gear trampling the defeated Turk). Mars' piled up weapons, Diana's foolish hounds (who have missed a hare) and the Emperor's caparisoned steed glitter in white and gold and green.

Nearby, the 13th-century castle at **Buchlov** provides a contrast, its uncompromising silhouette reflected by bare, basic interiors. It was owned and furnished by the Berchtold family (one of whom was the Austro-Hungarian foreign minister in 1914), whose less austere taste is to be seen at the frothy **Buchlovice** nearby: an 18th century pleasure-house in three parts, two half-circles and an octagonal pavilion.

At the southern foot of the Pavlovské vrchy (Pollauer Berge) where the famous 25,000-year-old 'Venus of Věstonice' was found, is the little district town of **Mikulov** (Nikolsburg) situated near the Austrian border along the river Dyje (Thaya), in the midst of fruit gardens, vineyards and vegetable fields. The settlement is mentioned for the first time in 1173, and by 1362 it had become a town. In 1526 Balthasar Hubmaier brought Anabaptists from Switzerland to Nikolsburg, where under the protection of the Liechtenstein family they spread the word, running a printing press, which published celebrated pamphlets about the Lord's Supper and free will, and making many converts. As the more fanatical elements among the Anabaptists led the movement towards a rejection of all civil authority, the established authorities throughout Europe felt threatened by social unrest. Hubmaier, although a moderate, was made a scapegoat. Less than a year after his arrival he was extradited by the Austrians to Vienna (which can be seen from Mikulov), where he was burnt at the stake and his wife drowned.

Mikulov is dominated by the massive Baroque *Schloss*, the towers and buildings of which loom over the town. Its origins lie in an early 13th-century Gothic castle of the Counts

Moravský kras (Moravian Karst region)

About 30 km north of Brno, near the little town of **Blansko** is the beginning of the region known ' as the **Moravský kras**, a wild, romantic, fissured terrain in the Drahan hills with magnificent gorges, chasms and dripstone caves. A whole day will be needed for a tour of the Karst region, which is a nature conservation area, (35 km starting from Blansko).

From Blansko road 380 runs down the Punkva valley (Punkevní udolí) to the *Punkva Cave* (Punkevní jeskyně) which has the biggest and most beautiful stalagmites and stalactites in the Moravian Karst. A visit – much of it by boat – can take up to 2 hours. The road then winds through the dry Pustý žleb (Ödes Tal; 'desolate valley') and then passes through the fertile valley Sloup. On the right is a limestone cliff 50 metres high with the prehistoric cave dwelling of Kůlna (Schuppen) and the massive Hřebenáč (Teufelsfelsen) and the extensive stalagmite caves of Sloup and Šošůvka (Sloupsko-šošůske jeskyně). The return journey goes through the village of Ostrov u Machocy down to the Balcar cave (Balcarka jeskyně) at the foot of massive Balcar cliff. 1 km further on a turning to the right goes to the *Macocha* (the name comes from *macecha*, stepmother), a chasm 281 metres long, 126 metres wide and 118 metres deep with almost perpendicular walls, the result of the collapse of a large limestone cave. A signposted path leads down to the bottom (about half an hour), where there are two small lakes. The road to Blansko then goes through the Suchý žleb (Dürres Tal; dry valley) to the Katherine Cave (Kateřinská jeskyně) in which there is a forest of wafer-thin stalagmites. Return to Blansko is along road 380.

Liechtenstein, but it was sold to the energetically Catholic Dietrichsteins at the end of the 16th century. Between 1611 and 1618 Adam von Dietrichstein had the castle converted into a Renaissance schloss, and after 1719 Gustav Oedel remodelled it in the Baroque style. The schloss was used by the SS during the Second World War as a depot for booty (including the costumes of the Vienna Opera), and it was the SS who blew it up in 1945, showering the town with stolen porcelain. Rebuilt between 1948 and 1961, the schloss now houses art collections and a museum of viticulture. The most interesting item is a wine barrel dating from 1643 with a capacity of 101,000 litres (the famous Heidelberg Barrel holds a mere 100,000 litres); it was designed to receive the tithes of the farmers. Below the schloss is the Jewish cemetery with graves from the 18th and 19th centuries.

In the small main square of Mikulov the Baroque *Trinity Column* was built in 1723 to a design by Anton Josef Preuner of Vienna. The grandiose façade of the church of *St Anne*, the burial church of the Dietrichsteins, faces the square. From 1623 a Loreto chapel stood here attached to the neighbouring Capuchin friary – the first Loreto shrine in Moravia. In the middle of the 17th century the Loreto chapel was enlarged by Giovanni Jacopo Tencalla into a hall-church with side chapels, and between 1704 and 1710 the church underwent a Baroque remodelling for Cardinal Leopold von Dietrichstein, when the great west front was built. Josef Kässmann designed the figure of Christ and the angels; Antonio Riga, Giovanni Mangoldi and Ignaz Lengelacher made the other façade figures. In 1784 the hall-church was destroyed by fire and was eventually rebuilt in Neo-Classical style by Heinrich Koch sixty years later. The final alterations to St Anne's were done between 1845 and 1852.

The Late Gothic town parish church of *St Wenceslas*, with its well-proportioned tower, was founded by Cardinal Franz von Dietrichstein around the middle of the 17th century as a collegiate church. In 1631 he summoned the Piarists to Nikolsburg who opened their first college in Moravia by the church of *St John* (Piarist church) in the lower town. In 1671 the Late Gothic church was baroquized and in 1768 its ceiling was painted with frescoes by Franz Anton Maulpertsch. To the north-east of the town the Dietrichsteins built a Way of the Cross leading up to the *Kopeček* (Heiliger Berg; 363 metres: good views of the Austrian plain) on which stands the Early Baroque chapel of St Sebastian (Kostel sv. Šebestiána; 1679).

South-east of Mikulov are two of the great Liechtenstein châteaux: **Valtice** (Feldsberg), an enormous Baroque structure (1668) built over 13th-century foundations, which contains interiors with very fine woodwork and ceiling paintings, and a handsome chapel. The overall effect, however, is a little cold. Their summer palace nearby at **Lednice** (Eisgrub), on the other hand, is a neo-Gothic extravaganza, with a romantic minaret in the garden.

Znojmo (Znaim)

The district town of **Znojmo** with a population of over 37,000, situated high above the river Dyje (Thaya), is the centre of south Moravian wine, fruit and vegetable growing. The most interesting buildings in the town are the Romanesque rotunda, the Gothic tower of the town hall and the massive parish church of St Nicholas.

In the 11th century the Přemyslid prince Břetislav I built a border castle on the rock above the Dyje, and in the following century German settlers arrived to occupy the area below the castle. In 1223 Znojmo became the first settlement in Moravia to receive a town charter. John of Luxemburg encouraged wine-growing by granting the town special privileges, and his son Charles IV supported the export of wine abroad. From the 15th to the 17th centuries large wine cellars were built beneath the market place and the houses that line it. In the 19th century another product besides the vine began to be cultivated: the famous Znojmo gherkin (originally brought from Hungary in 1571), mainly used for pickling, with a piquant flavour which made it the most sought-after vegetable in Moravia. History touched Znojmo briefly again when Napoleon and the Archduke Charles came to sign an armistice here in 1809 after the Battle of Wagram, the culmination of the campaign that humiliated Austria.

Its hill-top site and piecemeal development as a castle settlement are the reasons for the town's irregular street plan. In the centre, facing the market place, Masarykovo nám., stands a

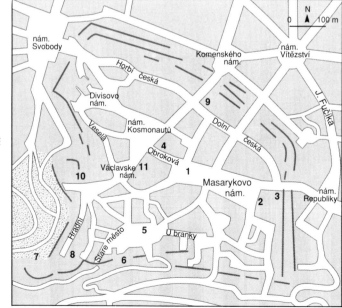

Znojmo (Znaim)
1 Town Hall Tower
2 Church of St John
  the Baptist
3 Wolf Tower (Vlková
  věž)
4 Goltz Palace
5 St Nicholas
6 St Wenceslas
7 South Moravian
  Museum
8 Rotunda
9 Church of the Holy
  Cross
10 Church of the
  Assumption
11 St Michael

modern supermarket which supports the finest *town hall tower* (radniční věž) in Moravia. The mid-15th-century town hall itself was destroyed in 1945 in the closing stages of the war, and only the Late Gothic tower, 80 metres high and built by Nikolaus of Edelspitz (1445–1448), survives. The diagonally placed cap lends an air of solid sophistication to this Gothic roof structure. The tower was reconstructed between 1951 and 1953. At the lower end of the square is the church of *St John the Baptist* (1623–1632), east of which, next to the Capuchin monastery, stands the medieval *Wolf Tower* (Vlková věž). The *Goltz Palace* (1606) at Obroková ul. 10 now contains the administrative offices of the town.

The church of *St Nicholas* (Kostel sv. Mikuláše) was built in 1338 to replace an earlier parish church. The Late Gothic three-aisled hall church has a net vault supported on round pillars. The square tower had to be demolished in 1837 and a Neo-Gothic replacement was built between 1848 and 1851. The painting of the *Glorification of St Nicholas* on the high altar (1759) and several of the pictures on the side altars are by Josef Daysinger, a Bamberg painter. The Late Gothic sacrament house dates from around 1500; its iron grilles have scenes from the life of the Virgin. The Late Gothic pulpit is in the form of a globe; the tester consists of a carving of God the Father with Adam and Eve, thought to be from the workshop of the local sculptor Josef Winterhalter (mid-18th century). The wall frescoes in the choir show scenes from the life of Christ and the Old Testament (second half of the 15th century).

Opposite St Nicholas's is the church of *St Wenceslas* (Kostel sv. Václava), a late 15th-century double church, where the lower chapel is dedicated to St Martin and the upper to St Anne. The upper chapel was given a Late Gothic net vault between 1500 and 1521.

Znojmo Castle belonged to the Margraves of Moravia and dates from the 11th century. In the 13th century it was replaced by a Gothic castle out of which a Baroque château developed which now houses the *South Moravian Museum* (Jihomoravské muzeum).

Part of the Přemyslid castle was the Romanesque *Rotunda* built before 1037 and decorated with remarkable wall paintings in 1134. Four anonymous artists created a work which combines spiritual and secular themes in a quite extraordinary way. The lowest register is a Marian cycle, the two registers above show the legend of the prophetess Libuše and the Přemyslid dynasty. At the very top of the vault are cherubim, four angels, the four evangelists and in the triumphal arch the donors, Margrave Konrad II of Moravia and his wife, Maria. Christ appears in the apse with the Virgin, John the Baptist and apostles. The Rotunda, now in the grounds of a brewery, is currently being restored. (The visitor who has acquired a taste for Czech muralism should visit Moravský Krumlov, 32km north east of Znojmo, where Alfons Mucha's great *Czech Epic* decorates the church.)

Three other churches in Znojmo are worth a visit: the Dominican church of the *Holy Cross* (1653–1677) with an altarpiece by Franz Anton Maulpertsch; the church of the *Assumption* attached to a double monastery of Friars Minor and Poor Clares, founded by Wenceslas I in the first half of the 13th century, and the church of *St Michael* taken over by the Jesuits in 1624 and given a Baroque remodelling.

On the edge of Znojmo stands the enormous unfinished abbey of **Louka** (Klosterbruck), a late work by Johann Lukas von Hildebrandt, now a barracks. The library here was transferred – books, shelves and floor – to the Strahov monastery in Prague when Louka was closed by Joseph II.

Another building near Znojmo worth a detour is the Renaissance mill at **Slip**, with its handsome double staircase and naive dormers.

Vranov Castle (Schloss Frain), set on a rock 60 metres above the Dyje, is one of the most beautiful and grandest Baroque châteaux in Moravia, and includes the earliest of J.B. Fischer von Erlach's architectural masterpieces. Its origins go back to a border castle built here by Břetislav I on the southern margin of the Přemyslid domains. After 1323 the castle, by now gothicized, passed as a fiefdom to several aristocratic families in turn, including the Lichtenbergs (from 1421) and the Althans (from 1618) who began the conversion of the castle into a magnificent Baroque schloss. In 1799 it was acquired by a Polish Count Mniszek who founded a stoneware factory whose products became famous as 'Frain Wedgwood'. In 1948 the

View of Znojmo (Znaim) from Merian's Topography

schloss became the property of the state and underwent an exemplary restoration between 1972 and 1979.

A high bridge leads to the former outer ward dating from the Renaissance period with its massive square tower. Parts of the Gothic fortifications, including a water tower and a watchtower on the east side known as the 'Crows' Tower', still survive. The original hall range with the round keep stood on the site of the present cour d'honneur. This is where tours of the château begin.

Fischer von Erlach's *Hall of Ancestors* on the east side of the cour d'honneur is approached up a mighty stairway with colossal statues of *Hercules and Antaeus* and *Aeneas and Anchises* by the Viennese sculptor Lorenzo Mattielli. These were a gift from the Emperor Charles VI to his mistress Maria Anna Althan, Princess Pignatelli by birth, and were in fact originally

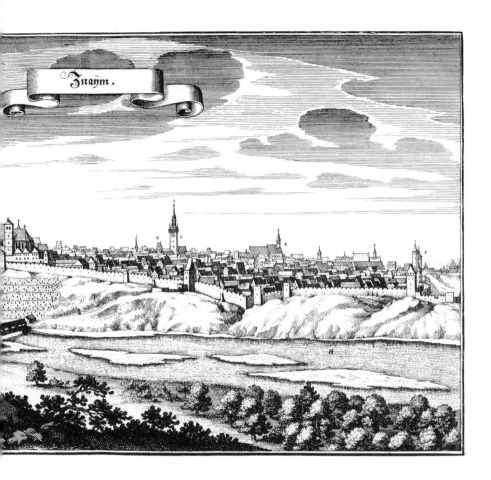

intended for the Imperial chancellery in Vienna. The giant statues are a fitting introduction to the Hall of Ancestors, one of the most splendid rooms in the country. Fischer von Erlach began work on this elliptical hall, 13 metres high, in 1688 as a free-standing building on the very edge of the cliff. In the niches between the windows of the hall stand statues of the fierce ancestors of the man who commissioned it, Count Johann Michael II von Althan; the sculptures, some of which are conscious pastiches were made by Adam Tobias Kracker of Vienna in 1694. The dome intersected by oval windows is covered with frescoes by the Salzburg painter, Johann Michael Rottmayr (1695), representing predominantly mythological scenes (*Labours of Hercules, Ulysses Blinding Polyphemus, Fall of the Giants*) and culminating in the *Glorification of the Althan Dynasty*. The predilection in this landlocked country for marine scenes is amply fulfilled with a threatening shark-dragon, and the deep scallops of the upper windows. The lower windows have Santinesque glazing bars.

The *castle church* (1698–1700), dedicated to the Holy Trinity, was also designed by Fischer von Erlach. It too stands on the cliff edge and consists of a round space with a dome surrounded by six elliptical chapels. After 1730 A.E. Martinelli added the two towers. Fischer von Erlach also designed the altar and the organ. The frescoes in the vault showing *Heaven, Hell* and *Paradise* are by Ignaz Crinitz. The west and south wings of the château were built in a transitional style between Late Baroque and Neo-Classicism between 1779 and 1787. The most interesting rooms are the Ballroom, the Napoleonic Salon, the Masonic Room, the Painting Gallery, Princess Pignatelli's flowered Bedroom with Neo-Classical stoves, and her Empire-style bath.

Every summer the splendid château and its park in the middle of the little town of **Jaroměřice** (Jarmeritz) are the centre for a festival of classical music. The structure goes back to a Gothic castle built by the Lords of Lichtenberg in the 14th century, which the Brno architect Giovanni Battista Erna transformed into a grand Renaissance château for the Counts Meziříčtí in the 16th century. In 1708 Count Johann Adam Questenberg commissioned a Baroque remodelling which was carried out to his designs by Domenico d'Angeli between 1711 and 1737, and he also started the tradition of music-making.

The building has three ranges with its main façade and cour d'honneur facing the town's main square. The two side wings surround a floral terrace. On the east side of the cour d'honneur is the theatre built between 1722 and 1730. A short passage links the main wing with the *castle church* which also serves as the parish church of the town and is dedicated to St Margaret (1715–1739). Built on an elliptical plan, it was designed by the great Baroque architect Johann Lukas von Hildebrandt, whose ambitious plans for rebuilding the château were not realized because of lack of money. Jakob Prandtauer may also have been involved.

More certain is that the remodelling of the interior of the château was carried out by Konrad Adolf Albrecht von Albrechtsburg (1728). The Hall, with its ceiling fresco showing the *Glorification of Jaroměřice*, occupies two storeys of the main wing. The Music and Ball Room in the west wing also has a magnificently frivolous ceiling and wall decoration. The *Chinese Cabinet* was designed by Tommaso Bella around 1731; the scarlet and lacquer decoration ingeniously combines Baroque forms with Chinese scenes. The floor has its original figural inlay in exotic woods. The *Gallery* has paintings by Veronese, van Honthorst, Bol, Rubens, Kupetzky, Brandl and others.

The *Park* was laid out in the style of the Baroque by the French designer, Jean Trehet; of the stone deities which populated it only six remain. The passage from the château to the park is formed by an illusionistically painted *sala terrena* on the west wing, and there is an equally lighthearted grotto.

Count Johann Adam Questenberg, Imperial Councillor and Treasurer, made the schloss a great centre of Baroque music. He organized his servants into an orchestra and put it under

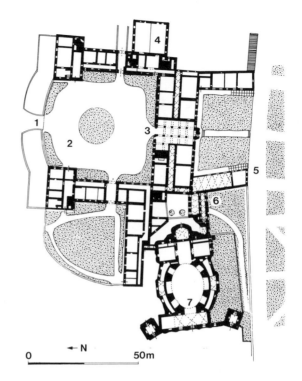

Jaroměřice (Jarmeritz) Castle, plan
1 Main Gate
2 Cour d'honneur
3 Vestibule
4 Castle Theatre
5 Park
6 Sala Terrena
7 Church of St Margaret

0   50m

the direction of his gifted valet František Václav Miča (1694–1744). Miča arranged the concert programmes at the château, studied Italian operas and Viennese singspiels and composed the first Czech opera *L'origine de Jarmeriz en Moravie*, first performed in the schloss theatre in 1730, which appeared in a Czech translation in the same year.

Telč (Teltsch)

The most beautiful medieval town in Czechoslovakia, **Telč**, surrounded by fishponds, has a historic town centre with sober churches and an attractive schloss which looks back to earlier, less peaceful times. The one street that breaches the almost undamaged town walls leads to the long market place surrounded by brightly coloured burghers' houses with their arcades and delightful gables (front cover and flap illustration). Because of its picturesque character Telč was one of the first towns to be given the status of a conservation area and since 1950 it has been lovingly restored. A new town was established beyond the ponds and the population is now about 7000.

Settlers moved into the marshy district in the 12th century. They formed three ponds from the water and built their houses between them. These ponds, or fish farms, were an important

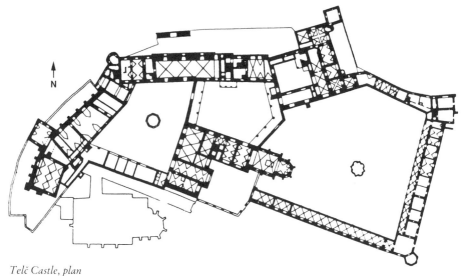

Telč Castle, plan

part of the medieval economy all over Europe, but particularly in lands far from the sea. At the beginning of the 13th century the Margrave of Moravia built a castle in Telč. Around the middle of the 14th century it duly received its town charter and shortly before 1400 an imposing aristocratic residence was built, in front of which the market place developed with its rows of houses. These were all destroyed in the great fire of 1530, and the rebuilding shows a medley of Renaissance and Baroque façades. The residence of the Margraves became a splendid Renaissance château. The appearance of Telč has hardly changed since.

Some of the arcaded houses in nám. Miru (colour plate 18), formerly the market, have sgraffito decoration, in particular the corner house (No. 15), which was given Renaissance features around the middle of the 16th century. The Late Romanesque tower of the church of the *Holy Ghost* (Kostel sv. Ducha) dates from the first quarter of the 13th century and was the keep of the princes' castle, on whose foundations the nave and chancel were eventually built. The parish church of *St James* (Chrám sv. Jakuba), built in the third quarter of the 14th century, is a two-aisled hall church which was given its Late Gothic appearance in the middle of the 15th century. Next to St James stands the 17th-century Jesuit College and the church of the *Assumption* (Kostel Nanebevzeti Panny Marie) dating from the 14th century and baroquized in the 17th century

The *Schloss* in the west corner of the market place goes back to the Gothic aristocratic residence of the 14th century, which was altered by Antonio Vlach (1553–1556) and Baldassare Maggi da Arogno (1566–1568) to form a splendid Renaissance château for a much-travelled connoisseur, Zacharias, Lord of Hradec, and his son Adam. The north and south wings were built in the 1560's and 1570's, as well as the two arcaded courtyards and the chapel of All Saints, in which Zacharias (d. 1589) and his wife, Katharina von Waldstein (d. 1571) are buried (marble sarcophagus behind a geometric wrought-iron grille). The courtyards are relatively plain, but inside the full force of Zacharias's fascination with Italy is obvious in the sumptuous Mannerist decoration. Nevertheless Telč also has a glittering lightness of touch not found south of the Alps.

Among the most interesting rooms in the château are the 'Treasury' with its lavish sgraffiti (perspective architecture and luxuriantly flowered ceilings; 1553); the *Dining Hall* with a splendid doorway, and sgraffiti of hunting scenes and of the Seven Deadly Sins; the *Knights' Hall* and Trophy Rooms with a whole stag triumphantly stuck to the ceiling; the *Golden Hall* with richly carved coffered ceiling (1591) reminiscent of the Doges' Palace; the *Blue Hall* with fine tapestries, and the *Arsenal* with a stellar vault, every compartment filled with grotesques. The tour also includes a glimpse of the bed of the 'Woman in White', Perchta (Berta) of Rožmberk, her portrait and that of her husband Hans von Liechtenstein (see pp. 205f). It was at Schloss Telč that the Austrian writer Franz Grillparzer (1791–1872) found the first inspiration for his ghost tragedy *Die Ahnfrau* ("The Ancestress", 1817).

30 km south of Telč, on the Austrian border, is the tiny Renaissance town of **Slavonice** (Zlabings). The houses here have remarkable sgraffiti, and some of the purest Gothic diamond vaulting in the country.

Jihlava (Iglau)

Mahler's birthplace, **Jihlava**, lies on a river of the same name – formerly called the Igel or Iglawa. It is a medieval town and the oldest mining town of the Bohemian Crown. The silver mines were developed by German miners, and the 'Iglauer Bergrecht' (Iglau mining law), later adopted as far away as South America, was drawn up by German lawyers. Until the Second World War Iglau was the centre of a German language-island, roughly diamond-shaped, extending 43 km north-south and 18 km east-west, in which more than half of the 80 communities had a German-speaking majority. Magnificent buildings of the Gothic, Renaissance and Baroque periods, including the unusual arcades of the burghers' houses with their mural paintings, and the well-preserved town fortifications, make Jihlava an interesting open-air museum.

In 1233 Hermann Balk, Commendator of the Teutonic Order of Knights, sold the properties around Jihlava and Humpolec as well as the tithes of thirteen villages for 100 silver marks to the Premonstratensian monastery of Želiv (Selau). The following year Wenceslas I gave the village of Iglau to the nunnery at Tišnov (Tischnowitz). However, when silver was unexpectedly discovered in 1240 the king quickly placed Iglau directly under royal administration and began exploiting the silver mines. The miners came from Saxony, while the craftsmen and farmers were from Bavarian territory, particularly the Upper Palatinate.

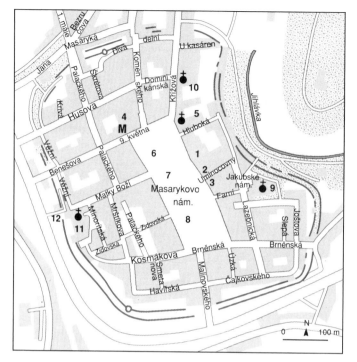

Jihlava (Iglau)
1 Town Hall
2 Miners' Court
3 Mint
4 Museum
5 St Ignatius
6 Plague Column
7 Poseidon Fountain
8 Amphitrite
  Fountain
9 St James
10 Dominican Church
   of the Holy Cross
11 Minorite Church
   of St Mary
12 Mother of God
   Gate

By 1249 Wenceslas I had made Iglau a town, and by 1269 it had been granted *Stapelrecht* by Otakar II Přemysl. In 1275 Iglau bought from the king the right to mint coins, and in 1294 the most important silver mining town in Europe, Freiberg in the Saxon Riesengebirge, adopted 'Iglauer Bergrecht', as 'established and written by burghers of the Ygla and the most noble miners' and confirmed with the seal of the town and the burghers. In 1304 Gozzius of Orvieto, a lawyer at the court of Wenceslas II, revised this law to form the *Jus regale montanorum*, which was adopted in large areas of Europe to regulate the dimensions and hiring out of mines, prospecting and tunnelling, protection from water and the selection of judges for miners' courts. In 1345 the upper court at Iglau became the final court of appeal for all mining matters throughout the Holy Roman Empire.

In 1421 Jihlava formed a confederation with Olomouc, Brno and Znojmo against the Hussites. Jan Žižka duly appeared before the walls of the town with his Hussite army the following year, but he was unable to capture it, and in fact it was here that negotiations between the Catholics and Hussites resulted in the 'Peace of Iglau' in 1436. Jihlava remained staunchly Catholic and was the only town to refuse to recognize the Utraquist King George of Poděbrady in 1458. After a five month siege and heavy bombardment the king finally persuaded Jihlava to recognize him, but when George was excommunicated by the pope,

Jihlava, together with Olomouc, Brno and Znojmo, withdrew its support from him. Not surprisingly, on his death, Jihlava took the lead and the Catholic Estates, the 'League of Grünberg', met in the parish church here in 1471 to elect the king of Hungary, Matthias Corvinus, as king of Bohemia and Moravia; the Utraquist federation in Prague was meanwhile electing Prince Władysław Jagiełło of Poland (Vladislav II of Bohemia). Finally it was in Jihlava, in 1486, that the two kings met and came to an agreement over the succession in an attempt to create a united front to counter the growing power of the Habsburgs. The signing of this was followed by ten days of celebration.

Gradually the veins of silver were worked out, but the citizens of Iglau kept their town flourishing by developing a new trade. From the 15th century on fulling houses and dyeing houses of the guilds of clothmakers and linen-weavers began to be built. Flemish weavers and dyers had brought this trade to Iglau, and now the high-quality Iglau cloth, dyed by a special process, conquered the central and southern European markets. Despite a fire (1523) and plague (1541) the hundred years from 1520 to 1620 mark the high point of the town's economic fortunes. The town's anti-Hussite attitude, did not prevent Luther's Reformation reaching Iglau as early as 1525, so that it was on the wrong side after the Battle of the White Mountain in 1620, which therefore put an end to the town's period of prosperity. In the same year Imperial troops occupied Iglau. In 1625 Cardinal Prince Dietrichstein of Brno gave the citizens six weeks to return to the Catholic faith or leave the country; most chose to emigrate. Jesuits took over the *Gymnasium* founded in 1561 (where Smetana and Mahler were later educated) and the other schools of the town. In 1645 the Swedes occupied Iglau, but it was retaken by the Imperial forces two years later. Of the 13,000 inhabitants only 299 were left at the end of the Thirty Years' War.

In the late 17th century mining was temporarily resumed, but water penetration in the galleries made it so expensive that it was no longer profitable, though it was not until 1783 that the Royal Moravian mining office in Iglau was closed and mining ceased. Clothmaking, however, continued to flourish and the population rose from 6246 in 1719 to 10,786 in 1798. Today Jihlava is a district town with a population of 54,000.

The main square of Jihlava, recently renamed Masarykovo nám., is 328 metres long and 114 metres wide, and covers an area of 3.7 hectares, making it the largest market place in the country. In the 13th century only Cologne, Breslau (Wrocław) and Cracow had bigger market places. Since 1426 the *Town Hall* has stood on the east side of the square; it has undergone several alterations and extensions and in 1786 was given an additional storey, a clock tower with a helm and a Baroque façade. Running beneath the square and the surrounding houses is a labyrinth of passageways built as store rooms, but which served as shelters for the population in time of war. Part of these 'catacombs' can be visited. The subterranean passages extend for about 25 km, linking together all the houses in the old town centre. They are now used to carry water, electricity, gas, heating, telecommunications and so on, making it unnecessary to dig up the pavement when extensions or repairs to the network are required.

The square is surrounded by patrician houses of two or three storeys with splendidly painted arcades. One of the oldest of these is No. 13/305 which has a Gothic core (1260); its Renaissance façade is decorated with most unusual sgraffiti. On the ground floor of No. 44/371 is a large hall (500 sq metres) in which the Diet used to meet. Until 1825 this was a famous inn, Zum wilden Mann, and from then for twenty-five years a theatre. The corner house No. 7/63 with an attractive oriel window extending through three storeys, is *U mincovny* (At the Mint) where the old miners' court used to meet. No. 57/488 with the Masters' Room on the first floor was the home of the clothmakers' guild from 1636. Together with the neighbouring house it now forms the Jihlava *Museum*. The Golden Lion Inn (No. 14/83) is decorated with a lion's head with a ring in its mouth. From 1796 to 1919 it was the hereditary post office and is still known as the 'Old Post Office'. The Renaissance doorway in the Late Baroque façade dates from the end of the 16th century, the balcony from the Rococo period.

In the north-east corner of the square stands the church of St *Ignatius* (Kostel sv. Ignáce), a Baroque Jesuit church built by Giovanni Jacopo Brasca between 1680 and 1689. Count Althan, an Imperial field marshal, donated the sites, where twenty-three buildings stood which had belonged to Protestant burghers, for the construction of a college with a church. The splendid frescoes were completed by Karl Töpper in 1717. The most precious object in the church is the 'Přemyslid Cross', a Gothic crucifix said to have been donated by Otakar II Přemysl. There is also a late 14th-century Gothic Pietà. The church changed hands several times: the Jesuits were followed by the Dominicans, and the Dominicans by the Premonstratensians. It served as a garrison church until 1918, and since then has been used by the Czechoslovak National Church. The neighbouring Jesuit college dating from 1699 is now the town library.

The *plague column* erected in 1679 is also the work of the Italian Giovanni Jacopo Brasca. The figures on the column, which is 15 metres high, were carved by Antonio Laghi: the Virgin at the very top, Sts Joseph, James, Sebastian and Francis Xavier at the foot. The *Poseidon* and *Amphitrite Fountains* in the square were made by the Jihlava sculptor, Václav Prchal. The modern textile supermarket in the centre of the square seems like an alien intruder, but the town planners were deliberately continuing the tradition of the old medieval 'staple-houses' which formerly stood on the site dominating the centre of the market place – and in which textiles were the main goods sold.

Farní ul. leads to the front of the church of St *James* (Kostel sv. Jakuba), the Gothic parish church with its asymmetrical towers. Construction of a Romanesque basilica began shortly after 1250; three years later the choir was complete and was consecrated by Bruno von Schaumburg, Bishop of Olomouc, in the presence of King Otakar II Přemysl. The three-aisled Early Gothic hall nave with its two west towers was built next and was completed in the second half of the 14th century. The interior decoration is Baroque: the high altar was made in 1771 by the sculptor Wenzel Kowanda, the altarpiece, *The Decollation of St James* is by Johann Nepomuk Steiner of Jihlava, Court Painter to the Empress Maria Theresa. There

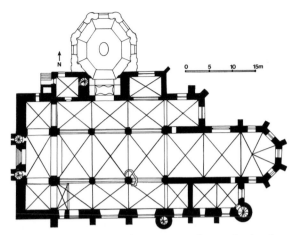

Jihlava (Iglau) St James, plan

is also a Gothic Madonna (mid–14th century) and a magnificent statue of St Katherine (late 14th century). The Nuremberg goldsmith, Hans Hirtz, made the great font in 1599, a Renaissance masterpiece with eight sides showing the Fall, Annunciation, Nativity, Circumcision, Baptism, the Way to Golgotha, Resurrection and Ascension. The Early Baroque chapel of the Virgin has an unusual story: it was built in 1702 by Jakob Kielmann, a doctor born in Jihlava who had made good in Vienna, to house a larger than life 14th-century pietà. This charming octagonal structure fits in neatly between two Late Gothic chapels. There is a superb wrought-iron grille in front of the chapel.

The Dominican church of the *Holy Cross* (Kostel sv. Kříž) in Křížová was founded in 1240 and completed in 1410. In 1784 Joseph II closed the friary and church, and they became a barracks and garrison church. Here the young Gustav Mahler, whose family moved in 1860, shortly after his birth, to Jihlava (where his father ran a distillery and several taverns), heard the military bands that echo thoughout his music. Since 1949 the Holy Cross church has belonged to the Czechoslovak National Church. The *Minorite Church* in Matky Boží is one of the three oldest churches in Jihlava. It was built around the middle of the 13th century as a three-aisled basilica. The tower, completed in 1412, has an octagonal stone helm above a gallery. The choir now has a Late Gothic appearance (1499–1508), while the façade was baroquized in the 18th century.

Matky Boží ends at *Brána Matky Boží* (Mother of God Gate; Frauentor) which dates from the 14th and 16th centuries, the only one of the five town gates to survive. South of the massive gate tower with its slightly make-believe crenellation, rise the remains of the town's fortifications (13th-15th centuries, strengthened with bastions 16th-17th centuries).

Žd'ár nad Sazavou (Saar)

On the Bohemian-Moravian uplands 30 km north-west of Jihlava lies the little town of Žd'ár nad Sazavou which developed around a Cistercian abbey founded in the early 13th century to colonize the border forest region. Fish-farming and ore-mining brought prosperity to the monastery and the adjoining settlement. The monastic buildings were burned down several times, the first occasion being during the Hussite Wars, but they were always rebuilt – in 1638 this was done with assistance from the monastery of Velehrad (see p. 319). The abbey's heyday was in the time of Abbot Václav Vejmluva (1705–1738), who became the most loyal client of J.B. Santini-Aichel, employing him to remodel the main abbey church, and to put up a number of the strangest buildings in Europe.

The abbey church of *St Mary* necessarily retains the appearance of a three-aisled Gothic basilica with Baroque decoration. The high altar (1734/35) and choir stalls were designed by the South Tyrolean sculptor, Gregor Theny, while the two paintings on the high altar are by Peter Johann Brandl. The *Prelature* attached to the church on the north side shows the influence of the great Baroque master Johann Bernhard Fischer von Erlach; a Museum of the Book (a department of the National Museum in Prague) is now installed here.

Santini-Aichel's most remarkable building is the chapel of St John of Nepomuk, on a slight rise rechristened *Zelená Hora* (Green Hill) after the hill at Nepomuk. The chapel was built in 1719, to celebrate not only the rediscovery of the saint's miraculously preserved tongue – for the holding of which he was martyred – but also the quincentenary of the abbey. Consequently tongue shapes and the number five recur, the latter also referring to the five stars that hovered around the saint's head as he drowned. The basic shape of the chapel is the star; and stars are used throughout the interior, with five-pointed ones referring to St John, six-pointed to the Virgin and eight-pointed to the Cistercians. Even the lancet windows are more than just gothicizing, since they allude to the saint's virtuous member both visually and metaphorically, it having been praised as the 'Sword of the Lord, Sword of Gideon'. The figure of St John of Nepomuk on the high altar and the evangelists on the side altars were made by Gregor Theny (1729). The cloister is decagonal, to echo the ancient fountain to which Žd'ár owed its Latin name, *Fons Mariae*.

View of Uherské Hradiště (Ungarisch-Hradisch)

Other Santini tours d'esprit are scattered in the countryside nearby: a courtyard shaped like a lyre and outbuildings in the shape of the abbot's (German) initials WW at **Ostrov nad Oslavou** (now an inn); and a chapel at **Obyčtov** in the shape of a turtle (a symbol of constancy).

At **Staré Město** (Altstadt), part of the district town of **Uherské Hradiště** (Ungarisch-Hradischt), archaeologists have discovered the oldest Slavic settlement yet found in Czechoslovakia. Together with its neighbouring settlements it covered an area of about 700 hectares, which has given rise to the suggestion that this was in fact the lost capital of the Great Moravian Empire (9th–10th centuries), *Veligrad*. A modern museum building was erected over the earliest stone architecture, the masonry foundations of a church, and several graves, in which a large quantity of gold and silver jewellery of local and Byzantine origin was found. It is now known as the *Památník Velké Moravy* (Monument of Great Moravia). As early as 1863 the first early Slavic objects were brought to light at Staré Město, but the systematic excavation of the site did not begin until 1948. More than 2000 urn burials of the 6th and 7th centuries have so far been examined in the *Na Valách* site alone. The largest of the buildings uncovered is the 8th-century two-storey cathedral in Sady (Derfle) on the opposite bank of the Morava.

The era of the Great Moravian Empire was also a period when the (putative) town of Veligrad flourished at the intersection of the north-south amber route, which here follows the right bank of the Morava, and the Slovak-Bohemian trade route. The Romans had maintained a base here at the ford and the Moravians used masonry from it to build their churches. The inhabitants of Veligrad built ramparts 4650 metres long to protect themselves on the land side. After the collapse of the Great Moravian Empire the town shrank to a size of a village, but in the first quarter of the 13th century this settlement, by now mainly inhabited by Germans, became a market town. The market place occupied what is now the village green of Staré Město. The Late Romanesque parish church of St Michael replaces an Early Romanesque rotunda also dedicated to the archangel.

In 1227 the royal town of *Nova Veligrad* was founded on the other side of the Morava, which was soon given the name *Redisch*, later *Hradiště*, while the market town of Velehrad was called *Antiqua civitas* or *Staré Město*. Hradiště, officially Uherské Hradiště, is now a district town with a population of 32,000 and the centre of Moravian Slovakia (Moravské Slovácko). The buildings in the town which merit a look are the Late Gothic Franciscan church of the *Annunciation*, founded in 1491 and given a Baroque remodelling in the 17th century; the Early Baroque Jesuit church of *St Francis Xavier*, built from 1670 to 1687; the Late Gothic *Town Hall*, and a Rococo *pharmacy* in the main square. The *Museum of Moravian Slovakia* (Slovacké muzeum) contains interesting ethnic and archaeological collections.

Vladislav Jindřich, Margrave of Moravia and brother of King Otakar I Přemysl founded the Cistercian abbey of **Velehrad** in 1205, 5 km from Staré Město. Every year on 5 July a colourful pilgrimage takes place to the monastery. The grandiose abbey church with its two towers, a basilica built between 1218 and 1238, is dedicated to the Apostles of the Slavs, Cyril and Methodios, because this was supposed to have been the site of St Methodios's bishopric. He died here in 885. Between 1684 and 1689 the church was given a Baroque renovation. The ceiling paintings in the nave are by Paolo Pagani and Franz Eckstein, the statues of *Sts John the Baptist* and *John the Evangelist* on the high altar are by Johann Josef Winterhalter (c. 1770) and those of *Cyril* and *Methodios* in front of the chapel of St Bernard are by Joseph Max (c. 1840) responsible for the many lifeless statues on the Charles Bridge in Prague. Beneath the church Romanesque crypts have been found. In the cloister on the south side of the church there are remains of Late Romanesque architecture, principally palmette capitals to the windows and compound piers. The monastery is now used as a nursing home. Pope John Paul II, who in 1980 had declared Cyril and Methodios the 'Patron Saints of Europe', came to Velehrad on 22 April 1990, in the course of his visit to Czechoslovakia, and announced the holding of a bishops' conference on the unification of Europe; half a million people came to see him.

Zlín

The development of Zlín (called Gottwaldov from 1949 to 1990: Klement Gottwald was born nearby) into a large town with a population of almost 90,000 is entirely due to shoemaking. In 1894 Tomáš Bat'a (1876–1932), the son of a shoemaker, started making *Batovky*, light linen shoes that everyone could afford, in the market place of Zlín. Soon Bat'a was producing his shoes in a factory, using mechanized production-line techniques and shared his profits with his fellow workers. Within a few years it was the largest shoe factory in the world, and when Tomáš Bat'a died in an air crash in 1932 he had 23,000 workers turning out 176,000 pairs of shoes a day. Bat'a influenced international fashions in shoes, dictated prices and left an indelible mark on the town of Zlín. Famous architects, including Le Corbusier and František Gahura of Prague, designed modern industrial, residential and shopping districts of concrete, bricks and glass. The centre of the town is the shoe factory and its main place of interest the shoe museum. After the nationalization of the Bat'a works in 1947 Tomáš's brother Antonín (1898–1965) continued to run the foreign branches of business from Brazil.

Besides being a monument to Bat'a's successful, caring capitalism (like Bourneville or Port Sunlight in England), and to his enlightened architectural patronage, Zlín is also Tom Stoppard's birthplace.

Northern Moravia (Severní Morava)

Ostrava (Ostrau)

Ostrava, with a population of 380,000 the fourth largest town in Czechoslovakia, is the regional capital of North Moravia. Of the old town centre at the confluence of the Ostravice and the Oder (Odra) scarcely anything has survived. Pithead towers, spoil heaps, blast furnaces and factories have dominated the town for the last hundred and fifty years. Nevertheless it is worth visiting this, the most important industrial town in the country, to admire the few remaining relics of the past and the first industrial buildings, which are protected as historic relics, or to see how this massive coal and steel centre is changing in the face of new technology and requirements.

Bruno von Schaumburg, Bishop of Olomouc, founded the town in 1267 as a Moravian border fortress. It soon gained a reputation as a clothmaking centre and in the Hussite Wars stood on the side of the 'Warriors of God'. In 1767 coal – 'black gold' – was discovered in neighbouring Slezská Ostrava (Schlesisch-Ostrau; Silesian Ostrava) and soon afterwards the local aristocracy began to have the coal extracted using primitive means. Then iron ore was found and in 1823 at nearby Vítkovice (Witkowitz) the first iron works in Moravia, the 'Rudolphshütte' belonging to the Bishop of Olomouc and Count Wlczek, began operating. The full transformation into an industrial town did not begin, however, until 1847 when the Vienna-Brno railway was extended as far as Ostrava. The banker Samuel Rothschild built a branch line to the mines and mills, acquired most of the mines and steelworks and changed the face of the town within a few decades. By 1880 only one of the 97 weaving mills working in 1834 was still in existence. Everything was turned over to coal and steel. Ivan Lendl was born at Ostrava and Leoš Janáček died here.

The nucleus of the town centre of Ostrava was known until recently as nám. Lidových milicí (People's Militia Square). It is the main square of one of the town's three districts, Moravská Ostrava, and has a garden in the middle surrounded by fine 16th-century burghers' houses and modern offices and shops. On the south side of the square stands the *Old Town Hall* (Stará radnice) which, together with its Baroque tower, dates from the 17th century. The town hall now contains the town museum (Městské muzeum) which concentrates mainly on the industrial development of the region.

In Kostelní nám. (Kirchplatz) east of the Old Town Hall stands the oldest extant building in Ostrava, the church of *St Wenceslas* (Kostel sv. Václava) built in the first half of the 14th century. The chancel with its polygonal apse dates from this period, while the three-aisled hall nave was built in the second half of the 15th century. A fine net vault rests on octagonal pillars. In the 17th century two Baroque chapels were added, one dedicated to the Virgin and the other to the Guardian Angels.

North west of Ostrava, but almost engulfed by the sprawling town, is **Hlučín** (Hultschin), the capital of Hlučín country (Hlučinsko), which has changed hands perhaps more often than any other area of Czechoslovakia, having belonged to the duchy of Troppau (Opava), the duchy of Ratibor, to Bohemia and to Prussia, before being given in 1919 to Czechoslovakia. It was repossessed by Germany as part of Upper Silesia between 1838 and 1945, before reverting after the war to Czechoslovakia.

Hukvaldy (Hochwald)

About 30 km south of Ostrava is the village of **Hukvaldy**, the birthplace of *Leoš Janáček* (1854–1928), born in the schoolhouse here where his father taught. Most of Janáček's professional life was spent at Brno, but in 1921 he returned to the pastoral calm of this village, and bought the cottage where he was to write his greatest works, including his opera of the countryside, *The Cunning Little Vixen* (Příhody Lišky Bystroušky). Here he entertained the woman who was his uncomprehending muse, Kamila Strösslová, pouring out his feelings for her in letters and music of ever greater intensity. Here too, looking for her son, lost in the woods near Hukvaldy, Janáček caught a fatal cold. The summerhouse is now a memorial (Památník Leoše Janáčka) and there is a music festival (Janáčkovo hudební Lašsko) held here every year.

The ruined *castle* of Hukvaldy, a popular excursion, rises on a wooded clifftop above the Ostravice, a tributary of the Oder (Odra). It was taken over by Bruno of Schaumburg, Bishop of Olomouc, after 1267, from the Rhine-Westphalian counts of Huckeswagen (hence its name). On the west side of its seven-sided courtyard was a round keep, and on the east a two-storey hall range (*palas*). Around this core further buildings were added in the 15th and 16th centuries. In the second half of the 17th century, long after fire arms had shown the pointlessness of castles, massive new bastions were built at the east end. In 1782 the castle burned down and fell into ruin.

In a park in the small town of **Rožnov pod Radhoštěm** on the E442 between Olomouc and Žilina is the *Wallachian Open-Air Museum* (Valašské přírodní muzeum) created in 1925, the first and most important such museum in Czechoslovakia. It has wooden buildings brought from the countryside all over Moravian Wallachia (Valašsko). Here the visitor will find a mayor's house (1770), a guest house (1660), a hundred-year-old village smithy, a saddlery, a pipe-maker's workshop and around eighty other village buildings.

Olomouc (Olmütz)

Olomouc lies on both sides of the middle Morava in the fertile low-lying areas called Haná. It was the capital of Moravia before Brno, and remains one of the oldest and most beautiful

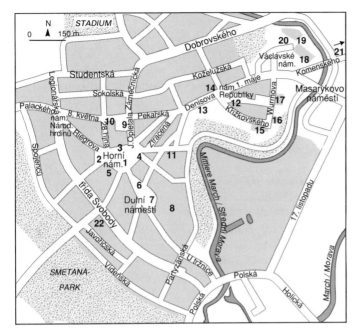

Olomouc (Olmütz)
1 Town Hall
2 Church of the
  Trinity
3 Hercules Fountain
4 Caesar Fountain
5 Theatre
6 Neptune Fountain
7 Jupiter Fountain
8 Capuchin Church
9 St Maurice
10 Mercury Fountain
11 St Michael
12 Trinity Fountain
13 Our Lady of the
   Snows
14 Town Museum
15 University
16 Archives
17 Archbishop's
   Palace
18 Cathedral of St
   Wenceslas
19 Palace of the
   Přemyslids
20 Cathedral Deanery
21 Hradisko Abbey
22 Theresa Gate

towns in Czechoslovakia, and an important centre of Catholicism – hence its nickname: 'Moravian Salzburg'. The passion for fountains, however, would make 'Moravian Rome' just as appropriate.

On Princes' Hill, now surmounted by the cathedral of St Wenceslas, there was already a Slavic castle in the 8th century; it was taken over by the Přemyslids in the 10th century. At the foot of the castle a settlement grew up whose name first appears in the sources in 1055 as *Olmuts*. In 1063 Olmütz was made the seat of a bishopric covering the whole of Moravia and Sudetan Silesia. The bishops of Olomouc sometimes had more influence than their colleagues in Prague. Bishop Jindřich Zdík (1126–1150) brought the colonizing Premonstratensian order to Moravia. A hundred years later Bishop Bruno von Schaumburg (1246–1281) brought German farmers, craftsmen and merchants to the country, and especially to Olomouc, which was given German town law. A little to the south-west of the castle a new urban centre developed with a trade court and market places. The old castle settlement gave way to a conglomeration of buildings for the clergy.

During the Hussite Wars the cathedral city of Olomouc naturally took the Catholic side. Between 1642 and 1650 it was occupied by the Swedes, which led to the removal of the administration of Moravia to Brno. Olomouc was never again to be the capital.

In the 18th century Maria Theresa furnished Olomouc with some magnificent buildings. When the diocese of Brno was created in 1777 for south Moravia, Olomouc was consoled by being made the see of an archbishop. But the following year neither the archbishop nor the town council could prevent the university, which had been founded in 1573 from the Jesuit college, from moving to Brno too. During the Revolution of 1848 the imperial family fled from Vienna to Olomouc, which remained faithful to the Habsburgs, and it was here that the Emperor Ferdinand announced his abdication on 2 December, naming his nephew Franz Joseph as his successor.

The centre of Olomouc is Horní nám. (Oberring), in the middle of which stands the fine *Town Hall* (ill. 48). The nucleus of this building goes back to a Gothic market hall and staple court. The tower was built after 1378, and it was given its graceful spire, which rises to a height of 70 metres, in 1443. The great astronomical clock was installed in 1420–1422, but was badly damaged in the Second World War, like the one at Prague; the modern mosaics and figures are the work of Karel Svolinsky (1945–1948). In 1564 the exterior staircase with a Late Renaissance loggia was built on the south side of the town hall; the stairs are decorated with the brilliantly carved arms of the lands of Bohemia and Moravia, below which is a

View of Olomouc (Olmütz) engraved by F. B. Werner

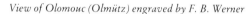

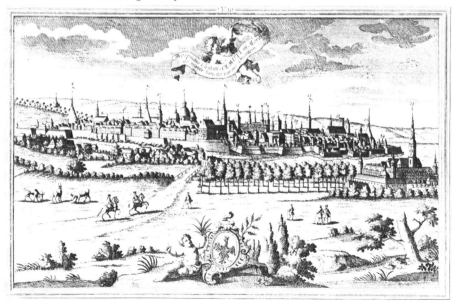

splendid Renaissance entrance doorway. Among the impressive features of the interior are the fine Renaissance staircase, the Gothic hall with scenes from the history of the town and the Late Gothic chapel of St Jerome (1488–1491) with a net vault supported on figural corbels. The oriel window on the south façade of the town hall belongs to this chapel.

In the north-west corner of Horní nám. rises the *Trinity Column*, 36 metres high, the largest and most magnificent Baroque monument of this kind in Czechoslovakia, built in the 18th century by Wenzel Reder and Andreas Zahner. Its base contains a tiny chapel. The column goes to contorted lengths to symbolize the Trinity by triangularizing the octagon, and at the very top no less than 18 figures represent the Three-in-One. The *Hercules Fountain* in the animated style of Bernini is the work of Michal Mandík of Znojmo (1687). The *Caesar Fountain* in the south-east corner of the square is also Baroque, made by the Olomouc sculptor Hans Georg Schauberger in 1724; its basin was designed by Wenzel Reder.

To the south of Horní nám. is the lower square, Dolní nám. with two fine fountains: the *Neptune Fountain* (1695) at the north end and the *Jupiter Fountain* (1707) to the south; both were made by Wenzel Reder. In the centre of the square stands a normal-sized plague column dating from 1720. To the right, on the corner of Lafayettova, is the *Hannscheld house* with its exuberant Baroque windows and lovely late 16th-century oriel with scenes from Ovid. The south-east side of the triangular square is occupied by the plain *Capuchin Church* with its former conventual buildings.

In the early middle ages the church of *St Maurice* (Kostel sv. Mořice) with its massive battlemented tower was already the main church of the burghers of Olomouc. The present three-aisled hall church was begun in 1412 and in 1453 badly damaged by fire shortly before its completion. By 1483 it was fully repaired, only to be partly destroyed again by fire in 1492. This last damage was repaired over the next fifty years. On the north side of the choir is the Renaissance funerary chapel of Wenzel Edelmann. The Baroque organ (1740–1745) by Michael Engler of Breslau has 2311 pipes, making it the biggest in the country. West of the church the visitor finds the beautiful *Mercury Fountain* designed by Philipp Sattler around 1730. The church of *St Michael* (Kostel sv. Michala) is also Gothic in origin, but underwent a Baroque remodelling between 1674 and 1700 when it was given its striking trio of domes.

Petařská ul. and Denisova ul. form the main traffic axis through the town, leading to the little nám. Republiky with its delightful *Triton Fountain* by Wenzel Reder (1709). The church of *Our Lady of the Snows* (Kostel Panny Marie Sněžné) was built by the Jesuits with the help of the architect Johannes Pirner between 1712 and 1719 in place of an earlier church. The town *Museum* (Městské muzeum) occupies rooms in the former nunnery of Poor Clares with its large church. The interested visitor will find extensive collections on egyptology, numismatics, ethnography, mineralogy, zoology and botany.

On the Princes' Hill stands the *Cathedral of St Wenceslas* (Chrám sv. Václava), built between 1107 and 1131 as a Romanesque basilica and extended in the 13th, 14th and 15th centuries. In 1617 the cathedral was given a new choir with crypt below, and between 1883 and 1890 it underwent a Neo-Gothic remodelling at the hands of Gustav Meretta when the east tower (100 metres high) was built. The bishops' tombs are of interest, especially that of Bishop Marcus Kuen (1565; Hans Strauberger of Nuremberg) with its curious blend of medieval layout, Renaissance vocabulary and Baroque moulding. Stranger still is one of the most bizarre monuments of the Counter-Reformation: Bishop Dietrichstein's memorial of 1603 to the the Přemyslid dukes who founded Olomouc. This consciously medievalizing slab is intended to serve as a reminder, on the eve of the Thirty Years' War, of a time when state and religion had appeared to be a seamless whole in Bohemia. The rich cathedral treasure is displayed in the crypt. To the left of the west door is the chapel of St Anne, a Venetian-looking Baroque building of 1593 nestling against the cathedral. The Gothic cloister was built in the late 13th century using parts of the Přemyslid castle. The magnificent wall paintings in the cloister were done c. 1500 by three German artists, one of them the famous Augsburg master, Jörg Breu the elder (c. 1475–1537) who was strongly influenced by Dürer. Restoration work in the last quarter of the 19th century revealed some sumptuously carved Romanesque windows (double and triple round arches on Corinthian capitals, mid–12th century) from the Přemyslid palace.

In the *Cathedral Deanery* (Domské děkanstív) next to the cathedral the eleven-year-old Wolfgang Amadeus Mozart lay ill with smallpox for six weeks in the autumn of 1767. Today the 17th-century arcaded building houses the Historical Institute of the Palacký University (named after the historian, who was born not far away at Hodslavice). A plaque recalls the ignominious murder of the sixteen-year-old Wenceslas III, the last of the Přemyslid kings, which took place on 4 August 1306 in the dean's rooms when he was staying at Olomouc before launching a military campaign against Poland. Who was responsible for the murder remains unclear, but uncertainty about the succession resulted in a period of upheaval in the Czech lands.

Olomouc was one of the richest sees in the Empire, and was used by the Dietrichsteins to build up a very fine art collection, remnants of which survive at Kroměříž. A later bishop was Beethoven's patron and friend, the Archduke Rudolph, for whose enthronement in 1818 the composer was commissioned to write a mass. By the time this mass – the Missa Solemnis – was completed several years later, the enthronement had gone ahead without it, and so the first performance took place not at Olomouc but at Vienna in 1824.

About 1 km north of the cathedral on the other side of the Morava lies the former Premonstratensian abbey of *Hradisko*. The present Baroque building is attributed to the Italian architect Domenico Martinelli. Founded as a Benedictine monastery in 1078 by one of the Přemyslids, it passed to the Premonstratensians in 1150. In 1241 the monastery was destroyed by the Tatars, and in 1643 by the Swedes, but on each occasion was rebuilt. In 1783 it was dissolved and since then the buildings have been used as a hospital. The decoration of Hradisko is of remarkable quality: reliefs and sculptures by Baldassare Fontana, Georg A. Heinz and Josef Winterhalter decorate the Prelature; the fresco of *The Israelites Fed in the Desert* is by Paul Troger.

Olomouc is also famous for *Olmützer Quargeln*, small round cheeses with a pungent aroma, which were first made in the then German-speaking village of Nebotein (Hněvotín) near Olomouc.

Kroměříž (Kremsier)

About 40 km south of Olomouc, on the right bank of the Morava, is **Kroměříž**, which began in the 12th century as a possession of the Bishops of Olomouc. Bruno of Schaumburg (c. 1205–1281), from 1247 Bishop of Olomouc and from 1253 the influential Chancellor of King Otakar II Přemysl, extended Kroměříž as his summer residence. At the king's behest he summoned German settlers to the country, who transformed Moravia into a flourishing agricultural region.

Kroměříž is now a busy district town with a population of 27,000. Set in the middle of the region of Haná, it is known as the 'Athens of Haná' because the richness of its cultural and architectural heritage. At its centre is the arcaded main square (Hlavní náměstí) with a Baroque Marian plague column (1725) and a delightful Triton Fountain. North-west of the square rises the *schloss* (Zámek), created for Bishop Bruno in 1260 out of an Early Gothic castle. In the 16th century, during the time of Bishop Stanislaus Thurzo, a Renaissance schloss developed with arcades and a corner tower 84 metres high. From 1666 the complex was rebuilt to designs by Filiberto Lucchese and Giovanni Pietro Tencalla in the Early Baroque idiom. It was here in 1848-49 that the Vienna Reichstag (Imperial Diet) – including František Palacký, then a deputy – met, since it no longer felt secure in the troubled Habsburg capital. But the constitution that it eventually invented was suppressed and the diet itself removed from Kremsier by the army.

The bishops held court in the Vassals' Hall, where they were separated from their vassals by a finely carved balustrade. The ceiling has an unusually fine fresco by the Viennese Franz Anton Maulpertsch. The Library (containing 55,000 books) also has a central balustraded reservation, now occupied by a collection of globes, and frescoes of *Parnassus* by the Brno master, Joseph Stern. Other rooms include the Throne Room, the Session Hall, the Audience Hall, the Tsar's Salon (where the Emperor Franz Joseph I and Tsar Alexander III met in 1885), the Hunting Hall, the Reichstag Hall and the Great Dining Hall. The schloss contains the second most important collection of paintings in Czechoslovakia (after the Prague National Gallery) including Titian's late masterpiece, *The Flaying of Marsyas*, part of Bishop Karl Liechtenstein-Kastelkorn's collection. In the park are several fine colonnades, fountains, ponds and a Chinese Pavilion.

The Parler workshop is thought to have have been involved in the building of the Early Gothic church of *St Maurice* (Kostel sv. Mořice). The church has several later alterations and additions, including a Baroque chapel that contains the tombs of several Bishops of Olomouc, among them the energetic Bruno of Schaumburg himself. The Baroque parish church of *St Mary* was built beween 1724 and 1736. The *Piarist church of St John the Baptist* (Chrám Jana Křtitele) and former Piarist school (*Gymnasium*) date from the same period.

The celebrated *Flower Garden* (Květná zahrada) about 500 metres south of the Piarist church and beyond the Kocářská brána (Smiths Gate), usually called Libosad ('pleasure garden'), is the setting for the annual summer festival of Kroměříž. Grottoes, mazes, artificial mounds, pavilions, and a splendid colonnade 233 metres long, are the highlights of these gardens, which were laid out in the 17th century for Prince Bishop Karl Liechtenstein-Kastelkorn.

Hrad Bouzov (Busau), the castle of the Teutonic Order, still stands in its medieval splendour – although much of this is thě result of Romantic historical restoration. Nevertheless there is perhaps no other place in Europe which better represents the traditions of this military order. Shortly after 1300 the Lords of Kunstadt (Kunštat) built Busau to defend their extensive domains. In the 16th century they remodelled the Early Gothic fortress in the Renaissance style. In the Thirty Years' War (1618–1648) Busau was devastated and fell into ruin, but in 1696 the Teutonic Order took it over together with its vast properties in north Moravia. Nothing much happened here until, at the turn of the present century, the Grand Master of the Order, Archduke Eugen, decided to turn Busau into a spectacle worthy of the Teutonic Knights. He engaged Georg Hauberisser, famous for his Town Hall in Munich, to rebuild the castle entirely in a Late Romantic, Neo-Gothic style that did not preclude occasional flashes of Secession purity. The result was decked out in banners, pictures, emblems and the finest furniture from the Order's properties throughout the Holy Roman Empire, which had all been secularized. This grandiose medievalism struck a chord with the Nazis, and Hitler presented Busau, which in 1938 had been made part of the Reichsgau of Sudetenland, to Himmler, though in the event the SS leader spent only a few days here. In 1945 Buzau was declared a national monument and restored.

The Teutonic Order had been founded as a hospitaller order in Palestine in 1190 by merchants of Lübeck and Bremen, and was transformed into a military religious order in 1198. In the 13th and 14th centuries, by means of conquest or bequests, the Order came into the possession of large tracts of land from Danzig to Estonia which it colonized and Christianized and developed into the 'Teutonic Order State'. But after its defeat at the hands of a Polish-Lithuanian army at Tannenberg in 1411, it had to give up most of its possessions in the Baltic. Like other medieval relics – the Venetian Republic, the Holy Roman Empire – the order was abolished by Napoleon, in 1809, though it was eventually restored in 1834 in Austria by the Emperor Francis I. One of the Archdukes was usually the Grand Master. Since the collapse of the Habsburg Monarchy in 1918 there have no longer been any Teutonic Knights, but the clerical branch of the order has continued, concentrating on charitable work. After a hiatus during the Nazi period, it resumed its activities in Austria and Germany in 1945, with its headquarters in Vienna.

Of the approximately 150 rooms, most of which preserve their original furnishings (including some superb Neo-Gothic stoves) the visitors are shown the most interesting, including the Column Hall, the Hunting Hall, the Knights' Hall, the Prince's Bedroom, the Hall of Arms, and the Chapel with the tombs of the Grand Masters.

The gateway to the Hruby jeseník ridge (Altvatergebirge, also formerly known as Hohes Gesenke), the eastern part of the Sudeten Mountains, is **Šumperk** (Mährisch-Schönberg), a lively district town with a 16th-century castle. The wooded region around Praděd (Altvater; 1492 metres) is popular for hiking and winter sports. At its summit is a television tower with a restaurant.

It was in Šumperk that a nasty series of witch hunts in the 17th century came to a climax with scores of women being burned at the stake. The trials themselves were conducted at **Velké Losiny** (Gross Ullersdorf), a beautiful Renaissance château 8 km north-east, little touched since the Žerotíns were expropriated after the Battle of the White Mountain. The château is the usual three-sided arcaded courtyard, fortified by some light rustication. Inside the rooms are fairly bare, though there are a few good pieces of furniture and tapestries, and some fine intarsia doorways. The Knights' Hall, or Dining Room, has a spiked ceiling, a majestic stove, and a remarkable credenza in a style that can only be called rustic Renaissance. The little balustrade around it is to protect the stored food 'in an age,' as one historian says, 'when poison was the best way of dealing with troublemakers.'

Beyond Velké Losiny are several small spas in the hills, and eventually the castle at **Javorník** (Jauernig), where Dittersdorf served both as a composer (operas for the castle's little theatre) and forest warden.

Opava (Troppau)

The present district town of **Opava** was formerly the residence of the Dukes of Troppau, and later the capital of Austrian Silesia. Despite heavy damage in the last days of the Second

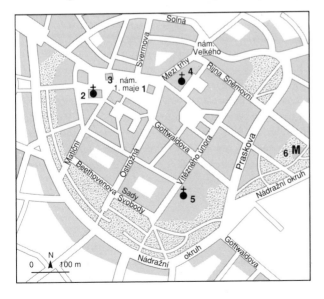

Opave (Troppau)
1 Schmetterhaus
2 Church of the
   Assumption
3 Theatre
4 St Adalbert
5 Minorite Church
6 Silesian Museum

The Vegetable Market in Opava
(Troppau), wood-engraving by
Erwin Ziegler

World War some interesting buildings have survived. Troppau was on the amber route, and a settlement first developed in the 10th century under the protection of a Slavic moated castle in the meadows (German: Aue) of the Oppa (Opava), a tributary of the Oder. In the last third of the 12th century German merchants and craftsmen from the Danube and from Lower Saxony settled there. A charter of Innocent III in 1204 mentions the lordship of Troppau as a commandery of the Teutonic Order. In 1222 King Otakar I Přemysl confirmed this donation and in 1224 raised Troppau to the status of a town. Under the protection of the powerful order the town's community grew, in spite of extensive fires, devastating floods and terrible plagues. The town walls protected it from the Mongol horde and the Hussites, but in the Thirty Years' War the town was helpless as it changed hands between the Swedes and the Imperial forces.

In 1318 Troppau became the capital of the duchy of the same name. Under Duke Nicholas II, also the Treasurer of the Bohemian Crown, the duchy separated from Moravia and became part of Silesia, though without breaking its legal connections with Prague. Silesian Diets were sometimes held at Troppau. In the Silesian Wars Lower Silesia, the county of Glatz and a large part of Upper Silesia were ceded to Prussia in 1742, but the southern part of

Upper Silesia – that is, the Duchy of Troppau – remained in the Habsburg Empire as 'Austrian Silesia'. The town of Troppau now enjoyed great importance as a regional capital, but Joseph II soon reduced its rights. A great highlight in the town's history occurred in 1820 when Prince Metternich invited representatives from almost all the states of Europe to the Congress of Troppau in an attempt to control the uprisings in Italy and quell the first stirrings of revolution in Europe.

In 1928 what was by now Czech Silesia was united with Moravia to form a single administrative area, but ten years later it was made part of 'Reichsgau Sudetenland'. After the end of the Second World War Opava was made the district capital of North Moravia.

The centre of the town is nám. 1 máje, formerly Horní nám. (Oberring), with the 72 metres high *Town Tower* (Městská věž) on the *Schmetterhaus*, a 'stapelplatz' for merchants passing through the town who had to offer their wares – mainly Flemish cloth – for sale for three days here. The Schmetterhaus also contained the council chamber and later the town scales. The tower, originally Gothic, was given its present form in 1618. The market hall has been altered many times with several extensions, the last of which was a tall Neo-Renaissance building of 1902-03.

The provostal parish church of the *Assumption* was built between 1360 and 1370 in a North German brick Gothic style. Its massive south tower is surmounted by an octagonal Renaissance bell chamber. The north tower was left unfinished. The interior of the church

---

Hřebečsko (Der Schönhengstau)

Until 1945 **Schönhengstau** was the biggest German language-island in the Bohemian-Moravian border region. At the king's command Bruno von Schaumburg, Bishop of Olomouc (c.1205–1281), invited German settlers from Bavaria, Franconia, Swabia and Saxony to the country. The settlers were mostly farmers, but there were also craftsmen and merchants. Several groups of these immigrants settled around a long range of hills which they called *Sintenhengst* – from *sinten* ('toil') and *hengst* ('slope'). This later became 'Schönhengst', so despite the literal meaning of the German it has nothing to do with 'fine stallions' – even though the Czech name for the hills is **Hřebec** ('stallion').

In 1930 the population of the six towns and 142 villages of Schönhengstau (1180 sq km) consisted of approximately 126,000 Germans and 6000 Czechs. In the Bohemian area were the towns of Mährisch-Trübau, Brüsau, Zwittau and Landskron; while on the Moravian side were the towns of Müglitz and Hohenstadt. Of these the most interesting today are **Moravská Třebová** (Mährisch Trübau) with fine Late Gothic, Renaissance and Baroque burghers' houses (good porches), a Gothic-Baroque parish church of the Assumption, the Late Gothic cemetery church of the Invention of the Cross connected with the old town by a shingle-covered flight of steps, and the Renaissance schloss of the Liechtensteins with its splendid arcaded courtyard; and **Svitavy** (Zwittau) with the Gothic church of St Giles (13th century), the church of the Visitation (18th century), a Renaissance town hall and fine arcaded houses of the 16th century.

Kravarsko (Das Kuhländchen)

In the upper course of the Oder (Odra) around the two towns of Fulnek and Nový Jičín lies the **Kuhländchen**, a German-speaking region from the 11th century until 1945. The German name of the region recalls the cattle-farming that flourished here. The main town is **Nový Jičín** (Neutitschein) which received its town charter and the right to levy tolls in 1313. The market place has arcaded houses, a Marian column (1710) and the delightful Peasants Fountain by the sculptor Franz Barwig (18th century). The schloss (16th-19th centuries) contains an interesting Hat Museum; in the 19th century the firm of Hückel (now Tonak), founded in 1799, was one of the biggest hat factories in the world with a workforce of over 2000.

8 km south of Nový Jičín is the little village of **Hodslavice**, the birthplace of František Palacký (1798–1876), the Czech nationalist, historian and naturalist, with a wooden church (1551); and 12 km northeast is **Příbor** (Freiberg), the birthplace of Sigmund Freud (1856–1939). Freud, born in rooms over a blacksmith's forge, was taken to Vienna at the age of three, but always insisted that his first years had been formative. He was less forthcoming about his later experience at Příbor, when he returned at the age of sixteen for a summer holiday. Yet this too was formative, since he promptly fell in love – his first romance – not only with the girl whose cot he had shared in those first three years, but also with her mother.

Fulnek in the north-west corner of the Kuhländchen, dominated by a large castle, received its charter as early as 1293. In the early 17th century it became the centre of the 'Bohemian Brethren', later known as the Moravian Brethren. The Late Gothic parish church (c.1407; altered in 1612 and 1748–1760) has a memorial to Jan Amos Comenius (Komenský; 1592–1670), the founder of modern educational theory, who was minister here from 1618 to 1621 and preached in the church, before being exiled after the Battle of the White Mountain. (In 1632 he became bishop of the Bohemian Brethren, and later travelled extensively throughout Europe, developing his educational ideas.) The Trinity church (1760) and the Gothic buildings of the Augustinian monastery (15th century) are also of interest.

was baroquized in the 17th and 18th centuries by Hans Georg Hausrucker and Jordan Zeller, though without detracting from the tall Gothic space. The Late Baroque high altar was made by Johann Schubert. Next to the provostal church the citizens of Troppau built their new *theatre* on the square in 1882-83. It was gutted by fire in 1909 but within a few months was open again with Neo-Baroque decoration. Lotte Lehmann was one of many famous performers who made their debut here.

On the south-east side of Dolní nám. (Niederring) stands the *Jesuit church* with the Jesuit college. From 1675 the Jesuits built a new Baroque church, after the model of the Gesù in Rome, on the site of the Gothic church of St Adalbert. On 30 March 1945 its frescoes and altarpieces were destroyed by fire bombs, but since then the church has been restored and in 1960 was reconsecrated to St Adalbert. The Jesuit college with its *Gymnasium* (grammar school) was built between 1711 and 1723 by Hans Georg Hausrucker and Josef Rieth. After the suppression of the order the Silesian Diet met here and until 1945 the building was known as the 'Altes Landhaus'. In front of the Jesuit church a *Marian column* was erected by Count Georg Stephan von Würben, taking as its model the column 'Am Hof' in Vienna.

Before the middle of the 13th century the Franciscans founded a *Minorite friary* with a church, though it was given its present appearance in the 18th century. This was where the Congress of Troppau took place from 20 October to 23 December 1820. The splendid interior and valuable library were destroyed in 1945 and today the building houses part of the Silesian Archives.

The *Minorite church* of the Holy Ghost is a three-aisled Gothic hall church with a plain tower which was given its Neo-Gothic roof in 1827. The church was the burial place of the Silesian Přemyslids and later of the Dukes of Troppau; in the 18th century it underwent a Baroque remodelling. The splendid façade with its porch is particularly striking. The town palaces also merit attention: the *Larisch Palace* (or Blücher Palace), the neighbouring *Gostheimb Palace* and the *Sobek-Skal Palace* opposite the Minorite church. The *Silesian Museum* in Komenského ul. contains fine collections covering archaeology, applied arts and natural history.

Schloss Hradec (Grätz) about 10 km south of Opava on the little Moravice river goes back to a Slavic fortification of the 10th century. This developed into a Gothic castle in the 13th century where Kunigunde, the widow of Otakar II Přemysl, held her court. Around 1600 the castle was transformed into a Renaissance château and rebuilt after the fire of 1796 in Empire style (*Weisses Schloss*). After 1880 brick pseudo-Gothic additions were built: a tower, a riding hall and a gatehouse (*Rotes Schloss*). The castle was destroyed by fire in 1971, but is now in the process of restoration.

The ownership of Hradec changed frequently, but the strongest influence on its development were the Princes Lichnowsky who resided there from 1777. Here they entertained the most famous composers of the age: Paganini and Franz Liszt were invited to give concerts, and Beethoven stayed here twice, in 1806 and 1811. He is commemorated by the Beethoven Room, containing the piano he played, and a plaque in the courtyard, but above all by the annual Beethoven Weeks held here.

Western Slovakia (Západní Slovensko)

Bratislava (Pressburg, Pozsony)

Bratislava on the north bank of the Danube (Dunaj) and at the foot of the Little Carpathians (Malé Karpaty) is on the very edge of Slovakia, near the Austrian and Hungarian borders, and only 60 km from Vienna. For two centuries the capital of Hungary, it is now the capital of Slovakia and administrative centre of the district of West Slovakia. The presence here of the Slovak Academy of Sciences, the Comenius University, numerous colleges and technical colleges, the National Gallery and National Museum make the town the cultural metropolis of Slovakia and the Slovaks. It is the second largest town in Czechoslovakia with a population of 420,000, mostly working in industry (chemicals, machinery, food). It is not generally realized that there are more than 1000 hectares of vineyards on the slopes of the Little Carpathians and that Bratislava is the largest wine-producing town in Czechoslovakia.

The 'Devín (Theben) Gate', through which the Danube passes between the Alps and the Carpathians, was already a crossing point of two great trade routes in prehistoric times: the east-west water route along the Danube and the overland route from the Baltic to the Mediterranean. The traffic along these routes was safeguarded by fortified hilltop settlements on what are now the castle hills of Bratislava and Devín. Around 15 BC, after the conquest of Raetia and Pannonia, the Romans reached the middle Danube and built numerous forts to protect the city of *Carnuntum* near present-day Deutsch Altenburg in Lower Austria. One of these was in the area of present-day Bratislava. The collapse of the Roman rule on the Danube was followed by the arrival of Goths, Herulians, Huns, Avars and finally in the 6th century, the Slavs.

In the 9th century the castle on the Devín served as a defence of the Great Moravian Empire against attacks from the Franks, and on the castle hill of Bratislava the Great Moravian prince Breslav built a mighty fortress in the second half of the 9th century which he chose as his residence. In 892 the Magyars together with Arnulf of Carinthia defeated the Great Moravian Empire and occupied Bratislava and Devín. In a document of 907 the place is called *Brezelauspurc*, 'Breslav's castle'. In the mouths of the German inhabitants this became *Pressburg*, while to the Slavs it was *Bratislava*. After the collapse of the Great Moravian Empire the town was for a time part of the territory of the Přemyslids, until King Stephen (István) I of Hungary (997–1038) incorporated it into his kingdom.

In 1217 Pressburg received its town charter, and a few decades later it was even granted the privileges of a Royal Hungarian free town. Around the year 1000 King Stephen had already settled some Bavarian colonists here, and after the Tatar attack in the 13th century (which the

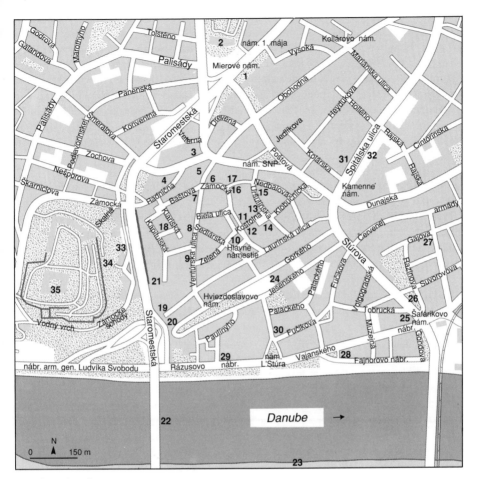

Bratislava (Pressburg)
1 *Interhotel Forum* 2 *Grassalkovich Palace* 3 *Holy Trinity Church* 4 *Capuchin Church*
5 *Michalská brána* 6 *Pharmaceutical Museum* 7 *Segner House* 8 *University Library* 9 *Academia*
Istropolitana 10 *Roland Fountain* 11 *Jesuit Church* 12 *Old Town Hall* 13 *New Town Hall*
14 *Primatial Palace* 15 *Ursuline Church* 16 *Franciscan Church* 17 *Mirbach Palace* 18 *Poor Clares*
Church 19 *Cathedral of St Martin* 20 *Trinity Column* 21 *Jesuit College and Provost's Palace*
22 *SNP Bridge* 23 *Janko Král' Park* 24 *Slovak National Theatre* 25 *Comenius University* 26 *Duck*
Fountain 27 *St Elizabeth* 28 *Slovak National Museum* 29 *Slovak National Gallery*
30 *Reduta* 31 *Church of Elizabethine Nuns* 32 *Aspremont Summer Palace* 33 *House of the Good*
Shepherd 34 *St Nicholas* 35 *Castle*

town itself had withstood) the Hungarian King Béla IV summoned more German and Italian
settlers to the depopulated country.

335

Between 1541 and 1784 Pressburg – or to give it its Hungarian name *Pozsony* – was the capital of Hungary after Buda had fallen to the Turks, and from 1563 until as late as 1830 the Hungarian kings were crowned here. In the carve-up of Habsburg dominions after the First World War, it became part of the new state of Czechoslovakia, and was known as Bratislava. In 1939 it was made the capital of the short-lived independent Slovak Republic, under its collaborationist leader Tiso. In 1945 it became the capital of Slovakia within a reunited Czechoslovakia. Slovaks have participated fully in Czechoslovak political life, the most notable example being Alexander Dubček, for many years a forestry inspector based in Bratislava.

In Mierové námestie, opposite the new Interforum Hotel, stands the *Grassalkovich Palace* (Grasalkovič palác) built between 1760 and 1765 as the summer residence of Prince Anton Grassalkovich, the president of the Hungarian Royal Chamber. The plans for this fine Rococo building were made by A. Mayerhoffer. There is a splendid staircase with four sandstone sculptures representing *Spring* and *Summer* (1760), and *David* and *Solomon*, and in the Spanish Hall on the second floor Haydn gave concerts with his orchestra in 1772.

Suché mýto ('Dry Toll') links Mierové nám, with Hurbanovo nám., on the west side of which stands *Trinity Church* (Kostol Najsvätejšej Trojice), a Baroque building on an elliptical plan with two flattened towers, built beween 1717 and 1727 for the Trinitarians. The rather plain exterior is relieved by a flamboyant doorway with winsome pilasters; but nothing suggests the real glory of the interior painted between 1736 and 1740 by Antonio Galli Bibiena, third son of the great set-designer who revolutionized theatrical illusionism. The church thrusts up through imaginary storeys to the eye of God. In 1844 Ignaz Feigler converted the adjoining Trinitarian monastery into a Komitat House (the *komitat* was an administrative division of Hungary, like an English county) which dominates the north side of Októbrové nám. (October Square, the Slovak names of the months being more familiar-sounding than the Czech). In the centre of the square stands a *Plague Column* of 1723. The south-west corner of the square is occupied by the Baroque *Capuchin Church* (Kostol kapucínov) built in 1717.

From Hurbanovo nám. the *Coronation Way* of the Hungarian kings (500 metres) leads across the old town centre along Michalská, Ventúrska and Straková ulica to Hviezdoslavovo nám. First a bridge spans the town moat with statues (1760) of St John of Nepomuk (left) and the Archangel Michael (right) holding a shield with the arms of Bratislava and the cypher of Maria Theresa. Beyond is a barbican with a bulwark and forward gate protecting the *Michalská brána* (colour plate 19, plate 52), the only one of the three original town gates that survives. The gatehouse itself dates from the 14th century, the octagonal structure on top was added between 1511 and 1517, and the Baroque onion dome with the statue of the Archangel Michael (Peter Eller) was not built until 1757. The gate tower contains an exhibition about the history of the fortifications of Bratislava.

Near the barbican is the former *Pharmacy at the Red Lobster* (U červeného raka) which now houses a *Pharmaceutical Museum* (Farmaceutiské múzeum) with original furniture,

49   BRNO (Brünn) Town Hall Doorway

◁ 48   OLOMOUC (Olmütz) Town Hall with Plague Column   50 TRNAVA (Tyrnau) Cathedral of St Nicholas

51 BRATISLAVA (Pressburg) Castle

52 BRATISLAVA (Pressburg) Old Town and Michalská brána

53 BRATISLAVA (Pressburg) Old Town

54 Trenčín (Trentschin) Market Square

55 Banská Bystrica (Neusohl) Market Square

56 View of Levoča (Leutschau)

57 BETLIAR Manor House

58 PIEŠŤANY (Pistyan)

59 PIEŠŤANY (Pistyan) Thermia Palace Sanatorium
60 Pilgrimage Church of St Ladislaus near SPIŠSKÝ ŠTURTOK (Donnersmarkt) in the Spiš (Zips) region ▷

61 ŽDIAR, a Goral village at the foot of the High Tatras

62 Village in the Slovak Ore Mountains

63 KOŠICE (Kaschau, Kassa) State Theatre

64 KOŠICE (Kaschau, Kassa) Market Square ▷

65 KOŠICE (Kaschau, Kassa) Cathedral of St Elizabeth, North Door

equipment, apparatus and containers from the last 700 years. The building was erected at the end of the 18th century on the site of the former town walls.

From Michalská brána the busy Michalská ul. with its many shops and some interesting houses, leads to the centre of the old town (Staré mesto). The *Segner House* (No. 7) was built in 1648 by Andreas Segner, a wealthy merchant. Its stone doorway is decorated with diamond rustication and a mermaid and merman in the spandrel, and the two broad oriel windows are supported by grotesque consoles. This was the birthplace of J.A. Segner (1707–1777), pioneer of hydraulics. The modest chapel of *St Catherine* (Kaplnka sv. Kataríny; No. 6) dates from 1311, though its façade was built in 1840. Between 1753 and 1756 Giovanni Battista Martinelli built the *Royal Chamber*, a Baroque palace that was extended to designs by Franz Anton Hillebrandt in 1772. From 1802 to 1848 the Diet of the Hungarian Estates met here, so it was also called the 'Landhaus'. Since 1953 it has contained the *University Library* (Univerzitná knižnica). Liszt gave recitals in the garden here as a nine-year-old, following the example another child prodigy, Mozart, who had performed a few doors away at the Pálffy Palace.

Michalská continues as Ventúrska ul. which is lined by a number of town palaces. The *Leopold de Pauli Palace* (No. 15) and the *Palace of Marshal Pálffy* (No. 10) date from the first half of the 18th century. The extremely plain *Academia Istropolitana* (No. 7) is the 15th-century building in which King Matthias I Corvinus founded the first, short-lived Hungarian university in 1467. After 1490 the building was used as an arsenal, mint office, residence, and from 1918 as a workers' academy. Since 1975 it has housed an Academy of Music.

Two medieval streets, Zelená ul. (Grünstüblgasse) and Sedlárska ul. (Sattlergasse) connect Ventúrska with Hlavné námestie (Main Square, until 1990 called nám. 4 apríla, to commemorate the day Soviet troops entered the city in 1945). In the centre of this square with its luxuriant greenery is the *Roland Fountain* (Rolandova fontána) designed in 1572 by Andreas Luttringer as a reservoir in case of fire. The *Jesuit Church* (Kostol jezuitov) in the north corner of the square is a towerless Late Renaissance building originally built by German Lutherans between 1636 and 1638. The Jesuits took it over in 1672 and decorated it with much magnificence. The pulpit by Ludwig Gode (1753) is one of the most splendid Rococo examples in Central Europe. In front of the Jesuit Church Leopold I built a *Marian Column* in 1675.

The *Old Town Hall* (Stará radnica) on the east side of Hlavné nám. developed in the 14th century (or possibly in the late 13th century) from a group of burghers' houses to form the unified Gothic 'House with the Tower'. The present roof dates from 1496-97, the façade frescoes were painted in 1533 by Hans Thiergarten, and the tower with its Baroque alterations seems something of an alien intruder. The rib-vaulted Late Gothic passage (1452) opens into a magnificent courtyard with Renaissance arcades, attics and miniature gables. The former Court Room has vigorous stucco work by Corati-Orseti, framing frescoes of biblical justice by J. Drentwett (1695). The 14th-century Gothic chapel was restored to its original state between 1967 and 1969. Since 1948, together with the neighbouring *Appónyi Palace* (1761-62), the town hall has housed the *Municipal Museum* (Mestské múzeum). Between the Old Town Hall and the Jesuit Church is Kostolná ul. (Kirchgasse) connecting Hlavné nám. with *Primaciálne nám.* On the north side of this square stands the *New Town Hall* (Mestský národný výbor) dating from 1947, while the west side is occupied by the rear of the Old Town Hall. The east side is dominated by the *Primatial Palace* (Primaciálne palác) built between 1777 and 1781 by Melchior Hefele for Archbishop Batthyányi. The Neo-Classical building was the winter residence of the Prince Primate and Archbishop of Esztergom, Hungary's highest ecclesiastical dignitary, who resided at Trnava (see p.360) and whose arms surmounted by a cardinal's cap crown the façade. The mosaic in the tympanum below is based on a fresco by Franz Anton Maulpertsch, to whom the fresco of *St Ladislas watering his horse* in the palace chapel is also attributed. Sculptures and paintings by Italian, Spanish and Flemish masters, and six English tapestries (c. 1630) which show scenes from the legend of *Hero and Leander*, decorate the Archbishop's state rooms. On 26 December 1805, after the Battle of Austerlitz, the 'Peace of Pressburg' was signed in the chaste splendour of the Palace's Hall of Mirrors between the Emperors Francis I and Napoleon. Venetia, Istria and Dalmatia were ceded to Napoleon, but Austria's permanent loss was her position of influence in Germany, for she was forced to recognize Bavaria, Baden and Württemberg as independent kingdoms. In 1903 the Town Council bought the palace for the local National Committee. Today the elegant building, now freshly restored, is used as the Municipal Gallery (Mestská galéria). Do not miss the Early Baroque fountain, a moustachioed St George killing a spouting dragon.

The *Ursuline Church* (Kostol uršulínok) on the corner of Nedbalova ul. (formerly Hummelgasse) and Uršulinska ul. was built around 1640 as a prayer house for the Slovak and Hungarian Protestants. In 1676 it was given to the Ursulines who built a convent with a school here. In the 18th century the order had the interior of the aisle-less church renovated.

The *Franciscan Church* (Kostol františkánov) and adjoining friary in Františkánské nám. were founded by King Ladislas IV of Hungary (1272–1290) in thanks for his victory at the Battle of the Marchfeld on 26 August 1278 when Hungarian and Habsburg troops defeated the army of the King of Bohemia, Otakar II Přemysl. The Early Gothic church was built between 1280 and 1297. In 1361 Mayor Jakub founded a High Gothic chapel dedicated to St John Elemosynarius (the Almsgiver), and in 1502 the Town Council followed suit with Chapel of St Sebastian. In the 18th century the church was partly baroquized; the Loreto chapel also dates from this period. After the earthquake of 1897 the tower of the church was in danger of collapse. It was demolished and replaced by a more stable copy, while the old Gothic tower was rebuilt by itself in the Janko Král' Park. Of the friary only the cloister and the chapel of St Rosalia survive. Opposite the Franciscan church stands the lovely Rococo *Mirbach Palace* (Mirbachov palác), built by Matthias Höllriegl between 1768 and 1770 for Michael Speck (Spech), a brewery owner. The delicious doorways lead to a courtyard with covered arcades. The palace was restored between 1972 and 1976 and now contains the

Bratislava (Pressburg) Castle and Pálffy Palace

Municipal Gallery (Mestská galéria). The Gothic *Poor Clares Church* (Kostel klarisiek) was built in the 13th century and the richly sculptured tower dates from about 1400. It is part of a convent dating from the beginning of the 13th century which has been altered many times in the course of the centuries and now houses the Slovak Pedagogical Library. The church was restored from 1966 to 1973 and is used as an exhibition space by the Municipal Gallery and as a hall for chamber concerts.

Looming over the south-west corner of the old town is *St Martin's Cathedral* (Dóm sv. Martina) with its tower, 85 metres high, and the glazed tiles of its roof glittering in the sun. Building work on the three-aisled hall church situated just next to the city walls lasted from the 13th century to the middle of the 15th. The Late Gothic form of the vaulting by Hans Puchspaum suggests a connection with the Cathedral workshop at Vienna. St Martin was consecrated in 1452, and was the coronation church of the kings of Hungary from 1563 until 1830. A plaque on the north-west wall of the sanctuary lists all the coronations that took place here; they are also commemorated by a stone cushion with a gilded crown built onto the spire between 1835 and 1847. In 1732–1734 Georg Raphael Donner built the chapel of St John the Almsgiver in the north aisle with the kneeling figure of the donor, Archbishop

Emmerich Esterházy. King Matthias Corvinus had been given the bones of the saint by the Turkish Sultan Mahmud I, and they now found their last resting place in this cathedral. Among the most remarkable objects in the cathedral are a late Gothic monstrance in the Treasury, and the equestrian statue of *St Martin* by G.R. Donner (1734/35), once the centre piece of a group of lead figures which formed the decoration of the high altar. The saint is curiously dressed in Magyar costume.

On the corner of Kapitulská ul. stands the Late Renaissance *Jesuit College* (Jezuitské kolégium) built by Jacopo Rava (1628–1635). Since 1936 it has been used by the Roman Catholic Theological Faculty named after Cyril and Methodios, the Apostles of the Slavs. Opposite is the *Provost's Palace* (Prepoštský palác) built in 1632, with a magnificent Renaissance gateway to its front garden which contains a monument to St Elizabeth of Thuringia, the Hungarian princess who was born at Pressburg in 1207 (see p. 384).

The new main road Starosmestská carries the traffic to Austria and crosses the bridge over the Danube (completed in 1972) to link the town centre of Bratislava with the southern town district of Petržalka (formerly Audorf or Engerau). The *Most SNP* (Most Slovenského národného povstania; Bridge of the Slovak National Uprising) is suspended from steel cables 72 mm thick fastened to a pylon which rises at an angle from the south bank. A fast lift takes the visitor up to the panoramic restaurant at the top of the pylon. The view back over Bratislava is slightly disappointing, since the construction of the bridge entailed destroying the entire Jewish quarter and the precincts of the cathedral.

The district between the old town and the Danube contains a number of grand public buildings such as the *Slovak National Theatre* (Slovenské národné divadlo) on the long Hviezdoslavovo nám., which was laid out as a park in the 19th century on the site of the town ramparts. The Neo-Renaissance theatre was built, of course, by the Viennese architects Ferdinand Fellner and Hermann Helmer between 1884 and 1886 on the site of the first Estates Theatre (Ständetheater; 1776); the interior is remarkable for its abundance of bare-breasted caryatids. Today it is used for opera and ballet performances. The *Ganymede Fountain* (Ganymedova fontána; 1888) in front of the theatre was made by V.O. Tilgner, who was also the creator of the *Hummel Memorial* (1887) a little further west. Johann Nepomuk Hummel (1778–1837), native of Pressburg, pupil and intimate friend of Mozart, successor to Haydn at Esterházy, is a major figure in the development of piano-playing. (He taught Czerny.) The cottage where Hummel was born, in Klobučnícka, is now a museum. Other buildings around the square are the *Carlton-Hotel*, the *Csomo Palace* (No. 13) of 1778, the *Pálffy Palace* (No. 18) of 1885 and the Rococo *Illésházy Palace* (No. 23) of 1769. The *Comenius University* (Univerzita Komenského) – the first Slovak university – is housed in a massive building completed in 1936, which dominates Šafárikovo nám. and the east end of Vajanského nábrežie (Vajanský Embankment). It was founded in 1914 as the successor to the *Academia Istropolitana* (see p.353). The little church of *St Elizabeth* (Kostol sv. Alžbety; also called the Modrý kostolík, 'Little Blue Church') in Bezručova ul. with its round belltower, was built between 1906–1908 by the idiosyncratic Hungarian architect Ödön Lechner. The style is Art Nouveau Romanesque: an attempt to create a Magyar poetic, now marooned in the Slovak capital.

The *Slovak National Museum* (Slovenské národné múzeum) at Vajanského nábrežie 2 has good natural history and archaeological collections. In Rázusova nábrežie 12 on the westward continuation of the embankment, in the former naval barracks (1759–1763), is the *Slovak National Gallery* (Slovenská národná galéria) with works by native and foreign artists of the 19th and 20th centuries. The Secessionist Baroque Revival *Reduta* in Mostová ul. was built between 1912 and 1914 and is the home of the Slovak Philharmonic Orchestra.

The city's northern fortifications were replaced by the long *nám. SNP* (nám. Slovenského národného povstania, Square of the Slovak National Uprising; formerly Marktplatz). From here Spitálska ul. runs north-east passing the *Church of the Elizabethine Nuns* (Kostol alžbetíniek) on the left hand side. This fine, if rather overblown, Baroque church was built by Franz Anton Pilgram between 1739 and 1742, with ceiling frescoes by the Tyrolean painter Paul Troger, and altarpieces by Franz Xaver Palko. A little further on is the *Aspremont Summer Palace* (Aspremontov letný palác) of the second half of the 18th century, now the medical faculty of the Comenius University. Not far from the Hotel Kyjev is the *Stará sladovňa* (Old Malt-House) which, with seating for more than a thousand, is now the second biggest beer hall in Europe (converted in 1976).

From St Martin's Cathedral the picturesque Zamocke schody (Castle Steps) lead through a Late Gothic gate (1480) up to the castle. A turning off at the corner of Mikulášska ul. takes the visitor to the *House at the Good Shepherd* (Dom U Dobrého pastiera) at Židovská ul. 1. This charming little corner house of around 1760, with its fragile Rococo decoration, contains a clock museum. Each storey consists of a single room; the figure of the Good Shepherd on the corner is protected by a fine canopy. Not far away a flight of steps lead from Mikulášska up to the small Russian Orthodox church of *St Nicholas* (Pravoslávný chrám sv. Mikuláša) which dates from the 17th century.

The *Castle* (Hrad), Bratislava's trademark, rises majestically 74 metres above the Danube. There was already a Slavic border castle here in the 9th century. It was extended by the Hungarians and then enlarged again in 1430 by the Emperor Sigismund. The Habsburgs strengthened it as a bulwark against Turkish attacks on Vienna. Between 1635 and 1649 the Hungarian Nádorispán (Palatine, or Viceroy) Paul Pálffy, with the help of Giovanni Battista Carlone, gave the castle its present square shape with the four corner towers. Maria Theresa had 'her Castle', in which the Hungarian Crown Jewels were kept, converted into a grandiose residence in 1761, but her successors did not share her liking for it. In 1784 a priests' seminary was established on the castle hill, and from 1802 the buildings were used as barracks. Destroyed by fire in 1811, they remained a ruin for 140 years until restoration began in 1953. The oratory has delicate stucco and paintwork. In the restored rooms the *National Museum* displays some interesting examples of Slovak culture.

The *Water Tower* near nábrežie armádneho generála Ludvíka Svobodu (Ludvík Svoboda Embankment) is evidence of nearly two thousand years of history: the foundations of the

The ruins at Devín (Theben)

walls which date from the 1st or 2nd centuries and are part of a Roman watch tower which controlled the strategically important ford over the Danube and with it the amber trade route. In the 13th century, the Cistercians restored the tower as a toll house, but in the 18th century the building disappeared under the poor-houses around it until it was rediscovered in the 1960's, when some of the dilapidated buildings were demolished.

More recent history is commemorated at the *Slavín Monument*, a mass grave of the Soviet soldiers who died in the liberation of the city in 1945. Its position high above the city affords it the prettiest views of Bratislava.

The road along the north bank of the Danube runs round the castle hill, passes the Park of Culture and Rest (Park kultúry a oddychu) and the Botanical Garden (Botanická zahrada) before taking the left hand fork at the village of Karlova Ves in the direction of **Devín** (Theben). The little village of Devín lies on the confluence of the Morava (March) and the Danube, the two rivers which here form the border between Austria and Czechoslovakia.

The castle rock, 212 metres high, had been settled without interruption since the 5th century BC. The 9th century was the most important period for Devín when under Prince Rastislav it was a border fortress of the Great Moravian Empire against the Franks. A chronicle of 864 says: 'King Louis emerged with his great army beyond the Danube, besieged

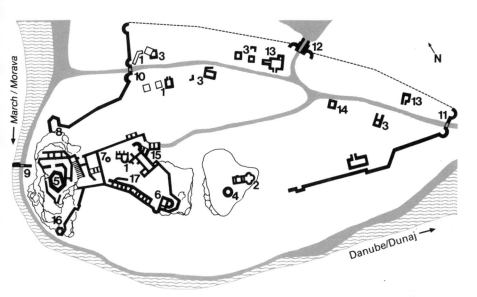

Devín (Theven) Castle Ruins
1 Roman buildings 2 Church (9th century) 3 Slavic settlement (10th-12th century) 4 Chapel
(10th-12th century) 5 Tower 6 Palace of Palatine Nicholas of Gara 7 Castle well 8 Bastion
9 Gate 10 West Gate 11 East Gate 12 North Gate (present entrance) 13 Guard Room (15th
century) 14 Building (15th century) 15 Renaissance Palace (16th century) 16 Watch tower ('the
Nuns'; 16th century) 17 Office buildings

Rastislav in a town which in the language of that country is called Dowina, meaning "maiden".' According to legend the castle was founded by a Moravian duke's daugher called Devoina. *Dowina* or *Devoina* became Devín. The mighty defensive ramparts of Rastislav's castle still survive on the north side of the precinct.

In the 13th century a polygonal residential tower was built on the steep rock and by the 15th century this had developed into an extensive Gothic castle. In 1527 Devín came into the possession of the Hungarian magnate – or warlord – Stephen Bathory who rebuilt the hall range in the Renaissance style and had little watchtowers, such as the 'Nun', built on the south slope down to the Danube. In 1809 Napoleon's soldiers blew up the castle and it has been in decay ever since. The first stirrings of Slovak nationalism gave the castle great symbolic value; it is particularly associated with the writer and agitator Ľudovít Štúr. Since 1945 the annual 'Peace Festival' has been held here in July.

Trnava (Tyrnau, Nagyszombat)

A motorway connects Bratislava with the town of **Trnava**, 45km away, which was formerly known to its German-speaking inhabitants as Tyrnau and to Hungarian-speakers as

Nagyszombat. Situated in the midst of vast vineyards and fertile fields, the town of Trnava celebrated its 750th anniversary in 1988. As the religious and intellectual centre of Hungary during the Turkish period the town had so many grand ecclesiastical buildings that it was called 'Slovak Rome'. Mechanical engineering and food production are now the most important industries for this regional town with a population of 70,000. Since 1989 the see of the Metropolitan Archbishop of Slovakia has once more had an occupant.

In 1238 King Béla IV of Hungary placed the township of *Zumbothel* directly under the crown and at the same time granted it the right to hold a market every Saturday; hence its Hungarian name which means 'Big Saturday'. The inhabitants could freely elect their magistrates and judges, did not have to provide military service and could use their wealth as they pleased, which was by no means guaranteed everywhere in the middle ages. At this intersection of two great European trade routes craftsmanship and trade flourished and expanded. In 1543 the Archbishop of Esztergom and Primate of Hungary, together with his cathedral chapter, moved his seat to Trnava because the greater part of Hungary was now under Turkish occupation; at the same time the kings established their capital at Bratislava. In 1635 the Primate founded a university on the model of the University of Graz (founded in 1586), with a theological and philosophical faculty. A faculty of law was added in 1667, and in 1669 a medical faculty. Trnava developed into the intellectual centre of Hungary; by the 17th century it had more than 40 printing houses. In 1777 Maria Theresa moved the university to Buda, and in 1820 the Primate returned to Esztergom. Trnava would have sunk back to its former provincial status had not some Slovak intellectuals made the town the seat of a 'Learned Fellowship' (Učené tovarišstvo), the most important scientific and literary society the land had yet seen, and one that greatly strengthened the national consciousness of the Slovaks. Finally the Vatican named Trnava as the residence of a Metropolitan Archbishop, the head of the Roman Catholic Church in Slovakia.

The two towers of the *Cathedral of St Nicholas* are surmounted by massive caps (plate 50). The three-aisled Gothic basilica with its long choir was built in 1380 on the site of a Romanesque basilica dating from before 1210. In 1629 Baroque side chapels were added and at the beginning of the 18th century a central chapel to the designs of the architect Franz Anton Hillebrandt. In the 18th century the two distinctive caps, shaped like Ottoman helmets with spires, were added to the west towers. The interior was restored in 1906.

The Early Baroque *University Church of St John the Baptist*, the largest religious building in Slovakia, was built for the Jesuits between 1629 and 1637 by Italian masters. Pietro and Antonio Spazzio provided the design for the long nave, which they built on the site of a 13th-century Dominican friary. The plasterwork of the interior is the work of Giovanni Battista Rosso, Giacomo Tornini and Pietro Antonio Conti, while the woodwork is by local masters. The neighbouring Rectorate and Medical Faculty were designed by F.A. Hillebrandt. More university buildings and the *Archbishop's Palace* of 1562 are to be found in Univerzitné nám. Other interesting churches are *St Elizabeth* of the mid–14th century, the *Trinitarian Church*

View of Trnava (Tyrnau)

of the 18th century, and the *Franciscan church* built in 1363 (the Gothic building was given a Baroque remodelling in the 17th century).

The Neo-Classical *Town Hall* now stands in all its recently restored glory on the long town square. It was built in 1793 and its pediment contains the arms of the town. The Late Renaissance *Town Tower* dates from 1574 and was baroquized about a hundred years later. Fine old burghers' houses can be found in Hollého ul. (Baroque houses: 1,2 and 3) and in Kapitulská ul. (Renaissance houses: 8,16 and 31). In Seminárska ul. the *West Slovak Museum* (Západoslovenské múzeum) occupies the former convent of Poor Clares: interesting local collections and a memorial to the Slovak composer Mikuláš Schneider-Trnavský (1881–1958) who was born in Trnava. The *Town Theatre*, built in 1831 in the Empire style, is the oldest theatre building in Slovakia.

The massive Gothic *town walls* to the west and east of the historic town centre are not to be missed. Built in the last third of the 13th century and in the 14th century they reinforced or replaced the earlier walls, and give an idea of the importance of the medieval town. The projecting tower bastions are also of brick and withstood all attacks. The fortifications were extended in 1435 during the Hussite Wars and again between 1553 and 1556, after the renewed outbreak of the Turkish wars when Ottoman reconnaissance parties were appearing before the walls of Trnava.

361

Piešt'any (Pistyan)

The motorway from Bratislava continues beyond Trnava and after another 33 km reaches **Piešt'any**, a spa which specializes in rheumatic disorders. Between the Little Carpathians (Malé Karpaty) and the Inovec mountains (Považský Inovec) the grand spa town extends along the bank of the Váh (Waag) and the Sĺňava reservoir with its modern water sports facilities and yacht marina. Radioactive thermal springs with a temperature of 67–69°C and a high mineral content, as well as sulphurous mud (sediment from a stopped branch of the Váh) are successful remedies for rheumatism, gout, sciatica and nervous disorders. The annual music festival attracts performers from all over the world.

It is possible that Neanderthal man was already using the hot springs since he left weapons and tools here, artefacts of the palaeolithic Moustérian Culture. In the district of Banka from 1941 to 1943 traces of the earliest huts in Central Europe (c. 36,000 BC) have been discovered. At Moravany, now also a district of Piešt'any, a statuette of a woman measuring 7.5 cm carved 23,000 years ago from a mammoth tooth was found here by a farmer in 1939; this is the famous 'Venus of Moravany', now in the National Museum in Bratislava. In the 4th century BC the Celts settled at the springs of Piešt'any. At the beginning of the present era they were driven out by the Quadi, who in their turn left the country in the 5th century. A hundred years later Slavs settled the banks of the Váh. In the 10th century they came under Hungarian rule which was to last about a thousand years.

Piešt'any is first mentioned as a spa in 1549 in a book entitled *De admirandis Hungariae aquis* (Concerning the Miraculous Waters of Hungary) by one Georg Wernher of Basle. The author praises the hot waters because of the extraordinary healing powers, far more effective than the other thermal springs in Hungary, and describes a bath in the thermal waters of Piešt'any, which involved digging oneself a pit by the bank of the Váh and filling it with hot water. As new water continually seeped into the pit, a constant temperature was maintained. The floor of the pit was covered with moss or branches. In 1599 a Turkish division attacked the spa, killed the sick, carried off the healthy and burned down the houses. Property disputes between the Hungarian feudal lords, revolts of the Estates

The Venus of Moravany

against the Habsburgs and the constant Turkish threat dominated the 17th century, yet more and more visitors came to the hot springs. In 1682 the Emperor Leopold I placed the spa under his protection.

In 1778 Count Johann Nepomuk Erdödy, whose family owned the town from 1720 until 1940, built the first bath house, a wooden building for tub baths. Most visitors, however, still had to be content with open holes in the ground. The beginning of the 19th century saw the start of a more rapid development: houses and hotels were built, spa gardens were laid out, craftsmen and businessmen arrived. In 1801 Beethoven, a friend of the Erdödys, wrote his famous letters to the mysterious 'Immortal Beloved' from Piešt'any. In 1821 Count Josef Erdödy began a drastic expansion of the town: new Neo-Classical bath houses sprang up, with a casino and a pharmacy. A spa park was created. In the 1850's several therapeutic facilities were added including the present Napoleon Bath, a second well was opened up, the spa gardens were extended with a music pavilion and an open-air theatre, and a spa doctor was appointed.

In 1889 the firm of Alexander Winter became the leaseholder of all the spa facilities and turned Piešt'any into a spa with a world reputation able to rival the famous West Bohemian spas and attract its share of prominent guests. In 1893 Winter founded a 'workers' boarding house' at which for the first time ever cures were financed by a health insurance scheme. This led to a massive expansion of the spa. Nationalized in 1940, it had a remarkable flowering under communism.

This is a working spa; the speciality is mud-wrapping. There is a music festival in June and July in the modern *House of Art* (Dom umenia). Little survives of the earlier spa

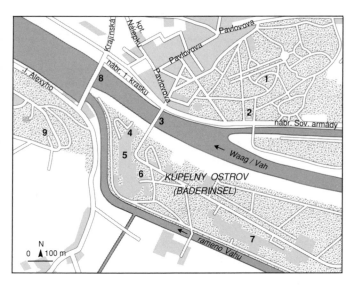

Piešt'any (Pistyan)
1 Spa Park
2 House of Art
3 Colonnade Bridge
4 Thermia Palace
5 Irma
6 Napoleon Bath
7 Balnea
8 Krajinský Bridge
9 Red Tower

beyond two fashionable hotels at the entrance to the spa gardens on *Kúpelní ostrov* (Bathers Island), the *Thermia Palace* (plate 59) and the *Irma*, both built in the Vienna Secession style by the Budapest architects Armin Hegedüs and Heinrich Böhm between 1910 and 1912. The sculptural decoration is by Alexander Krisztián of Budapest; in the frieze a portrait of the great Art Nouveau master Alfons Mucha can be seen.

In a niche on the outside of the Irma Sanatorium stands a statue of the Empress Elisabeth ('Sissi'), Queen of Hungary (1837–1898). The little park in front of the Thermia Palace is populated with Graeco-Roman deities. The oldest spa building still standing is the *Napoleon Bath* (Napoleonské kúpele), formerly called the Franz-Joseph-Bad (or Franzensbad for short), a Neo-Classical building with three wings built between 1822 and 1862. Beyond it is the main spring (Pramen Adam Trajan). The gardens on the island are filled each year with new works by modern sculptors forming the largest open-air art exhibition in the world. The most famous sculpture here, however, is the larger-than-life bronze 'Man Breaking his Crutches' (Robert Kühmayer, 1933), the optimistic trademark of Piešťany.

Trenčín (Trentschin)

Between the forested Stražovská hills (Stražovská vrchy) and the river Váh lies the busy district town of **Trenčín**, loomed over by a mighty castle, which once guarded the trade route through the Váh valley at the Hungarian-Moravian frontier. The town is now best known for the nearby thermal spa of Trenčianske Teplice.

During the Marcomanni wars Roman soldiers arrived here in 179 AD. After a victory over the Germanic Quadi they built the fortified military camp of *Laugaricio* as winter quarters. We know who they were – 855 soldiers of the Second Auxiliary Legion under their commander Marcus Valerius Maximianus, based at *Aquincum* (Budapest) – thanks to an inscription carved on the castle rock, the earliest piece of written evidence found on Czechoslovak soil.

A gap in the records follows, before the Slavs began to settle on the Váh in the 6th century. They built a castle on the high rock, which served in the 11th century as a royal watch castle. At its foot a market settlement developed in the 12th century and received its town charter in 1412. In 1302 the Hungarian magnate Maté Čák (or in Hungarian Mátyás Csák) seized the castle and built a grand crenellated palace on the castle rock. Čák ruled western Slovakia and attempted to be a king-maker in Hungary and Bohemia too. Not until his death in 1321 was the castle reclaimed by the king and it was the scene of important meetings on several occasions: in 1335 John of Luxemburg came here with his son Charles to negotiate with King Casimir III (the Great) of Poland and King Charles I Robert of Hungary; and in 1362 Charles IV met Louis I of Hungary (later called the Great) at Trenčín Castle.

The fortifications which King Sigismund added in 1387 were strong enough to withstand all the attacks of the Hussites from neighbouring Moravia. After Sigismund's death in 1437 Trenčín changed hands several times until in 1477 it came into the possession of the Voivode

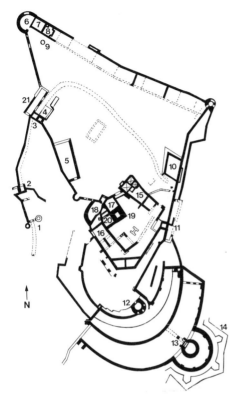

Trenčín (Trentchin) Castle, plan
1 Outer Gate 2 First Gate 3 Second Gate
4 Clock Tower 5 Accommodation for castle
garrison 6 Artillery bastion 7 Mill 8 Chapel
9 Well 10 Artillery bastion 11 Gate to outer
ward 12 Jeremy Tower 13 Hunger Tower
14 Baroque fortifications 15 Barbara fortifications 15 Barbara Palace 16 Zápolya Palace 17 Ľudovít Palace 18 Great Bastion
19 Matúš Tower 20 Chapel 21 Administrative
offices

of Transylvania, Stephen Zápolya (Zá-pol'sky). When the Habsburg Ferdinand I was elected king of Bohemia and Hungary in 1526, the Hungarian aristocracy set up Stephen's grandson John Zápolya (1487–1540) as a rival king. With Turkish help John Zápolya managed to gain possession of most of Hungary, but after his death in 1540 the Hungarian crown passed to the Habsburgs for good.

In 1594 the Emperor Rudolph II gave the lordship of Trenčín, including the castle and the neighbouring sulphurous spa of *Aqua Teplica* (now Trenčianske Teplice), to the Counts Illésházy first as a fiefdom and soon afterwards as an inheritance. The Illésházys rebuilt the castle to the latest standards in fortifications, adding artillery bastions and strengthening the masonry. In 1835 the last scion of the Illésházy family sold the lordship of Trenčín to a Greek businessman, Georg Sina, who mainly concerned himself with developing the spa. His granddaughter, Iphigénie d'Harcourt, gave the castle to the town of Trenčín, because of the cost of securing the ruins, and busied herself with the beautification of Bad Teplitz. After the Second World War the district town of Trenčín experienced an extraordinary period of prosperity. Mechanical engineering flourished and textile works made Trenčín the 'town of fashion'. Trenčianske Teplice is now one of the most important spas in Czechoslovakia.

Mierové nám. (plate 54), the long main square of old Trenčín, with its plague column of 1713, is lined with fine Renaissance burghers' houses (late 16th and early 17th centuries), often with baroquized façades, as well as many 19th-century houses. Among these rise the two towers of the Early Baroque Piarist church of *St Francis* (1653–1657) with frescoes by the Viennese painter Christoph Tausch (1712), which are among the most beautiful examples of Baroque art in Slovakia. The Late Baroque building which was once the headquarters of the Ispán (in Slovak: Župan; High Sheriff) now houses the interesting local collections of the *District Museum* (Trenčianske múzeum). Nearby is the octagonal *Town Tower* with a passageway running through it, with the sturdy 19th-century synagogue immediately behind.

The town's *parish church* stands at the foot of the castle rock. It was built in 1324 and given Renaissance alterations in 1528. In the adjoining Baroque funerary chapel is a splendid alabaster altar which has been attributed to the sculptor Georg Raphael Donner, but in fact is probably the work of L. Gode (1750–1753), and the Early Baroque tomb of Kaspar Illésházy carved in black marble to designs by Kaspar Menneler of Augsburg (1649). The *charnel house* next to the parish church dates from the middle of the 15th century and is the only purely Gothic building in the town. In the parish house is a Gothic monstrance which was presented by Charles IV to the Hungarian King Louis I (the Great) in 1362.

The mighty *castle* (Trenčianske hrad) high above the town has its origins in the 11th century. Parts of the main tower (33 metres high) date from this period, though it was extended by Matúš Čák in the 13th century and so bears his name (Matúš Tower). Also dating from the 11th century is a Romanesque *Rotunda*, a castle chapel, which was only discovered in 1973. In the 15th and 16th century the castle was considerably enlarged and strengthened. The road to the castle rises steeply through the Renaissance outer gateway (16th century) and the first castle gateway (15th century). Beyond the second castle gateway with the adjacent clock-tower (15th century, renovated in the 17th century) is the accommodation for the castle personnel (15th and 16th centuries). The projecting artillery bastion dates from the 16th century and contains a chapel and a mill. According to legend the well, 142 metres deep, was struck into the rock in the 15th century by a Turkish prince in order to pay for the release of his bride who was being held prisoner by the lord of the castle, which is why it is known as the 'Lovers' Well'. Around 1430 King Sigismund built the Barbara Palace, decorated with blind arcading, for his wife Barbara (Barbora Celjská). The Zápolya Palace was built in the 16th century, while the Ľudovit Palace (the palace of Louis the Great) dates from the 14th century, but was renovated in the 16th century.

About 15 km north-east of Trenčín, in the picturesque valley of the Teplička, in the midst of the wooded Stražovská hills, lies the spa of **Trenčianske Teplice**, formerly known throughout Europe as Trentschin-Teplitz (or in Hungarian Trencsénteplic). The warm sulphur and lime springs are used especially to treat rheumatism, gout and nervous disorders.

As early as 1247 a charter of the Hungarian King Béla IV mentions the healing springs as *Aqua Teplica*. In 1579 a Moravian country doctor, Thomas Jordan, described the spa, which then consisted of only 'a few dilapidated wooden huts and two little thermal lakes', one reserved as a 'bath for the gentry' and the other as a 'paupers' bath', for the people. In the late 17th century wooden houses were built over the springs and a master of the baths supervised their use, but it was not until 1729 when the Hungarian magnate Joseph Illésházy built his summer residence on the Teplička, that the spa came to the attention of society. A magnificent 'Castellum' was built next to the springs, and hotels, sanatoria and boarding houses followed. Nationalization in 1948 marked the beginning of an unparalleled expansion.

In all there are eleven *mineral springs* in Trenčianske Teplice. Ten are alkaline-muriatic and one sulphurous. The most delightful building in the spa is the *Hammam*. Iphigenie d'Harcourt, the proprietress of the spa, saw a design by the architect Franz Schmoranz at the Paris World Exhibition of 1878 and was so taken with it that she arranged to have it executed at Trenčianske Teplice. Thus between 1886 and 1888 on the banks of the Teplička there arose a luxuriously appointed oriental bath in Moorish style. A double row of columns divides the central hall from the 33 cubicles, which are decorated with tiles and originally had thermal water basins. The bath is illuminated by glazed openings in the three domes. Today the Hammam is used as a men's changing room by the adjacent Sina Sanatorium.

The *Schloss* (Kaštiel') was built around 1750 for Count Joseph Illésházy after the model of Italian Renaissance palaces. Here the most eminent guests at the spa once stayed. Today the complex houses the three main springs as well as spa facilities.

Nitra (Neutra; Nyitra)

A broad loop of the river Nitra (Neutra), a tributary of the Váh, surrounds the ancient core of **Nitra**, probably the oldest urban site in Czechoslovakia. It is dominated by a medieval castle,

Nitra (Neutra) in the 19th century

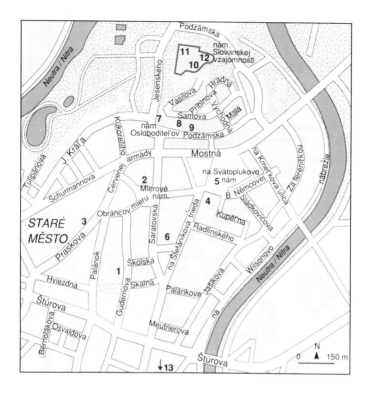

Nitra (Neutra)
1 Piarist Church and
  School
2 Chapel of St
  Michael
3 Chapel of St
  Stephen
4 Regional Museum
5 Andrej Bagar
  Theatre
6 Synagogue
7 Nitranska-štatná
  Galerie
8 Franciscan Church
9 Slovak
  Agricultural
  Museum
10 Plague Column
11 Castle
12 Cathedral with
  Church of St
  Emmeram
13 Town Hall

the earliest beginnings of which certainly go back to the 11th century, perhaps even to the 9th. Around 830 Archbishop Adalram of Salzburg consecrated the first Christian church in Slovakia, within the palace of Pribina, Prince of Nitra. Pribina, a Slav and the first ruler of Slovakia known to history, was not himself a Christian, but was careful to tolerate the faith of his Germanic neighbours. When, a few years later, he was driven from Nitra by Prince Mojmir I who incorporated the town into the Great Moravian Empire, the Germans duly gave Pribina asylum and he eventually converted, becoming a zealous proselytizer in Pannonia (present-day Hungary). In 880 Pope John VIII raised the town of *Nitrava* to the first episcopal see on Slovak territory – this was about as far as the writ of Rome was to run. Crafts and trade flourished at Nitra; its ceramics, metalwork, glass and jewellery were in demand far beyond the country's boundaries.

After the collapse of the Great Moravian Empire Nitra came alternately under the control of the Czech Přemyslids and the Polish Piast dynasty. Not until the reigns of the Hungarian Kings Béla I (1060–1063) and Géza I (1074–1077), when its bishops were also rulers of a komitat, did Nitra again experience a period of flowering. The bishop resided at the castle with his administration, the upper town at the foot of the castle was a fortified patrician quarter, while in the unwalled lower town lived the Slav craftsmen and Jewish merchants.

From the end of the 13th century until the 18th century Nitra stagnated; it was overshadowed by other towns and gradually lost the privileges of a free royal town. Looting and fires were the characteristic events of the 14th and 15th centuries. After the conquest of Buda by the Turks in 1526 Nitra found itself in a border area which was constantly under threat. At the beginning of the 18th century it was the scene of the battles between the imperial troops and the rebellious Hungarian magnates under Prince Ferenc Rákóczi II, as well as being seriously damaged by Turkish assaults.

The old town centre (Staré mesto) is a harmonious ensemble of historic buildings and architecture of our own time. The two towers of the Baroque *Piarist Church* in Gudernova ul. deserve a look, as does the neighbouring grammar school (*Gymnasium*) of the same period. The present Piarist church was built between 1742 and 1748 and restored in 1940. In the same year Edmund Massányi also painted the frescoes on the theme of the *Christianizing of Nitra*.

The little *Chapel of St Matthew* (1739) in the middle of Mierové nám. commemorates those who died in the cholera epidemics of 1710 and 1739. The friendly *garden tavern* of the Hotel Slovan is a meeting place for students from the town's colleges.

The aisle-less *Chapel of St Stephen* in Párovská ul. near the new grammar school, dates from the 11th century. The main street of the lower town, na Štefánikova trieda (formerly Dlhá ul, Long Street), runs south from Svätoplukovo nám. In the middle ages this was Nitra's main square, and until 1786 the parish church of St James stood here. The *Town Hall* (Mestský národný výbor; Municipal National Committee) was built in a revivalist style and completed in 1912. The imposing building in the centre of the square is the brand new *Andrej Bagar Theatre* (Divadlo Andrej Bagara), completed in 1990. The architects were J. Hlavica, Š Rosincová and M. Žitňanský, with decoration by Tíbor Bártfay, J. Marth, K. I. Sujanová and others. The curtain is decorated with the perennially popular *Vision of the Great Moravian Empire* (here, after M. Peršnajder).

The *Synagogue* in Gorazdova ul. was built in 1910-11, and when restoration work is completed (probably in 1993) will be used as a concert hall; it has excellent acoustics. In Štúrova trieda, the main traffic route through Nitra, stands the gloomy building of the former *Župa Tribunal* (1902/03), which now contains law courts, state administration and the central library of agriculture.

Saratovská ul. leads up to the upper town and the castle. It ends at nám. Osloboditel'ov (Liberators Square), where there was once a moat around the walled upper town. The underpass near what is now the Nitranska-Štatná Gallery and the Academy of Art, formerly the office of the Župan (or Ispán), the district administrator, was the only gateway to the fortress of Nitra. The office was built in 1823 in a Late Baroque style and its historicizing extension dates from between 1903 and 1908.

At the beginning of Samova ul., stands the *Franciscan Friary and Church* dating from around 1630, which contains 33 remarkable wooden reliefs with scenes from the life of the

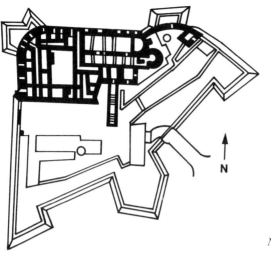

Nitra (Neutra) Castle, plan

founder of the order. Above the doorway to the Chapel of St Anthony is a 16th-century relief showing the Resurrection. Another relief near the doorway is dedicated to the Apostles Peter and Paul. (The other half of this relief is in the National Museum in Budapest.) The *Pol'nohospodárske múzeum* that it houses is the Slovak Agricultural Museum. A little further on stands the *Great Seminary* built in 1770 and extended between 1876 and 1878. The building is in a transitional style between Late Baroque and Neo-Classicism. It now houses the *Regional Museum* with its remarkable archaeological collection. Here too is the Diocesan Library with 78 precious incunabula and many manuscripts, among them the famous Nitra Codex of the 11th century. Opposite stands the three-storey *Canons' House* (1818–1821) with a muscular Atlas at the corner. He is called *Corgoň*, or 'rogue', since despite all his apparent effort this corner in fact requires no structural support. Samova, Pribinova and Východná ul. form a triangular square with a modern fountain in the middle.

Vasilova, Východná and Hradná ul. lead up to the *Castle* and all end at nám. Slovanskej vzájomnosti (Slavic Cooperation Square) in which stands a Rococo *Marian column* made by the Austrian sculptor Martin Vogerl in 1750, commemorating the two great cholera epidemics of 1710 and 1739; it was restored in 1989-90. Crossing a stone bridge set with 18th-century figures of saints, the visitor reaches the first gateway of the castle which has a Latin inscription commemorating those who commissioned it. The second gateway is part of the Mosóczi Palace, the residence of the commandant of the fortress (18th century). The round tower is a relic of the medieval fortifications; its Neo-Gothic restoration dates from 1857. Ascending a broad stairway the visitor reaches the *Cathedral*, built between 1333 and 1355 as an aisleless Gothic church, and altered and extended between 1622 and 1642. The famous Italian architect Domenico Martinelli directed the baroquization of the building between

1710 and 1718, including the weak cupola of the tower. Its frescoes were painted by Gottlieb Anton Galliardi in 1720.

Attached to the cathedral is the late 11th-century church of *St Emmeram*, built as an aisleless Romanesque church and dedicated to Sts Svorad and Benedict, as well as St Emmeram. When Matúš Čák laid waste the town and castle in 1317, the little church suffered damage and was incorporated into the building of the Gothic cathedral. It was only identified in 1930/31.

Two hills offer the visitor a superb view over the town: the Zobor and the Kalvária. The *Zobor* (588 metres) is on the south-east edge of the Tribeč hills, a famous wine-growing area. Of the friendly wine taverns at the top, the 'Zoborská perla' probably has the best view. The *Kalvária* (213 metres), 1.5 km south of the old town centre has a chapel of the Holy Cross on its summit. About 300 metres northwards is a little 14th-century church whose pietà has been a focus of pilgrimages since the 18th century.

In the *Dražovce* district of the town an Early Romanesque church dating from the beginning of the 12th century has survived. It was built on the site of an old Slavic fortification and its ground plan in particular still shows the influence of Great Moravian architectural traditions. In the *Párovské Háje* district stands another Early Romanesque church, the 11th-century St Stephen, originally dedicated to the Virgin, which has undergone many alterations in the course of the centuries.

Central Slovakia (Střední Slovensko)

Banská Bystrica (Neusohl; Besztercebanya)

At the point where the river Bystrica joins the Hron, a tributary of the Danube, lies **Banská Bystrica**, in a splendid location between the foothills of the Low Tatra (Nízké Tatry), the Slovak Ore Mountains (Slovenské rudohorie), the Great Fatra mountains (Veľká Fatra) and the Kremnica hills (Kremnické pohorie). Its history as a famous mining town, whose copper trade was controlled by the fabulously wealthy Fuggers of Augsburg, bankers to Charles V, around 1500, is recalled by many buildings which are now protected as historic monuments. Today Banská Bystrica (population: 85,000) is the administrative capital of Central Slovakia, a flourishing industrial town (mechanical engineering, textiles and pharmaceuticals) and a cultural centre with a college, radio station and theatre. In the winter the slopes of the Turíčka (556 metres) south of the town are ideal for skiing and tobogganing (ski lifts, ski-jump ramps).

At the beginning of the 13th century when the rich silver mines and deposits of copper ore were discovered, German miners – who were granted royal privileges – moved there from nearby Altsohl (Zvolen) further up the Bystrica to extract the precious ore. They settled at Bystrica and called the place 'Neusohl'. The Altsohlers were joined by miners and craftsmen from Thuringia who had been summoned to the country by King Andrew II. In 1255 Neusohl received its town charter. Its greatest period was at the beginning of the 16th century when Jakob Fugger II of Augsburg ('the Rich'; 1459–1525) acquired most of the mines in the vicinity of Neusohl and created a European monopoly in copper, in which the Thurzo family of Hungarian magnates was also involved. The town was the administrative centre for the mining and processing of the ore and for the lucrative trade in precious metals, to which the town's wealth was in fact principally due.

The heart of the old town centre of Banská Bystrica is its great market place decorated with fountains and flower beds, now called the nám. Slovanského národného povstania (Square of the Slovak National Uprising), or nám. SNP for short (plate 55). The square was formed in the 13th century and of the splendid burghers' and patricians' houses which surround it, only a few are much more recent. Most were built in the Gothic period, but given a Renaissance remodelling between 1480 and 1520. Some art nouveau elements were added in the 19th and 20th centuries.

The *Thurzo House* on the south-east side of the square was formed by the Thurzo family in 1495 by joining together two older burghers' houses. It was intended as a representative building for the all-powerful Fugger-Thurzo mining and metallurgical company. In the early

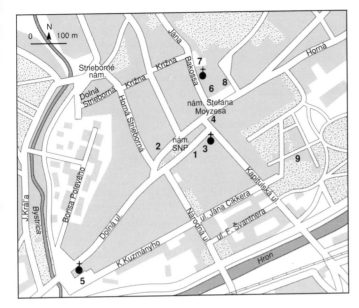

Banská Bystrica
(Neusohl)
1 Thurzo House
2 Benicky House
3 Protestant Church
4 Clock Tower
5 St Elizabeth
6 Castle
7 St Mary
8 Town Hall
9 Pamätník SNP

16th century Master Oswald gave the building a Renaissance façade with rich sgraffito decoration. The building is now a *museum* housing collections illustrating town history and folk culture. The visitor should look particularly at the *Green Hall* with its Late Gothic painted decoration showing themes from Aesop's fables, the Last Judgment, Susanna and the Elders, and the local legend of the miner Knapius. The vault is painted with the royal arms of the Anjou and Hunyadi families – the families of the Hungarian kings Louis I (the Great; 1342–1382) and Matthias I Corvinus (1458–1490) respectively.

The *Benicky House* was also created from running together two Gothic burghers' houses in the last third of the 16th century and remodelling them in the Renaissance style. The arcaded loggia with its decorative tuscan columns was added in the 17th century by the Italian architect, Jacopo di Pauli. No. 22 has a splendid oriel window, made in 1636 by the sculptor Johann Weinhardt of Wallendorf (now Spišské Vlachy). The burgher's house underwent Romanticizing alterations in the late 19th century. The Baroque *Bishop's Palace* was built in the last years of the 18th century.

On the corner of Kapitulská ul. stands the Neo-Classical *Protestant Church* (of the Augsburg Confession) built by Michael Pollack of Budapest. The north-west corner of the long market place is dominated by the *Clock Tower* (Hodinová veža) dating from 1567. At the end of Dolná ul. which runs southwards from the square stands the little Gothic church of *St Elizabeth* of 1303 with a 14th-century carved altarpiece.

Nám. Štefana Moyzesa (until recently nám. Červenej armády, Red Army Square) which extends northwards beyond the market place, sloping slightly up to the *castle*, is typical of all

373

Slovak mining towns. It is necessary to examine the unimpressive-looking buildings closely to identify the parts which belonged to the medieval castle. In the 13th century, when the first silver and copper ore was extracted at Neusohl, a Romanesque parish church stood here together with the house of the royal official who was charged with overseeing the mining and payment of part of the ore as tax. Over the following centuries the church grew, first taking on a Gothic and then a Baroque appearance. The royal official's house, which also served as a storeplace for the extracted ore, increased in height until eventually it had five storeys. Since the late 15th century it has been called the *Matthias House* because the Hungarian King Matthias I Corvinus used to reside here. The king's arms can still be seen next to those of the town on the wall. At that time the Gothic gate tower and church of the Holy Cross for the miners (now known as the *Slovak Church*) were built within the castle precincts. The barbican was built in 1521, when solid stone walls replaced the palisades and ramparts built of wooden beams, rubble and earth. After the town fire of 1761 the town tower was raised a storey and given a Baroque cap and lantern. The steward of the castle lived in the barbican, which with the gate tower was called the 'Petermann Bastion'.

St Mary, the parish church of Neusohl, was first built before 1255 as a Romanesque building. Vestiges from this period can be seen in the tower and outer walls. In the first half of the 14th century the church was enlarged in the Gothic style, and in 1473 the chapels of St Andrew and Corpus Christi were added. The Late Gothic altarpiece in the *Chapel of St Barbara* (1478) – the patron saint of miners – is the work of Master Paul of Leutschau, who also made the famous altarpiece of the church of St James at Levoča (Leutschau; see pp. 397f). It has life-size figures of the Virgin and Child, St Barbara and St Jerome (after 1500). The *Chapel of St John the Evangelist* was founded after 1500 by the rich mine-owner, Michael Königsberger. The oratory of the chapel (with its Late Gothic vault) and the sculptures on the pillars were designed by Anton Pilgram, the architect of St Stephen's Cathedral in Vienna. On one of the pillars the master himself is to be seen leaning for a moment, set-square in hand, looking contendedly at his work.

After the 1761 fire the church was given a new Baroque interior and furnishings. The high altar was erected by the architect Peter Grossmann, with figures carved by Joseph Hebenstreit, and and altarpiece of the Assumption painted by Johann Lucas Kracker (1774).

The *Town Hall* (Bývalá radnica) was built in 1510 by Veit Mühlstein, a mine-owner and the gespan of Neusohl, on the very edge of the castle precincts. This square building, which was then called the *Prätorium*, is in a mixture of Gothic and Renaissance styles and rises above the castle walls. In time of war it was used as a bastion. The sides facing the castle had an open loggia in the Italian Renaissance style. Today the town hall contains the *District Art Gallery* (Oblastná galéria).

The modern *Pamätník SNP* (Múzeum SNP) at Š. Moyzesa 23 is the memorial to the Slovak National Uprising, which started here (see p. 32). It is a building of distinctive beauty, completed in 1969 and designed by the architect Dušan Kuzma and the sculptor Jozef Jankovič.

In the *Sásová* district, 2.5 km north of nám. SNP stands the small Gothic church of the *Hermit Saints Anthony and Paul* dating from the first half of the 14th century. Alterations in the first half of the 16th century were undertaken under the direction of Master Anton Pilgram; his is the wonderful vault in the nave and chancel. The Late Gothic high altar is the combined work of the great sculptor Master Paul (or Pavol) and the painter Master Nicholas, both of Levoča (c. 1500).

Zvolen (Altsohl; Zólyom)

18 km south of Banská Bystrica in the middle of the hills at the point where the Slatina flows into the Hron, lies the district town of **Zvolen**, once the capital of the Komitat of Zólyom (Altsohl) and the summer residence of the kings of Hungary. Already in the 12th century Altsohl was a German mining settlement, mainly extracting silver, and in 1244 King Béla IV of Hungary granted the growing settlement a town charter. Between 1370 and 1382 King Louis (Ľudovít) the Great built a magnificent hunting lodge in the style of an Italian castello on the hill above the Slatina. Zvolenský zámok became the favourite residence of King Matthias Corvinus (1458–1490). After his death Johann Thurzo, a Hungarian magnate and mine-owner, took over the *castello* and converted it into a fortress with diminutive corner towers. Inside he set up a Late Gothic chapel. As the Turkish threat became ever greater, the fortifications were strengthened again in the mid–15th century and linked with the town's fortifications. In 1628 the noble Esterházy family aquired the castle and converted it into a residence which was representative of their status. The Gothic ashlar façades were replaced with sgraffito decorations, and swallow-tail crenellations formed the cresting to the walls. In

The castle at Zvolen (Altsohl)

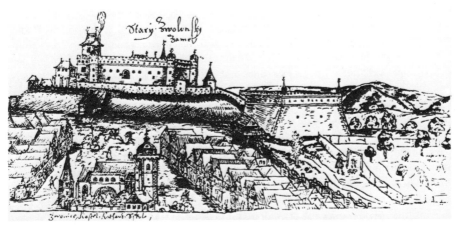

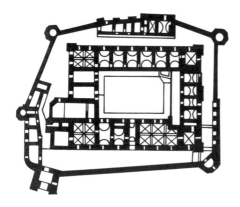

Zvolen (Altsohl) Castle, plan

1712 the Esterházys created a central hall in the west wing with a coffered ceiling in which each of the 78 fields was filled with the naive and earnest head of a Holy Roman Emperor – up to the reigning Charles VI. In 1784 the chapel was given Baroque decoration. Between 1956 and 1971 the castle was thoroughly restored, and since then has housed a valuable collection of medieval Slovak art.

In the gardens west of the castle an *armoured train* commemorates the Slovak National Uprising of 29 August 1944. Workers and railway staff at Zvolen put together three armoured trains to safeguard the landing of Soviet transport planes at Tri Duby air field. On the long main square of Zvolen (nám. SNP) is another memorial to the uprising. The Gothic church of *St Elizabeth* dates from 1381–1390 and was altered after 1500, when it was given charming Renaissance decoration.

Kremnica (Kremnitz; Körmöcbanya)

Amongst the gold and silver towns of Upper Hungary, **Kremnica** in the middle of the Kremnica hills (Kremnické pohorie) has the most glorious history. Gold coins and medals have been struck at the mint here for more than 650 years. The old appearance of Kremnica is largely preserved and the town is now a conservation area. Precious metals are mined only from a single shaft here, but this is also a flourishing centre of lace and ceramic production.

The Slavic settlement of *Kremnychbana* began here in the early 12th century at the intersection of two mountain valleys. Soon miners from Thuringia and Silesia were settling there to prospect for gold and silver. In 1328 the Hungarian King Charles I Robert granted the settlement a charter as a royal free town, and its heyday lasted from the 14th to the 16th centuries. The miners' court, Kammerhof, which had originally met at Banská Štiavnica (Schemnitz; see p. 378), had its seat here between 1328 and 1587. In 1335 Kremnica was even granted the right to mint gold ducats and silver groschen.

The nucleus of old Kremnica is *nám. 1. mája*, a long rectangular square sloping down to the valley, with Trinity column and gardens. It has existed in its present shape since the foundation of the town in the early 14th century and is surrounded with the Gothic houses of mine-owners and merchants, which have taken on Renaissance and Baroque features over the centuries. The town wall runs just behind it. In the 18th century the *Town Hall* (No. 1) was joined to the neighbouring Late Gothic burgher's house, which has a passageway to the

View of Kremnica (Kremnitz)

courtyard with unusual, delicately interlocking groin vaulting. No. 7 is now the *Municipal Museum*. The *Trinity Column* was erected between 1765 and 1772.

The topmost corner of the square abuts the precincts of the *castle*, the storage place of the precious metals extracted here and the seat of the royal court. Since the 15th century it has also been the centre of the municipal and ecclesiastical administration. In the 14th century a four-storey gate tower, an outer ward and three bastions (Parish Bastion, Miners' Bastion and Clock Tower) were built to strengthen the double walls, up to 12 metres high and with a water-filled moat between. The round 13th-century Romanesque charnel house next to the gate tower consists of an ossuary with a sexpartite vault and above it a chapel of St Andrew, which received Gothic alterations in the 14th century. A covered stairway leads up to the Parish Bastion. An underground passageway links the castle with several burghers' houses in the town. Around the massive keep, the 13th-century residential tower, there developed in the Gothic period a *church* which was first dedicated to St Michael and then since 1488 to St Catherine. The two-aisled hall church with two central piers is built on a square plan. At the east end is a spacious chancel, while to the west stands the majestic former castle keep, now the bell tower. In the 16th and 17th centuries the church belonged to the Protestants, but the 18th century brought restitution of the church to the Roman Catholics with the inevitable baroquization. The interior has since regained its original Gothic appearance.

The *town fortifications* date from the period before 1441. Of the three gates only the Dolná bràna (Lower Gate) survives. From 1539 it was strengthened by a barbican which also consisted of a gate tower. A semi-circular Renaissance oriel and an armorial niche decorate the gate façade. Four of the defensive towers of the wall are extant, including the *Červená veža* (Red Tower) to the south-east of the town, which was for a long time used as the town prison. The *Mint* has been in existence since 1335 and still produces gold coins, medals and plaques. The working mint can be visited in Horná ul.

Banská Štiavnica (Schemnitz; Selmecbánya)

In the middle of the Štiavnické pohorie (Schemnitz hills) stands the ancient mining town of Schemnitz, now **Banská Štiavnica**, picturesquely laid out on a number of terraces. From the 14th to the 16th centuries it was the most important mining town in Hungary, a source of gold and silver for the Magyar kings and the Fuggers of Augsburg. Today its inhabitants work in tourism and there are a few moderately sized textile, leather and food producing concerns.

There were prospectors for gold and silver in the Schemnitz hills, part of the Slovak Ore Mountains (Slovenské rudohorie), in prehistoric times, but the first documentary mention of a mining settlement is in 1075. At that time there was already a castle surrounded with earthworks. In the 12th century German miners arrived and replaced the open-cast mining used until then with underground mining. Towards the end of the 12th century Schemnitz received its town charter from King Béla III, and in 1244 it became a royal free town. From 1217 Schemnitz mining law was binding for all Hungarian mining towns. The town's fortunes reached a zenith between the 14th and 16th centuries, when first gold and then silver were mined here. In the 16th century the Fuggers took a lease on the productive mines. In 1627 Schemnitz miners were the first in the world to use gunpowder to make their galleries, and in 1732 the miners scored another first with their use of steam-driven machines to pump out water. The water was pumped into 40 large basins where it was left to evaporate so that it would not seep into the ground again. In the second half of the 18th century the town had a population of 20,000 and was the third largest town in Hungary. From 1735 it had a school of mines which developed in 1763 into an Academy of Mining and Metallurgy (closed in 1918, when the extraction of precious metals had ceased).

Looming over the old town centre of Banská Štiavnica is the *Old Castle* (Starý zámok), which was created out of a medieval church dedicated to the Virgin. At the beginning of the 13th century a three-aisled Romanesque basilica with a two-storey charnel house was built near the entrance. Between 1497 and 1515 it was replaced by a Late Gothic hall church. Between 1546 and 1559, with the Turkish menace increasing, the inhabitants of the town converted this church into a Renaissance fortress with reinforced outer walls and small corner towers. The nave became an open courtyard and the whole building was surrounded with a massive wall with five towers. The castle was where the precious metal was stored and it also provided protection for the townspeople during attacks by the Turks. In 1717 the tall west tower was given a Baroque copper roof. Today the Old Castle contains the history and art sections of the Slovak Mining Museum. A Late Gothic statue of St Catherine dating from the beginning of the 16th century belongs to the group understandably known as 'Beautiful Madonnas' and its drapery already shows the influence of the approaching Renaissance.

The small *Trojičné nám.* (Trinity Square) is the main square of the historic town centre. Here stood the houses of the rich burghers, called the 'Forest Burghers' because they owned the forests and the treasures beneath them. Some of the houses, for example No. 27 on the corner of Leninova ul., have remains of Romanesque masonry, but most are Gothic buildings of the 14th and 15th centuries which were remodelled in the Renaissance and Baroque periods. All the houses of the Forest Burghers were plain and modest from the outside but lavishly decorated within. The Renaissance house (No. 47) was once the *Miners' Court* (Berggericht). Now it is used by the *Slovak Mining Museum* to show its mineralogical collections and models of ore deposits. From here a medieval tunnel, which has been left in its original state, runs straight into the hillside for 76 metres. The *Trinity Column* in the middle of the square was made by Dionysius Stanetti between 1755 and 1764.

The third section of the Mining Museum is in the *Kammerhof* (Leninova ul. 18) and deals with mining technology. Around the middle of the 15th century the royal mining chamber (*Bergwerkskammer*) purchased several Romanesque houses and joined them together to form a Renaissance building with beautiful arcades around a central courtyard. This was to be the administrative centre of the Bergwerkskammer, whose main task it was to oversee the quantities of ore extracted in all the surrounding mines. The Bergwerkskammer was based in Schemnitz from the early 13th century until 1328, then moved to Kremnitz (Kremnica), returning eventually to Schemnitz in 1587.

The two most notable churches in the town are the parish church of *St Nicholas*, built in the 13th century as a Late Romanesque basilica and given a Neo-Classical transformation in the 18th century, and *St Catherine*, built between 1488 and 1491 and formerly called the 'Slovak Church' because the priests there preached in Slovak. The *Old Town Hall* dates back to the Gothic period and was renovated in the Renaissance style in the 16th century. Another survival is the *Piargská brána*, a gate with Renaissance and Baroque features, now some way out of the town. From the *Klopačka* tower built in 1681 the miners were called to their shifts by banging on a wooden panel. Today this is still done in the summer months at 10 am every day.

The *New Castle* (Nový zámok) on the Jungfrauenberg was built between 1554 and 1571 as a fortification to guard against the Turks. The six-storey fortress, built on a square ground plan, has round bastions protecting its corners. The New Castle now contains a Museum of the Turkish Wars (16th and 17th centuries).

About 2 km east of the town centre rises the Kalvária hill (727 metres) with a group of religious buildings dating from between 1744 and 1751. A sequence of seventeen Stations of the Cross along a *scala santa* links a chapel at the foot of Scharffenberg with the church on the hill with a Crucifixion tableau. Next to a medieval water-basin, the *Klingersee* (Klinger Lake), is a reconstruction of the part of an old ore mine that was above ground.

5 km south of Banská Štiavnica is the village of **Antol** above which rises the *St. Anton Château*, a magnificent Baroque building set in the middle of a well-kept park and full of unusual furniture and extremely interesting collections. In 1744 the Hungarian Nádorispán (Palatine, or Viceroy) General Andreas J. Kohar built the house on the site of a medieval castle of refuge which in the 16th century had still barred the way of the Turks to the mining town of Schemnitz. Opposite the main doorway stands the castle chapel with illusionistic frescoes by Anton Schmidt (late 18th century) and a Baroque, shingle-covered belltower. All the rooms, are decorated with works by Dutch, French and German masters, valuable old prints, chromolithographs, daguerreotypes and around 2000 hunting trophies, with forests of antlers lining the corridors. The most interesting rooms, which have largely preserved their original decoration, are the great Louis XVI-style Audience Room, the Golden Salon with its stove shaped as a seated oriental, the Chinese Salon with Rococo furnishings from the first half of the 18th century, the little Gaming Room with a gaming table made by the Augsburg master Johann Mann, and the Blue Salon. The *park* covers 30 hectares and merges with the surrounding forest; there are some fine trees, including a magnificent sequoia.

Rising above the little spa of **Bojnice** a few kilometres west of Prievidza (Priewitz), in the middle of forests, stands one of the oldest and most interesting castles in Slovakia: *Bojnice Castle* (Bojnický hrad). Nothing remains of either the first wooden fortress (1113) or the stone castle built by the Hungarian warlord and king-maker Matúš Čák (1321), but the present Neo-Gothic building preserves features of the massive fortifications of the 15th and 16th centuries. Between 1899 and 1910 the much-travelled Count Johann Pálffy, whose family had taken over the ownership of the property from the Thurzos in 1649, had the castle remodelled in the French Gothic style by Josef Hubert, creating a Romantic, fairy-tale castle, which was acquired in 1938 by the shoe manufacturer Ján Bat'a. Today the castle has a wide-ranging, not to say eclectic collection of furnishings and works of art from various periods, most of which were brought together by the last Count Pálffy.

Žilina (Sillein)

The district town of **Žilina** surrounded by hills at the confluence of the Kysuca and the Váh is notable for its successful mixture of medieval and modern buildings. Žilina is the economic and cultural centre of northern Slovakia, the home of important industries (wood, textiles, mechanical engineering, chemicals), the biggest railway junction in Slovakia and the seat of a college of transport and communications. The tourist, however, will encounter it mainly as a useful centre for exploring the Malá Fatra mountains.

In the 12th century Žilina was already a Slavic settlement, but under King Béla IV many German settlers moved there, and in 1312 it was granted a town charter under the name of *Sillein*. In 1378 the German town councillors began compiling the famous 'Silleiner Buch'

(Žilinká kniha), recording legal precedents. In 1381 the Slovak citizens received an edict from the king which guaranteed them equal rights in the town parliament (*Privilegium pro Slavis*). From 1451 the Book of Žilina was kept in two languages and soon afterwards only in Slovak. Arcaded Renaissance houses, some of them built on Gothic foundations, line the *nám. Dukla*, the centre of the historic town centre, which is encircled by ring-roads. House No. 1 on the corner of Radnička ul. is the *Old Town Hall* (Stará radnica). Dominating the south-west corner of the square is the former *Jesuit monastery* with a church dating from 1743. The Baroque statue of the Virgin in the square was erected in 1738. To the north-east of the market place, in Fučikova ul., stands the stately *parish church*. It was built around the middle of the 13th century as a Romanesque basilica, given a Gothic renovation around 1400 and a free-standing Renaissance belltower in 1540. *Trinity Church* (Kostol sv. Trojice) in Dolný val (Lower Rampart) dates from the Gothic period. The northern edge of the old town is marked by the Baroque *Franciscan Church* dating from 1723–1730.

At the point where the Kycisa flows into the Váh stands the medieval fortified customs post called *Budatín* (Budatínsky zámok). It was originally built as a moated Romanesque castle in the first half of the 13th century. Between 1545 and 1551 the residential tower was extended by the Hungarian magnate György Sunyog who built a Renaissance palace with three wings. The castle underwent Baroque alterations in 1713. It now houses a museum of the Váh Valley (Považské múzeum) with a collection of paintings and local crafts.

The little fortified church of *St Stephen* (Kostol sv. Štefana) on the Závodská cesta beyond the little Rajčanka river dates from the 13th century. It is one of the earliest Romanesque buildings in Slovakia and may stand on the site of the earliest Slavic settlement. The church is famous for its 14th-century wall paintings.

One of the most delightful tourist regions in all Czechoslovakia is the **Orava** (Arva) district in the northernmost tip of central Slovakia. The White Orava (Biela Orava) winds its way through many ranges of hills to join the water of the Black Orava (Czerna Orawa) from Poland at the Vodná nádrž Orava reservoir (35 sq km) before turning south-west towards the Váh. The reservoir with its plentiful fish and many campsites forms a single large resort area.

The main tourist sight in the region is *Orava Castle* (Oravský hrad), one of Slovakia's most beautiful border castles, which for more than 700 years has seemed to hover over the village of Oravský Podzámok on a limestone cliff 122 metres above the river. The castle is thought to date from the beginning of the 13th century, but is first mentioned in documentary sources in 1267, as *Castrum Arva*, the property of King Béla IV. At that time it guarded the trade traffic and the Polish frontier. After frequent changes of ownership it passed in 1532 to Jan of Dubova (Dubovec), who modernized and strengthened the defences to cope with the Turkish threat and built a new five-storey palace. Finally the powerful magnate and mine-owner Ferenc Thurzo made the castle his property. He and his son György further extended the fortifications from 1556 to 1574 and 1606 to 1611, adding bastions for heavy artillery. They also remodelled all the buildings in the Renaissance style. The well-bearded György is

The Castle at Orava

commemorated in the castle chapel by a fine tomb sculpture (G. Mevinola, 1616). The Baroque high altar (1752) is charming. Count Edmund Zichy (1842–1894) and after him Johann Pálffy (1895–1904) carried out Gothicizing restorations – the castle had been damaged by fire in 1800 – and created a folk museum. Between 1953 and 1968 Oravský hrad was completely restored and since then has contained collections illustrating the history of the Orava region.

Malá Fatra (Little Fatra Mountains)

From Žilina a side road leads eastwards via Teplicka nad Váhom (Teplitz an der Waag) and Belá to **Terchová**, the birthplace of the Slovak folk hero Juro Jánosík (1688–1713), by turns a rebel fighter in Rakoczi's anti-Habsburg uprising, a priest and a Robin Hood. After only a couple of years brigandage, however, he was captured and hanged by a spit thrust through his left ribs – which did not prevent him jibing at his tormenters. As R.W. Seton-Watson wrote in 1908, 'Jánosík is a name which lives in the mouth of every Slovak: wherever injustice is done, there his name is to be found, and there is hardly a river, a valley, a cave or a precipice in all Slovensko with which it is not connected.'

At Terchová we take a turning southwards and after a few kilometres reach the enchanting **Vrátna Valley** (Vrátna dolina) through which flows the Vrátnanka. This is the centre of the Malá Fatra, a popular region for winter sports and hiking. A chair lift takes visitors up to near the summit of Vel'ky Kriván (1709 metres), the highest mountain in the range.

Eastern Slovakia (Východní Slovensko)

Košice (Kaschau; Kassa)

Only 25 km or so from the Hungarian border, in the broad valley of the Hornád (Kundert; Hernad) lies the city of **Košice**, the administrative centre of the region of East Slovakia. With a population of 240,000 it is the second largest city in Slovakia and has a university, technical college and a large iron works. Košice is a bishop's see and was for many centuries a predominantly German town under Hungarian kings.

The earliest documents mentioning *Kaschau* or *Kassa* date from the 13th century: in 1216 a monastery was founded here; in 1230 the parish church of the *'villa'* was established, and in 1244 King Béla IV of Hungary granted special privileges to 'Our guests at Kassa' (*hospites nostri de Cassa*), that is, the Saxon colonists. In 1261 King Stephen V rewarded the loyal services of two Germans, Samphleben and Obel, with the old castle of Kaschau and all the lands belonging to it if 'they paid the King half a ferton in good gold once a year on St George's Day'. Around 1290 King Andrew III raised Kaschau to a town, and in 1342 it received from King Louis I the status of a royal free town, which brought with it further privileges, such as the right to elect judges and parish priests freely, to hold annual markets within the walls at their own discretion, to forbid the selling of foreign wines in Kaschau and to be exempt from tithes. In 1369 Louis I granted the town a coat of arms – the first civic coat of arms in Europe.

In the 14th century flourishing trade with Hungary and Poland, made Kaschau grow to become the second largest town in Hungary (after Buda). With the other royal free towns in East Slovakia (Leutschau, Bartfeld, Preschau and Sabinov) it formed the *Pentapolis*, a loose federation created for exchanging views and coming to common decisions. From 1459 Kaschau was permitted to mint its own coins, at first sporadically, but on a regular basis from 1511 onwards. Towards the end of the 15th century the town had 635 houses and more than 4000 inhabitants.

In 1657 Leopold I, King of Hungary and Bohemia, and later also Holy Roman Emperor, founded the University of Kaschau (Academia Casoviensis), which was in continual existence until 1921. A university printing house was started in 1674, and later published the famous 'Kaschau Calendar' in four languages (German, Hungarian, Slovak and Latin). The Turkish Wars, the Rebellion of the Estates and the Peasants' Revolts resulted in the economic decline of the town, and in the 18th century Kaschau lost its importance in Hungary's external trade. It was not until the building of the railway (1860) that the local economy experienced a modest revival.

View of Košice (Kaschau, Kassa)

From 1918 Kaschau and the East Slovak regions became part of Czechoslovakia for two decades, until the 'Vienna Decision' of 2 November 1938 returned the Kaschau region, where the population was overwhelmingly Magyar, to Hungary, where it languished for the next few years as an insignificant border town with no hinterland. On 19 January 1945 Soviet troops marched into Kassa, and eleven days later the Slovak National Council established itself at Kassa/Košice. The 'Košice Programme' promulgated on 5 April was the basis of a new Czechoslovak constitution. In the following decades the population of the town increased fivefold, and Košice became a city. In 1952 the Technical College opened to be followed in 1959 by the Pavol Jozef Šafárik University. Today Košice has a student population of almost 20,000.

The main street follows the ancient trade route through the middle of the town, widening to form the lozenge-shaped nám. Slobody (Freedom Square; plate 64). On the south side of the square stands *St Elizabeth's Cathedral* (Dóm sv Alžbety), one of the biggest churches in Slovakia and one of the easternmost (and most interesting) Gothic churches in Europe. At the west front the north tower rises to a height of 59 metres while the south tower was left unfinished. The present cathedral was built around the turn of the 15th century, to replace the old Romanesque parish church which had undergone Gothic alterations between 1380 and 1385 before finally being demolished in 1420. The new cathedral was built in a number of separate campaigns, and with each break in construction the new architects changed the design. The last phase was between 1504 and 1508, though the cathedral was not finally to achieve its present form until 1877–1896.

The magnificent north door, the 'Golden Gate' (*porta aurea*) of 1460 is particularly impressive (plate 65). Between the two doors stands a statue of St Elizabeth, to whom the cathedral is dedicated. This Hungarian princess, born in Bratislava, was the daughter of King Andrew II; after the death on crusade of her husband, Landgrave Ludwig of Thuringia, she

Košice (Kaschau,
Kassa)
 1 Cathedral of St
   Elizabeth
 2 Urban Tower
 3 Chapel of St
   Michael
 4 Bishop's Palace
 5 Forgách Palace
 6 Black Eagle
 7 State Theatre
 8 Komitat House
 9 Café Slavia
10 Leutschau
   (Levoča) House
11 Premonstratensian
   Church
12 Plague Column
13 East Slovak
   Gallery
14 East Slovak
   Museum
15 Executioner's
   Bastion
16 Nicholas Prison
17 Ursuline Convent
18 Dominican Church
19 Franciscan Church
20 Technical Museum

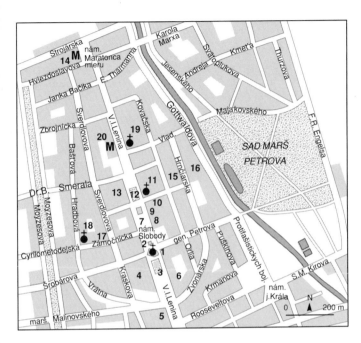

devoted her life to caring for the sick, poor and old, and was canonized in 1235, only four years after her death. Her acts of mercy are shown in the two reliefs flanking the tympanum, which contains a carving of the Last Judgement.

The interior of the five-aisled church is dominated by the St Elizabeth altar with one of the largest panelled *altarpieces* in Europe, 11 metres high and 8 metres wide (1474–1477). The 48 panels, 12 of which show scenes from the life of the saint, are attributed to Stephen and Alexander of Kaschau. The sculptural parts of the altarpiece, larger than life-size figures of the Madonna, St Elizabeth of Hungary, and St Elizabeth, the mother of John the Baptist, are by Master Erhard of Ulm. In 1906 the remains of Ferenc Rákóczi II (1676–1735) were brought home to Kassa from the Turkish town of Tekirdağ on the Sea of Marmara, where the great fighter for Hungarian freedom had spent the last 18 years of his life, and were buried together with those of his comrades-in-arms in a crypt specially built for the purpose. The Chapel of St Stephen to the left of the sacristy and the Chapel of St John are also of interest.

Next to the cathedral rises the free-standing *Urban Tower* (Urbanova věža), a 14th-century belltower given Renaissance alterations by Martin Lindner in 1628. In 1912 arcades replaced the old market booths on the tower. Grave stones from the cathedral graveyard, some of them dating from the 13th century, now cover the walls of the arcade. Beyond the cathedral stands *St Michael's Chapel* (Kaplnka sv. Michala; 1260). From about 1400 the building was used as a cemetery chapel. A relief on the gable of the doorway dating from around that time shows the Archangel Michael weighing the souls of the dead.

West of St Michael's the *Bishop's Palace* (1901-02) makes an attempt with its mixture of historical styles to fit in with the medieval buildings around the main square. The grandiose palace façade imitates Baroque forms, but elements of the Vienna Sezession crop up here and there in the plasterwork. South of it stands the Neo-Classical *Forgách Palace* built in the 1830's for the Hungarian magnate family of Forgács. On the opposite side of the square is the famous hotel *U čierneho orla* (Zum schwarzen Adler; The Black Eagle), a Neo-Classical building of 1782.

The other dominant feature in the square is the imposing *State Theatre* (Štátne divadlo; plate 63), built between 1897 and 1899 by Adolf A. Lany in an eclectic Renaissance-Baroque style. Kaschau's first permanent theatre building was established in 1789, at a time when plays or operas were performed here in German or Italian.

It was in the *Komitat House* (Dom Košického vládneho programmu, or Bývalý župný dom) that the provisional coalition Czechoslovak government proclaimed the 'Košice Programme' on 5 April 1945, which set the agenda for post-war Czechoslovakia. Among its provisions were some autonomy for Slovakia (now reunited with the Czech lands), the expulsion of Germans and Magyars, the redistribution of land, the nationalization of industry, retribution for wartime collaborators, and close cooperation with the Soviet Union. The Komitat House is a Late Baroque and Neo-Classical building with a splendid central frontispiece, built by Johann Langer in 1779 as the residence of the Hungarian Palatine (in Hungarian, nádorispán: the local administrator). A relief on the wall commemorates the fact that the Russian Marshal Mikhail I. Kutuzov stayed at this house from 30 December 1805 to 4 January 1806, returning from Austerlitz (see p. 303), where he had watched the army he had so carefully shepherded thrown away by the Tsar.

Next to the tall Art Nouveau house with pastel-coloured paintings, now the *Café Slávia* (Kaviareň Slávia), stands the Late Gothic *Levoča House* (Levočský dom), which the Hungarian magnate Alexius Thurzo gave in 1442 to Leutschau (Levoča), the capital of the Zips region, as its headquarters in Kaschau for envoys and merchants. In 1469 the town council of Kaschau acquired the building and converted it into an elegant inn which remains a popular meeting place today. The *Premonstratensian Church* (Kostol Premonštrátov; 1671–1684) with its massive twin-towered ashlar façade was originally part of a Jesuit monastery and until the suppression of the order served as the university church. In 1773 it passed to the Premonstratensians. The *Marian column* north of the theatre dates from 1723.

The *East Slovak Gallery* (Východoslovenská galéria) in an old palace in Leninova is part of the *East Slovak Museum* (Východoslovenské múzeum) which has its main building in nám. Maratónu mieru (Freedom Marathon Square) with interesting collections of folklore and applied arts, including the 'Košice Treasure', a hoard of gold coins dating from the 15th to 17th centuries minted at Kremnica, hidden by the town council during the Thököly rebellion in the 1670's and only rediscovered in 1935.

To the right of the former Jesuit church we come to the *Executioner's Bastion* (Katova bašta), a remnant of the 13th-century town fortifications. A little further east is the *Nicholas Prison* (Miklušova veznica), converted in the 16th century from two Late Gothic burghers' houses, which was still being used for prisoners until 1909. The cells, underground passages and torture chambers are open to the public.

Almost 30 km north-east of Košice is the **Herl'any** geyser. Every 32 to 34 hours the water under a mushroom-shaped concrete slab begins to seeth and rumble, and a jet of 40,000 to 60,000 litres of warm (14°C) water shoots out of an opening 35 metres into the air. This lasts for approximately half an hour, after which the water and carbon dioxide have to accumulate again before the next outburst. In the 18th century Herl'any (Herlein) was a popular spa which was successful in treating a wide variety of ailments. However, the spring did not produce enough water. Boring in the 1870's revealed the unusual geyser, but also showed that the quantity of water would never be sufficient for a viable spa. By telephoning Košice 116 the visitor can find out when the next eruption is due.

About 25 km west of Košice is the little town of **Jasov** (Jossau) set in the middle of delightful countryside with a former *Premonstratensian abbey*, which is the largest monastery in Slovakia and one of the finest Baroque buildings in Czechoslovakia. A Romanesque monastery is recorded here at the turn of the 12th century. Gothic alterations were made in the 14th century and it was fortified in the 15th. Around the middle of the 18th century Abbot Andreas Schauberer had the old monastery demolished and between 1750 and 1766 built a new Late Baroque building to designs by Franz Anton Pilgram with a church dedicated to St John the Baptist. The plain-speaking Baroque of the façade has one unusual element: the ball decoration of the first-storey capitals. The illusionistic wall paintings are the work of Johann Lucas Kracker, who also painted the impressive ceiling painting of the *Allegory of the Arts and Sciences* in the famous library. The plasterwork is by Johann Hennevogel, the sculptures by Johann Anton Krauss, who also carved the extremely expressive statue of *Bishop Friedrich* and the statues of *St Philip the Apostle* and *St Gilbert of Sempringham* (a Lincolnshire man) in the church. The enormous monastery now contains an old people's home and a museum of handicrafts, but is closed at present for restoration. Behind the monastery is a French Baroque garden with a hothouse in a transitional style between Rococo and Neo-Classicism.

A high cliff on the bank of the River Bodva on the northern edge of Jasov is the location of the **Jasovská jaskyňa** karst cave, which was already inhabited in neolithic times. During the Mongol invasions and the Hussite troubles the inhabitants of Jasov took refuge in this network of caves. Of the 2122 metres of the cave system so far explored, 618 metres are open to visitors.

8 km east of the town of Rožňava (Rosenau) stands **Krásna Hôrka Castle** perched on a rocky hilltop. Count Dedrich, called Bebek, built the first residential tower with defensive walls in the 13th century to guard the roads between Zips, the Gemer (Gömer) region and the Košice basin. In 1318 this fortified residence passed to the noble family of Mariássy who built a hall range (*palas*) and extended the castle ward. In 1352 the castle returned to the possession of the Bebeks, who commissioned the Italian architect Alessandro da Vedano to convert the property into a strong Renaissance fortress between 1539 and 1545. However, because of the Bebek family's activities as counterfeit coiners, King Maximilian confiscated the castle and gave it to Peter Andrássy. The Andrássys added further domestic buildings, modernized the fortifications and in 1903 even set up a richly appointed family museum which they opened to visitors. Since 1945 Krásna Hôrka has belonged to the state. In 1961 it was declared a National Cultural Monument. Many of the rooms still contain their original furnishings: the castle kitchen, the dining hall, the residential apartments, the music room, and the audience hall. The artillery bastion and the fine collection of arms are also of interest.

Within sight of the castle, near Krásnohorské Podhradie on the road to Košice, stands the *Andrássy Mausoleum*, built by the Hungarian Count Dénes Andrássy in 1903-04 for his beloved Bohemian wife Františka Hablavcová (Franziska Hablawetz). Their marriage was considered a *mésalliance*, since the beautiful Františka was a celebrated singer at the Vienna Opera and not of noble blood. The count was disowned by his family and he followed his wife round the great cities of the world. The mausoleum, a Jugendstil masterpiece designed and executed mainly by Munich artists, combines the most precious materials – marbles of various colours from all over the world, polished agate and Venetian glass.

Nearly every village in the beautiful countryside of what was Upper Hungary (now Slovakia) has its manor house, in a more or less good state of repair, a sort of secondary residence for the Hungarian aristocracy, often a hunting lodge and usually smaller than a full-sized schloss. Many of these houses have been used, since their Hungarian owners were expropriated, for institutional purposes, as old people's homes, youth hostels, holiday homes for trade unions, homes for the handicapped or mentally ill. The finest and most interesting houses have been carefully restored and with their contents – often supplemented with additional exhibits – are open to the public.

One such is **Betliar** situated on the edge of village with a population of 2000 (plate 57). Originally a medieval fort, it came into the possession of the Andrássy family in the 16th century and was remodelled several times over the centuries to suit prevailing tastes: first Renaissance, then Baroque, then Neo-Classical (1792–1795), before undergoing its final eclectic transformation between 1880 and 1886. Some of the original furnishings dating from the 17th to the 20th centuries survive in the grander rooms, such as the music salon, gaming room, hunting salon, dining hall, library (with about 20,000 books) and the great entrance hall. Among the contents of the house is a wonderful wedding chest from the Zips region (1653). The English park attached to the house was laid out around the turn of the century with fountains (e.g. the Psyche Fountain in front of the house), pavilions and sculptures. Betliar is currently under restoration.

Probably the finest dripstone cave in Slovakia – perhaps in all Czechoslovakia – is the **Domica jaskyňa** on the Hungarian border (10 km from Plešivec in the direction of the frontier). The cave system with its extraordinary drip shields, sinter drums and cascades extends for 21 km, far into Hungary, following the course of the River Styx. When buying a ticket be sure to take a tour which includes a boat trip on the Styx.

Spiš (Zips)

The historic region extending from the High Tatras to the Slovak Ore Mountains was called *Zips* by its German inhabitants, *Spiš* by its Slovak population and *Szepes* by the Hungarian magnates. The origin of the name is disputed: some believe it to be derived from the *Gepiden*, an East Germanic people who settled here before the Slavs, others from the Latin *saepes* ('fence'), while Slovak philologists find its root in the Slavonic word *zepish* ('collection of tithes').

King Géza II of Hungary (1141–1162) encouraged German colonists to settle here and already in 1249 King Béla IV granted the two largest Zips settlements, Leutschau and Käsmark, the privileges of royal free towns. From then on the two towns were in continual competition with each other for the leading economic position in the region; Leutschau was usually slightly ahead. In 1271 the 'Zipser Sachsen' ('Zips Saxons'), as the German settlers called themselves, had their privileges confirmed by King Stephen V. At the same time they joined to form the 'Federation of the 24 Free Towns of Zips', which elected its own count, had its own jurisdiction, took care of its own hunting, fishing, land-clearance and prospecting rights and chose its judges and parish priests. Much to the chagrin of the Käsmarkers, the federation chose the Royal Town of Leutschau (Levoča) as the residence of its count, and hence the capital of Zips. In 1370 the federation produced its own code of law, called the 'Zipser Willkür', with 95 articles derived from the German Sachsenspiegel and Hungarian law. A second federation of towns was formed in 1276 in Lower Zips, the 'Gründner Boden' in the Zipser Erzgebirge (now Slovenské rudohorie, Slovak Ore Mountains), where six mining towns gathered around the royal free town of Göllnitz (Gelnica) and proclaimed themselves the 'Federation of the Seven Zips Mining Towns'.

In 1412 the Emperor Sigismund (who was also King of Hungary) needed money for his war against Venice, and so mortgaged 13 Zips towns for 37,000 Bohemian silver groschen to his brother-in-law Władisław Jagiełło of Poland. These 13 mortgaged towns which now belonged to Poland joined with three other towns to form the 'Federation of the 16 Towns', which although they were placed under a *starost*, or Royal governor, continued to enjoy their old Zips privileges. The 'Federation of the Eleven Towns' remained in Hungary.

Over the following centuries the position of the Zips towns worsened. The anti-Habsburg rebellions of the Hungarian nobles and the Turkish Wars often brought trade to a standstill, and mining declined. After the Thirty Years' War the rigorous re-Catholicizing of the region drove many Germans away. The towns of Hungarian Zips came under increasingly severe pressure from the Magyar aristocracy, and the influence of the magnate families – Zápolya, Thurzo, Csáky, Thököly and the rest – increased. For the mortgaged towns, where the Polish starosts exerted arbitrary rule, things were even harder. At the request of the townspeople the Austrians under Count Imre Eszterházy finally occupied the Polish-held towns in 1769, and thus after an interval of 357 years Zips was once again a single state.

The towns which had been thus regained were 'peculiar Crown property' and from then on formed a province of 16 Zips crown towns with the capital at Neudorf (Hungarian: Igló; now Spišska Nová Ves). The seven Zips mining towns with their capital at Göllnitz also had their own laws, and the two royal free towns, Leutschau and Käsmark, at first retained their privileges. The Federation of the Eleven Towns had meanwhile collapsed, to be replaced by the rule of the Hungarian aristocracy.

In 1876 the last Zips towns lost their autonomy and the rest of their privileges. They were all incorporated into the newly

Typical houses of the Spiš (Zips) region

created Komitat of Zips. There were few protests, since most Zips Saxons supported the efforts of Hungary to create a uniform state. From then on Hungarian was the only language spoken in secondary schools, and those wishing to escape Magyarization emigrated to America. When the Germans emigrated the Slovaks moved in. In the aftermath of the First World War and the breakup of the Habsburg Monarchy, Hungary gained its independence, but lost the regions of Upper Hungary to Czechoslovakia. The Czechoslovak government put an end to the process of Magyarization and the German-speakers once again had their own schools. In 1920 the creation of a 'Zipser Deutsche Partei' was permitted. Zips continued to be a German language-island, although the proportion of German-speakers had

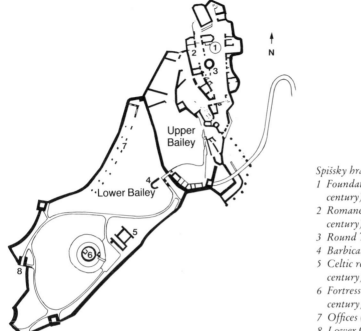

Spišsky hrad (Zipser Burg) plan
1 *Foundations of tower (11th century)*
2 *Romanesque Palace (13th century)*
3 *Round Tower (13th century)*
4 *Barbican (14th century)*
5 *Celtic religious building (2nd century)*
6 *Fortress of Ján Jiskra (15th century)*
7 *Offices (17th century)*
8 *Lower Gate (15th century)*

dropped between 1847 and 1919 from 33 per cent to 23 per cent. In 1944-45 nearly all Zips Saxons were forced to leave the country.

In the 11th century Zips was still part of royal fiefdom ruled by the Ispán (High Sheriff) of Torna, but in the first half of the 12th century the royal komitat of Zips was created with its administrative centre at an early Slavic castle, which gradually developed into **Zips Castle (Spišský hrad)**, the largest castle in Slovakia, indeed one of the largest castles in the whole of Europe.

The nucleus of the early medieval fortress was a large round tower, the foundations of which have only recently come to light. At the beginning of the 13th century the Romanesque hall range (*palas*) was built, with a great hall on the first floor and private rooms on the second. After the collapse of the original tower it was replaced by a new round tower in the Lombard style. From 1209 the palas was the residence of the Ispán of Zips. The castle survived the Mongol invasion of the 13th century largely unscathed, and further buildings were added: an outer ward with the residence of the chapter provost and a Romanesque castle chapel. The most extensive building work was undertaken in the 15th century under Ján Jiskra, who surrounded the western slope, an area measuring 285 by 115 metres, with a strong wall, and built a separate fortress in the middle of the military camp thus created. This camp below the castle (known as the Lower Castle) had its own gateway protected by massive towers facing the new town of Kirchdrauf (now Spišské Podhradie).

Soon after Jiskra's death Zips Castle came into the possession of King Matthias I Corvinus of Hungary who gave it to the brothers István and Imre Zápolya (Zápol'ský). They remodelled the Romanesque palas in the Gothic style and built a new chapel as well as several residential buildings. In 1540 the castle passed to the Thurzo family who made alterations in the Renaissance style and at the same time reinforced the fortifications in line with the latest military techniques. In 1710 Habsburg troops forced the Rákóczi rebels who held the castle to capitulate.

In 1945 the state took over Spišský hrad and in 1969 a lengthy process of research and conservation began. Today the visitor can view the extensive fortifications and rooms, and there is a small museum showing arms and armour from Zips's past, and some instruments of medieval punishment. Even more impressive than the mighty ruins is the view from the castle of the little town of Spišské Podhradie at its foot, the village of Spišská Kapitula with the Romanesque double tower of the cathedral and the magnificent Zips countryside.

The Provostry of Zips was established in 1202 just next to Zips Castle on Pažit' hill as the centre of ecclesiastical administration for the region; it is now a bishopric. The foundations of an 11th-century Augustinian monastery were used for the new buildings, which were erected around 1209 by the provost on the orders of the Archbishop of Esztergom. They comprised the Provost's residence and a capitular church in the form of a Romanesque rotunda. Around this nucleus an ecclesiastical township developed which became known as **Zipser Kapitel (Spišská Kapitula)**. Also in 1209 the 24 parish priests of the Zips towns joined together to form a fraternity. In 1569 the Zips Chapter went over en masse to the teachings of Martin Luther.

The most important building in the little walled town is the *Cathedral of St Martin*, the handsome principal church of the Zips Chapter, built between 1245 and 1273 in the Late Romanesque style, and converted in the 15th century into a three-aisled Late Gothic hall church, though without losing its muscular simplicity. On the south side of the cathedral the Gothic funerary chapel of the Zápolya family was built from 1488 to 1493. Two red marble Renaissance tomb slabs commemorate the lords of the Komitat of Zips and Hungarian Palatines Imre (d. 1487) and István (d. 1499) Zápolya. On the north door to the cathedral is a Gothic fresco (1317) showing the coronation of Charles Robert of Anjou as King of Hungary on 20 August 1310. Probably the earliest wall painting in Zips, it was commissioned by the Provost of Zips from one of the Italian artists who were already working for the Anjou family in Naples. The portal is guarded by a lion dating from the second half of the 13th century. The fine altarpiece has a Coronation of the Virgin surrounded by several restored panels that are masterpieces of late 15th-century painting. In 1989 the state finally agreed to the appointment of a new Bishop of Spiš after the see had been vacant for several decades.

5 km south-east of Spišský hrad is the little village of **Žehra**, with a tiny, frescoed Romanesque church and an onion dome that seems more like a pumpkin.

The present district town of **Spišská Nová Ves** (Neudorf) is worth visiting mainly for the Gothic parish church of the *Assumption* built in the second half of the 14th century to replace an earlier Romanesque church. The tympanum of the south doorway with a relief showing the Coronation of the Virgin dates from this period. After an earthquake the nave and aisle were given a new cross-rib vault around 1445. The elegant tower has Neo-Gothic alterations and only reached its present height of 86 metres in the late 19th century. Inside the church the *Crucifixion* group was made by Master Paul of Leutschau (Levoča) and the *Man of Sorrows* by Master Nicholas of Leutschau, while the Gothic reliquary *cross* is a work of the Neudorf goldsmith Mikuláš Galica.

The *Zips House* (No. 58) was the administrative centre of the Federation of the 16 Towns. Its core is a Gothic house built in the 14th century which was later remodelled in the 17th century and given Rococo alterations between 1763 and 1765. The façade is decorated with splendid stucco ornaments. The austerely beautiful *Redoute*, now the Theatre, is a jewel of the Vienna Sezession style built between 1900 and 1905 by Kálmán Gerster. The Neo-Classical *Town Hall* of Spišská Nová Ves was erected in the 18th century.

The road from Levoča to Poprad passes the small town of **Spišský Štvrtok** (Donnersmarkt), a member of the Federation of 24 Towns. Just outside the town in the midst of fertile fields stands *St Ladislas*, a Gothic church incorporating some Romanesque remains, which was consecrated in 1263. Beside it is the *funerary chapel* of the Palatine István Zápolya, built by Master Hans Puchsbaum, one of the builders of St Stephen's Cathedral in Vienna. The adjacent monastery dates from 1668. Near the church archaeologists have discovered the fortified bronze age settlement of *Mysia Hôrka* (1500 BC), where objects related to Mycenean culture have been found.

The town of **Poprad**, the 'Gateway to the High Tatras', lies on the river Poprad (Popper) which flows via the Dunajec (Dunajetz) to the Vistula. It is an industrial town (carriage works), with a population of 38,000. Founded in the 12th century by settlers from Middle Germany as 'Deutschendorf', it received its town charter in 1221 and fifty years later joined the 'Federation of the 24 Free Towns of Zips'.

The main square of Poprad is lozenge-shaped, an indication that the town was founded on a major road. The Early Gothic church of *St Giles* was built in the 13th century and was given its Renaissance appearance in the 15th century, as was the free-standing belltower with its impressive spire. The sgraffito decoration on the tower façade, at present obscured by plaster, is to be uncovered by restorers in the near future.

The district town of Poprad includes the town once known as *Forum Sabathi* or *Georgenberg* but now called **Spišská Sobota**, another of the 24 towns of the Zips Federation. The Late Romanesque church of *St George* (mid–13th century) was transformed into a

Gothic building between 1460 and 1464 by the architect Josef Steinmetz. The winged altarpiece was made by Paul of Leutschau (Pavol of Levoča) in 1516 and the paintings are the work of Master John from Neusohl (Banská Bystrica). This German craftsmen's town has retained much of its Zips character, as shown for instance in the five burghers' houses with overhanging eaves which stand side by side on the main square. They were built from the middle of the 16th to the beginning of the 17th century.

The little town of **Gelnica** (Göllnitz) in the south-east corner of the Zips region, in what was known as the 'Gründner Boden', has a central importance in the history of the Zips towns. Its location in the Slovak Ore Mountains attracted miners, particularly from Bavaria. In 1264 it was granted a mining privilege and thereafter provided a supreme court for matters of mining law for the surrounding six mining towns. From 1276 Göllnitz was a royal Hungarian free town and capital of the 'Seven Zips Mining Towns': Göllnitz, Jekelsdorf, Kochseifen, Margaretendorf, Einsiedeln, Wagendrüssel and Krompach. The Göllnitz mining law (Göllnitzer Bergrecht) of the first half of the 15th century was valid for all Hungarian mines. Places of interest in the town include the 14th-century Gothic *Parish Church*, the royal *Castle* built between the 13th and 15th centuries (a ruin since 1527), the *Old Town Hall*, Baroque and Neo-Classical burghers's houses, typical miners' houses and a museum of mining.

Slovenský raj (Slovak Paradise)

South-west of Spišská Nová Ves stretches the wild romantic beauty of **Slovenský raj**, the 16 km long gorge of the Hornád and its tributary, the Hnilec, with steeply rising cliffs reaching a height of 150 metres. Platforms and iron gangways have made even the steepest sections climbable. In 1988 the area was declared a national park.

The most remarkable sight in Slovensky raj is the **Dobšiná ice cave** (Dobsinská l'adová jaskyna) on the road from Poprad to Rožňava. An underground area of about 7000 sq metres is covered with bizarre ice shapes. Even in the summer months the temperature in the cave is minus 7°C, so warm clothes should be worn for the guided tours, which last almost an hour.

Levoča (Leutschau; Löcse)

The capital of Zips and the best preserved medieval town in Slovakia is **Levoča**, once known as the 'Königin der Zips', the 'Queen of Zips' (plate 56). The old walled town is like a magnificent museum. It has been called the 'Nuremberg of Slovakia' and the 'Rothenburg of Zips', but neither of these comparisons really does justice to the delightful Slovak town, which once had a reputation throughout Europe as a centre of trade.

Levoča, High Altar of Church of St James, Attempted Martyrdom of St John. ▷

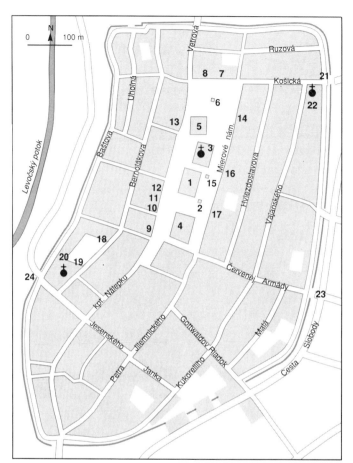

Levoča (Leutschau,
Löcse)
1 Town Hall
2 Pillory
3 St James
4 Lutheran Church
5 School
6 L'udovít Štúr
  Memorial
7 Little Komitat
  House
8 Great Komitat
  House
9 Burgher's House
  No. 40 (Lyceum)
10 Mariássy House
11 Krupek House
12 Spillenberg House
13 Municipal Inn
14 Thurzo House
15 Soviet Army
  Memorial
16 House of Master
  Paul
17 Breuer's Printing
  House
18 Grammar School
  (Gymnázium)
19 Minorite Friary
20 School Church
  (Gymnázialny
  Kostol)
21 Košice Gate
22 New Minorite
  Church
23 Menhard Gate
24 Polish Gate

A Slavic settlement at the crossing of two important trade routes between Cracow, Hungary, Nuremberg, Prague and Vienna was probably in existence by the 12th century. At the beginning of the 13th century German merchants and craftsmen settled there and soon brought commercial prosperity to the town. According to an unlikely story in the chronicle of Caspar Hain (see p. 399) the name is supposed to have originated in 1245 when occasional groups of Mongol raiders passed through Zips and the sentries warned the people: '*Leuth schaut*, gebt achtung, stellet euch zur Wehre, der Feind kombt!' ('People look, watch out, be on guard, the enemy is coming!'). In 1249 Leutschau received its town charter and all the privileges which could be useful to a trading centre. In 1271 the Zips Saxons chose Leutschau as the head of their Federation of 24 Towns, in effect the capital of Zips.

In the 16th century neither the Turkish wars nor the struggles for the throne hindered the economic and cultural flourishing of Leutschau. Indeed it was during this Renaissance period that the most splendid buildings were erected. In 1550, however, almost the whole town, including the town hall containing the Zips archives, was consumed by a great fire, and in 1600 half the population was wiped out by the plague. In the 17th century conspiracies among the Estates reduced the political importance of the town.

In the 19th century Leutschau was still the administrative centre of Zips, and it became the residence town of the Komitat of Zips, though it had by then ceased to be an important centre economically. Its conservative inhabitants prevented the founding of new businesses, its councillors opposed its integration into the railway system. Present-day Levoča has no industry to speak of, and its population earns its living mainly from tourism.

The 'Ring' (town square) of old Leutschau is now the Mierové nám. (Peace Square) of present-day Levoča. It was large enough to contain a large number of public buildings: the parish church, town hall, market hall and customs house, and more recently a second church for the Protestants. A series of magnificent patrician and burghers' houses surround the square, one of the most beautiful in all Czechoslovakia. The *Town Hall* (colour plate 21) also deserves a superlative: with its arcades, decorative gables and massive clock tower it is one of the finest Renaissance town halls in Europe. It was built between 1551 and 1559, after its predecessor was destroyed by fire. The frescoes on the façade depict the civic virtues (1615). Between 1656 and 1661 the mighty clock tower was added. The clock, a work of Master Nicholas, is the oldest in what was then Hungarian territory. The grand Council Chamber with a carved and painted wooden ceiling and panelled walls, contains portraits of the judges of Leutschau. The *Zips Museum* (Spišské múzeum) shows documents (mostly in German) relating to the political, economic and cultural development of the town. In front of the town hall stands the *Chain House*, a pillory for women (*Klietka hanby*, 'cage of shame') dating from the second half of the 16th century.

The church of *St James* (Kostol sv. Jakuba), a Gothic hall church of the 14th century (1332–1342), was renovated in the 15th century. The most outstanding of its furnishings is the Late Gothic *high altar*. This is the tallest Gothic altarpiece in the world, and also one of the most beautiful and elaborate, easily the equal of the famous altarpieces of Pacher, Stoss and Riemenschneider in the magnificence of its architectural conception and its decoration. Its creator was Master Paul of Leutschau (Pavol z Levoče), whose works are found in numerous churches in Slovakia and Hungary. The high standing of the altarpiece in Late Gothic art is an indication of the status Leutschau enjoyed in medieval Europe as a trade centre between Cracow and Budapest, Kiev and Nuremberg.

Its central panel measuring 6 by 4 metres contains the larger than life-size statues of the Virgin, St James and St John. The inner faces of the two wings each have four reliefs with scenes from the life of St James and St John, while the outer faces have eight panel paintings showing a Passion cycle, probably painted by Hans Moler of Leutschau or Theophil Stanzel of Bartfeld, who used woodcuts by Lucas Cranach the elder and Hans Schäufelein as models. The carvings on the altarpieces of St Nicholas, St Anne, the Nativity and the Four Sts John are also attributed to Master Paul. The Gothic bronze font was cast towards the end of the 14th century by a foundry in Zipser Neudorf. The Renaissance pulpit was made in 1626 by the Leutschau woodcarver Karl Kollmitz. The altars of St Catherine (c. 1460), the Man of Sorrows (1480) and St Mary in the Snow (1494) are also of interest, as is the 16th-century organ and the tombs of the powerful Thurzo family.

South of the town hall is the Neo-Classical *Protestant Church* (Evanjelický kostol) built by

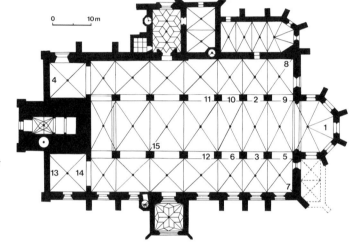

Levoča (Leutschau) St James, plan
1 *High Altar*
2 *Altar of St Nicholas*
3 *Altar of St Anne*
4 *Altar of the Nativity*
5 *Altar of the Four Sts John*
6 *Altar of St Catherine*
7 *Altar of the Man of Sorrows*
8 *Altar of Our Lady of the Sorrows*
9 *Altar of Sts Peter and Paul*
10 *Altar of the Fourteen Auxiliary Saints* 11 *Altar of the Good Shepherd* 12 *Altar of the Archangel Michael* 13 *Altar of St Elizabeth* 14 *Gothic font* 15 *Renaissance pulpit*

Anton Povolný between 1825 and 1837 on the site of a wooden church. It has a Greek cross plan with a central space surmounted by a mighty dome. The rich furnishings of the old wooden church were retained by its successor, which today houses an extensive craft collection and the valuable Zips library.

The building to the north of St James's was created around 1588 by joining together several storehouses to form a large market hall, or arsenal. This was where the town scales were kept and the finance office was housed. The town arms above the entrance indicate the former importance of the building, which was modernized first in 1810 and again between 1858 and 1862. It is now used as the *Town School*. At the northern end of the square a monument in the middle of a garden commemorates the writer Ľudovít Štúr (1815–1856), the leader of the Slovak uprising in 1848 and the creator of the Slovak literary language. Opposite the monument stands the *Little Komitat House* (Malý župný dom; No. 60) with the arms of Zips in sgraffito work. The neighbouring Neo-Classical *Great Komitat House* (Vel'ký župný dom; No. 59) was built in the first half of the 19th century by Anton Povolný.

One of the most splendid of the Renaissance houses which line the square is the *burgher's house* at No. 40, which was formed out of two Gothic houses after the 1431 fire. It was given an Early Renaissance appearance in 1530. In the 17th century it belonged to Caspar Hain, the town judge (Stadtrichter) and councillor of Leutschau, who also ran the German Latin School and wrote the famous *Zipserische oder Leutscherische Chronika undt Zeitbeschreibung*, which tells of the troubles surrounding the conspiracies among the Hungarian aristocracy against the Habsburgs and the Counter-Reformation under Leopold I. Hain's son presented the house to the Lutheran church which established its Lyceum here in the second half of the 18th century. Since 1982 the building has been used as a department of the Zips Museum which displays a most interesting exhibition of 'the Figurative Arts in Zips' with exhibits dating from the 14th to the 19th centuries, including the wooden figure of St Mary Magdalene from Danišovce (wood; c. 1410).

The *Thurzo House* (Turzov dom; No. 7; colour plate 22) with its exotic Renaissance attic was formed in the 16th century when two Gothic burghers' houses were combined. In 1903-04 István Groh, a professor of art from Budapest, and his pupils covered the façade with pretty sgraffiti in the Renaissance manner.

In the *House of Master Paul* (Dom Majstra Pavla; No. 20) the artist who carved the great St James altarpiece lived and worked. From 1515 to 1525 he was even a town councillor of Leutschau. The house now contains an exhibition (mostly copies and photographs) giving a survey of his work.

In Bernolákova ul. stands the grandiose building of the *Grammar School (Gymnasium)* (Gymnázium) dating from 1913. The adjacent *Minorite Friary* (Starý kláštor minoritov), with its Gothic cloister, goes back to a foundation by a nobleman named Dončo in 1309. It was built during the 14th century and remodelled at the beginning of the 16th. In the 16th and 17th centuries it was in the hands of the Protestants, until in 1671 the Jesuits took it over for a short time. The Gothic *Gymnasium Church* (Gymnaziálny kostol), first built between 1310 and 1320 was renovated in the 14th century and baroquized in 1671. The *town fortifications* of the 14th and 15th centuries largely survive. Of the thirteen or so bastions five are still extant, as well as two of the original three town gates, the *Menhard Gate* (Menhardská brána) and the *Košice Gate* (Košická brána), the main entrance to the town. The remains of the *Polish Gate* (Pol'ská brána) can still be seen.

Kežmarok (Käsmark)

On the right bank of the river Poprad (Popper) at the foot of the High Tatras lies **Kežmarok**, one of the towns founded by the Zips Saxons and the capital of Upper Zips. It has a medieval

Eathquake in the Snow
Mountains, 1660,
recorded in the
Leutschau Chronicle

town centre, now a conservation area, and is a good base for excursions into the High Tatras (see pp. 402f) and the Spišská Magura (see p. 405).

The settlement of Käsmark was founded around the middle of the 12th century, probably in the reign of King Géza II, by German colonists. It was made a royal free town in the 13th century. In 1433 the Hussites seized the town and remained here until 1460, when they were driven out by Matthias I Corvinus. Like Leutschau Käsmark enjoyed the privileges of an independent town subject only to the King, within the Zips federations of towns. The legal code established by the 'Zipser Willkür' (see p. 389) did not apply to the two royal towns, which had their own law codes. They vied with one another for leadership of Zips, with Leutschau usually supporting the cause of the emperor and Käsmark that of the Estates. In the 17th and 18th centuries nearly all revolts started at Käsmark. Imre Thököly, lord of Käsmark castle, led the great rebellion of 1678–1686 (see p. 402). In 1876 the crown placed all the towns of Zips, including Käsmark, under the government of the Komitat of Zips, which had its seat at Leutschau.

The old town square of Käsmark, until recently called nám. Sovietskej armády, broadens at its south end, where the *Town Hall* stands at the entrance to the wide Dukelská ul. (Dukla Street). After a fire the original Gothic building was restored in 1515 and again between 1541 and 1553 in the Renaissance style. In 1799 another storey was added and the building was given a Neo-Classical appearance. The clock tower and central frontispiece were also built in 1799. The square has some fine old *burghers' houses* with Gothic cores and Renaissance frontages. Their wooden gables with overhanging eaves and the round-arched gateways are reminiscent of rural house types.

At the east end of the elongated square, stands the *Town Castle* (Tökölyho hrad), named after its former owners, the Hungarian Counts Thököly. Here, at the point where the Tvarožniansky potok river joins the Poprad, a castle was created around 1348 out of a 12th-century nunnery, with its walls attached to the stone ramparts of the town. Between 1433 and 1460 the fortress was a stronghold of the Hussites, then it was occupied by Imre Zápolya, the Palatine (Nádorispán: the Royal Governor) of Zips. At the end of the 16th century Count Sebastian Thököly took it over and converted it into a Renaissance palazzo in the Italian style. The outer walls were given elaborate cresting and rich sgraffito decoration. Artistic plasterwork and fine furniture adorn the rooms. The Gothic chapel was given its Baroque appearance in 1657-58.

In 1678 the Hungarian Estates under the leadership of Count Imre Thököly (1656–1705) rose in rebellion here against Habsburg rule with the aim of creating a free Hungarian state. Together with his *Kuruczok* (Freedom-Fighters) Thököly had conquered the whole of Upper Hungary (i.e. present-day Slovakia) by 1682. The Ottoman Sultan Mehmed IV

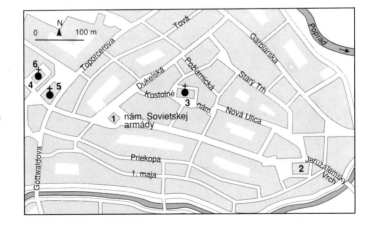

Kežmarok (Käsmark)
1 *Town Hall*
2 *Castle*
3 *Parish Church of*
  the Holy Cross
4 *Articular Church*
5 *Lutheran Church*
6 *Latin School*

appointed him Prince of Upper Hungary and later Prince of Transylvania. The Turks, of course, supported the Hungarian freedom struggle against the Habsburgs for their own ends: in 1683 they were once again outside the walls of Vienna. However, the defeat at Kahlenberg broke the power of the Ottomans, and the Habsburgs regained their power in Hungary and the Kurucz rebellion collapsed. A magnanimous amnesty exempted the Hungarian aristocracy from punishment; only their leader, Imre Thököly, was sentenced to death. He, however, went into exile and died in 1705 at Izmit in Turkey. His town castle at Käsmark was confiscated by the Imperial court and later passed into the possession of the town. It fell increasingly into decay; in the 19th century it was used as barracks, and in 1902 it even became a textile factory. Some of the rooms, since restored, were opened as a museum.

In Kostolné nám. (Kirchplatz) stands the Roman Catholic parish church of the *Holy Cross* (Kostol sv. križa), a Gothic hall church dating from the beginning of the 15th century. A magnificent net vault spans the nave and choir. Between 1589 and 1591 Master Ulrich Materer introduced Renaissance features and built the massive belltower (1586–1591) with crenellations and naïve sgraffito decoration typical of Zips towers ('Zips Renaissance').

The Articles of the Sopron (Ödenburg) Diet of 1681 allowed the Protestants in what was then Hungary to build churches again – but they had to be built outside the town walls and entirely of wood, without stone foundations. At Käsmark the carpenter Georg Müttermann of Deutschendorf (Poprad) built one such *Articular Church* (Artikularkirche) of red spruce and yew. The altar, pulpit and four columns which support the barrel vault were carved by Johann Lerch of Käsmark. The pew to the left of the altar was intended for the higher clergy, while in the pews with wooden railings below the gallery sat the town councillors and master craftsmen. When the houses nearby caught fire in 1922 the fire brigade doused the wooden ceiling with so much water that the ceiling paintings suffered considerable damage, though on the walls they have survived rather better and still have great charm. The church is one of only four surviving Articular Churches in Slovakia and is the most important example of this type of Protestant ecclesiastical architecture. (At present it is closed for restoration.)

Near the Articular Church the Viennese architect Theophil Hansen built a new *Lutheran Church* (of the Augsburg Confession) between 1879 and 1892. It is in an eclectic style mixing Renaissance and Moorish elements and measures 80 metres long, 20 metres wide and 30 metres high. The ceiling is decorated with arabesques. Above the plain wooden altar stands a figure of Christ blessing, and the building is surmounted by a high dome. On the south side of the church is the mausoleum of Imre Thököly, whose remains were brought here in 1906. The plain house behind the Articular Church is the famous *Latin School* of Käsmark, founded 400 years ago and now containing a library with more then 100,000 books.

The High Tatras (Vysoké Tatry)

The High Tatras in the northern border region of Slovakia are the most important tourist area in Czechoslovakia and the 'smallest' high mountain range in the world (just 26 km long and

17 km wide at their broadest point). A fifth of the area is in Poland and the remaining four fifths in Czechoslovak territory. About twenty peaks rise above 2500 metres, the highest being Gerlachovský štít (Gersdorfer Spitze). Ice-age glaciers, long since melted, formed the valleys and ravines, and filled the lakes. There are 35 such mountain lakes (*pleso*) on the Slovak side, popularly known as 'sea eyes' (*Morské oko*) because it used to be believed that they were connected by subterranean passages with the sea. 'The sight of anyone who bathes in them becomes bright and clear, the whole world is revealed to him; he can see through doors and walls, even the human heart lies open to him,' the story goes, 'but the eyes of anyone whose heart is sullied by sins, are covered with blindness.' Whether or not one believes the legend the water is certainly very cold and deep. The largest and deepest Slovak sea eye, the Vel'ké Hincovo pleso (Grosse Hinzensee) at a height of 1946 metres, covers an area of 20 hectares and is 53 metres deep.

In his book *Medulla Geographiae Practica* published in 1639, David Fröhlich of Käsmark praised the 'Schneegebirge' which 'surpassed the Alps of Italy, Switzerland and the Tyrol for wildness and steepness'. At the age of 15, in 1615 (a surprisingly early date for mountaineering), he had climbed the Lomnitzer Spitze (Lomnický štít; 2634 metres) together with two schoolfriends. However, it was not until 1870 that Otto Still, a teacher

The High Tatras

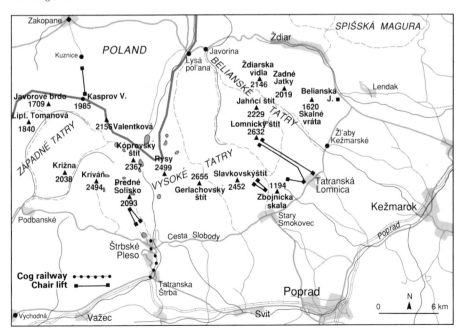

from Zips, succeeded in scaling the difficult Gersdorfer Spitze, the highest mountain in the Tatras. The first tourists appeared on the scene at the turn of the 18th century; in 1797 the spa of Schmecks (now Starý Smokovec) was founded at a mineral spring. In 1820 Count Stephen Csáky opened the first 'Tourist home as a base for researchers and agile mountain climbers'. The building of the railway to the High Tatras in 1871 led to the development of other tourist centres besides Schmecks (or Altschmecks as it became): in 1875 Neuschmecks (Nový Smokovec), in 1877 Tschirmer See (Štrbské Pleso), and in 1892 Tatra-Lomnitz (Tatranská Lomnica). In the 1870's the High Tatras began to be opened up by the creation of footpaths and mountain shelters. Between 1885 and 1893 a highway 71 km long (since the Second World War called Cesta Slobody, Freedom Road) was built around the Tatras. It connects the tourist centres between Podbanské in the west and Lysá Pol'ana in the east, and gives magnificent views of the Tatra peaks. The number of walkers, mountaineers, skiers and tobogganers has since grown to such an extent that the Slovak National Council created the *Tatras National Park* covering an area of 50,965 hectares and placed large parts of the West Tatras (Západné Tatry) and the whole of the White Tatras (Belianske Tatry) under protection. Although around 300 km of excellently signposted footpaths are still accessible, a number of popular paths are periodically closed (usually until 30 June) in the interests of conservation.

Tatranská Lomnica is the tourist centre of the High Tatras, with the headquarters of administration of the Tatras National Park (Tatranský národný park, TANAP), the centre of the rescue service and the extremely interesting National Park *museum* containing a great herbarium with plants of the Spišská Magura assembled by Cyprian, a monk and physician at the Červený Kláštor (see p. 406) in the last century. From Tatranská Lomnica two cable cars run up to *Skalnaté pleso* (Steinbachsee; 1750 metres) with the Encián mountain hotel and an observatory. From here the visitor can continue his ascent by cable car to *Lomnický štít* (2632 metres), the second highest mountain in the High Tatras, or by chair lift to *Lomnický hrebeň* (Lomnitzer Kamm; 2200 metres). In the summer of 1989 another cable car between Skalnaté pleso and Lomnický štít was opened.

Starý Smokovec (Altschmecks) lies at the foot of *Slavkovský štít* (Schlagendorfer Spitze; 2452 metres) in the midst of quiet coniferous forests. A cable car runs up to *Hrebionok* (Kämmchen; 1280 metres), a massive moraine embankment. From here a footpath goes through the *Malá studená dolina* (Kleines Kohlbach-Tal) to *Pät' Spišských plies* (Five Zips Lakes) in a valley surrounded by steeply rising mountain peaks (5–6 hours there and back).

Štrbské Pleso (Tschirmer See) is the highest town in Czechoslovakia, 1335 metres above sea-level. Its name comes from the most famous and most often visited of the 'sea eyes'. In 1875 the Kaiserlich-Königlich Karpaten-Verein (Imperial-Royal Carpathian Club) built a hikers' hostel here. It was soon followed by other hotels and pensions, until in 1877 the village of Tschirmer See was founded. As early as 1896 a cog railway linked the village with Tschirm (Štrba) railway station. One of the most beautiful walks in the High Tatras goes

Starý Smokovec (Altschmecks)

along the *Mengusovká dolina* (Mengsdorfer Tal) to the fairy-tale beauty of *Popradské pleso* (Poppersee; 1513 metres; colour plate 23) and on to *Rysy* (Meeraugspitze; 2499 metres) which has one of the most splendid views in the High Tatras (6-7 hours there and back).

The **White Tatras** (Belianske Tatry) border the High Tatras on the north-east side and include a number of peaks above 2000 metres. The highest is Havran (2152 metres). The main village is **Ždiar** (plate 61), founded 500 years ago by *Gorals*, as the Polish mountain dwellers are called, though the present population of 1600 now think of themselves as Slovaks. They still wear their beautiful old national costume, however, and not only at folkloric events laid on for tourists but also on Sundays and festivals and for ceremonial occasions. Recently new wooden houses in traditional style have been built next to the old black, shingle-roofed cottages. The interiors of many of the houses resemble folk museums, and the old craft techniques are flourishing everywhere. At house No. 326, for example, the visitor can admire a collection of beautiful folk costumes – and even try them on and be photographed in them.

To the north west of the Belianske Tatry along the border with Poland lies the **Spišská Magura** (Zipser Magura) with the National Park of *Pieniny* (Pieninský národný park). The River Dunajec, a tributary of the Vistula, is here squeezed between gigantic limestone cliffs.

405

The most interesting and popular point in the rocky district of Pieninen (Penin) is Červený Kláštor (Rotes Kloster), which is the starting point for a pleasant 8.5 km raft trip along the Polish border. The return journey is made on foot and includes a visit to the restored early 14th-century Carthusian monastery.

Bardejov (Bartfeld, Bartfa)

High in the north of eastern Slovakia, at the foot of Východné Beskydy mountains, lies the old cloth-making town of **Bardejov**, now a busy little town with the best preserved medieval town centre in Slovakia. German weavers settled here in the 12th century next to a Slavic village on the Topl'a and within a few decades their settlement had developed into an important trading centre for linen and wine between Hungary and Poland. At the end of the 14th century it was made a royal Hungarian free town.

In the middle of the large, slightly sloping market square, now called nám. Oslobiditel'ov (Liberators' Square), stands the two-storey *Town Hall*. The ground floor with its two Gothic portals was built by Master Alexander in 1505. The building was continued in a Renaissance spirit by Alexius, an Italian. His are the staircase and the oriel on the south wall and also the steep gables with their figure decoration. The south gable is surmounted by a bronze Roland. (The original is in the Town Hall Museum.)

The square is dominated by the grand parish church of *St Giles* (Kostol sv. Egidia), a three-aisled basilica completed in 1415 on the site of a Cistercian abbey church. The polygonal choir, together with the sacristy, the oratory and the chapel of St Catherine above, were all built by Master Nicholas (Mikuláš) of Bartfeld between 1448 and 1458. The net vault in the nave is the work of Master Urban, who also designed the chapels of the Virgin, St Andrew and St Elizabeth on the south side of the church. The top-heavy tower was completed in 1486-87 by Master Johann Stelmasshek of Anspach. The Neo-Gothic high altar by Moritz Hölzel dates from the re-gothicizing restoration of the church between 1886 and 1899. The Late Gothic *altarpieces* on the eleven side altars are particularly important. They all date from the period between 1460 and 1510. The most interesting are the altarpiece of the Nativity (c. 1480–1490) by Master Stefan Tarner, the altarpiece of the Man of Sorrows (c. 1500–1510; colour plate 24) and the altarpiece of St Barbara (c. 1450–1460). The Crucifixion group over the crossing is attributed to Veit Stoss himself.

The *burghers' houses* which line the square mostly date from the first quarter of the 14th century, though they were rebuilt after town fires in the 17th and 18th centuries in the style of the Renaissance or the Baroque. The last great fire, in 1878, destroyed almost all the roofs and gables, but since 1953 these have been replaced with the help of old engravings. Among the few houses to survive the last great fire is the *Rhody House* in the neighbouring Rhodyho ul. (Nos. 1 and 2). The core of the house is Gothic but it was given its Renaissance appearance at the beginning of the 17th century. It now contains a museum with folk collections from the Šariš (Scharosch) region. The medieval *town fortifications* are splendidly preserved. *Horná*

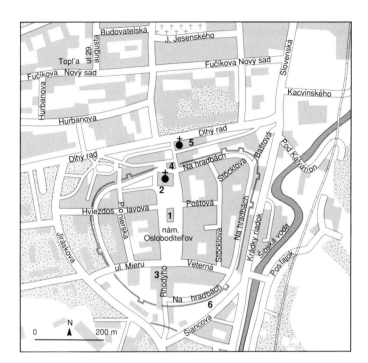

Bardejov (Bartfeld)
1 Town Hall
2 Parish Church of St Giles
3 Rhody House
4 Grammar School (Gymnázium)
5 Franciscan Church
6 Town Walls

Brána (Upper Gate) was restored by Master Matthias of Nuremberg between 1405 and 1407, though the building was altered many times in the 15th and 16th centuries. Eight of the bastions are still extant, mostly on the eastern and southern ramparts.

In a picturesque wooded valley about 5 km north of Bardejov is the spa of **Bardejovské Kúpele** (Bad Bartfeld). The mineral springs of Bardejov were mentioned in a charter of King Béla IV of Hungary (1247), but it was not until towards the end of the 18th century and the beginning of the 19th, and then again at the turn of the present century, that the spa flourished. At that time the Neo-Baroque *Alžběta Sanatorium* (now the Branisko House) was erected as the central building in the spa. In 1893 the first train went from Preschau to Bartfeld and thereafter Bad Bartfeld rose to become one of the most popular spas in Hungary. Since the 1970's and 1980's the most modern facilities have been built at this well-kept spa, which is now able to provide its guests with every convenience besides the charm of its wooded surroundings. The interesting *Museum of Vernacular Architecture* was established in 1964 as an open-air museum with many wooden buildings from Upper Šariš, including a wooden Russian Orthodox church of 1766 with a collection of East Slovak icons.

Prešov (Preschau; Eperjes)

The district town of **Prešov** on the Torysa, a tributary of the Hornád (Kundert), is in the middle of the Šariš (Scharosch) region and the cultural and ecclesiastical centre of the

407

Prešov (Preschau)

Ruthenian (Ukrainian) minority. The town centre, with its beautiful churches and splendid burghers' houses, is a conservation area. Prešov is the see both of a Roman Catholic and a Ruthenian Uniate bishop, as well as being the seat of the Philosophical and Pedagogical Faculty of the University of Košice. Besides the Jonáš Záborsky Theatre it is also the home of the Ukrainian National Theatre with its folk ensemble.

The Prešov region has been inhabited since neolithic times, and archaeological evidence has been found of a Slavic settlement in the 9th century Here at the beginning of the 13th century, on the trade route between the Baltic and the Black Sea, German colonists founded a market which they called *Eperies*, from its Hungarian name *Eperjes*. In 1247 King Béla IV granted the German inhabitants ownership of the town together with lucrative privileges. In 1299 it was created a town with the laws of Zips, and in 1374 given the status of a royal Hungarian free town. This marked the beginning of its economic and cultural rise to become an important centre in Upper Hungary. In the 17th and 18th centuries the rebellions of the Estates against the Habsburgs started here. After the imperial general Antonio Caraffa had put down the Thököly rebellion (see p. 401), he held the notorious 'Eperjes Bloody Tribunal' here on 3 March 1687, after which 24 Protestant town councillors were executed. A revolt of the Upper Hungarian peasants, supported by the poorer inhabitants of the town (now called *Preschau*) against the aristocracy was likewise bloodily suppressed. On 16 June 1919 the Slovak Republic of Councils, a Soviet-style state, was proclaimed here, but dissolved only three weeks later, since Czechs and Slovaks had meanwhile joined to form the single state of Czechoslovakia.

The nucleus of the historic old town centre of Prešov is the long lozenge-shaped main square, now called nám. Slovenskej republiky rád (or nám. SRR for short: Square of the Slovak Republic of Councils), which contains a Marian column (17th–18th century) and the Neptune Fountain (19th century). The parish church of *St Nicholas* (Kostol sv. Mikuláš), also in the square, originally an aisle-less Romanesque building, was completed in 1347 in the Gothic style and extended with two Late Gothic aisles on the south side between 1501 and 1515. The architects were Master Nicholas of Leutschau (Levoča), a town councillor in Eperies (Preschau) and Master Paul from Leutschau. Master Johann of Preschau (Ján Brengisejn) created the tracery of the windows and the impressive star- and net-vaults. In 1642 the church was given a Renaissance gallery. The Neo-Classical south doorway dates from 1788 and the Neo-Classical loggia on the north side is early 19th century.

The Baroque high altarpiece of 1696 with statues by the woodcarver Josef Hartmann repays careful attention. The central panel is Gothic in origin (1490–1506), with figures carved by Johann Weiss; the sculptures on the cornice are from the workshop of Master Paul from Leutschau, while some groups, such as the Annunciation, St Michael and the Calvary, are from the hand of Master Paul himself.

Several of the burghers' houses surrounding the square date back to the Gothic period. They were given a Renaissance appearance in the 16th century, and in the 18th century Neo-Classical features were also added. A particularly notable example is the freshly restored *Rákócki House* (Rákócziho dom; No. 86), a town palace built for Prince Sigmund Rákócki at the end of the 16th century by joining together two burghers' houses. The decorative attic is characteristic of Renaissance architecture in Upper Hungary (East Slovakia). Since 1955 it has housed the Museum of the Slovak Republic of Councils. The visitor should also take a

The Dukla Pass (Dukelský priesmyk)

For 35 km the road from Bardejov winds through the Východné Beskydy mountains to **Svidník**, a little town destroyed in 1944 during the fighting around the Dukla Pass, but since rebuilt. A massive monument at the entrance to the town commemorates the 80,000 Soviet soldiers who fell here. The road continues northwards along the Ladomirka valley towads the **Dukla Pass** on the Polish border. Almost every village here has a pretty wooden church. Reminders of the events of 1944 follow in quick succession marking important events in the battle for the pass: 'Soviet tanks block the way of German tanks', 'Plane awaits deployment', 'Guns take aim at the road'. Finally a mighty stone monument marks the large Czechoslovak war cemetery, for the 6500 dead among the Czechoslovak troops under General Ludvík Svoboda, later President of the ČSSR, who fought side by side with the Red Army. On 29 August 1944, when the Soviet Army stood on the border to Slovakia, the Slovak National Uprising was declared. It was intended to bring about the collapse of the Fascist Slovak-German Front. However, the German troops put up fierce resistance at the Dukla Pass and brutally suppressed the uprising. Thus the entry of the Soviet troops was delayed for several weeks.

look at the burghers' houses at Nos. 75 and 107, both of which have retained the distinctive style of the East Slovak Renaissance. The *Town Hall* in nám. SNP (nám. Slovenského národného povstania; Square of the Slovak National Uprising) was built by Johann of Preschau, his brother Albert, and Master Nicholas of Leutschau between 1511 and 1520. Later in the 16th century the original Late Gothic gable was replaced by a Renaissance attic. In 1788, after a fire, the building was given three Baroque windows. Its present appearance dates from 1887. It was from the town hall balcony that Antonín Janoušek, President of the Revolutionary Government Council, proclaimed the Slovak Republic of Councils in June 1919.

The Solivar district of the town contains the medieval *Leopold Shaft salt mine* with its unusual wooden buildings. It was still in operation in the 19th century but is now an open-air museum. Salt was being mined here as early as the 13th century. In the 17th century the mine was full of water and new technical installations and buildings had to be constructed: the tower (*klopačka*), the whim, a kind of mining windlass (*gápel*), the reservoirs of the brine (*četerna*) of 1815, the place for evaporating the brine with salt pans and what was called the *Kammern* (chambers), an enormous Baroque storehouse built in 1674. In 1780 another storey was added and an arcaded hall built for loading the salt. The tower was built in 1810.

Chronology of the history of Czechoslovakia

623   Samo, a Frankish merchant, founds the first empire of the Slavs

833   The Moravian princes Mojmir I and Rastislav form the Great Moravian Empire

c. 879   The Czech duke Bořivoj and his wife Ludmila (later canonized) are baptized by Methodius, Apostle of the Slavs

907   The Hungarians defeat the allied Bavarian-Moravian army at Bratislava; end of the Great Moravian Empire

921–929   Duke Wenceslas I (St Wenceslas) converts Bohemia to Christianity. He is assassinated c. 930

972   Boleslav II founds the bishopric of Prague

1029   Duke Břetislav I unites Moravia with Bohemia

1085   Emperor Henry IV crowns Vratislav II at Mainz as the first king of Bohemia

1173   Soběslav II grants German settlers special rights

1198–1230   Foundation of German towns in the reign of Otakar II Přemysl

after 1241   German colonization of Slovakia (Zips, Spiš)

1306   End of the Přemyslid dynasty; beginning of Luxemburg dynasty with election of John of Luxemburg

1346   Charles IV elected King of the Holy Roman Empire

1348   Charles IV founds the first university in central Europe at Prague

1355   Pope Innocent VI crowns Charles IV Emperor

1356   Charles IV issues the basic law of the Empire ('Golden Bull') which remains in force until the dissolution of the Empire in 1806

1415   Jan Hus, the Czech religious reformer and nationalist, is burned at the stake as a heretic

1419–1435   Hussite Wars

1439   George of Poděbrady, leader of the Hussite Utraquists, is made Regent (1439–1458), and then King (1458–1471) of Bohemia

1526   Ferdinand I begins the rule of the Habsburg dynasty, uniting the Bohemian, German and Imperial crowns

1576–1612   Emperor Rudolph II makes the Imperial capital at Prague the artistic and intellectual treasure-house of Europe

1618   The Second Defenestration of Prague triggers off the Bohemian Wars which turn into the Thirty Years' War

1634   Albrecht von Waldstein (Wallenstein), the Imperial commander, is murdered at Eger (Cheb)

1648   The Peace of Westphalia ends the Thirty Years' War

1743   Maria Theresa is crowned Queen of Bohemia at Prague

1782   Joseph II issues the 'Edict of Tolerance', dissolves many religious houses and makes German the only official language of the Habsburg Empire

1805   In the Battle 'of the Three Emperors' at Austerlitz in southern Moravia Napoleon defeats the troops of the Russian Tsar Alexander I and the Austrian Emperor Francis I

1848   The new Austrian constitution 'guarantees all peoples the inviolablility of their nationality and language'

1866   At Königgrätz in eastern Bohemia Prussian troops under Helmuth von Moltke defeat the Austrians. The 'German War' of 1866 results in the exclusion of Austria from the German Union and strengthens the position of Prussia

1867   Austria forms the Dual Monarchy of Austria-Hungary; the Vienna government rejects Czech claims for similar status

1876 Hungary abolishes self-government of the German-speaking towns in Zips (Spiš) and 'Magyarizes' the German population

1882 Prague University is divided into German Czech sections

1908 Karel Kramář, leader of the Young Czechs demands a Czech state and union with Slovakia, which is part of Hungary

1916 Tomáš Garrigue Masaryk and Edvard Beneš found a Czechoslovak National Council

1918 The 'Pittsburgh Agreement' provides for the union of Czechs and Slovaks in a single state

28.10.1918 The Czechoslovak Republic (ČSR) is proclaimed in Prague

29.9.1938 Incorporation of the German-speaking areas of Bohemia into the German Reich following the 'Munich Agreement'; at the same time Poland and Hungary 'correct' their borders with Czechoslovakia

6.10.1938 Slovakia becomes an autonomous state within 'Czecho-Slovakia'

14.3.1939 Slovakia proclaims its full autonomy; Jozef Tiso becomes its President

15.3.1939 The 'Reich Protectorate of Bohemia and Moravia' is formed

Autumn 1939 Edvard Beneš in London forms a 'Czechoslovak National Committee' as a provisional government

May 1942 Assassination of the 'Deputy Protector of the Reich' Reinhard Heydrich by Czech exiles

5.4.1945 The Czechoslovak National Council proclaims the 'Košice Programme'

1946 The Communist party of Czechoslovakia (KPČ) received the majority of votes in the election

9.5.1948 The Constitution establishes the ČSR as a 'centralized popular democratic republic'

11.6.1960 A change in the Constitution makes the popular republic a Socialist Republic (ČSSR)

1968 Reformers Alexander Dubček, Ludvík Svoboda and Oldřich Černik present a new programme before the KPČ, promising 'Socialism with a human face' (the 'Prague Spring'). In accordance with the Brezhnev Doctrine troops of the Warsaw Pact march into the ČSSR and force the Czechoslovak state and party leadership to rescind all reforms

1969 The reformers are replaced with orthodox Communists

1970 Federal Constitution. Agreement of Friendship and Cooperation with the Soviet Union

1977 Founding of the civil rights movement 'Charter 77'

1988 Beginning of student demonstrations

19.11.1989 Founding of 'Civic Forum', a union of all democratic groups, with Václav Havel as its spokesman

9.12.1989 Marián Čalfa forms a government in which for the first time Communists are in the minority; at the same time President Husák resigns. His successor is Václav Havel

29.3.1990 The name of the ČSSR is changed to the 'Czecho-Slovak Federative Republic' (ČSFR)

8/9.6.1990 Elections confirm the Czech 'Civic Forum' and the Slovak 'Public against Violence' as the strongest party groupings in the ČSFR. Marián Čalfa remains prime minister

5.7.1990 The Federative Assembly re-elects Václav Havel as president

Czechoslovakia in brief

Area: 128,000 km² (UK 244,103km²). Greatest length: 767 km; greatest width: 276 km. Czechoslovakia borders five states: Federal Republic of Germany (815 km), Poland (1391 km), USSR (98 km), Hungary (679 km), Austria (570 km).
Population: 15,560,000 (UK 57,000,000)
Population density: 121 inhabitants per km² (UK: 231 inhabitants per km²)
Capital: Prague

Economy

Czechoslovakia is an industrialized country with industry accounting for about 60% of the national income, construction work c. 11% and agriculture only 8%. The most important industrial centres are in northern and southern Moravia and in the Prague area. The biggest industries are mechanical engineering (25%), followed by the food and alcohol production (14%), electrical engineering (12%) and textiles, clothing and leather (10%).

Of the total area of Czechoslovakia 6.8 million ha (i.e. more than half) is used for agriculture, of which 4.8 million ha is under cultivation, 1.6 million ha is pasture, 48,000 ha is vineyards and 13,000 ha is hop gardens. Besides the farmland there is 4.6 million ha of forest and 53,000 ha of fishponds.

Administrative regions

	capital	area (km²)	pop.(m)
Czech Republic	Praha (Prague)	78,864	10.4
Prague	Praha	496	1.3
Central Bohemia	Praha	10,994	1.1
South Bohemia	České Budějovice	11,345	0.7
West Bohemia	Plzeň	10,875	0.9
North Bohemia	Ústí nad Labem	7,819	1.2
East Bohemia	Hradec Králové	11,240	1.2
South Moravia	Brno	15,028	2.0
North Moravia	Ostrava	11,067	2.0
Slovak Republic	Bratislava	49,036	5.2
Bratislava	Bratislava	367	0.5
West Slovakia	Bratislava	14,492	1.7
Central Slovakia	Banská Bystrica	17,986	1.6
East Slovakia	Košice	16,191	1.4
Czechoslovakia total:		**127,900**	**15.6**

Geography

Bohemia owes its identity to a well-circumscribed geographical position. The **Bohemian Basin** in the west of Czechoslovakia is surrounded by the Bohemian Forest (Šumava), the Ore Mountains (Krušne hory), the Jizera Mountains (Jizerské hory) and the Giant Mountains (Krkonoše) with Sněžka (1602 metres), and is drained into the North Sea by the river Elbe (Labe) with its tributaries the Jizera (Iser), Vltava (Moldau) and Ohře (Eger). Moravia which borders it to the east forms the watershed between the Baltic and the Black Sea: the Odra (Oder) flows northwards, the Morava (March) southwards to the Danube (Dunaj). Slovakia rises from the Hungarian plain, or *puszta* country in the south to the High Tatras (Vysoké Tatry) mountains which reach heights of up to 2655 metres. In between are the Little Carpathians (Malé Karpaty), the White Carpathians (Bílé Karpaty), the Little and Great Fatra (Malá Fatra, Vel'ka Fatra), the Slovak Ore Mountains (Slovenské Rudohorie) and the Lower Tatras (Nízke Tatry). Except for the Poprad which flows via the Dunajec to the Vistula, all Slovak rivers, the Váh (Waag), Nítra (Neutra), Hron (Gran) and Hornád (Kundert) flow southwards to the Danube (Dunaj) which forms the border with Hungary for 172 km of its length.

Climate

Bohemia and Moravia are more under the influence of the central European maritime climate with mild winters and rainy summers, while in Slovakia the East European continental climate prevails with cold winters and dry summers.

July is the warmest but also the wettest month of the year. In Prague the average annual rainfall is 476 mm, while the observatory on Lomnicky štit in the High Tatras measures 1665 mm. The lowest rainfall occurs in January to March.

Vegetation

35% of Czechoslovakia is covered by forest, which has suffered particularly serious damage from acid rain in north-western Bohemia because of the many power stations fuelled by brown coal (70% of trees are affected).

Fauna

In the national parks of the Fatra and White Carpathians, the High Tatras and the Lower Tatras, there are wolves, lynxes, forest and rock martens, chamois and marmots, otters, eagle owls, capercaillies and blackcocks, and around 700 brown bears. The bears have increased in numbers to such an extent in recent years that they now come to mountain huts and hotels to search the dustbins for food. A fixed number is designated annually for shooting.

Average air temperatures in °C (mid-month average daytime extremes)

	January		July	
Karlovy Vary	−2.1	0.2	16.9	23.4
Praha	−0.9	1.1	19.0	24.8
České Budějovice	−2.1	0.6	17.4	24.1
Brno	−2.1	0.2	18.4	25.3
Bratislava	−1.6	0.6	20.1	26.6
Zvolen	−4.0	−0.6	18.8	26.0
Košice	−3.4	−0.7	19.1	26.0
Stary Smokovec	−5.2	−1.0	14.3	19.5

Ethnic groups

The population of Czechoslovakia consists of the following nationalities:

Czechs	9,805,000	(63.0%)
Slovaks	4,924,000	(31.6%)
Magyars	593,000	(3.8%)
Germans	56,000	(0.4%)
Ukrainians and Russians	56,000	(0.4%)
Poles	74,000	(0.5%)
Others	52,000	(0.3%)
	15,560,000	

The gypsies (Sinti and Roma), approximately 380,000 in number, are officially listed with the ethnic groups to which they claim to belong.

Religion

The constitution guarantees freedom of religion, but since 1945 a large part of the population has left religious groups. The largest religious group is the Roman Catholic Church (approx. 8.7 million communicants), most of whose members are in the Czech and Moravian area. In Slovakia the Protestants predominate (approx. 1.2 million): Lutherans of the Augsburg Confession (c. 550,000), Moravian Brethren (c. 425,000) and Reformed (c. 215,000). The Czechoslovak Church which developed from Hussitism is the third largest denomination (c. 700,000). There is also an Orthodox minority in the extreme east of Slovakia.

Glossary

Atlas Architectural support in the form of a male figure, named after the Atlas who held up the heavens in classical mythology

Attic Windowless superstructure above the main cornice of a building, built to hide the roof and often with vases or sculptures placed on it

Auxiliary Saints, the Fourteen Prayed to in times of need, and also known as the Fourteen Holy Helpers. They include St George, St Vitus and St Christopher

Barbican Outwork set in front of a fortress or city gate

Basilica Form of church with a central nave taller than its flanking aisles

Calvary Representation of the Crucifixion at the end of a Way of the Cross

Capital Upper part of a column, pier or pilaster

Casemate Room built within ramparts of a fortification

Cenotaph Tomb or memorial for someone who, for whatever reason, is buried elsewhere

Chapter College of priests attached to a cathedral or collegiate church

Chapter house Room where the leading members of a religious house met

Charnel house Two-storey cemetery chapel, the lower part of which is used to contain the bones that appear when new graves are dug ·

Console Projecting element on wall or pier, to support vault, figure etc.

Commandery Headquarters of medieval military orders (Hospitallers, Teutonic Knights)

Czech Lands Bohemia and Moravia

Diet Parliament in the Holy Roman Empire and Austro-Hungarian Empire

Fresco Painting on fresh (still wet) plaster

Groin vault Vault composed of two intersecting barrel vaults

German King Elective title of the Holy Roman Emperor. Also borne by his son as elected heir. 'King of the Romans' is sometimes used instead

Hall church Church in which the aisles are the same height as the nave and/or choir

Incunable/incunabulum Book printed before 1500

Ispán (Slavic: Župan) Hungarian local administrator (High Sheriff)

Komitat Old administrative division of Hungary

Land Records Official register in which all the important decisions of the Bohemian diet, together with changes in ownership of land among the higher nobility, clergy and towns were recorded

Lokator Medieval official, usually a nobleman, entrusted with attracting foreign settlers to the country, and with the founding of villages and towns

Minorites Franciscans (First Order of St Francis)

Ossuary Cemetery building containing bones

Palas German term for the residential part of a medieval castle, containing the hall and private rooms

Palatine Hungarian viceroy in a komitat, until 1848 (Hungarian: Nadorispán)

Pietà Representation of the Virgin Mary lamenting over the body of the dead Christ

Pinnacle Slender, pointed spirelet surmounting flying buttresses

Plague Column Column with statuary, usually dedicated to the Virgin or the Trinity, set up as a thanks offering for the end of a plague; common in Central European towns

Roland Figure of an armed man set up usually in the market square, as a symbol of a town's mercantile rights and legal status

Sala terrena Garden hall of a Baroque schloss, usually situated below the banqueting hall

Schöner Stil A Late Gothic style of sculpture and painting characterized by flowing forms and attractive physiognomy (also known as the 'International Style')

Sezession Variant of Art Nouveau found in Austria-Hungary

Sgraffito Façade decoration scratched into layers of coloured plaster when still wet

Stapelrecht Market privilege of a town, whereby all passing merchants were compelled to put their wares on sale there for a specified length of time

Triptych Altarpiece in three parts, consisting of the central panel and two wings

Triforium In a church, the passage below the clearstorey with arcades open to the choir or nave

Road Distances in Kilometres

	Praha	Karlovy Vary	Plzeň	České Budějovice	Liberec	Špindlerův Mlýn	Brno	Olomouc	Ostrava	Bratislava	Banská Bystrica
Karlovy Vary	126										
Plzeň	88	79									
České Budějovice	148	216	137								
Liberec	109	213	197	257							
Špindlerův Mlýn	139	257	227	283	83						
Brno	226	352	292	190	248	232					
Olomouc	254	380	342	267	255	239	77				
Ostrava	343	469	431	358	343	317	168	99			
Bratislava	364	490	430	322	386	370	138	213	277		
Banská Bystrica	499	625	565	463	514	498	273	259	216	205	
Poprad	539	665	627	545	540	524	386	285	242	329	124

Practical Information

Accommodation

Though Lady Mary Wortley Montagu carried her own bed with her (and even then she 'could not sometimes find a place to set it up in') in 1716, today's visitor should have relatively little trouble finding suitable accommodation. Čedok will organize bookings not only at Interhotels of the highest categories (3 to 5 stars), such as the *Inter-Continental* (*****), the *Palace* (****), the *Forum* (****), the *Paříž* (****) and the *Evropa* (***) in **Prague**; the *Forum* (****) and the *Kyjev* (***) in **Bratislava**; the *International* (****) in **Brno**; the *Grandhotel Pupp* (*****) in **Karlovy Vary**, but also holiday apartments, and rooms in private houses.

The independent traveller planning his own itinerary should have no real difficulty finding places to stay. Except during the summer holidays and at the main tourist centres there is always reasonably priced accommodation available.

Camping

At all Czechoslovakia's most beautiful places, by rivers and lakes, in mountain valleys, the traveller will find approx. 250 camp-sites which are divided into two categories (A and B). Most sites also have bungalows which must be reserved during the high season. Some sites are open all year round, but most from the beginning/middle of May to the middle/end of September. A detailed list of camp-sites with a map is available from Čedok.

Clothing

Czechoslovakia has a continental climate, and greater seasonal extremes than are usual in the British Isles. The rainfall is high, so waterproof clothing and an umbrella are essential, even in July and August; and visitors to mountainous regions such as the High Tatras or Riesengebirge (Krknoše), should remember to take warm clothing: temperatures can drop to low levels even in summer.

Customs Regulations

On entry
Duty is not charged on items brought into the country for personal use. It is in traveller's interest to declare any valuables (jewellery, cameras, camcorders etc.) at the

customs control at the border; if anything is lost or stolen it must be reported immediately to the police and then to the customs authorities. The following (for personal consumption) may be brought into the country without paying duty: 3kg of food, 250 cigarettes or 250 gm of other tobacco products, 2 l of wine, 1 l of spirits. Pure alcohol may not be imported.

Presents for friends and relatives cannot exceed a total value of 1000 kčs (Czechoslovak market price) for each person entering the country. Foreign automobile clubs will provide the latest information regarding the bringing in of CB radios and car phones. Hunting weapons and their ammunition can only be brought in with a weapons certificate (information from Čedok).

On leaving

The following goods may be taken out of the country without paying duty: things needed on the journey in reasonable quantities, 250 cigarettes or an equivalent quantity of other tobacco products, 2 l of wine and 1 l of spirits, objects with a total value of 500 kčs, all goods bought at Tuzex or Artia shops for foreign currency (receipts needed), glass and porcelain, souvenirs and other gifts.

For certain goods, e.g. leather gloves and sports goods, an export licence is needed and fee equal to the cost price of goods must be paid. The export of leather clothing, natural furs, shoes, coffee and tea, gold and silver goods and antiques is forbidden, unless they have been purchased with foreign currency. Further information can be obtained from the Customs authorities of the ČSFR and Čedok.

Festivals

Early January *Prague Winter* Music and theatre festival; Prague

May/June *Prague Spring* Music festival with concerts, opera and ballet; Prague

June *Kmochs Kolín* International brass band festival; Kolín, central Bohemia

Last weekend in June *Jánošík Festival* in the Malá Fatra (Little Fatra) Commemorating the legendary Slovak robber leader and folk hero Juro Jánošík (1688–1713); Terchová, central Slovakia

Late June *Hungarian Folk Festival* Gombasek (Hungarian: Gombaszög) near Rožňava, eastern Slovakia

Late June *Ukrainian Festival* Svidník, eastern Slovakia

Late June *Folk Festival* Strakonice, Bohemian Forest, western Bohemia

Late June/early July *Strážnice Folk Festival* gathering of Czechoslovak and foreign national costume groups; Strážnice, southern Moravia

July *Marionette Festival* Chrudim, eastern Bohemia

Mid-July *Folk Festival* Železný Brod, eastern Bohemia

Mid-July *Royal Banquet* historical knights tournament; Znojmo, southern Moravia

July/August *Folk Festival* the most important national costume festival in Slovakia with folk music, singing and dancing; Východná, central Slovakia

July/August *Summer Concerts* Jaroměřice nad Rokytnou, southern Moravia

Mid-August *Festival of the Chods* with national costumes, folk dancing and bagpipe playing; Domažlice, western Bohemia

Mid-September *Hop Festival* Žatec, northern Bohemia

September/October *Hanácké dožinky* harvest festival; Náměšt' na Hané, northern Moravia

October *Grand Pardubice Steeplechase* international horse race; Pardubice, eastern Bohemia

Late October *International Jazz Festival* Bratislava

Further information about dates and other folk festivals can be obtained from Čedok which also handles bookings (hotels, tickets etc.)

Embassies

Czechoslovak Embassies

UK and Eire: 28 Kensington Palace Gardens, London W8 4OX tel: 07-1727-3966

USA: 3900 Linnean Ave NW, Washington DC 20008 tel: 202-363-6315

Canada: 50 Rideau Terrace, Ottawa, Ontario K1M 1A1 tel: 514-849-4495

Australia: 169 Military Road, Dover Heights, Sydney NSW 2030 tel: 02-371-8878

New Zealand: 12 Anne Street, Wadesdown, PO Box 2843, Wellington tel: 04-723-142

Embassies in Czechoslovakia

UK and Eire: 12500 Praha 1, Thunovská 14 tel: 53-33-47

USA: 12548 Praha 1, Třiště 15 tel: 53-66-41

Canada: 12533 Praha 6, Mickiewiczova 6 tel: 32-47-15

Australia: Hotel Praha, 166 35 Praha 6, Sušicka 20 tel: 333-8111

New Zealand: Emergencies dealt with by British Embassy. Otherwise 1 Vienna 1, P.O. Box 1471, A-1011, Vienna, Austria, tel: 222-512-6636

Food and Drink

Since the times of the Habsburg Monarchy Bohemian cuisine has been famous for its solid and extremely tasty dishes, similar to South German and Austrian cooking. Bread dumplings, roast pork and sauerkraut are now the main fare offered on menus from Aš to Znojmo. There is also delicious roast goose, sauerbraten, Rahmbeuschel (finely chopped lung in a cream sauce) and other dishes. Perhaps the tastiest dishes are the many kinds of soups. Dumplings appear in many forms: made from raw or boiled potatoes; filled with plums, apricots or other fruit. Slovak dishes have not lost their Hungarian character. They are hotter, flavoured with paprika, but no less delicious.

The following is a short selection of Czechoslovak specialities which the visitor should try, if they are on the menu (*jídelní lístek*). First, the incomparable soups (*polévky*): *bramborová polévka* (potato soup with mushrooms), *zelná polévka* (white cabbage soup), *hrachová polévka* (pea soup with garlic), *ledvinková polévka* (piquant kidney soup), *rybi polévka* (fish soup with carp roe). Then the main courses: Moravian *klobasen* (sausages) with sour lentils, lean leg of pork with caraway in a beer sauce, *zadéjávané drsky* (strips of tripe with minced ham), Znojmo goulash with chopped spiced gherkins, fillets of carp à la abbé Tucka on asparagus tips. Lastly the excellent desserts: Bohemian fritters, *powideldatschgerl*, cakes and tarts (*koláče*), and pancakes (*lívance*), not forgetting the stuffed pancakes (*palačinky*). In Slovakia there are tempting *haluški* (dumplings with sheep's milk quark and roasted bacon cubes). With afternoon coffee – especially in the west of Czechoslovakia – there is a delicious range of patisserie, cakes, tarts, soufflés and strudels. Specialities include the Karlsbad *oblátky* (wafers), Prague nut tart, Bohemian *bublanina*, an incomparable cherry soufflé, and many other specialities.

There is a saying that Bohemia produces the best beer, Moravia the best wine and Slovakia the best schnaps in the world. This is arguable as far as wine and schnaps are concerned but not as regards beer, especially the world famous Pilsner Urquell (sold in Czechoslovakia as *Plzeňský Prazdroj*), the Queen of Beers. But Prazdroj is only one of hundreds of beers, dark and light, bitter and sweet, brewed by the Czechs and Slovaks. In every town and village in Czechoslovakia even early in the morning men can be seen drinking beer in taverns. Prague alone has more than 1300 pubs/taverns. One of them, 'U Fleků, gets through more than three and a half million pints a year alone.

Less well known abroad are the excellent wines from Mělník, white and red wine from southern Moravia and the area around Bratislava.

Visitors who want to try something stronger will go for *slivovitz* of which the best is the aromatic plum schnapps from Vizovice in Moravia, or Moravian *borovička*, the mildly aromatic juniper spirit from Spiš (Zips). Or – as a digestif after a rich meal – Bohemian *Becherovka*, the world famous tonic from Karlovy Vary.

Getting to Czechoslovakia

Visitors may travel to Czechoslovakia from the UK by air, train, coach or car. There are frequent BA and ČSA (Czechoslovak Airlines) flights to Prague. Rail connections may be made via Ostende-Cologne, or Calais-Paris. An infrequent direct coach link is also available. Motorists can cover the distance (approximately 1200km) in under 24 hours, but it is more advisable to allow two or more days. Travel to Czechoslovakia from other English-speaking countries is most easily done via London.

Package holidays are provided by all travel agents through Čedok, the Czechoslovak travel bureau. There are trips by plane, rail or bus to Prague, Bratislava or Brno, to Karlovy Vary or Plzeň lasting four to eight days, as well a longer tours of Bohemia, Moravia and Slovakia lasting two to four weeks. At all towns day or half-day excursions to places of particular interest are offered.

Information is available from Čedok Travel:

London: 17–18 Old Bond Street, London W1 tel: 071-629-6058

New York: 10 East 40th Street, New York City, NY 10157 tel: 212-689-9720

There are no restrictions on independent travel; this can be done by plane, rail, bus or private car. Cars (self-drive or with driver) can be hired from Čedok. Most major cities will have a branch of Pragocar (in Prague at Štěpánská 42, tel: 02–352–825) or Brnocar (in Brno at Solnički 6, tel: 05–24039).

Border crossings (for private cars)
The main border crossings to Czechoslovakia are:

From Austria:
Berg / Petržalka Vienna-Bratislava
Reinthal
Drasenhofen Vienna-Brno
Laa an der Thaya
Kleinhaugsdorf Vienna-Prague
Retz
Hardegg
Riegersburg
Thürnau
Fratres
Grametten
Neu-Nagelberg (Vienna-Prague)
Gmünd
Wullowitz (Linz-České Budějovice)
Weigetschlag (Linz-Vyšší Brod)

From Germany:
Bavaria:
Philippsreut
Bayrisch Eisenstein
Eschlkam
Furth im Wald (Regensburg-Plzeň)
Waldmünchen
Waidhaus (Nürnberg-Plzeň)
Mähring
Waldsassen

Schirnding (Bayreuth-Karlovy Vary)
Selb

Saxony:
Schönberg (Plauen-Cheb)
Johanngeorgenstadt
Oberwiesthal (Chemnitz-Karlovy Vary)
Reitzenhain
Zinnwald-Georgenfeld (Dresden-Prague)
Hellendorf
Schmilka (Dresden-Děčín)
Sebnitz
Seifhennersdorf
Großschönau

From Poland
Kudowa Slone
Chalupki
Lysa Polana
Jakuszyce
Chyzne
Piwniszna
Barwinek
Ceiszyn

From the USSR
Uzhgorod

From Hungary
Komárom
Sátoraljaújhely
Hidasnmeti
Balassagyarmat
Parassapuszta
Rajka

Information

Much tourist information is provided by the state travel bureau Čedok, which can also make bookings for all journeys. Information can also be obtained from most travel agents, some of which will arrange holidays – even combined bicycle and coach tours.

Language

The official languages are Czech and Slovak, two closely related West Slavic tongues which are divided into several dialect groups. English is occasionally useful, and German is still widely understood.

Pronunciation

c as in its
č as in cheap
ch as in loch
d' as in duty
g as in good
j as in yet
l' as in million
ň as in onion
p as in spin
ř as in Dvořák (a combination of r and ž)
s as in sun
š as in shun
t' as in stew
z as in zero
ž as in pleasure
a as in up
á as in father
ä as in set
e as in bet
é as in air
i,y as in bit
í,ý as in beat

o as in not
ó as in nor
ô as in pure
u as in took
ů,ú as in tool

Diphthongs are pronounced by gliding from one vowel to another:
ou = o + u
au = a + u
eu = e + u

Note: The accent on a vowel denotes its length; it does not indicate where the stress falls in a word, which is always on the first syllable.

Essential words

	Czech	Slovak
please	prosím	prosím
thank you	děkuji	d'akujem
good day	dobrý den	dobrý deň
good morning	dobré ráno	dobré ráno
good evening	dobrý večer	dobrý večer
good night	dobrou noc	dobrou noc
goodbye	na shledanou	do videnia
yes	ano	áno
no	ne	nie
sorry	pardon	pardón
where is ...?	kde je ...?	kde je ...?
main street	třída	trieda
smaller street	ulice	ulica
square	náměstí	námestie
church	kostel	kostol
town hall	radnice	radnica
château, schloss	zámek	zámok
castle	hrad	hrad
theatre	divadlo	divadlo
museum	muzeum	múzeum
house	dům	dom

	Czech	Slovak
bridge	most	most
gate	brána	brána
park	sady	sady
hotel	hotel	hotel
restaurant	restaurace	rěstaurácia
inn	hostinec	hostinec
toilet	záchod	záchod
gents	muži	muži
ladies	ženy	ženy
pharmacy	lékárna	lekáreň
doctor	lékař	lekár
entrance	vchod	vchod
exit	východ	východ
menu	jidelní listek	jedalny listok
coffee	káva	káva
tea	čaj	čaj
water	voda	voda
beer	pivo	pivo
white wine	bílé víno	bílé víno
red wine	červené víno	červené víno
soup	polévka	polievka
meat	maso	mäso
chicken	kuře	kurča
fish	kapr	kapor
bread	chléb	chlieb
butter	máslo	maslo
salt	sůl	sol'
sugar	cukr	cukor
glass	sklenice	pohár
plate	talíř	tanier
fork	vidlička	vidlička
spoon	lžíce	lyžica
knife	nůž	nôž
napkin	ubrousek	servítka
one	jeden, jedna, jedno	jeden, jedna, jedno
two	dva, dvě, dvě	dva, dve, dvaja
three	tři	tri, traja

	Czech	Slovak
four	čtyři	štyri
five	pět	pät'
six	šest	šest'
seven	sedm	sedem
eight	osm	osem
nine	devět	devät'
ten	deset	desat'
twenty	dvacet	dvadsat'

days of the week:

Monday	pondělí	pondelok
Tuesday	úterý	uterok
Wednesday	středa	streda
Thursday	čtvrtek	štvrtok
Friday	pátek	piatok
Saturday	sobota	sobota
Sunday	neděle	nedeľa

months:

January	Leden	Január
February	Únor	Február
March	Březen	Marec
April	Duben	Apríl
May	Květen	Máj
June	Červen	Jún
July	Červenec	Júl
August	Srpen	August
September	Zaří	September
October	Říjen	Október
November	Lístopad	November
December	Prosinec	December

Medical Assistance

In case of accidents or sudden illness out-patients' departments and hospitals are open to any foreign traveller, and there are now registered practitioners. Medical care corresponds to the standards in western Europe. Doctors understand English.

Innoculations are not required. You should take usual medicaments with you, if not you can obtain all necessary medicines at hospitals (*Klinika*) or pharmacies (*Lékárna*).

Money

The Czechoslovak currency is the **Crown** (Kčs). 1 crown (*koruna*) makes 100 heller (*haléřů*). There are 5, 10, 20 and 50 heller and 1, 2 and 5 crown coins, and notes for 10, 20, 50, 100, 500 and 1000 crowns. It is not permitted to take crowns in or out of the country. This is also true of other eastern European currencies, but does not apply to other currencies.

Currency can only be changed at banks, state bureaux de change, and hotels. Travellers cheques (American Express, Visa etc.) and credit cards (Access, American Express, Carte Blanche, Diners Club, Eurocard, JCB, Master Card, Visa) can also be cashed, but Eurocheques must be cashed at state banks.

Money should never be exchanged on the street, although the offers may be tempting. Unofficial exchange is still against the law and may result in prosecution. Besides, the unwary tourist can often be duped in black-market exchange and receive notes that are no longer legal tender or worthless notes of other currencies (dinars, zloty, etc.).

Motoring

Driving in Czechoslovakia is a delight; the roads are in excellent condition and are still relatively empty. In all the smaller towns it is possible to park in the large main square (market place) or nearby. Parking is only a problem in the larger towns and cities. Guarded city car parks are mostly for the short-term parker: after one or two hours the fees rise sharply.

You must carry the vehicle's registration document, and, if you are not the owner, a letter of permission from the owner authenticated by a motoring organization or other official body. You must also carry your national driving licence; an international green card for insurance is recommended. First aid equipment, spare bulbs and a red warning triangle are compulsory, as is a national identification sticker.

The **speed limit** in built up areas is 60 km/h, outside towns it is 90 km/h and on motorways 110 km/h. Motor cycles and cars with trailers must be driven under 90 km/h, even on motorways. Before level crossings the speed limit for all vehicles is 30 km/h. The traffic police use radar to check that the speed limits are being observed. Safety belts must be worn by anyone more than 150cm (4'11") tall.

When parking, at least 3 metres width of road must be left free for traffic in both directions. Parking is forbidden 15 metres on either side of level crossings. A distance of at least 3.5 metres must be kept between parked cars and tram lines. **The consumption of alcohol by drivers is absolutely forbidden.** If your car has high-level brake lights these must be covered or disconnected before you reach the border.

In case of *breakdown* the emergency road services (Silniční Služba) can be contacted on the **Police Emergency number 158**. In the

Prague area the emergency service provides a round-the-clock service, which can be called on 02/77 34 55. UK motoring organizations can provide full cover.

Vehicles with visible **damage to bodywork** may only leave the country again with a police certificate of damage. This certificate is given at the site of the accident. People entering Czechoslovakia with damage to the bodywork of their car must obtain a certificate at the border.

Road accidents must be reported to the police immediately, and nothing must be changed at the site of the accident.

Fuel vouchers for special (90 octane), unleaded (95 octane) and super (96 octane) can be bought at Čedok, at the Živnostenská Bank, 18 King William Street, London EC4N 7BY tel. 071–283–3333 (9.30am–3.30pm) and in Czechoslovakia at the border crossings and at state banks. Fuel is not cheap: approximately 60p ($1) a litre. At present tourists can only buy diesel at petrol stations with the sign 'TT-Diesel'. Unused fuel coupons cannot be refunded. No duty is charged on petrol in the tank on entry into Czechoslovakia, but on leaving the country tanks should contain no more than 10 litres of petrol and the full duty is to be paid.

Unleaded petrol can be obtained in all larger towns. Motorists should bear in mind that most petrol stations close in the early evening and are closed on Sundays and holidays. Every larger town has at least one petrol station which is open round the clock.

National Holidays

Official holidays are: 1 January (New Year), Easter Monday, 1 May (International Workers' Day), 5 July (SS Cyril and Methodius Day), 6 July (Anniversary of the Martyrdom of Jan Hus), 28 October (Republic Day), and 25 and 26 December (Christmas and Boxing Day).

Photography and Filming

Photography and filming are permitted everywhere, unless the usual signs prohibiting the use of cameras are displayed. Only areas near the border are excluded from this rule. Photography is prohibited in certain museums, castles, country houses, galleries and some churches (even outside the times of services). Visitors should bring films etc. with them since the popular western brands of film are often not stocked.

Public Transport

Because of the high cost of petrol Czechoslovaks in towns mostly use public transport, rail, bus and in Prague the metro. These cover most districts and run at short intervals. For several decades the fare for travelling in the town limits has been 1 Kčs.

425

Opening times

Museums, castles, country houses, galleries etc. are mostly open from 10.00 am to 5.00 pm from Tuesday to Sunday, and some are open from 8.00 am to 12.00 noon and from 1.00 pm to 5.00 pm. On Mondays and the days following national holidays they are closed. Most castles and country houses are closed from November to March and in October and April many open only at the weekends.

It cannot be too strongly emphasized that many of the sights listed in this book may be closed for a number of reasons, often described as 'restoration'. The situation with churches has improved considerably since the return to democracy, but some churches will now be out of bounds to non-worshippers.

Seasons

Every season has its attractions in Czechoslovakia. From mid-April the hills of Bohemia are very attractive with their millions of blossoming fruit trees. The period from mid-May to mid-September is the main tourist season for all parts of the country, especially the holiday months of July and August, the warmest, sunniest, stormiest and most over-crowded of the year. Long periods of fine weather which can extend into November are characteristic of the colourful autumn. January to the end of March is the winter sports season in the mountains. In the Slovak mountains, above

all the High Tatras, snow lies until May, and in high places until June or even July. The spas are popular all year round, as are the cities, Prague, Bratislava and Brno.

Shopping and Souvenirs

With Czechoslovak crowns (koruny; Kčs) the visitor can make full use of the relatively well-stocked shops and department stores. Except during the main shopping hours in the late afternoon, queues are rare. The stringent export regulations are seldom enforced.

The most popular gifts are pieces of **Bohemian glass** in traditional or modern shapes, magnificent works from the renowned glass factories of the Bohemian Forest and the Jizera Mountains. This is now generally available, but in case of difficulty look for the state-owned *Tuzex shops*.

Also much sought after is white **porcelain** with its famous cobalt blue decoration and its classic onion decoration. In 1864 the Meissen kiln and porcelain factory, formerly C. Teichert, founded a branch factory at Dubí near Teplice because of the kaolin deposits nearby. Hence the onion-pattern porcelain comes not only from Meissen but also from Dubí.

Lastly, **garnet jewellery** and other jewellery from Jablonec nad Nisou (formerly Gablonz an der Neisse) are also popular souvenirs. Lace, leather goods, metalwork and woodwork, ceramics, records and books, especially art books, are very good value. And it is always worth looking in the many second-hand bookshops.

Shops are open from Monday to Friday from 8.30 or 9.00 am to 6.00 pm, and on Saturdays until 12.00 noon (department stores until 4.00 pm). On certain days some large stores stay open until 8.00 pm. Food shops often open at 6.00 am. Smaller shops close at midday for two hours.

Spas

The presence of a large number of natural springs, mineral waters, healing mud and spring gas has given rise to a centuries-old tradition of spas. Combined with the pleasant climate and varied, delightful countryside this has made Czechoslovakia an ideal country for a cure. There are 57 spas in all, 36 in Bohemia and Moravia and 21 in Slovakia. The following is a selection:

Bardejovské Kúpele (Bad Bartfeld), eastern Slovakia: ailments of the digestive traact, diabetes

Františkovy Lázně (Franzensbad), western Bohemia: gynaecological disorders, infertility, heart disease

Jáchymov (St. Joachimsthal), western Bohemia: muscular illnesses, nervous ailments, metabolic diseases

Janské Lázně (Johannesbad), northern Bohemia: nervous disorders, muscular ailments

Karlovy Vary (Karlsbad), western Bohemia: digestive disorders and metabolic diseases

Luhačovice (Luhatschowitz), southern Moravia: respiratory and digestive disorders, diabetes

Mariánské Lázně (Marienbad), western Bohemia: renal disorders, respiratory ailments, skin diseases, metabolic disorders

Nový Smokovec (Neuschmecks in der Hohen Tatra), eastern Slovakia: disorders of internal secretion and metabolism

Piešt'any (Pistyan), western Slovakia: rheumatic ailments, nervous disorders

Poděbrady, central Bohemia: heart disease

Štrbské Pleso (Tschirmer See in der Hohen Tatra), eastern Slovakia: asthma, industrial poisoning

Teplice (Teplitz), northern Bohemia: muscular disorders, vascular diseases

Třeboň (Wittingau), southern Bohemia: muscular disorders

Trenčianské Teplice (Trentschin-Teplits), western Slovakia: muscular disorders, rheumatic diseases

Further information about individual spas can be obtained from the spa authorities or (for spas in Bohemia and Moravia) from *Balnea*, 11001 Praha 1, Pařížská 11, and (for spas in Slovakia) *Slovakoterma*, 88141 Bratislava, Radlinského 13; or from Čedok.

Sports

Angling

Almost half a million Czechoslovaks are anglers in the rivers, streams, lakes and ponds. A plentiful supply of fish is ensured by the fish-breeding complex at the south Bohemian town of Tábor, which provides 50 million young pike a year alone for home and abroad. Fishing reserves are organized by local angling clubs. Information can be obtained from Čedok. Carp, tench, bass, bream, barbel, grayling, chub, pike, perch, pike-perch, catfish, eels and trout are fished.

Hunting

Čedok can supply a hunting permit for certain types of game (red deer, fallow deer, roe deer, mouflon, wild boar, pheasants, hare, wild duck – even brown bears). Besides the not inconsiderable fees the huntsman has also to pay for a ghillie and possibly an interpreter. If he is successful there is a trophy fee to pay too, which can run to several hundred pounds. Accomodation for sportsmen is in mountain hotels or forest lodges.

Mountaineering

Czechoslovakian mountaineers take part in Himalaya expeditions and climb mountains of all levels of difficulty all over the world. They learn their skills at training cliffs in Bohemian Paradise (Český raj), Bohemian Switzerland (České Švýcarsko), Slovak Paradise (Slovensky raj), the Little Fatra (Malá Fatra) and of course in the High Tatras (Vysoké Tatry). All these ranges are also open to foreign mountaineers.

Rambling

Czechoslovakia is a paradise for ramblers, with 50,000 km of signposted footpaths through a wide variety of landscapes, from Moravian karst to the High Tatras. German speakers will find Otakar Mohyla's Kompass-Wanderführer *Tschechoslowakei* useful.

Telephone

Long distant calls abroad can be made from almost all telephone boxes and major post offices. Public telephones take 1 Kčs coins. The code for the United Kingdom is 0044, for Eire 00353, for the US and Canada 001, for Australia 0061 and for New Zealand 0064.

Tipping

Officially there is no tipping and service is included in the bill at restaurants and hotels. If you are pleased with the service, however, 5–10% can be added to the total. It is difficult to tip waiters in taverns because there is a single waiter to collect all payments.

Visas

Visas are not required for UK, Eire, US and Canadian nationals with a valid full passport. UK nationals are permitted to stay for six months, Eire, US and Canadian nationals for three months. New Zealand and Australian nationals require a visa, valid for 30 days. Extensions may be obtained at police stations.

Photographic Acknowledgements

Colour plates
Christel Gorys, Krefeld 1–22, 24
Werner Neumeister, Munich 23

Black and white plates
Jiří Doležal, Prague 1–4, 8, 11, 14, 17–20
Erhard Gorys, Krefeld 5–7, 9–10, 12–13, 15–16, 21, 24, 29, 31–33, 40–42, 47–51, 57, 59, 61, 63, 65
Max Grönert, Cologne 22–23, 25–28, 30, 34–39, 43, 46, 52–56, 58, 60, 62, 64

Text illustrations
Archiv für Kunst und Geschichte, Berlin pp. 18, 62, 73, 207
Erhart Gorys, Krefeld pp. 31, 128, 250, 262
Max Grönert, Cologne pp. 40, 49, 53
Ullstein Bilderdiest, Berlin pp. 20, 23, 25, 27, 171, 228, 263

Maps
Berndtson und Berndtson, Fürstenfeldbruck

Plans
DuMont Buchverlag, Cologne

All information in this book has been provided to the best of the author's knowledge and has been checked by him and the publisher with the greatest possible care. However, no responsibility can be taken for any possible inaccuracies.

We are always most grateful to readers who can draw our attention to errors and omissions. Please write to: Pallas Athene (publishers), 59 Linden Gardens, London W2 4HJ.

Prague Metro

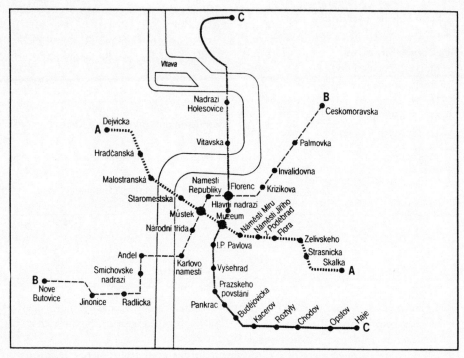

Booklist

General

Garton Ash, T. The Uses of Adversity, London 1989

We the People: the Revolutions of 89, London 1990

Glenny, M. The Rebirth of History: Eastern Europe in the Age of Democracy, London 1990

Havel, V. Living in Truth, London 1989

Letters to Olga, London 1989

Disturbing the Peace, London 1990

Open Letters – Selected Prose 1965–1990, London 1991

Masaryk, T.G. The Meaning of Czechoslovak History (ed. R. Wellek), London 1974

Rokyta, H. Die böhmischen Länder: Handbuch der Denkmäler und Gedenkstätten europäischer Kulturbeziehungen in den böhmischen Ländern, Salzburg 1970

Rechcígl, M. (ed.) The Czechoslovak Contribution to World Culture, The Hague etc. 1964

History

Brock, P. The Slovak National Awakening, Toronto 1976

Brock, P. and H. G. Skilling The Czech Renascence of the nineteenth century, Toronto 1970

Dekan, J. Moravia Magna: the Great Moravian Empire, London 1979

Dvornik, F. The Slavs in European History and Civilization, New Brunwick 1962

Evans, R.J.W. Rudolf II and his World, Oxford 1973

Heřman, J. Jewish Cemeteries in Bohemia and Moravia, Prague n.d.

Hillel, J.K. The Making of Czech Jewry: National Conflict and Jewish Society, Oxford 1988

Jarret, B. The Emperor Charles IV, London 1935

Kamensky, H. A History of the Hussite Revolution, Berkeley 1967

Koestler, A. The Sleepwalkers: A History of Man's changing vision of the Universe, London 1959

Krejčí, J. Czechoslovakia at the Crossroads of European History, London 1990

Lettrich, J. History of Modern Slovakia, Toronto 1985 (first publ. 1955)

Mamety, V.S. and R. Luža A History of the Czechoslovak Republic 1918–1948, Princeton 1973

Odložlík, O. The Hussite King, New Brunswick 1965

Renner, H. A History of Czechoslovakia, London 1988

Ross, J. The Winter Queen, London 1979

Shawcross, W. Dubček and Czechoslovakia, London 1990

Seton-Watson, R.W. Racial Problems in Hungary, London 1908 (on Slovakia)

A History of the Czechs and Slovaks, London 1943

Spinka, M. John Hus: a Biography, Princeton 1968

Taylor, A.J.P. The Habsburg Monarchy, London 1948 (and later editions)

Vyšný, P. Neo-Slavism and the Czechs 1898–1914, Cambridge 1977

Wiskemann, E. Czechs and Germans, London 1938

Wedgwood, C.V. The Thirty Years War, London 1957

Zeman, Z. Prague Spring: A Report on Czechoslovakia, Harmondsworth 1969

Zeman, Z. The Masaryks: The Making of Czechoslovakia, London 1970 (repr. 1990)

Memoirs

Charles IV, Vita Karoli Quarti, Hanau 1979

Davenport, M. Too Strong for Fantasy, London 1968

Glanville Baker, B. From a Terrace in Prague, London 1923

Leigh Fermor, P. A Time for Gifts, London 1977

Margolius Kovaly, H. Prague Farewell, London 1988

Martin, N. Prague Winter, London 1990

Parrott, C. The Serpent and the Nightingale, London 1977

Travel

Bassett, R. Guide to Central Europe, London 1987

Burke, M.J. Czechoslovakia, London 1976

Druce, G. Wanderings in Czechoslovakia, London 1930

Robson, E.I. A Wayfarer in Czecho-Slovakia, London 1935

White, W. A July Holiday in Saxony, Bohemia and Silesia, London 1857

Art and architecture

Baroque in Bohemia: an exhibition of Czech art organized by the National Gallery Prague, (exh. cat. Arts Council), London 1969

Bialostocki, J. The Art of the Renaissance in Eastern Europe, Oxford 1976

Blažíček, O.J. Baroque Art in Bohemia, Feltham 1968

Buxton, D. The Wooden Churches of Eastern Europe: an introductory survey, Cambridge 1981

Cannon-Brookes, P. Czech Sculpture 1800–1938 (exh. cat. National Gallery of Wales), London 1983

Czech Functionalism 1918–1938 (exh. cat. Architectural Association), London 1987

Damas, J. Giovanni Santini Aichel, architecte gothico-baroque en Bôhème, Paris 1989

Devětsil: Czech Avant-Garde Art, Architecture and Design of the 1920s and 30s (exh. cat. Museum of Modern Art Oxford), 1990

Dvořáková, V. et al. Gothic Mural Painting in Bohemia and Moravia 1300–1378, Oxford 1964

Haupt, H. et al. Le Bestiaire de Rodolphe II, Paris 1990

Hempel, E. Baroque Art and Architecture in Central Europe (Pelican History of Art), Harmondsworth 1965

Knox, B. The Architecture of Prague and Bohemia, London 1962

Norberg-Schulz, C. Late Baroque and Rococo Architecture, London 1979

Margolius, I. Cubism in Architecture and the Applied Arts – Bohemia and France 1910–1914, London 1979

Merhautová, A. and D. Třešík Románské Umění v Čechách a na Moravě (Romanesque Art in Bohemia and Moravia), Prague 1984 (with good illustrations and a summary in English)

Petrová, S. and J.-L. Olivié, Bohemian Glass, Paris 1990

Seibt, F. (ed.) Renaissance in Böhmen, Munich 1985

Součková, M. Baroque in Bohemia, Ann Arbor 1980

Stejskal, K. L'Empereur Charles IV: L'art en Europe au XIVe siècle, Paris 1980

Swoboda, K. (ed.) Barock in Böhmen, Munich 1964

Gotik in Böhmen, Munich 1969

Trevor-Roper, H. Princes and Artists: Patronage and Ideology at Four Habsburg Courts 1517–1633, London 1976

Prague

Burian, J. and J. Svoboda, Prague Castle, Prague 1973

Burkhardt, F., et al. Jože Plečnik, architect 1872–1957, Cambridge, Mass. and London 1989

Flegl, M. Prague, Prague 1989

Lion, J. The Prague Ghetto, London 1959

Neumann J. Rudolphine Prague, Prague 1984

Pavlík, M. and V. Uher Dialogue of Forms: Prague Baroque Architecture, London and New York 1977

Prag um 1600: Kunst und Kultur am Hofe Rudolfs II. (exh. cat.), Essen 1988

Wirth, Z. Prag in Bildern aus fünf Jahrhunderten, Prague 1954

Literature

Brod, M. Tycho Brahe's Path to God, Munich (1925)

Comenius, J.A. The Labyrinth of the World, Ann Arbor 1972

Čapek, K. RUR and The Insect Play, Oxford 1961

Čapek, K. Towards a Radical Centre, London 1990

Gruša, J. Franz Kafka of Prague, London 1983

Hašek, J. The Good Soldier Švejk (trans. C. Parrot), London (Penguin) 1973

Hrabal, B. I Served the King of England, London 1989

The Death of Mr Baltisberger (1966), London 1990

Kafka, F. Complete Novels, London 1983

Complete Short Stories, London 1983

Diary, London 1969

Klíma, I. A Summer Affair, London 1987

Love and Garbage, London 1991

Kundera, M. The Joke (1983),

The Book of Laughter and Forgetting (1982)

The Unbearable Lightness of Being (1984)

Lustig, A. Diamonds of the Night (1958), London 1978

Meyrink, G. The Golem, Munich 1915, London 1928/1985

Mörike, E. Mozart's Journey to Prague (1855), London 1957

Němcová, B. Granny: Scenes from Country Life, Westport Conn. 1976

Neruda, J. Tales of the Little Quarter (1878), London 1957

Škvorecký, J. The Cowards (1958), London 1970

The Bass Saxophone (1967), London 1978

Stifter, A. Brigitta (and other stories), London 1990

Wellek, R. Essays on Czech Literature, London 1963

Poetry

Holub, M. The Fly, Newcastle (Bloodaxe) 1987

Poems Before and After, Newcastle (Bloodaxe) 1990

Vanishing Lung Syndrome, London (Faber) 1990

The Jingle Bell Principle, Newcastle (Bloodaxe) 1991

Čejka, J. et al. The New Czech Poetry, Newcastle (Bloodaxe) 1991

Fischerová, S. The Tremor of Racehorses, Newcastle (Bloodaxe) 1990

Hanzlík, J. Selected Poems, Newcastle (Bloodaxe) 1991

Janovic, V. The House of the Tragic Poet, Newcastle (Bloodaxe) 1988

Rilke, R.M. Selected Poems, Harmondsworth 1964

Seifert, J. The Plague Column, London 1979

Selected Poetry, London 1986

Music

Burney, C. The Present State of Music in Germany, the Netherlands and United Provinces, London 1773

Clapham, J. Dvořák, London 1979

Kristek, J. Mozart's Don Giovanni in Prague, Prague 1987

Newmarch, R. The Music of Czechoslovakia, Oxford 1942 (repr 1969)

Tyrrell, J. Czech Opera, Cambridge 1988

Vogel, J. Leoš Janáček: a biography, London 1981

Large, B. Smetana, London 1970

Persons

Figures in *italics* refer to illustrations

Abelles, Shimon Abrams 49
Abraham, Patriarch 20
Adalbert (Vojtěch), Bishop of Prague 16, 60, 92, 138
Adalram, Archbishop of Salzburg 368
Adamec, Ladislav 35
Adamites 203
Adela of Eger, wife of Frederick Barbarossa 217
Adelaide (Adelheid), wife of Soběslav I 71
Adler, Dr. Bernhard Vinzens 220
Agnes (Anežka) of Bohemia, Saint 54, 67, 68
Aichbauer, Johann Georg 120
Aichel, Johann Santini- see Santini
Alagrav, Johannes 198
Albenreuth, Wilhelm Lamminger von, called Lomikar 216
Albert I, German King 18
Albert II, King of Bohemia and Hungary, German King 22
Albrecht von Albrechtsberg, Konrad Adolf 310
Aleš, Mikoláš 46, 47, 51, 68, 71, 124, 136, 139, 165, 212, 264
Aleš of Malkovice 121
Alexander I, Tsar 26, 247, 248, 283, 303, 386, 411
Alexander III, Tsar 327
Alexander of Bardejov 406
Alexander of Košice 385
Alexius of Bardejov 406
Alliprandi, Giovanni Battista 25, 43, 76, 81, 117, 217, 284, 294
Althan family 308, 309
Althan, Count Johann Michael II 309, 316
Althan, Maria Anna (Princess Pignatelli) 309, 310
Altomonte, Andrea 168
Andrássy family 388
Andrássy, Count Dénes 388
Andrássy, Peter 388
André, Matthias 168
Andrew II, King of Hungary 372, 384
Andrew III, King of Hungary 383

Angeli, Domenico d' 310
Angelus, apothecary 43
Anhalt-Cöthen, Duke of 225
Anjou family 373
Anna Jagiełło, wife of Ferdinand I 90, 115
Anne of Bohemia, wife of Richard II of England 20
Anne of Foix, wife of Vladislav II Jagiello 90
Anne of Schweidnitz, third wife of Charles IV 143
Anton of Klatovy 214
Aostali, Giovanni Battista 294
Aostali, Udalrico (Avostalis, Ulrich) 115, 117, 141, 294
Arcimboldo, Giuseppe 87
Arnošt see Ernest
Arnulf of Carinthia, East Frankish king 15, 16, 334
Arogno, Baldassare Maggi da 167, 312
Asam, Cosmas Damian 138, 139
Asam, Peter the elder 47
Aspelt, Peter, Archbishop of Mainz 18
Augustin of Kutná Hora 154
Auguston, Jakob 213
Augustus III, King of Saxony and Poland 224
Avostalis see Aostali

Babenberg family 17
Bach, Johann Christian 80
Bach, Johann Sebastian 225
Baier (Charles IV's physician) 223
Balk, Hermann 313
Balko, Franz Xaver 154
Balli, Ambrosio 239
Balšánek, Antonín 42, 264
Barbara Celjská, wife of Sigismund 366
Bärenstein see Pernštejn
Barrault, Jean Louis 158
Bártfay, Tíbor 369
Bartoň, Josef 292
Barwig, Franz 332
Bat'a, Antonín 320

Bat'a, Ján 380
Bat'a, Tomáš 320
Bathory, Stephen 359
Batthányi, Archbishop of Esztergom 354
Bauer, Johann Baptist 246
Baugut, F. 153, 155
Bauer, Felice 231
Bavor I of Strakonice 201
Bayer, Paul Ignaz 25, 131, 138, 164
Bebek family 388
Bebek, Count Dedrich 388
Becher, Joseph 226
Bechteller, Kasper 92
Becquerel, Antoine 233
Beer, Franz 164
Beethoven, Ludwig van 80, 223, 225, 247, 290,
    326, 333, 363
Béla I, King of Hungary 368
Béla III, King of Hungary 378
Béla IV, King of Hungary 335, 360, 366, 375,
    380, 381, 383, 389, 407, 408
Běhounek, František 234
Bella, Tommaso 310
Benda, František 295
Bendl, Johann Georg 54, 87
Benedek, General Ludwig August von 260
Beneš, Edvard 29, 30, 31, 32, 33, 34, 412
Benešov family 158
Berchtold family 303
Berger, V. A. 159
Berka, Hynek 115
Berka of Dubá family 149, 243, 254, 257
Berka of Dubá, Zdislav 243
Berlioz, Hector 70, 127
Bernini, Gian Lorenzo 118, 325
Bezruč, Petr 256
Bianco, Baccio 83
Biberstein family 257, 284
Bibiena, Antonio Galli 336
Biemann, Dominik 290
Bílek, Jakub 146
Birk, Georg 299
Bismarck, Otto von 80, 225, 303
Blanche de Valois, first wife of Charles IV 18,
    130, 143, 146
Blažek, mason 294
Blücher, Prince 225
Böhm, Heinrich 364
Böhm, Josef Kamil 58
Bol, Ferdinand 310
Boleslav I the Cruel, Duke of Bohemia 16, 37, 90

Boleslav II the Pious, Duke of Bohemia 16, 37,
    113, 138, 149, 411
Boleslav I Chrobry the Bold, Duke of Poland 17
Bolla, Abondio 68
Bolzano, Bernard 151
Bořivoj I, Duke of Bohemia 16, 36, 83, 149, 411
Bořivoj II, Duke of Bohemia 92
Bossi, Carlo Giuseppe 292
Bouda, Cyril 89
Brahe, Tycho 23, 49, 50, 115, 118, 121, 152
Brahms, Johannes 125
Brandl, Peter Johann 53, 81, 138, 154, 157, 205,
    247, 258, 262, 282, 310, 318
Brasca, Giovanni Jacopo 316
Brath, Anton 292
Bratoněk, Vojtěch 123
Braun, Anton 47, 134
Braun, Matthias Bernhard 25, 44, 51, 53, 58, 61,
    77, 79, 81, 90, 91, 118, 133, 134, 159, 247, 249,
    256, 262, 282, 284, 285, 292, 293
Brázda, Jan 153
Brengisejn, Albert 410
Brengisejn, Jan, (Master Johann of Preschau)
    409, 410
Brentano, Clemens von 247
Breslav, Prince 334
Breu, Jörg the elder 326
Breuer, printer 398
Brezhnev, Leonid 34, 412
Brixi 153
Brod, Max 74, 125
Broggio, Giulio 240
Broggio, Ottavio 25, 236, 239, 240, 249, 250, 251
Brokoff, Ferdinand Maximilian 58, 70, 77, 80, 82,
    113, 115, 249
Brokoff, Johann 57, 116, 132, 145
Brožík, Václav 46, 129
Bruckner, Anton 231
Brüderle, J.M. 120
Brunner, Vratislav Hugo 89
Brus, Antonín, Archbishop of Prague 117
Břetislav I, Duke of Bohemia 17, 92, 216, 306,
    308, 411
Břetislav II, Duke of Bohemia 62,92
Buchar, Jan 291
Bünau family 252
Buquoy, General 78, 197
Burebista, Dacian king 13
Burkhart of Janovitz, see Purkart
Burney, Charles 80, 295
Butler, Colonel 218

Caesar, Gaius Julius 13
Callot, Jacques 293
Campion, Giovanni 139
Canevale, Giovanni Domenico 54
Capestrano, Johannes 298
Caraffa, General Antonio 408
Caratti, Francesco 25, 52, 54, 80, 93, 118, 205
Caretto de Millesimo, Count Johann 43
Carloman, German prince 15
Carlone, Carlo 51
Carlone, Giovanni Battista 357
Carracci, Annibale 154
Casanova, Giacomo 77, 248, 249
Casimir III the Great, King of Poland 364
Casimir IV, King of Poland 22
Cervantes, Miguel 160
Chamberlain, Neville 31, 228
Charlemagne (Charles I), Holy Roman Emperor
  14, 18, 134
Charles IV, Holy Roman Emperor 18, 19, *19*, 20,
  23, 37, 38, 40, 42ff, 51, 55, 56, 65, 69, 70, 72,
  85, 87ff, 96, 115, 123, 124, 127, 130, 132ff,
  141ff, 146, 149, 151, 153, 157, 161, 200, 223,
  227, 229, 238, 245, 281, 296, 301, 302, 306, 308,
  364, 366, 411
Charles V, Holy Roman Emperor 22, 303, 372
Charles VI, Holy Roman Emperor 26, 376
Charles I, Emperor of Austria 30
Charles IV the Fair, King of France 18
Charles V, King of France 20
Charles X, King of France 80
Charles I Robert, King of Hungary 364, 376, 392
Charles, Archduke 306
Chateaubriand, François-René de 80
Chods 215, 216
Chopin, Frédéric 225, 231, 247
Chotek, Countess Sophie 158
Christine, Queen of Sweden 206
Clam-Gallas family see Gallas
Clare of Assisi, Saint 67
Clary-Aldringen, Count Franz Wenzel 248
Claudel, Paul 78
Clemenceau, Georges 225
Clement VI, Pope 87
Cola di Rienzo 19
Colin, Alexander 90
Collins, Chris 281
Comenius, Jan Amos see Komenský
Cometa, Antonio 205
Cometa, Domenico Battista 205
Conrad IV, German King 229

Conrad see also Konrad
Constantine the Philosopher, Saint see Cyril,
  Saint
Constantine VII Porphyrogenitus, Byzantine
  Emperor 15
Conti, Pietro Antonio 360
Copernicus, Nicolas 80
Corati-Orseti, stuccadore 353
Corbellini, Giacomo Antonio 251
Cornelius, Peter 67
Corradini, Antonio 92
Cranach, Lucas the elder 398
Cranach, Lucas the younger 240, 298
Crinitz, Ignaz 310
Csák, Maté see Čak, Matúš
Csáky family 390
Csáky, Count Stephen 404
Cubr F. 137
Curie, Pierre 233
Curie-Skłodowska, Marie 233
Cyprian 404
Cyril, Saint 14, 15, 132, 320, 356
Cyrus, Andrea 292
Czernín family 93
Czernín of Chudenice, Heřman 149
Czernín von Chudenice, Count Jan Humprecht
  25, 92, 118
Czernín-Morzin family 289
Czerny, Carl 356

Čák, Matúš of Trenčín 364, 366, 380
Čalfa, Marián 35, 412
Čapek, Josef 81
Čapek, Karel 125, 136
Čech 151
Čech, Jan 239
Černik, Oldřich 34, 35, 412
Černín, see Czernin
Černý, František M. 132

Daladier, Edouard 31
Dalibor, knight 114
Damajan, Deodat 77
Daun, Count Leopold Josef von 158
Daysinger, Josef 307
Debureau, Jean Gaspard 157, 158
Debureau, Philippe Germain 157
Dee, Arthur 206
Dee, John 23, 206
Dee, Mrs. John 206
Delmedigo, Josef Salomon 66

Descartes, René 139
Devereux, Walter 218
Devoina 359
Deworetzky, Ferdinand Damian 164
Dientzenhofer, Christoph 25, 47, 74, 75, 80,
    119f, 138, 220
Dientzenhofer, Georg 75
Dientzenhofer, Johann 75
Dientzenhofer, Kilian Ignaz 25, 43, 47, 48, 53,
    75, 75, 76, 81, 87, 117, 119, 120, 132ff, 138,
    145, 153, 215, 227, 291
Dientzenhofer, Leonhard 75
Dientzenhofer, Wolfgang 75
Dietrich, Josef 162
Dietrichstein family 79, 297, 305, 326
Dietrichstein, Adam von 305
Dietrichstein, Cardinal Prince Franz von 119,
    297, 305, 315, 326
Dietrichstein, Leopold von 305
Dittersdorf, Karl Ditters von 206, 295, 329
Dittmann, Kristián 95
Dobner, J 54
Dobrovský, Josef 80, 151
Dollinger, F. 240
Dončo, nobleman 400
Donndorf, Adolf 228
Donne, John 53
Donner, Georg Raphael 355, 356, 366
Dostoevsky, Feodor Mikhailovich 125
Drahomíra of Stodor 37
Drentwett, Jonas 353
Dryák, A. 127
Dubček, Alexander 34, 336, 412
Dubova (Dubovec), Jan of 381
Dürer, Albrecht 117, 256, 326
Dušek, Jan Ladislav 139, 295
Dvořák, Antonín 125, 134, 136, 152, 226
Dvořák, Dominik 294
Dvořák, František 157
Dvořák, Karel 58, 59
Dyck, Anthonis van 249

Eberle, Jakob 193, 227
Ebert, Karl Egon 151
Eckstein, Franz Gregor 320
Edelmann, Wenzel 325
Edelspitz, Nikolaus von 307
Edward the Confessor, King of England, Saint
    89
Edward, Prince of Wales 18
Edward VII, King-Emperor 225, 231

Efeldar, Hans 154
Eggenberg family 166, 168, 193
Eggenberg, Baron Johann Ulrich 166
Eigler, Kaspar 154
Einstein, Albert 46, 66
Elizabeth of Bavaria, wife of Franz-Joseph I 364
Elizabeth of Pomerania, fourth wife of Charles
    IV 20, 89
Elizabeth of Thuringia, Saint 59, 67, 356, 384
Elizabeth Přemysl, wife of John of Luxemburg
    18, 301
Elizabeth Rejscka (Ryksa), wife of Wenceslas II
    and of Rudolph I 260, 261
Elizabeth Stuart, wife of Frederick, Elector
    Palatine 24, 139
Eller, Peter 335
Engler, Michael 325
Erdödy family 363
Erdödy, Count Johann Nepomuk 363
Erdödy, Count Josef 363
Erhard of Ulm 385
Eritzer, Antonio 167
Erna, Andrea 301
Erna, Giovanni Battista 310
Erna, Otto 298
Ernst August, Duke of Hanover 224
Ernst, Wolf 56
Esterházy family 375, 376
Esterházy, Emmerich, Archbishop of Esztergom
    356
Esterházy, Count Imre 390
Eugen, Archduke 328
Eugene of Savoy, Prince 294

Fabricius, Philipp 44, 94
Faconi, Giovanni Maria 205
Falkenstein, Záviš of 164, 195
Fanta, Josef 129
Faustus, Doctor Johann 44, 131
Feigler, Ignaz 336
Felicissimus, Saint 120
Fellner, Ferdinand 228, 256, 259, 301, 356
Ferdinand I, Holy Roman Emperor 22, 24, 28,
    38, 52, 85, 89, 90, 115, 139, 214, 239, 365, 411
Ferdinand II, Holy Roman Emperor 24, 25, 166,
    218, 223, 291
Ferdinand III, Holy Roman Emperor 26, 56, 82
Ferdinand I, Emperor of Austria 85, 283, 324
Ferdinand, Archduke of the Tyrol 85, 114, 139,
    146, 223
Ferenc II Rákoczi see Rákoczi

Ferrabosco, Pietro 303
Fibich, Zdeněk 136
Fichte, Johann Gottlieb 247
Fierlinger, Zdeněk 33
Filippi, Giovanni Maria 80
Fischer von Erlach, Johann Bernhard 25, 51, 68, 90, 92, 120, 282, 296, 308, 309, 310, 318
Foerster, Josef Bohuslav 78
Fontana, Baldassare 326
Forgács family 386
Fragner, Jaroslav 69
Francis of Assisi, Saint 67
Francis I, Holy Roman Emperor 43
Francis I (II), Emperor of Austria (Holy Roman Emperor) 26, 220, 247, 283, 303, 328, 354, 411
Franz Joseph I, Emperor of Austria 28, 60, 62, 87, 124, 225, 324, 327
Franz Ferdinand, Archduke 158, 242
Frederick I Barbarossa, Holy Roman Emperor 19, 217, 220, 302
Frederick II, Holy Roman Emperor 17, 67, 217
Frederick II, the Great, King of Prussia 39, 158, 240, 242, 296
Frederick William III, King of Prussia 247
Frederick III, Elector of Brandenburg 224
Frederick, Elector Palatine 24, 139
Freud, Sigmund 332
Friček, Martin 131
Frick, Wilhelm, Reichsprotektor 33
Fritigil, Marcoman princess 13
Frobzig, Dr 226
Fröhlich, David 403
Fugger family 372, 378
Fugger, Jakob II, the Rich 372
Fürstenberg family 146, 148
Fux, Jan 77

Gablenz, Field Marshal Ludwig von 286
Gahura, Fratišek 320
Galica, Mikuláš 393
Galilei, Galileo 53
Gall, Saint 70
Gallas (Clam-Gallas) family 256, 257
Gallas, Count Johann Wenzel 51
Gallas, Count Matthias 257, 258
Galliardi, Gottlieb Anton 371
Gans, David 66
Garbi, Pietro 303
Garrigue, Charlotte 29
Geiger, Ferdinand 76
Gendorf, Christoph von 289

George of Litoměříce 238
George of Poděbrady, King of Bohemia 22, 38, 41, 42, 49, 62, 90, 149, 210, 212, 314, 411
Gerster, Kálmán 393
Géza I, King of Hungary 368
Géza II, King of Hungary 389
Glaubic, mayor of Malá strana 72
Glaubner, Johann Rudolf 222
Gluck, Christoph Willibald 50, 243, 295
Gočar, Josef 261
Gode, Ludwig 353, 366
Godyn, Abraham and Isaak 138
Goethe, Johann Wolfgang von 74, 220, 225, 228, 230, 232, 245, 247, 248, 286, 290
Golem 65, 66
Goltz, Count Johann Ernst 48
Gorbachev, Mikhail 35
Gordon, John 218
Gottman, Č. V. 199
Gottwald, Klement 34, 40, 48, 70, 140, 320
Gozzius of Orvieto 314
Granovsky of Granov, Jakob 50
Grassalkovich, Prince Anton 336
Gregory VII, Pope 135
Gregory XIII, Pope 250, 251
Griesbach, Florian 117, 152
Grillparzer, Franz 261, 313
Grimm, Mauritz 298, 299, 301
Groh, István 399
Grossmann, Peter 374
Grotte, Alfred 65
Gschwendt, Josef 215
Guarini, Guarino 25, 75, 77
Gustavus II Adolphus, King of Sweden 24
Gustav IV, King of Sweden 225
Guta of Habsburg see Jitka
Guta II Přemysl 68
Gutenberg, Johannes 198

Haas, Willy 74
Hablavcova, Františka see Hablawetz
Hablawetz, Franciska 388
Habsburg family 20, 22, 25ff, 40, 73, 85, 89, 139, 164, 202, 211, 257, 315, 324, 357, 363
Hácha, Emil 32
Hadrian II, Pope 15
Haffenecker, Anton 69, 80, 85
Hähnel, Ernst Julius 55
Hain, Caspar 396, 399, 400
Hájek, Jiří 35
Hamilton, Johann Georg de 165

Hansen, Theophil 402
Hanuš of Růže 45, 155
Hanuš of Mühlheim, Johann 71
Hapsburgs see Habsburgs
Harcourt, Iphigénie d' 365, 367
Harrach family 290, 291
Harrach, Ernst 41
Harrach, Count 291
Harrachov see Harrachsdorf
Harrachsdorf, Dorothea 160
Hartmann, Josef 409
Hašek, Jaroslav 134
Hauberisser, Georg 328
Hausrucker, Hans Georg 332
Havel, Václav 35, 40, 127, 164, 412
Haydn, Joseph 336, 356
Hebenstreit, Joseph 374
Heermann, Johann Georg 138
Heermann, Paul 138
Hefele, Melchior 354
Hegedüs, Armin 364
Heilmann, Jakob 246
Heinrich (Jindřich) 209
Heinrick C.G. 258
Heintsch, Johann Georg 131, 254
Heinz, Georg A. 326
Helmer, Hermann 228, 256, 259, 301, 356
Hemma, Princess 149
Henlein, Konrad 30, 31, 33, 245, 255
Hennevogel, Johann 387
Henry I, the Fowler, Holy Roman Emperor 90
Henry II, German King 17
Henry III, Holy Roman Emperor 17, 216
Henry IV, German King 17, 411
Henry VI, Holy Roman Emperor 217
Henry VII, Holy Roman Emperor 18
Henry III, King of England 67, 89
Henry of Carinthia 18, 211
Hermann, Johann 227
Heroldt, Wolff Hieronymus 57
Heydrich, Reinhard 32, 89, 133, 148, 412
Hiebl, Johann 52, 53
Hilbert, Kamil 89, 147, 148
Hildebrandt, Johann Lukas von 25, 134, 308, 310
Hillebrandt, Franz Anton 353, 360
Himmler, Heinrich 328
Hirtz, Hans 317
Hitler, Adolf 31, 328
Hlavica, J. 369
Hnátek, František 153
Hodějovský family 158, 160

Hodějovská, Dorota 160
Hodějovský, Přech 160
Hodža, Milan 31
Hoffmann, Bernard 227
Hofmann, Vladislav 130
Höger, Bernhard 297
Holbein, Hans 197
Höllriegl, Matthias 354
Hölzel, Moritz 406
Honthorst, Gerrit van 310
Hötzendorf, Conrad von 225
Hradec, Adam of 312
Hradec, Katharina of (Waldstein) 313
Hradec, Zacharias of 312, 313
Hrbek, Markus 120
Hrubý, J. 137
Hubáček, Karel 257
Hubert, Josef 380
Hubmaier, Balthasar 304
Huckeswagen family 322
Hudeček, Antonín 293
Humboldt, Wilhelm von 225
Hummel, Johann Nepomuk 356
Hunyadi family 373
Hurvínek 213
Hus, Jan 20f, *21*, 38, 46, 47, 48, 52, 70, 71, 153, 197, 201, 203, 411
Husák, Gustav 34, 35, 412

Ibrahim Ibn Jakub 40, 62
Illeshazy family 365
Illéshazy, Count Josef 366, 367
Illéshazy, Count Kaspar 366
Ilow (Illo), Field Marshall Freiherr von 220
Innocent III, Pope 330
Innocent VI, Pope 19, 411
Isaac, Patriarch 20
Iswolsky 231

Jacob, Patriarch 20
Jäckel, Matthäus Wenzel 54, 58
Jagiełło family 149, 155 and see Vladislav II and Anna
Jakeš, Miloš 35
Jakub, mayor of Pressburg 354
James I, King of England 24
Jan Augusta, Bishop 146, 147
Janáček, Leoš 125, 301, 321, 322
Janák, Pavel 118, 127, 130
Jankovič, Jozef 374
Jánošík, Juro 382

Janoušek, Antonín 410
Janowitz see Purkart
Janscha, Lorenz *194, 285*
Jaroš, Tomáš 115
Jedlička, Josef 156
Jehuda ben Bezalel, see Löw, Rabbi
Jenzenstein, John of, Archbishop of Prague 56
Jerome of Prague 203
Jindřich, Jindřich 216
Jirásek, Alois 139, 216, 293
Jiří Poděbradský see George of Poděbrady
Jiskra, Ján 391, 392
Jitka (Guta) of Habsburg, wife of Wenceslas II 282
Joanna, wife of King Charles IV of France 18
Joanna of Bavaria, wife of Wenceslas IV 49
Johann Friedrich I, Elector of Saxony 239
Johann Georg III, Elector 224
Johann of Preschau see Brengisejn, Jan
Johannes von Saaz (or Tepl) 245
John VIII, Pope 15, 368
John XIII, Pope 37, 113
John V Palaeologus, Byzantine Emperor 20
John of Banská Bystrica (Neusohl) 394
John of Luxemburg, King of Bohemia 18, 40, 44, 48, 88, 146, 212, 237, 250 285, 305, 411
John of Nepomuk, Saint 56, 57, 91, 156, 318
John Henry, Margrave of Bohemia 51, 301, 302
John Paul II, Pope 320
Jordaens, Jacob 292
Jordan, Thomas 366
Joseph I, Holy Roman Emperor 26, 224
Joseph II, Holy Roman Emperor 26, 39, 62, 63, 68, 81, 87, 113, 122, 193, 240, 250, 256, 301, 308, 317, 331, 411
Judith of Thuringia, wife of Vladislav II Přemysl 56, 247
Jungmann, Josef 130, 237
Jurkovič, Dušan 292

Kafka, Bohumil 93, 137, 140
Kafka, Franz 46, 47, 48, 50, 62, 74, 81, 114, 125, 128
Känischbauer, Johann 120
Kaňka, František Maximilián 25, 43, 52, 53, 54, 69, 81, 90, 92, 118, 124, 133, 151, 153, 159
Karo, Selicha Abigdor 65
Kässmann, Josef 305
Kastner, Jan 153
Kaunitz family 303
Kazimierz, Kings of Poland, see Casimir

Kelley, Edward 23, 114, 131
Kepler, Johannes 23, 49, 50, 53, 121
Kern, Antonín 120
Kielmann, Jakob 317
Kinský family 247, 281
Kinský, Baron 220
Kinský, Klaus 48
Kinský, Nastassia 48
Kinský, Prince Rudolf 220
Kisch, Egon Erwin 69
Kitzinger, Abraham Felix 252
Klausenburg, George of 87
Klausenburg, Martin of 87
Kleist, Heinrich von 247
Koch, Heinrich 305
Koch, Johann Wenzel 252
Koestler, Arthur 152
Kofránek, Ladislav 93
Kohar, General Andreas J. 380
Kohl, Johann (Jan) Friedrich 58, 119
Kollař, Jan 28
Kollmitz, Karl 398
Kolostuj, knight 247
Komenský, Jan Amos (Comenius) 83, 332
Königsberger, Michael 374
Konrad I Otto, King of Bohemia 136
Konrad II, Margrave of Moravia 307
Konrad see also Conrad
Körner, Theodor 252
Kosch, Johann Christoph 246
Kotěra, Jan 127, 261, 262
Kotzebue, August von 225
Kovař, Karel 132
Kowanda, Wenzel 316
Kozina, Jan Sladký 216
Kracker, Adam Tobias 297, 309
Kracker, Johann Lucas 76, 374, 387
Krakonoš see Krkonoš
Kramář, Karel 29, 412
Kramolín, Josef 283
Kranner, Josef 89
Kraus, Karl 282
Krauss, Johann Anton 387
Krčín of Jelčany, Jakob 207
Krisztián, Alexander 294
Krkonoš 285, 286
Kubelík, Jan 127, 137
Kubin, Alfred 237
Kuen, Franz Anton 251
Kuen, Markus, Bishop 326
Kuhn, master baker 233

Kühmayer, Robert 364
Kunhuta (Kunigunde), wife of Otakar II 68, 149, 164, 333
Kunigunde see Kunhuta
Kunštat (Kunstadt) family
Kunz, František 120
Kunz, Johann Josef 256
Kupetzky, Johann 282, 310
Kurland, Duke Peter of 292
Kurz von Senftenau, Jakob 121
Kurz, Anton 85
Kutuzov, Mikhail I., Marshal 386
Kuzma, Dušan 374
Kysela, František 89
Kysela, Ludvík 127

Lábler, Ludvík 155
Lachhofer, Johann 122
Ladislas IV, King of Hungary 354
Ladislas Postumus 22, 90
Laghi, Antonio 316
Landek, Lucretia of 283
Langer, Baron Joseph 43
Langer, Johann 386
Lany, Adolf A. 386
Lara, Maria Manriques de 81
Lauermann, Josef 122
Lawrence of Brindisi 121
Le Corbusier 320
Lechner, Ödön 356
Lederer, Hugo 298
Lederer, Josef 168
Lehmann, Lotte 332
Leibnitz, Baron Gottfried Wilhelm 225
Leipa family 254
Lendl, Ivan 321
Lengelacher, Ignaz 305
Lennon, John 79
Leo XII, Pope 225
Leopold I, Holy Roman Emperor 26, 114, 118, 197, 260, 353, 363, 383, 399
Leopold II, Holy Roman Emperor 26, 295
Leopold William, Archduke 206
Lerch, Johann 402
Lesley, Captain 218
Lessing, Gotthold Ephraim 69
Leuthner, Abraham 75, 229
Leux, Franz 258
Levetzow, Ulrike von 229, 230
Levý, Václav 136
Libuše 16, 36, 134, 137, 256, 307

Lichnowsky family 80, 333
Lichtenberg family 308, 310
Lidický, Karel 69
Liebig, Johann 255, 256
Liebscher, Adolf 123
Liebscher, Karl 123
Liechtenstein family 304, 305, 331
Liechtenstein, Hans 205
Liechtenstein, Karl von 73
Liechtenstein-Kastelkorn, Karl von, Bishop of Olomouc 327, 328
Lindner, Martin 385
Linhart of Aldeberg 193
Lischka, Johann Christoph 54, 251
Liszt, Franz 70, 125, 225, 247, 248, 333, 353
Liška, O. 261
Lobkowicz family 81, 149, 158, 237, 243, 244, 284
Lobkowicz, Princess Benigna Kateřina 119, 120
Lobkowicz, Jan of 115
Lobkowicz, Johann of 246
Lobkowicz, Polyxena of 81
Lobkowicz, Wenzel Eusebius of 114, 237
Lobkowicz, Zdeněk Popel of 81, 114
Loew, Rabbi see Löw
Lohelius, Jan, Abbot 121
Lomikar see Albenreuth
Loos, Adolf 302
Lothar, Holy Roman Emperor 151
Lothar, King of Saxony and German King 251
Louis the German, King of the East Franks 14, 15, 359
Louis IV, German King 217
Louis (Ludvík) II, King of Bohemia 22, 146, 166, 232
Louis I (Ludwik, Ludvík, Ľudovít, Lajos) the Great, King of Hungary and Poland 20, 359, 364, 366, 373, 375, 383
Löw, Jehuda ben Bezalel, Rabbi 65, pl.16
Lucchese, Filiberto 327
Lucchese, Giovanni 139
Lučan family 245
Lucian, Augustin 50
Ludmila of Pšov, Saint 16, 37, 143, 149, 411
Ludwig IV, Landgrave of Thuringia 384
Lukešová, J. 131
Lurago, Anselmo 48, 76, 85, 87, 113, 118
Lurago, Carlo 25, 52, 54, 75, 76, 80, 114, 131, 136, 145, 215, 244, 262, 291, 292
Lurago, Francesco 117
Luther, Martin 52

Luttringer, Andreas 353
Luxemburg dynasty 56, 89, 411 and see John of Luxemburg, Charles IV and Wenceslas IV

Mácha, Karl Hynek 151
Mahler, Gustav 295, 313, 315, 317
Mahmud I, Sultan of Turkey 356
Maisel, Mordechai 62, 65, 66
Makh, Laurenz 168
Malejovský, Josef 72
Mandík, Michal 325
Mandl, Michael Bernhard 58
Mánes, Josef 45, 67, 68
Mann, Johann 380
Mangoldi, Giovanni 305
Marbod, Germanic king 13
Marceau, Marcel 158
Marchant, gardener 160
Marchetti, architect 200
Marchetti, Francesco 138
Marcia, Saint 120
Maria, wife of Konrad II of Moravia 307
Maria Amalie, Princess 90
Maria Theresa, Holy Roman Empress 26, 27, 39, 43, 62, 85, 90, 92, 113, 158, 240, 260, 316, 324, 336, 357, 360, 411
Mariássy family 388, 398
Marie Louise, wife of Napoleon 123, 247
Marth, J. 369
Martinelli, Anton Erhard 162, 167, 310
Martinelli, Domenico 117, 326, 370
Martinelli, Giovanni Battista 353
Martinic, Jaroslav 90, 94
Martinic, Count Jiří Adam 118
Martriola, Pietro 205
Marx, Karl 225
Mařák, Julius 293
Mařatka, Josef 66
Masaryk, Jan 34, 40, 48, 119, 127
Masaryk, Tomáš Garrigue 22, 29, 29, 30, 31, 33, 39, 40, 80, 85, 127, 148, 412
Massányi, Edmund 369
Master I.W. 90
Master of the Emmaus Cycle 132
Master of the Family Tree 141
Master of the Hradec Králové (Königgrätz) Altarpiece 262
Master of the Litoměřice (Leitmeritz) Altarpiece 90, 93, 239, 240
Master of the Třeboň (Wittingau) Altarpiece 165, 207, 208

Master of the Vyšši Brod (Hohenfurt) Altarpiece 195
Master of the Zvíkov (Klingenberg) Lamentation 197, 198, 201
Materer, Ulrich 402
Mathauser, Josef 145
Mathey, Jean-Baptiste 25, 54, 82, 114, 117, 121, 122, 123, 137, 214, 248
Matthias I, Holy Roman Emperor 23, 24, 86, 299
Matthias I Corvinus, King of Hungary 22, 315, 353, 356, 373, 375, 392
Matthias of Arras 88, 92, 93, 141
Matthias of Nuremberg 407
Mattielli, Lorenzo 308
Maulbronn, Jörg von 246
Maulpertsch, Franz Anton 122, 258, 298, 299, 301, 305, 307, 327, 354
Max, Emanuel 58, 59, 91
Max, Josef 58, 59, 320
Maximilian I of Bavaria 24, 117, 139
Maximilian II, Holy Roman Emperor 23, 90, 237, 388
Maximianus, Marcus Valerius 364
Mayer, Johann Ulrich 51, 58, 76
Mayer, Václav, Abbot 122
Mayerhoffer, A. 336
Mehmed IV, Sultan 401
Melana, Antonio 166
Melantrich of Aventino, Jiří 68
Mendel, Gregor Johann 301
Menneler, Kaspar 366
Menzel, Otto 225
Meretta, Gustav 325
Merian, Matthäus 203, 212, 226, 244, 308
Merkel, Leo 168
Methodios, Saint 14, 15, 16, 36, 132, 320, 356, 411
Metternich, Prince Klemens Wenzel 225, 331
Metzner, Franz 256
Mevinola. G 382
Meyrink, Gustav 66
Meytens, Martin von 27
Mezières, architect 240
Meziříčtí family 310
Miča, František Václav 311
Michael III, Byzantine Emperor 14
Michelberg family 243
Michna of Vacinov, Count Jan Vacláv 133
Mikš, František 136
Miksch, architect 232
Mikuláš of Kadaň 45

Mikuláš of Písek 200
Mikuláš see also Nicholas
Milič of Kroměříž, Jan 47, 49, 70
Milleschau, Mras of 239
Mitrovsky family 303
Mlada, sister of Boleslav II, Abbess 37, 113
Mniszek, Count 308
Mocker, Josef 42, 56, 89, 96, 136, 141, 147, 155, 158, 200
Modena, Tommaso da 142, 145
Mojmir I, Moravian prince 14, 368, 411
Moler, Hans 398
Molitor, Johann Peter 251
Moltheim, Humbert Walcher von 147
Moltke, Helmut von 225
Moltke, Helmuth von 28, 260, 411
Moryson, Fynes 138, 260
Mössmer, gardener 160
Mosto, Ottavio 68, 116
Mozart, Wolfgang Amadeus 54, 69, 71, 77, 80, 82, 122, 139, 295, 326, 353, 356
Mucha, Alfons Maria 42, 92, 137, 307
Mühlstein, Veit 374
Müntzer, Thomas 71
Münzberger, Bedřich 137
Mussolini, Benito 31
Müttermann, Georg 402
Myslbek, Josef Václav 92, 125, 127, 137, 293

Náchod, Count Hron of 291
Napoleon Bonaparte, Emperor of the French 26, 27, 123, 225, 247, 283, 296, 301, 303, 306, 328, 354, 359, 411
Napoleon III 231
Navrátil, Josef 68, 151
Nehr, Josef, Dr 230
Nepomuk, see John of Nepomuk
Neruda, Jan 76, 136
Netolický, Josef Štěpanek 206, 207
Neumann, Balthasar 219
Neumann, Captain 220
Neumann, Franz von 256
Neunherz, Georg Wilhelm 122
Nezval, Vítěslav 228
Nicholas II, Duke of Troppau 330
Nicholas (Mikuláš) of Bardejov (Bartfeld) 406
Nicholas of Levoča (Leutschau) 375, 393, 409, 410
Nicholas of Levoča (Leutschau), clockmaker 397
Nicholas see also Mikuláš
Niederöcker, Leopold 286

Niedzielski, architect 232
Nikolaus see also Mikuláš and Nicholas
Nobel, Alfred 48
Norbert of Xanten (or Magdeburg), Saint 121
Nortmann, Benjamin Magnus 258
Nosecký, Siard 123
Novák, Karl 42
Novotný, Antonín 34
Novotný, Otakar 127
Nugent, Thomas 118, 225

Obel 383
Oedel, Gustav 305
Oemlichen, Kaspar von 118
Ohmann, Friedrich 154
O'Kelly, Countess 160
Oppenheim, David 66
Orsi, Giovanni Battista 120
Orsi, Giovanni Domenico 52, 70, 74, 123, 131, 154, 215
Oswald of Banská Bystrica (Neusohl) 373
Oswald of Prague 90, 132, 372
Otakar I Přemysl, King of Bohemia 17, 92, 146, 156, 229, 319, 330
Otakar II Přemysl, King of Bohemia 17, 37, 42, 64, 66, 68, 72, 92, 96, 146, 149, 161ff, 193, 194, 198, 200, 214f, 235, 250, 285, 296, 301, 314, 316, 327, 333, 354, 411
Otto the Great, Holy Roman Emperor 16, 143
Ottersdorf, Sixt von 44
Ovid 167, 325
Oybin, Vinzenz 254

Pacassi, Baron Nikolaus von 25, 83, 85, 86, 87, 88, 113, 114
Pachelbel, mayor of Eger 218
Pacher, Michael 397
Pachta of Rajov family 43
Pachta, František Joseph 43
Pagani, Paolo 320
Paganini, Niccoló 247, 333
Palacký, František 28, 127, 326, 327, 332
Palach, Jan 67, 127
Pálffy, Count Johann 380, 382
Pálffy, Paul, Nádorispán 357
Palko, Franz Xaver 76, 357
Palliardi, Ignaz Johann 72, 122
Pambio, Andrea Avostalis del 139
Pambio, Juan Maria del 139
Pánek, Jan Šimon (also called Panetius) 68
Panetius see Pánek

Paracelsus, physician 220, 247
Pardubice, Arnošt (Ernest) of, Archbishop of Prague 141, 144
Paris, Abraham 82
Parler family 85, 91, 92, 93, 113, 154, 163, 193, 201, 301, 327
Parler, Heinrich the elder 91
Parler, Heinrich the younger 90, 91, 302
Parler, Heinrich of Gmünd 91
Parler, Johann 88, 91
Parler, Michael 87
Parler, Paul 89
Parler, Peter *19*, 45, 49, 55, 56, 88, 89, 91, 92, 93, *93*, 95, 118, 157, 302
Parler, Wenzel 87, 88, 91
Patočka, Jan 35
Patton, General George S. 211
Paul II, Pope 210
Paul (Pavol) of Leutschau (Levoča) 374, 375, 393, 394, *395*, 397, 398, 399, 409
Paul of Litoměřice (Leitmeritz) 238
Pauli, Jacopo di 373
Payer, Wenzel, Dr 223
Pellico, Silvio, Count 301
Pernstein, see Pernštejn
Pernštejn family 263, 264, 292, 293, 294, 302
Pernštejn, Jan of 263
Pernštejn, Polyxena of see Lobkowicz, Polyxena of
Pernštejn, Vilem (Wilhelm) of 164, 263, 302
Pernštejn, Vratislav of 81, 92, 114, 294
Peršnajer, M. 369
Peter the Great, Tsar 80, 224, 228, 247
Peter of Brüx (Most) 246
Petrarch, Francesco 19, 44
Pettenberg-Mietingen, Reichsgraf von und zu 226
Pfeiffer, Antonín 127–128
Pfrogner, Chrysostomus, Abbot 230
Philip VI, King of France 18
Philippi, G. M. 86
Philippot, Karl 193
Piast family 368
Piccolomini family 292
Piccolomini-Pieri, Ottavio I 291, 292
Pierroni, Giovanni Battista 83, 283, 301
Pignatelli, Princess Maria Anna 308
Pilgram, Anton 298, 299, 300, 374
Pilgram, Franz Anton 357, 387
Pinkas 66
Pirner, Johannes 325

Pitrolf, royal lokator 72
Pius II, Pope (Aeneas Silvius Piccolomini)
Pláchy, J. 55
Platzer, Ignaz Franz 76, 86, 87, 92, 93, 122
Platzer, Ignaz Michael 122
Platzer, Josef 295
Plečnik, Jože 77, 85, 86, 87, 114
Pokorný, Karel 69
Pokorný, Z 137
Polívka, Osvald 42, 66, 70, 124
Pollack, Michael 373
Ponte, Lorenzo da 70
Postl, K. *194*, *285*
Povolný, Anton 398, 399
Prachner, Peter 76
Prachner, Richard Georg 54, 76, 120
Prachner, Václav 67
Praetorius, Johannes 286
Prager, Karel 125
Prandtauer, Jakob 310
Prchal, Václav 316
Preuner, Anton Josef 305
Pribina, Prince of Nitra 368
Princip, Gavrilo 242
Procopius, Saint 60, 95
Procopius (Prokop) the Great (or Bald) 22, 203, 216, 235
Procopius (Prokop) the Less 22
Přemysl 16, 36, 256
Přemyslid dynasty 16, 17, 18, 36, 40, 68, 87, 89, 90, 92, 113, 123, 134, 136, 146, 148, 149, 214, 245, 252, 307, 326, 334, 368, 411
Puchsbaum, Hans 355, 393
Pupp, Johann Georg 228
Purkart of Janovic (Burkhart of Janowitz) 198
Pytlich, Jan 51

Questenberg, Count Johann Adam 295, 310
Questenberg, Kaspar, Abbot 121
Quittainer, Andreas Philipp 54, 119, 145
Quittainer, Johann Anton 121, 122

Raas von Tirol, Johann 82
Radetzky, Josef, Count Radetz 74
Raduit, Count of Souches 300
Raimund II, Abbot 230
Rákóczi, Prince Ferenc II 369, 382, 385, 392
Rákóczi, Prince Sigmund 409
Rastislav, Prince 14, 358, 359, 411
Rattay, J. *199*
Rauchmüller, Matthias 57

Rava, Jacopo 356
Rechtskron, Count 204
Reder, Wenzel 325
Redern family 254, 257, 258
Redern, Baron Christoph von 257, 258
Redern, Baron Friedrich von 257, 258
Redl, Colonel Alfred 73
Reimboth, Leopold 246
Reiner, Wenzel Lorenz 54, 68, 81, 95, 113, 118,
   120, 130, 133, 139, 247, 249, 251, 258
Reitenberger, Karl, Abbot 230, 232
Rejchl, V. 261
Rejscka, Eliška, see Elizabeth, wife of Wenceslas
   II
Rejsek, Matuš 42, 45, 50, 153, 155, 262
Richard II, King of England 20
Richter, Edmund Johann 251
Richter, Ludwig *236*
Ried, Heinrich 301
Riedl, Georg 154
Riemenschneider, Tilman 397
Rieth, Benedikt 90, 94 96, 113, 114, 155, 156,
   201, 244, 245, 246
Rieth, Josef 332
Riga, Antonio 305
Rilke, Rainer Maria 80, 168
Rodero, Panacius 65
Roders, Pancraz see Rodero
Rodin, Auguste 56
Roentgen, Theodor 233
Rohe, Ludwig Mies van der 302
Rokycana, Jan 43
Roland 58, 239, 406
Ronovec, knight 257
Rosenberg see Rožmberk
Rosincová, Š 369
Rossi, Domenico 292
Rössler, J. 129
Rosso, Giovanni Battista 360
Rothe, Johann 235
Rothschild, Samuel 321
Rotlev see Rotlöw
Rotlöw, Johlin (Rotlev, Jan) 69
Rotter, Guido 288
Rothmayer, O. 86
Rottmayr, Johann Michael 309
Rousseau, Théodore
Rozdražov family 201
Rozínek, gardener 160
Rožmberk family 113, 115, 166, 193, 195, 197,
   198, 206, 207

Rožmberk, Henry of 166
Rožmberk, Jan of 78
Rožmberk, Perchta (Berta) of 205, 313
Rožmberk, Peter of 193
Rožmberk, Peter Vok of 50, 113, 115, 166, 193,
   194, 206
Rožmberk, Vílem of 166, 167, 197
Rožmital family 201
Rožmital, Johanka of 149
Rubens, Sir Peter Paul 82, 298, 310
Rübezahl see Krkonoš
Rudolph I, German King, 17, 38, 91, 250, 260
Rudolph II, Holy Roman Emperor 23, *23*, 49,
   62, 66, 83, 85, 87, 89, 90. 96, 113, 114, 115, 117,
   121, 132, 138, 146, 166, 211, 212, 254, 299, 365,
   411
Rudolph, Archduke 326
Runciman, Lord 31
Russ, Willy 229
Rutský, Caspar 114
Ryksa Elzbieta see Elizabeth, wife of Wenceslas
   II

Saaz, Johann von, see Johann
Sagan, Duchess of 247
Salhausen family 252
Salm, Wilhelm Florentin von, Archbishop of
   Prague 115
Samo, Frankish merchant 14, 411
Samphleben 383
Santini, Giovanni Battista (or Santini-Aichel,
   Johann Blasius) 25, 43, 70, 77, 81, 134, 155,
   156, 214, 262, 282, 302, 310, 318, 319
Sattler, Philipp 325
Sayers, jockey 281
Schaffgotsch, Count 290
Schatzmann, Christian 68
Schauberer, Andreas, Abbot 387
Schauberger, Hans Georg 325
Schauberger, J.G. 301
Schaumberger, Johann M. 168
Schaumburg, Bruno von, Bishop of Olomouc
   316, 321, 322, 323, 327, 331
Schäufelein, Hans 398
Schedel, cartographer *37*
Scheffler, Felix A. 292
Scheiwl, Josef 262
Schellenberg family 284
Scheuffler, Otto 49
Schiele, Egon 166
Schiller, Friedrich von 218, 228, 257

Schlansovský, J. J. 134
Schlesinger, Josef 65
Schlick, Count Leopold 90, 232
Schmelzer, Peter 49
Schmidt, Anton 380
Schmidt, Friedrich 141
Schmoranz, Franz 158, 367
Schneider-Trnavský, Mikuláš 361
Schnirch, Bohuslav 124
Schönherr, Matthias 68
Schopenhauer, Arthur 247
Schöpf, Johann Anton 120, 139
Schor, Johann Ferdinand 81, 134
Schremmel, Josef 244
Schubert, Johann 332
Schulz, Damian 230
Schulz, Josef 67, 129
Schumann, Robert 225
Schwanberg family 206
Schwanthaler, Ludwig 129
Schwarz, Karl 299
Schwarzenberg family 164, 165, 166, 193, 198,
    200, 206, 242
Schwarzenberg, Eleonore von 165
Schwarzenberg, Friedrich Josef, Cardinal
    Archbishop 92
Schwarzenberg, Johann Adolf von 164, 206, 290
Schwarzenberg, Prince Joseph Adam 168
Schwarzenberg, Prince Karl 164
Schwarzenberg, Prince Karl Philipp 115
Schwarzenberg, Maria Ernestine, Princess 166
Schwenckfeldt, Caspar 247
Scotti, Bartholomäus 79
Sebregondi, architect 283
Seeberg, Count 42
Segner, Andreas 353
Segner, J. A. 353
Seifert, Jaroslav 114, 125
Seton-Watson, R. W. 382
Sigismund, Saint 92
Sigismund, Holy Roman Emperor 20, 21, 139,
    146, 210, 357, 364, 366, 389
Sina, Georg 365
Skupa, Josef 213
Slanský, Rudolph 34
Slavata von Chlum, Wilhelm 94
Slavibor, Prince of Pšov 149
Slavíček, Antonín 68
Slavnik family 16, 293
Smetana, Bedřich 28, 36, 47, 71, 114, 124, 125,
    134, 136, 195, 293, 293, 295, 315

Smiřic, Zikmund of 282
Smiřicky family 282, 292
Smiřický, Eliška Kateřina 282
Smiřický, Jindřich 282
Smiřický, Markéta Salomena 282
Smrkovský, Josef 34
Smyly, P. 281
Soběslav I, Duke of Bohemia 71, 85, 96, 136, 151,
    251
Soběslav II, Duke of Bohemia 17, 70, 411
Sochor, Eduard 151
Soldati, Tommaso 120, 131
Soldier, Unknown 140
Solimena, Francesco 76
Spatio, Marco 257
Spazzio, Antonio 360
Spazzio, Pietro 360
Speck (Spech), Michael 354
Speed, John 203
Spejbl 213
Spezza, Andrea 25, 82, 283
Spiess, Hans 90, 147, 150
Spineta, Bernardo 240
Spinetti, Bernardo 47, 133
Spitihněv I 16, 83
Spitihněv II 17, 92, 237
Spohr, Louis 231
Spontini, Gasparo Luigi Pacifico 231
Sporck, Count Franz Anton 25, 258, 283, 284,
    295
Spranger, Bartholomäus 87
Stalin, Joseph 34, 137
Stamitz, Johann 295
Stanetti, Dionysius 379
Stanzel, Theophil 398
Starburg, Špaček von 151
Statio, Giovanni de 212
Stegner, Matthias 120
Steiner, Johann Nepomuk 316
Steinfels, Johann Jakob 138, 251
Steinmetz, Josef 394
Steinmetz, Karl Friedrich von 303
Stella, Paolo della 115
Stelmasshek, Johann 406
Stephen (István) I, King of Hungary 334
Stephen (István) V, King of Hungary 383, 389
Stephen of Košice (Kaschau) 385
Stern, Joseph 327
Sternberg family 158, 205, 210, 212
Sternberg, Count Kaspar 74
Sternberg, Count Wenzel Adalbert 117, 137

Stevens, Anton 245
Stevens, John Jacob see Steinfels, Johann Jakob
Stifter, Adalbert 166, 193, 195, *195*, 196, 198
Stilicho, Vandal ruler 13
Still, Otto 403
Stoppard, Tom 320
Storař, Severin 292
Stoss, Veit 397, 406
Strachovský, Josef 202
Strahovský, M. 204
Stransy, Paul 240
Strauberger, Hans 326
Strösslová, Kamila 322
Styrl, Veit 245
Sucharda, Jan 283
Sucharda, Stanislav 66, 89, 127
Sucharda, Vojtěch 45, 262
Sujanová, K. I. 369
Suk, Josef the elder 125
Suk, Josef the younger 125
Sunyog, Georg 381
Suttner, Bertha von 48
Süssner, C. M. 54
Süssner, J. 54
Svatopluk, Moravian prince 15
Svatovit 132
Svoboda, Ludvík 43, 409, 411
Svolinský, Karel 89, 324
Sychra, Vladimír 69

Šalda, František Xaver 256
Šaloun, Ladislav 42, 46, 66, 124, 137
Široky, Villem 34
Škréta, Karel 49, 70, 80, 131, 133, 154, 205, 240, 243, 258, 282
Škoda 214
Škroup, F.J. 66
Španiel, Otakar 89, 136, 295
Špillar, Karel 42
Špork, see Sporck
Šternberk see Sternberg
Štrougal, Lubomir 35
Štúr, Ľudovít 29, 359, 398
Štursa, Jan 293
Šujanová, K. 369
Šultys, Jan 153
Švabinský, Max 89, 293
Švejk, the Good Soldier 134

Tarner, Stefan 406
Tauch, Simon 300

Tausch, Christoph 365
Temple-Black, Shirley, Ambassador 81
Tencalla, Giovanni Jacopo 305
Tencalla, Giovanni Pietro 327
Teniers, David the younger 298
Teplý, Jakub 264
Terzio, Francesco 115
Theny, Gregor 318
Theodoric, painter 113, 144
Thiergarten, Hans 353
Thierhier, V. 128
Thietman, Bishop of Prague 16
Thököly family 390, 401
Thököly, Count Imre 400, 401, 402, 408
Thököly, Count Sebastian 401
Thun-Hohenstein family 252, 253
Thun-Hohenstein, Count Maximilian 252
Thun-Hohenstein, Michael Oswald, Count 116
Thurzo family 372, 380, 392, 398, 399, 400
Thurzo, Alexius 386
Thurzo, Ferenc 381
Thurzo, György 381
Thurzo, Johann 375
Thurzo, Stanislaus, Bishop 327
Tilgner, V.O. 356
Tilly, General Johann Tserclaes 24, 139
Tirpitz, Admiral 160
Tiso,Jozef 31, 32, 33, 336, 412
Titian, Tiziano Vecellio called 327
Tomášek, Václav 82
Tommaso da Modena see Modena, Tommaso da
Tornini, Giacomo 360
Töpper, Karl 316
Trauttmansdorff family 294
Trauttmansdorff, Countess Eleonora 153
Trauttmansdorff, Count 294
Trčka family 282
Trčka, Count 220
Trehet, Jean 310
Trenck, Franz, Freiherr von der 298, 301
Trnka, Jiří 213
Troger, Paul 326, 357
Troppau, Dukes of 329; and see Nicholas
Tugendhat family 302
Tuka, Vojtěch 30
Tuscany, Grand Duchess Maria Anna of 116
Tyl, Josef Kajetán 70, 213
Tyl, Oldřich 124

Urban II, Pope 62
Urban VI, Pope 20

Urban, František 154, 264
Urban of Bardejov 406
Úprka, František 293

Václav, see Wenceslas
Vajce, Josef 121
Vandamme, Dominique-René 251
Van Dyck, Anthonis see Dyck
Vaněk of Kutná Hora 155
Vedano, Alessandro da 388
Veith, Baron 151
Vejmluva, Václav, Abbot 318, 319
Věnava, charcoal burner 264
Venus of Moravany 362, *362*
Venus of Věstonice 11, *12*
Verle, Heinrich von 166
Veronese, Paolo Cagliari called 310
Vetter, Johann Karl 246
Veverka, Václav 281
Veverka, František 281
Viollet-le-Duc, Eugène 56
Virgil 168
Vischer, Hans 90
Vitek (Witigo) 166, 204, 206
Vitek, Henry 204
Vitus, Saint 20, 87
Vlach, Antonio 312
Vlach, Augustin 115
Vlach, Hans 200
Vladislav II, duke of Bohemia, later Vladislav I
    Přemysl, King of Bohemia 56, 79, 96, 135, 247,
    302
Vladislav II Jagiello, King of Bohemia 22, 38, 41,
    42, 49, 85, 88, 90, 94, 96, 146, 147, 153, 315
Vladislav Jindřich, Prince, Margrave of Moravia
    300, 319
Vogerl, Martin 370
Voget, Franz Guido 68
Vojtěch, Saint see Adalbert, Bishop of Prague
Vratislav I, Duke of Bohemia 16, 37, 83, 113
Vratislav II, Duke of Bohemia, later Vratislav I,
    King of Bohemia 17, 96, 135, 136, 411
Vratislav of Mitrovic, Count Jan Václav 68
Vries, Adriaen de 83, 87
Vries, Hans Vredeman de 92
Vrtba family 81, 158
Vtrba, Jan Josef of 81

Wackher von Wackenfels 53
Wagner, Anton 129
Wagner, Otto 114

Wagner, Richard 82, 231, 237, 247, 248
Waldhauser, Konrad 49, 70
Waldstein family 146, 246, 284
Waldstein, Albrecht Wenzel Eusebius, see
    Wallenstein
Waldstein, Count Karl Josef 248
Waldstein, Katharina von see Hradec
Waldstein-Wartenberg, Count Georg Josef 294
Wallenstein, Count Albrecht Wenzel Eusebius
    24, 25, 39, 82, 83, 211, 217, 218, *219*, 248, 249,
    254, 256f, *258*, 282f, 291, 411
Wartenberg family 252, 284
Wartenberg, Otto von 282
Weber, Carl Maria von 70, 225, 231
Weinhardt of Wallendorf, Johann 373
Weiss, F. I. 92
Weiss, Johann 409
Weizenhofen, Count Johann Wenzel M. von see
    Michna
Welser, Philippine 146
Wenceslas (Václav) I, Saint, Duke of Bohemia 16,
    37, 83, 87, 89, 91, 149, 411
Wenceslas I, King of Bohemia 54, 67, 68, 72, 114,
    164, 200, 250, 296, 307, 313, 314
Wenceslas II, King of Bohemia 17, 18, 68, 81,
    154, 193, 209, 260, 261, 282, 296, 314
Wenceslas III, King of Bohemia 18, 326
Wenceslas IV, King of Bohemia 20, 21, 38, 40,
    49, 56, 69, 71, 85, 90, 131, 153, 154, 159
Wenda, Oswald 229
Wenzel see Wenceslas
Werfel, Franz 57, 74
Werle, Georg 164
Werner, F. B. *300*, *324*
Wernher, Georg 362
Wetschel, Johann 168
White, Walter 66, 85, 223
Wiching, Bishop of Nitra 15
Widemann, Christian 213
Widmann, Georg 166
Wiehl, Antonín 70, 71
Wilgefortis, Saint 120
Wilhelm I, Emperor of Germany 225
Wilhelm II, Emperor of Germany 160
Willmann, Michael 251
Wilson, President Woodrow 129
Windischgrätz, Prince General Alfred 28, 43, 73
Windischgrätz, Princess 43
Winter, Alexander 363
Winter, Karl 259
Winterhalter, Johann Josef 320

Winterhalter, Josef 307, 326
Wirch, Johann Joseph 43, 117
Witigo see Vitek
Władisław II Jagiełło, King of Poland 389
Władisław see also Vladislav
Wlczek, Count 321
Wohlmut, Bonifaz 88, 92, 96, 115, 134
"Woman in White" see Rožmberk, Perchta of
Worath, Johann 193
Wölflin vom Steine (Kámen) 44
Würben, Count Georg Stephan von 332
Wurmser, Nikolaus 132, 142
Würth, J. J. 92
Wurzelbauer, Benedikt 83
Wycliffe, John 20, 52

Zahner, Andreas 325
Zápolya (Zápol'sky) family 390, 392
Zápolya (Zápol'sky), Imre 391, 392, 401
Zápolya (Zápol'sky), John (János) 365

Zápolya (Zápol'sky), Stephen (István) 365, 391, 392, 393
Zapotocký, Antonín 34
Zasche, Joseph 130, 259
Zdík, Jindřich 323
Zeller, Jordan 332
Zichy, Count Edmund 382
Ziegler, Erwin 330
Zinner, Johann Anton 168
Zítek, Josef 67, 124, 225
Zrinský, Jan, Abbot 194

Želivsky, Jan 38, 46, 130, 131
Ženíšek, František 71, 129
Žerotín family 329
Žitňanský M. 369
Žižka of Trocnov, Jan 21, 139, 140, 197, 201f, 202, 209, 210, 243, 260, 314
Žumbera, knight 212

Prague place names

Figures in **bold** refer to principal entries
Figures in *italic* refer to illustrations

Prague 16ff., 23ff., **36ff.**, *37*, *78*, *128*, *135*, 149,
    153, 161, 199, 202f., 238, 260, 283, 290, 295,
    315, 323, 330, 395, 414, 417, 418, 420, pls. 1–
    21, col. pls. 1–8

Bilá Hora (White Mountain) 24, 216
Bridges
    Charles 38, 54, **56ff.**, *61*, 71f., *77*, 80, 91, 136,
        157 col. pl. 7
    Jiraskův 127
    Judith 54, 56
    Legion (most Legii) **127**
    Mánes 56, **67**
    Palacký 137
Belvedere, see Castle
Břevnov 75

Cafés
    Malostranská kavárna 74
    Café Slavia 125
Canons' Houses, Hradčany 117
Carolinum, see University, Charles
Castle 21, 25f., 37, 41, 82, **83ff.**, 134f., pl. 2, col.
    pl. 2
    All Saints' Chapel **95**, 113
    Art Gallery **88**
    Belvedere (Summer Palace) **115**
    Black Tower 114
    Bohemian Chancellery 94
    Daliborka Tower **114**
    Deanery 96
    Deer Moat **114**
    Diet Hall 95
    Ferdinand Stables **114**
    First Courtyard **85f.**
    Gardens 77, 114f.
    Golden Alley **114**
    Golden Gate 87
    Holy Cross Chapel 86

Imperial Court Council Room 95
Lobkowicz Palace **114**
Ludvík Wing **94**, 95
Matthias Gate 82, 84, **85**
Mihulka Tower 96
New White Tower **114**
Old Land Records 96
Old Provost's Lodge **87**, 89
Old Registry 96
Old Royal Palace **93ff.**
Palace of Charles IV 96
Plečnik Hall of Columns 86
Powder Bridge 85, **114**
Riding School 114
Royal Gardens **115**
Rožmberk Palace **113**
Rudolph Gallery **87**
Second Courtyard **86f.**
Spanish Hall **87**
St George's Square 96
St George's Basilica 37, 85, **96f.**
St George's Convent **247**
Third Courtyard **87**
Vladislav Hall 38, **94**, 95, *95*, 113, 134
Wenceslas IV Hall of Columns 96
Cathedral, St Vitus 19f., 26, 37, 74, 83, 85, **87ff**,
    88, 91,113, 130, 136, 141, 144, 147, 157, 195,
    pls. 1, 3–5, col. pl. 4
    Golden Gate 87, 90, pls. 3, 4
    Crown Chamber 90
    Royal Mausoleum 90
    Royal Oratory 91f., 147
    Treasury of St Vitus 87
    St Wenceslas Chapel 90
Cemeteries
    National Cemetery, Vyšehrad **136**
    Old Jewish Cemetery *63*, *65f*, pls. 16, 17, 18
    Slavín 136
Churches
    Assumption, Strahov 122
    Bethlehem Chapel **71**
    Calvary Chapel 123

Holy Sepulchre Chapel 124
Italian Chapel, Clementinum **53**
Nativity, Loreto 120
Our Lady in the Fortifications **136**
Our Lady of the Snows **130**
Our Lady of Victory **80f.**
Our Lady see also St Mary
Our Lady see also Týn
St Bartholomew 54
St Benedict **116**
St Catherine **133**
St Clement 52, **53**
Sts Cyril and Methodios **133**, 148
St Francis 25, **54**
St Gall **70**
St George's Basilica, see Castle
St Ignatius **131**
St James **68**
St John of Nepomuk **117**
St John of Nepomuk on the Rock (Vyšehrad)
   57, 75, **132**, 227
St Joseph **82**
St Lawrence, Petřin **123**
St Lawrence, Vyšehrad **136**
St Longinus **133**
St Martin in the Wall 71
St Mary below the Chain **79**
St Mary 'Na Slupi' **133**
St Mary of Altötting 27
St Mary see also Our Lady
St Mary see also Theatine
St Mary see also Týn
St Nicholas, Old Town **47f.**, pl. 9
St Nicholas in the Lesser Town (Malá strana)
   72, **74f.**, pls. 19, 20
Sts Peter and Paul 136
St Roch, Strahov 121f.
St Saviour **53f.**
St Stephen **133**
St Thomas 74, **82**
Theatine (St Mary) 27, **77**
Týn (Our Lady before Týn) 40, 47, **49f**, pls. 2,
   21
Vlašské kapl, see Italian Chapel
Clementinum see Monasteries
Clock, Astronomical (Orloj) **45f.**, col. pl. 3
Country houses, see Villas
Customs House (former) Malá strana

Čertovka **78f**

Exhibition grounds and pavilions see
   VystavištéFaust's House **131**, 132

Federal Assembly Building **129**
Fountain
   Vltava ('Tereska') 67

Gall District (Havelské město) 70f.

Hotels
   Adria 127
   Evropa 127
   Forum 137
   Tatran 127
House
   of Artists, see House of Artists
   Black Rose 124
   Blue Bunch of Grapes 118
   Blue Star **47**
   Faust **131**, 132
   French Crown **53**
   Golden Cup 76
   Golden Griffin 118
   Golden Horseshoe 76
   Golden Jug **68**
   Golden Key 76
   Golden Lily **51**
   Golden Lion 76
   Golden Pear 118
   Golden Stag **82**
   Golden Unicorn **46ff.**
   Golden Vulture **43**
   Golden Well **51**
   Green Lobster 76
   Kaňka's 124
   Leaping Horse pl. 6
   at the Minute **43**, pl. 13
   Municipal (Obecní dům) see Municipal House
   Painters' **80**
   Pezold **51**
   Red Eagle 76
   Red Lion 76
   Richter **51**
   Rott **51**
   St John Nepomuk 76
   Sixt **43**
   Stone Bell **48**
   Štorch **46**
   Three Kings **43**
   Three Little Fiddles 76, pl. 7
   Three Ostriches **77**

Three Storks 82
Three White Roses **51**
Two Golden Bears **69**, pl. 8
Two Suns 76
White Lion **45**
White Swan 76
White Unicorn **48**
Horse Market 127
House of Artists (Rudolfinum) **67**
Hradčany 27, 36, 37, 41, 62, 72, 76ff., 82,
  83ff.,132, 135, 137, col. pl. 2
Hradschin, see Castle, Hradčany
Hunger Wall 115, 121, **123**

Jesuit College **74**
Jewish Town, see Josefov
Jewish Town Hall 62
Josefov 47, **62ff.**

Kampa 59, **77f.**
Kotce 70

Lesser Town see Malá strana
Libraries:
  Clementinum **52**
  Municipal People's **66**
  Nostitz 80
  Strahov **122f.**

Malá strana 36, 37, 54, 59, 71, **72ff.**, 121, 124
  Lesser Town Bridge Towers 62, col. pl. 7
Memorials:
  Jan Hus **46f.**, pl. 21
  Brahe and Kepler 121
  Charles IV 55
  Wenceslas 127
  Jan Želivský **131**
  Palacký 127
  Smetana 72
Mincovna see Mint
Mint (Mincovna) **43**
Monasteries and religious institutions
  Capuchin **121**
  Clementinum 23f., 25, **51f.**, 55, 67
  Emmaus **132**
  Karlov **134**
  Loreto 115, 118, **119ff.**, pl. 11
  St Agnes **67**
  Strahov **121ff**, 250, 308, col. pl. 8
    St Roch 121f
    Assumption 122

Municipal House (Obecní dům) **40ff.**
Museums and Galleries
  Applied Arts (UPM) 67
  City of Prague 43, **130**
  Czech Literature (Strahov) **121ff.**
  Dvořák **134**
  Jewish **64**
  Interior Ministry (former) 134
  Lapidarium 137
  Military History 115
  Mozart 139
  National Gallery (Prints and Drawings,
    Kinský Palace) 48
  National Gallery (St Agnes Convent) **67f**
  National Gallery (St George's Convent) 51,
    57, 67, **113**, 165, 195, 208
  National Gallery (Sternberg Palace) 82, **117**
  National Museum 11, 39, **128**
  National Museum Music Archive (Grand
    Prior's Palace) 79
New Town see Nové město
Nové město (New Town) 36, 38, 72, **124ff**, 201
Nový Svět **117**
Novotného lávka 71

Obecní dům, see Municipal House
Old Town see Stará město
Old TownBridge Tower 42, **55**, *56*, 87
Old Town Mills 71, col. pl. 5

Palace of Culture 137
Palaces (see also Villas)
  Archbishop's **117**
  Bretfeld **77**
  Buquoy 78
  Caretto-Millesimo **43**
  Clam-Gallas 25, **51**, 67
  Černin 25, 93, **118f.**, 119
  Grand Priory **78f.**
  Grömling **74**
  Hrzán, Stará město **43**
  Hrzán, Hradčany **118**
  Kinský **48**, pl. 12
  Kučera **121**
  Lažanský **125**
  Liechtenstein **73**
  Lobkowicz 25, **81**, 83, and see Castle **114**
  Martinic, Hradčany Square **117**
  Martinic, Loretánská ul. **118**
  Menhart **43**
  Morzin **77**

Muscon 77
Nostitz 80
Pachta 42
Rohan 80
Rosenberg, see Rožmberk
Rožmberk 113
Salm 115
Schonborn 81
Schwarzenberg 113, 115
Smiřický 73
Sporck (Špork) 80
Sternberg, Hradčany 117
Sternberg, Malá strana 73
Thun-Hohenstein 77
Trauttmannsdorff 118
Tuscan 116
Valdštejnský see Waldstein
Vrtba 81, pl. 20
Waldstein 25, 39, 82f
Petřin 39, 81, 115, 123f., 125
Powder Tower 42, 90, pl. 14

Railway Station 129
Royal Court 40ff
Royal Way 44ff., 72
Rozhlada Viewing Tower 123

St Gall Market 70
Shops and Offices
    Adria Palace (Riunione Adriatica di Sicurta)
        130
    Assicuriazone Generali 128
    Dům elegance 124
    Dům obuv (House of Shoes) 127
    Máj 124
    National Bank 124
    Palác Koruna 128
    Peterka House 127
    Rapid 124
    Topič 124
Squares
    Betlémské nám. 71
    Charles 130ff., 135
    Grand Priory, see Velkopřevorské nám.
    Hradčanské nám. 85, 115ff.
    Karlovo nám., see Charles Square
    Jana Palacha nám. 67
    Jiráskovo nám. 130
    Jungmannova nám. (Malostranské nám.) 130
    Křižovnické nám. 54
    Lesser Town 72ff., 82

Loretánské nám. 118ff.
Malé náměstí (Little Square) 45, 50f., 69
Malostranské nám., see Lesser Town Square
Maltézské nám. 79f.
Mariánské nám. 66
Old Town 39f., 44ff., 44, 68, 135, col. pl. 6
Pohořelec 121
Staroměstské nám., see Old Town Square
Václavské nám. see Wenceslas
Valdštejnské nám. 82
Velkopřevorské nám. 78
Wenceslas 33, 35, 68, 127ff, 130
Stará město (Old Town) 36, 38, 40ff., 85, 125,
    137
Stará pošta (Old Post Office) 80
Streets
    17. listopadu 67
    28. řijna 124
    Celetna 42ff., 46
    Červená 65
    Dlabacov 121
    Harantova 80
    Havelská 70
    Husova 51
    Janský všek 76
    Jilské 51
    Josefská 82
    Jungmannova 130
    Kanovnická 117
    Karlova 50ff.
    Karmelitská 80f.
    Ke hradu 77
    Ke Karlovu 133
    Kožná 69
    Křižovnická 52, 54
    Lázeňská 79, 80
    Letenská 82, 83
    Loretánská 118
    Maislova 65
    Malá Štupartská 50
    Melantřichova 68, 69
    Michalská 69
    Mostecká 72
    Na Přikopě 124
    Na slupi 132
    Národní třída 124, 127
    Nerudová 76ff.
    New Castle Steps see Zámecké schody
    Ovocný trh 70
    Pařižká třída 63, 64
    Platnéřská 52

Prokopská 80
Resslova
Rytiřská 70
Seminářská **51**
Široká 66
Štěpánská 133
Štupartská 50
Týnská 50
U Kasáren 115
U starého hřbitova 65
Uhelný trh 70
Újezd 123
Uvoz 77
V kotcích 70
Vlašska 81
Vodičkova 131
Vyšehradská 132
Wilsonova **129**
Zámecké schody (New Castle Steps) 77, 85
Železna **47**, 69
Žitná 133

Střelecký ostrov (Marksmen's Island) 127

Synagogues
  High (Town Hall Synagogue) **65**
  Klausen 65
  Maisel 65
  Old-New 62, **64**, 65, pl. 15
  Pinkas **66**
  Spanish **66**

Taverns/pubs
  U Fleků 420
  U Bindrů 47
  U Glaubiců 72
  U Mecenaše 72

U sv. Tomáše (St Thomas's Brewery) 82
U Schnellů 82
U Kalicha 134
Theatres
  Laterna Magica 130
  National 40, 67, 124, 125, 129, 225, pl. 10
  Tyl **69**, 70, 77
  Smetana **129**
Town Halls
  Hradčany (Castle Town) **118**
  Jewish 63, **65**, pl. 15
  Lesser Town (Malá strana) **74**
  New 66
  New Town 20, 38, 131
  Old Town 24, **45ff.**, col. pl. 1, 3
Týn see Ungelt
Týn Presbytery (Týnská fara) **43**
Týn School **48f.** 50

Ungelt **49**, 68, 69
University, Charles (Carolinum) 20, 23, 26, 29,
  30, 38, 39, 43, 55, **69**, 129, 131, 133, 153, 230

'Venice' 78
Villas and Country Houses
  Villa Amerika **134**
  Villa Bertramka **139**
  Hvězda (Star) **138f.**
  Troja 25, **137**
Vítkov see Žižkov
Vystavište 137
Vyšehrad 62, 124, 127, 132, **134ff.**

Zoological Gardens 137

Žižkov (Vítkov) 22, **139**, 201

Place names

Figures in **bold** refer to principal entries
Figures in *italic* refer to illustrations

Abraham 12
Adamov 13
Adersbach see Adršpach
Adršpach 286, col. pl. 16
Alt-Pilsenetz see Starý Plzenec
Altbunzlau see Stará Boleslav
Altschmecks see Starý Smokovec
Altsohl see Zvolen
Altvater see Praděd
Altvatergebirge see Hruby jeseník
Antol 380
Arva see Orava
Aš 419
Aunjetitz see Únětice
Auscha see Úštěk
Aussig see Ústí nad Labem
Austerlitz see Slavkov u Brna

Bad Bartfeld see Bardejovské Kúpele
Banka 362
Banská Bystrica 32, **372ff.**, pl. 55
Banská Štiavnica (Schemnitz) 376, **378ff.**, 380
Bardejov (Bartfeld) 383, **406f.**, 409, col. pl. 24
Bardejovské Kúpele **407**, 427
Bartfeld see Bardejov
Belá 382
Belianské Tatry (White Tatras) 404, **405**
Benátky 152
Beroun (Beraun) 13
Berounka (Beraun) river 36, 209
Betlém 283
Betliar **388f.**, pl. 57
Bilé Karpaty 414
Bilé Labe (White Elbe) river 291
Bílina (Biela) river 235, 246
Bistritz, see Bystrica
Blansko 232, 304
Blanskýles 166
Blatná **201**, col. pl. 20

Bohemian Forest see Šumava
Bohemian Paradise see Český ráj
Böhmerwald see Šumava
Böhmisch-Leipa see Česká Lípa
Böhmisches Paradies see Český ráj
Bojnice **380**
Bouzov **328f.**
Bratislava 15, 25, 33, 35, **334ff.**, *355*, 360, 362, 384, 417, 420, 426, pls. 51, 52, 53, pls. 51, 52, 53, col. pl. 19
Břevnov, near Prague 75
Brno 11, 13, 29, 125, 232, 264, **296ff.**, *300*, 314f., 322, 324, 327, 417, 426, pl. 49
Broumov (Braunau) **291**
Brünn see Brno
Brüx see Most
Buchlov 303
Buchlovice 304
Bučovice 303
Budatín Castle 381
Budweis see České Budějovice
Bürglitz see Křivoklát
Busau see Bouzov
Bylani 11
Bystrica, river 372

Carlsbad see Karlovy Vary
Cesta Slobody 404
Cheb 24, 31, 75, 211, **216ff.**, 220, 221, 291, pls. 26, 27, 29, 44
Chlum **262f.**
Chlumec (Kulm) 151, **251f.**
Chlumec nad Cidlinou **281f.**
Chlumetz see Chlumec nad Cidlinou
Chodsko **216**
Chomutov **243f.**, *244*, 246
Chrudim 418
Chrudimka, river 263
Cidlina, river 282

Čáslav 21
Černá hora 195, **290**

Červená Lhota **206**
Červený Kláštor 404, 406
Česká Les 196
Česká Lípa **253f.**
České Budějovice **161ff.**, *163*, 166, 197
České středohoří (Central Bohemian Range) 242
České Švycarsko 428
Český Krumlov 165, **166ff.**, *194*, 294
Český ráj (Bohemian Paradise) 282, **284**, 428

Danube, river see Dunaj
Děčín (Tetschen) **252ff.**, *253*, 256, pl. 34
Děčínské stěny 252, **254**
Deschtna see Deštna
Deštna 206
Deutsch-Brod see Havličkův Brod
Deutschendorf see Poprad
Devín 334, 356, 357, *358*
Divoká souteška (Wilde Klamm) 254
Dobšinská ľadová jaskyňa, ice cave, **394**
Dolní soutěska (Edmunds Klamm) 254
Dolní Věstonice 11
Domažlice 215, **216**, 419
Domica jaskyňa, cave 389
Donnersmarkt see Spišský Stvrtok
Doubravska Castle 248
Doubravská horn (Eichenwaldberg) 248
Duchcov (Dux) 246, **248f.**
Dukelský priesmyk see Dukla Pass
Dukla Pass 410
Důl Bilého Labe 287
Dunaj (Danube), river 13, 22, 330, 332, 356, 357, 359, 372, 414
Dunajec, river 393, 405, 414
Dux see Duchcov
Dyje (Thaya), river 306. 308

Edmundskamm see Dolní soutěska
Eger (river) see Ohře
Eger (town) see Cheb
Einsiedeln 394
Elbe (Labe), river 19, 148, 150, 235, 237, 240, 252, 254, 256, 260, 282, 283, 284, 287, 414, pl. 45
Elbe, source of **291**
Elbfall see Labská vodopad
Elbogen see Loket
Elbsandsteingebirge see Děčínské stěny
Eperjes see Prešov
Erzgebirge see Krušne hory

Frain see Vranov nad Dyjí

Františkovy Lázně **220ff.**, 290, 427, pls. 32, 33
Franzensbad see Františkovy Lázně
Frauenberg see Hluboká nad Vltavou
Friedland see Frýdlant
Frýdlant **257f.**, 282
Fulnek **332**

Gablonz see Jablonec nad Nisou
Gánovce 11
Gelnica (Göllnitz) 389, 390, **394**
Gemer (Gömer) 388
Georgsberg see Říp
Gerlachovský štít (Gersdorfer spitze) 403f.
Goldenkron see Zlatá Koruna
Göllnitz see Gelnica
Gottwaldov see Zlín
Gran see Hron
Grätz see Hradec
Great Fatra see Veľká Fatra
Gründner Boden 394

Haná 327
Harrachov 47, 287, **290**
Harrachsdorf see Harrachov
Havlíčkův Brod 202
Havran 405
Herľany, geyser **387**
Hermankovice 291
Herrenhausfelsen, see Panská skála
High Tatras see Vysoké Tatry
Hluboká nad Vltavou **164f.**, col. pl. 12
Hlučín **322**
Hněvotin (Nebotein) 327
Hodslavice 326, **332**
Hohenelbe see Vrchlabí
Hohenfurt see Vyšší Brod
Holašovice 166
Hornád, river 383, 407, 414
Horní Planá **195**
Hradec **333**
Hradec Králové (Königgrätz) **260ff.**, 283, pls. 42, 46
Hradisko, Olomouc 326
Hrebionok (Kämmchen) 404
Hron, river 372, 414
Hrubá Skála 284
Hrubčice 12
Hruby jeseník 329
Hřebečsko 293, **331**
Hřensko 245, pl. 45
Hukvaldy **322**

Hultschin see Hlučín
Humpolec 213
Humprecht Hunting Lodge 284
Hůrka 209, 214
Husinec 197

Iglau see Jihlava
Iser see Jizera
Isergebirge see Jizerské hory

Jablonec nad Nisou (Gablonz) **258f.**
Jáchymov **232ff.**, 427
Janské Lázně 287, **290**, 427
Jarmeritz see Jaroměřice
Jaroměřice nad Rokytnou 25, 295, 418
Jasov (Jossau) **387**
Jasovská jaskyňa, cave 387
Javorník (Jauernig) 329
Jekelsdorf 394
Jeschken see Ještěd
Ještěd **257**
Jičín 25, **282f.**, pl. 43
Jihlava 17, 295, **313ff.**
Jihlava, river 313
Jilemnice 291
Jindřichův Hradec **204ff.**, 295
Jitschin see Jičín
Jizera, river 152, 414
Jizerské hory (Jizera Mountains) 254, 257, 414, 426
Johannesbad see Janské Lázně
Jossau see Jasov

Kaaden see Kadaň
Kadaň 217, **246**
Kamenice (Kamnitz) 254
Karlova Koruna (Karlskrone) 281f.
Karlovy Vary 27, 75, 138, **223ff.**, *226*, *229*, 417, 420, 427, pls. 30, 31
Karlsbad see Karlovy Vary
Karlstein see Karlštejn
Karlštejn 20, 93, 113, **141ff.**, *145*, pl. 23
Kaschau see Košice
Käsmark see Kežmarok
Kežmarok 389, 390, **399ff.**
Kirchdrauf see Spišske Podhradie
Kladruby (Kladrau) 25, **214**
Klatovy **214ff.**
Klattau see Klatovy
Klingenberg see Zvíkov
Klínovec (Keilberg) 232

Klosterbruck see Louka
Kochseifen 391
Kokořín **151**
Kokorschin, see Kokořín
Kolín 39, **156f.**, *156*, 418
Komotau see Chomutov
Königgrätz see Hradec Králové
Konopischt see Konopiště
Konopiště **158f.**, *159*, col. pl. 17
Kost Castle 284
Košice 33, **383ff.**, *384*, 408, pls. 63, 64, 65
Kotnov 201
Kouřím **158f.**
Krásna Hôrka Castle **388**
Kratochvíle (Kurzweil) **166**
Kravarsko (Kühlandchen) **332**
Krečhoř 158
Kremnica (Kremnitz) 376, *377*
Kremnické pohorie (Kremnica Hills) 372, **376ff.**, 379
Kremnitz see Kremnica
Kremsier see Kroměříž
Krkonoše 195, 257, **287ff.** 414, 417, pls. 35, 37, 46
Kroměříž 12, 28, 326, **327f.**
Krompach 394
Krumau see Český Krumlov
Krušné Hory (Ore Mountains) 195, 217, 232, 243, 246, 414
Křivoklát **146ff.**, pl. 24
Křtiny (Kiritein) 302
Kuhländchen see Kravařsko
Kuks 25, **283ff.**, 295
Kumburk 282
Kutná Hora 11, 17, 91, **152ff.**, *154*, 156, pl. 25
Kysuca, river 380, 381

Labe, see Elbe
Labská bouda 287, 291
Labská důl 287, 291
Labská studanka 291
Labská vodopád 291
Lany 148
Laun see Louny
Lednice (Eisgrub) 13, 299
Leitmeritz see Litoměřice
Leitomischl see Litomišl
Leutschau see Levoča
Levoča 374, 375, 383, 386, 389, 390, 393, **394ff.**, *395*, *400*, 400, 408, pl. 56, col. pls. 21, 22
Levý Hradec 16, 83
Liběchov **151**

Liberec 27, 31, **254ff.**, 291, pl. 39
Libín Mountain 195
Liboch see Liběchov
Libosad 283
Lidice **148**
Lipan see Lipany
Lipany 22, 38
Lipno Reservoir (Udolní nádrž Lipno) 195
Litoměřice 25, 114, 236, **237ff.**, *238*, 250, col. pl. 15
Litomyšl 264, **293f.**, *294*
Lobositz see Lovosice
Loket (Elbogen) 223, **228ff.**, col. pl. 9
Lomnice, river 201
Lomnický štít (Lomnitzer spitze) 403, 404, 414
Louka (Klosterbruck) 122, 123, **308**
Louny (Laun) 240, **244ff.**
Lovosice (Lobositz) 242f.
Luhačovice 427
Lužická Nisa (Lausitzer Neisse), river 254
Lužnice, river 207
Lysa Pol'ana 404

Mährisch-Budweis see Moravské Budějovice
Mährisch-Schönberg see Šumperk
Mährisch-Trübau see Moravská Třebová
Malá Fatra (Little Fatra) 380, **382**, 414, 428
Malé Karpaty (Little Carpathians) 334, 362, 414
Malše, river 161, 163
March see Morava
Margaretendorf 394
Mariánské Lázně (Marienbad) 75, 229, **230ff.**, 427, col. pl. 10
Marienbad see Mariánské Lázně
Maschau see Maštov
Maštov (Maschau) 249
Melnik see Mělník
Mělník **148ff.**, 420, col. pl. 18
Mengusovká dolina (Mengsdorfer Tal) 405
Metuje (Mettau), river 292
Mikulov 11, 13, 28, 119, **304f.**
Mísečky 291
Mnichnovo Hradište (Münchengrätz) 283
Mohra see Moravice
Moldau see Vltava
Morava (March), river 319, 326, 327, 359, 414
Moravany 362, *362*
Moravice,river 333
Moravská Třebová (Mährisch-Trübau) **331**
Moravské Budějovice (Mährisch-Budweis) 161
Moravský kras (Moravian Karst) **304**, 428

Moravský Krumlov 307
Most (Brüx) **246ff.**, 250
Mšecké Zehrovice 13
Mühlhausen see Nelahozeves
Mumlava (Mummel), river 290
Music, Museum of Czech 295
Mysia Hôrka 393
Mže, river 209

Náchod **291ff.**
Náměšt' na Hané 419
Nelahozeves (Mühlhausen) **152**
Neudorf see Spišská Nová Ves
Neuhaus see Jindřichův Hradec
Neuschmecks see Nový Smokovec
Neusohl see Banská Bystrica
Neustadt see Nové Město nad Metuji
Neutitschein see Nový Jičín
Neutra see Nitra
Nežarka, river 202
Nikolsburg see Mikulov
Nitra 15, **367ff.**, *367*
Nitra, river 367, 414
Nízke Tatry (Low Tatras) 372, 414
Nové Město nad Metuji (Neustadt) **292**, *292*, 293
Nový Bor (Haida) 253
Nový Jičín **332**
Nový Smokovec (Neuschmecks) 404, 427
Nový Svět (Neuwelt) 290

Oberplan, see Horní Planá
Obořiště 75
Obřany 13
Obří důl 290
Obyčtov 319
Ochoz 11
Oder (Odra) 321, 322, 332, 414
Ohrada **165**
Ohře (Eger), river 13, 14, 216, 223, 237, 241, 242, 244, 246, 414
Olmütz see Olomouc
Olomouc 18, 28, 296, 314f., **322ff.**, *324*, pl. 48
Oparany 75
Opava 31, **329ff.**, *330*
Opava (Oppa), river 330
Orava Castle 381, *382*
Orava district **381f.**
Orlice (Adler), river 260
Orlické hory (Adlergebirge) 292
Orlík Reservoir 200
Osek 247, **249ff.**, pl. 41

Osseg see Osek
Ostrau see Ostrava
Ostrava **321f.**
Ostravice 321, 322
Ostrov nad Oslavou 319

Pancava (Pantsche) 287
Panenský Týnec 13
Panská skála (Herrnhausfelsen) **253**, pl. 34
Pardubice (Pardubitz) **263f.**, *281*, 419, pls. 40, 47, col. pl. 13
Pardubitz see Pardubice
Pavlovské vrchy (Pollauer Berge) 304
Pec pod Sněžkou 287, 290, pl. 37
Pernštejn **302f.**
Petrov (Petersburg), Brno 296, 298
Petržalka (Audorf, Engerau), Bratislava 356
Pieniny, national park 405f.
Piešťany (Pistyan) **362ff.**, 427, pls. 58, 59
Pilsen see Plzeň
Písek **199f.**, *199*
Pistyan see Piešťany
Plaňany 158
Plasy (Plass) **214**, 254
Platten see Blatná
Plechý (Böhmischer Plöckenstein) 196, 198
Plešivec 389
Plešné jezero (Plöckensteinsee) 198
Plzeň 161, **209ff.**, *211*, *212*, 216, pls. 22, 28
Podbanské 404
Poděbrady 427
Podmokly (Bodenbach) 252, **253**
Poprad **393**, 402
Poprad (Popper), river 393, 399. 401
Popradské pleso, lake 405, col. pl. 23
Považský Inovec (Inovec Mountain) 362
Prachatice **195ff.**, 200
Prachatitz see Prachatice
Prachovské skály 284
Prachower Felsen see Prachovské skály
Praděd 329
Pravčická brána 254
Prebischtor see Pravčická brána
Preschau see Prešov
Pressburg see Bratislava
Prešov (Preschau) 383, **407ff.**, *408*
Prossnitz see Prostějov
Prostějov 12, 13
Příbor (Freiberg) **332**
Příbram **144f.**, col. pl. 11
Pškova, river 151

Pšov 149
Punkva cave 304
Pürglitz see Křivoklát

Radbuza, river 209, 213
Rakonitz, see Rakovník
Rakovník 146
Rajčanska river 381
Rajhrad (Raigern) 302
Reichenberg see Liberec
Riesengebirge see Krkonoše
Rochlitz an der Iser see Rokytnice nad Jizerou
Rokytnice nad Jizerou 287
Rothlhota see Červená Lhota
Rožmberk Pond, near Třeboň 207
Rožnov pod Radhoštěm **322**
Rožňava (Rosenau) 388, 418
Rybník Svět (World Pond) 207
Rysy (Meeraugspitze) 405
Rýžmburk (Riesenburg, Hrad Osek) 249, **251**

Říp 151

Saaz see Žatec
Sabinov 383
Sadova 260, **262**, 286
Sady (Derfle) 319
St. Joachimsthal, see Jachymov
Sázava 95
Schemnitz, see Banská Štiavnica
Schlan, see Slaný
Schneekoppe, see Sněžka
Schönhengstgau, see Hřebečsko
Schreckenstein, see Střekov
Schwarzberg, see Černá hora
Sedlec 25, **155**, 214
Selau see Želiv
Semtin 263
Sillein, see Žilina
Skalnaté pleso 404
Slaný (Schlan) 13, 245
Slatina, river 375
Slavkov u Brna (Austerlitz) 26, 296, **303**, 354
Slavkovský štít (Schlagendorfer Spitze) 404
Slavonice (Zlabings) **313**
Slip 308
Sloup 254
Slovak Ore Mountains see Slovenské rudohorie
Slovenské rudohorie (Slovak Ore Mountains) 372, 378, 389, 394, 414, pl. 62
Slovenský raj (Slovak Paradise) **394**, 428

Smědá (Wittig) 257
Sněžka 257, 287, **290f.**, 414
Spindlermühle see Špindlerův Mlýn
Spiš 17, 386, 388, **389ff.**, *390*, 420, pl. 60
Spišská Kapitula (Zipser Kapitel) **392**
Spišská Magura 400, 404, **405f.**
Spišská Nová Ves (Neudorf) 390, **393**, 398
Spišská Sobota (Georgenberg) **393f.**
Spišské Podhradie (Kirchdrauf) 392
Spišské Vlachy (Wallendorf) 373
Spišský hrad **392**, pl. 36
Spišský Štvrtok (Donnersmarkt) **393**, pl. 60
Stanovice (Stangendorf) 285
Stará Boleslav 90
Staré Brno (Alt Brünn) 302
Staré Hradisko 13
Staré Město, Uherské Hradiště 319
Starkenbach, see Jilemnice
Starý Plzenec 209, **214**
Starý Smokovec **404**, *405*
Stradonice 13
Strakonice **198f.**, 418
Strakonitz, see Strakonice
Strážnice 418
Střekov (Schreckenstein) **236–7**, *236*
Střelice 12
Stupava 13
Styx, river 389
Sudeten Mountains 329
Svatá Hora **144**
Svidník 409, 418
Svitava (Zwittawa) 296
Svitavy (Zwittau) 331
Svratka (Schwarzawa) 296, 299

Šanov (Schönau) 247
Šariš (Scharosch) region 407
Špilberk (Spielberg), Brno 296ff., 301
Špindlerův Mlýn 287, 289, **290**, 291
Štiavnické pohorie (Schemnitz Hills) 378
Štramberk 11
Štrba 404
Štrbské Pleso 404, **405**, 427
Šumava 195, **196**, *196*, 197f., 215, 217, 414, 426
Šumperk 329

Tábor 21, **201ff.**, *203*, 427
Tatra-Lomnitz, see Tatranská Lomnica
Tatranská Lomnica **404**
Taus see Domažlice
Telč **311ff.**, col. pl. 14, front cover and inside
    front cover

Teplá (Tepl) 75, 230
Teplá (Tepl), river 223
Teplice (Teplitz) **246f.**, 427, pl. 38
Teplice nad Metuji 286
Teplice nad Váhom (Teplitz an der Waag) 382
Teplicko-adršpašske skalý **286**
Teplička, river 366f.
Terchová **382**, 418
Terezín 63, 65, **240ff.**
Tetschen, see Děčín
Theben, see Devín
Theresienstadt, see Terezín
Tisá (Tyssa) 252
Tiské sedlo (Nollendorfer Pass) 251
Tiské stěny (Tyssauer Wände) 252
Tisza (Theiss), river 13
Tišnov (Tischnowitz) 303, 313
Topl'a, river 406
Torna 390
Torysa, river 497
Trabschitz 240
Trautenau, see Trutnov
Trenčíanské Teplice 364f., **366f.**, 427
Trenčín **364ff.**, pl. 54
Tri Duby, airfield 376
Trhanov 216
Trnava 354, **359ff.**, *361*, pl. 50
Troppau, see Opava
Trosky, castle 284, *285*
Trutnov 283, **285f.**, 291
Třebon 166, **206ff.**, 427
Tschaslau, see Čáslav
Tschirm, see Štrba
Tschirmer See, see Štrbské Pleso
Tvarožniansky potok 401
Tyrnau, see Trnava

Uherské Hradiště *318*, **319**
Uhlava, river 209
Únětice 12, 217
Ungarisch-Hradisct, see Uherské Hradiště
Unterwisternitz, see Dolni Věstonice
Úslava, river 209
Ústí nad Labem 31, **235f.**, 243, 252
Úštěk 243

Váh (Waag), river 362, 364, 367, 380, 381, 414
Vajgar, lake 204
Valdice (Walditz) 282, **283**
Valdštejn Castle 284
Valtice (Feldsberg) 305

Velké Losiny (Gross Ullersdorf) 329
Vel'ká Fatra (Great Fatra Mountains) 372, 414
Vel'ke Hincovo pleso 403
Vel'ký Krivan 382
Velehrad 318, **319f.**
Veligrad 319
Vernerovice 291
Věstonice 12, 297, 304
Vimperk 198
Vítězov 158
Vítkovice (Wittkowitz) 321
Vizovice 420
Vltava (Moldau), river 19, 23, 36, 38, 40, 44, 55,
    56, 63, 67, 71, 72, 83, 124, 125, 127, 133, 134,
    148, 150, 152, 161, 163, 164, 166, 195, 209, 414
Volary **197f.**
Volyňka, river 198
Vranov nad Dyjí 25, **308f.**
Vrátna valley 382
Vrátnanka, river 382
Vrchlabí 287, 288f.
Vrchlice, river 152, 15.
Východná 418
Východné Beskydy 406, 409
Vysoká, near Kolín 158
Vysoké Tatry (High Tatras) 389, 399, **402ff.**, *403*,
    414, 417, 426, 428, pl. 61, col.pl. 61
Vyšší Brod **193ff.**

Waag, see Váh
Wagendrüssel 394
Walditz, see Valdice
Wallachian Open-air Museum 322
Wallern, see Volary

Wekelsdorf, see Teplice nad Metuji
Westonitz, see Věstonice
White Carpathians see Bilé Karpaty
White Mountain see Prague, Bilé hora
White Tatras see Belianske Tatry
Wilde Klamm see Divoká soutěska
Winterberg see Vimperk
Wittingau see Třeboň
Wogatisburg 13

Západné Tatry (West Tatras) 404
Závist 13
Zbraslav 129
Zips see Spiš
Zipser Burg see Spišsý hrad
Zipser Magura see Spišská Magura
Zlatá Koruna 91, **193**
Zlatá stoka (Golden Canal) 207
Zlín **320**
Znaim, see Znojmo
Znojmo (Znaim) 12, **306ff.**, *308*, 313f., 418, 419
Zvíkov **200f.**
Zvolen 372, **375ff.**, *375*
Zwittau, see Svitavy

Žatec (Saaz) 217, 240, 244, **245f.**, 419
Žd'ár nad Sázavou 25, **317f.**
Ždiar **405**, pl. 61
Žehra 393
Železný Brod 418
Želiv (Selau) 313
Žlutica (Luditz) 227
Žilina 322, **380f.**, 382